Annual Editions:
Social Problems,
Fortieth Edition

Kurt Finsterbusch

M000251905

http://create.mheducation.com

Copyright 2016 by McGraw-Hill Education. All rights
reserved. Printed in the United States of America. Except as
permitted under the United States Copyright Act of 1976, no part
of this publication may be reproduced or distributed in any form
or by any means, or stored in a database or retrieval system,
without prior written permission of the publisher.

This McGraw-Hill Create text may include materials submitted to
McGraw-Hill for publication by the instructor of this course.
The instructor is solely responsible for the editorial content of such
materials. Instructors retain copyright of these additional materials.

ISBN-10: 125935959X   ISBN-13: 9781259359590

Contents

Preface

The reason we study social problems is so that we can do something about them. Corrective action, however, is not taken until the situation is seen as a problem and the fire of concern is kindled in a number of citizens. A democratic country gives those citizens means for legally trying to change things, and this freedom and opportunity is a great pride for our country. In fact, most college students have already given time or money to some cause in which they believe. This is necessary because each generation will face struggles for rights and justice. Daily forces operate to corrupt, distort, bias, exploit, and defraud as individuals and groups seek their own advantage at the expense of others and the public interest. Those dedicated to a good society, therefore, constantly struggle against these forces. Furthermore, the struggle is often complex and confusing. Not always are the defenders of the status quo wrong and the champions of change right. Important values will be championed by both sides. Today there is much debate about the best way to improve education. Opposing spokespersons think that they are serving the good of the children and of the United States. In a similar manner, conscientious students in the same college class and reading the same material will hotly disagree. Therefore, solving problems is usually not a peaceful process. First, it requires information and an understanding of the problem, and we can expect disagreements on both the facts and the interpretations. Second, it requires discussion, compromise, and a plan with majority support, or at least the support of the powerful groups. Third, it requires action. In a democratic society, this process should involve tolerance and even goodwill toward one's opponents as long as they act honestly, fairly, and democratically. Class discussions should involve respect for each other's opinions.

In some ways, the study of social problems is easy and in some ways it is hard. The easy aspect is that most people know quite a lot about the problems that this book addresses; the hard part is that solving those problems is very difficult. If the solutions were easy, the problems would have been solved by now, and we would not be studying these particular issues. It may be easy to plan solutions, but it is hard to implement them. In general, however, Americans are optimistic and believe in progress; we learn by our mistakes and keep trying until conditions are acceptable. For instance, the members of Common Cause, including myself, have worked for campaign finance reform since 1970. Our efforts failed until Watergate created a huge public demand for it, and both campaign finance reform and public-right-to-know laws were passed. The reform, however, led to the formation of PACs (Political Action Committees) to get around the law and buy influence legally.

In 2002 a new campaign finance reform law, the McCain-Feingold Act, was passed. Nevertheless, the role of big money in campaign finances is today larger than it has been for many decades. This will eventually precipitate yet another major reform effort. It could be that at the end of the twenty-first century, Americans will still be struggling with many of the same problems as today. But it is reasonable to believe that things will be somewhat better at that point because throughout this century people will mobilize again and again to improve our society; some will even do this at considerable cost to themselves.

The articles presented here were selected for three reasons: (1) their attention to important issues, (2) the value of the information and ideas they present, and/or (3) their ability to move the reader to concern and possibly even action toward correcting social problems. This edition of *Annual Editions: Social Problems* begins by broadly describing the United States and recent changes in forces that affect our lifestyles. It then examines some big issues in the political and economic systems that have society-wide impacts, as well as issues of inequality and injustice that challenge basic American values. The next section considers how well the various institutions of society work. Most institutions are being heavily criticized. These articles help to explain why. The proceeding section studies the traditional problem of crime and law enforcement. Fortunately, there is some good news here. Finally, the last section focuses on the future and problems of population, environment, technology, globalization, community, and long-term change.

Editor

Kurt Finsterbusch received a bachelor's degree in history from Princeton University in 1957 and a bachelor of divinity degree from Grace Theological Seminary in 1960. His PhD in sociology, from Columbia University, was conferred in 1969. Dr. Finsterbusch is the author of several books, including *Understanding Social Impacts* (Sage Publications, 1980), *Social Research for Policy Decisions* (Wadsworth Publishing, 1980, with Annabelle Bender Motz), and *Organizational Change as a Development Strategy* (Lynne Rienner Publishers, 1987, with Jerald Hage). He is currently teaching at the University of Maryland, College Park, and, in addition to serving as editor for *Annual Editions: Social Problems,* he is also editor of *Annual Editions: Sociology,* McGraw-Hill's *Taking Sides: Clashing Views on Controversial Social Issues,* and *Sources: Notable Selections in Sociology.*

Dedication
Dedicated to the many heroes and heroines who are trying to fix the various social problems addressed here.

Academic Advisory Board
Members of the Academic Advisory Board are instrumental in the final selection of articles for each edition of ANNUAL EDITIONS.

    Their review of articles for content, level, and appropriateness provides critical direction to the editors and staff. We think that you will find their careful consideration well reflected in this volume.

Pamela Altman,
Georgia Southern University

Thomas E. Arcaro,
Elon University

Sylven Beck,
The George Washington University

Heather Boone,
Atlantic Cape Community College

Mamie Bridgeforth,
Essex County College

M. Jennifer Brougham,
Arizona State University

Shakira Cain-Bell,
Jackson State University

Judy Chiasson,
California State University

Elizabeth F. Cohen,
Syracuse University

Lynn Connolly,
Chestnut Hill College

Maria Cuevas,
Yakima Valley Community College

T. Jesse Dent,
Johnson C. Smith University

Roger G. Dunham,
University of Miami

Kathy Edwards,
KCTCS—Ashland Community & Tech College

Leslie Elrod,
University of Cincinnati Ray Walters

Nancy Federman,
San Diego State University

Sylvia Haith,
Forsyth Technical Community College

Gary Heath,
Ashford University

Elizabeth Hegeman,
John Jay College—CUNY

Raymond A. Helgemoe,
University of New Hampshire

Mark Killian,
University of Cincinnati

Rosalind Kopfstein,
Western Connecticut State University

Timothy LaFountaine,
Quinsigamond Community College

Celia Lo,
University of Alabama

John P. Lynxwiler,
University of Central Florida, Orlando

James F. MacNair,
Atlantic Cape Community College

Karith Meyers,
Moorpark College

Christopher P. Morley,
SUNY Upstate Medical University

Kathryn S. Mueller,
Baylor University

Robert G. Newby,
Central Michigan University

Wendy Parker,
Albany College of Pharmacy

Dean G. Rojek,
University of Georgia

Larry Rosenberg,
Millersville University

Goldie Satt-Arrow,
Empire State College

Leretta Smith,
North Dakota State University

Joseph L. Victor,
Mercy College

Casey Welch,
Flagler College

Signe Whitson,
The LSCI Institute

Unit 1

UNIT
Prepared by: Kurt Finsterbusch, *University of Maryland, College Park*

Introduction: Clashing Values and Problematic Transformations of Social Life

This unit offers an introduction to the study of American social problems. It looks at American culture that provides the value system by which we decide what are the significant social problems. Immediately we recognize that people have different values. Some of these value differences are related to different positions in the social structure and different experiences. Racial, religious, gender, income, occupational, and age differences lead to different experiences, and therefore, different perspectives. For example, all races in America will share a common culture but also have different subcultures. Same with each generation. Some of these differences will be explored in this unit.

We propose a perspective that should be helpful as we observe value differences. We suggest that most people share roughly the same set of values. They differ however, on how these values should be ranked. For example, almost all Americans are both materialists and environmentalists. Even the business person who pollutes the environment while producing products for sale and profits wants to live in a clean and healthy environment. Even an environmentalist drives a car to work and uses air conditioning in warm weather. Both have the same values but rank them differently and therefore act differently. In this unit, we try to get a general picture of American culture and then select specific areas for closer examination. Some of the areas examined are civic virtue, Facebook impacts, and generational differences.

Article

Prepared by: Kurt Finsterbusch, *University of Maryland, College Park*

The American Narrative: Is There One & What Is It?

WILLIAM H. CHAFE

Learning Outcomes

After reading this article, you will be able to:

- Trace the role of the culture of serving the public good and the role of the culture of individual freedom in American history.

- Analyze how these two value systems are opposing each other today.

- Discuss the importance of balance between these sets of values and the danger of destroying that balance today.

Who are we? Where have we been? Where are we going? Can we even agree on who "we" includes? At no time in our history have these questions been more relevant. The American political system seems dysfunctional, if not permanently fractured. A generational gap in technological expertise and familiarity with the social network divides the country to an even greater extent than the culture wars of the 1960s and 1970s. Soon, more "Americans" will speak Spanish as their first language than English. For some, access to health care is a universal right, for others, a privilege that must be earned. Rarely—and certainly not since the Civil War—have we been so divided on which direction we should be heading as a country. How can there be an American narrative when it is not clear what it means to talk about an American people or nation? Two overriding paradigms have long competed in defining who we are. The first imagines America as a community that places the good of the whole first; the second envisions the country as a gathering of individuals who prize individual freedom and value more than anything else each person's ability to determine his own fate.

When the Puritans arrived in the Massachusetts Bay Colony in 1630, their leader, John Winthrop, told his shipmates aboard the *Arabella* that their mission was to create a "city upon a hill," a blessed society that would embody values so noble that the entire world would admire and emulate the new colony. Entitled "A Modell of Christian Charity," Winthrop's sermon described what it would take to create that beloved community: "We must love one another. We must bear one another's burdens . . . make others' conditions our own. We must rejoice together, mourn together, labor, and suffer together, always having before our eyes a community [where we are all] members of the same body."

Consistent with Winthrop's vision, Massachusetts was governed in its early decades by a sense of communal well-being. While the colony tolerated differences of status and power, the ruling norm was that the common good took precedence. Thus, "just prices" were prescribed for goods for sale, and punishment was imposed on businesses that sought excess profits. Parents who mistreated their children were shamed; people who committed adultery were exposed and humiliated.

Soon enough, a surge of individualism challenged the reigning norms. Entrepreneurs viewed communal rules as shackles to be broken so that they could pursue individual aspirations—and profits. The ideal of a "just price" was discarded. While religion remained a powerful presence, secularism ruled everyday business life, and Christianity was restricted to a once-a-week ritual. Class distinctions proliferated, economic inequality increased, and the values of *laissez-faire individualism* displaced the once-enshrined "common wealth." Aid to the poor became an act of individual charity rather than a communal responsibility.

Not surprisingly, the tensions between those who put the good of the community first and those who value individual freedom foremost have reverberated throughout our history. Thomas Jefferson sought to resolve the conflict in the Declaration of Independence by embracing the idea of "equal opportunity" for all. Note that he championed not equality of results, but equality of opportunity. Every citizen might have an "inalienable" right to "life, liberty, and the pursuit of happiness," but what happened to each person's "equal opportunity" depended on the performance of that particular individual. Success was not guaranteed.

Throughout American history, the tensions between the value of the common good and the right to unbridled individual freedom have resurfaced. The federal government sought to build roads and canals across state lines to serve the general good. The nation fought a Civil War because slavery contradicted the belief in the right of equal citizenship. In the aftermath of the war, the Constitution guaranteed all males the right to vote, and its Fourteenth Amendment promised each citizen "equal protection" under the law.

But by the end of the nineteenth century, rampant economic growth had created myriad enterprises that threatened the common good. In *The Jungle,* Upton Sinclair highlighted the danger of workers falling into vats of boiling liquid at meatpacking plants. The influx of millions of immigrants brought new dangers of infectious disease. As sweatshops, germ-filled tenements, and unsafe factories blighted American cities, more and more Americans insisted on legislation that fostered the general welfare. Led by women reformers such as Jane Addams and Florence Kelley, social activists succeeded in getting laws passed that ended child labor, protected workers from injury from dangerous factory machines, and created standards for safe meat and food. The Progressive Era still left most people free to pursue their own destiny, but under President Theodore Roosevelt, the government became the ultimate arbiter of minimal standards for industry, railroads, and consumer safety.

The tensions between the two narratives continued to grow as the nation entered the Great Depression. Nearly a million mortgages were foreclosed, the stock market crashed, 25 percent of all American workers were chronically unemployed, and banks failed. When Franklin Roosevelt was elected president, he promised to use "bold, persistent experimentation" to find answers to people's suffering. The legislation of the first 100 days of his presidency encompassed unprecedented federal intervention in the regulation of industry, agriculture, and the provision of welfare payments to the unemployed. The good of the whole reemerged as a dominant concern. By 1935, however, the American Liberty League, a political group formed by conservative Democrats to oppose New Deal legislation, was

indicting **fdr** as a socialist and demanding a return to laissez-faire individualism. But the New Deal rolled on. In 1935, Congress enacted Social Security, the single greatest collective investment America had ever made, for *all* people over 65, and the Wagner Labor Relations Act gave unions the right to organize. Roosevelt ran his 1936 reelection campaign on a platform emphasizing that "one third of [our] nation is ill-housed, ill-clothed, and ill-fed."

This focus on the good of the whole culminated during World War II, a time when everyone was reminded of being part of a larger battle to preserve the values that "equal opportunity" represented: the dignity of every citizen, as well as the right to freedom of religion, freedom from want, and freedom of political expression. For the first time since Reconstruction, the government acted to prohibit discrimination against African-Americans, issuing an executive order to allow blacks as well as whites to be hired in the war industries. Similarly, it supported policies of equal pay to women workers while leading a massive effort to recruit more women into the labor force to meet wartime demands. From wage and price controls to the universal draft, government action on behalf of the good of the whole reached a new height.

After the war ended, the tension between the competing value systems returned, but, significantly, even most Republicans accepted as a given the fundamental reforms achieved under the New Deal. Anyone who suggested repeal of Social Security, President Dwight Eisenhower wrote to his brother Milton midway through his term in office, was "out of his mind." Eisenhower even created a new Cabinet department to oversee health and welfare.

The stage was set for the revolutions of the 1960s: that is, the civil rights movement, the women's movement, the student movement, and the War on Poverty. Blacks had no intention of accepting the status quo of prewar Jim Crow segregation when they returned from serving in World War II. Building on the community institutions they had created during the era of Jim Crow, they mobilized to confront racism. When a black woman was raped by six white policemen in Montgomery, Alabama, in the late 1940s, the Women's Political Council, organized by local black women, and the Brotherhood of Sleeping Car Porters, an all-black union, took on the police and forced a trial. That same network of black activists sought improvements in the treatment of blacks at downtown department stores and on public transport. Thus, when one of their members, Rosa Parks, was arrested in 1955 for refusing to give up her seat on a city bus to a white person, both groups took action. By initiating a phone tree and printing 4,000 leaflets, they organized a mass rally overnight. Held at a local

Baptist church to consider a bus boycott, the rally featured an address by Martin Luther King, Jr., who later became the embodiment of the movement (though it should be noted that the movement created King and not vice versa). After that night, Montgomery's black community refused to ride the city buses for 381 consecutive days, until the buses were desegregated.

A few years later, four first-year students at the all-black North Carolina Agricultural and Technical College in Greensboro, North Carolina, carried the movement a step further. Although they had come of age after the Supreme Court outlawed school segregation, little had changed. Now that their generation was reaching maturity, they asked what they could do. The young men had gone to an all-black high school where their teachers had asked them to address voter registration envelopes to community residents and encouraged them to think of themselves as first-class citizens. They had participated in an **naacp** youth group in which weekly discussions had centered on events such as the Montgomery Bus Boycott. They attended a Baptist church where the pastor preached the social gospel and asked for "justice now." Embittered by how little the status of black Americans had improved, they sought new ways of carrying forward what they had learned.

Their solution was simple: highlight the absurdity of segregation by going to a downtown department store and acting like regular customers. At the Woolworth's in Greensboro, they bought notebooks at one counter, purchased toothpaste at another, then sat down at the lunch counter and ordered a cup of coffee. "We don't serve colored people here," they were told. "But you served us over there," they responded, showing their receipts. Opening their school books, they sat for three hours until the store closed. The next day, they returned to the lunch counter with 23 of their classmates. The day after there were 66, the next day 100. On the fifth day, 1000 black students and adults crowded the streets of downtown Greensboro.

The direct-action civil rights movement had begun. Within two months, sit-ins occurred in 54 cities in nine states. By April 1960, the Student Nonviolent Co-ordinating Committee (sncc) had been founded. Soon, *The New York Times* was devoting a special section each day to civil rights demonstrations in the South. On August 28, 1963, a quarter-million people came together for the March on Washington. There, Martin Luther King, Jr., gave his "I Have a Dream" speech, a contemporary version of what John Winthrop had said 238 years earlier that celebrated the same idea of a "beloved community" where "neither Jew nor Gentile, black man, or white man" could be separated from each other.

At long last, the government responded. The Civil Rights Act of 1964 ended Jim Crow. The Voting Rights Act of 1965 restored the franchise to black Americans. The War on Poverty gave hope to millions who had been left out of the American dream. Medicare offered health care to all senior citizens, and Medicaid offered it to those who could not otherwise afford to go to the doctor. Federal Aid to Education created new and better schools. The Model Cities Program offered a way for blighted neighborhoods to be revitalized.

The narrative of progress toward the common good reached a new crescendo. With the civil rights movement as an inspiration, women started their own movement for social equality. Access to previously closed careers opened up under pressure. By 1990, half of all medical, law, and business students were women. Young girls grew up with the same aspirations as young boys. Latinos, gay Americans, and other minorities soon joined the march demanding greater equality. It seemed as though a permanent turning point had occurred.

But the counternarrative eventually rediscovered its voice. Millions of white Americans who might have supported the right of blacks to vote or eat at a lunch counter were appalled by affirmative action and demands for Black Power. When the war in Vietnam caused well-off students to take to the streets in protest against their country's military actions, thousands of ordinary workers were angered by the rebellion of the young against authority. Traditional families were outraged when feminists questioned monogamy and dared to challenge male authority.

By 1968, the nation was divided once more, and the events of that election year crystallized the issues. Incumbent Lyndon Johnson withdrew from the presidential race at the end of March. Martin Luther King, Jr., was assassinated in April, with riots spreading like wildfire across the country in response. Student protestors took over Columbia University in May, making a mockery of the idea of civil discourse and respect for authority. Robert F. Kennedy was assassinated in June, just as he seemed ready to move decisively toward the Democratic presidential nomination. And when the Democratic party met for its convention in Chicago, thousands of protestors were pummeled by police as they demonstrated against conventional politics.

At the same time, Richard Nixon was nominated by the Republican party on a platform of "law and order" and respect for authority. Adopting a "Southern strategy," he appealed for white Southern votes by opposing forced desegregation of schools. Lambasting students who protested the war, he pleaded for a return to respect for traditional institutions. Nixon claimed to speak on behalf of "the silent majority" who remained proud to be American citizens, who celebrated the flag rather than mocked it, and who affirmed the rights of individuals to do as they wished.

Richard Nixon's election in Fall 1968 launched the resurgence of a conservative consensus in American politics. Though on issues such as the environment Nixon pursued many policies consistent with the "good of the whole" framework, on most issues he moved in the opposite direction. He opposed busing as a tool to create greater school desegregation, started to dismantle War on Poverty programs, based his 1972 reelection campaign on attacking the "collectivism" of the Democratic party, and insisted on defending the values of "traditional" Americans against attacks by the young, minorities, and women.

As social issues provided a rallying point for those set against further social change, the conservative narrative gained new proponents. Those opposed to gay rights mobilized to curtail further efforts to make sexuality a civil rights issue. Evangelical Christians joined groups such as Jerry Falwell's Moral Majority or Pat Robertson's "Praise the Lord" clubs to lobby against advances for minority rights. Direct mail campaigns and the use of cable television helped the Right galvanize new audiences of potential supporters.

Presidential politics also continued on a conservative path. Even though Richard Nixon was compelled to resign in shame over his illegal activities in the Watergate scandal, each of his successors—even Democrats—advanced the conservative agenda he initiated. Gerald Ford vetoed more legislation in two years than most presidents veto in eight. Jimmy Carter, though a liberal on gender equality and black civil rights, proved conservative on most economic issues. Ronald Reagan personified the conservative revival. He not only celebrated patriotism, but also revived the viewpoint that the best America was one without government intervention in the economy, and one that venerated the ideal of individualism.

Even Democrat Bill Clinton, excoriated by the Right as a demonic embodiment of counterculture values, was in practice more a Dwight Eisenhower Republican than a Lyndon Johnson Democrat. Dedicated to cultivating the political mainstream, he achieved legislative victories primarily on traditionally Republican issues: deficit reduction; the North American Free Trade Agreement; an increased police presence on the streets; welfare reform that took people off the public dole after two years; and the use of V-chips to allow parents to control their children's television viewing habits. Only his failed health care proposal acted in tune with the ideology of fdr and lbj.

George W. Bush simply extended the conservative tradition. With massive tax cuts, he created lower rates for the wealthy than had been seen in more than a half-century. His consistent support of deregulation freed up countless companies and investment capital firms to pursue profits without restriction. He made nationalism a cherished part of his political legacy, including the pursuit of a doctrine that emphasized unilateral initiatives defined as in the best interests of the United States, and downplayed multilateral cooperation that would subject America to constraint by the wishes of its partners and allies.

From 1968 to 2008, the American political and ideological trajectory hewed to a conservative narrative that celebrates individualism over collective action and criticizes government activity on behalf of the common good.

In recent years, the tension between the two narratives has escalated to an alarming degree. Barack Obama's 2008 election appeared to revitalize a focus on the common good. More people voted, embracing the idea of change, and elected a black American who seemed to embody those values. The fact that Obama became the first president in 100 years to successfully pass national health care reform—albeit without the provision of a public alternative to private insurance companies—appeared to validate that presumption.

But with the midterm elections of 2010, the rejection of Democratic politics—especially state intervention on behalf of the common good—resulted in the most dramatic electoral turnaround since 1946, when President Harry Truman's Democrats lost 81 seats in the House of Representatives. "Tea Party" Republicans not only stood for conservative positions on most social issues, but most dramatically, they insisted that all taxes should be cut, that federal expenditures for Medicare, Social Security, and other social programs must be slashed, and that it is preferable for the government to default on its financial responsibilities than to raise the national debt ceiling.

A backward glance through United States history would reveal no clearer example of the tension between the two competing American narratives, existing side by side, seemingly irreconcilable. The moment is historic, particularly at a time when climate change, stalled immigration reform, and a depressed global economy cry out for action. Thus, the conflict between the good of the whole and the ascendancy of individualist freedom has reached new heights. The choice that voters make in the 2012 presidential election will define our country's political future. Which narrative will we pursue? Are health care and quality education universal rights or privileges reserved for only those with the means to pay? Do we wish to bear "one another's burdens . . . make others' conditions our own . . . mourn together [and] labor and suffer together?" Or do we wish to make each individual responsible for his or her own fate? These questions are not new. But now, more than ever, they challenge us to find an answer: Who are we? In which direction do we wish to go?

Despite the trend over the past three-and-a-half centuries toward legislation that creates a safety net to protect the larger community, millions of Americans appear committed to dismantling government, slashing federal spending, and walking away from previous commitments to the good of the whole. A number of candidates running for the

Republican presidential nomination in 2012 wish to curtail federal responsibility for Social Security for senior citizens. Every Republican candidate seeks to repeal Obama's national health insurance program. Cutting taxes has become a holy mantra. While it is true that in the coming decades demographic change will dramatically increase the number of Latino voters, who historically have favored legislation on behalf of the common good, it is not inconceivable that a reversal of social welfare legislation will happen first.

The tension between these two narratives is as old as the country itself. More often than not, it has been a healthy tension, with one set of values checking and balancing the other. But the polarization of today is unparalleled. The decisions the electorate makes in 2012 are of historic importance in determining which direction the country will take.

Critical Thinking

1. How does the value system focused on the public good benefit American society and how might it hurt American society?

2. How does the value system focused on individual freedom benefit American society and how might it hurt American society?

3. How can balance between these two value systems be maintained?

Create Central

www.mhhe.com/createcentral

Internet References

New American Studies Web
www.georgetown.edu/crossroads/asw
Social Science Information Gateway
http://www.sosig.esrc.bris.ac.uk
Sociosite
http://www.topsite.com/goto/sociosite.net
Socioweb
http://www.topsite.com/goto/socioweb.com
Sociology—Study Sociology Online
http://edu.learnsoc.org
Sociology Web Resources
http://www.mhhe.com/socscience/sociology/resources/index.htm

WILLIAM H. CHAFE, a Fellow of the American Academy since 2001, is the Alice Mary Baldwin Professor of History at Duke University. His publications include *Private Lives/Public Consequences: Personality and Politics in Modern America* (2005) and *The Rise and Fall of the American Century: The United States from 1890 to 2008* (2008). His current project is titled *Behind the Veil: African American Life During the Age of Segregation.*

From *Daedalus*, Winter 2012, pp. 11–17. Copyright © 2012 by MIT Press Journals/American Academy of Arts and Sciences. Reprinted by permission via Rightslink.

Article Prepared by: Kurt Finsterbusch, *University of Maryland, College Park*

Nice Places Finish First

The economic returns of civic virtue.

JOHN M. BRIDGELAND AND ALAN KHAZEI

Learning Outcomes

After reading this article, you will be able to:

- Understand the importance of civic virtue.
- Understand the reduction of social mobility in the United States and be able to explain it.
- Understand the relationship between civic virtue and social mobility.

The American Dream is a core part of our national ethos. It is the idea that anyone can advance up the economic ladder with hard work and determination, regardless of where they come from or what zip code they're born into.

Over the last few years, however, the American Dream has taken a beating, and not just because of the Great Recession. A number of careful studies have found that there is less upward mobility in America than in other wealthy countries, such as Germany, Demark, Sweden, and the UK. In fact, only 8 percent of Americans born in the lowest fifth of the income scale ever make it to the top fifth in our so-called classless society, while the percentage is 11 to 14 percent in these "Old European" countries.

These new revelations would have shocked Alexis de Tocqueville, the French aristocrat who traveled through the United States in the 1830s and was among the first to write about the restive, egalitarian scramble for material success that then characterized America, so different from the class-bound Europe of his day.

Fortunately, America may be able to get back in the upward mobility game by paying greater attention to another phenomenon that struck Tocqueville about Americans in the 1830s: our propensity to join groups and volunteer our time for the public good.

"Americans of all ages, all conditions, and all dispositions, constantly form associations," the Frenchman observed in his famous book *Democracy in America*. Americans, he continued, banded together not only to advance their political and commercial interests but also "to found establishments for education, to build inns, to construct churches, to diffuse books . . . and in this manner they found hospitals, prisons, and schools." Whereas in Europe such civic endeavors were typically controlled by wealthy individuals or the state, in the US average citizens worked together to drive these organizations.

Today, Tocqueville would be writing about our nonprofit sector, or civil society. It is comprised of a vast array of different kinds of groups—local sports leagues and PTAs, church-based charities, labor unions, business and professional societies, fraternal organizations like the Elks and the NAACP, and national cause-oriented membership groups like the Humane Society—that operate in the space between the individual and the government.

This sector gained renewed attention in 1995, when Harvard's Robert Putnam published an article (later a book) called "Bowling Alone," in which he posited that the tradition of voluntary association was in steep decline in America. Citizens, he argued, were increasingly apt to spend their time watching TV rather than attending Rotary Club meetings. Many academics questioned Putnam's thesis—old-line fraternal organizations might be losing members, they observed, but youth soccer leagues are burgeoning and social media like Facebook provide alternative ways to connect.

Still, Putnam's work galvanized academic interest in "social capital"—the phrase sociologists use for the benefits that complex networks of friendships and connections bring to individuals and societies. Further studies showed, for instance, that levels of social capital varied greatly across the country. In some regions (the Northeast and the Upper Midwest), citizens are far more engaged in civic activities and connected with each other than in other areas (the Deep South and Nevada). Other studies found that communities with higher levels of social capital suffer less unemployment during recessions. As evidence of a link between civic engagement and economic health accumulated, the group Opportunity Nation included indicators of social capital among the 16 indicators of local economic health in its Opportunity Index (see page 43).

Then, this summer, a much-discussed study from a team of economists from Harvard and the University of California at Berkeley showed, for the first time, how rates of upward mobility vary geographically across the United States. The study from the Equality of Opportunity Project found that children born in the bottom quarter of the income scale in, for instance, the Denver metro area were twice as likely to rise to the top quarter as those born in Charlotte, and those born in the San Francisco Bay Area were three times as likely. Even in areas with similar average incomes, the rates of upward mobility dramatically differ. On average, lower-income children in metro Seattle who grew up in the bottom 25th percentile of income do similarly well as middle-class children in metro Atlanta.

Though the researchers couldn't prove what causes these geographic disparities in social mobility, they showed correlations. Among the strongest correlations—higher even than the quality of local high schools or the availability and affordability of local colleges—turned out to be social capital. Literally, the more bowling leagues, nonprofits, and similar groups per 10,000 residents, the more likely the area's young people were to rise economically. And this was true not just for those whose parents were involved in these groups, but for all young people in the community.

What might account for the connection between a place's social capital and the economic success of its children? No one can say for sure, but Putnam, who is writing a book on the subject, puts it this way: "Upward mobility is aided when everyone in a community thinks of other people's kids as 'their' kids." In other words, in civic-minded communities with thick webs of interpersonal connections, individuals help not only their friends but also others in the community whom they might not know—with a basket of food, or a summer job offer, or inside information on who are the best teachers and counselors at the local high school.

Social capital, in other words, expands our notion of "we."

If social capital is a critical component of social mobility, what can be done to increase its stock? Part of the answer is to be found in two other attributes that correlate with upward mobility: middle-class wages, and families with involved parents. Places with lots of both also tend to have high rates of social capital, which makes sense: two-parent households with sufficient incomes are more likely to be able to be involved in civic affairs. So anything that generally allows families to enter or stay in the middle class, and specifically policies that help them cope with the stresses of modern life—like more-flexible work schedules that free parents to invest more time in their families and communities—will likely strengthen social capital.

Another way to grow social capital is to expand programs of national and community service. These programs strengthen civil society in three ways.

First, they act as a force multiplier of people and resources. Take AmeriCorps, the federal domestic national service program that provides a modest living stipend and education award to those who give a year of full-time service to their country. AmeriCorps members are mostly detailed to nonprofit organizations like Habitat for Humanity, where, instead of swinging hammers themselves, they typically organize armies of unpaid part-time volunteers. They make sure hammers and drywall are at the housing site, that volunteers get the right training, and that food and water are at the ready. In other words, they build the capacity of nonprofits to engage with the broader community. The federal agency that runs AmeriCorps, the Corporation for National and Community Service (CNCS), also smartly ensures that government resources to the nonprofit leverage a private-sector commitment.

The second way service programs build social capital is by opening up opportunities for lower-income young people who are disconnected from school and work. YouthBuild, for instance, a nonprofit service initiative partially funded by federal grants, employs disadvantaged young people in community construction projects while helping them complete their education and get jobs. In 2010, 78 percent of YouthBuild enrollees completed the program, 63 percent obtained their GEDs or high school diplomas, and 60 percent went on to postsecondary education or decent-paying jobs.

A third way national and community service builds social capital is by expanding our notion of "we." Programs like AmeriCorps typically bring individuals from different geographies, races, ethnicities, party affiliations, and income levels together in common national purpose. It's no accident that one of the greatest periods of both civic involvement and upward mobility in America came in the years after World War II. A generation of Americans had grown up having witnessed the Civilian Conservation Corps, which put three million young unemployed men to work on our public lands over a decade. That generation went on to serve in the war, when the universal draft and the experience of fighting beside soldiers from widely different geographic, ethnic, and income backgrounds broadened the nation's sense of collective identity. Not surprisingly, the "Greatest Generation" volunteered more, joined organizations more, gave more in charitable contributions, attended church, school, and community activities more, and were active neighbors, helping those in need more than the generations before or after it. Interestingly, during the same period when our civic stocks rose, Americans also voted more, entered public service in greater numbers, and had much lower levels of political polarization than we see today. Even the gap between rich and poor was smaller.

That willingness to give something back isn't unique to the Greatest Generation. Millennials, who grew up during a time of war and economic stress, are showing such strong civic inclinations that the demand for service opportunities far outstrips supply. Applications to AmeriCorps soared from 359,000 in 2009 to more than 580,000 in 2011 (the latest year for which numbers are available) for only about 80,000 slots, half of which are full-time. There were 150,000 requests for applications to the Peace Corps for the 4,000 annual openings in 2011. Other service programs are similarly oversubscribed, like Teach for America (48,000 applications for 5,800 positions). This gap represents wasted democratic energy and social capital that could be put to work at very low cost to improve our country.

Recognizing this growing demand, a strong bipartisan majority in Congress passed, and Barack Obama signed, the Edward M. Kennedy Serve America Act in 2009, which authorized a tripling of AmeriCorps from 75,000 to 250,000 members. But with the budget wars that commenced after the 2010 midterms, little of those extra funds materialized. The House even voted to eliminate all funding for the CNCS and the programs it administers, like AmeriCorps (thankfully, those cuts didn't become law, although Senior Corps was cut dramatically).

In response to congressional paralysis, Obama in July issued a presidential memorandum instructing federal departments and agencies to use existing recourses to create their own service programs to support their missions. These agency-specific service initiatives will be modeled after programs like FEMA Corps, a new partnership between the Federal Emergency Management Agency and the CNCS that trains and deploys teams for 10 months to aid in disaster relief.

The outside momentum for national service is also building. Groups like Voices for National Service, which leads the effort to boost funding for AmeriCorps, and ServiceNation, which championed the passage of the Serve America Act, are keeping the service field together right at a time when the country needs their advocacy and creativity most. And this summer, the Aspen Institute established the Franklin Project, led by retired General Stanley McChrystal, to help realize the goal of engaging more than one million young Americans between the ages of 18 and 28 in a year of civilian national service, on par with the more than one million Americans on active duty in our military.

To help reach that goal, the Franklin Project will challenge private-sector institutions, be they universities or nonprofits, to create, fund, and manage new opportunities for national service. These new positions will be certified by a new entity and advertised on a digital site listing all national service programs and positions. The site will effectively serve as a combination of Monster.com and Kickstarter—that is, it will make it easy for young people to apply for a wide variety of national service positions, while also enabling corporate and other sources of support for such service opportunities. The system will take advantage of technology, social networks, and civil society to democratize and modernize national service.

The challenges and opportunities facing this country are big. And we need bold solutions to deal with them. For more than 80 years, national service programs have shown that they can strengthen communities, transform service participants, and build the social capital we need to make the American Dream a reality for all. Millennials are clamoring to serve their country, and such service could boost their economic mobility in a tough economy. We should give them that chance.

Critical Thinking

1. What role should the federal government have in helping to create more civic virtue?
2. What forces hinder the development of civic virtue?
3. Why has social mobility decreased and inequality increased in the United States in the past few decades?

Create Central

www.mhhe.com/createcentral

Internet References

Social Science Information Gateway
   http://sosig.esrc.bris.ac.uk
Sociology—Study Sociology Online
   http://edu.learnsoc.org
Sociology Web Resources
   http://www.mhhe.com/socscience/sociology/resources/index.htm

Sociosite
http://www.topsite.com/goto/sociosite.net

Socioweb
http://www.topsite.com/goto/socioweb.com

The American Studies Web
http://lamp.georgetown.edu/asw

JOHN M. BRIDGELAND is CEO of Civic Enterprises, former director of the White House Domestic Policy Council under President George W. Bush, and a member of the White House Council for Community Solutions under President Barack Obama. **ALAN KHAZEI** is CEO of the Action Tank and cofounder of City Year. They are cochairs of the Franklin Project at the Aspen Institute.

Bridgeland, John M.; Khazei, Alan, "Nice Places Finish First: The Economic Returns of Civic Virtue," *Washington Monthly*, November/December 2013 pp. 50–52. Copyright © 2013 by Washington Monthly. All rights reserved. Used with permission.

Article   Prepared by: Kurt Finsterbusch, *University of Maryland, College Park*

Is Facebook Making Us Lonely?

Social media—from Facebook to Twitter—have made us more densely networked than ever. Yet for all this connectivity, new research suggests that we have never been lonelier (or more narcissistic)—and that this loneliness is making us mentally and physically ill. A report on what the epidemic of loneliness is doing to our souls and our society.

STEPHEN MARCHE

Learning Outcomes

After reading this article, you will be able to:

- Know the trends in loneliness over the past several decades.
- Understand the role of Facebook in present-day loneliness.
- Understand the effects of loneliness on the mental and physical health of individuals and on society.

Yvette Vickers, a former *Playboy* playmate and B-movie star, best known for her role in *Attack of the 50 Foot Woman,* would have been 83 last August, but nobody knows exactly how old she was when she died. According to the Los Angeles coroner's report, she lay dead for the better part of a year before a neighbor and fellow actress, a woman named Susan Savage, noticed cobwebs and yellowing letters in her mailbox, reached through a broken window to unlock the door, and pushed her way through the piles of junk mail and mounds of clothing that barricaded the house. Upstairs, she found Vickers's body, mummified, near a heater that was still running. Her computer was on too, its glow permeating the empty space.

The *Los Angeles Times* posted a story headlined "Mummified Body of Former Playboy Playmate Yvette Vickers Found in Her Benedict Canyon Home," which quickly went viral. Within two weeks, by Technorati's count, Vickers's lonesome death was already the subject of 16,057 Facebook posts and 881 tweets. She had long been a horror-movie icon, a symbol of Hollywood's capacity to exploit our most basic fears in the silliest ways; now she was an icon of a new and different kind of

horror: our growing fear of loneliness. Certainly, she received much more attention in death than she did in the final years of her life. With no children, no religious group, and no immediate social circle of any kind, she had begun, as an elderly woman, to look elsewhere for companionship. Savage later told *Los Angeles* magazine that she had searched Vickers's phone bills for clues about the life that led to such an end. In the months before her grotesque death, Vickers had made calls not to friends or family but to distant fans who had found her through fan conventions and Internet sites.

Vickers's web of connections had grown broader but shallower, as has happened for many of us. We are living in an isolation that would have been unimaginable to our ancestors, and yet we have never been more accessible. Over the past three decades, technology has delivered to us a world in which we need not be out of contact for a fraction of a moment. In 2010, at a cost of $300 million, 800 miles of fiber-optic cable was laid between the Chicago Mercantile Exchange and the New York Stock Exchange to shave three milliseconds off trading times. Yet within this world of instant and absolute communication, unbounded by limits of time or space, we suffer from unprecedented alienation. We have never been more detached from one another, or lonelier. In a world consumed by ever more novel modes of socializing, we have less and less actual society. We live in an accelerating contradiction: the more connected we become, the lonelier we are. We were promised a global village; instead we inhabit the drab cul-de-sacs and endless freeways of a vast suburb of information.

At the forefront of all this unexpectedly lonely interactivity is Facebook, with 845 million users and $3.7 billion in revenue last year. The company hopes to raise $5 billion in an initial public offering later this spring, which will make it by far the largest Internet IPO in history. Some recent estimates put the company's potential value at $100 billion, which would make it larger than the global coffee industry—one addiction preparing to surpass the other. Facebook's scale and reach are hard to comprehend: last summer, Facebook became, by some counts, the first website to receive one trillion page views in a month. In the last three months of 2011, users generated an average of 2.7 billion "likes" and comments every day. On whatever scale you care to judge Facebook—as a company, as a culture, and as a country—it is vast beyond imagination.

Despite its immense popularity, or more likely because of it, Facebook has, from the beginning, been under something of a cloud of suspicion. The depiction of Mark Zuckerberg, in *The Social Network,* as a bastard with symptoms of Asperger's syndrome, was nonsense. But it felt true. It felt true to Facebook, if not to Zuckerberg. The film's most indelible scene, the one that may well have earned it an Oscar, was the final, silent shot of an anomic Zuckerberg sending out a friend request to his ex-girlfriend, then waiting and clicking and waiting and clicking—a moment of superconnected loneliness preserved in amber. We have all been in that scene: transfixed by the glare of a screen, hungering for response.

When you sign up for Google+ and set up your Friends circle, the program specifies that you should include only "your real friends, the ones you feel comfortable sharing private details with." That one little phrase, *Your real friends—* so quaint, so charmingly mothering—perfectly encapsulates the anxieties that social media have produced: the fears that Facebook is interfering with our real friendships, distancing us from each other, making us lonelier; and that social networking might be spreading the very isolation it seemed designed to conquer.

Facebook arrived in the middle of a dramatic increase in the quantity and intensity of human loneliness, a rise that initially made the site's promise of greater connection seem deeply attractive. Americans are more solitary than ever before. In 1950, less than 10 percent of American households contained only one person. By 2010, nearly 27 percent of households had just one person. Solitary living does not guarantee a life of unhappiness, of course. In his recent book about the trend toward living alone, Eric Klinenberg, a sociologist at NYU, writes: "Reams of published research show that it's the quality, not the quantity of social interaction, that best predicts loneliness." True. But before we begin the fantasies of happily eccentric singledom, of divorcées dropping by their knitting circles after work for glasses of Drew Barrymore pinot grigio, or recent college graduates with perfectly articulated, Steampunk-themed, 300-square-foot apartments organizing croquet matches with their book clubs, we should recognize

that it is not just isolation that is rising sharply. It's loneliness, too. And loneliness makes us miserable.

We know intuitively that loneliness and being alone are not the same thing. Solitude can be lovely. Crowded parties can be agony. We also know, thanks to a growing body of research on the topic, that loneliness is not a matter of external conditions; it is a psychological state. A 2005 analysis of data from a longitudinal study of Dutch twins showed that the tendency toward loneliness has roughly the same genetic component as other psychological problems such as neuroticism or anxiety.

Still, loneliness is slippery, a difficult state to define or diagnose. The best tool yet developed for measuring the condition is the UCLA Loneliness Scale, a series of 20 questions that all begin with this formulation: "How often do you feel . . . ?" As in: "How often do you feel that you are 'in tune' with the people around you?" And. "How often do you feel that you lack companionship?" Measuring the condition in these terms, various studies have shown loneliness rising drastically over a very short period of recent history. A 2010 AARP survey found that 35 percent of adults older than 45 were chronically lonely, as opposed to 20 percent of a similar group only a decade earlier. According to a major study by a leading scholar of the subject, roughly 20 percent of Americans—about 60 million people— are unhappy with their lives because of loneliness. Across the Western world, physicians and nurses have begun to speak openly of an epidemic of loneliness.

The new studies on loneliness are beginning to yield some surprising preliminary findings about its mechanisms. Almost every factor that one might assume affects loneliness does so only some of the time, and only under certain circumstances. People who are married are less lonely than single people, one journal article suggests, but only if their spouses are confidants. If one's spouse is not a confidant, marriage may not decrease loneliness. A belief in God might help, or it might not, as a 1990 German study comparing levels of religious feeling and levels of loneliness discovered. Active believers who saw God as abstract and helpful rather than as a wrathful, immediate presence were less lonely. "The mere belief in God," the researchers concluded, "was relatively independent of loneliness."

But it is clear that social interaction matters. Loneliness and being alone are not the same thing, but both are on the rise. We meet fewer people. We gather less. And when we gather, our bonds are less meaningful and less easy. The decrease in confidants—that is, in quality social connections—has been dramatic over the past 25 years. In one survey, the mean size of networks of personal confidants decreased from 2.94 people in 1985 to 2.08 in 2004. Similarly, in 1985, only 10 percent of Americans said they had no one with whom to discuss important matters, and 15 percent said they had only one such good friend. By 2004, 25 percent had nobody to talk to and 20 percent had only one confidant.

In the face of this social disintegration, we have essentially hired an army of replacement confidants, an entire class of professional carers. As Ronald Dworkin pointed out in a 2010 paper for the Hoover Institution, in the late 40s, the United States was home to 2,500 clinical psychologists, 30,000 social workers, and fewer than 500 marriage and family therapists. As of 2010, the country had 77,000 clinical psychologists, 192,000 clinical social workers, 400,000 nonclinical social workers, 50,000 marriage and family therapists, 105,000 mental-health counselors, 220,000 substance-abuse counselors, 17,000 nurse psychotherapists, and 30,000 life coaches. The majority of patients in therapy do not warrant a psychiatric diagnosis. This raft of psychic servants is helping us through what used to be called regular problems. We have outsourced the work of everyday caring.

We need professional careers more and more, because the threat of societal breakdown, once principally a matter of nostalgic lament, has morphed into an issue of public health. Being lonely is extremely bad for your health. If you're lonely, you're more likely to be put in a geriatric home at an earlier age than a similar person who isn't lonely. You're less likely to exercise. You're more likely to be obese. You're less likely to survive a serious operation and more likely to have hormonal imbalances. You are at greater risk of inflammation. Your memory may be worse. You are more likely to be depressed, to sleep badly, and to suffer dementia and general cognitive decline. Loneliness may not have killed Yvette Vickers, but it has been linked to a greater probability of having the kind of heart condition that did kill her.

And yet, despite its deleterious effect on health, loneliness is one of the first things ordinary Americans spend their money achieving. With money, you flee the cramped city to a house in the suburbs or, if you can afford it, a McMansion in the exurbs, inevitably spending more time in your car. Loneliness is at the American core, a by-product of a long-standing national appetite for independence: The Pilgrims who left Europe willingly abandoned the bonds and strictures of a society that could not accept their right to be different. They did not seek out loneliness, but they accepted it as the price of their autonomy. The cowboys who set off to explore a seemingly endless frontier likewise traded away personal ties in favor of pride and self-respect. The ultimate American icon is the astronaut: Who is more heroic, or more alone? The price of self-determination and self-reliance has often been loneliness. But Americans have always been willing to pay that price.

Today, the one common feature in American secular culture is its celebration of the self that breaks away from the constrictions of the family and the state, and, in its greatest expressions, from all limits entirely. The great American poem is Whitman's "Song of Myself." The great American essay is Emerson's "Self-Reliance." The great American novel is Melville's *Moby-Dick,* the tale of a man on a quest so lonely that it is incomprehensible to those around him. American culture, high and low, is about self-expression and personal authenticity. Franklin Delano Roosevelt called individualism "the great watchword of American life."

Self-invention is only half of the American story, however. The drive for isolation has always been in tension with the impulse to cluster in communities that cling and suffocate. The Pilgrims, while fomenting spiritual rebellion, also enforced ferocious cohesion. The Salem witch trials, in hindsight, read like attempts to impose solidarity—as do the McCarthy hearings. The history of the United States is like the famous parable of the porcupines in the cold, from Schopenhauer's *Studies in Pessimism*—the ones who huddle together for warmth and shuffle away in pain, always separating and congregating.

We are now in the middle of a long period of shuffling away. In his 2000 book *Bowling Alone,* Robert D. Putnam attributed the dramatic postwar decline of social capital—the strength and value of interpersonal networks—to numerous interconnected trends in American life: suburban sprawl, television's dominance over culture, the self-absorption of the Baby Boomers, and the disintegration of the traditional family. The trends he observed continued through the prosperity of the aughts, and have only become more pronounced with time: the rate of union membership declined in 2011, again; screen time rose; the Masons and the Elks continued their slide into irrelevance. We are lonely because we want to be lonely. We have made ourselves lonely.

The question of the future is this: Is Facebook part of the separating or part of the congregating; is it a huddling-together for warmth or a shuffling-away in pain?

Well before facebook, digital technology was enabling our tendency for isolation, to an unprecedented degree. Back in the 1990s, scholars started calling the contradiction between an increased opportunity to connect and a lack of human contact the "Internet paradox." A prominent 1998 article on the phenomenon by a team of researchers at Carnegie Mellon showed that increased Internet usage was already coinciding with increased loneliness. Critics of the study pointed out that the two groups that participated in the study—high-school journalism students who were heading to university and socially active members of community-development boards—were statistically likely to become lonelier over time. Which brings us to a more fundamental question: Does the Internet make people lonely, or are lonely people more attracted to the Internet?

The question has intensified in the Facebook era. A recent study out of Australia (where close to half the population is active on Facebook), titled "Who Uses Facebook?," found a complex and sometimes confounding relationship between loneliness and social networking. Facebook users had slightly lower levels of "social loneliness"—the sense of not feeling bonded with friends—but "significantly higher levels of family loneliness"—the sense of not feeling bonded with family. It may be that Facebook encourages more contact with people outside of our household, at the expense of our family relationships—or it may be that people who have unhappy family relationships in the first place seek companionship through other means, including Facebook. The researchers also found that lonely people are inclined to spend more time on Facebook: "One of the most noteworthy findings," they wrote, "was the tendency for neurotic and lonely individuals to spend greater amounts of time on Facebook per day than nonlonely individuals." And they found that neurotics are more likely to prefer to use the wall, while extroverts tend to use chat features in addition to the wall.

Moira Burke, until recently a graduate student at the Human-Computer Institute at Carnegie Mellon, used to run a longitudinal study of 1,200 Facebook users. That study, which is ongoing, is one of the first to step outside the realm of self-selected college students and examine the effects of Facebook on a broader population, over time. She concludes that the effect of Facebook depends on what you bring to it. Just as your mother said: you get out only what you put in. If you use Facebook to communicate directly with other individuals—by using the "like" button, commenting on friends' posts, and so on—it can increase your social capital. Personalized messages, or what Burke calls "composed communication," are more satisfying than "one-click communication"—the lazy click of a like. "People who received composed communication became less lonely, while people who received one-click communication experienced no change in loneliness," Burke tells me. So, you should inform your friend in writing how charming her son looks with Harry Potter cake smeared all over his face, and how interesting her sepia-toned photograph of that tree-framed bit of skyline is, and how cool it is that she's at whatever concert she happens to be at. That's what we all want to hear. Even better than sending a private Facebook message is the semi-public conversation, the kind of back-and-forth in which you half ignore the other people who may be listening in. "People whose friends write to them semi-publicly on Facebook experience decreases in loneliness," Burke says.

On the other hand, nonpersonalized use of Facebook—scanning your friends' status updates and updating the world on your own activities via your wall, or what Burke calls "passive consumption" and "broadcasting"—correlates to feelings of disconnectedness. It's a lonely business, wandering the labyrinths of our friends' and pseudo-friends' projected identities,

trying to figure out what part of ourselves we ought to project, who will listen, and what they will hear. According to Burke, passive consumption of Facebook also correlates to a marginal increase in depression. "If two women each talk to their friends the same amount of time, but one of them spends more time reading about friends on Facebook as well, the one reading tends to grow slightly more depressed," Burke says. Her conclusion suggests that my sometimes unhappy reactions to Facebook may be more universal than I had realized. When I scroll through page after page of my friends' descriptions of how accidentally eloquent their kids are, and how their husbands are endearingly bumbling, and how they're all about to eat a home-cooked meal prepared with fresh local organic produce bought at the farmers' market and then go for a jog and maybe check in at the office because they're so busy getting ready to hop on a plane for a week of luxury dogsledding in Lapland, I do grow slightly more miserable. A lot of other people doing the same thing feel a little bit worse, too.

Still, Burke's research does not support the assertion that Facebook creates loneliness. The people who experience loneliness on Facebook are lonely away from Facebook, too, she points out; on Facebook, as everywhere else, correlation is not causation. The popular kids are popular, and the lonely skulkers skulk alone. Perhaps, it says something about me that I think Facebook is primarily a platform for lonely skulking. I mention to Burke the widely reported study, conducted by a Stanford graduate student, that showed how believing that others have strong social networks can lead to feelings of depression. What does Facebook communicate, if not the impression of social bounty? Everybody else looks so happy on Facebook, with so many friends, that our own social networks feel emptier than ever in comparison. Doesn't that *make* people feel lonely? "If people are reading about lives that are much better than theirs, two things can happen," Burke tells me. "They can feel worse about themselves, or they can feel motivated."

Burke will start working at Facebook as a data scientist this year.

John Cacioppo, the director of the Center for Cognitive and Social Neuroscience at the University of Chicago, is the world's leading expert on loneliness. In his landmark book, *Loneliness,* released in 2008, he revealed just how profoundly the epidemic of loneliness is affecting the basic functions of human physiology. He found higher levels of epinephrine, the stress hormone, in the morning urine of lonely people. Loneliness burrows deep: "When we drew blood from our older adults and analyzed their white cells," he writes, "we found that loneliness somehow penetrated the deepest recesses of the cell to alter the way genes were being expressed." Loneliness affects not only the brain, then, but the basic process of DNA transcription. When you are lonely, your whole body is lonely.

To Cacioppo, Internet communication allows only ersatz intimacy. "Forming connections with pets or online friends or even God is a noble attempt by an obligatorily gregarious creature to satisfy a compelling need," he writes. "But surrogates can never make up completely for the absence of the real thing." The "real thing" being actual people, in the flesh. When I speak to Cacioppo, he is refreshingly clear on what he sees as Facebook's effect on society. Yes, he allows, some research has suggested that the greater the number of Facebook friends a person has, the less lonely she is. But he argues that the impression this creates can be misleading. "For the most part," he says, "people are bringing their old friends, and feelings of loneliness or connectedness, to Facebook." The idea that a website could deliver a more friendly, interconnected world is bogus. The depth of one's social network outside Facebook is what determines the depth of one's social network within Facebook, not the other way around. Using social media doesn't create new social networks; it just transfers established networks from one platform to another. For the most part, Facebook doesn't destroy friendships—but it doesn't create them, either.

In one experiment, Cacioppo looked for a connection between the loneliness of subjects and the relative frequency of their interactions via Facebook, chat rooms, online games, dating sites, and face-to-face contact. The results were unequivocal. "The greater the proportion of face-to-face interactions, the less lonely you are," he says. "The greater the proportion of online interactions, the lonelier you are." Surely, I suggest to Cacioppo, this means that Facebook and the like inevitably make people lonelier. He disagrees. Facebook is merely a tool, he says, and like any tool, its effectiveness will depend on its user. "If you use Facebook to increase face-to-face contact," he says, "it increases social capital." So if social media let you organize a game of football among your friends, that's healthy. If you turn to social media instead of playing football, however, that's unhealthy.

"Facebook can be terrific, if we use it properly," Cacioppo continues. "It's like a car. You can drive it to pick up your friends. Or you can drive alone." But hasn't the car increased loneliness? If cars created the suburbs, surely they also created isolation. "That's because of how we use cars," Cacioppo replies. "How we use these technologies can lead to more integration, rather than more isolation."

The problem, then, is that we invite loneliness, even though it makes us miserable. The history of our use of technology is a history of isolation desired and achieved. When the Great Atlantic and Pacific Tea Company opened its A&P stores,

giving Americans self-service access to groceries, customers stopped having relationships with their grocers. When the telephone arrived, people stopped knocking on their neighbors' doors. Social media bring this process to a much wider set of relationships. Researchers at the HP Social Computing Lab who studied the nature of people's connections on Twitter came to a depressing, if not surprising, conclusion: "Most of the links declared within Twitter were meaningless from an interaction point of view." I have to wonder: What other point of view is meaningful?

Loneliness is certainly not something that Facebook or Twitter or any of the lesser forms of social media is doing to us. We are doing it to ourselves. Casting technology as some vague, impersonal spirit of history forcing our actions is a weak excuse. We make decisions about how we use our machines, not the other way around. Every time I shop at my local grocery store, I am faced with a choice. I can buy my groceries from a human being or from a machine. I always, without exception, choose the machine. It's faster and more efficient, I tell myself, but the truth is that I prefer not having to wait with the other customers who are lined up alongside the conveyor belt: the hipster mom who disapproves of my high-carbon-footprint pineapple; the lady who tenses to the point of tears while she waits to see if the gods of the credit-card machine will accept or decline; the old man whose clumsy feebleness requires a patience that I don't possess. Much better to bypass the whole circus and just ring up the groceries myself.

Our omnipresent new technologies lure us toward increasingly superficial connections at exactly the same moment that they make avoiding the mess of human interaction easy. The beauty of Facebook, the source of its power, is that it enables us to be social while sparing us the embarrassing reality of society—the accidental revelations we make at parties, the awkward pauses, the farting and the spilled drinks, and the general gaucherie of face-to-face contact. Instead, we have the lovely smoothness of a seemingly social machine. Everything's so simple: status updates, pictures, your wall.

But the price of this smooth sociability is a constant compulsion to assert one's own happiness, one's own fulfillment. Not only must we contend with the social bounty of others; we must foster the appearance of our own social bounty. Being happy all the time, pretending to be happy, actually attempting to be happy—it's exhausting. Last year a team of researchers led by Iris Mauss at the University of Denver published a study looking into "the paradoxical effects of valuing happiness." Most goals in life show a direct correlation between valuation and achievement. Studies have found, for example, that students who value good grades tend to have higher grades than those who don't value them. Happiness is an exception. The study came to a disturbing conclusion:

Valuing happiness is not necessarily linked to greater happiness. In fact, under certain conditions, the opposite is true. Under conditions of low (but not high) life stress, the more people valued happiness, the lower were their hedonic balance, psychological well-being, and life satisfaction, and the higher their depression symptoms.

The more you try to be happy, the less happy you are. Sophocles made roughly the same point.

Facebook, of course, puts the pursuit of happiness front and center in our digital life. Its capacity to redefine our very concepts of identity and personal fulfillment is much more worrisome than the data mining and privacy practices that have aroused anxieties about the company. Two of the most compelling critics of Facebook—neither of them a Luddite—concentrate on exactly this point. Jaron Lanier, the author of *You Are Not a Gadget,* was one of the inventors of virtual-reality technology. His view of where social media are taking us reads like dystopian science fiction: "I fear that we are beginning to design ourselves to suit digital models of us, and I worry about a leaching of empathy and humanity in that process." Lanier argues that Facebook imprisons us in the business of self-presenting, and this, to his mind, is the site's crucial and fatally unacceptable downside.

Sherry Turkle, a professor of computer culture at MIT who in 1995 published the digital-positive analysis *Life on the Screen,* is much more skeptical about the effects of online society in her 2011 book, *Alone Together:* "These days, insecure in our relationships and anxious about intimacy, we look to technology for ways to be in relationships and protect ourselves from them at the same time." The problem with digital intimacy is that it is ultimately incomplete: "The ties we form through the Internet are not, in the end, the ties that bind. But they are the ties that preoccupy," she writes. "We don't want to intrude on each other, so instead we constantly intrude on each other, but not in 'real time.'"

Lanier and Turkle are right, at least in their diagnoses. Self-presentation on Facebook is continuous, intensely mediated, and possessed of a phony nonchalance that eliminates even the potential for spontaneity. (Look how casually I threw up these three photos from the party at which I took 300 photos!) Curating the exhibition of the self has become a 24/7 occupation. Perhaps not surprisingly, then, the Australian study "Who Uses Facebook?" found a significant correlation between Facebook use and narcissism: "Facebook users have higher levels of total narcissism, exhibitionism, and leadership than Facebook non-users," the study's authors wrote. "In fact, it could be argued that Facebook specifically gratifies the narcissistic individual's need to engage in self-promoting and superficial behavior."

Rising narcissism isn't so much a trend as the trend behind all other trends. In preparation for the 2013 edition of its diagnostic manual, the psychiatric profession is currently struggling to update its definition of narcissistic personality disorder. Still, generally speaking, practitioners agree that narcissism manifests in patterns of fantastic grandiosity, craving for attention, and lack of empathy. In a 2008 survey, 35,000 American respondents were asked if they had ever had certain symptoms of narcissistic personality disorder. Among people older than 65, 3 percent reported symptoms. Among people in their 20s, the proportion was nearly 10 percent. Across all age groups, one in 16 Americans has experienced some symptoms of NPD. And loneliness and narcissism are intimately connected: a longitudinal study of Swedish women demonstrated a strong link between levels of narcissism in youth and levels of loneliness in old age. The connection is fundamental. Narcissism is the flip side of loneliness, and either condition is a fighting retreat from the messy reality of other people.

A considerable part of Facebook's appeal stems from its miraculous fusion of distance with intimacy, or the illusion of distance with the illusion of intimacy. Our online communities become engines of self-image, and self-image becomes the engine of community. The real danger with Facebook is not that it allows us to isolate ourselves, but that by mixing our appetite for isolation with our vanity, it threatens to alter the very nature of solitude. The new isolation is not of the kind that Americans once idealized, the lonesomeness of the proudly nonconformist, independent-minded, solitary stoic, or that of the astronaut who blasts into new worlds. Facebook's isolation is a grind. What's truly staggering about Facebook usage is not its volume—750 million photographs uploaded over a single weekend—but the constancy of the performance it demands. More than half its users—and one of every 13 people on Earth is a Facebook user—log on every day. Among 18 to 34-year-olds, nearly half check Facebook minutes after waking up, and 28 percent do so before getting out of bed. The relentlessness is what is so new, so potentially transformative. Facebook never takes a break. We never take a break. Human beings have always created elaborate acts of self-presentation. But not all the time, not every morning, before we even pour a cup of coffee. Yvette Vickers's computer was on when she died.

Nostalgia for the good old days of disconnection would not just be pointless, it would be hypocritical and ungrateful. But the very magic of the new machines, the efficiency and elegance with which they serve us, obscures what isn't being served: everything that matters. What Facebook has revealed about human nature—and this is not a minor revelation—is that a connection is not the same thing as a bond, and that instant and total connection is no salvation, no ticket to a happier, better world or a more liberated version of humanity. Solitude used to be good for self-reflection and self-reinvention. But now we are left thinking about who we are all the time, without ever really thinking about who we are. Facebook denies us a pleasure whose profundity we had underestimated: the chance to forget about ourselves for a while, the chance to disconnect.

Critical Thinking

1. What are the advantages of social media for mental health?
2. What are the tradeoffs for time using social media?
3. What in your opinion are the best ways to use social media?

Create Central

www.mhhe.com/createcentral

Internet References

Global X Social Media Index ETF
http://www.globalxfunds.com/SOCL

Social Science Information Gateway
http://sosig.esrc.bris.ac.uk

Sociology Web Resources
http://www.mhhe.com/socscience/sociology/resources/index.htm

Sociology—Study Sociology Online
http://edu.learnsoc.org

Sociosite
http://www.topsite.com/goto/sociosite.net

Socioweb
http://www.topsite.com/goto/socioweb.com

The American Studies Web
http://lamp.georgetown.edu/asw

© 2014 The Atlantic Media Co., as first published in The Atlantic Magazine. All rights reserved. Distributed by Tribune Content Agency, LLC.

Unit 2

UNIT

Prepared by: Kurt Finsterbusch, *University of Maryland, College Park*

Problems of the Political Economy

Since the political system and the economy interpenetrate each other to a high degree, it is now common to study them together under the label political economy. The political economy is the most basic aspect of society, and it should be studied first. The way it functions affects how problems in other areas can or cannot be addressed. Here, we encounter issues of power, control, and influence. It is in this arena that society acts corporately to address the problems that are of public concern. It is important, therefore, to ascertain the degree to which the economic elite control the political system. The answer determines how democratic America is. Next, we want to know how effective the American political economy is. Can government agencies be effective? Can government regulations be effective? Can the economy be effective? Can the economy make everyone, and not just the owners and top administrators, prosper and be happy?

The first section of this unit covers the political system. The most basic issue is the extent that the economic elite and major corporations control the government. If their control is tight, then democracy is a sham. The following section includes topics such as the degree that the governing institutions can provide for the common good, the question of whether American organizations and institutions have gotten so big that they have become unaccountable, and what should be done about the welfare system. The next section deals with the type of capitalism that is dominate today, the devolution of the relations between capitalism and labor, and the general conditions of the working class. The final section covers urbanism and immigration policy.

Article   Prepared by: Kurt Finsterbusch, *University of Maryland, College Park*

The Rule of the Rich

BILL MOYERS

Learning Outcomes

After reading this article, you will be able to:

- Understand the considerable influence that the rich have over the US political system.

- Identify the many mechanisms utilized by the rich to influence the government.

- Try to discern what is necessary to counter the influence of the rich.

Howard Zinn helped us see how big change can start with small acts. He championed grassroots social change and famously chronicled its story as played out over the course of our nation's history. More, those stirring sagas have inspired and continue to inspire countless people to go out and make a difference. The last time we met, I told him that the stories in *A People's History of the United States* remind me of the fellow who turned the corner just as a big fight broke out down the block. Rushing up to an onlooker he shouted, "Is this a private fight, or can anyone get in it?" For Howard, democracy was one big public fight and everyone should plunge into it. That's the only way, he said, for everyday folks to get justice—by fighting for it.

So let's begin with some everyday folks.

When she heard the news, Connie Brasel cried like a baby. For years she had worked at minimum-wage jobs, until 17 years ago, when she was hired by the Whirlpool refrigerator factory in Evansville, Indiana. She was making $18.44 an hour when Whirlpool announced in early 2010 that it was closing the operation and moving it to Mexico. She wept. I'm sure many of the other 1,100 workers who lost their jobs wept, too; they had seen their ticket to the middle class snatched from their hands. The company defended its decision by claiming high costs, underused capacity, and the need to stay competitive. Those excuses didn't console Connie

Brasel. "I was becoming part of something bigger than me," she told Steven Greenhouse of *The New York Times*. "Whirlpool was the best thing that ever happened to me."

She was not only sad, she was mad. "They didn't get world-class quality because they had the best managers. They got world-class quality because of the United States and because of their workers."

Among those workers were Natalie Ford, her husband, and her son; all three lost their jobs. "It's devastating," she told the *Times*. Her father had worked at Whirlpool before them. Now "there aren't any jobs here. How is this community going to survive?"

And what about the country? Between 2001 and 2008, about 40,000 US manufacturing plants closed. Six million factory jobs have disappeared over the past dozen years, representing one in three manufacturing jobs. Natalie Ford said to the *Times* what many of us are wondering: "I don't know how without any good-paying jobs here in the United States people are going to pay for their health care, put their children through school."

In polite circles, among our political and financial classes, this is known as "the free market at work." No, it's "wage repression," and it's been happening in our country since around 1980. Economists Thomas Piketty and Emmanuel Saez have found that from 1950 through 1980, the share of all income in America going to everyone but the rich increased from 64 percent to 65 percent. Because the nation's economy was growing handsomely, the average income for 9 out of 10 Americans was growing, too: from $17,719 to $30,941. That's a 75 percent increase in income in constant 2008 dollars. But then it stopped. Since 1980 the economy has also continued to grow handsomely, but only a fraction at the top have benefitted. The line flattens for the bottom 90 percent of Americans. Average income went from that $30,941 in 1980 to $31,244 in 2008. Think about that: the average income of Americans increased just $303 in 28 years.

Another story in the *Times* caught my eye a few weeks after the one about Connie Brasel and Natalie Ford. The headline read: "Industries Find Surging Profits in Deeper Cuts." Nelson Schwartz reported that despite falling motorcycle sales, Harley-Davidson profits are soaring—with a second quarter profit of $71 million, more than triple what it earned the previous year. Yet Harley-Davidson has announced plans to cut 1,400 to 1,600 more jobs by the end of 2011—this on top of the 2,000 jobs cut in 2009.

The story noted: "This seeming contradiction—falling sales and rising profits—is one reason the mood on Wall Street is so much more buoyant than in households, where pessimism runs deep and unemployment shows few signs of easing."

There you see the two Americas: a buoyant Wall Street and a doleful Main Street. The Connie Brasels and Natalie Fords—left to sink or swim on their own. There were no bailouts for them.

Or, as the chief economist at Bank of America Merrill Lynch, Ethan Harris, told the *Times*: "There's no question that there is an income shift going on in the economy. Companies are squeezing their labor costs to build profits."

Yes, Virginia, there is a Santa Claus. But he's run off with all the toys.

L ate in August, I clipped another story from *The Wall Street Journal*. Above an op-ed piece by Robert Frank the headline asked: "Do the Rich Need the Rest of America?" The author didn't seem ambivalent about the answer. He wrote that as stocks have boomed, "the wealthy bounced back. And while the Main Street economy" [where the Connie Brasels and Natalie Fords and most Americans live] "was wracked by high unemployment and the real-estate crash, the wealthy—whose financial fates were more tied to capital markets than jobs and houses—picked themselves up, brushed themselves off, and started buying luxury goods again."

Citing the work of Michael Lind at the Economic Growth Program of the New America Foundation, the article went on to describe how the super-rich earn their fortunes with overseas labor, selling to overseas consumers, and managing financial transactions that have little to do with the rest of America, "while relying entirely or almost entirely on immigrant servants at one of several homes around the country."

So the answer to the question "Do the Rich Need the Rest of America?" is as stark as it is ominous: Many don't. As they form their own financial culture increasingly separated from the fate of everyone else, it is "hardly surprising," Frank and Lind concluded, "that so many of them should be so hostile to paying taxes to support the infrastructure and the social programs that help the majority of the American people."

W hen Howard came down to New York last December for what would be my last interview with him, I showed him this document published in the spring of 2005 by the Wall Street giant Citigroup, setting forth an "Equity Strategy" under the title (I'm not making this up) "Revisiting Plutonomy: The Rich Getting Richer."

Now, most people know what plutocracy is: the rule of the rich, political power controlled by the wealthy. Plutocracy is not an American word and wasn't meant to become an American phenomenon—some of our founders deplored what they called "the veneration of wealth." But plutocracy is here, and a pumped up Citigroup even boasted of coining a variation on the word—"plutonomy," which describes an economic system where the privileged few make sure the rich get richer and that government helps them do it. Five years ago, Citigroup decided the time had come to "bang the drum on plutonomy."

And bang they did. Here are some excerpts from the document "Revisiting Plutonomy":

"Asset booms, a rising profit share, and favorable treatment by market-friendly governments have allowed the rich to prosper . . . [and] take an increasing share of income and wealth over the last 20 years. . . . The top 10 percent, particularly the top 1 percent of the United States—the plutonomists in our parlance—have benefited disproportionately from the recent productivity surge in the U.S. . . . [and] from globalization and the productivity boom, at the relative expense of labor. . . . [And they] are likely to get even wealthier in the coming years. Because the dynamics of plutonomy are still intact."

I'll repeat that: *"The dynamics of plutonomy are still intact."*

That was the case before the Great Collapse of 2008, and it's the case today, two years after the catastrophe. But the plutonomists are doing just fine. Even better in some cases, thanks to our bailout of the big banks. (To see just how our system was rigged by the financial, political, and university elites, run, don't walk, to the theater nearest you showing Charles Ferguson's new film, *Inside Job*. Take a handkerchief because you'll weep for the republic.)

As for the rest of the country, listen to this summary in *The Economist*—no Marxist journal—of a study by Pew Research: "More than half of all workers today have experienced a spell of unemployment, taken a cut in pay or hours or been forced to go part-time. . . . Fewer than half of all adults expect their children to have a higher standard of living than theirs, and more than a quarter say it will be lower. For many Americans, the Great Recession has been the sharpest trauma since the Second World War, wiping out jobs, wealth, and hope itself."

Let that sink in: For millions of garden-variety Americans, the audacity of hope has been replaced by a paucity of hope.

Time for a confession. The legendary correspondent Edward R. Murrow told his generation of journalists that bias is OK as long as you don't try to hide it. Here is mine: Plutocracy and democracy don't mix. Plutocracy too long tolerated leaves democracy on the auction block, subject to the highest bidder.

Socrates said to understand a thing, you must first name it. The name for what's happening to our political system is corruption: a deep, systemic corruption. The former editor of *Harper's,* Roger D. Hodge, brilliantly dissects how democracy has gone on sale in America. Today, he says, voters still "matter," but only as raw material to be shaped by the actual form of political influence—money. Hodge's new book, *The Mendacity of Hope,* describes how America's founding generation especially feared the kind of corruption that occurs when the private ends of a narrow faction succeed in capturing the engines of government. James Madison and many of his contemporaries knew this kind of corruption could consume the republic. So they attempted to erect safeguards against it, hoping to prevent private and narrow personal interests from overriding those of the general public.

They failed. Hardly a century passed after the ringing propositions of 1776 before America was engulfed in the gross materialism and political corruption of the First Gilded Age, when Big Money bought the government right out from under the voters. In their magisterial work, *The Growth of the American Republic,* the historians Morison, Commager, and Leuchtenburg describe how in that era "privilege controlled politics," and "the purchase of votes, the corruption of election officials, the bribing of legislatures, the lobbying of special bills, and the flagrant disregard of laws" threatened the very foundations of the country.

As one of the plutocrats crowed: "We are rich. We own America. We got it, God knows how, but we intend to keep it."

And they have never given up. The Gilded Age returned with a vengeance in our time. It slipped in quietly at first, back in the early 1980s, when Ronald Reagan began a "massive decades-long transfer of national wealth to the rich."

As Roger Hodge makes clear, under Bill Clinton the transfer was even more dramatic, as the top 10 percent captured an ever-growing share of national income.

The trend continued under George W. Bush—those huge tax cuts for the rich, remember, which are now about to be extended because both parties have been bought off by the wealthy—and by 2007 the wealthiest 10 percent of Americans were taking in 50 percent of the national income.

Today, a fraction of people at the top earns more than the bottom 120 million Americans.

People say, "Come on, this is the way the world works." No, it's the way the world is *made* to work.

This vast inequality is not the result of Adam Smith's invisible hand; it did not just happen; it was no accident.

As Hodge drives home, it is the result of a long series of policy decisions "about industry and trade, taxation and military spending, by flesh-and-blood humans sitting in concrete-and-steel buildings." And those policy decisions were paid for by the less than 1 percent who participate in our capitalist democracy by making political contributions.

Over the past 30 years, with the complicity of Republicans and Democrats alike, the plutocrats (or plutonomists, as Citigroup calls them) have used their vastly increased wealth to assure that government does their bidding. Looking back, it all seems so clear that it's amazing that we could have ignored the warning signs at the time.

Yet here we are at a moment, says the new chairman of Common Cause and former Labor Secretary Robert Reich, that "threatens American democracy: an unprecedented concentration of income and wealth at the top; a record amount of secret money flooding our democracy; and a public becoming increasingly angry and cynical about a government that's raising its taxes, reducing its services, and unable to get it back to work." We are losing our democracy, Reich says, to an entirely different system, one where political power derives from wealth.

Its ratification came in January 2010, when the five reactionary members of the Supreme Court ruled that corporations are "persons" with the right to speak during elections by funding ads like those now flooding the airwaves. It was the work of legal fabulists. Corporations are not people; they are legal fictions, creatures of the state, born not of the womb, not of flesh and blood. They're not permitted to vote. They don't bear arms (except for the nuclear bombs they can now drop on a Congressional race without anyone knowing where it came from). Yet thanks to five activist conservative judges, they have the privilege of "personhood" to "speak"—and not in their own voice, mind you, but as ventriloquists, through hired puppets.

Our government has been bought off. Welcome to the plutocracy.

Obviously, Howard Zinn would not have us leave it there. Defeat was never his counsel. Look at this headline from one of his articles he published in *The Progressive* prior to *Citizens United*: "It's Not Up to the Supreme Court." The Court was lost long ago, he said. Don't go there looking for justice: "The Constitution gave no rights to working people; no right to work less than 12 hours a day, no right to a living wage, no right to safe working conditions. Workers had to organize, go on strike, defy the law, the courts, the police, create a great movement which won the eight-hour day, and caused such commotion that Congress was forced to pass a minimum wage law, and Social Security, and unemployment insurance. . . . Those rights only come alive when citizens organize, protest, demonstrate, strike, boycott, rebel, and violate the law in order to uphold justice."

So what are we to do about Big Money in politics buying off democracy?

I can almost hear him throwing that question back at us: "What are we to do? ORGANIZE! Yes, organize—and don't count the costs."

Some people already are mobilizing. There's a rumbling in the land. All across the spectrum, people oppose the escalating power of money in politics. Fed-up Democrats. Disillusioned Republicans. Independents. Greens. Even tea partiers, once they wake up to realize they have been sucker-punched by their bankrollers who have no intention of sharing the wealth.

Veteran public interest groups like Common Cause and Public Citizen are aroused. There are the rising voices, from web-based initiatives such as freespeechforpeople.org to grassroots initiatives such as Democracy Matters on campuses across the country. Moveon.org is looking for a million people to fight back in a many-pronged strategy to counter the Supreme Court decision.

In taking on Big Money, we're talking about something more than a single issue. We're talking about a broad-based coalition to restore American democracy—one that is trying to be smart about the nuts-and-bolts of building a coalition, remembering that it has a lot to do with human nature.

Some will want to march.

Some will want to petition.

Some will want to engage through the web.

Some will want to go door-to-door: many gifts, but the same spirit. A fighting spirit.

As Howard Zinn would tell us: No fight, no fun, and no results.

Let's be clear: Even with most Americans on our side, the odds are long. We learned long ago that power and privilege never give up anything without a struggle. Money fights hard, and it fights dirty. Think Karl Rove, the Chamber of Commerce, the Brothers Koch. And we may lose.

But hear out Baldemar Velasquez on this. He and his Farm Labor Organizing Committee took on the Campbell Soup Company—and won. They took on North Carolina growers—and won. And now they're taking on no less than R. J. Reynolds Tobacco and one of its principal financial sponsors, JPMorgan Chase.

"It's OK if it's impossible," Velasquez says. "It's OK! The object is not to win. The object is to do the right and good thing. If you decide not to do anything, because it's too hard or too impossible, then nothing will be done, and when you're on your deathbed, you're going to say, 'I wish I had done something.' But if you go and do the right thing NOW, and you do it long enough, good things will happen."

Shades of Howard Zinn!

Critical Thinking

1. The rich have great influence in all societies. What is Bill Moyers saying about the influence of the US rich that is beyond normal?
2. What specific government actions or nonactions have the rich achieved?
3. Is this a story of corruption?

Create Central

www.mhhe.com/createcentral

Internet References

National Center for Policy Analysis
   www.ncpa.org
Social Science Information Gateway
   http://sosig.esrc.bris.ac.uk
Sociology—Study Sociology Online
   http://edu.learnsoc.org
Sociology Web Resources
   http://www.mhhe.com/socscience/sociology/resources/index.htm
Sociosite
   http://www.topsite.com/goto/sociosite.net
Socioweb
   http://www.topsite.com/goto/socioweb.com

BILL MOYERS is the veteran PBS broadcaster. This article is adapted from remarks he made on October 29, 2010, at Boston University as he inaugurated the Howard Zinn Lecture Series.

Reprinted by permission from *The Progressive*, February 2011, pp. 20–23. Copyright © 2011 by The Progressive, 409 E Main St, Madison, WI 53703. www.progressive.org

Article

Prepared by: Kurt Finsterbusch, *University of Maryland, College Park*

Finding the Common Good in an Era of Dysfunctional Governance

Thomas E. Mann and Norman J. Ornstein

Learning Outcomes

After reading this article, you will be able to:

- Understand the role of the government according to the Constitution.

- Be able to compare what the Constitution says about the role of government and the present state of affairs.

From Federalist No. 1 on, the framers of the American political system showed a deep concern about the role of government as a trustee of the people, grappling with questions about the power, structural stability, and credibility of government. In that first Federalist paper, Alexander Hamilton defended a vigorous role for government: "[It] will be equally forgotten that the vigor of government is essential to the security of liberty; that, in the contemplation of a sound and well-informed judgment, their interests can never be separated; and that a dangerous ambition more often lurks behind the specious mask of zeal for the rights of the people than under the forbidding appearance of zeal for the firmness and efficiency of government."[1]

In Federalist No. 46, James Madison wrote, "The federal and state governments are in fact but different agents and trustees of the people, constituted with different powers and designed for different purposes."[2] And in Federalist No. 62, Madison, outlining and defending the special role of the Senate, reflected at length on the need for stable government and the danger of mutable policy: "[G]reat injury results from an unstable government. The want of confidence in the public councils damps every useful undertaking, the success and profit of which may depend on a continuance of existing arrangements."[3]

Stable government, to Madison, included an underlying and enduring legitimacy in the legislative process. This meant both a disciplined government that did not spew out a plethora of unnecessary and careless laws, and a government that did not produce contradictory laws or reversals of laws so frequently that citizens questioned the content and legitimacy of the standing policies affecting their lives. Madison wrote in Federalist No. 62 of mutable policy: "It will be of little avail to the people, that the laws are made by men of their own choice, if the laws be so voluminous that they cannot be read, or so incoherent that they cannot be understood; if they be repealed or revised before they are promulgated, or undergo such incessant changes that no man, who knows what the law is today, can guess what it will be tomorrow."[4]

Madison ended Federalist No. 62 with a warning that resonates today: "But the most deplorable effect of all is that diminution of attachment and reverence which steals into the hearts of the people, toward a political system which betrays so many marks of infirmity, and disappoints so many of their flattering hopes. No government, any more than an individual, will long be respected without being truly respectable; nor be truly respectable without possessing a certain portion of order and stability."[5]

The actions and functions of government, a vibrant political process and system, were thus essential for the common good of a society. The framers saw several challenges peculiar to the new American country. It was, as they wrote, an "extended republic," a huge geographic expanse and a society containing dramatically diverse populations, including people living in rural areas so remote that they literally might not see other human beings for months, and others living in urban areas far more densely packed than today's Manhattan. How could the new government build consensus and legitimacy around policies that would affect all citizens, in light of their different interests, lifestyles, and backgrounds? The demands of the American political system differed from those in Britain, a much smaller and far more homogeneous culture and society. Instead of a parliamentary system, the framers carefully constructed a system that would be practicable and desirable for their nation, built around the following elements:

Debate and deliberation. The legislative branch was called Congress—not parliament. This was not simply a different word, but reflective of a different approach to governance. The word *congress* comes from the Latin word *congredi,* meaning to come together; *parliament* comes from the French word *parler,* meaning to talk. In a parliament, the legislators vote on a program devised by the government; the majority members reflexively vote for it, the minority members reflexively vote against. Citizens accept the legitimacy of the actions, even if they do not like them, because within four or five years, they have the opportunity to hold the government accountable at the polls. The minority expresses its power by publicly questioning government actions and intentions during regular periods of "Question Time."

In contrast, the American framers wanted a system in which representatives of citizens from disparate regions would come together and meet face to face, going through extended periods of debate and deliberation across factional and partisan lines. This model would enable the representatives to understand each other's viewpoints and ultimately reach some form of consensus in policy-making. Those who lost out in the deliberative process would be satisfied that they had been given ample time to make their case, adding to the likelihood that they would accept the legitimacy of the decisions made, and communicate that acceptance back to their constituents. Of course, in contrast to a parliament, it was a process that made swift action extremely difficult. But the trade-off was that government power would be constrained and that Americans would be more likely to accept the decisions and implement them fairly and smoothly.

Debate and deliberation could not be limited to governmental actors. For the system to work and be perceived as legitimate, there had to be debate and deliberation among citizens, via local and national "public squares," and in campaigns, where candidates and their partisans could press their cases and voters could weigh the viewpoints and preferences of their alternatives for representation.

Divided powers competing with one another. America's unusual system of the separation of powers did not offer a clean and pure division between the executive, legislative, and judicial branches, nor between the House of Representatives and Senate. Instead, as constitutional scholar Edward Corwin put it, it was an "invitation to struggle" among the branches and chambers. But that invitation to struggle, which anticipated vibrant, assertive, and proud branches, also was infused with *the spirit of compromise,* as eloquently analyzed by Amy Gutmann and Dennis Thompson in this volume and in their recent book on the subject.[6] A political system with separation of powers and separate elections for House, Senate, and president could easily have institutions at loggerheads. The system, and the culture supporting it, required safeguards to enable the government to act when necessary and desirable, without getting caught in stalemate or gridlock.

Regular order. To make the processes work and to foster legitimacy, legislative, and executive procedures had to be regularized and followed. This would in turn enable real debate by all lawmakers, opportunity for amendments, openness and reasonable transparency, and some measure of timeliness. Executive actions, including crafting and implementing regulations to carry out policy, would also require elements of transparency, responsiveness to public concerns, and articulated purpose. Similarly, judicial actions would have to allow for fairness, access to legal representation, opportunities for appeal, and a parallel lack of arbitrariness.

Avenues to limit and punish corruption. Public confidence in the actions of government—a sense that the processes and decisions reflect fairness and enhance the common good—demands that the cancer of corruption be avoided or at least constrained. If small groups of special interests or wealthy individuals can skew decisions in their favor, it will breed cynicism and destroy governmental legitimacy. Thus, it is necessary to find ways to constrain the role of money in campaigns, to build transparency around campaign finance and lobbying, to discourage "old boy networks" and revolving doors, to investigate and prosecute bribery, and to impeach and remove government officials who commit high crimes and misdemeanors, which include corrupt behavior.

On all these fronts, there is ample reason to be concerned about the health and function of America's current political institutions. Of course, no political system operates exactly as intended. Politics and policy-making are inherently messy, occurring at the intersection of power, money, and ambition, and leading to temptations and imperfections. We have been immersed in these processes in Washington for more than 43 years, and we have observed frequent governmental failures, deep tensions, and challenges to the political system—from profound societal divisions over wars like Vietnam to the impeachment proceedings against two presidents. But those challenges were modest compared to what we see today: a level of political dysfunction clearly greater than at any point in our lifetimes.

Fundamentally, the problem stems from a mismatch between America's political parties and its constitutional system. For a variety of reasons, all recounted in our book *It's Even Worse Than It Looks: How the American Constitutional System Collided With the New Politics of Extremism,* the two major political parties in recent decades have become increasingly homogeneous and have moved toward ideological poles.[7] Combined with the phenomenon of the permanent campaign, whereby political actors focus relentlessly on election concerns and not on problem-solving, the parties now behave more like parliamentary parties than traditional, big-tent, and pragmatic American parties.

Parliamentary parties are oppositional and vehemently adversarial, a formula that cannot easily work in the American political system. The parliamentary mindset has been particularly striking in recent years with the Republican Party, which has become, in its legislative incarnation especially, a radical insurgent, dismissive of the legitimacy of its political opposition. Of course, substantial majorities in the House and Senate, along with the presidency, can give a majority party the opportunity to behave like a parliamentary majority. But that phenomenon, which occurred for Democrats in the first two years of the Obama administration, resulted in major policy enactments but not a smoothly functioning political system. It featured neither a widespread sense of legitimacy nor deep public satisfaction.

Why? The processes of debate and deliberation were disrupted first by the Republicans' unprecedented use of the filibuster and the threat of filibuster as purely obstructionist tools. This deluge was designed to use precious floor time without any serious discussion of the reasons behind the filibusters, or any real debate on differences in philosophy or policy. Second, when Democrats were able to pass legislation, it was against the united and acrimonious opposition of the minority. America's political culture does not easily accept the legitimacy of policies enacted by one party over the opposition of the other— much less the continued, bitter unwillingness of the minority party to accept the need to implement the policies after lawful enactment. But this dynamic, which accompanied the economic stimulus package in 2009, the health care reform law of 2010, and the financial regulation bill in 2010, among others, resulted in greater divisions and public cynicism, not less.

The approach of the minority party for the first two years of the Obama administration was antithetical to the ethos of compromise to solve pressing national problems. The American Recovery and Reinvestment Act of 2009, a plan which included $288 billion in tax relief, garnered not one vote from Republicans in the House. The Affordable Care Act, essentially a carbon copy of the Republican alternative to the Clinton administration's health reform plan in 1994, was uniformly opposed by Republican partisans in both houses. A bipartisan plan to create a meaningful, congressionally mandated commission to deal with the nation's debt problem, the Gregg/Conrad plan, was killed on a filibuster in the Senate; once President Obama endorsed the plan, seven original Republican co-sponsors, along with Senate Republican Leader Mitch McConnell, joined the filibuster to kill it. McConnell's widely reported comment that his primary goal was to make Barack Obama a one-term president—a classic case of the permanent campaign trumping problem-solving—typified the political dynamic.

The succeeding midterm election brought a backlash against the status quo—which meant divided government once Republicans captured a majority in the House of Representatives. As a result, the 112th Congress had the least productive set of sessions in our lifetimes, enacting fewer than 250 laws, more than 40 of which were concerned with naming post offices or other commemoratives.[8] The major "accomplishment" of the 112th Congress was the debt limit debacle, which marked the first time the debt limit had been used as a hostage to make other political demands. The result was not just the first ever downgrade in America's credit, but another blow to the public's assessment of its government's capacity to act on behalf of the common good.

The 2012 elections were in most respects a clear expression of public will. President Obama earned reelection with a majority of popular votes, as did Democrats in elections for the House and in the 33 contests for the Senate. But in the House, a concentration of Democratic voters in high-density urban areas, contributing to a more efficient allocation of Republican voters across congressional districts, and a successful partisan gerrymander in the redistricting process left Republicans with a majority of seats, and hence control. Despite the election, the dysfunction in the policy process continued in the succeeding lame duck session of Congress, as efforts to resolve America's fiscal problems before a January 1, 2013, deadline were thwarted until after the deadline had passed. House Speaker John Boehner was himself undermined by members of his own party when he tried to devise an alternative to the president's plan. In this case, a substantial share of safe House Republican seats were immune to broader public opinion and to their own Speaker, but were more sensitive to threats from well-financed challenges in their next primaries—from the Club for Growth and other ideological organizations—and to incendiary comments from radio talk show hosts and cable television commentators popular among Republican voters in their districts.

Tribal politics and vehement adversarialism has also led to deterioration of the regular order. In recent years, there have been more and more closed rules in the House, denying opportunities for amendments from the minority, and more uses of a majority tactic in the Senate called "filling the amendment tree," in which the majority leader precludes amendments, usually as a way to forestall or limit the impact of filibusters.

There have been more omnibus bills, pooling action across areas because of the increased difficulty in getting legislation enacted; and fewer real conference committees to iron out differences between bills passed by each house of Congress. There have been fewer budget resolutions adopted and appropriations bills passed; fewer authorizations of programs and agencies; and less oversight of executive action. Fewer treaties have gained the two-thirds vote needed for ratification in the Senate, leading to more executive actions. There have been more holds and delays in the Senate in executive nominations. All of these pathologies lead to more acrimony inside Congress and between Congress and the executive, and a diminished sense of confidence by Americans in their political and policy institutions.

At the same time, the administration of elections has been politicized. Partisan legislatures have passed stringent voter ID laws to narrow the vote; several of these laws have been thrown out by courts for targeting or unfairly affecting minorities. In other cases, shortened voting hours and restrictions on early voting, in states such as Florida and Ohio, were also aimed at constraining minority voters. Fortunately, the 2012 election was not close; had it been more like the 2000 election, it is very likely that it would have further reduced public trust in the fundamentals of democratic elections.

The world of money and politics has also taken an alarming turn toward at least the appearance of corruption, of democracy driven by big money and large interests. A combination of factors—the Supreme Court's *Citizens United* decision, an appeals court decision called *SpeechNow,* a Federal Election Commission that is unable or unwilling to enforce campaign finance laws, and an Internal Revenue Service that allows the operation of faux social-welfare organizations set up to influence elections but not required to disclose donors—has given wealthy individuals, corporations, and other entities an overweening influence on elections and on the policy process. If super PACs did not determine the outcome of the presidential election, their impact did expand as one moved down through Senate and House elections and on to state, local, and judicial elections. In states like Kansas, North Carolina, and Arkansas, large donations from a handful of individuals and groups targeted moderate Republicans and replaced them with reactionary conservatives, creating more division and polarization, not to mention politicians beholden to those whose money put them in power.

Organizations such as the American Legislative Exchange Council (ALEC) have used large and often anonymous contributions from corporations and individuals to write laws, including the voter ID laws and laws favoring the corporate sector, that many state legislatures have simply enacted as written, obviating their independent role. And inside Congress, many lawmakers have told us about the intimidating effect that occurs when a lobbyist tells them that if they do not support a bill or amendment, they might face a multimillion dollar independent attack days or weeks before the election, which they will be unable to counter due to a lack of time or fundraising limitations. Such threats can result in the passage of bills or amendments without any money even being spent. By any reasonable standard, this is corruption.

All of this exhibits a level of dysfunction in American political institutions and processes that is dangerous to the fundamental legitimacy of decisions made by policy-makers, not to mention the ability of those policy-makers to act at all. Tribal politics at the national level has metastasized to many states and localities, and has affected the broader public as well. The glue that binds Americans together is in danger of eroding. What can be done about these problems?

There is no easy answer, no panacea. The problems are as much cultural as structural. But if structural change inside and outside Washington cannot solve the problems, it can ameliorate them, and perhaps also begin to change the culture.

One strategy for structural change is to accept the emergence of parliamentary-style polarized parties and try to adapt our political institutions to operate more effectively in that context. This is easier said than done. Eliminating or constraining the Senate filibuster would give unified party governments a better shot at putting their campaign promises into law.[9] But separate elections for the presidency and Congress, as well as the midterm congressional elections, often conspire to produce divided party government, which has become more a basis of parliamentary opposition and obstruction than consensus-building and compromise. Shifting more power to the presidency, which is already under way, may produce more timely and coherent policies but at a considerable cost to deliberation, representation, and democratic accountability. A president is, of course, elected by the entire nation. Especially on national security issues, Americans are willing to tolerate and even embrace many unilateral presidential actions; think Grenada and Abbottabad. But America's political culture has ingrained in the public a sense that legitimate policies more often call for some form of broad leadership consensus and institutional buy-in. A series of unilateral actions by the president would not necessarily result in public acceptance of the decisions as being made for the common good. The same can be said for other forms of delegation, from Congress to fed-like independent agencies, or boards that encourage more expert and evidence-based decision-making that is at least somewhat removed from the clash of polarized parties. Each of these ideas has some limited promise, but none can be the basis of constructively reconciling a fundamental mismatch between parliamentary-like political parties and the American constitutional system.

Another approach emphasizes trying to bring the warring parties together: by reaching for consensus through increased social interaction (the House experiment with civility retreats); encouragement of or pressure on politicians to come together to make a deal (Fix the Debt); the mobilization of centrists in the citizenry to create political space for more collegial and collaborative policy-making (No Labels); the use of outside bipartisan groups to map policy solutions that split the differences between the polarized parties (Committee for a Responsible Federal Budget); and the support of independent presidential candidates or third parties to lay claim to the allegedly abandoned political "center" (Americans Elect). These efforts by and large seek to create a spirit of compromise, an atmosphere of civility and mutual respect, and a focus on problem-solving—outcomes which are indeed commendable.

But we believe that these well-intentioned efforts are limited by the strength and reach of party polarization, which is buttressed not only by genuine ideological differences among elected officials, but also by like-minded citizens clustered in safe districts, committed activists, a partisan media, a tribal culture, interest groups increasingly segregated by party, a party-based campaign funding system that now encompasses allegedly independent groups, and a degree of parity in party strength that turns legislating into strategic political campaigning. Most of these efforts also suffer from an unwillingness to acknowledge the striking asymmetry between today's political parties, which in the process gives a pass to obstructionist and dysfunctional behavior.

A more promising strategy of reform is to bring the Republican Party back into the mainstream of American politics and policy as the conservative, not radical, force. Ultimately, this is the responsibility of the citizenry. Nothing is as persuasive to a wayward party as a clear message from the voters. The 2012 election results and the widespread speculation of the diminishing prospects of the Republican coalition in presidential elections may be the start of that process. But it can be boosted and accelerated by the groups discussed above speaking clearly and forthrightly about the damage caused to constructive public policy by tax pledges, debt limit hostage-taking, the abuse of the filibuster, climate change denial, the demonization of government, and ideological zealotry. The mainstream press could also do its part by shedding its convention of balancing the conflicting arguments between the two parties at the cost of obscuring the reality. Voters cannot do their job holding parties and representatives accountable if they do not have the necessary information. Some in the media think it is biased or unprofessional to discuss the many manifestations of our asymmetric polarization. We think it is simply a matter of collecting the evidence and telling the truth.

More significant, for both parties, would be to enlarge the electorate to dilute the overweening influence of narrow, ideologically driven partisan bases that dominate party primaries. As a result, these bases have an outsized role in choosing candidates, who often do not reflect the views of their broader constituencies; and as a means of heading off primary challenges, the bases can intimidate lawmakers searching for compromise or a common good into moving away from solutions. Meanwhile, the enlarged influence of party bases pushes campaign operatives and candidates away from broader appeals and toward strategies to turn out one's own base (often by scaring them to death), and to suppress the other side's base. The politics of division trump the politics of unity.

To counter this set of problems, we propose adoption of the Australian system of mandatory attendance at the polls, where voters who do not show up (they do not have to vote for specific candidates, but can cast unmarked ballots) and do not have a written excuse are subject to modest fines, the equivalent of a parking ticket. This system moved Australian turnout from around 55 percent, similar to the United States, to over 90 percent.[10] Most important, it changed Australian campaign discourse. Politicians of all stripes have told us that when they know that their own base will turn out en masse, and will be balanced by the other party's base, they shift their efforts to persuading voters in the middle. That means talking less about wedge issues, like abortion or guns, and more about larger issues like education and jobs; and it means using less of the fiery or divisive rhetoric that excites base voters but turns off those in the middle.

Another option is to expand the use of open primaries and combine them with preference voting. Several states, including California, now use open primaries, in which all candidates from all sides run together; the top two finishers go on the ballot for the general election. Add in preference voting, whereby voters rank their choices in order of preference (something also done in Australia), and it reduces the chances of an extreme candidate winning a top-two finish because multiple nonextreme candidates divide the votes of the more populous, moderate electorate. Another advantage of an open primary is that lawmakers who cast contentious votes would be less intimidated by threats of a primary challenge funded by ideological organizations if they knew the primary electorate would be expanded beyond a small fringe base. If we could combine these changes with redistricting reform, using impartial citizen commissions to draw district lines as we have seen operate in states like Iowa and California, we might get somewhere.

Of course, the enhanced leverage that smaller groups possess over the sentiments of the larger populace has other roots, including especially the post—*Citizens United* campaign finance world. When groups like the Club for Growth, wealthy individuals, or "social welfare" organizations funded by anonymous sources threaten lawmakers with massive negative campaigns sprung in the final weeks of the election season, or threaten to finance primary opponents against them, it gives immense leverage to the well-heeled few against the viewpoints of the many. Absent a new Supreme Court, a multiple public match for contributions from small donors would give additional leverage to the broader population.

The pull toward tribal politics and away from a focus on the common good has also been shaped by the emergence of tribal media, via cable television and talk radio. The tribal media have established lucrative business models built on apocalyptic rhetoric and divisive messages that guarantee regular audiences within select demographics. These business models have emerged in large part because of the dramatic technological changes that have created hundreds or thousands of alternative information outlets, which are amplified by the emergence of social media. All of this has devastated the concept of a public square, where most Americans could get their information, share a common set of facts, and debate vigorously what to do about common problems. Having real debate and deliberation at the public level, much less the governmental level, depends on sharing a common set of facts and assumptions.

Recreating a public square is a Herculean task given the contemporary media and technology landscape. But it must be attempted. Public media would be the best venue; finding a way to fund a public/private foundation that would focus on innovative ways to use public media for straightforward analysis and discourse, including vigorous debate based on common understanding of the facts, should be a priority here. One way to do so would be to apply a rental fee to broadcasters and others for their use of the public airwaves, in return for erasure of the public-interest requirements that now have little impact.[11]

Most of these changes will be hard to implement in the short run. The best we can hope for is a more tempered Republican Party willing to do business (that is, deliberate, negotiate, and compromise without hostage-taking or brinksmanship) with their Democratic counterparts. Over the long haul, both political parties in the United States need to depolarize to some degree. The parties may maintain clear differences in philosophy and policy, to be sure, but they must also cultivate enough agreement on major issues to permit the government to work as designed. The parties must also serve an electorate that shares a common vision and common facts, even with sharp differences in philosophy, lifestyles, and backgrounds. Despite the obstacles, we must think big about changing the structures and the culture of our partisan government and populace; the stakes are high.

Notes

1. Alexander Hamilton, "Federalist No. 1," *The Federalist Papers,* http://thomas.loc.gov/home/histdox/fed_01.html.

2. James Madison, "Federalist No. 46," *The Federalist Papers,* http://thomas.loc.gov/home/histdox/fed_46.html.

3. James Madison, "Federalist No. 62," *The Federalist Papers,* http://thomas.loc.gov/home/histdox/fed_62.html.

4. Ibid.

5. Ibid.

6. See Amy Gutmann and Dennis Thompson, *The Spirit of Compromise: Why Governing Demands It and Campaigning Undermines It* (Princeton, N.J.: Princeton University Press, 2012).

7. See Thomas E. Mann and Norman J. Ornstein, *It's Even Worse Than It Looks: How the American Constitutional System Collided With the New Politics of Extremism* (New York: Basic Books, 2012).

8. Amanda Terkel, "112th Congress Set To Become Most Unproductive Since 1940s," *The Huffington Post,* December 28, 2012, http://www.huffingtonpost.com/2012/12/28/congress-unproductive_n_2371387.html.

9. For more on this topic, see Norman J. Ornstein, "A Filibuster Fix," *The New York Times,* August 27, 2010, http://www.aei.org/article/politics-and-public-opinion/legislative/afilibuster-fix/.

10. Australian Electoral Commission, "Who Voted in Previous Referendums and Elections," October 26, 2012, http://www.aec.gov.au/Elections/Australian_Electoral_History/Voter_Turnout.htm. Compulsory voting was implemented in Australia in 1924.

11. For in-depth discussion of the recreation of a public square, see Norman J. Ornstein with John C. Fortier and Jennifer Marsico, "Creating a Public Square in a Challenging Media Age: A White Paper on the Knight Commission Report on *Informing Communities: Sustaining Democracy in the Digital Age*," American Enterprise Institute White Paper, June 23, 2011, http://www.knightcomm.org/wp-content/uploads/2011/06/CreatingaPublicSquare.pdf.

Critical Thinking

1. Why is the US government currently dysfunctional according to the authors?
2. What does the common good mean and why is the government not providing it very well today?
3. What should the United States do to fix this problem?

Create Central

www.mhhe.com/createcentral

Internet References

National Center for Policy Analysis
  www.ncpa.org

New American Studies Web
  www.georgetown.edu/crossroads/asw

Sociology—Study Sociology Online
  http://edu.learnsoc.org

Sociology Web Resources
  http://www.mhhe.com/socscience/sociology/resources/index.htm

Sociosite
  http://www.topsite.com/goto/sociosite.net

Socioweb
  http://www.topsite.com/goto/socioweb.com

THOMAS E. MANN, a Fellow of the American Academy since 1993, is the W. Averell Harriman Chair and Senior Fellow in Governance Studies at the Brookings Institution. He previously served as the Director of Governmental Studies at Brookings and as the Executive Director of the American Political Science Association. His publications include *It's Even Worse Than It Looks: How the American Constitutional System Collided With the New Politics of Extremism* (with Norman J. Ornstein, 2012), *The Broken Branch: How Congress is Failing America and How to Get It Back on Track* (with Norman J. Ornstein, 2006), and *Party Lines: Competition, Partisanship and Congressional Redistricting* (2005). NORMAN J. ORNSTEIN, a Fellow of the American Academy since 2004, is Resident Scholar at the American Enterprise Institute for Public Policy Research. He also writes the weekly column "Congress Inside Out" for *Roll Call*. His publications include *It's Even Worse Than It Looks: How the American Constitutional System Collided With the New Politics of Extremism* (with Thomas E. Mann, 2012), *The Broken Branch: How Congress is Failing America and How to Get It Back on Track* (with Thomas E. Mann, 2006), and *The Permanent Campaign and Its Future* (edited with Thomas E. Mann, 2000). He is chair of the Academy's Stewarding America project.

Mann, Thomas E.; Ornstein, Norman J., "Finding the Common Good in an Era of Dysfunctional Governance," *Daedalus*, Spring 2013, pp. 15–24. Copyright © 2013 by MIT Press Journals. All rights reserved. Used with permission.

The End of Welfare as I Knew It

How Temporary Assistance for Needy Families failed the test of the Great Recession.

DIANA SPATZ

Learning Outcomes

After reading this article, you will be able to:

- Determine what TANF has accomplished.
- Determine what TANF has not accomplished.
- Identify administrative problems of the current welfare system.

I'll always remember the day President Clinton signed Temporary Assistance to Needy Families (TANF), or welfare reform, into law. It was August 1996, and I was reading the morning paper in Barstow, California, completing the last leg of a crosscountry road trip I'd taken with my daughter to celebrate my finishing school. Having just earned my bachelor's degree from the University of California, Berkeley, I would finally earn enough to get my family off welfare—and out of poverty—for good. As I read the news that the Personal Responsibility and Work Opportunity Reconciliation Act had become law, I hung my head and cried. I felt like I'd crossed a bridge just as it collapsed behind me, and worried what would become of mothers who remained trapped on the other side.

Since 1996, politicians have bragged about passing welfare reform. Even House Speaker John Boehner recently praised TANF as a bipartisan success. But successful at what? If kicking low-income children and their families off welfare is the measure, then TANF was a huge success. States were given bonuses for reducing their caseloads rather than reducing poverty. As long as families were off the rolls, it didn't matter how or why. Studies show that parents were 10 times more likely to get cut off welfare because of punitive sanctions than because they got jobs paying enough to "income off." In many

states, "full family" sanctions cut low-income children off welfare along with their parents. Under the "work first" mantra, TANF caseloads plummeted by almost 70 percent, as nearly 9 million low-income parents and children were purged from the national welfare rolls by 2008. Given the four goals of TANF—promoting low-wage work, encouraging marriage, reducing caseloads, and curtailing out-of-wedlock births—these outcomes are no surprise. But if the measure of success is poverty reduction, TANF has failed.

To start, its restrictions on postsecondary education and training—the most effective pathway out of poverty for parents on welfare—make earning a bachelor's degree nearly impossible. Even earning an associate degree is difficult. "Any job is a good job" was the slogan emblazoned on the walls of county welfare agencies across the country, as tens of thousands of low-income mothers were made to quit college to do up to 35 hours per week of unpaid "workfare": sweeping streets, picking up trash in parks, and cleaning public restrooms in exchange for benefits as low as $240 a month.

9: Number, in millions, purged from the welfare rolls by 2008.

$\frac{1}{5}$: proportion of poor children served by TANF today.

Contrary to "welfare queen" stereotypes, like most welfare mothers, I worked first. Work wasn't the problem; it was the nature of the work—low-wage, dead-end jobs with no benefits, and little chance for advancement—that kept families like mine on the welfare rolls. Investing in my education enabled me to break that cycle and earn a solid upper-middle-class income.

I now pay three times more in taxes than I used to earn working full time in a low-wage, dead-end job.

This trajectory is what motivated mothers like Rya Frontera and Melissa Johnson to pursue nursing degrees, despite being sanctioned: having their families' cash grants cut off and losing childcare and transportation assistance when they refused to quit school. Whereas mothers in "work first" programs earn less than $9,000 a year, after completing her BS in nursing Melissa graduated off welfare to a career-path job as a registered nurse making $90,000 a year. Similarly, Rya is now a full-time nurse with full benefits working for Kaiser. Not only are they off welfare permanently; both women are filling a crucial labor market need, as our nation faces a nursing shortage with no end in sight. Isn't that how welfare should work?

It is also time to end the arbitrary rules under TANF that imposed a lifetime limit of 60 months for receiving benefits, and that allowed states to enact shorter time limits. It took me 10 years to overcome a lifetime of physical, emotional, and sexual abuse; depression; and posttraumatic stress disorder, one or more of which have been experienced by most mothers on welfare as girls or adults—or in my case, both. In to one-third of welfare families nationally—the experience of "timed off" families clearly challenges the notion that five years is enough; TANF's work-first emphasis relegated many parents to low-wage jobs that didn't pay enough to get their families off welfare, let alone out of poverty. Consequently, in 2003 the vast majority of parents in California's CalWORKs program who reached their 60-month limit were working and playing by the rules when they timed off welfare for the rest of their lives. And this year, like many states, California shortened its lifetime limit to 48 months in response to budget shortfalls, despite having the second-highest unemployment rate in the country. As a result, 22,500 parents were permanently cut off the welfare rolls on July 1.

22,500 Number of parents cut off in July after California shortened its lifetime limit to 48 months.
80 percent of mothers in California's welfare system who are victims of domestic violence.

Ashley Proctor, a young single mother in Oakland, was doing her 32-hour weekly work requirement when she timed off. Her benefits were cut to a "child only" grant of $320 per month. "My son and I are sleeping on a friend's sofa," she says. "On the weekends I take him to our storage unit so he can

play with his toys." That's better than what mothers faced in other states, where time limits as short as 21 months were enacted. How unfortunate that Congress, in its infinite wisdom, didn't put a time limit on poverty instead.

While states like California curtailed much-needed benefits, under welfare reform billions in federal funds were invested in unproven "marriage promotion" programs to marry poor women off the welfare rolls. Never mind that in some of California's most populous counties in 2003, most timed-off parents were already in two-parent families where one was working. And in a cruel twist, while billions were spent on marriage promotion programs that were mandatory for the states, the Family Violence Option let states choose whether to provide domestic violence services in their TANF programs, including waivers of time limits and welfare-to-work rules. Furthermore, although research shows that women who receive welfare experience domestic violence at double the rate of all American women, not a dime in federal funding was provided for family violence services. Even in California, which adopted the FVO, studies show that as many as 80 percent of CalWORKs mothers are domestic violence victims. Of these, less than 1 percent get family violence counseling and services, and less than one-quarter of 1 percent get waivers from welfare work requirements that could save their lives.

This includes mothers like Felicia Jones, whom my agency, Low-Income Families' Empowerment Through Education, or LIFETIME, was helping when she went into hiding after her ex threatened to kill her and their children. While on the run, Felicia got a notice of a mandatory welfare-to-work appointment, which had been scheduled on the same day and time as the hearing for her restraining order. When she called to say she couldn't make the appointment, her caseworker said she couldn't help her and hung up the phone, and later sanctioned Felicia for missing that appointment. Despite my urging, Felicia was too afraid to request a state appeals hearing and later disappeared. To this day, I don't know what happened to her and her children.

Fifteen years of welfare reform, and what do we have to show for it? Poverty is at its highest level in nearly 20 years. The number of children living in deep poverty—in families with income less than 50 percent of the poverty line—is at its highest level in 35 years. The unemployment rate for single mothers, who represent 90 percent of parents in the welfare system, has nearly doubled, to a 25-year high. Welfare rolls are rising for the first time since TANF was passed, despite efforts by states to tighten time limits and make it harder for families to get help. In Georgia, for example, families applying for TANF have faced "wait periods" before they can get cash assistance—the welfare equivalent of a poll tax or literacy test—with caseworkers offering to send children into foster care or put them up for adoption to ease the burden. Consequently, since 2002 Georgia increased TANF spending on child welfare—related services by 245 percent. According to Clare Richie, a senior policy analyst with the Georgia Budget and Policy Institute, the state now spends more on adoption services and foster care (58 percent) than it does on assistance to families.

This trend is alarming to people like Georgia State Senator Donzella James, who has been getting calls from constituents whose children are being taken away by the Department of Family and Child Services, the state's welfare agency. "One woman told me, 'I'm not a bad mother. I'm just unemployed,'" she said. Similarly, Arizona, Rhode Island, and Texas spend nearly half their TANF block grants on child welfare–related services. One has to wonder if this was the plan all along, given the proposal by Newt Gingrich, who was House speaker when TANF was created, to use orphanages to reduce the welfare rolls.

The Great Recession was the first true test of welfare reform during an economic downturn, and TANF failed the grade miserably. The proof is in the numbers: in 1995 the old welfare program served at least 8 out of every 10 low-income children, including mine. Today TANF serves only 2 out of every 10 poor children nationwide. In passing TANF, Congress and Bill Clinton made good on their promise to "end welfare as we know it." It's time to end welfare reform as we know it instead.

Critical Thinking

1. Poverty is at its highest level in nearly 20 years. Does that mean that TANF has failed?
2. Why are welfare rolls now rising?
3. Does TANF address the incentives problem of welfare?

Create Central

www.mhhe.com/createcentral

Internet References

Joint Center for Poverty Research
    www.jcpr.org
Sociology—Study Sociology Online
    http://edu.learnsoc.org
Sociology Web Resources
    http://www.mhhe.com/socscience/sociology/resources/index.htm
Sociosite
    http://www.topsite.com/goto/sociosite.net
Socioweb
    http://www.topsite.com/goto/socioweb.com

Diana Spatz is executive director of LIFETIME, a statewide organization of low-income parents in California who are pursuing postsecondary education and training as their pathway out of poverty.

Reprinted by permission from the January 2, 2012 issue of *The Nation*. Copyright © 2012 by The Nation. For subscription information, call 1-800-333-8536. Portions of each week's Nation magazine can be accessed at www.thenation.com

Article   Prepared by: Kurt Finsterbusch, *University of Maryland, College Park*

Predatory Capitalism: Old Trends and New Realities

C.J. POLYCHRONIOU

Learning Outcomes

After reading this article, you will be able to:

- Understand the evolution of capitalism into its present system of predatory capitalism.

- Be able to explain how globalization has affected the evolution of capitalism.

- Understand the past and present relation of capitalism and labor to each other.

In seeking to understand the nature of contemporary capitalism, it is important to realize that the whole is indeed greater than the sum of its parts. It is also pertinent that we recognize the importance of structural causality in making sense of contemporary capitalist developments while avoiding methodological reductionism.

Thus, in trying to come to terms with the nature of the beast at hand, a capitalist system running amok, we need to look at the overall structure of the system; that is, we need to comprehend the different constitutive parts of the system that keep it together and running in ways which are harmful to the interests of the great majority of the population, dangerous to democracy and public values, and detrimental to the environment and earth's ecosystem. Focusing on one element of the system while ignoring other things (perhaps because we think that they constitute incidental outcomes or processes of secondary nature) may limit our understanding by creating a flawed perspective about the dynamics and the contradictions of contemporary capitalism and thereby undermine our ability to propose sound and realistic solutions.

Capitalism as a socioeconomic system is neither egalitarian nor democratic

In considering the central question, why contemporary capitalism pursues goals which benefit almost exclusively big capital and the rich (this is the underlying issue behind virtually all recent studies dealing with inequality), it should be clear from the outset that capitalism as a socioeconomic system is neither egalitarian nor democratic. Capitalism is not an economic system designed to cater to the needs of the common folk, and, left to its own devices—especially the financial component—it can wreak havoc on societies. As for the so-called trickle-down theory, or the horse-and-sparrow theory, as John Kenneth Galbraith referred to it[1], it is nothing more than a propaganda tool used by those who seek to justify policies favoring the rich.

Some Notes on the Dynamics and Contradictions of Capitalism

Capitalism represents a specific, historically determined mode of production. It is a ruthless economic system, representing the most advanced form of commodity production. In this system, the extraction of profit is the driving force of capitalist commodity production, with exploitation and inequality representing structural necessities. Capital itself is nothing but a sort of self-expanding value, that is, value that generates surplus value.

The production of surplus value is the fundamental law of capitalism. Capitalist production has as its objective aim and goal not the production of use-values as such, but rather that of surplus value. Under capitalism, it is of course the workers themselves who create new value, which is greater than the value of their labor power. This is the essence of surplus value.

Capital accumulation is an anarchic and contradictory process. The logic of the accumulation of capital leads to enormous wealth (there is no other known economic system which can match capitalism's inherent capacity to generate wealth), on the one hand, and to the relative impoverishment of the working population on the other. Unemployment is a structural element of capitalism. The manifold activities of capitalist accumulation also tend to accelerate the process of the concentration and centralization of capital, eventually giving rise to the dominance of finance capital and to the emergence of financialization as a possible new stage in the evolution of capitalism.[2]

Capitalism is an expansionist socioeconomic system. Capitalist expansion has taken place in the course of history via different venues, ranging from plunder and exploitation, through trade, to investment in industry and the financialization of assets. There is no point in going into details here about the history of global capitalism, but suffice to say that capitalism has a long and brutal history of expansion, exploitation, and injustice, dating back to the 15th century and to the subsequent rise of imperial powers across Europe and North America, with the subjugation and the exploitation of people and resources from the periphery providing the growth engine for the economies of the imperial centers.[3]

It is only in the postwar era that the most destructive tendencies of capitalism are contained (at least inside the advanced capitalist economies), thanks to the spread of progressive economic thinking, the influence of socialism and the power exerted by trade unions. However, since the late 1970s, capitalism is seeking to return with a vengeance to its cruel, brutal, and barbaric past by breaking the social contract and intensifying the rate of exploitation in order to shift increasingly greater amounts of wealth from the bottom to the top.[4] A study released in early 2014 by the British humanitarian group Oxfam International shows that the richest one percent had 65 times the total wealth of the bottom half of the population. Stating the case of inequality in more dramatic terms, the report reveals that the richest 85 individuals on the planet share a combined wealth that is equal to that owned by the bottom half of the world's population.[5]

Along with increasing inequality, mass unemployment is once again displaying itself as an intrinsic feature of capitalism and poverty rates are sharply on the rise. There is a consensus that today's young people in the Western world will be worse off than their parents' generation.[6]

Why is capitalism fouling things up again by returning to the more ugly practices of the past? Is it because today's capitalists are greedier than those of the past? Even if we assume that this rather silly suggestion is true, greed alone can hardly explain away why capitalism is running amok in our own time.

For a convincing answer to the question of why capitalism has embarked on a journey back toward the future (and perhaps in the process is making the money class even greedier), we need to come to terms with the structural changes in the operation of the capitalist economy.

Resurrecting Anarcho-Capitalism

Contemporary capitalism is characterized by a political economy which revolves around finance capital, is based on a savage form of free market fundamentalism and thrives on a wave of globalizing processes and global financial networks that have produced global economic oligarchies with the capacity to influence the shaping of policymaking across nations.[7] As such, the landscape of contemporary capitalism is shaped by three interrelated forces: financialization, neoliberalism and globalization. All three of these elements constitute part of a coherent whole which has given rise to an entity called predatory capitalism.[8] Under this system, as Henry A. Giroux has consistently pointed out, democracy and the social state are under constant attack and "citizens are now reduced to data, consumers and commodities."[9]

In this regard, Pope Francis hit the nail on the head when he described today's capitalism as "a new tyranny."[10] Today's brand of capitalism is particularly antidemocratic and simply incapable of functioning in a way conducive to maintaining sustainable and balanced growth. By waging the most vicious class warfare in the entire postwar period, the economic elite and their allies have managed to roll back progress on the economic and social fronts by resurrecting the predatory, free-market capitalism that immiserated millions in the early twentieth century while a handful of obscenely wealthy individuals controlled the bulk of the wealth.

As indicated in the report on inequality by Oxfam International cited earlier, evidence in support of this dramatic state of affairs has been growing for a number of years, and the latest work to underscore this point, Thomas Piketty's publishing sensation, *Capital in the Twenty-First Century,* does it with such powerful impact that, as Paul Krugman said, writing in *The New York Review of Books,* it may very well "change both the way we think about society and the way we do economics."[11]

But let's take things from the start. The capitalist order we have in place today has its roots in the structural changes that took place in the accumulation process back in the mid-to-late 1970s. The 1970s was a decade of economic slowdown and inflationary pressures in the advanced capitalist world. The crisis, brought about by new technological innovations, declining rates of profit, and the dissolution of the social structures of accumulation that had emerged after World War II, led to sluggish growth rates, high inflation and even higher rates of unemployment, bringing about a phenomenon that came to be known as "stagflation." From a policy point of view, "stagflation" signaled the end of an era in which there was a trade-off between inflation and unemployment (shown by the Phillips curve) and, by extension, the end of the dominance of the Keynesian school of thought.

As with all other capitalist crises in the past, the crisis of the 1970s compelled capital, and the economic elite to restructure the way the capitalist economy had functioned up to that time. The restructuring process unfolded in several ways, which included, among other things, increasing the pace of market liberalization, attacking the traditional welfare state, and the interests of unionized workers in an attempt to eliminate social programs and suppress wages and create greater flexibility in the labor market, respectively, and initiating a new wave of globalization under the aegis of both industrial and financial capital.

The new economic orthodoxy (which came to be known as the "Washington Consensus") called for open markets, deregulation, privatization, labor flexibility, short-term optimization as a more attractive way to ensure competition and growth, low taxation for corporations and the rich, and a minimum welfare state. The desire was to return to an era in which capitalism functioned unfettered by government and social constraints, in other words, back to the age when capital grew by running roughshod over labor.

Indeed, a counterrevolution was under way, and it seemed to be global in nature and scope. The radical paradigm shift in economics was taking place in highly diverse economic environments, ranging from Chile under Augusto Pinochet's reign of terror to liberal democracies in the Anglo-Saxon world (in the UK under Margaret Thatcher and in the United States under Ronald Reagan) and to communist China under Deng Xiaoping. By the mid-1980s, most capitalist nations around the world, including many Western European countries with long traditions with social democratic policies, had shifted from Keynesianism to neoliberalism.

The march to "economic freedom," which is how the neoliberal counterrevolution was celebrated by arch-conservative thinkers (such as Thomas Sowell, for example) captivated by the nonsense of Austrian economics, did not take place on the basis of some abstract entity known as the "free market." On the contrary, it required active intervention by the capitalist state across society and the economy. Indeed, how else was the welfare state going to be reduced and the power of the labor unions weakened? How else could policies be introduced that increased the upward flows of income, created new investment sites, promoted a new wave of privatization and permitted banks and other financial institutions to practice financial chicanery? How else could failed financial institutions be bailed out with public funds if governments and elected officials had not been turned into the minions of the money class?

The capitalist state everywhere resorted to the use of both hard (i.e., repression) and soft (propaganda) power in order to secure the transition to the new economic and social order commanded by finance capital and big business interests. International organizations such as the International Monetary Fund and the World Bank, but also countless nongovernmental organizations throughout the world, were mobilized for the promotion of this goal. The corporate-owned mainstream media and the overwhelming majority of academics and intellectuals also joined the show as cheerleaders of the neoliberal vision.

In sum, the return to predatory capitalism was prompted by a crisis in the workings of the postwar capitalist regime and realized through active political intervention, i.e., class politics, by the capitalist state and international organizations, and the support provided by the intellectual elite and mass media.[12]

On the Links Between Financialization, Neoliberalism, and Globalization

The three pillars on which contemporary capitalism is structured around—financialization, neoliberalism, and globalization— need to be understood on the basis of a structural connectivity model, although it is rather incorrect to reduce one from the other. Let me explain.

The surge of financial capital long predates the current neoliberal era, and the financialization of the economy takes place independently of neoliberalism, although it is greatly enhanced by the weakening of regulatory regimes and the collusion between finance capital and political officials that prevails under the neoliberal order. Neoliberalism, with its emphasis on corporate power, deregulation, the marketization of society, the glorification of profit and the contempt for public goods and values, provides the ideological and political support needed for the financialization of the economy, and the undermining of the real economy. Thus, challenging neoliberalism—a task of herculean proportions given than virtually every aspect of the economy and of the world as a whole, from schools to the workplace and from post offices to the IMF, functions today on the basis of neoliberal premises— does not necessarily imply a break on the financialization processes under way in contemporary capitalist economies. Financialization needs to be tackled on its own terms, possibly with alternative finance systems and highly interventionist policies, which include the nationalization of banks, rather than through regulation alone. In any case, what is definitely needed in order to constrain the destructive aspects of financial capitalism is what the late American heterodox economist Hyman Minsky referred to as "big government." We shall return to Minsky later in the analysis.

The surge of finance capital can be traced at least since the beginning of the twentieth century. In a major study addressing "the economic characteristics of the latest phase of capitalist development,"[13] published in 1910, Rudolf Hilferding, an Austrian-born Marxist economist and main theoretician for the Social Democratic Party of Germany during the Weimar Republic, devoted special attention to the processes of the concentration and centralization of capital, and outlined a theory of imperialism as a necessary development in the evolution of capitalism.[14] In the course of this process he also made it clear that systematic investigation of the role of money and credit, the expansion of capitalist enterprises into corporations and their conversion into corporations was of the outmost importance for the understanding of the evolution of capitalism.

Hilferding demonstrated that the rise of the industrial corporation reflects an objective "change in the function of the industrial enterprise."[15] The industrial corporation, or the joint-stock company, allows anyone in possession of money to become a money capitalist. In effect, what Hilferding was observing was the phenomenon of the separation of ownership of capital from control in the joint-stock company. According to him, this process not only accelerated the concentration of capital, but also provided the joint-stock company with the ability to expand far more rapidly than the individually owned enterprise, thereby leading to the centralization of capital.

For Hilferding, however, it was the emergence of financial institutions and banks, in particular, that truly intensified the processes toward concentration. He stressed that in the mature stage of capitalism, banks, which were quite necessary to the growth of industry, had become fully dominant and directly controlled the economic life of the system. Through its vast resources of liquid capital, banks were able to obtain control of major trusts in industry, since the latter needed idle capital in order to increase and expand the production process. Viewed from this perspective, industrial capital was inextricably intertwined with banking capital and wholly dependent on money capital.

The merging process between industrial and banking capital gives rise to a new form of capital: finance capital. Moreover, the establishment of an intimate relationship between banking capital and industrial capital results in an increased tendency toward the export of capital. The concentration of capital, which leads to monopolization, encourages the export of capital by virtue of the fact that the over-accumulation of capital can no longer find profitable investment opportunities at home.

While it is true that Hilferding mistakenly considered the dependence of industrial capital on banking capital as a permanent state of affairs (the great monopolistic corporations became independent of banking capital and today's large corporations use their own retained profits to finance investment), there can be no mistake that the transition "from the domination

of capital in general to the domination of finance capital"[16] emerged as a key feature of "modern" capitalism even before the outbreak of World War I. Indeed, the Great Depression of the 1930s revealed in unmistaken terms the extent to which finance and financial capitalism had taken central stage, reshaping in a profound way the United States' economy and affecting dramatically developments across the world.

While Hilferding, Lenin, and many other Marxist thinkers provided important insights regarding the evolution of capitalism, the significance of financial arrangements in "modern" capitalism was scrutinized and analyzed most insightfully and more thoroughly perhaps than anyone else in the postwar period by the American heterodox economist Hyman Minsky. Although he focused purely on the domestic economy, Minsky based his analysis on the claim that financial capitalism is inherently unstable, leading inevitably to financial crises as those produced by the stock market crash of 1929.

Relying on both empirical observations and theoretical analysis, Minsky underscored the point that the financial component of capitalism was the single most important aspect behind capitalism's inherent tendencies toward crises. Building upon Keynes' *General Theory,* Minsky wrote:

The capital development of a capitalist economy is accompanied by exchanges of present money for future money. The present money pays for resources that go into the production of investment output, whereas the future money is the "profits" which will accrue to the capital asset owning firms (as the capital assets are used in production). As a result of the process by which investment is financed, the control over items in the capital stock by producing units is financed by liabilities—these are commitments to pay money at dates specified or as conditions arise. For each economic unit, the liabilities on its balance sheet determine a time series of prior payment commitments, even as the assets generate a time series of conjectured cash receipts.[17]

In this manner,

" . . . in a capitalist economy the past, the present, and the future are linked not only by capital assets and labor force characteristics but also by financial relations. The key financial relationships link the creation and the ownership of capital assets to the structure of financial relations and changes in this structure. Institutional complexity may result in several layers of intermediation between the ultimate owners of the communities' wealth and the units that control and operate the communities' wealth."[18]

Minsky's analysis of financial capitalism clearly points the way to the development of the financialization of the economy:

In the modern world, analyses of financial relations and their implications for system behavior cannot be restricted to the liability structure of businesses and the cash flows they entail.

Households (by the way of their ability to borrow on credit cards for big ticket consumer goods such as automobiles, house purchases, and to carry financial assets), governments (with their large floating and funded debts), and international units (as a result of the internationalization of finance) have liability structures which the current performance of the economy either validates or invalidates.[19]

Consistent with both Marx's and Keynes' analysis, and "in spite of the greater complexity of financial relations," Minsky treats profits as a "key determinant of system behavior"[20], with aggregate demand determining profits.

In Minsky's analysis, the role of banks as profit-seeking institutions is granted special attention. Noting that banks realize the importance of innovation in the pursuit of profits (he calls bankers "merchants of debt who strive to innovate in the assets they acquire and the liabilities they market"[21]), thus rejecting the orthodox quantity theory in which the circulation of money is treated as constant, Minsky identified three distinct financing positions: hedge, speculative, and Ponzi.

Hedge financing units are those that can fulfill all of their contractual payment obligations by their cash flows: the greater the weight of equity financing in the liability structure, the greater the likelihood that the unit is a hedge financing unit. Speculative finance units are units that can meet their payment commitments on "income account" on their liabilities, even as they cannot repay the principle out of income cash flows. Such units need to "roll over" their liabilities: (e.g., issue new debt to meet commitments on maturing debt. Governments with floating debts, corporations with floating issues of commercial paper, and banks are typically hedge units.

For Ponzi units, the cash flows from operations are not sufficient to fulfill either the repayment of principle or the interest due on outstanding debts by their cash flows from operations. Such units can sell assets or borrow. Borrowing to pay interest or selling assets to pay interest (and even dividends) on common stock lowers the equity of a unit, even as it increases liabilities and the prior commitment of future incomes. A unit that Ponzi finances lowers the margin of safety that it offers the holders of its debts.[22]

This description of lending is closer to the real world of finance that leads to crises than anything available in the existing literature. For Minsky, it is the stability in the system that breeds instability as investors, banks, and financial institutions become complacent and begin to embark on a riskier approach, which results in rising asset prices and eventually financial crashes when people begin to sell en-masse upon the realization that the accumulated debt cannot be paid off. This development is known as a "Minsky moment."

Minsky's "financial instability hypothesis" provides a useful explanation of financial crises, but also carries practical

consequences. Essentially, Minsky felt that the internal contradictions of financial capitalism could be constrained by the establishment of strong institutions. He argued that the reason there had been no financial crises in the first few decades of the postwar era was because of the presence of "big government."[23]

The task of stabilizing financial capitalism's inherent tendency towards instability has clearly been severely undermined since the onset of the neoliberal era, with the global financial crisis of 2008 to 2009 representing just the latest act in a long series of financial crises since 1966[24], and with each new crisis getting bigger and becoming more severe than the previous one. Yet, it is equally clear that financial crises have occurred prior to the installation of a neoliberal regime. Moritz Schularick of the Free University of Berlin identified more than 70 "systemic banking crises" that took place in the past 140 years prior to the global financial crisis of 2008 to 2009.[25] Moreover, because of globalization, "big government" action is restrained and the challenges posed to central banking from globalized finance are quite severe, with financial globalization leading "to growing frequency and severity of systemic financial crises."[26] Thus, globalization is in itself a contributing factor to the spread of financial crises while also providing a greater impetus for the deepening of neoliberalism.

Although finance is at the forefront of globalization, there is hardly an aspect of contemporary life that is not affected by globalization, making it a very elusive concept indeed, while adding new levels of complexity to the task of forming appropriate economic and political responses to a system bent on instability and prone to large-scale crises. Globalization creates new systemic risks[27] which we are simply uncertain how to address given the existing power structure in the global political economy where a plutocracy reigns supreme as national governments have capitulated to the whims of the corporate and financial elite and the formal global governance structure needed is missing. Yet, this is precisely the environment that makes predatory capitalism thrive, and one can be certain that its insatiable appetite for more and more profits will only intensify problems in the years ahead if it is not stopped.

Where to Go from Here

Unsurprisingly, given how dysfunctional and dangerous the neoliberal order has proven to be, proposed solutions for the problems stemming from unfettered capitalism are not in short supply. They extend from short-range (proposals for tax reform in order to close the gap between rich and poor) and medium-range goals (reregulation and even nationalization) to some rather long-range structural reforms (redesigning the architecture of the global financial system). *The Stiglitz Report* is a prime example of the latter set of proposals.[28] Controlling climate change also represents a long-range goal, in fact of vital importance for the stability of any future social and economic order.[29]

Nevertheless, proposals for major reforms that fail to incorporate a vision of alternative social orders must be treated with skepticism. The same goes for approaches that rely purely on reforms undertaken by the elite without citizen involvement and participation. By the same token, progressive forces bent on social change must re-embrace fundamental political principles and courses of social action. Building and sustaining a mass movement remains the best route to challenging the practices of predatory capitalism. However, progressive forces need to stop being constantly on the defensive in order to protect basic and fundamental values from neoliberal jackals and vultures and seek, instead, to sharpen strategic abilities in order to go on the offensive. Narrow ideological blinders must be dropped and joining forces with kindred groups is an absolute necessity in today's world.

Theoretically, we need an eclectic political economy approach which relies on Marxian, Keynesian and post-Keynesian traditions in order to understand contemporary capitalist developments. There are no intellectual giants in the neoliberal tradition. We still need to look to Marx, Keynes, and Minsky for great insights into the true workings of capitalism.

On the political front, the task of recapturing the state would seem to be a necessary first step in the drive of any progressive movement or political party seeking to reestablish balance in the relationship between labor and capital, resurrect democracy, redress social injustice, and reorient the economy toward sustainable and balanced growth. Still, such undertakings are likely to fail if they are pursued in the absence of a solid understanding of the nature of the current system and without having captured the public imagination, with ignorance of political and social developments and activist practices in other advanced capitalist countries and elsewhere around the world, and without a vision towards a new global order. A long-term vision should not stand in the way of pursuing immediate reforms that alleviate human pain and suffering, and short-term goals should not block the imagination from opening up a world of new possibilities for human relations.

As this article may have made clear, a major advantage that predatory capitalism has over alternative social orders, especially in the direction of a truly democratic future where the economic system produces wealth for the benefit of society as a whole is that it has managed to (a) break free from national government control, (b) shift the balance of power between labor and capital overwhelmingly towards the latter, (c) establish ideological hegemony, and (d) globalize the environment in which it operates. The future of a progressive social order probably requires nothing short of the reversal these trends.

Notes

1. "If you feed the horse enough oats, some will pass through to the road for the sparrows," Galbraith quipped in response to Ronald Reagan's supply-side economics. See John Kenneth Galbraith, "Recession Economics." *The New York Review of Books* (February 4, 1982) at http://www.nybooks.com/articles/archives/1982/feb/04/recession-economics/

2. See Costas Lapavitsas, *Profiting Without Producing: How Finance Exploits Us All.* New York: Verso Books, 2013.

3. A classic work on this topic, unrivalled in its scope, narration and clarity, is L. S. Stavrianos's *Global Rift: The Third World Comes of Age.* New York: William Morrow and Co., 1981.

4. See C. J. Polychroniou, "Actually Existing Capitalism: Wrecking Societies for the Benefit of Big Capital and the Super-Rich." *Truthout* (December 12, 2013) at http://truth-out.org/opinion/item/20558-actually-existing-capitalism-wrecking-societies-for-the-benefit-of-big-capital-and-the-super-rich

5. Graeme Wearden, "Oxfam: 85 richest people as wealthy as poorest half of the world." *The Guardian* (January 20, 2014) at http://www.theguardian.com/business/2014/jan/20/oxfam-85-richest-people-half-of-the-world

6. See Daniel Boffey, "Middle-class young 'will fare worse than their parents.'" *The Guardian* (October 12, 2013) at http://www.theguardian.com/society/2013/oct/12/middle-class-young-people-future-worse-parents; also Eugene Steuerle, Signe-Mary McKernan, Caroline Ratcliffe, and Sisi Zhang, "Lost Generations? Wealth Building among Young Americans." Urban Institute (March 2013) at http://www.urban.org/publications/412766.html

7. While the existence of a global capitalist class and its power in influencing government policies across the world is undeniable, the analysis advanced here does not subscribe to the instrumentalist and conspiratorial view of a global elite running the world. What it suggests, instead, is that the links that have been created in the global economy have produced a global plutocracy whose vast wealth and control of major corporations and organizations impact heavily on the shaping of domestic economic and social policies. The way national governments bend over backwards in order to accommodate the needs and wants of big corporations and the global rich via low taxation is but one example of the way this influence is carried out. So is the demand placed on national governments by global financial markets for the adoption of austerity measures when deficits and debt ratios are seen as running out of control. The much revered notion of "competitiveness"—national economies undergoing structural reforms in their labor markets in order to reduce unit labor costs—is yet another example of how the global environment shapes domestic policymaking.

8. See C. J. Polychroniou, "The Political Economy of Predatory Capitalism." *Truthout* (January 12, 2014) at http://truth-out.org/opinion/item/21138-the-political-economy-of-predatory-capitalism

9. Henry Giroux, "Neoliberalism and the Machinery of Disposability." *Truthout* (April 8, 2014) at http://truth-out.org/opinion/item/22958-neoliberalism-and-the-machinery-of-disposability

10. Heather Saul, "'A new tyranny': Pope Francis attacks unfettered capitalism and says rich should share wealth." *The Independent* (November 26, 2013) at http://www.independent.co.uk/news/uk/home-news/pope-francis-unfettered-capitalism-is-a-new-tyranny-and-rich-should-share-wealth-8965045.html

11. Paul Krugman, "Why We're in a New Gilded Age." *The New York Review of Books* (May 8, 2014) at http://www.nybooks.com/articles/archives/2014/may/08/thomas-piketty-new-gilded-age/

12. For an interesting and insightful analysis of the ideological factors leading to the making and consolidation of the neoliberal counterrevolution, see Daniel Stedman Jones, *Masters of the Universe: Hayek, Friedman, and the Birth of Neoliberal Politics.* Princeton, NJ: Princeton University Press, 2012.

13. Rudolf Hilferding, *Finance Capital: A Study of the Latest Phase of Capitalist Development,* edited with an Introduction by Tom Bottomore. London: Routledge & Kegan Paul, 1981), p. 21.

14. The discussion on Hilferding draws freely here from the author's own work titled *Marxist Perspectives on Imperialism: A Theoretical Analysis.* New York: Praeger, 1991, pp. 53–58.

15. Rudolf Hilferding, *Finance Capital,* p. 107.

16. V. I. Lenin, *Imperialism: The Highest Stage of Capitalism,* in *Selected Works* in one volume (New York: International Publishers, 1976), p. 200.

17. Hyman P. Minsky, "The Financial Instability Hypothesis." Working Paper No. 74. Annandale-on-Hudson, New York: Levy Economics Institute (May 1992), pp. 2–3 at http://www.levyinstitute.org/pubs/wp74.pdf

18. Ibid., p. 4.

19. Ibid., pp. 4–5.

20. Ibid., p. 5.

21. Ibid., p. 6.

22. Ibid., p. 7.

23. See Dimitri B. Papadimitriou and L. Randall Wray, "Minsky's Analysis of Financial Capitalism. Working Paper No. 275. Annandale-on-Hudson, New York: Levy Economics Institute (July 1999) at http://www.levyinstitute.org/pubs/wp/275.pdf

24. L. Randall Wray, "The 1966 Financial Crisis: A Case of Minskian Instability?" Working Paper No. 262. Annandale-on-Hudson, New York: Levy Economics Institute, January 1999. Available at SSRN: http://dx.doi.org/10.2139/ssrn.150728.

25. Moritz Schularick, "140 Years of Financial Crises: Old Dog, New Tricks." Freie Universität Berlin (August 2010) at http://www.jfki.fu-berlin.de/faculty/economics/team/Ehemalige_Mitarbeiter_innen/schularick/Old_Dog_New_Tricks_Schularick.pdf?1376087682

26. Piero C. Ugolini, Andrea Schaechter, and Mark R. Stone, "Introduction." In Piero C. Ugolini, Andrea Schaechter, and Mark R. Stone (eds.), *Challenges to Central Banking from Globalized Financial Systems.* Washington, DC.: International Monetary Fund, March 2004.

27. See Ian Goldin and Mike Mariathasan, *The Butterfly Defect: How Globalization Creates Systemic Risks and What to Do About It.* Princeton, NJ.: Princeton University Press, 2014.

28. See Joseph E. Stiglitz, *The Stiglitz Report: Reforming the International Monetary and Financial Systems in the Wake of the Global Crisis.* New York: New Press, 2010.

29. See, for example, Bert Metz, *Controlling Climate Change.* Cambridge: Cambridge University Press, 2012.

Critical Thinking

1. How does current capitalism impact on government?
2. What role does ideology have in current institutional arrangements?
3. Is the current form of capitalism harmful to the economy?

Create Central

www.mhhe.com/createcentral

Internet References

National Center for Policy Analysis
   www.ncpa.org
New American Studies Web
   www.georgetown.edu/crossroads/asw
Social Science Information Gateway
   http://sosig.esrc.bris.ac.uk
Sociology—Study Sociology Online
   http://edu.learnsoc.org
Sociology Web Resources
   http://www.mhhe.com/socscience/sociology/resources/index.htm
Sociosite
   http://www.topsite.com/goto/sociosite.net
Socioweb
   http://www.topsite.com/goto/socioweb.com

C.J. POLYCHRONIOU is a research associate and policy fellow at the Levy Economics Institute of Bard College and a columnist for a Greek daily national newspaper. His main research interests are in European economic integration, globalization, the political economy of the United States, and the deconstruction of neoliberalism's politico-economic project. He has taught for many years at universities in the United States and Europe and is a regular contributor to *Truthout* as well as a member of *Truthout*'s Public Intellectual Project. He has published several books and his articles have appeared in a variety of journals and magazines. Many of his publications have been translated into several foreign languages, including Greek, Spanish, Portuguese, and Italian. The views expressed in this article do not necessarily represent those of the Levy Economics Institute or those of its board members.

Polychroniou, C.J., ''Predatory Capitalism: Old Trends and New Realities,'' *Truthout*, July 14, 2014. Copyright © 2014 by Truthout. All rights reserved. Used with permission.

Article   Prepared by: Kurt Finsterbusch, *University of Maryland, College Park*

The Bargain at the Heart of Our Economy Has Frayed

The trend toward growing inequality is not unique to America's market economy. But this increasing equality is most pronounced in our country, and it challenges the very essence of who we are as a people.

BARACK OBAMA

Learning Outcomes

After reading this article, you will be able to:

- Understand how social programs helped build the middle class.

- Understand the complexity of the functioning of society in terms of the many interacting factors that are involved in the evolution of society.

- Begin to consider how the identified economic problems could be addressed.

Well, thank you, Neera, for the wonderful introduction and sharing a story that resonated with me. There were a lot of parallels in my life, and probably resonated with some of you.

You know, over the past 10 years, the Center for American Progress has done incredible work to shape the debate over expanding opportunity for all Americans. And I could not be more grateful to CAP not only for giving me a lot of good policy ideas but also giving me a lot of staff. My friend John Podesta ran my transition. My chief of staff, Denis McDonough, did a stint at CAP. So you guys are obviously doing a good job training folks.

I also want to thank all of the members of Congress and my administration who are here today for the wonderful work that they do. I want to thank Mayor Gray and everyone here at THEARC for having me.

This center, which I've been to quite a bit and have had a chance to see some of the great work that's done here, and all the nonprofits that—that call THEARC home offer access to everything from education to health care to a safe shelter from the streets, which means that you're—you're harnessing the power of community to expand opportunity for folks here in DC. And your work reflects a tradition that runs through our history, the belief that we're greater together than we are on our own. And—and that's what I've come here to talk about today.

Now, over the last two months, Washington's been dominated by some pretty contentious debates, I think that's fair to say. And between a reckless shutdown by congressional Republicans in an effort to repeal the Affordable Care Act and, admittedly, poor execution on my administration's part in implementing the latest stage of the new law, nobody has acquitted themselves very well these past few months. So it's not surprising that the American people's frustrations with Washington are at an all-time high.

But we know that people's frustrations run deeper than these most recent political battles. Their frustration is rooted in their own daily battles, to make ends meet, to pay for college, buy a home, save for retirement. It's rooted in the nagging sense that no matter how hard they work, the deck is stacked against them. And it's rooted in the fear that their kids won't be better off than they were.

They may not follow the constant back-and-forth in Washington or all the policy details, but they experience, in a very personal way, the relentless decades long trend that I want to spend some time talking about today, and that is a dangerous and growing inequality and lack of upward mobility that has jeopardized middle-class America's basic bargain that if you work hard, you have a chance to get ahead. I believe this is the defining challenge of our time: making sure our economy works for every working American. That's why I ran for president. It was the center of last year's campaign. It drives everything I do in this office.

And I know I've raised this issue before, and some will ask why I raise the issue again right now. I do it because the outcomes of the debates we're having right now, whether it's health care or the budget or reforming our housing and financial systems—all these things will have real practical implications for every American. And I am convinced that the decisions we make on these issues over the next few years will determine whether or not our children will grow up in an America where opportunity is real.

Now, the premise that we're all created equal is the opening line in the American story. And while we don't promise equal outcomes, we've strived to deliver equal opportunity—the idea that success doesn't depend on being born into wealth or privilege, it depends on effort and merit. And with every chapter we've added to that story, we've worked hard to put those words into practice.

It was Abraham Lincoln, a self-described poor-man's son who started a system of land-grant colleges all over this country so that any poorman's son could go learn something new. When farms gave way to factories, a rich-man's son named Teddy Roosevelt fought for an eight-hour work day, protections for workers and busted monopolies that kept prices high and wages low.

When millions lived in poverty, FDR fought for Social Security and insurance for the unemployment and a minimum wage. When millions died without health insurance, LBJ fought for Medicare and Medicaid. Together we forged a new deal, declared a war on poverty and a great society, we built a ladder of opportunity to climb and stretched out a safety net beneath so that if we fell, it wouldn't be too far and we could bounce back.

And as a result, America built the largest middle class the world has ever known. And for the three decades after World War II, it was the engine of our prosperity. Now, we can't look at the past through rose-colored glasses. The economy didn't always work for everyone.

Racial discrimination locked millions out of opportunity. Women were too often confined to a handful of often poorly paid professions. And it was only through painstaking struggle that more women and minorities and Americans with disabilities began to win the right to more fairly and fully participate in the economy.

Nevertheless, during the post-World War II years, the economic ground felt stable and secure for most Americans. And

the future looked brighter than the past. And for some, that meant following in your old man's footsteps at the local plant. And you knew that a blue-collar job would let you buy a home and a car, maybe a vacation once in a while, health care, a reliable pension.

For others it meant going to college, in some cases maybe the first in your family to go to college. And it meant graduating without taking on loads of debt, and being able to count on advancement through a vibrant job market.

Now, it's true that those at the top, even in those years, claimed a much larger share of income than the rest. The top 10 percent consistently took home about one-third of our national income. But that kind of inequality took place in a dynamic market economy where everyone's wages and incomes were growing. And because of upward mobility, the guy on the factory floor could picture his kid running the company someday.

But starting in the late '70s, this social compact began to unravel. Technology made it easier for companies to do more with less, eliminating certain job occupations.

A more competitive world led companies ship jobs anyway. And as good manufacturing jobs automated or headed offshore, workers lost their leverage; jobs paid less and offered fewer benefits.

As values of community broke down and competitive pressure increased, businesses lobbied Washington to weaken unions and the value of the minimum wage. As the trickle-down ideology became more prominent, taxes were slashes for the wealthiest while investments in things that make us all richer, like schools and infrastructure, were allowed to wither.

And for a certain period of time we could ignore this weakening economic foundation, in part because more families were relying on two earners, as women entered the workforce. We took on more debt financed by juiced-up housing market. But when the music stopped and the crisis hit, millions of families were stripped of whatever cushion they had left.

And the result is an economy that's become profoundly unequal and families that are more insecure. Just to give you a few statistics: Since 1979, when I graduated from high school, our productivity is up by more than 90 percent, but the income of the typical family has increased by less than 8 percent. Since 1979 our economy has more than doubled in size, but most of the growth has flowed to a fortunate few. The top 10 percent no longer takes in one-third of our income; it now takes half. Whereas in the past, the average CEO made about 20 to 30 times the income of the average worker, today's CEO now makes 273 times more.

And meanwhile, a family in the top 1 percent has a net worth 288 times higher than the typical family, which is a record for this country.

So the basic bargain at the heart of our economy has frayed. In fact, this trend towards growing inequality is not unique to America's market economy; across the developed world, inequality has increased. Some—some of you may have seen just last week, the pope himself spoke about this at eloquent length. How could it be, he wrote, that it's not a news item when an elderly homeless person dies of exposure, but it is news when the stock market loses two points?

But this increasing inequality is most pronounced in our country, and it challenges the very essence of who we are as a people. Understand, we've never begrudged success in America; we aspire to it, we admire folks who start new businesses, create jobs and invent the products that enrich our lives, and we expect them to be rewarded handsomely for it. In fact, we've often accepted more income inequality than many other nations for one big reason, because we were convinced that America is a place where, even if you're born with nothing, with a little hard work, you can improve your own situation over time and build something better to leave your kids.

As Lincoln once said: "While we do not propose any war upon capital, we do wish to allow the humblest man an equal chance to get rich with everybody else."

The problem is that alongside increased inequality, we've seen diminished levels of upward mobility in recent years. A child born in the top 20 percent has about a 2-in-3 chance of staying at or near the top. A child born into the bottom 20 percent has a less than 1-in-20 shot at making it to the top. He's 10 times likelier to stay where he is. In fact, statistics show not only that our levels of income inequality rank near countries like Jamaica and Argentina, but that it is harder today for a child born here in America to improve her station in life than it is for children in most of our wealthy allies, countries like Canada or Germany or France. They have greater mobility than we do, not less.

You know, the idea that so many children are born into poverty in the wealthiest nation on Earth is heart-breaking enough. But the idea that a child may never be able to escape that poverty because she lacks a decent education or health care or a community that views her future as their own—that should offend all of us. And it should compel us to action. We are a better country than this.

So let me repeat: The combined trends of increased inequality and decreasing mobility pose a fundamental threat to the American dream, our way of life and what we stand for around the globe. And it is not simply a moral claim that I'm making here. There are practical consequences to rising inequality and reduced mobility.

For one thing, these trends are bad for our economy.

One study finds that growth is more fragile and recessions are more frequent in countries with greater inequality.

And that makes sense. You know, when families have less to spend that means businesses have fewer customers and households rack up greater mortgage and credit card debt. Meanwhile, concentrated wealth at the top is less likely to result in the kind of broadly based consumer spending that drives our economy and, together with lax regulation, may contribute to risky, speculative bubbles.

And rising inequality and declining mobility are also bad for our families and social cohesion, not just because we tend to trust our institutions less but studies show we actually tend to trust each other less when there's greater inequality. And greater inequality is associated with less mobility between generations. That means it's not just temporary. The effects last. It creates a vicious cycle.

For example, by the time she turns three-years old, a child born into a low-income home hears 30 million fewer words than a child from a well-off family, which means by the time she starts school, she's already behind. And that deficit can compound itself over time.

And finally, rising inequality and declining mobility are bad for our democracy. Ordinary folks can't write massive campaign checks or hire high-priced lobbyists and lawyers to secure policies that tilt the playing field in their favor at everyone else's expense. And so people get the bad taste that the system's rigged. And that increases cynicism and polarization and it decreases the political participation that is a requisite part of our system of self-government.

So this is an issue that we have to tackle head-on.

And if, in fact, the majority of Americans agree that our number one priority is to restore opportunity and broad-based growth for all Americans, the question is, why has Washington consistently failed to act? And I think a big reason is the myths that have developed around the issue of inequality.

First, there is the myth that this is a problem restricted to a small share of predominantly minority poor. This isn't a broad-based problem; this is a black problem or Hispanic problem or a Native American problem.

Now, it's true that the painful legacy of discrimination means that African-Americans, Latinos, Native Americans are far more likely to suffer from a lack of opportunity—higher unemployment, higher poverty rates. It's also true that women still make 77 cents on the dollar compared to men.

So we're going to need strong application of anti-discrimination laws. We're going to need immigration reform that grows the economy and takes people out of the shadows. We're going to need targeted initiatives to close those gaps.

But—but here is an important point. The—the decades-long shifts in the economy have hurt all groups, poor and middle class, inner city and rural folks, men and women, and Americans of all races.

And as a consequence, some of the social patterns that contribute to declining mobility, that were once attributed to the urban poor—you know, that's a—that's a particular problem for the inner city, you know, single-parent households, or drug abuse or—it turns out now we're seeing that pop up everywhere.

A new study shows that disparities in education, mental health, obesity, absent fathers, isolation from church, and isolation from community groups—these gaps are now as much about growing up rich or poor as they are about anything else. The gap in test scores between poor kids and wealthy kids is now nearly twice what it is between white kids and black kids. Kids with working-class parents are 10 times likelier than kids with middle-or upper-class parents to go through a time when their parents have no income.

So the fact is this: The opportunity gap in America is now as much about class as it is about race. And that gap is growing. So if we're going to take on growing inequality and try to improve upward mobility for all people, we've got to move beyond the false notion that this is an issue exclusively of minority concern. And we have to reject a politics that suggests any effort to address it in a meaningful way somehow pits the interests of a deserving middle class against those of an undeserving poor in search of handouts.

Second, we need to dispel the myth that the goals of growing the economy and reducing inequality are necessarily in conflict when they should actually work in concert.

We know from our history that our economy grows best from the middle out when growth is more widely shared. And we know that beyond a certain level of inequality growth actually slows altogether.

Third, we need to set aside the belief that government cannot do anything about reducing inequality. It's true that government cannot prevent all the downsides of the technological change and global competition that are out there right now—and some of those forces are also some of the things that are helping us grow. And it's also true that some programs in the past, like welfare before it was reformed, were sometimes poorly designed, created disincentives to work, but we've also seen how government action time and again can make an enormous difference in increasing opportunity and bolstering ladders into the middle class. Investments in education, laws establishing collective bargaining and a minimum wage these all contributed to rising standards of living for massive numbers of Americans.

Likewise, when previous generations declared that every citizen of this country deserved a basic measure of security, a floor through which they could not fall, we helped millions of Americans live in dignity and gave millions more the confidence to aspire to something better by taking a risk on a great idea. Without Social Security nearly half of seniors would be living in poverty—half. Today fewer than 1 in 10 do. Before Medicare, only half of all seniors had some form of health insurance. Today virtually all do. And because we've strengthened that safety net and expanded pro-work and pro-family tax credits like the Earned Income Tax Credit, a recent study found that the poverty rate has fallen by 40 percent since the 1960s.

And these endeavors didn't just make us a better country; they reaffirmed that we are a great country.

So we can make a difference on this. In fact, that's our generation's task, to rebuild America's economic and civic foundation to continue the expansion of opportunity for this generation and the next generation. And like and like Neera, I take this personally. I'm only here because this country educated my grandfather on the GI Bill. When my father left and my mom hit hard times trying to raise my sister and me while she was going to school, this country helped make sure we didn't go hungry. When Michelle, the daughter of a shift worker at a water plant and a secretary, wanted to go to college, just like me this country helped us afford it until we could pay it back.

So what drives me, as a grandson, a son, a father, as an American, is to make sure that every striving, hardworking, optimistic kid in America has the same incredible chance that this country gave me. It has been the driving force between everything we've done these past five years. And over the course of the next year and for the rest of my presidency, that's where you should expect my administration to focus all our efforts.

Now, you'll be pleased to know this is not a State of the Union address.

And many of the ideas that can make the biggest difference in expanding opportunity, I've presented before. But let me offer a few key principles, just a road map that I believe should guide us in both our legislative agenda and our administrative efforts.

To begin with, we have to continue to relentlessly push a growth agenda. And it may be true that in today's economy, growth alone does not guarantee higher wages and incomes. We've seen that. But what's also true is we can't tackle inequality if the economic pie is shrinking or stagnant. The fact is if you're a progressive and you want to help the middle class and the working poor, you've still got to be concerned about competitiveness and productivity and business confidence that spurs private sector investment.

And that's why from day one, we've worked to get the economy growing and help our businesses hire. And thanks to their resilience and innovation, they've created nearly 8 million new jobs over the past 44 months. And now we've got to grow the economy even faster, and we got to keep working to make America a magnet for good middle-class jobs to replace the ones that we've lost in recent decades, jobs in manufacturing and energy and infrastructure and technology.

And that means simplifying our corporate tax code in a way that closes wasteful loopholes and ends incentives to ship jobs overseas. We can—by broadening the base, we can actually lower rates to encourage more companies to hire here and use some of the money we save to create good jobs rebuilding our roads and our bridges and our airports and all the infrastructure our businesses need.

It means a trade agenda that grows exports and works for the middle class.

It means streamlining regulations that are outdated or unnecessary or too costly. And it means coming together around a responsible budget, one that grows our economy faster right now and shrinks our long-term deficits, one that unwinds the harmful sequester cuts that haven't made a lot of sense—and then frees—frees up resources to invest in things like the scientific research that's always unleashed new innovation and new industries.

When it comes to our budget, we should not be stuck in a stale debate from two years ago or three years ago. A relentlessly growing deficit of opportunity is a bigger threat to our future than our rapidly shrinking fiscal deficit. So that's step one towards restoring mobility, making sure our economy is growing faster.

Step two is making sure we empower more Americans with the skills and education they need to compete in a highly competitive global economy. We know that education is the most important predictor of income today, so we launched a Race to the Top in our schools, we're supporting states that have raised standards in teaching and learning, we're pushing for redesigned high schools that graduate more kids with the technical training and apprenticeships, the in-demand high-tech skills that can lead directly to a good job and a middle-class life.

We know it's harder to find a job today without some higher education, so we've helped more students go to college with grants and loans that go farther than before, we've made it more practical to repay those loans and today, more students are graduating from college than ever before.

We're also pursuing an aggressive strategy to promote innovation that reins in tuition costs.

We've got to lower costs so that young people are not burdened by enormous debt when they make the right decision to get higher education. And next week, Michelle and I will bring together college presidents and nonprofits to lead a campaign to help more low-income students attend and succeed in college.

But while higher education may be the surest path to the middle class, it's not the only one. We should offer our people the best technical education in the world. That's why we've worked to connect local businesses with community colleges, so that workers, young and old, can earn the new skills that earn them more money.

And I've also embraced an idea that I know all of you at the Center for American Progress has championed, and by the way, Republican governors in a couple of states have championed, and that's making high-quality pre-school available to every child in America. We know that kids in these programs grow up are likelier to get more education, earn higher wages, form more stable families of their own. It starts a virtuous cycle, not a vicious one. And we should invest in that. We should give all of our children that chance.

And as we empower our young people for future success, the third part of this middle-class economics is empowering our workers. It's time to ensure our collective bargaining laws function as they're supposed to so unions have a level playing field to organize—to organize for a better deal for workers and better wages for the middle class.

It's time to pass the Paycheck Fairness Act so that women will have more tools to fight pay discrimination. It's time to pass the non-Employment non-Discrimination Act so workers can't be fired for who they are or who they love.

And even though we're bringing manufacturing jobs back to America, we're creating more good-paying jobs in education and health care and business services, we know that we're going to have a greater and greater portion of our people in the service sector. And we know that there are airport workers and fast-food workers and nurse assistance and retail salespeople who work their tails off and are still living at or barely above poverty. And that's why it's well past the time to raise a minimum wage that, in real terms right now, is below where it was when Harry Truman was in office.

This shouldn't be an ideological question. You know, it was Adam Smith, the father of free-market economics, who once said, "They who feed, clothe, and lodge the whole body of the people should have such a share of the produce of their own labor as to be themselves tolerably well-fed, clothed and lodged." And for those of you who don't speak old English let me translate. It means if you work hard, you should make a decent living. If you work hard, you should be able to support a family.

Now, we all know the arguments that have been used against the higher minimum wage. Some say it actually hurts low-wage workers; business will be less likely to hire them. There's no solid evidence that a higher minimum wage costs jobs, and research shows it raises incomes for low-wage workers and boosts short-term economic growth.

Others argue that if we raise the minimum wage, companies will just pass those costs on to consumers, but a growing chorus of businesses small and large argue differently and already there are an extraordinary companies in America that provide decent wages, salaries and benefits, and training for their workers, and deliver a great product to consumers.

SAS in North Carolina offers child care and sick leave. REI, a company my secretary of interior used to run, offers retirement plans and strives to cultivate a good work balance. There are companies out there that do right by their workers. They recognize that paying a decent wage actually helps their bottom line, reduces turnover. It means workers have more money to spend, to save, maybe eventually start a business of their own.

A broad majority of Americans agree we should raise the minimum wage. That's why last month voters in New Jersey decided to become the 20th state to raise theirs even higher. That's why yesterday the DC Council voted to do it too. I agree with those voters. I agree with those voters and I'm going to keep pushing until we get a higher minimum wage for hardworking Americans across the entire country. It will be good for our economy. It will be good for our families.

Number four, as I alluded to earlier, we still need targeted programs for the communities and workers that have been hit hardest by economic change in the Great Recession. These communities are no longer limited to the inner city. They're found in neighborhoods hammered by the housing crisis, manufacturing towns hit hard by years of plants packing up, land-locked rural areas where young folks oftentimes feel like they've got to leave just to find a job. There are communities that just aren't generating enough jobs anymore.

So we've put new forward new plans to help these communities and their residents because we've watched cities like Pittsburgh or my hometown of Chicago revamp themselves, and if we give more cities the tools to do it—not handouts, but a hand up—cities like Detroit can do it too.

So in a few weeks we'll announce the first of these Promise Zones, urban and rural communities where we're going to support local efforts focused on a national goal, and that is a child's course in life should not be determined by the ZIP code he's born in but by the strength of his work ethic and the scope of his dreams.

And we're also going to have to do more for the long-term unemployed. You know, for people who've been out of work for more than six months, often through no fault of their own, life is a Catch-22. Companies won't give their resume an honest look because they've been laid off so long, but they've been laid off so long because companies won't give their resume an honest look. And that's why earlier this year I challenged CEOs from some of America's best companies to give these Americans a fair shot. And next month, many of them will join us at the White House for an announcement about this.

Fifth, we've got to revamp retirement to protect Americans in their golden years, to make sure another housing collapse doesn't steal the savings in their homes.

We've also got to strengthen our safety net for a new age so it doesn't just protect people who hit a run of bad luck from falling into poverty, but also propels them back out of poverty.

Today nearly half of full-time workers and 80 percent of part-time workers don't have a pension or a retirement account at their job. About half of all households don't have

any retirement savings. So we're going to have to do more to encourage private savings and shore up the promise of Social Security for future generations. And remember, these are promises we make to one another. We—we don't do it to replace the free market, but we do it reduce risk in our society by giving people the ability to take a chance and catch them if they fall.

One study shows that more than half of Americans will experience poverty at some point during their adult lives. Think about that. This is not an isolated situation. More than half of Americans at some point in their lives will experience poverty. That's why we have nutrition assistance, or the program known as SNAP, because it makes a difference for a mother who's working but is just having a hard time putting food on the table for her kids.

That's why we have unemployment insurance, because it makes a difference for a father who lost his job and is out there looking for a new one that he can keep a roof over his kids' heads. By the way, Christmas time is no time for Congress to tell more than 1 million of these Americans that they have lost their unemployment insurance, which is what will happen if Congress does not act before they leave on their holiday vacation.

The point is, these programs are not typically hammocks for people to just lie back and relax.

These programs are almost always temporary means for hardworking people to stay afloat while they try to find a new job, or going to school to retrain themselves for the jobs that are out there, or sometimes just to cope with a bout of bad luck.

Now, progressives should be open to reforms that's actually strengthen these programs and make them more responsive to a 21st-century economy. For example, we should be willing to look at fresh ideas to revamp unemployment disability programs, to encourage faster and higher rates of reemployment without cutting benefits. We shouldn't weaken fundamental protections built over generations because given the constant churn in today's economy, and the disabilities that many of our friends and neighbors live with, they're needed more than ever. We should strengthen and adapt them to new circumstances so they work even better. But understand that these programs of social insurance benefit all of us, because we don't know when we might have a run of bad luck. We don't know when we might lose a job.

Of course, for decades there was one yawning gap in the safety net that did more than anything else to expose working families to the insecurities of today's economy, namely, our broken health care system. That's why we fought for the Affordable Care Act, because 14,000 Americans lost their health insurance every single day, and even more died each year because they didn't have health insurance at all. We did it because millions of families who thought they had coverage were driven into bankruptcy by out-of-pocket costs that they didn't realize would be there.

Tens of millions of our fellow citizens couldn't get any coverage at all.

You know, Dr. King once said, "Of all the forms of inequality, injustice in health care is the most shocking and inhumane." Well, not anymore, because in the three years since we passed this law, the share of Americans with insurance is up, the growth of health care costs are down to their slowest rate in 50 years, more people have insurance, and more have new benefits and protections, a 100 million Americans who've gained the right for free preventive care like mammograms and contraception, the more than 7 million Americans who've saved an average of $1,200 on their prescription medicine, every American who won't go broke when they get sick because their insurance can't limit their care anymore. More people without insurance have gained insurance, more than 3 million young Americans who've been able to stay on their parents' plan, the more than half a million Americans and counting who are poised to get coverage starting on January 1st, some for the very first time.

And it is these numbers, not the ones in any poll, that will ultimately determine the fate of this law. It's the measurable outcomes and reduced bankruptcies and reduced hours that have been lost because somebody couldn't make it to work and healthier kids with better performance in schools and young entrepreneurs who have the freedom to go out there and try a new idea. Those are the things that will ultimately reduce a major source of inequality and help ensure more Americans get the start that they need to succeed in the future.

I've acknowledged more than once that we didn't roll out parts of this law as well as we should have. But the law's already working in major ways that benefit millions of Americans right now, even as we've begun to slow the rise in health care costs, which is good for family budgets, good for federal and state budgets and good for the budgets of businesses, small and large.

So this law's going to work. And for the sake of our economic security, it needs to work. Andas people in states as different as California and Kentucky sign up every single day for health insurance, signing up in droves, they're proving they want that economic security. You know, if the Senate Republican leader still thinks he's going to be able to repeal this someday, he might want to check with the more than 60,000 people in his home state who are already set to finally have coverage that frees them from the fear of financial ruin and lets them afford to take their kids to see a doctor.

So let me end by addressing the elephant in the room here, which is the seeming inability to get anything done in Washington these days. I realize we are not going to resolve all of our political debates over the best ways to reduce inequality and increase upward mobility this year or next year or in the next five years.

But it is important that we have a serious debate about these issues, for the longer that current trends are allowed to continue, the more it will feed the cynicism and fear that many Americans are feeling right now that they'll never be able to repay the debt they took on to go to college, they'll never be able to save enough to retire, they'll never see their own children land a good job that supports a family.

And that's why, even as I will keep on offering my own ideas for expanding opportunity, I'll also keep challenging and welcoming those who oppose my ideas to offer their own. If Republicans have concrete plans that will actually reduce inequality, build the middle class, provide moral ladders of opportunity to the poor, let's hear them. I want to know what they are. If you don't think we should raise the minimum wage, let's hear your idea to increase people's earnings. If you don't think every child should have access to preschool, tell us what you'd do differently to give them a better shot.

If you still don't like "Obamacare"—and I know you don't—even though it's built on market-based ideas of choice and competition and the private sector, then you should explain how exactly you'd cut costs and cover more people and make insurance more secure. You owe it to the American people to tell us what you are for, not just what you're against. That way, we can have a vigorous and meaningful debate. That's what the American people deserve. That's what the times demand. It's not enough anymore to just say we should get our government out of the way and let the unfettered market take care of it, for our experience tells is that's just not true.

Look, I've never believed that government can solve every problem, or should, and neither have you. We know that ultimately, our strength is grounded in our people, individuals out there striving, working, making things happen.

It depends on community, a rich and generous sense of community. That's at the core of what happens at the THEARC here every day. You understand that turning back rising inequality and expanding opportunity requires parents taking responsibility for their kids, kids taking responsibility to work hard. It requires religious leaders who mobilize their congregations to rebuild neighborhoods block by block, requires civic organizations that can help train the unemployed, link them with businesses for the jobs of the future. It requires companies and CEOs to set an example by providing decent wages and salaries and benefits for their workers and a shot for somebody who's down on his or her luck. We know that's our strength: our people, our communities, and our businesses.

But government can't stand on the sidelines in our efforts, because government is us. It can and should reflect our deepest values and commitments. And if we refocus our energies on building an economy that grows for everybody and gives every child in this country a fair chance at success, then I remain confident that the future still looks brighter than the past and that the best days for this country we love are still ahead.

Thank you, everybody.

Critical Thinking

1. Do you agree with Obama's analysis of the current economy?
2. According to Obama, what has caused the middle class to decline?
3. Do you agree that our economy is coming apart?

Create Central

www.mhhe.com/createcentral

Internet References

National Center for Policy Analysis
www.ncpa.org

New American Studies Web
www.georgetown.edu/crossroads/asw

Social Science Information Gateway
http://sosig.esrc.bris.ac.uk

Sociology—Study Sociology Online
http://edu.learnsoc.org

Sociology Web Resources
http://www.mhhe.com/socscience/sociology/resources/index.htm

Sociosite
http://www.topsite.com/goto/sociosite.net

Socioweb
http://www.topsite.com/goto/socioweb.com

Obama, Barack, "The Bargain at the Heart of Our Economy has Frayed," *Vital Speeches of the Day*, vol. 80, 2, February 2014 pp. 54–61.

Article   Prepared by: Kurt Finsterbusch, *University of Maryland, College Park*

The Plight of the U.S. Working Class

FRED MAGDOFF AND JOHN BELLAMY FOSTER

Learning Outcomes

After reading this article, you will be able to:

- Understand the evolution of capitalism and how that has affected its treatment of workers.

- Understand the role of financialization in increasing affluence but also the risks it causes.

- Explain the vast increase in inequality in the United States in the past three decades.

Modern capitalism, sociologist Max Weber famously observed early in the twentieth century, is based on "the rational capitalistic organization of (formally) free labor." But the "rationality" of the system in this sphere, as Weber also acknowledged, was so restrictive as to be in reality "irrational." Despite its *formal* freedom, labor under capitalism was *substantively* unfree.[1]

This was in accordance with the argument advanced in Karl Marx's *Capital*. Since the vast majority of individuals in the capitalist system are divorced from the means of production they have no other way to survive but to sell their labor power to those who own these means, that is, the members of the capitalist class. The owner capitalists are the legal recipients of all the value added that is socially produced by the labor in their employ. Out of this the owners pay the wages of the workers, while retaining for themselves the residual or surplus value generated by the social process of production. This *surplus* then becomes the basis for the further accumulation of capital, leading to the augmentation of the means of production owned by the capitalist class. The result is a strong tendency to the polarization of income and wealth in society. The more the social productivity of labor grows the more it serves to promote the wealth and power of private capital, while at the same time increasing the relative poverty and economic dependency of the workers.

A crucial element in this process is what Marx called "the reserve army of labor" or "relative surplus population." With the exception of extraordinary situations such as major wars that mobilize millions of people or epoch-making expansions resulting from special historical factors, the capitalist economic system does not produce enough jobs for everyone. Although there are certainly better times, during upturns, and worse times, during downturns, there are almost always large numbers of people who need jobs but who cannot easily find employment. Many of the jobs that are created pay low wages—below those necessary to afford basic needs like decent housing and a good diet.

The unemployed, the underemployed, and those with only tenuous holds on their jobs, constitute the reserve army of labor, necessary to the functioning of capitalism. The reserve army is created and maintained as a means to capital accumulation, which requires that a surplus labor force be constantly available to facilitate expansion and at the same time to hold down the wages of workers and to make them less recalcitrant.[2]

Workers in the reserve army are characterized by "extremely irregular employment."[3] They are easily fired if the economy slows a bit, but ready for hiring when the economy picks up. This group of workers includes all those that have given up looking for jobs in weak labor markets, along with those working part-time but wanting full-time employment—on top of those officially designated as unemployed. It also includes the chronically impoverished.[4] It is the existence of this reserve army of "surplus" workers that makes it difficult for those in the active labor army to increase their wages or improve their working conditions without a united effort involving labor union struggles.

Marx defined the general condition of workers, particularly those in the reserve army, as one of *precariousness*. As he put it, "the higher the productivity of labor, the greater is the pressure of the workers on the means of employment, the more precarious therefore becomes the condition for their existence, namely sale of their own labor-power for the increase of alien wealth, or in other words the self-valorization of capital." With the current mobility of capital and modern material handling and rapid shipping techniques, the reserve army available to capital in any one country has become truly global in scope.[5]

There have of course been periods of time when strong union movements or pro-labor political parties (especially in Europe) have allowed for improved working conditions and higher wages. Although capital gave nothing away without a struggle by workers, the Cold War added a new dimension. Governments in the wealthy countries at the center of the capitalist world economy that needed to ensure the support of their workers as part of a Cold War compact were a bit more likely to take labor's wishes into account. This was later reversed. While there have been ups and downs since the late 1970s the conditions of labor have generally deteriorated over the period as a whole.

Workers in the United States are currently under extreme pressure—unlike any other period since the Great Depression of the 1930s. Conditions in today's phase of monopoly-finance capital, dominated by neoliberal policy, are the culmination of a long process of lopsided class war—with capital continually gaining strength in its battle to limit and control labor. During this period, and especially since the beginning of the Great Recession, capital has squeezed labor ever harder—doing more with less, as they say—in order to increase profits.

At the same time, the economy has been characterized by deepening stagnation—with real GDP growth declining from around 4 percent a year in the 1950s and 1960s to around 3 percent a year in the 1970s–1990s to 1.8 percent a year for the last decade (2002–2012). Financialization, arising in response to deepening stagnation from the 1970s to the present, has served to preserve and promote wealth at the top and temporarily to lessen stagnation in the economy as a whole—but at the cost of even greater economic instability over the long run.

As economic growth has slowed so has net job creation—from around a 2 percent increase per annum in the 1970s and 1980s to less than 0.3 percent per year for the last decade, 2002–2012 (and 1 percent a year over the last two decades).[6] The economic trend toward greater stagnation and capital's response to it—including the turn to finance, outsourcing and offshoring, and increasing pressure on workers and their organizations—have combined to undermine the overall condition of the U.S. working class.

Open War on Labor

The decline in circumstances of workers in the United States goes back to long before the Great Recession—to capital's concern over the upsurge of labor militancy following the Second World War, specifically a wave of strikes in 1946. Some 4.5 million workers went on strike during that year—from the Hawaiian sugar plantations to Oakland (a general strike) to General Motors to the railroad, steel, and coal industries. The Taft-Hartley Act, passed by a Republican Congress with some Democratic support in 1947 over President Truman's veto, was a clear offensive against labor. Workers and unions had been given a boost by the Depression-era National Labor Relations Act (1936), which restricted a number of antiunion employer practices such as

interfering with workers trying to form a union. Taft-Hartley, however, placed severe restrictions on labor—for example, outlawing the very effective sympathy strikes and boycotts. It also required union leaders to submit affidavits indicating that they were neither Communist Party members nor had any connection with what were considered to be subversive organizations, thereby excluding some of the most militant leaders.[7]

Taft-Hartley commenced a new phase of the class war of capital against labor, which was interrupted briefly in the 1960s, but was ramped up again with the economic slowdown of the 1970s. A full-scale, organized class war against the U.S. working class and against all progressive government policies was unleashed beginning on August 23, 1971, with corporate lawyer Lewis Powell's confidential memorandum to the U.S. Chamber of Commerce (only two months before he was nominated by President Nixon to the U.S. Supreme Court) calling on corporations and their CEOs to organize a concerted attack on labor, the left academy, and the liberal media—and to use their financial leverage to dominate government. The memo, which came to light only after Powell's Supreme Court appointment, galvanized business and the wealthy, leading to what Jacob Hacker and Paul Pierson in *Winner-Take-All Politics* described as a "domestic version of Shock and Awe." As Bill Moyers has written, "we look back on it now as a call to arms for class war waged from the top down." It inspired the establishment of the powerful Business Roundtable (which has only CEOs as members), the American Legislative Exchange Council (ALEC), the Heritage Foundation, the Cato Institute, and Citizens for a Sound Economy (the forerunner of Americans for Prosperity). Within a decade the number of firms with lobbyists expanded by almost 15-fold. Corporate PACs quadrupled in number between 1976 and the mid–1980s.[8]

Next to Powell the most influential figure in initiating the new corporate-based assault on workers during the 1970s was William E. Simon, Treasury Secretary in the Nixon and Ford administrations and a former top executive at Salomon Brothers. Simon's 1978 book, *A Time for Truth,* included a preface by Milton Friedman and a foreword by Friedrich von Hayek, and called for a business crusade against labor, environmentalists, and the left. Simon insisted that "multimillions" of dollars were needed for conservative causes to overthrow the legacy of the New Deal. These attacks set the stage for President Carter's sharp turn to the right in 1979, marked by the appointment of Paul Volcker as Chairman of the Federal Reserve Board.[9]

President Reagan's 1981 breaking of the PATCO (air traffic controllers') strike contributed a major blow to the prestige and power of organized labor. National Labor Relations Board and court appointees became yet more favorable to the view of capital and less inclined to adopt even the appearance of neutrality. Other aspects of the class war today include the attack on pensions of public workers at the city and state level and the decline in workplace safety enforcement. At present Occupational Safety and Health Administration inspectors are estimated to be able to visit each workplace in the United States once every 99 years. It had been more than a quarter-century since inspectors made their last visit to the Texas fertilizer plant where an April 2013 explosion killed 14 and injured over 200.[10]

In the aftermath of the Great Financial Crisis, and the rise of the Tea Party as a right-wing adjunct to the Republican Party, the assault on workers intensified still further. A report by the Economic Policy Institute that reviewed state-level legislative changes in labor policy and labor standards since 2010 found that "the changes undermine the wages, working conditions, legal protections, or bargaining power of either organized or unorganized employees. . . . The consequence of this legislative agenda is to undermine the ability of workers to earn middle-class wages and to enhance the power of employers in the labor market. These changes did not just happen but were the results of an intentional and persistent political campaign by business groups."[11]

Multibillionaire Warren Buffet, who is in a position to know a thing or two about what has been happening, declared in 2006: "There's class warfare, all right, but it's my class, the rich class, that's making war, and we're winning."[12] With unions crushed to the point that they now account for only 6.6 percent of private-sector employees, the lowest level in a century, the class war from above has shifted more and more to attacking state and local government workers, particularly teachers' unions, which are seen as standing in the way of the privatization of public education.[13]

This class war from above has taken on a toxic dimension in the form of an open attack on the officially designated "poor," now encompassing about 50 million people, according to government figures. There has long been a dimension of racism and blaming the poor for their condition, but it has now become a continuous refrain. After all, the argument goes, if they would only have done this, that, or the other thing—usually gotten more education, not had children, or not had children out of wedlock—then they would not be poor. It is their own fault, so why should society help them? In this distorted logic children are made to suffer for the alleged mistakes their parents made. Twenty-one Republican state governors have refused to accept the part of the Affordable Care Act that expands health-care access for the poor through extension of Medicaid. Since this starts out as fully funded by the federal government and then becomes 90 percent federally funded, the explanation for their actions seems to be something other than not wanting to spend money. As John Kasich, the Republican Governor of Ohio, who *is* implementing the enhanced Medicaid program, put it, "I'm concerned about the fact there seems to be a war on the poor. That, if you're poor, somehow you're shiftless and lazy."[14]

International Agreements Against Labor

The various bilateral and multilateral trade agreements that are now in effect—such as NAFTA, CAFTA, and the WTO—did not spring up out of thin air in response to a new ruling-class ideology.

Rather they are the result of a continuing process in which imperial capital has created a post-Second World War, postcolonial economic structure favorable to its interests. Designed to give maximum flexibility to capital, it has ensured a more docile workforce, rightfully afraid that jobs could be "offshored" to countries with lower wages and other costs of production. An earlier trend that happened within the United States, in which factories from the Northeast (textiles) and Midwest (automobiles) moved to the South, now occurs on an international scale.

What is referred to in financial circles as "the global labor arbitrage," or the increasing shift of multinational corporate production to the global South in order to exploit workers with the lowest worldwide unit labor costs, was made possible through an international political process, spurred by U.S. imperialism, that opened up the periphery of the world system to unrestricted flows of global capital.[15] This meant a two-pronged attack on labor and its political power in both the global South and in the global North—of which the 1994 North American Free Trade Agreement (NAFTA) was to emerge as emblematic.

Writing in *Monthly Review* in 1998, Harry Magdoff described the developments as follows:

> The road to NAFTA began early on in the postwar period. At a 1948 conference in Bogota, 20 American nations signed agreements to facilitate foreign investment. Bilateral Treaties of Friendship, Commerce, and Navigation, were negotiated with countries on other continents to pave the way for the unrestricted investment of U.S. capital. Enlargements of markets and private investment opportunities were key objectives of the World Bank and the IMF from day one. The IMF in particular assumed the robes of the colonial overseer, enforcing the rules of the game, including the discipline of austerity for the masses, in order to assure an uninterrupted flow of profits and debt service to the centers of the capitalist world. The difference between the so-called Keynesian period and today is that in earlier days there was a hush-hush aspect to the discipline imposed on the third world, whereas now neo-liberal principles are loudly proclaimed as the true faith.[16]

There were numerous indications of the decline of organized labor's fortunes and power relative to capital in the United States from the 1970s to the onset of the Great Recession in late 2007. For example, there was a decreased percentage of the workforce that was unionized, a decreased esteem in which union workers were viewed by many in society, and a lower frequency of major strikes (only a few per year compared to literally hundreds per year in the 1950–1980 period). There is no doubt that the increased surrender of workers in the face of the assault by capital was due to the fact that they were understandably concerned that the bosses would either hire replacement workers or close the facility and move the jobs to another location in the United States or to another country.

Given the pre-existing problems and negative trends for labor, the Great Recession (officially considered to have run from December 2007 to June 2009) and the deep stagnation that followed have made the situation of workers in the United States ever more precarious. As far as workers are concerned the Great Recession has turned into the Great Stagnation, the slowest "recovery" from a downturn in the post-Second World War era. Wages have stagnated, with the real median family income in 2012 below that of 1996, and the economy has yet to produce enough activity to regain all the jobs lost during the Recession.

The effects of the Great Recession and the Great Stagnation have thus only served to worsen the conditions associated with the loss of worker power under the prolonged attack on labor. There are a number of important trends occurring simultaneously in this respect—(1) the decline of employment, (2) erosion of health associated with job loss, (3) wage stagnation, (4) growth of the working poor, (5) increased exploitation of labor on the job, and (6) the drop in the labor share of income. It is important to discuss these separately, but also in relation to each other, in order to get a better grasp of the extent of the problems.

The Decline of Employment

Workers do not need anyone to tell them that the general employment situation is bad. The overall condition is best depicted not in term of official unemployment data, where the unemployment rate is now hovering around 7 percent, but by looking at the numbers of those without jobs as a share of the civilian noninstitutional population. This is sometimes known as the "jobless rate" or as the "nonemployment rate" (not to be confused with the common reference to the unemployment rate in these terms, and hence here referred to as the "real jobless rate"). Some of those who are jobless may not want to work or may not be able to do so. There are those raising families on a spouse's income or others who are students and some who are disabled—plus of course a very few who are independently wealthy. Nevertheless, long-term data on the real jobless rate allows one to capture more broadly the actual employment gap, as compared to more limited unemployment data (which excludes a wide variety of those without work).[17]

As shown in Chart 1 (using five-year moving averages) the percentage of the total male civilian noninstitutional population, ages 25 to 54—constituting prime working ages—lacking

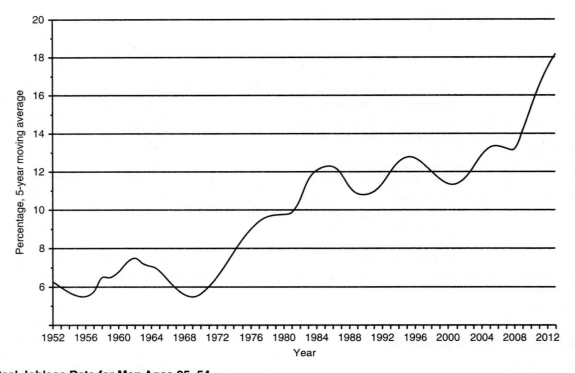

Chart 1   Real Jobless Rate for Men Ages 25–54.

Notes: The real jobless rate is calculated as 1-employed/civilian non institutional population for a given age group. It is the inverse of what the BLS terms the "Employment-Population Ratio."

Sources: U.S. Bureau of Labor Statistics (BLS), "Employment Level" and "Population Level," series LNU02000061 and LNU00000061, http://data.bls.gov.

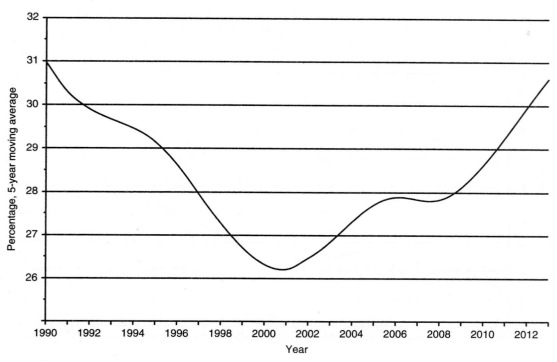

Chart 2   Real Jobless Rate for Women Ages 25–54.

Sources: BLS, "Employment Level" and "Population Level," series LNU02000062 and LNU00000062. Also see note to Chart 1.

Notes: The real jobless rate is calculated as 1-employed/civilian non institutional population for a given age group. It is the inverse of what the BLS terms the "Employment-Population Ratio."

employment of any kind has trended upward from 5 percent in 1968 to 18 percent in 2013.

Although women's labor force participation rose steadily over the last decades of the twentieth century, and hence the real jobless rate for women declined for decades, this trend has now reversed. For women ages 25 to 54 in the 1990–2013 period (shown in Chart 2 with five-year moving averages) the real jobless rate trend takes the form of a sharp V-curve, dramatically reversing in the early 2000s, and increasing to over 30 percent in 2013. As compared to two decades ago many more of these jobless women are in a position where they need jobs simply to maintain themselves and their families.

For younger workers, the picture is even worse. Chart 3 shows the trends in the real jobless rates for men and for women ages 18 to 24 since 1990. These rates rose to 44 percent for men in 2013 and 46 percent for women. Increasingly young people are being driven out of the job market altogether. They are finding themselves in a particularly untenable situation with it being so difficult even to enter the ranks of the employed. About 15 percent of people aged 16 to 24—some 6 million of them—are neither working nor in school.[18] And their future prospects are questionable given the findings of

studies showing that once workers get behind their cohort in the job market they rarely catch up.

The situation for the long-term unemployed—"now one of the defining realities of the American workforce"—is truly discouraging. A *New York Times* article, describing one woman's quest for a job after being laid off from a university professional position, quoted her as follows: "I've been turned down from McDonald's because I was told I was too articulate . . . I got denied a job scrubbing toilets because I didn't speak Spanish and turned away from a laundromat because I was 'too pretty.' I've also been told point-blank to my face, 'We don't hire the unemployed.' And the two times I got real interest from a prospective employer, the credit check ended it immediately."[19]

At the depths of the Great Recession, some 8.6 million jobs had been lost. However, the situation was actually even more serious than that—since even though there were more than 11 million *full-time* jobs lost, the increase in *part-time* employment during the Recession made the job-loss situation appear less severe than it was (Chart 4). At the time of this writing, there are still about 2 million fewer employed workers today, four years after the official end of the Great Recession, than were employed before the recession began. But there are some

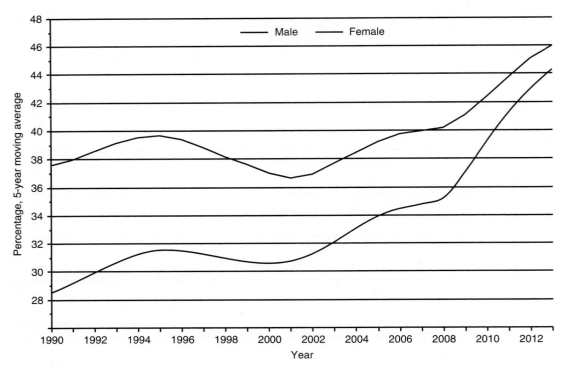

Chart 3   Real Jobless Rate for Men and Women Ages 18–24.

Sources: BLS, "Employment Level" and "Population Level," series LNU02000152, LNU02000317, LNU02024885, LNU02024886, LNU00024886, LNU00000317, LNU00000061, LNU00000152, and LNU00024885. Also see note to Chart 1.

Notes: The real jobless rate is calculated as 1-employed/civilian non institutional population for a given age group. It is the inverse of what the BLS terms the "Employment-Population Ratio."

5.5 million fewer full-time jobs. At the same time that millions of jobs lost in the Great Recession have still not been regained, the population has also been growing—so many more jobs are now needed than before. In 2007–2012 the number of people ages 25 to 54, most of whom presumably need jobs, increased by about 6 million.

The precarious employment conditions affecting workers in the United States are even more apparent if we look at the data derived from what the Bureau of Labor Statistics (BLS) refers to as "alternative measures of unemployment," encompassing part-time workers desiring full-time work and workers who are discouraged, having given up looking for work—along with those who are otherwise "marginally attached." Such data gets closer to what Marx meant when he wrote of the reserve army of labor.

Although the population of working age people has increased in what is still a very weak labor market, a large number of people have stopped looking for work while others have taken part-time employment although desiring full-time work. Therefore, the number of those classified as unemployed (you must be actively looking for work to be counted as officially unemployed) is a vast under-assessment of the jobless situation.

The 7.2 percent official unemployment rate in September 2013 increases to 13.6 percent unemployed when "discouraged" and other workers "marginally attached to the labor force," and part-timers wanting full-time jobs, are included. (It should be noted that even by the narrow gauge of official unemployment accounting, 15 percent of the labor force was unemployed *at some point* during the year in 2011.[21])

The increase in discouraged workers began even before the onset of the Great Recession, going back to the previous recession (2001) following the bursting of the dotcom bubble. The percent of the population that is actually employed or looking for work (the labor force participation rate) dropped from 67.3 percent in 2000 to 63.2 percent in September of 2013. Although the population is aging and increasing numbers are retiring (the baby boomers are reaching retirement age), even when looking at only those considered to be in the prime working ages of 25 to 54 years old, participation rates dropped from 84.6 percent in 1999 to 80.4 percent in September 2013. Although these percentage-point changes may seem small, the implication is that there are nearly 10 million *extra* people, including 1.5 million in the 25 to 54 year old age group, who

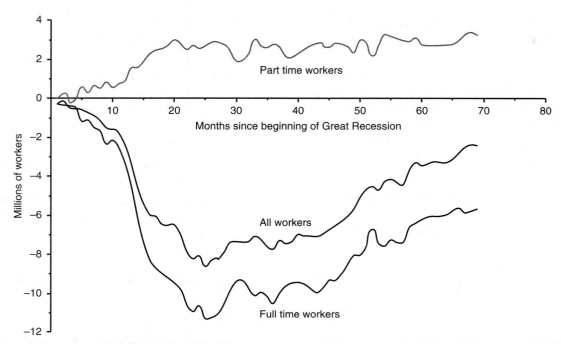

Chart 4   Full, Part-Time, and All Workers (in Millions) Relative to Number in November 2007—Prior to Great Recession.
Sources: St. Louis Federal Reserve Fred Database, series LNS12500000 and LNS12600000.

would have been in the labor force if participation rates had not declined.

The BLS's estimate of those "marginally attached" to the labor force plus people working part-time but wanting full-time work is approximately another 9 million people. Thus there are over 20 million people who are "officially" unemployed, or "marginally attached," or working part-time but wanting full-time jobs (Table 1). But the BLS counts in its alternative measurements of unemployment merely 1.2 million of those not in the labor force—including among the marginally attached *only* those who looked for work in the last year (but not during the last four weeks). But what about people who gave up looking for work more than a year ago or, if young, have never looked for work because they feel that they will not find a job?

One way to get at this issue is to use the estimate (in Table 1) of the number of "missing workers" that would have been in the labor force if the labor force participation rate had remained at its 2000 level.[22] If they are added in (minus those already counted by the BLS in their estimate of un- and underemployment), the total number of jobs needed to reach full employment is close to 30 million (Table 1). To put this into perspective, the total private-sector employment (in September 2013) was

113 million. Thus the jobs needed for full employment by this count represent more than a quarter again as many as the private sector currently provides.

It is important to recognize that enormous levels of racial/ethnic inequality lie hidden behind aggregate figures on unemployment and underemployment. Approximately, one in five Hispanic (18.9 percent) and black (22.4 percent) workers are either officially unemployed, part-time wanting full-time work, or "marginally attached."[23]

Increasing use of part-time workers commonly occurs during recessions and decreases with recoveries. However, since the 1960s there has been a general upward trend in the use of part-timers, increasing from about 14 percent of all employed workers in 1970 to close to 20 percent in 2013. During and after the Great Recession some 36 percent of all new jobs were part-time jobs. Although some people prefer to work part-time jobs, many (and indeed a rapidly growing proportion) of part-timers desire full-time work—with a significant percentage of part-timers, given the shortage of full-time employment, trying to hold down multiple part-time jobs. (There is some concern that hiring part-time employees is being made even more common by implementation of the new Affordable Care Act, which

Table 1 Estimate of Jobs Needed for Full Employment (September 2013)

Unemployed	11.3 million
Marginally attached to labor force—did look for work in last year but not in last four weeks because	
a) thought none was available	0.4 million
b) of illness, lack of transportation, lack of daycare, etc.	0.8 million
c) working part-time for economic reasons	7.9 million
Total BLS Estimate *Un*- and *Under*employment	**20.4 million**
Number of people that would be in the labor force *if* participation rate had not declined from 67.3 to 63.2 percent (minus the 1.2 million not in labor force but counted above as marginally attached).	8.8 million
Total jobs needed for full employment	**29.2 million**

Notes: If the incarcerated population—consisting of some 2 million people at the end of 2012, the greater portion of which constitute hidden unemployment (and well over half of whom are racial/ethnic minorities)—were added to this total, it would come to over 31 million.[20]

obligates businesses with more than 50 employees to participate in providing health care options for full-time employees. However, there is currently no evidence to support this assertion. The large increase in the percent of workers in part-time employment occurred during the early stages of the Great Recession.)

Another growing phenomenon is the increased use of non-permanent workers, hired for a specified time period or to complete particular tasks. Referred to as contingent employees—a category that includes temporary hires (frequently from temp agencies), contract workers, freelancers, and consultants—their number has risen sharply and is now estimated at upwards of one-third of all employees; some believe it will rise to one-half of all workers as soon as 2020.[24] What this means is described in some detail in the *Time* magazine article, "The 4 A.M. Army":

> In cities across the country, workers stand on corners, line up in alleys or wait in a neon-lighted beauty salon for rickety vans to whisk them off to warehouses miles away. Workers say the 15-passenger vans often carry 22 people. They sit on the wheel wells, in the trunk space or on milk crates or paint buckets. Female workers complain that they are forced to sit on the laps of strangers. Some workers must lie on the floor, other passengers' feet on top of them.
>
> This is not Mexico. It is not Guatemala or Honduras. This is Chicago, New Jersey, Boston.
>
> The people here are not day laborers looking for an odd job from a passing contractor. They load the trucks and stock the shelves for some of the U.S.'s largest companies—Walmart, Nike, PepsiCo's Frito-Lay division—but they are not paid by them; instead they work for temp agencies. On June 7, 2013 the Labor Department reported that the nation had more temp workers than ever before: 2.7 million. Almost one-fifth of the total job growth since the recession has been in the temp sector. One list of the

biggest U.S. employers placed Kelly Services second only to Walmart.

> Outsourcing to temp agencies has cut deep into the U.S. job market: one in five manual laborers who move and pack merchandise is now a temp, as is one in six team assemblers, who often work at auto plants. This system insulates companies from workers' compensation claims, unemployment taxes, union drives and the duty to ensure that their workers are legal immigrants. Meanwhile, the temps suffer high injury rates, and many of them endure hours of unpaid waiting and face fees that depress their pay below the minimum wage. Many get by renting rooms in run-down houses, eating dinners of beans and potatoes and surviving on food banks and taxpayer-funded health care. They almost never get benefits and have little opportunity for advancement.[25]

The Health Effects of Job Loss

About 16–18 million workers losing their jobs each year is about "normal" (this rose to 25 million at height of the Great Recession)—though most quickly find work. This number does not include those that quit or leave for other reasons such as retirement. The private sector, as previously noted, has only about 113 million workers altogether. Thus, although those precariously attached to the economy (essentially the reserve army) lose their jobs more frequently than others, over a period of a few years a high percentage of all workers either have experienced unemployment or know someone who has.

Studies in both the United States and Europe have documented severe health effects associated with losing one's job. Some of these occur even if the unemployed person quickly gets another job. A study funded by the U.S. National Institutes of Health concluded "that unemployment was associated with a substantially increased risk of death among broad segments of the population."[26] Compared to people who have not lost their jobs, heart disease, high blood pressure, and diabetes occurs more frequently in the unemployed (even if it was only a short duration of unemployment).[27] In a summary of data from Sweden, despite its strong social safety net, researchers found that "becoming unemployed [in] 1992–4 and experiencing 90 days or more of unemployment was . . . significantly associated with an increased risk of all-cause mortality from natural causes, including CVD [cardiovascular disease], as well as from external causes, both from suicide and from causes other than suicide."[28] Another study in Europe found that:

> the incidence of mental disorders has increased in Greece and Spain, and self-reported general health and access to health-care services have worsened in Greece. The number of suicides among people younger than 65 years has grown in the European Union (EU) since 2007, reversing a steady decrease in many countries. In the member states that joined the EU in or after 2004, suicides peaked in 2009 and remained high in 2010, whereas a further increase was noted in 2010 in the 15 pre-2004 countries of the EU. In England, the increase in suicides in 2008–10 was significantly associated with increased unemployment, and resulted in an estimated 1000 excess deaths.[29]

Wage Stagnation

Increased unemployment and underemployment affects workers as a whole, not just those lacking work or full-time jobs—pulling down wages, leading to a decline in the labor share, and resulting in increased exploitation on the job. Starting with the lowest paid workers, approximately 75 million workers (out of approximately 128 million wage and salary earners) are paid on an hourly basis. Some 3.5 million of these were paid at or below the federal minimum wage of $7.25 an hour. Another 5 million are estimated to earn wages not far above the minimum wage. A person working for 40 hours a week for a full 52 weeks at this wage would earn only $15,080, less than the 2013 poverty threshold for a two-person family. The federal minimum wage is not indexed for inflation and is raised only sporadically by Congress. The real minimum wage (adjusted for inflation) is lower today than it was in 1956 during Eisenhower's first administration.[30]

Real wages for all workers, corrected for inflation, have actually declined since the 1970s and are more than 10 percent below their level over 40 years ago. Even when considering real median family income that includes many two-earner households there has been a decrease of around 9 percent from 1999 to 2012.[31]

Even when employed, many workers are struggling just to get by. Part of the explanation as to how people manage is the dependence of low-income working people on social (government) programs such as Medicaid, Children's Health Insurance Program, the earned income tax credit, Supplemental Nutritional Assistance Program (which replaced food stamps), as well as on private charities, especially for food assistance. It has been estimated that about 50 percent of all the fast food workers participate in government programs—amounting to a $7 billion annual subsidy to the fast food industry.[32] But it is not just fast food workers that need to participate in social programs in order to get by—other sectors with high rates of worker participation in government social programs include restaurants and food services (44 percent of workers with families are enrolled), agriculture, forestry, and fisheries (35 percent), construction (30 percent), retail trade (30 percent), and other leisure and hospitality (30 percent). All told, some 63 percent of the total amount of families' benefit-programs funds (about $240 billion) goes to worker families.[33]

Senator Bernie Sanders, an independent from Vermont, explained the situation with Walmart workers as follows:

> The wealthiest family in this country is the Walton family. They are worth about a 100 billion dollars. That's more wealth than the bottom 40 percent of the American people. One of the reasons that the Walton family, the owners of Walmart, are so wealthy is that they receive huge subsidies from the taxpayers of this country. . . . When you pay, at Walmart, starvation wages, you don't provide benefits to your workers, who picks up the difference? The answer is that many of the workers in Walmart end up getting Medicaid, they get food stamps, they get affordable housing paid for by the taxpayers of this country while the Walton family remains the wealthiest family in America.[34]

Thus while profits of the fast food industry and giant companies that use mainly low-wage labor like Walmart are definitely private, a portion of their labor costs—the difference between what they pay and what a person needs to survive in this country—have been socialized. In Marx's terms, private companies are not paying the full value of labor power (the cost of reproduction of the worker) but are requiring society to pick up the tab through a welfare system that is at the same time punitive and demoralizing.

The Working Poor

Given the long-term pressure on labor generated by the one-sided class warfare from above, the result has been that many in the United States—both working and nonworking families—are simply unable to make ends meet. As discussed previously, there are large monetary costs for social programs to support workers earning inadequate incomes to support their families. But the uncounted costs of poverty in terms of quality of human lives, and health and life expectancy, are enormous.

The sheer number of poor people in the United States, and the number that are near poverty—perhaps a single paycheck away from losing housing or from hunger—is truly staggering. About 15 percent of the population, 46 million people, live below the poverty level, which is around $14,000 for a two-person household and $23,492 for a four-person household.[35] Twenty million of those living in poverty (close to half) are relying on an income that is less than 50 percent of the poverty level—$7,000 for a two-person household and $12,000 for a family of four. Over 100 million people (one-third of the U.S. population) are existing below twice the poverty income, close to $47,000 for a family of four.

The poor include a large number of individuals or family members that are working while not earning enough to escape poverty because of low wages and/or lack of full-time hours. The BLS estimates that 10 million individuals were among the "working poor" in 2011. This is defined as a person who spent at least 27 weeks in the labor force (i.e., working or looking for work), but whose income still fell below the official poverty level. In 2011, the working-poor rate—the ratio of the working poor to all individuals in the labor force for at least 27 weeks—was 7 percent.[36]

Minorities have the highest rates of working people living in poverty. One BLS report said, "Blacks and Hispanics were more likely than Whites and Asians to be among the working poor. In 2011, 13.3 percent of Blacks and 12.9 percent of Hispanics were among the working poor, compared with 6.1 percent of Whites and 5.4 percent of Asians."[37]

Increased Exploitation of Employed Workers

The Great Recession resulted in a drop of aggregate output of U.S. industry by about 7 percent in 2007–2009. But at the same time aggregate hours worked declined by 10 percent. This meant that labor productivity (or output per labor hour) shot up. According to a 2013 study by the National Bureau of Economic Research (NBER), this was because workers, afraid of losing their jobs, were compelled to work harder, producing greater economic surplus and profits for their employers. In the language of establishment economics, workers who see a decline in the overall demand for their labor—who recognize that there are fewer jobs, but more unemployed workers looking for them—have responded by increasing their "supply of effort" on the job. According to the NBER study, "When the alternatives

are poorer, say because the job search is less likely to result in success, it is optimal for a worker to respond with increased effort." Indeed, in economic hard times, the report indicated, it is not necessary for management to use higher wages as incentives to get workers to increase their productivity, since the lack of any viable alternative jobs will do just as well—and increase profit margins even faster.[38] As the *Washington Post* stated in 2010: "Workers were in a panic of their own in 2009. Fearful of losing their jobs, people seem to have become more and more willing to stretch themselves to the limit to get more done in any given hour of work. And they have been tolerant of furloughs and cutbacks in hours, which in better times would drive them to find a new employer." Facing continuing economic stagnation (including a long jobless recovery), a vast reserve army of the unemployed and underemployed, wage stagnation, household debt, and the loss of health insurance if unemployed—the alternatives to employed workers continue to shrink and hence they have no choice but to submit to higher levels of exploitation in their present jobs.[39]

Labor's Declining Share

In a previous article (Class War and Labor's Declining Share), we discussed the falling share of the GDP "pie" that goes to workers.[40] As we pointed out, there are many ways to approach this concept and different sources of data that can be used. Nevertheless, it is clear from a number of government sources—publications of the Cleveland and San Francisco Federal Reserve Banks, the Congressional Budget Office, and the *Economic Report of the President, 2013*, written by the president's Council of Economic Advisers—that not only is the labor share declining, but that it has capitalists and their representatives concerned, perhaps because they fear that the inequality of wealth and income that has accompanied the decline might lead to political instability at some future time.[41] Even Wall Street is beginning to worry about the lopsided income and wealth: "Some big investors have worried increasing income and wealth gaps threaten the economy's ability to expand. They also fret that public anger over it, which Democrat Bill de Blasio tapped in his successful run for New York City mayor, is creating dangerous political tensions."[42]

In our previous article on this topic, we showed that the decline in wages and salaries as a percent of the GDP is especially severe for those approximately 80 percent of private-sector workers that are classified as "production and nonsupervisory" employees. But research recently published by the Federal Reserve Bank of San Francisco indicates that just removing the highest of earners is sufficient to change things drastically—"the measured decline in the labor share [including all forms of compensation of wage and salary earners] would be much larger if not for the gains of the top

1 percent of payroll and self-employment income. By 2010, the labor share of the bottom 99 percent of taxpayers had fallen to approximately 50 percent from just above 60 percent prior to the 1980s."[43] In other words, including the compensation of the highest paid people—literally, the top 1 percent—adds enough to national labor compensation to skew the data for the entire labor force and make it appear that the declining share of the economy going to labor is not really that dramatic. This makes sense when we consider that in 2012 the top 1 percent took home an income estimated at 80 cents to "almost a dollar out of every $4 generated by the American economy."[44]

So, while the share of income going to most workers is declining in the stagnating economy, the wealthiest are receiving an increasing share of the pie. It should come as no surprise to *Monthly Review* readers that corporate profits account for an increasing proportion of total income (which, of course, mainly end up in the pockets of the rich). Between 1986 and 2012, after-tax corporate profits increased over 7 percentage points in relation to GDP. In 2012 corporate profits reached a record high for the last half-century of 10.8 percent of GDP (domestic corporate profits alone set a record of 8.2 percent of GDP).[45]

During the economic recovery from the Great Recession the top 1 percent of income earners in the United States has captured 95 percent of the total growth of income in the economy. In 2002–2012, the bottom 90 percent of the population saw their average family income (excluding capital gains) drop by 11 percent, while those in the top to 0.1 to 0.01 percent saw theirs rise by 30 percent and those in the top 0.01 percent, that is, one in every 10,000 people, enjoyed a 76 percent increase in average family income (excluding capital gains).[46]

The Class War: Is it Necessarily One-Sided?

In the present period of monopoly-finance capital the U.S. economy has been increasingly prone to stagnation. This is reflected in stunted growth rates, coupled with rising unemployment, underemployment, and unutilized productive capacity. Similar conditions exist throughout the triad of the United States/Canada, Europe, and Japan.

With the increased financialization of the economy the fates of the haves and the have-nots have more and more diverged. For a large portion of the working class, these are the worst of times. However, for the 1 percent in general, the 0.1 percent more specifically, and especially for the exclusive 0.01 percent at the very top of society, these are the best of times. And it has not been too bad for those near the upper echelons, even somewhat below the top 1 percent. Unable to prevent the deepening stagnation of the monopoly capitalist economy, the wealthy were nonetheless able to transform it to meet their own "needs" by financializing the system and their own wealth, and diverting more and more of the monetary flows of the economy, including state-sector funds, into their own deep pockets.

The enormous expansion of the reserve army of labor over the last 30 years, which has weakened the working class and undermined its traditional organizations such as labor unions, coupled with an organized, one-sided class war from above, has resulted in a massive and continuing redistribution of income and wealth to the top of the pyramid. Even before the Great Recession, between 2001 and 2006, more than half of the income gains in the United States were going to the top 1 percent of income earners, and around 20 percent to the top 0.1 percent.[47] Under these circumstances, economic growth can slow down and yet the rich can get relatively (and absolutely) richer faster—precisely because the poor are getting relatively (and absolutely) poorer faster. The combination of stagnation, financialization, and austerity all work to reinforce the power and wealth of capital and to place workers in a weaker and more dependent position. The economy as a whole may not be doing well but the rich are seeing their income and wealth rise hand over fist.

This situation—one in which the amassing of wealth at the top is no longer as directly dependent on the growth of capital accumulation/investment or of production (which increasingly take second place to financial speculation)—is bound to create ever larger contradictions in the system as a whole. This is related within the world economy to the relative shift in industrial production to the global South, with multinational corporations in the center gaining the lion's share of the surplus generated through the global labor arbitrage, or the migration of production worldwide to regions with the lowest wages (and safety and environmental protection) costs—the highly exploited export zones in the global South.

What should the response of the U.S. working class and the working class in the rest of the advanced capitalist world—not to mention the rapidly emerging working-class of the periphery—be in these circumstances? It hardly needs to be said. The only possible answer to capital's unlimited decades-long assault on labor is to unleash a class struggle from below in response. But economic resistance alone is never sufficient; and all the less so in those cases where workers are economically hemmed in as at present. The "very necessity of *general political action*," Marx wrote in *Value, Price and Profit*, "affords the proof that in its merely economic action capital is the stronger side."[48] The revolt of the underlying population therefore must take the form of a general political offensive against what is an unequal and irrational system. If the future of humanity and that of capitalism can be said to have coincided at one time, this is certainly no longer the case today. All reality and all hope demand a new system of production and consumption, *beyond capital and beyond mere wage labor.*

Notes

1. Max Weber, *The Protestant Ethic and the Spirit of Capitalism* (New York: Charles Scribners, 1958), 21, and *Economy and Society* (Berkeley: University of California Press, 1978), 85–86, 138, 1156.

2. Karl Marx, *Capital*, vol. 1 (London: Penguin, 1976), 781–802.

3. Marx, *Capital*, vol. 1, 796.

4. Broader conceptions of the reserve army would include most of those incarcerated and in the military since these soak up the surplus labor of society and show how far the society is from using the productive labor at its disposal.

5. Marx, *Capital*, vol. 1, 798; Harry Braverman, *Labor and Monopoly Capital* (New York: Monthly Review Press, 1998), 264–277. For a detailed empirical discussion of the modern reserve army of labor see Fred Magdoff and Harry Magdoff, "Disposable Workers: Today's Reserve Army of Labor," *Monthly Review* 55, no. 11 (April 2004). On the global aspects of the reserve army see John Bellamy Foster and Robert W. McChesney, *The Endless Crisis* (New York: Monthly Review Press, 2012), 125–154. For a recent dissertation on Marx's reserve army and its significance for the sociology of unemployment see R. Jamil Jonna, "Toward a Political-Economic Sociology of Unemployment: Renewing the Classical Reserve Army Perspective," PhD dissertation, University of Oregon, June 2013.

6. Calculated from St. Louis Federal Reserve FRED database, series PAYEMS, all nonfarm employees.

7. See David Milton, *The Politics of U.S. Labor* (New York: Monthly Review Press, 1982), 154–167.

8. Lewis Powell, "Memo to U.S. Chamber of Commerce," August 23, 1971, http://reclaimdemocracy.org; Bill Moyers, "How Wall Street Occupied America," *Nation*, November 21, 2011, http://thenation.com; Jacob S. Hacker and Paul Pierson, *Winner-Take-All Politics* (New York: Simon and Schuster, 2010), 117–120.

9. William E. Simon, *A Time for Truth* (New York: McGraw Hill, 1978), 195–201, 219–221, 230–238; Moyers, "How Wall Street Occupied America"; Hacker and Pierson, *Winner-Take-All Politics*, 123–124; W. Carl Biven, *Jimmy Carter's Economic Policy* (Chapel Hill: University of North Carolina Press, 2002), 237–252.

10. Kris Maher, "House Bill Would Boost Federal Authority Over Workplace Safety," *Wall Street Journal*, April 18, 2013, http://online.wsj.com.

11. Gordon Lafer, *The Legislative Attack on American Wages and Labor Standards, 2011–2012*, Economic Policy Institute Briefing Paper #364, October 31, 2013, http://epi.org.

12. Ben Stein, "In Class Warfare, Guess Which Class Is Winning," *New York Times*, November 26, 2006, http://nytimes.com.

13. See Doug Henwood and Liza Featherstone, "Marketizing Schools," *Monthly Review* 65, no. 2 (June 2013): 58–70.

14. Paul Krugman, "A War on the Poor," *New York Times*, October 31, 2013.

15. On the global labor arbitrage see Foster and McChesney, *The Endless Crisis*, 137–143.

16. Harry Magdoff, "A Letter to a Contributor: The Same Old State," *Monthly Review* 49, no. 8 (January 1998): 1–10.

17. See Floyd Norris, "Many More Are Jobless Than Are Unemployed," *New York Times*, April 12, 2008, http://nytimes.com. Related to the real jobless or nonemployment rate is the employment-population ratio. See Paul Krugman, "The Employment Situation," *New York Times Opinion Pages*, September 7, 2012, http://krugman.blogs.nytimes.com.

18. Philip Elliott, "Study: 15 percent of US Youth Out of School, Work," Associated Press, October 21, 2013, http://bigstory.ap.org.

19. Annie Lowrey, "Caught in a Revolving Door of Unemployment," *New York Times*, November 16, 2013, http://nytimes.com.

20. Bruce Western, Jeffrey Kling, and David F. Weiman, "The Labor Market Consequences of Incarceration," *Crime & Delinquency* 47, no. 3 (2001): 410–427; Bureau of Justice Statistics, "Prisoners in 2012," http://bjs.gov; Hannah Holleman, Robert W. McChesney, John Bellamy Foster, and R. Jamil Jonna, "The Penal State in an Age of Crisis," *Monthly Review* 61, no. 2 (June 2009): 1–17.

21. Heidi Shierholz, "A Projected 13.1 Percent of Workers Will Be Unemployed at Some Point in 2013," *Economic Policy Institute*, December 19, 2012, http://epi.org.

22. On this topic see Heidi Shierholz, "The Missing Workers: How Many Are There and Who Are They?," *Economic Policy Institute*, April 30, 2013, http://epi.org.

23. Heidi Shierholz, "Roughly One in Five Hispanic and Black Workers are 'Underemployed,'" *Economic Policy Institute*, August 22, 2013, http://epi.org.

24. Carol Hazard, "Hiring Explodes in Part-time and Contract Work," *Richmond Times-Dispatch*, September 2, 2013, http://timesdispatch.com.

25. Michael Grabell, "The 4 A.M. Army," *Time*, June 27, 2013, http://nation.time.com.

26. David J. Roelfs, Eran Shor, Karina W. Davidson, and Joseph E. Schwartz, "Losing Life and Livelihood: A Systematic Review and Meta-Analysis of Unemployment and All-Cause Mortality," *Social Science and Medicine* 72, no. 6 (March 2011): 840–854, http://ncbi.nlm.nih.gov.

27. Kate W. Strully, "Job Loss and Health in the U.S. Labor Market," *Demography* 46, no. 2 (May 2009): 221–246.

28. A. Lundin, I. Lundberg, L. Hallsten, J. Ottosson, and T. Hemmingsson, "Unemployment and mortality—a longitudinal prospective study on selection and causation in 49321 Swedish middle-aged men," *Journal of Epidemiology and Community Health* 64 (2010): 22–28.

29. Marina Karanikolos, Philipa Mladovsky, Jonathan Cylus, Sarah Thomson, Sanjay Basu, David Stuckler, Johan P Mackenbach, and Martin McKee, "Financial Crisis, Austerity, and Health in Europe," *Lancet* 381 (2013): 1323–1331.

30. "Federal Minimum Wage Rates, 1955–2013," http://infoplease.com.

31. Calculated from St. Louis Federal Reserve FRED database, Real Median Household Income in the United States (MEHOINUSA672N).

32. Sylvia Allegretto, Marc Doussard, Dave Graham-Squire, Ken Jacobs, Dan Thompson, and Jeremy Thompson, *Fast Food, Poverty Wages: The Public Cost of Low-wage Jobs in the Fast-food Industry*, University of California, Berkeley, Center for Labor Research and Education and the University of Illinois at Urbana-Champaign Department of Urban & Regional Planning, October 15, 2013, http://laborcenter.berkeley.edu.

33. Carl Bialik, "Public Cost of Fast-Food Industry's Low Pay Remains Unclear," *Wall Street Journal*, November 1, 2013, http://online.wsj.com.

34. David Ferguson, "Bernie Sanders: Walmart Family's 'Obscene' Wealth Subsidized by Taxpayers," *Raw Story*, August 3, 2013, http://rawstory.com.

35. "Poverty," U.S. Census, http://census.gov.

36. *A Profile of the Working Poor, 2011*, U.S. Bureau of Labor Statistics Report 1041, April 2013, http://bls.gov.

37. *A Profile of the Working Poor, 2011*.

38. Edward P. Lazear, Kathryn L. Shaw, and Christopher Stanton, "Making Do With Less: Working Harder During Recession," NBER Working Paper No. 19328, National Bureau of Economic Research, August 2013, http://nber.org; "Why Productivity Increased During the Downturn," *CNN Money*, October 3, 2013, http://management.fortune.cnn.com/.

39. "Workers' Awesome Output," *Washington Post*, March 31, 2010, http://washingtonpost.com.

40. Fred Magdoff and John Bellamy Foster, "Class War and Labor's Declining Share," *Monthly Review* 64 no. 10 (March 2013): 1–11. It should be noted that our article contained a small error. In the comparison of private-sector employees and all employees in Charts 1 and 2 the difference between the two was incorrectly said to be government workers instead of government and nonprofit workers. However, this did not materially affect the argument in any significant way, because the argument clearly was that the small decline in the wage share in the 1970s did not occur within the private/profit sector and was instead attributable to the growth of nonprivate/nonprofit sector employment.

41. Margaret Jacobson and Filippo Occhino, "Labor's Declining Share of Income and Rising Inequality," Commentary, Federal Reserve Bank of Cleveland, 2012, http://clevelandfed.org; Michael W.L. Elsby, Bart Hobijn, and Aysegul Sahin, *The Decline of the U.S. Labor Share*, Federal Reserve Bank of San Francisco Working Paper 2013-27, 2013, http://frbsf.org; Congressional Budget Office, *What Accounts for the Slow Growth of the Economy After the Recession?*, 2012, http://cbo.gov, 14; *Economic Report of the President*, 2013, http://gpo.gov, 60–61.

42. Justin Lahart, "Worry Over Inequality Occupies Wall Street," *Wall Street Journal*, November 10, 2013, http://online.wsj.com.

43. *The Decline of the U.S. Labor Share*, 31.

44. Eduardo Porter, "Rethinking the Rise of Inequality," *New York Times*, November 12, 2013, http://nytimes.com; "How the 1 Percent Won the Recovery, in One Table," *Washington Post*, September 11, 2013, http://washingtonpost.com/; "Worry Over Inequality Occupies Wall Street."

45. Calculated from NIPA Tables 1.1.5. Gross Domestic Product and 6.19D. Corporate Profits After Tax by Industry, U.S. Department of Commerce, Bureau Economic Analysis, http://bea.gov.

46. "Worry Over Inequality Occupies Wall Street."

47. Hacker and Pierson, *Winner-Take-All Politics*, 3.

48. Karl Marx, *Value, Price and Profit* (New York: International Publishers, 1935), 59.

Critical Thinking

1. Evaluate the authors' thesis that capitalism has involved class warfare against workers over the past century.
2. Judge the consequences of extreme inequality.
3. Explore solutions to the identified problems.

Create Central

www.mhhe.com/createcentral

Internet References

grass-roots.org
   www.grass-roots.org
Joint Center for Poverty Research
   www.jcpr.org
National Center for Policy Analysis
   www.ncpa.org
New American Studies Web
   www.georgetown.edu/crossroads/asw
Social Science Information Gateway
   http://sosig.esrc.bris.ac.uk
Sociology—Study Sociology Online
   http://edu.learnsoc.org
Sociology Web Resources
   http://www.mhhe.com/socscience/sociology/resources/index.htm
Sociosite
   http://www.topsite.com/goto/sociosite.net
Socioweb
   http://www.topsite.com/goto/socioweb.com

FRED MAGDOFF is professor emeritus of plant and soil science at the University of Vermont. **JOHN BELLAMY FOSTER** is editor of *Monthly Review* and professor of sociology at University of Oregon. They are coauthors of *The Great Financial Crisis* (2009) and *What Every Environmentalist Needs to Know About Capitalism* (2011)—both published by Monthly Review Press.

Magdoff, Fred; Foster, John Bellamy, "The Plight of the U.S. Working Class," *Monthly Review: An Independent Socialist Magazine*, vol. 65, 8, January 2014. Copyright © 2014 by Monthly Review. All rights reserved. Used with permission.

Article   Prepared by: Kurt Finsterbusch, *University of Maryland, College Park*

Urban Legends
Why Suburbs, Not Cities, Are the Answer

Joel Kotkin

Learning Outcomes

After reading this article, you will be able to:

- Discuss the prospects of cities, suburbs, and rural areas given current and future demographics.

- Explain the ways that megacities are dysfunctional.

- Understand the many dimensions that cities are to be evaluated on and consider whether that dimension is better served by a big city or a small city.

The human world is fast becoming an urban world—and according to many, the faster that happens and the bigger the cities get, the better off we all will be. The old suburban model, with families enjoying their own space in detached houses, is increasingly behind us; we're heading toward heavier reliance on public transit, greater density, and far less personal space. Global cities, even colossal ones like Mumbai and Mexico City, represent our cosmopolitan future, we're now told; they will be nerve centers of international commerce and technological innovation just like the great metropolises of the past—only with the Internet and smart phones.

According to Columbia University's Saskia Sassen, megacities will inevitably occupy what Vladimir Lenin called the "commanding heights" of the global economy, though instead of making things they'll apparently be specializing in high-end "producer services"—advertising, law, accounting, and so forth—for worldwide clients. Other scholars, such as Harvard University's Edward Glaeser, envision universities helping to power the new "skilled city," where high wages and social amenities attract enough talent to enable even higher-cost urban meccas to compete.

The theory goes beyond established Western cities. A recent World Bank report on global megacities insists that when it comes to spurring economic growth, denser is better: "To try to spread out economic activity," the report argues, is to snuff it. Historian Peter Hall seems to be speaking for a whole generation of urbanists when he argues that we are on the cusp of a "coming golden age" of great cities.

The only problem is, these predictions may not be accurate. Yes, the percentage of people living in cities is clearly growing. In 1975, Tokyo was the largest city in the world, with over 26 million residents, and there were only two other cities worldwide with more than 10 million residents. By 2025, the U.N. projects that there may be 27 cities of that size. The proportion of the world's population living in cities, which has already shot up from 14 percent in 1900 to about 50 percent in 2008, could be 70 percent by 2050. But here's what the boosters don't tell you: It's far less clear whether the extreme centralization and concentration advocated by these new urban utopians is inevitable—and it's not at all clear that it's desirable.

Not all Global Cities are created equal. We can hope the developing-world metropolises of the future will look a lot like the developed-world cities of today, just much, much larger—but that's not likely to be the case. Today's Third World megacities face basic challenges in feeding their people, getting them to and from work, and maintaining a minimum level of health. In some, like Mumbai, life expectancy is now at least seven years less than the country as a whole. And many of the world's largest advanced cities are nestled in relatively declining economies—London, Los Angeles, New York, and Tokyo. All suffer growing income inequality and outward migration of middle-class families. Even in the best of circumstances, the new age of the megacity might well be an era of unparalleled human congestion and gross inequality.

Perhaps we need to consider another approach. As unfashionable as it might sound, what if we thought less about the benefits of urban density and more about the many possibilities for proliferating more human-scaled urban centers; what if healthy growth turns out to be best achieved through dispersion, not concentration? Instead of overcrowded cities rimmed by hellish new slums, imagine a world filled with vibrant smaller cities, suburbs, and towns: Which do you think is likelier to produce a higher quality of life, a cleaner environment, and a lifestyle conducive to creative thinking?

So how do we get there? First, we need to dismantle some common urban legends.

Perhaps the most damaging misconception of all is the idea that concentration by its very nature creates wealth. Many writers, led by popular theorist Richard Florida, argue that centralized urban areas provide broader cultural opportunities and better access to technology, attracting more innovative, plugged-in people (Florida's "creative class") who will in the long term produce greater economic vibrancy. The hipper the city, the mantra goes, the richer and more successful it will be—and a number of declining American industrial hubs have tried to rebrand themselves as "creative class" hot spots accordingly.

But this argument, or at least many applications of it, gets things backward. Arts and culture generally do not fuel economic growth by themselves; rather, economic growth tends to create the preconditions for their development. Ancient Athens and Rome didn't start out as undiscovered artist neighborhoods. They were metropolises built on imperial wealth—largely collected by force from their colonies—that funded a new class of patrons and consumers of the arts. Renaissance Florence and Amsterdam established themselves as trade centers first and only then began to nurture great artists from their own middle classes and the surrounding regions.

Even modern Los Angeles owes its initial ascendancy as much to agriculture and oil as to Hollywood. Today, its port and related industries employ far more people than the entertainment business does. (In any case, the men who built Hollywood were hardly cultured aesthetes by middle-class American standards; they were furriers, butchers, and petty traders, mostly from hardscrabble backgrounds in the czarist *shtetls* and back streets of America's tough ethnic ghettos.) New York, now arguably the world's cultural capital, was once dismissed as a boorish, money-obsessed town, much like the contemporary urban critique of Dallas, Houston, or Phoenix.

Sadly, cities desperate to reverse their slides have been quick to buy into the simplistic idea that by merely branding themselves "creative" they can renew their dying economies; think of Cleveland's Rock and Roll Hall of Fame, Michigan's bid to market Detroit as a "cool city," and similar efforts in the washed-up industrial towns of the British north. Being told you live in a "European Capital of Culture," as Liverpool was in 2008, means little when your city has no jobs and people are leaving by the busload.

Even legitimate cultural meccas aren't insulated from economic turmoil. Berlin—beloved by writers, artists, tourists, and romantic expatriates—has cultural institutions that would put any wannabe European Capital of Culture to shame, as well as a thriving underground art and music scene. Yet for all its bohemian spirit, Berlin is also deeply in debt and suffers from unemployment far higher than Germany's national average, with rates reaching 14 percent. A full quarter of its workers, many of them living in wretched immigrant ghettos, earn less than 900 euros a month; compare that with Frankfurt, a smaller city more known for its skyscrapers and airport terminals than for any major cultural output, but which boasts one of Germany's lowest unemployment rates and by some estimates the highest per capita income of any European city. No wonder Berlin Mayor Klaus Wowereit once described his city as "poor but sexy."

Culture, media, and other "creative" industries, important as they are for a city's continued prosperity, simply do not spark an economy on their own. It turns out to be the comparatively boring, old-fashioned industries, such as trade in goods, manufacturing, energy, and agriculture, that drive the world's fastest-rising cities. In the 1960s and 1970s, the industrial capitals of Seoul and Tokyo developed their economies far faster than Cairo and Jakarta, which never created advanced industrial bases. China's great coastal urban centers, notably Guangzhou, Shanghai, and Shenzhen, are replicating this pattern with big business in steel, textiles, garments, and electronics, and the country's vast interior is now poised to repeat it once again. Fossil fuels—not art galleries—have powered the growth of several of the world's fastest-rising urban areas, including Abu Dhabi, Houston, Moscow, and Perth.

It's only after urban centers achieve economic success that they tend to look toward the higher-end amenities the creative-classers love. When Abu Dhabi decided to import its fancy Guggenheim and Louvre satellite museums, it was already, according to *Fortune* magazine, the world's richest city. Beijing, Houston, Shanghai, and Singapore are opening or expanding schools for the arts, museums, and gallery districts. But they paid for them the old-fashioned way.

Nor is the much-vaunted "urban core" the only game in town. Innovators of all kinds seek to avoid the high property prices, overcrowding, and often harsh antibusiness climates of the city center. Britain's recent strides in technology and design-led manufacturing have been concentrated not in London, but along the outer reaches of the Thames Valley and the areas around Cambridge. It's the same story in continental Europe, from the exurban Grand-Couronne outside of Paris to the "edge cities" that have sprung up around Amsterdam and Rotterdam. In India, the bulk of new tech companies cluster in campus-like developments around—but not necessarily in—Bangalore, Hyderabad, and New Delhi. And let's not forget that Silicon Valley, the granddaddy of global tech centers and still home to the world's largest concentration of high-tech workers, remains essentially a vast suburb. Apple, Google, and Intel don't seem to mind. Those relative few who choose to live in San Francisco can always take the company-provided bus.

In fact, the suburbs are not as terrible as urban boosters frequently insist.

Consider the environment. We tend to associate suburbia with carbon dioxide-producing sprawl and urban areas with sustainability and green living. But though it's true that urban residents use less gas to get to work than their suburban or rural counterparts, when it comes to overall energy use the picture gets more complicated. Studies in Australia and Spain have found that when you factor in apartment common areas, second residences, consumption, and air travel, urban residents can easily use more energy than their less densely packed neighbors. Moreover, studies around the world—from Beijing and Rome to London and Vancouver—have found that packed concentrations of concrete, asphalt, steel, and glass produce what are known as "heat islands," generating 6 to 10 °C more heat than surrounding areas and extending as far as twice a city's political boundaries.

When it comes to inequality, cities might even be the problem. In the West, the largest cities today also tend to suffer the most extreme polarization of incomes. In 1980, Manhattan ranked 17th among U.S. counties for income disparity; by 2007 it was first, with the top fifth of wage earners earning 52 times what the bottom fifth earned. In Toronto between 1970 and 2001, according to one recent study, middle-income neighborhoods shrank by half, dropping from two-thirds of the city to one-third, while poor districts more than doubled to 40 percent. By 2020, middle-class neighborhoods could fall to about 10 percent.

Cities often offer a raw deal for the working class, which ends up squeezed by a lethal combination of chronically high housing costs and chronically low opportunity in economies dominated by finance and other elite industries. Once the cost of living is factored in, more than half the children in inner London live in poverty, the highest level in Britain, according to a Greater London Authority study. More than 1 million Londoners were on public support in 2002, in a city of roughly 8 million.

The disparities are even starker in Asia. Shenzhen and Hong Kong, for instance, have among the most skewed income distributions in the region. A relatively small number of skilled professionals and investors are doing very well, yet millions are migrating to urban slums in places like Mumbai not because they've all suddenly become "knowledge workers," but because of the changing economics of farming. And by the

way, Mumbai's slums are still expanding as a proportion of the city's overall population—even as India's nationwide poverty rate has fallen from one in three Indians to one in five over the last two decades. Forty years ago, slum dwellers accounted for one in six Mumbaikars. Now they are a majority.

To their credit, talented new urbanists have had moderate success in turning smaller cities like Chattanooga and Hamburg into marginally more pleasant places to live. But grandiose theorists, with their focus on footloose elites and telecommuting technogeniuses, have no practical answers for the real problems that plague places like Mumbai, let alone Cairo, Jakarta, Manila, Nairobi, or any other 21st-century megacity: rampant crime, crushing poverty, and choking pollution. It's time for a completely different approach, one that abandons the long-held assumption that scale and growth go hand in hand.

Throughout the long history of urban development, the size of a city roughly correlated with its wealth, standard of living, and political strength. The greatest and most powerful cities were almost always the largest in population: Babylon, Rome, Alexandria, Baghdad, Delhi, London, or New York.

But bigger might no longer mean better. The most advantaged city of the future could well turn out to be a much smaller one. Cities today are expanding at an unparalleled rate when it comes to size, but wealth, power, and general well-being lag behind. With the exception of Los Angeles, New York, and Tokyo, most cities of 10 million or more are relatively poor, with a low standard of living and little strategic influence. The cities that do have influence, modern infrastructure, and relatively high per capita income, by contrast, are often wealthy small cities like Abu Dhabi or hard-charging up-and-comers such as Singapore. Their efficient, agile economies can outpace lumbering megacities financially, while also maintaining a high quality of life. With almost 5 million residents, for example, Singapore isn't at the top of the list in terms of population. But its GDP is much higher than that of larger cities like Cairo, Lagos, and Manila. Singapore boasts a per capita income of almost $50,000, one of the highest in the world, roughly the same as America's or Norway's. With one of the world's three largest ports, a zippy and safe subway system, and an impressive skyline, Singapore is easily the cleanest, most efficient big city in all of Asia. Other smaller-scaled cities like Austin, Monterrey, and Tel Aviv have enjoyed similar success.

It turns out that the rise of the megacity is by no means inevitable—and it might not even be happening. Shlomo Angel, an adjunct professor at New York University's Wagner School, has demonstrated that as the world's urban population exploded from 1960 to 2000, the percentage living in the 100 largest megacities actually declined from nearly 30 percent to closer to 25 percent. Even the widely cited 2009 World Bank report on megacities, a staunchly prourban document, acknowledges that as societies become wealthier, they inevitably begin to deconcentrate, with the middle classes moving to the periphery. Urban population densities have been on the decline since the nineteenth century, Angel notes, as people have sought out cheaper and more appealing homes beyond city limits. In fact, despite all the "back to the city" hype of the past decade, more than 80 percent of new metropolitan growth in the United States since 2000 has been in suburbs.

And that's not such a bad thing. Ultimately, dispersion—both city to suburb and megacity to small city—holds out some intriguing solutions to current urban problems. The idea took hold during the initial golden age of industrial growth—the English nineteenth century—when suburban "garden cities" were established around London's borders. The great early twentieth century visionary Ebenezer Howard saw this as a means to create a "new civilization" superior to the crowded, dirty, and congested cities of his day. It was an ideal that attracted a wide range of thinkers, including Friedrich Engels and H.G. Wells.

More recently, a network of smaller cities in the Netherlands has helped create a smartly distributed national economy. Amsterdam, for example, has low-density areas between its core and its corporate centers. It has kept the great Dutch city both livable and competitive. American urbanists are trying to bring the same thinking to the United States. Delore Zimmerman, of the North Dakota-based Praxis Strategy Group, has helped foster high-tech-oriented development in small towns and cities from the Red River Valley in North Dakota and Minnesota to the Wenatchee region in Washington State. The outcome has been promising: Both areas are reviving from periods of economic and demographic decline.

But the dispersion model holds out even more hope for the developing world, where an alternative to megacities is an even more urgent necessity. Ashok R. Datar, chairman of the Mumbai Environmental Social Network and a longtime advisor to the Ambani corporate group, suggests that slowing migration to urban slums represents the most practical strategy for relieving Mumbai's relentless poverty. His plan is similar to Zimmerman's: By bolstering local industries, you can stanch the flow of job seekers to major city centers, maintaining a greater balance between rural areas and cities and avoiding the severe overcrowding that plagues Mumbai right now.

Between the nineteenth century, when Charles Dickens described London as a "sooty spectre" that haunted and deformed its inhabitants, and the present, something has been lost from our discussion of cities: the human element. The goal of urban planners should not be to fulfill their own grandiose visions of megacities on a hill, but to meet the needs of the people living in them, particularly those people suffering from overcrowding, environmental misery, and social inequality. When it comes to exporting our notions to the rest of the globe, we must be aware of our own susceptibility to fashionable theories in urban design—because while the West may be able to live with its mistakes, the developing world doesn't enjoy that luxury.

Critical Thinking

1. Why do some analysts think that megacities are the wave of the future?
2. Why does Kotkin think that smaller cities, suburbs, and towns are the best prospects for the future?
3. What size places sustain the best quality of life?

Create Central

www.mhhe.com/createcentral

Internet References

New American Studies Web
www.georgetown.edu/crossroads/asw
Sociology—Study Sociology Online
http://edu.learnsoc.org
Sociology Web Resources
http://www.mhhe.com/socscience/sociology/resources/index.htm
Sociosite
http://www.topsite.com/goto/sociosite.net
Socioweb
http://www.topsite.com/goto/socioweb.com

Reprinted in entirety by McGraw-Hill with permission from *Foreign Policy,* September/October 2010. www.foreignpolicy.com. © 2010 Washingtonpost.Newsweek Interactive, LLC.

Article   Prepared by: Kurt Finsterbusch, *University of Maryland, College Park*

America's Immigration Policy Fiasco: Learning from Past Mistakes

DOUGLAS S. MASSEY

Learning Outcomes

After reading this article, you will be able to:

- Know the ways that immigration policies have failed.
- Be able to discuss the difficulty of controlling illegal immigration.
- Understand both the support for and the opposition to immigration.

Following the landmark immigration reforms of 1965, which sought to eliminate the taint of racism from U.S. immigration law, America's immigration and border policies took an increasingly restrictive turn. For the first time, hard numerical limits were imposed on immigration from the Western Hemisphere. These limits were tightened in subsequent years, drastically reducing opportunities for legal entry from Mexico, our neighbor and the largest contemporary source of immigrants to the United States. Inevitably, these restrictions gave rise to mass undocumented migration.[1] In response to the rising tide of apprehensions, U.S. policy-makers increased border enforcement exponentially, scaling up deportations to record levels. The immigration enforcement industry presently costs the U.S. government an estimated $18 billion per year; employs more than 20,000 Border Patrol Officers (an all-time high); and deports an unprecedented 400,000 undocumented migrants per year.[2]

Despite the astounding enforcement effort of the past several decades, net immigration from Latin America has only accelerated. From 1970 to 2010, the percentage of foreign-born rose from 4.7 percent to 13 percent of the U.S. population, the undocumented population rose from a few 1,000 to a current total of 11 million persons, and Latinos climbed from 4.7 percent to 16.3 percent of the total population.[3] If the goal of U.S. policy was to limit the number of Latin Americans living in the United States, it clearly failed. Although the 1965 liberalization of restrictions on Asian, African, and Southern/Eastern European immigration generally worked as expected—bringing in a diverse array of new immigrants in manageable numbers, many of whom were highly educated—the tightening of restrictions on immigration from the Americas backfired.

This failure derives from the fact that the immigration policies implemented in 1965 and thereafter were not founded on any rational, evidence-based understanding of international migration. Instead, they were enacted for domestic political purposes and reveal more about America's hopes and aspirations—and its fears and apprehensions—than anything having to do with immigrants or immigration per se. When policies are implemented for symbolic political purposes, and massive interventions are undertaken with no real understanding of how they might affect a complex social system such as immigration, the results are not only likely to be unanticipated, but counterproductive. And that is exactly what transpired in North America. The unintended consequences of U.S. immigration policy unleashed a chain reaction of events that produced an unprecedented boom in Latin American immigration to the United States, despite monumental enforcement efforts.

Our story begins with the crest of the civil rights movement in the 1960s, as legislators pushed to right the historical wrong of racial segregation. The 1964 Civil Rights Act outlawed discrimination in hiring and service provision and put teeth into school desegregation; the 1965 Voting Rights Act guaranteed black suffrage and prohibited the various subterfuges by which African Americans historically had been disenfranchised; the 1968 Fair Housing Act prohibited discrimination in the rental or sale of housing; and the 1974 Equal Credit Opportunity Act banned discrimination in mortgage lending. Within a brief decade, the vestiges of racism were purged from the American legal code.

In the context of an expanding civil rights movement, the provisions within U.S. immigration policy that openly discriminated against Asians, Africans, and Southern/Eastern Europeans came to be seen as intolerably racist. In 1965, over vociferous Southern objections, Congress amended the Immigration and Nationality Act to create a new immigration system that allocated residence visas on the basis of skills and family ties to U.S. residents, rather than national origins.[4] The legislation initially created separate numerical quotas for the Eastern and Western Hemispheres, but in 1978, the hemispheric caps were abandoned in favor of a single worldwide ceiling of 290,000 visas, with each nation eligible for up to around 20,000 visas per year. Immediate relatives of U.S. citizens were exempt from these numerical limits, however.[5]

Mexican immigration to the United States had averaged around 50,000 persons per year prior to 1965. In addition to this sizable inflow of legal immigrants, Mexico enjoyed access to a large temporary worker program that, from 1942 to 1964, enabled short-term visas for work in the United States, mostly in agriculture. At the program's height, some 450,000 Mexicans were entering each year as temporary laborers. As the civil rights era gained momentum, however, the program came to be seen as exploitive and discriminatory, on par with Southern sharecropping. Congress began to cut back the number of work visas in 1960 and unilaterally terminated the program in 1965, despite strong protests from the Mexican government.[6]

The repeal of the discriminatory quotas and the termination of the temporary worker program had been undertaken for the laudable goal of ending racism in U.S. immigration policy; but in neither case did Congress give any consideration to what the consequences might be for the system of Mexican migration, which had evolved to become fully institutionalized by 1965. In the late 1950s, the United States was admitting a half-million Mexican migrants per year (all in legal status), roughly 90 percent for temporary work and 10 percent for permanent residence. By 1960, these flows were sustained by well-developed social networks that connected households and communities in Mexico to jobs and employers in the United States. Economic expectations and structures on both sides of the border were adapted to this reality.[7]

What would happen to this deeply entrenched, thoroughly institutionalized flow of migrants once opportunities for legal entry from Mexico were terminated? Congress did not address or even seriously consider this question; but migration theory and research yield the strong conclusion that immigration flows tend to acquire an obdurate momentum once they are supported by an institutionalized social infrastructure of networks, practices, and expectations, especially when conditions of labor supply and demand remain unchanged. As a result, when opportunities for legal entry disappeared after 1965, the massive inflow from Mexico simply reestablished itself under undocumented auspices. Undocumented migration steadily rose in subsequent years until, by 1979, it roughly equaled the volume observed in the late 1950s, only now the overwhelming majority of migrants were "illegal."[8]

Although little had changed except the documentation of the migrants, the rise of illegal migration after 1965 offered a golden opportunity for ambitious bureaucrats and cynical politicians to garner financial resources and political support; for by definition, illegal migrants were "criminals" and "lawbreakers," and thus readily portrayed as a grave threat to the nation. Magazine articles on immigration published between 1970 and 2000 were characterized by the rise of a distinct "Latino threat narrative" that framed Latin Americans in general, and Mexicans in particular, using one of two threatening metaphors. On the one hand, migrants from the south were portrayed as a brown "flood" that would "inundate" American culture and "drown" its society. On the other hand, undocumented migrants were portrayed as "invaders" who "swarmed" across the border in "banzai charges" to overrun "outgunned" Border Patrol Agents who fought vainly to "hold the line" against the "alien invasion."[9]

As the Cold War climaxed, the war on drugs accelerated, and the war on terror came to dominate public rhetoric, martial metaphors overtook marine metaphors. As the number of border apprehensions rose each year, press releases, news articles, and political speeches heralded the increase as confirmation of the ongoing invasion. Although the steady drumbeat of the Latino threat narrative inflamed public opinion and pushed it in a more conservative, restrictionist direction,[10] from 1965 to 1979, the rise in apprehensions stemmed from actual increases in undocumented traffic at the border, because formerly legal temporary migration was restored under undocumented auspices as circular illegal migration. After 1979, however, the number of undocumented entries stabilized and the rise in apprehensions was pushed forward by the intensifying enforcement effort.[11]

The 1976 *Reader's Digest* article "Illegal Aliens: Time to Call a Halt!"—written by the Commissioner of the U.S. Immigration and Naturalization Service—reflects the popularized Latino threat narrative. In it, the commissioner alleges that his agency is "out-manned, under-budgeted, and confronted by a growing, silent invasion of illegal aliens" that "threatens to become a national disaster."[12] Through such scare tactics, he and other immigration officials and their political allies were successful in channeling ever-greater resources and personnel to combat the alleged invasion. The number of apprehensions began to rise in self-feeding fashion, even though the underlying traffic at the border was no longer increasing. Each new release of apprehension statistics was accompanied by a demand for more enforcement resources, which indeed produced more apprehensions, which justified still more enforcement resources. As a result, during the 1980s and 1990s, border enforcement increased exponentially in a manner that was completely detached from the actual number of undocumented migrants attempting to cross the border.[13]

From 1980 to 2000, the Border Patrol increased from 2,500 to 9,200 officers, and its budget rose from $83 million to $1.1 billion. In response, apprehensions surged from 817,000 to 1.7 million, even though independent estimates indicate the volume of undocumented entries was roughly constant. Despite the massive increase in border enforcement, the number of migrants entering the United States without authorization changed little; but the sharp upward surge in the costs and risks of border crossing did alter the behavior of migrants, though not in ways expected by policy-makers. As enforcement personnel and matériel accumulated in the two busiest border sectors, migratory flows were diverted away from El Paso and, especially, San Diego, and toward the Sonoran desert and new crossing points on the Arizona border. This shift increased the average cost of crossing from roughly $500 to $3,000 per trip and tripled the death rate of undocumented migrants attempting the crossing. Having been forcibly pushed away from California, migrants continued on to new destinations, such as North Carolina, South Carolina, Georgia, Nebraska, and Iowa, states which in the 1990s came to house the most rapidly growing Latino populations.[14]

In addition to changing crossing and destination points, rising border enforcement also altered the propensity of migrants to circulate back and forth. Given the rising costs and risks of unauthorized border crossing, migrants quite logically minimized crossing—not by remaining in Mexico, but by settling more permanently in the United States. The principal effect of the progressive militarization of the Mexico–U.S. border was to reduce the rate of undocumented out-migration back to Mexico; it did not lower the rate of undocumented migration into the United States.[15] The end result was a doubling of the net rate of illegal migration and a sharp increase in undocumented population growth through the 1990s and into the new century. In the course of two decades, the North American migration system was transformed from a circular flow of male workers going to California and a few other states into a settled population of families living in all 50 states. From 1988 to 2008, the number of unauthorized residents of the United States grew from 1.9 million to 12 million, while the share residing in California dropped from 40 percent to 25 percent.[16]

Illegal migration has always been confounded in the public mind with threats to the nation's security—be they from Jacobins, papists, or Communists—and the 1980s were no exception. In the context of the Cold War and the proxy confrontation with the Soviet Union in Central America, President Reagan warned Americans that "terrorists and subversives are just two days' driving time from [the border crossing at] Harlingen, Texas," and in response to such rhetoric, the 1986 Immigration Reform and Control Act contained a host of provisions enacted to manage a potential "immigration emergency." In another speech, Reagan predicted that extremist groups would "feed on the anger and frustration of recent Central and South American immigrants who will not realize their own version of the American dream."[17]

With the collapse of the Soviet Union, illegal immigrants lost their value as a trope in the Cold War; however, they were quickly co-opted symbolically in the war on terror. In response to the 1993 attack on the World Trade Center and the 1995 bombing in Oklahoma City, Congress in 1996 passed the Anti-Terrorism and Effective Death Penalty Act and the Illegal Immigration Reform and Immigrant Responsibility Act. Following the 1998 bombing of the USS *Cole* in Yemen, the 2000 bombings of American embassies in Kenya and Tanzania, and the catastrophic attacks of September 11, 2001, Congress enacted the USA PATRIOT Act. These measures not only strengthened border enforcement, but very deliberately increased pressure on both legal and illegal immigrants within the United States.[18]

The 1996 legislation, for example, authorized removals from ports of entry without judicial hearings, declared undocumented migrants ineligible for public benefits, restricted access of documented migrants to certain means-tested programs, granted local agencies the power to assist in immigration enforcement, declared any alien who had *ever* committed a crime immediately deportable, authorized the "expedited exclusion" of any alien who had *ever* crossed the border without documents, granted authority to the State Department to designate any organization as "terrorist" and render all its members deportable, added alien smuggling to the list of crimes covered by the antimafia RICO statute, and severely limited the possibilities for judicial review of all deportations. The 2001 legislation granted executive authorities additional powers to deport, without presentation of evidence, any alien—legal or illegal—that the attorney general had "reason to believe" might commit, further, or facilitate acts of terrorism. It also authorized the arrest, imprisonment, and deportation of noncitizens upon the orders of the attorney general, again without judicial review.[19]

The cumulative result of these actions was a massive escalation of roundups in immigrant neighborhoods, raids at employment sites, "stop and frisk" actions on city streets, and traffic stops along public roadways. The end result was an exponential increase in immigrant detentions and deportations that threatened not only undocumented migrants, but any foreigner who was not a U.S. citizen. From 1990 to 2010, deportations from the United States rose from 30,000 to around 400,000 per year. In response, millions of legal immigrants rushed to undertake *defensive naturalization:* petitioning for U.S. citizenship in order to protect their rights and safeguard their ability to remain in the United States.[20]

Historically, Latin American and, especially, Mexican immigrants had displayed very low rates of naturalization. In the 1990s, however, citizenship applications surged in response to the rising tide of internal enforcement and cumulative restriction of liberties. Among Mexicans, the number of naturalizations had never exceeded 30,000 per year prior to 1990, and the total number in the two decades between 1970 and 1990 stood at just 233,000. However, Mexican naturalizations surged to 255,000 in 1996, with plateaus of 208,000 in 1999 and 232,000 in 2008, yielding a cumulative total of 2.1 million new citizens between 1990 and 2010.[21]

The surge in naturalizations is key to understanding the acceleration of legal immigration from Mexico that has unfolded in recent years, despite the annual cap of 20,000 visas per country; for as noted earlier, immediate relatives of U.S. citizens are exempt from numerical limits. Although legal permanent residents are authorized to petition for the entry of their spouses and minor children, these visas fall under the annual cap, and their relatives must wait until a visa becomes available—which for an oversubscribed country such as Mexico takes years. In contrast, if permanent residents naturalize to become U.S. citizens, their spouses and minor children are eligible for immediate entry, along with the immigrant's parents. Moreover, their adult children and siblings acquire the right to enter, subject to numerical limitation.

In sum, each new citizen creates new entitlements within the U.S. immigration system and produces more legal immigrants down the road. As a result, when Congress began to strip away the rights and privileges of permanent residents and threaten them with deportation for a growing number of infractions, it unwittingly created hundreds of thousands of new entitlements for permanent resident visas that pushed legal immigration well above the statutory cap of 20,000 visas per year. To be sure, the exemption offered to citizen relatives had long pushed legal immigration from Mexico above the 20,000 visa limit. During the 1970s, for example, arrivals of Mexican legal residents averaged 63,000 per year despite the cap. By the latter half of the 1990s, however, the average more than doubled to reach

136,000, and from 2000 through 2010, it stood at 170,000 per year. Whereas only 5 percent of all legal Mexican immigrants entered as relatives of U.S. citizens in 1990, that figure rose to nearly two-thirds by 2010. In its zeal to increase pressure on foreigners in the name of the war on terror, Congress inadvertently increased legal immigration from Mexico by a factor of nearly three.[22]

Up to now I have focused on Mexico, by far the leading contributor of migrants to the United States. Since 1970, Mexico alone has accounted for approximately 20 percent of documented and 60 percent of undocumented immigrants to the United States—and half of all documented and three-quarters of all undocumented immigrants from Latin America. After Mexico, the second major source region in Latin America is Central America, which accounts for around 15 percent of documented and 20 percent of undocumented migrants from the region. Immigration from Central America was minimal prior to 1980, with legal entries totaling just 114,000 during the 1970s. But entries by Central Americans grew rapidly thereafter, totaling around 325,000 in the 1980s and around 600,000 in both the 1990s and 2000s.[23]

The surge in Central American immigration stemmed from the U.S.-Contra intervention, which raised levels of violence and social disorder in the region and pushed thousands of people northward as refugees. Although Nicaraguans, escaping a left-wing, pro-Soviet regime, were readily accepted as refugees and ultimately admitted to permanent residence, other Central Americans—Salvadorans, Guatemalans, and Hondurans—were labeled "economic migrants," and were not welcomed. U.S. officials relegated these migrants to temporary protected status at best, and more commonly undocumented status, adding a significant Central American component to America's Latin American population boom.[24]

Over the past four decades, the United States has undergone a mass immigration not seen since the early twentieth century. The new wave has yielded a progressive Latinization of the U.S. population and a rising prevalence of illegality among the foreign born. From 1970 to 2010, the foreign-born population rose from 9.6 to 40 million persons, while the Latino population grew from 9.6 million to 50.5 million, now making up 16.3 percent of the total population. Among Latinos, the foreign-born population rose from 30 percent to 40 percent, and Central Americans and Mexicans together increased their share of the population from two-thirds to three-quarters. (Caribbeans fell from 25 percent to about 15 percent.) Among Latinos present in 2010, nearly a third lacked documents, and nearly 60 percent of immigrant Latinos were unauthorized.[25]

For the most part, these developments were unintended consequences of U.S. immigration and border policies enacted without regard for realities on the ground. By curtailing opportunities for legal entry from the Americas after 1965, the United States transformed a well established and largely circular flow of legal migrants into an equally well established, circular flow of illegal migrants. The increase in illegal migration led, in turn, to the rise of the Latino threat initiative and a shift toward increasingly restrictive policies. The resultant militarization of the Mexico–U.S. border transformed the geography of border crossing and led to a proliferation of new destinations, while at the same time reducing rates of return migration and accelerating the undocumented population growth. Finally, U.S. political and military interventions in Central America during the 1980s generated outflows of émigrés that further augmented Latin American population growth in the United States. As a result, since 1970, the foreign-born population has quadrupled, the United States became substantially more Latino, national origins among Latinos have shifted decisively toward Mexico and Central America, and the share present without authorization has risen to unprecedented heights.

The evidence thus suggests that the turn toward restrictive immigration policies after 1965 was counterproductive, to say the least. Particularly in the case of Mexico, the contradictions are glaring. In 1994, the United States and Mexico entered into a free trade agreement designed to reduce barriers to crossborder movements of goods, capital, resources, information, services, and many categories of people. Not only was free movement of labor excluded from the otherwise integrated North American market being established, but that same year, the United States launched Operation Gatekeeper to block the flow of migrants through the busiest border sector—part of a two-decade-long process of border militarization. Apparently, the contradiction between the stated goal of integrating all factor markets in North America and the exclusion of Mexican labor from participating never occurred to leaders in Washington.

The simple reality is that, as a practical matter, it is virtually impossible to stop the movement of people between two countries that share a 3,000-mile border, are linked together in a free trade agreement, are among one another's largest trading partners, and are bound by a joint history of social, economic, and political interpenetration. If one tries unilaterally to block flows of people that are the natural outgrowth of broader processes of social and economic integration, moreover, the results are dysfunctional and counterproductive, as we have seen. Rather than seeking to suppress migratory flows that merely reflect the powerful forces binding North America together, the alternative is to accept the flows and seek to manage them in

ways that are beneficial to Americans, Mexicans, and the immigrants themselves.

In North America, the stars might finally be aligned for such a transition, moving away from unilateral repression toward bilateral strategies of management. With the conspicuous help of Latino voters, President Obama won a second term and need not worry again about reelection. In Mexico, meanwhile, new President Enrique Peña Nieto has taken charge and is looking for a way forward on issues with its northern neighbor. Should the two presidents seek to cooperate in managing international migration more effectively, they will benefit from a unique political moment when the pressure is off: undocumented migration from Mexico has fallen to a net of zero and has remained there since 2008. Indeed, the net immigration rate may even be negative.[26]

One reason for this development is the quiet return of temporary worker migration. Whereas only 3,300 Mexicans entered the United States on temporary work visas in 1980, in 2010 the number reached 517,000.[27] Though the latter figure is inflated by new measurement efforts at the border, in 2008, before these new efforts were implemented, the number of entries stood at 361,000, the largest number since 1959. When added to the average of 170,000 Mexicans who entered each year as permanent residents, we see that substantial opportunities for legal entry have opened up in the U.S. immigration system, with numbers fluctuating around the half-million level last observed in the late 1950s. Although labor demand in the United States faltered in the great recession of 2008, the demand that remains is currently being met by legal migration in various categories.

In Mexico, meanwhile, the conditions that have for so long driven immigrants northward have shifted. Birth rates have fallen dramatically, the rate of labor force growth is rapidly decelerating, and the Mexican population is aging as rural populations continue to dwindle. Rural dwellers, long the source of a disproportionate share of Mexican immigrants, dropped from 35 percent of the population to roughly 20 percent today. At the same time, real wages have stabilized even as they have fallen in the United States, while education levels among younger cohorts have steadily risen and the middle class has grown.[28] The young migrants leaving Mexico today are increasingly well-educated people of metropolitan origin who are migrating in response to the rhythms of development in an ever-more integrated North American economy.[29]

In sum, the conditions that supported mass undocumented migration in the past appear to be disappearing, and what needs to be done now is to find ways to better manage the flows that will inevitably occur in the course of North American economic integration. We must facilitate the entry and return of the large majority of migrants who prefer circulation to settlement, while opening up opportunities for legal permanent residence for the minority of migrants who acquire strong social or economic connections to the United States and wish to remain permanently.

In recent years, politicians in the United States have referred to four "pillars" of comprehensive immigration reform: gain control of the border, create a sizable guest worker program, increase the quotas for immigration from Mexico (and Canada), and enact a pathway to legalization for undocumented U.S. residents. Of these, three have already been achieved in de facto terms: illegal migration has been at a net of zero since 2008; temporary worker entries are at levels not seen since the late 1950s; and through defensive naturalization, Mexicans themselves have in practical terms increased the size of their quotas for legal immigration.

Although the current system of temporary worker migration could certainly benefit from improvements to protect workers from exploitation, the most serious task remaining for immigration reformers is the legalization of the 11 million persons who are currently unauthorized, especially the 3 million or more persons who entered as minors and grew up in the United States. The lack of legal status constitutes an insurmountable barrier to social and economic mobility, not only for the undocumented immigrants themselves, but for their citizen family members. Not since the days of slavery have so many residents of the United States lacked the most basic social, economic, and human rights.

The transition to a minority–majority U.S. population is now well under way, and is inevitable in demographic terms. Although the U.S. population is currently 16 percent Latino, 14 percent black, 5 percent Asian, and 3 percent mixed race, among births, 25 percent are to Latino mothers, 15 percent are to African Americans, and 7 percent are to Asians, making up almost half the total. Our failure to arrange for the legalization of the 11 million persons currently out of status will not change the demographic transition under way in the United States; it will only render it more contentious, problematic, and costly to society. In 2013, the United States, Mexico, and Canada have a unique opportunity to break with the failed policies of the past and enter a new era of cooperation to manage, rather than suppress, the ongoing flow of migrants who will inevitably move within the free trade zone that has been created among the three countries.[30]

Notes

1. Aristide R. Zolberg, *A Nation by Design: Immigration Policy in the Fashioning of America* (New York: Russell Sage Foundation, 2006); and Douglas S. Massey, Jorge Durand, and Nolan J. Malone, *Beyond Smoke and Mirrors: Mexican Immigration in an Age of Economic Integration* (New York: Russell Sage Foundation, 2002).

2. Doris Meissner, Donald M. Kerwin, Muzaffar Chishti, and Claire Bergoni, *Immigration Enforcement in the United States: The Rise of a Formidable Machinery* (Washington, D.C.: Migration Policy Institute, 2013).

3. Yesenia D. Acosta, G. Patricia de la Cruz, Christine Gambino, Thomas Gryn, Luke J. Larsen, Eward N. Trevelyan, and Nathan P. Walters, *The Foreign-Born Population in the United States: 2010* (Washington, D.C.: U.S. Census Bureau, 2012); and Sharon R. Ennis, Merarys Ríos-Vargas, and Nora G. Albert, *The Hispanic Population: 2010* (Washington, D.C.: U.S. Census Bureau, 2011).

4. Gabriel J. Chin, "The Civil Rights Revolution Comes to Immigration Law: A New Look at the Immigration and Nationality Act of 1965," *North Carolina Law Review* 75 (1996–1997): 279–345.

5. Zolberg, *A Nation by Design;* and Guillermina Jasso and Mark R. Rosenzweig, *The New Chosen People: Immigrants in the United States* (New York: Russell Sage Foundation, 1990), 2–97.

6. Massey, Durand, and Malone, *Beyond Smoke and Mirrors.*

7. Douglas S. Massey, Rafael Alarcón, Jorge Durand, and Humberto González, *Return to Aztlan: The Social Process of International Migration from Western Mexico* (Berkeley: University of California Press, 1987).

8. Douglas S. Massey and Karen A. Pren, "Origins of the New Latino Underclass," *Race and Social Problems* 4 (2012): 5–17.

9. Leo R. Chavez, *Covering Immigration: Population Images and the Politics of the Nation* (Berkeley: University of California Press, 2001); Otto Santa Ana, *Brown Tide Rising: Metaphors of Latinos in Contemporary American Public Discourse* (Austin: University of Texas Press, 2002); and Leo R. Chavez, *The Latino Threat: Constructing Immigrants, Citizens, and the Nation* (Stanford, C.A.: Stanford University Press, 2008).

10. Massey and Pren, "Origins of the New Latino Underclass."

11. Douglas S. Massey and Karen A. Pren, "Unintended Consequences of U.S. Immigration Policy: Explaining the Post—1965 Surge from Latin America," *Population and Development Review* 38 (2012): 1–29.

12. Leonard F. Chapman, "Illegal Aliens: Time to Call a Halt!" *Reader's Digest,* October 1976, 188–192.

13. Massey and Pren, "Unintended Consequences of U.S. Immigration Policy."

14. Massey, Durand, and Malone, *Beyond Smoke and Mirrors;* and Douglas S. Massey, *New Faces in New Places: The New Geography of American Immigration* (New York: Russell Sage Foundation, 2008).

15. Massey, Durand, and Malone, *Beyond Smoke and Mirrors;* Massey and Pren, "Unintended Consequences of U.S. Immigration Policy."

16. Ruth E. Wasem, *Unauthorized Aliens Residing in the United States: Estimates Since 1986* (Washington, D.C.: Congressional Research Service, 2011).

17. Quoted in Al Kamen, "Central America is No Longer the Central Issue for Americans," *Austin American Statesman,* October 21, 1990. See also, Timothy J. Dunn, *The Militarization of the U.S.-Mexico Border, 1978–1992: Low-Intensity Conflict Doctrine Comes Home* (Austin: Center for Mexican American Studies, University of Texas at Austin, 1996).

18. Zolberg, *A Nation by Design.*

19. Douglas S. Massey and Magaly Sánchez R., *Brokered Boundaries: Creating Immigrant Identity in Anti-Immigrant Times* (New York: Russell Sage Foundation, 2010).

20. Massey and Pren, "Unintended Consequences of U.S. Immigration Policy."

21. U.S. Office of Immigration Statistics, *2010 Yearbook of Immigration Statistics* (Washington, D.C.: U.S. Department of Homeland Security, 2011).

22. Massey and Pren, "Unintended Consequences of U.S. Immigration Policy."

23. U.S. Office of Immigration Statistics, *2010 Yearbook of Immigration Statistics.*

24. Jennifer H. Lundquist and Douglas S. Massey, "Politics or Economics? International Migration During the Nicaraguan Contra War," *Journal of Latin American Studies* 37 (2005): 29–53.

25. Michael Hoefer, Nancy Rytina, and Bryan C. Baker, *Estimates of the Unauthorized Immigrant Population Residing in the United States: January 2010* (Washington, D.C.: Office of Immigration Statistics, U.S. Department of Homeland Security, 2010).

26. Jeffrey Passel, D'Vera Cohn, and Ana Gonzalez-Barrera, *Net Migration from Mexico Falls to Zero—and Perhaps Less* (Washington, D.C.: Pew Research Hispanic Center, 2012).

27. U.S. Office of Immigration Statistics, *2010 Yearbook of Immigration Statistics.*

28. Instituto Nacional de Estadística y Geografía, Gobeirno de México, http://www.inegi.org.mx/.

29. Filiz Garip, "Discovering Diverse Mechanisms of Migration: The Mexico-U.S. Stream from 1970 to 2000," *Population and Development Review* 38 (2012): 393–433.

30. Douglas S. Massey, "Caution: NAFTA at Work," *Miller-McCune Magazine* 1 (1) (2008): 2–9; and Patricia Fernández Kelly and Douglas S. Massey, "Borders for Whom? The Role of NAFTA in Mexico-U.S. Migration," *Annals of the American Academy of Political and Social Science* 610 (2007): 98–119.

Critical Thinking

1. Why is the Latino population at the center of the immigration debate?
2. What should be done about illegal immigration into the United States?
3. What are the pros and cons about a path to citizenship for illegal immigrants?

Create Central

www.mhhe.com/createcentral

Internet References

Immigration Facts
www.immigrationforum.org

New American Studies Web
www.georgetown.edu/crossroads/asw

Sociology—Study Sociology Online
http://edu.learnsoc.org

Sociology Web Resources
http://www.mhhe.com/socscience/sociology/resources/index.htm

Sociosite
http://www.topsite.com/goto/sociosite.net

Socioweb
http://www.topsite.com/goto/socioweb.com

DOUGLAS S. MASSEY, a fellow of the American Academy since 1995, is the Henry G. Bryant Professor of Sociology and Public Affairs at Princeton University. His publications include *Brokered Boundaries: Creating Immigrant Identity in Anti-Immigrant Times* (with Magaly Sánchez R., 2010), *Categorically Unequal: The American Stratification System* (2007), and *Beyond Smoke and Mirrors: Mexican Immigration in an Age of Economic Integration* (with Jorge Durand and Nolan J. Malone, 2002).

Massey, Douglas S., "America's Immigration Policy Fiasco: Learning from Past Mistakes," *Daedalus,* Summer, 2013. Copyright © 2013 by MIT Press Journals. All rights reserved. Used with permission.

Unit 3

UNIT

Prepared by: Kurt Finsterbusch, *University of Maryland, College Park*

Problems of Poverty and Inequality

America is famous as the land of opportunity, and people from around the world have come to its shores in pursuit of the American dream. But how is America living up to this dream today? It is still a place for people to get rich, but it is also a place where people are trapped in poverty. This unit tells a number of stories of Americans dealing with advantages and disadvantages, opportunities and barriers, power, and powerlessness.

The first section of this unit deals with income inequality and the hardships of the poor. It documents that poverty is widespread in America. It explores the impacts of globalization on our economy detailing both the positive and the negative impacts. It examines the culture of poverty thesis and finds that it is a myth. The next section examines racial and ethnic issues. Racism continues to exist and one of the causes of the present strength of racism are the misperceptions embedded is a racist culture. Finally, the harmful attitudes toward Arab and Muslim Americans since 9/11 are appraised. The last section covers gender inequalities and issues. A major issue is whether women can have it all, meaning success both at work and raising children at home. This section also presents the facts on human sex trafficking in America, LGBT rights, and sexism against boys.

Article   Prepared by: Kurt Finsterbusch, *University of Maryland, College Park*

Overwhelming Evidence That Half of America Is In or Near Poverty

PAUL BUCHHEIT

Learning Outcomes

After reading this article, you will be able to:

- Have a good understanding of the definitions and extent of poverty in the United States.

- Understand which policies have reduced poverty.

- Know why so many people are poor.

The Charles Koch Foundation recently released a commercial that ranked a near poverty level $34,000 family among the Top one percent of poor people in the world. Bud Konheim, CEO and cofounder of fashion company Nicole Miller, concurred: "The guy that's making, oh my God, he's making $35,000 a year, why don't we try that out in India or some countries we can't even name. China, anyplace, the guy is wealthy."

Comments like these are condescending and self-righteous. They display an ignorance of the needs of lower-income and middle-income families in America. The costs of food and housing and education and health care and transportation and child care and taxes have been well defined by organizations such as the Economic Policy Institute, which calculated that a U.S. family of three would require an average of about $48,000 a year to meet basic needs; and by the Working Poor Families Project, which estimates the income required for basic needs for a family of four at about $45,000. The median household income is $51,000.

The following discussion pertains to the half of America that is in or near poverty, the people rarely seen by Congress.

1. The Official Poverty Threshold Should Be Much Higher

According to the Congressional Research Service (CRS), *"The poverty line reflects a measure of economic need based on living standards that prevailed in the mid-1950s . . . It is not adjusted to reflect changes in needs associated with improved standards of living that have occurred over the decades since the measure was first developed. If the same basic methodology developed in the early 1960s was applied today, the poverty thresholds would be over three times higher than the current thresholds."*

The original poverty measures were (and still are) based largely on the food costs of the 1950s. But while food costs have doubled since 1978, housing has more than *tripled,* medical expenses are *six times higher,* and college tuition is *eleven times higher.* The Bureau of Labor Statistics and the Census Bureau have calculated that food, housing, health care, child care, transportation, taxes, and other household expenditures consume nearly the *entire* median household income.

CRS provides some balance, noting that the threshold should also be impacted by safety net programs: *"For purposes of officially counting the poor, noncash benefits (such as the value of Medicare and Medicaid, public housing, or employer provided health care) and 'near cash' benefits (e.g., food stamps.) are not counted as income."*

But many American families near the median are not able to take advantage of safety net programs. Almost all, on the other hand, face the housing, health care, child care, and transportation expenses that point toward a higher threshold of poverty.

2. Almost Half of Americans Own, on Average, NOTHING

The bottom half of America own just 1.1 percent of the country's wealth, or about $793 billion, which is the same amount owned by the 30 richest Americans. ZERO wealth is owned by approximately the bottom 47 percent.

This nonexistent net worth is due in great part to the overwhelming burden of debt for Americans, which now includes college graduates entering the work force. The average student loan balance has risen 91 percent in the past 10 years.

3. Half of Americans are "Poor" or "Low-Income"

This is based on the Census Department's *Relative Poverty Measure* (Table 4), which is "most commonly used in developed countries to measure poverty." The Economic Policy Institute uses the term "economically vulnerable." With this standard, 18 percent of Americans are below the poverty threshold and 32 percent are below twice the threshold, putting them in the *low-income* category.

The official poverty rate increased by 25 percent between 2000 and 2011. Seniors and children feel the greatest impact, with 55 percent of the elderly and almost 60 percent of children classified as poor or low-income under the relative poverty measure. *Wider Opportunities for Women* reports that "sixty percent of women age 65 and older who live alone or live with a spouse have incomes insufficient to cover basic, daily expenses."

4. It's Much Worse for Black Families

Incredibly, while America's total wealth has risen from $12 trillion to $77 trillion in 25 years, the median net worth for black households has GONE DOWN over approximately the same time, from $7,150 to $6,446, adjusted for inflation. *State of Working America* reports that almost half of black children under the age of six are living in poverty.

5. Nearly Half of American Households Don't Have Enough to Hold Them for Three Months

That's according to the Corporation for Enterprise Development. Even more striking, a survey by Bankrate.com concluded that only *one in four* Americans has "six months' worth of expenses for use in emergency, the minimum recommended by many financial planning experts."

It Would Be Much Worse without the Safety Net

The Center on Budget and Policy Priorities estimates that without food stamps and other safety net initiatives, the poverty rate would be *double* the official rate. Economist Jared Bernstein quantifies the importance of Social Security, arguing that without retirement benefits the elderly poverty rate would be *five times* the current rate.

The Koch Foundation and Mr. Konheim need to look beyond their own circles of privilege before making insulting comments about the lower-income half of America.

Critical Thinking

1. What are the different views about the extent of poverty?
2. What evidence does Buchheit provide to show that almost half of Americans are poor?
3. How should poverty be addressed?

Create Central

www.mhhe.com/createcentral

Internet References

Joint Center for Poverty Research
www.jcpr.org
New American Studies Web
www.georgetown.edu/crossroads/asw
Social Science Information Gateway
http://sosig.esrc.bris.ac.uk
Sociology—Study Sociology Online
http://edu.learnsoc.org
Sociology Web Resources
http://www.mhhe.com/socscience/sociology/resources/index.htm
Sociosite
http://www.topsite.com/goto/sociosite.net
Socioweb
http://www.topsite.com/goto/socioweb.com

PAUL BUCHHEIT is a college teacher, a writer for progressive publications, and the founder and developer of social justice and educational websites (UsAgainstGreed.org, PayUpNow.org, RappingHistory.org.

Buchheit, Paul, "Overwhelming Evidence That Half of America Is In or Near Poverty," *AlterNet*, March 23, 2014. Copyright © 2014 by Paul Buchheit. All rights reserved. Used with permission.

Article   Prepared by: Kurt Finsterbusch, *University of Maryland, College Park*

The Impact of Globalization on Income and Employment: The Downside of Integrating Markets

MICHAEL SPENCE

Learning Outcomes

After reading this article, you will be able to:

- Understand how globalization has affected Americans' economic situation.

- Understand that globalization means that American workers in most areas of production must compete against workers in poor countries who receive very low wages.

- Better understand the role of technology in transforming world economies.

Globalization is the process by which markets integrate worldwide. Over the past 60 years, it has accelerated steadily as new technologies and management expertise have reduced transportation and transaction costs and as tariffs and other man-made barriers to international trade have been lowered. The impact has been stunning. More and more developing countries have been experiencing sustained growth rates of 7–10 percent; 13 countries, including China, have grown by more than 7 percent per year for 25 years or more. Although this was unclear at the outset, the world now finds itself just past the midpoint in a century-long process in which income levels in developing countries have been converging toward those in developed countries. Now, the emerging economies' impact on the global economy and the advanced economies is rising rapidly. Until about a decade ago, the effects of globalization on the distribution of wealth and jobs were largely benign. On average, advanced economies were growing at a respectable rate of 2.5 percent, and in most of them, the breadth

and variety of employment opportunities at various levels of education seemed to be increasing. With external help, even the countries ravaged by World War II recovered. Imported goods became cheaper as emerging markets engaged with the global economy, benefiting consumers in both developed and developing countries.

But as the developing countries became larger and richer, their economic structures changed in response to the forces of comparative advantage: they moved up the value-added chain. Now, developing countries increasingly produce the kind of high value-added components that 30 years ago were the exclusive purview of advanced economies. This climb is a permanent, irreversible change. With China and India—which together account for almost 40 percent of the world's population—resolutely moving up this ladder, structural economic changes in emerging countries will only have more impact on the rest of the world in the future.

By relocating some parts of international supply chains, globalization has been affecting the price of goods, job patterns, and wages almost everywhere. It is changing the structure of individual economies in ways that affect different groups within those countries differently. In the advanced economies, it is redistributing employment opportunities and incomes.

For most of the postwar period, U.S. policymakers assumed that growth and employment went hand in hand, and the U.S. economy's performance largely confirmed that assumption. But the structural evolution of the global economy today and its effects on the U.S. economy mean that, for the first time, growth and employment in the United States are starting to diverge. The major emerging economies are becoming more competitive in areas in which the U.S. economy has histori-cally been dominant, such as the design and manufacture of semiconductors, pharmaceuticals, and information technology services. At the same time, many job opportunities in the United States are shifting away from the sectors that are experiencing the most growth and to those that are experiencing less. The result is growing disparities in income and employment across the U.S. economy, with highly educated workers enjoying more opportunities and workers with less education facing declining employment prospects and stagnant incomes. The U.S. government must urgently develop a long-term policy to address these distributional effects and their structural underpinnings and restore competitiveness and growth to the U.S. economy.

Jobless in the U.S.

Between 1990 and 2008, the number of employed workers in the United States grew from about 122 million to about 149 million. Of the roughly 27 million jobs created during that period, 98 percent were in the so-called nontradable sector of the economy, the sector that produces goods and services that must be consumed domestically. The largest employers in the U.S. nontradable sector were the government (with 22 million jobs in 2008) and the health-care industry (with 16 million jobs in 2008). Together, the two industries created 10 million new jobs between 1990 and 2008, or just under 40 percent of total additions. (The retail, construction, and hotel and restaurant industries also contributed significantly to job growth.) Meanwhile, employment barely grew in the tradable sector of the U.S. economy, the sector that produces goods and services that can be consumed anywhere, such as manufactured products, engineering, and consulting services. That sector, which accounted for more than 34 million jobs in 1990, grew by a negligible 600,000 jobs between 1990 and 2008.

Dramatic, new labor-saving technologies in information services eliminated some jobs across the whole U.S. economy. But employment in the United States has been affected even more by the fact that many manufacturing activities, principally their lower value-added components, have been moving to emerging economies. This trend is causing employment to fall in virtually all of the U.S. manufacturing sector, except at the high end of the value-added chain. Employment is growing, however, in other parts of the tradable sector—most prominently, finance, computer design and engineering, and top management at multinational enterprises. Like the top end of the manufacturing chain, these expanding industries and positions generally employ highly educated people, and they are the areas in which the U.S. economy continues to have a comparative advantage and can successfully compete in the global economy.

In other words, the employment structure of the U.S. economy has been shifting away from the tradable sector, except for the upper end of the value-added chain, and toward the nontradable sector. This is a problem, because the nontradable sector is likely to generate fewer jobs than is expected of it in the future.

Moreover, the range of employment opportunities available in the tradable sector is declining, which is limiting choices for U.S. workers in the middle-income bracket. It would be unwise to assume that under present circumstances, employment in the government and health care in the United States will continue to grow as much as it had been growing before the recent economic crisis. If anything, it is remarkable that the U.S. economy did not have much of an employment problem until the recent economic crisis. If the nontradable sector continues to lose its capacity to absorb labor, as it has in recent years, and the tradable sector does not become an employment engine, the United States should brace itself for a long period of high unemployment.

For What It's Worth

One way to measure the size of a company, industry, or economy is to determine its output. But a better way is to determine its added value—namely, the difference between the value of its outputs, that is, the goods and services it produces, and the costs of its inputs, such as the raw materials and energy it consumes. (Value added comes from the capital and labor that turn the inputs into outputs.) Goods and services themselves are often purchased as intermediate inputs by other companies or industries, legal services purchased by a corporation being one example. The value added produced by all the industries in all the sectors of an economy adds up to that country's GDP. Unlike employment, value added in the tradable and nontradable parts of the U.S. economy has increased at a similar rate since 1990. In the nontradable sector, which experienced rapid employment growth, this means that value added grew slightly faster than employment: value added per employee increased modestly, by an annual average of 0.7 percent since 1990. On the tradable side of the U.S. economy, where employment levels barely increased, both value added overall and value added per employee rose very swiftly as the U.S. tradable sector moved up the value-added chain and grew in sync with the global economy. Whereas in the nontradable sector, value added per employee grew from $72,000 to over $80,000 between 1990 and 2008, in the tradable sector it grew from $79,000 to $120,000—in other words, it grew by just about 12 percent in the nontradable sector but by close to 52 percent in the tradable sector.

Most striking are the trends within the tradable sector. Value added rose across that sector, including in finance, where employment increased, and in manufacturing industries, where employment mostly declined. In fact, at the upper end of the manufacturing chain, value added increased so much that it outweighed the losses at the lower end caused by the movement of economic activity from the United States to other countries.

Value added represents income for someone. For employed people, it means personal income; for shareholders and other owners of capital, profit or returns on investment; for the government, tax revenues. Generally, the incomes of workers are closely correlated with value added per employee (this is not the case in the mining industry and utilities, however, where value added per employee is much higher than wages because these activities are very capital intensive and most value added is a return on capital). Since value added in the nontradable part of the U.S. economy did not rise much, neither did average incomes in that sector. In the tradable sector, on the other hand, incomes rose rapidly along with value added per employee thanks both to rising productivity gains in some industries and the movement of lower-income jobs to other countries. And since most new jobs were created in the nontradable part of the economy, in which wages grew little, the distribution of income in the U.S. economy became more uneven. The overall picture is clear: employment opportunities and incomes are high, and rising, for the highly educated people at the upper end of the tradable sector of the U.S. economy, but they are diminishing at the lower end. And there is every reason to believe that these trends will continue. As emerging economies continue to move up the value-added chain—and they must in order to keep growing—the tradable sectors of advanced economies will require less labor and the more labor-intensive tasks will shift to emerging economies.

Highly educated U.S. workers are already gravitating toward the high value-added parts of the U.S. economy, particularly in the tradable sector. As labor economists have noted, the return on education is rising. The highly educated, and only them, are enjoying more job opportunities and higher incomes. Competition for highly educated workers in the tradable sector spills over to the nontradable sector, raising incomes in the high value-added part of that sector as well. But with fewer jobs in the lower value-added part of the tradable sector, competition for similar jobs in the nontradable sector is increasing. This, in turn, further depresses income growth in the lower value-added part of the nontradable sector. Thus, the evolving structure of the global economy has diverse effects on different groups of people in the United States. Opportunities are expanding for the highly educated throughout the economy: they are expanding in the tradable sector because the global economy is growing and in the nontradable sector because that job market must remain competitive with the tradable sector. But opportunities are shrinking for the less well educated.

Faced with an undesirable economic outcome, economists tend to assume that its cause is a market failure. Market failures come in many forms, from inefficiencies caused by information gaps to the unpriced impacts of externalities such as the environment. But the effects on the U.S. economy of the global economy's structural evolution is not a market failure: it is not an economically inefficient outcome. (If anything, the global economy is generally becoming more efficient.) But it is nonetheless a cause for concern in that it is creating a distributional problem in the advanced economies. Not everyone is gaining in those countries, and some may be losing.

Although everyone does benefit from lower-priced goods and services, people also care greatly about the chance to be productively employed and the quality of their work. Declining employment opportunities feel real and immediate; the rise in real incomes brought by lower prices does not. For example, according to recent surveys, a substantial number of Americans believe that their children will have fewer opportunities than they have had. The slow recovery from the recent economic crisis may be affecting these perceptions, which means that they might dissipate as the situation improves and growth returns. But the long-term structural evolution of the U.S. and global economies suggests that distributional issues will remain. These must be taken seriously.

Making It Work

Analysts have been quick to point out that not all the structural changes under way in the U.S. economy should be attributed to greater openness in the global economy. Some important changes in employment patterns and income distribution are the result of labor-saving information technology and the automation of transactions. Automation has undoubtedly cut jobs in the information- and transaction-intensive parts of value-added chains throughout the U.S. economy, in both the tradable and the nontradable sectors. But if that were the only trend, why would employment decline so much more in manufacturing than in other industries?

One answer might be that information processing and automation occupy a more significant fraction of the value-added chain in manufacturing. But this is not true. Information-processing technology, for example, has eliminated jobs throughout the U.S. economy, including in finance, retail, and the government—all areas in which employment has grown. The structural trends affecting the U.S. economy cannot be explained by changes in technology alone. To think otherwise tends to yield the misleading conclusions that technology, not the global economy, is the principal cause of the United States' employment challenge and that the most important forces operating on the structure of the U.S. economy are internal, not external. In fact, all these factors are relevant, with some more significant in some sectors of the economy than in others.

If giving technology as the preferred explanation for the U.S. economy's distributional problems is a way to ignore the structural changes of the global economy, invoking multinational companies (MNCs) as the preferred explanation is a way to overstate their impact. MNCs are said to underpay and otherwise exploit poor people in developing countries, exporting jobs that should have stayed in the United States.

MNCs do, indeed, play a central role in managing the evolution of the global economy. They are the principal architects of global supply chains, and they move the production of goods and services around the world in response to supply-chain and market opportunities that are constantly changing. MNCs have generated growth and jobs in developing countries, and by moving to those countries some lower value-added parts of their supply chains, they have increased growth and competitiveness in advanced economies such as the United States. A June 2010 report by the McKinsey Global Institute estimated that U.S.-based MNCs accounted for 31 percent of GDP growth in the United States since 1990.

With ample labor available in various skill and educational categories throughout the tradable sector globally, companies have little incentive to invest in technologies that save on labor or otherwise increase the competitiveness of the labor-intensive value-added activities in advanced economies. In short, companies' private interest (profit) and the public's interest (employment) do not align perfectly. These conditions might not last: if growth continues to be high in emerging economies, in two or three decades there will be less cheap labor available there. But two or three decades is a long time.

In the meantime, even though public and private interests are not perfectly aligned today, they are not perfectly opposed either. Relatively modest shifts at the margin could bring them back in sync. Given the enormous size of the global labor force, the dial would not need to be moved very much to restore employment growth in the tradable sector of the U.S. economy. Specifically, the right combination of productivity-enhancing technology and competitive wage levels could keep some manufacturing industries, or at least some value-added pieces of their production chains, in the United States and other advanced countries. But accomplishing this will require more than a decision from the market; it must also involve labor, business, and governments. Germany, for one, has managed to retain its advanced manufacturing activities in industrial machinery by removing rigidities in the labor market and making a conscious effort to privilege employment over rapid rises in incomes. Wages may have increased only modestly in Germany over the past decade, but income inequality is markedly flatter there than in the United States, where it is higher than in most other industrial countries and rising steadily.

Conditioning access to the domestic market on domestic production is a form of protectionism and a way to try to limit the movement out of the country of jobs and of value-added components in the supply chain. This is more common than might be supposed. It exists in the aerospace industry; and in the 1970s and 1980s, in the car industry, quotas on Japanese imports to the United States led to an expansion of the manufacture of Japanese cars in the United States. However, if the large economies—such as China, the European Union, Japan, or the United States—pursue protectionist measures on a broad front, the global economy will be undermined. Yet that may be exactly what happens if employment challenges such as the ones affecting the United States are not tackled differently. With pressure on government budgets at all levels, rapidly rising health-care costs, a fragile housing market, the postcrisis effort to curb excess consumption and boost savings, and the risk of a second economic downturn, it is highly unlikely that net employment in the nontradable sector of the U.S. economy will continue to grow as rapidly as it has been.

The drop in domestic consumption in the United States has left the country with a shortage of aggregate demand. More public-sector investment would help, but the fiscal consolidation currently under way may make expanding government investment difficult. Meanwhile, because private-sector investment responds to demand and currently there is a shortfall in demand caused by the economic crisis and increased savings by households, such investment will not return until domestic consumption or exports increase. Therefore, the United States will need to focus on increasing job growth in the tradable sector. Some growth will naturally come from the high value-added part of that sector. The question is whether there will be enough growth and whether the educational attainment of U.S. workers will keep pace with rising job requirements at that level. There are reasons to be skeptical.

The Big Tradeoff

It is a common view that the market will solve the disparities in employment and incomes once the economic crisis recedes and growth is restored. Warren Buffett and other very smart, experienced, and influential opinion-makers say so clearly. But as this analysis suggests, they may not be right. And as long as their view dominates U.S. public policy and opinion, it will be difficult to address the issues related to structural change and employment in the United States in a systematic way.

What is needed instead of benign neglect is, first, an agreement that restoring rewarding employment opportunities for a full spectrum of Americans should be a fundamental goal. With that objective as a starting point, it will then be necessary to develop ways to increase both the competitiveness and the inclusiveness of the U.S. economy. This is largely uncharted territory: distributional issues are difficult to solve because they require correcting outcomes on the global market without doing too much damage to its efficiency and openness. But admitting that not all the answers are known is a good place to begin. With considerable uncertainty about the efficacy of various policy options, a multistakeholder, multipronged approach to addressing these distributional problems is best. The relevant knowledge about promising new technologies and market opportunities is dispersed among business, the government, labor, and universities, and it needs to be assembled and turned into initiatives. President Barack Obama has already appointed a commission, led by Jeffrey Immelt, the CEO of General Electric, to focus on competitiveness and employment issues in the U.S. economy. This is an important step forward. But it will be hugely difficult to invest in human capital, technology, and infrastructure as much as is necessary at a time of fiscal distress and declining government employment. And yet restoring opportunities for future generations requires making sacrifices in the present.

Given the structural changes under way in the U.S. economy—especially the growing premium on highly educated workers at the top end of the value-added chain—education should be boosted. As many people as possible should be able to compete in that part of the economy. But if this goal is clear, the ways to achieve it are less so. Improving the performance of the educational system has been a priority for some years, yet the results are in doubt. For example, the Organization for Economic Cooperation and Development administers a set of standardized tests, the Program for International Student Assessment, across more than 60 countries, advanced and developing, to measure the cognitive skills of teenage students. The United States ranks close to the average in reading and science and well behind most countries in math.

The problems in the quality and effectiveness of parts of the U.S. educational system have been recognized for some time. Numerous attempts to improve matters, including administering national standardized tests and providing merit-based compensation, have thus far yielded inconclusive results. And the problem extends beyond the school system. A lack of commitment to education in families and in communities makes the entire field of education seem unattractive, demoralizing dedicated teachers and turning off talented students from teaching. That, in turn, reduces the incentives of communities to value the primacy of education. To break this pattern, it will be necessary to shift communities'—and the country's—values about education through moral leadership, at both the community and the national levels. Creating attractive employment opportunities conditional on educational success is another important incentive. One comes full circle, in other words: increased educational effectiveness is needed for the United States to be competitive, and the promise of rewarding employment is a necessary incentive for committing to improving education.

As important as education is, it cannot be the whole solution; the United States will not educate its way out of its problems. Both the federal and state governments must pursue complementary lines of attack. They should invest in infrastructure, which would create jobs in the short term and raise the return on private-sector investment in the medium to longer term. They should also invest in technologies that could expand employment opportunities in the tradable sector of the U.S. economy at income levels other than the very top. The private sector will have to help guide these investments because it has much of the relevant knowledge about where these opportunities might lie. But this effort will also require the participation of the public sector. The U.S. government already invests heavily in science and technology but not with job creation as its primary focus; that has generally been viewed only as a beneficial side effect. It is time to devote public funding to developing infrastructure and the technological base of the U.S. economy with the specific goal of restoring competitiveness and expanding employment in the tradable sector. The tax structure also needs to be reformed. It should be simplified and reconfigured to promote competitiveness, investment, and employment. And both loopholes and distorting incentives should be eliminated. For example, corporate tax rates and tax rates on investment returns should be lowered in order to make the United States more attractive for business and investment. MNCs with earnings outside the United States currently have a strong incentive to keep their earnings abroad and reinvest them abroad because earnings are taxed both where they are earned and also in the United States if they are repatriated. Lower tax rates would mean a loss in revenue for the U.S. government, but that could be replaced by taxes on consumption, which would have the added benefit of helping shift the composition of demand from domestic to foreign—a necessary move if the United States wants to avoid high unemployment and an unsustainable current account deficit.

But even these measures may not be sufficient. Globalization has redefined the competition for employment and incomes in the United States. Tradeoffs will have to be made between the two. Germany clearly chose to protect employment in the industries of its tradable sector that came under competitive threat. Now, U.S. policymakers must choose, too.

Some will argue that global market forces should simply be allowed to operate without interference. Tampering with market outcomes, the argument goes, risks distorting incentives and reducing efficiency and innovation. But this is not the only approach, nor is it the best one. The distribution of income across many advanced economies (and major emerging economies) differs markedly. For example, the ratio of the average income of the top 20 percent of the population to the average income of the bottom 20 percent is four to one in Germany and eight to one in the United States. Many other advanced countries have flatter income distributions than the United States, suggesting that tradeoffs between market forces and equity are possible. The U.S. government needs to face up to them.

Experimenting the Way Forward

The massive changes in the global economy since World War II have had overwhelmingly positive effects. Hundreds of millions of people in the developing world have escaped poverty, and more will in the future. The global economy will continue to grow—probably at least threefold over the next 30 years. One person's gain is not necessarily another's loss; global growth is not even close to a zero-sum game. But globalization hurts some subgroups within some countries, including the advanced economies.

The late American economist Paul Samuelson once said, "Every good cause is worth some inefficiency." Surely, equity and social cohesion are among them. The challenge for the U.S. economy will be to find a place in the rapidly evolving global economy that retains its dynamism and openness while providing all Americans with rewarding employment opportunities and a reasonable degree of equity. This is not a problem to which there are easy answers. As the issue becomes more pressing, ideology, and orthodoxy must be set aside, and creativity, flexibility, and pragmatism must be encouraged. The United States will not be able to deduce its way toward the solutions; it will have to experiment its way forward.

Source

Spence, Michael. "The impact of globalization on income and employment: the downside of integrating markets." *Foreign Affairs* 90.4 (2011): 28. *General OneFile*. Web. 20 Dec. 2011.

Critical Thinking

1. How does globalization affect income and employment in America?
2. How does globalization increase inequality?
3. Why does Spence believe that the American economy will be in serious trouble for a long time?

Create Central

www.mhhe.com/createcentral

Internet References

Joint Center for Poverty Research
www.jcpr.org
National Center for Policy Analysis
www.ncpa.org
New American Studies Web
www.georgetown.edu/crossroads/asw
Social Science Information Gateway
http://sosig.esrc.bris.ac.uk
Sociology—Study Sociology Online
http://edu.learnsoc.org
Sociology Web Resources
http://www.mhhe.com/socscience/sociology/resources/index.htm
Sociosite
http://www.topsite.com/goto/sociosite.net
Socioweb
http://www.topsite.com/goto/socioweb.com

MICHAEL SPENCE is Distinguished Visiting Fellow at the Council on Foreign Relations and the author of *The Next Convergence: The Future of Economic Growth in a Multispeed World*. He received the Nobel Prize in Economics in 2001.

From *Foreign Affairs*, 90(4), July–August, 2011, pp. 28. Copyright © 2011 by Council on Foreign Relations, Inc. Reprinted by permission of Foreign Affairs. www.ForeignAffairs.com

Article   Prepared by: Kurt Finsterbusch, *University of Maryland, College Park*

The Myth of the "Culture of Poverty"

Instead of accepting myths that harm low-income students, we need to eradicate the systemwide inequities that stand in their way.

PAUL GORSKI

Learning Outcomes

After reading this article, you will be able to:

- Assess the role of culture in the condition of the poor.

- Discuss the role of opportunity structures in contributing to the conditions of the poor.

- Evaluate how different the poor are from the middle class.

As the students file out of Janet's classroom, I sit in the back corner, scribbling a few final notes. Defeat in her eyes, Janet drops into a seat next to me with a sigh. "I love these kids," she declares, as if trying to convince me. "I adore them. But my hope is fading."

"Why's that?" I ask, stuffing my notes into a folder.

"They're smart. I know they're smart, but . . ."

And then the deficit floodgates open: "They don't care about school. They're unmotivated. And their parents—I'm lucky if two or three of them show up for conferences. No wonder the kids are unprepared to learn."

At Janet's invitation, I spent dozens of hours in her classroom, meeting her students, observing her teaching, helping her navigate the complexities of an urban midwestern elementary classroom with a growing percentage of students in poverty. I observed powerful moments of teaching and learning, caring, and support. And I witnessed moments of internal conflict in Janet, when what she wanted to believe about her students collided with her prejudices.

Like most educators, Janet is determined to create an environment in which each student reaches his or her full potential. And like many of us, despite overflowing with good intentions,

Janet has bought into the most common and dangerous myths about poverty.

Chief among these is the "culture of poverty" myth—the idea that poor people share more or less monolithic and predictable beliefs, values, and behaviors. For educators like Janet to be the best teachers they can be for all students, they need to challenge this myth and reach a deeper understanding of class and poverty.

Roots of the Culture of Poverty Concept

Oscar Lewis coined the term *culture of poverty* in his 1961 book *The Children of Sanchez.* Lewis based his thesis on his ethnographic studies of small Mexican communities. His studies uncovered approximately 50 attributes shared within these communities: frequent violence, a lack of a sense of history, a neglect of planning for the future, and so on. Despite studying very small communities, Lewis extrapolated his findings to suggest a universal culture of poverty. More than 45 years later, the premise of the culture of poverty paradigm remains the same: that people in poverty share a consistent and observable "culture."

Lewis ignited a debate about the nature of poverty that continues today. But just as important—especially in the age of data-driven decision making—he inspired a flood of research. Researchers around the world tested the culture of poverty concept empirically (see Billings, 1974; Carmon, 1985; Jones & Luo, 1999). Others analyzed the overall body of evidence regarding the culture of poverty paradigm (see Abell & Lyon, 1979; Ortiz & Briggs, 2003; Rodman, 1977).

These studies raise a variety of questions and come to a variety of conclusions about poverty. But on this they all agree: *There is no such thing as a culture of poverty.* Differences in values and behaviors among poor people are just as great as those between poor and wealthy people.

In actuality, the culture of poverty concept is constructed from a collection of smaller stereotypes which, however false, seem to have crept into mainstream thinking as unquestioned fact. Let's look at some examples.

Myth: Poor people are unmotivated and have weak work ethics.

The Reality: Poor people do not have weaker work ethics or lower levels of motivation than wealthier people (Iversen & Farber, 1996; Wilson, 1997). Although poor people are often stereotyped as lazy, 83 percent of children from low-income families have at least one employed parent; close to 60 percent have at least one parent who works full-time and year-round (National Center for Children in Poverty, 2004). In fact, the severe shortage of living-wage jobs means that many poor adults must work two, three, or four jobs. According to the Economic Policy Institute (2002), poor working adults spend more hours working each week than their wealthier counterparts.

Myth: Poor parents are uninvolved in their children's learning, largely because they do not value education.

The Reality: Low-income parents hold the same attitudes about education that wealthy parents do (Compton-Lilly, 2003; Lareau & Horvat, 1999; Leichter, 1978). Low-income parents are less likely to attend school functions or volunteer in their children's classrooms (National Center for Education Statistics, 2005)—not because they care less about education, but because they have less access to school involvement than their wealthier peers. They are more likely to work multiple jobs, to work evenings, to have jobs without paid leave, and to be unable to afford child care and public transportation. It might be said more accurately that schools that fail to take these considerations into account do not value the involvement of poor families as much as they value the involvement of other families.

Myth: Poor people are linguistically deficient.

The Reality: All people, regardless of the languages and language varieties they speak, use a full continuum of language registers (Bomer, Dworin, May, & Semingson, 2008). What's more, linguists have known for decades that all language varieties are highly structured with complex grammatical rules (Gee, 2004; Hess, 1974; Miller, Cho, & Bracey, 2005). What often are assumed to be *deficient* varieties of English—Appalachian varieties, perhaps, or what some refer to as Black English Vernacular—are no less sophisticated than so-called "standard English."

Myth: Poor people tend to abuse drugs and alcohol.

The Reality: Poor people are no more likely than their wealthier counterparts to abuse alcohol or drugs. Although drug sales are more visible in poor neighborhoods, drug use is equally distributed across poor, middle class, and wealthy communities (Saxe, Kadushin, Tighe, Rindskopf, & Beveridge, 2001). Chen, Sheth, Krejci, and Wallace (2003) found that alcohol consumption is significantly higher among upper middle class white high school students than among poor black high school students. Their finding supports a history of research showing that alcohol abuse is far more prevalent among wealthy people than among poor people (Diala, Muntaner, & Walrath, 2004; Galea, Ahern, Tracy, & Vlahov, 2007). In other words, considering alcohol and illicit drugs together, wealthy people are more likely than poor people to be substance abusers.

The Culture of Classism

The myth of a "culture of poverty" distracts us from a dangerous culture that does exist—the culture of classism. This culture continues to harden in our schools today. It leads the most well intentioned of us, like my friend Janet, into low expectations for low-income students. It makes teachers fear their most powerless pupils. And, worst of all, it diverts attention from what people in poverty *do* have in common: inequitable access to basic human rights.

The most destructive tool of the culture of classism is deficit theory. In education, we often talk about the deficit perspective—defining students by their weaknesses rather than their strengths. Deficit theory takes this attitude a step further, suggesting that poor people are poor because of their own moral and intellectual deficiencies (Collins, 1988). Deficit theorists use two strategies for propagating this world view: (1) drawing on well-established stereotypes, and (2) ignoring systemic conditions, such as inequitable access to high-quality schooling, that support the cycle of poverty.

The implications of deficit theory reach far beyond individual bias. If we convince ourselves that poverty results not from gross inequities (in which we might be complicit) but from poor people's own deficiencies, we are much less likely to support authentic antipoverty policy and programs. Further, if we believe, however wrongly, that poor people don't value education, then we dodge any responsibility to redress the gross education inequities with which they contend. This application of deficit theory establishes the idea of what Gans (1995) calls the *undeserving poor*—a segment of our society that simply does not deserve a fair shake.

If the goal of deficit theory is to justify a system that privileges economically advantaged students at the expense of working-class and poor students, then it appears to be working marvelously. In our determination to "fix" the mythical culture of poor students, we ignore the ways in which our society cheats them out of opportunities that their wealthier peers take for granted. We ignore the fact that poor people suffer disproportionately the effects of nearly every major social ill. They lack access to health care, living-wage jobs, safe and affordable housing, clean air and water, and so on (Books, 2004)—conditions that limit their abilities to achieve to their full potential.

Perhaps most of us, as educators, feel powerless to address these bigger issues. But the question is this: Are we willing, at the very least, to tackle the classism in our own schools and classrooms?

The myth of a "culture of poverty" distracts us from a dangerous culture that does exist—the culture of classism.

This classism is plentiful and well documented (Kozol, 1992). For example, compared with their wealthier peers, poor students are more likely to attend schools that have less funding (Carey, 2005); lower teacher salaries (Karoly, 2001); more limited computer and Internet access (Gorski, 2003); larger class sizes; higher student-to-teacher ratios; a less-rigorous curriculum; and fewer experienced teachers (Barton, 2004). The National Commission on Teaching and America's Future (2004) also found that low-income schools were more likely to suffer from cockroach or rat infestation, dirty, or inoperative student bathrooms, large numbers of teacher vacancies and substitute teachers, more teachers who are not licensed in their subject areas, insufficient or outdated classroom materials, and inadequate or nonexistent learning facilities, such as science labs.

Here in Minnesota, several school districts offer universal half-day kindergarten but allow those families that can afford to do so to pay for full-day services. Our poor students scarcely make it out of early childhood without paying the price for our culture of classism. Deficit theory requires us to ignore these inequities—or worse, to see them as normal and justified.

What does this mean? Regardless of how much students in poverty value education, they must overcome tremendous inequities to learn. Perhaps the greatest myth of all is the one that dubs education the "great equalizer." Without considerable change, it cannot be anything of the sort.

What Can We Do?

The socioeconomic opportunity gap can be eliminated only when we stop trying to "fix" poor students and start addressing the ways in which our schools perpetuate classism. This includes destroying the inequities listed above as well as abolishing such practices as tracking and ability grouping,

segregational redistricting, and the privatization of public schools. We must demand the best possible education for all students—higher-order pedagogies, innovative learning materials, and holistic teaching and learning. But first, we must demand basic human rights for all people: adequate housing and health care, living-wage jobs, and so on.

Of course, we ought not tell students who suffer today that, if they can wait for this education revolution, everything will fall into place. So as we prepare ourselves for bigger changes, we must

- Educate ourselves about class and poverty.
- Reject deficit theory and help students and colleagues unlearn misperceptions about poverty.
- Make school involvement accessible to all families.
- Follow Janet's lead, inviting colleagues to observe our teaching for signs of class bias.
- Continue reaching out to low-income families even when they appear unresponsive (and without assuming, if they are unresponsive, that we know why).
- Respond when colleagues stereotype poor students or parents.
- Never assume that all students have equitable access to such learning resources as computers and the Internet, and never assign work requiring this access without providing in-school time to complete it.
- Ensure that learning materials do not stereotype poor people.
- Fight to keep low-income students from being assigned unjustly to special education or low academic tracks.
- Make curriculum relevant to poor students, drawing on and validating their experiences and intelligences.
- Teach about issues related to class and poverty—including consumer culture, the dissolution of labor unions, and environmental injustice—and about movements for class equity.
- Teach about the antipoverty work of Martin Luther King Jr., Helen Keller, the Black Panthers, César Chávez, and other U.S. icons—and about why this dimension of their legacies has been erased from our national consciousness.
- Fight to ensure that school meal programs offer healthy options.
- Examine proposed corporate-school partnerships, rejecting those that require the adoption of specific curriculums or pedagogies.

Most important, we must consider how our own class biases affect our interactions with and expectations of our students. And then we must ask ourselves, Where, in reality, does the deficit lie? Does it lie in poor people, the most disenfranchised people among us? Does it lie in the education system itself—in, as Jonathan Kozol says, the savage inequalities of our schools? Or does it lie in us—educators with unquestionably good intentions who too often fall to the temptation of the quick fix, the easily digestible framework that never requires us to consider how we comply with the culture of classism.

References

Abell, T., & Lyon, L. (1979). Do the differences make a difference? An empirical evaluation of the culture of poverty in the United States. *American Anthropologist,* 6(3), 602–621.

Barton, R. E. (2004). Why does the gap persist? *Educational Leadership,* 62(3), 8–13.

Billings, D. (1974). Culture and poverty in Appalachia: A theoretical discussion and empirical analysis. *Social Forces,* 53(2), 315–323.

Bomer, R., Dworin, J. E., May, L., & Semingson, R. (2008). Miseducating teachers about the poor: A critical analysis of Ruby Payne's claims about poverty. *Teachers College Record,* 110(11). Available: www.tcrecord.org/PrintContent .asp?ContentID=14591

Books, S. (2004). *Poverty and schooling in the U.S.: Contexts and consequences.* Mahway, NJ: Erlbaum.

Carey, K. (2005). *The funding gap 2004: Many states still shortchange low-income and minority students.* Washington, DC: Education Trust.

Carmon, N. (1985). Poverty and culture. *Sociological Perspectives,* 28(4), 403–418.

Chen, K., Sheth, A., Krejci, J., & Wallace, J. (2003, August). *Understanding differences in alcohol use among high school students in two different communities.* Paper presented at the annual meeting of the American Sociological Association, Atlanta, GA.

Collins, J. (1988). Language and class in minority education. *Anthropology and Education Quarterly,* 19(4), 299–326.

Compton-Lilly, C. (2003). *Reading families: The literate lives of urban children.* New York: Teachers College Press.

Diala, C. C., Muntaner, C., & Walrath, C. (2004). Gender, occupational, and socioeconomic correlates of alcohol and drug abuse among U.S. rural, metropolitan, and urban residents. *American Journal of Drug and Alcohol Abuse,* 30(2), 409–428.

Economic Policy Institute. (2002). *The state of working class America* 2002–03. Washington, DC: Author.

Galea, S., Ahern, J., Tracy, M., & Vlahov, D. (2007). Neighborhood income and income distribution and the use of cigarettes, alcohol, and marijuana. *American Journal of Preventive Medicine,* 32(6), 195–202.

Gans, H. J. (1995). *The war against the poor: The underclass and antipoverty policy.* New York: BasicBooks.

Gee, J. R (2004). *Situated language and learning: A critique of traditional schooling.* New York: Routledge.

Gorski, R. C. (2003). Privilege and repression in the digital era: Rethinking the sociopolitics of the digital divide. *Race, Gender and Class,* 10(4), 145–176.

Hess, K. M. (1974). The nonstandard speakers in our schools: What should be done? *The Elementary School Journal,* 74(5), 280–290.

Iversen, R. R., & Farber, N. (1996). Transmission of family values, work, and welfare among poor urban black women. *Work and Occupations,* 23(4), 437–460.

Jones, R. K., & Luo, Y. (1999). The culture of poverty and African-American culture: An empirical assessment. *Sociological Perspectives,* 42(3), 439–458.

Karoly, L. A. (2001). Investing in the future: Reducing poverty through human capital investments. In S. Danzinger & R. Haveman (Eds.), *Undemanding poverty* (pp. 314–356). New York: Russell Sage Foundation.

Kozol, J. (1992). *Savage inequalities. Children in America's schools.* New York: Harper-Collins.

Lareau, A., & Horvat, E. (1999). Moments of social inclusion and exclusion: Race, class, and cultural capital in family-school relationships. *Sociology of Education,* 72, 37–53.

Leichter, H. J. (Ed.). (1978). *Families and communities as educators.* New York: Teachers College Press.

Lewis, O. (1961). *The children of Sanchez: Autobiography of a Mexican family.* New York: Random House.

Miller, R. J., Cho, G. E., & Bracey, J. R. (2005). Working-class children's experience through the prism of personal story-telling. *Human Development,* 48, 115–135.

National Center for Children in Poverty. (2004). *Parental employment in low-income families.* New York: Author.

National Center for Education Statistics. (2005). *Parent and family involvement in education:* 2002–03. Washington, DC: Author.

National Commission on Teaching and America's Future. (2004). *Fifty years after* Brown v. Board of Education: *A two-tiered education system.* Washington, DC: Author.

Ortiz, A. T., & Briggs, L. (2003). The culture of poverty, crack babies, and welfare cheats: The making of the "healthy white baby crisis." *Social Text,* 21(3), 39–57.

Rodman, R. (1977). Culture of poverty: The rise and fall of a concept. *Sociological Review,* 25(4), 867–876.

Saxe, L., Kadushin, C., Tighe, E., Rindskopf, D., & Beveridge, A. (2001). *National evaluation of the fighting back program: General population surveys, 1995–1999.* New York: City University of New York Graduate Center.

Wilson, W. J. (1997). *When work disappears.* New York: Random House.

Critical Thinking

1. What features of American society greatly benefit some people and hold back other people?

2. Family background is so important to a child's life chances. Are there ways to make life chances more equal?

3. If discrimination were completely removed would society be completely fair?

Create Central

www.mhhe.com/createcentral

Internet References

Human Rights and Humanitarian Affairs
www.etown.edu/vl/humrts.html

Joint Center for Poverty Research
www.jcpr.org

Sociology—Study Sociology Online
http://edu.learnsoc.org

Sociology Web Resources
http://www.mhhe.com/socscience/sociology/resources/index.htm

Sociosite
http://www.topsite.com/goto/sociosite.net

Socioweb
http://www.topsite.com/goto/socioweb.com

PAUL GORSKI is Assistant Professor in the Graduate School of Education, Hamline University, St. Paul, Minnesota, and the founder of EdChange (www.edchange.org).

From *Educational Leadership*, April 1, 2008. Copyright © 2008 by ASCD. Reprinted by permission. The Association for Supervision and Curriculum Development is a worldwide community of educators advocating sound policies and sharing best practices to achieve the success of each learner. To learn more, visit ASCD at www.ascd.org.

Article   Prepared by: Kurt Finsterbusch, *University of Maryland, College Park*

Somewhere Between Jim Crow & Postracialism

Reflections on the Racial Divide in America Today

LAWRENCE D. BOBO

Learning Outcomes

After reading this article, you will be able to:

- Describe the extent to discrimination between racial and ethnic groups in the United States today.

- Understand the progress that has been made in the past in race relations.

- Understand the significance of the *Brown vs. Board of Education* Supreme Court Decision in 1954.

In assessing the results of the Negro revolution so far, it can be concluded that Negroes have established a foothold, no more. We have written a Declaration of Independence, itself an accomplishment, but the effort to transform the words into a life experience still lies ahead.

—Martin Luther King, Jr.,
Where Do We Go From Here? (1968)

By the middle of the twentieth century, the color line was as well defined and as firmly entrenched as any institution in the land. After all, it was older than most institutions, including the federal government itself. More important, it informed the content and shaped the lives of those institutions and the people who lived under them.

—John Hope Franklin,
The Color Line (1993)

This is where we are right now. It's a racial stalemate we've been stuck in for years. Contrary to the claims of some of my critics, black and white, I have never been so naive as to believe that we can get beyond our racial divisions in a single election cycle, or with a single candidacy—particularly a candidacy as imperfect as my own.

—Barack H. Obama,
"A More Perfect Union" (May 18, 2008)[1]

The year 1965 marked an important inflection point in the struggle for racial justice in the United States, underscoring two fundamental points about race in America.[2] First, that racial inequality and division were not only Southern problems attached to Jim Crow segregation. Second, that the nature of those inequalities and divisions was a matter not merely of formal civil status and law, but also of deeply etched economic arrangements, social and political conditions, and cultural outlooks and practices. Viewed in full, the racial divide was a challenge of truly national reach, multilayered in its complexity and depth. Therefore, the achievement of basic citizenship rights in the South was a pivotal but far from exhaustive stage of the struggle.

The positive trend of the times revolved around the achievement of voting rights. March 7, 1965, now known as Bloody Sunday, saw police and state troopers attack several 100 peaceful civil rights protestors at the Edmund Pettus Bridge in Selma, Alabama. The subsequent march from Selma to

Montgomery, participated in by tens of thousands, along with other protest actions, provided the pressure that finally compelled Congress to pass the Voting Rights Act of 1965. A triumphant Reverend Martin Luther King, Jr., and other activists attended the signing in Washington, D.C., on August 6, 1965. It was a moment of great triumph for civil rights.

The long march to freedom seemed to be at its apex, inspiring talk of an era of "Second Reconstruction." A decade earlier, in the historic *Brown v. Board of Education* decision of 1954, the U.S. Supreme Court repudiated the "separate but equal" doctrine. Subsequently, a major civil rights movement victory was achieved with the passage of the Civil Rights Act of 1964, which forbade discrimination in employment and in most public places. With voting rights now protected as well, and the federal government authorized to intervene directly to assure those rights, one might have expected 1965 to stand as a moment of shimmering and untarnished civil rights progress. Yet the mood of optimism and triumph did not last for long.

The negative trend of the times was epitomized by deep and explosive inequalities and resentments of race smoldering in many Northern, urban ghettos. The extent to which the "race problem" was not just a Southern problem of civil rights, but a national problem of inequality woven deep into our economic and cultural fabric, would quickly be laid bare following passage of the Voting Rights Act. Scarcely five days after then-President Johnson signed the bill into law, the Los Angeles community of Watts erupted into flames. Quelling the disorder, which raged for roughly six days, required the mobilization of the National Guard and nearly 15,000 troops. When disorder finally subsided, 34 people had died, more than 1,000 had been injured, well over 3,000 were arrested, and approximately $35 million in property damage had been done. Subsequent studies and reports revealed patterns of police abuse, political marginalization, intense poverty, and myriad forms of economic, housing, and social discrimination as contributing to the mix of conditions that led to the riots.

It was thus more than fitting that in 1965, *Dædalus* committed two issues to examining the conditions of "The Negro American." The essays were wide ranging. The topics addressed spanned questions of power, demographic change, economic conditions, politics and civil status, religion and the church, family and community dynamics, as well as group identity, racial attitudes, and the future of race relations. Scholars from most social scientific fields, including anthropology, economics, history, law, political science, psychology, and sociology, contributed to the volumes. No single theme or message dominated these essays. Instead, the volumes wrestled with the multidimensional and complex patterns of a rapidly changing racial terrain.

Some critical observations stand out from two of those earlier essays, which have been amplified and made centerpieces

of much subsequent social science scholarship. Sociologist and anthropologist St. Clair Drake drew a distinction between what he termed *primary victimization* and *indirect victimization*. Primary victimization involved overt discrimination in the labor market that imposed a job ceiling on the economic opportunities available to blacks alongside housing discrimination and segregation that relegated blacks to racially distinct urban ghettos. Indirect or secondary victimization involved the multidimensional and cumulative disadvantages resulting from primary victimization. These consequences included poorer schooling, poor health, and greater exposure to disorder and crime. In a related vein, sociologist Daniel Patrick Moynihan stressed the central importance of employment prospects in the wake of the civil rights victories that secured the basic citizenship rights of African Americans. Both Drake and Moynihan expressed concern about a black class structure marked by signs of a large and growing economically marginalized segment of the black community. Drake went so far as to declare, "If Negroes are not to become a permanent lumpen-proletariat within American society as a result of social forces already at work and increased automation, deliberate planning by governmental and private agencies will be necessary." Striking a similar chord, Moynihan asserted: "[T]here would also seem to be no question that opportunities for a large mass of Negro workers in the lower ranges of training and education have not been improving, that in many ways the circumstances of these workers relative to the white work force have grown worse." This marginalized economic status, both scholars suggested, would have ramifying effects, including weakening family structures in ways likely to worsen the challenges faced by black communities.[3]

If the scholarly assessments of 1965 occurred against a backdrop of powerful and transformative mass-based movement for civil rights and an inchoate sense of deep but imminent change, the backdrop for most scholarly assessments today is the election of Barack Obama as president of the United States, the rise of a potent narrative of postracialism, and a sense of stalemate or stagnation in racial change. Many meanings or interpretations can be attached to the term *postracial*. In its simplest and least controversial form, the term is intended merely to signal a hopeful trajectory for events and social trends, not an accomplished fact of social life. It is something toward which we as a nation still strive and remain guardedly hopeful about fully achieving. Three other meanings of postracialism are filled with more grounds for dispute and controversy. One of these meanings attaches to the waning salience of what some have portrayed as a "black victimology" narrative. From this perspective, black complaints and grievances about inequality and discrimination are well-worn tales, at least passé if not now pointedly false assessments of the main challenges facing blacks in a world largely free of the dismal burdens of overt racial divisions and oppression.[4]

A second and no less controversial view of postracialism takes the position that the level and pace of change in the demographic makeup and the identity choices and politics of Americans are rendering the traditional black-white divide irrelevant. Accordingly, Americans increasingly revere mixture and hybridity and are rushing to embrace a decidedly "beige" view of themselves and what is good for the body politic. Old-fashioned racial dichotomies pale against the surge toward flexible, deracialized, and mixed ethnoracial identities and outlooks.[5]

A third, and perhaps the most controversial, view of postracialism has the most in common with the well-rehearsed rhetoric of color blindness. To wit, American society, or at least a large and steadily growing fraction of it, has genuinely moved beyond race—so much so that we as a nation are now ready to transcend the disabling racial divisions of the past. From this perspective, nothing symbolizes better the moment of transcendence than Obama's election as president. This transcendence is said to be especially true of a younger generation, what *New Yorker* editor David Remnick has referred to as "the Joshua Generation." More than any other, this generation is ready to cross the great river of racial identity, division, and acrimony that has for so long defined American culture and politics.

It is in this context of the first African-American president of the United States and the rise to prominence of the narrative of postracialism that a group of social scientists were asked to examine, from many different disciplinary and intellectual vantage points, changes in the racial divide since the time of the *Dædalus* issues focusing on race in 1965 and 1966.

The context today has points of great discontinuity and of great similarity to that mid-1960s inflection point. From the viewpoint of 1965, the election of Obama as the first African-American president of the United States, as well as the expansion and the cultural prominence and success of the black middle class of which Obama is a member, speak to the enormous and enduring successes of the civil rights era. Yet also from the standpoint of 1965, the persistence of deep poverty and joblessness for a large fraction of the black population, slowly changing rates of residential segregation by race, continued evidence of antiblack discrimination in many domains of life, and historically high rates of black incarceration signal a journey toward racial justice that remains, even by superficial accounting, seriously incomplete.

In order to set a context for the essays contained in this volume, I address three key questions in this introduction. The first concerns racial boundaries. In an era of widespread talk of having achieved the postracial society, do we have real evidence that attention to and the meaning of basic race categories are fundamentally breaking down? The second set of questions concerns the extent of economic inequality along the racial divide. Has racial economic inequality narrowed to a point where we need no longer think or talk of black disadvantage? Or have the bases of race-linked economic inequality changed so much that, at the least, the dynamics of discrimination and prejudice no longer need concern us? The third question is, how have racial attitudes changed in the period since the mid-1960s *Dædalus* issues?

To foreshadow a bit, I will show that basic racial boundaries are not quickly and inevitably collapsing, though they are changing and under great pressure. Racial economic inequality is less extreme today, there is a substantial black middle class, and inequality *within* the black population itself has probably never been greater. Yet there remain large and durable patterns of black-white economic inequality as well, patterns that are not overcome or eliminated even for the middle class and that still rest to a significant degree on discriminatory social processes. In addition, I maintain that we continue to witness the erosion and decline of Jim Crow racist attitudes in the United States. However, in their place has emerged a new pattern of attitudes and beliefs, variously labeled *symbolic racism, modern racism, color-blind racism,* or as I prefer it, *laissez-faire racism.* The new form of racism is a more covert, sophisticated, culture centered, and subtle racist ideology, qualitatively less extreme and more socially permeable than Jim Crow racism with its attendant biological foundations and calls for overt discrimination. But this new racism yields a powerful influence in our culture and politics.[6]

Consider first the matter of group boundaries. The 2000 Census broke new ground by allowing individuals to mark more than one box in designating racial background. Indeed, great political pressure and tumult led to the decision to move the Census in a direction that more formally and institutionally acknowledged the presence of increasing mixture and heterogeneity in the American population with regard to racial background. Nearly seven million people exercised that option in 2000. The successful rise of Obama to the office of president, the first African American to do so, as a child of a white American mother and a black Kenyan father, has only accelerated the sense of the newfound latitude and recognition granted to those who claim more than one racial heritage.[7]

Despite Obama's electoral success and the press attention given to the phenomenon, some will no doubt find it surprising that the overwhelming majority of Americans identify with only one race. Less than 2 percent of the population marked more than one box on the 2000 Census in designating their racial background. Fully 98 percent marked just one. I claim no deep rootedness or profound personal salience for these identities. Rather, my point is that we should be mindful that the level of "discussion" and contention around mixture is far out of proportion to the extent to which most Americans actually designate and see themselves in these terms.

Moreover, even if we restrict attention to just those who marked more than one box, two-thirds of these respondents designated two groups other than blacks (namely, Hispanic-white, Asian-white, or Hispanic and Asian mixtures). Some degree of mixture with black constituted just under a third of mixed race identifiers in 2000. Given the historic size of the black population and the extended length of contact with white Americans, this remarkable result says something powerful about the potency and durability of the historic black-white divide.

It is worth recalling that sexual relations and childbearing across the racial divide are not recent phenomena. The 1890 U.S. Census contained categories for not only "Negro" but also "Mulatto," "Quadroon," and even "Octoroon"; these were clear signs of the extent of "mixing" that had taken place in the United States. Indeed, well over one million individuals fell into one of the mixed race categories at that time. In order to protect the institution of slavery and to prevent the offspring of white slave masters and exploited black slave women from having a claim on freedom as well as on the property of the master, slave status, as defined by law, followed the mother's status, not the father's. For most of its history, the United States legally barred or discouraged racial mixing and intermarriage. At the time of the *Loving v. Virginia* case in 1967, 17 states still banned racial intermarriage.[8]

Formal, legal definitions of who was black, and especially the development of rules of "hypodescent," or the one-drop rule, have a further implication that is often lost in discussions of race: these practices tended to fuse together race and class, in effect making blackness synonymous with the very bottom of the class structure. As historian David Hollinger explains:

The combination of hypodescent with the denial to blacks residing in many states with large black populations of any opportunity for legal marriage to whites ensured that the color line would long remain to a very large extent a property line. Hence the dynamics of race formation and the dynamics of class formation were, in this most crucial of all American cases, largely the same. This is one of the most important truths about the history of the United States brought into sharper focus when that history is viewed through the lens of the question of ethnoracial mixture.[9]

Still, we know that today the ethnoracial landscape in the United States is changing. As of the 2000 Census, whites constituted just 69 percent of the U.S. population, with Hispanics and blacks each around 12 percent. This distribution represents a substantial decline in the percentage of whites from 20 or, even more so, 40 years ago.

With continued immigration, differential group fertility patterns, and the continued degree of intermarriage and mixing, these patterns will not remain stable. . . .

Does that pressure for change foretell the ultimate undoing of the black-white divide? At least three lines of research raise doubts about such a forecast. First, studies of the perceptions of and identities among those of mixed racial backgrounds point to strong evidence of the cultural persistence of the one-drop rule. Systematic experiments by sociologists and social psychologists are intriguing in this regard. For example, sociologist Melissa Herman's recent research concluded that "others' perceptions shape a person's identity and social understandings of race. My study found that part-black multiracial youth are more likely to be seen as black by observers and to define themselves as black when forced to choose one race."[10]

Second, studies of patterns in racial intermarriage point to a highly durable if somewhat less extreme black-white divide today. A careful assessment of racial intermarriage patterns in 1990 by demographer Vincent Kang Fu found that "one key feature of the data is overwhelming endogamy for blacks and whites. At least 92 percent of white men, white women, black women and black men are married to members of their own group."[11] Rates of intermarriage rose for blacks and whites over the course of the 1990s. However, subsequent analysts continued to stress the degree to which a fundamental black-white divide persists. As demographers Zhenchao Qian and Daniel Lichter conclude in their analyses of U.S. Census data from 1990 and 2000:

[O]ur results also highlight a singularly persistent substantive lesson: African Americans are least likely of all racial/ethnic minorities to marry whites. And, although the pace of marital assimilation among African Americans proceeded more rapidly over the 1990s than it did in earlier decades, the social boundaries between African American and whites remain highly rigid and resilient to change. The "one-drop" rule apparently persists for African Americans.[12]

Third, some key synthetic works argue for an evolving racial scheme in the United States, but a scheme that nonetheless preserves a heavily stigmatized black category. A decade ago, sociologist Herbert Gans offered the provocative but well-grounded speculation that the United States would witness a transition from a society defined by a great white–nonwhite divide to one increasingly defined by a black–nonblack fissure, with an in-between or residual category for those granted provisional or "honorary white" status. As Gans explained: "If current trends persist, today's multiracial hierarchy could be replaced by what I think of as a dual or bimodal one consisting of 'nonblack' and 'black' population categories, with a third 'residual' category for the groups that do not, or do not yet, fit into the basic dualism." Most troubling, this new dualism would, in Gans's expectations, continue to bring a profound sense of undeservingness and stigma for those assigned its bottom rung.[13]

Gans's remarks have recently received substantial support from demographer Frank Bean and his colleagues. Based on their extensive analyses of population trends across a variety of indicators, Bean and colleagues write: "A black-nonblack divide appears to be taking shape in the United States, in which Asians and Latinos are closer to whites. Hence, America's color lines are moving toward a new demarcation that places many blacks in a position of disadvantage similar to that resulting from the traditional black-white divide."

If basic racial categories and identities are not soon to dissolve, then let me now address that second set of questions, concerning the degree of racial economic inequality. I should begin by noting that there has been considerable expansion in the size, security, and, arguably, salience and influence of the black middle class. . . .[14]

The official black poverty rate has fluctuated from two to three times the poverty rate for whites. Recent trend analyses suggest that this disparity declined during the economic boom years of the 1990s but remained substantial. As public policy analyst Michael Stoll explains: "Among all black families, the poverty rate declined from a 20 year high of about 40 percent in 1982 and 1993 to 25 percent in 2000. During this period, the poverty rate for white families remained fairly constant, at about 10 percent." That of 25 percent remains true through more recent estimates. In addition, the Great Recession has taken a particularly heavy toll on minority communities, African Americans perhaps most of all. As the Center for American Progress declared in a recent report: "Economic security and losses during the recession and recovery exacerbated the already weak situation for African Americans. They experienced declining employment rates, rising poverty rates, falling home-ownership rates, decreasing health insurance and retirement coverage during the last business cycle from 2001 to 2007. The recession that followed made a bad situation much worse."[15]

Overall trends in poverty, however, do not fully capture the cumulative and multidimensional nature of black economic disadvantage. Sociologist William Julius Wilson stresses how circumstances of persistently weak employment prospects and joblessness, particularly for low-skilled black men, weaken the formation of stable two-parent households and undermine other community structures. Persistent economic hardship and weakened social institutions then create circumstances that lead to rising rates of single-parent households, out-of-wedlock childbearing, welfare dependency, and greater risk of juvenile delinquency and involvement in crime.

Harvard sociologist Robert Sampson points to an extraordinary circumstance of exposure to living in deeply disadvantaged communities for large segments of the African American population. This disadvantage involves living in conditions that expose residents to high surrounding rates of unemployment, family breakup, individuals and families reliant on welfare, poor-performing schools, juvenile delinquency, and crime. As Sampson explains:

> [A]lthough we knew that the average national rate of family disruption and poverty among blacks was two to four times higher than among whites, the number of distinct ecological contexts in which blacks achieve equality to whites is striking. In not one city of 100,000 or more in the United States do blacks live in ecological equality with whites when it comes to these basic features of economic and family organization. Accordingly, racial differences in poverty and family disruption are so strong that the "worst" urban contexts in which whites reside are considerably better than the average context of black communities.[16]

Recent work published by sociologist Patrick Sharkey assesses race differences in the chances of mobility out of impoverished neighborhoods. The result is a very depressing one. He finds evidence of little upward social mobility for disadvantaged blacks and a fragile capacity to maintain advantaged status among even the most well-off African Americans. He writes: "[M]ore than 70 percent of black children who are raised in the poorest quarter of American neighborhoods will continue to live in the poorest quarter of neighborhoods as adults. Since the 1970s, more than half of black families have lived in the poorest quarter of neighborhoods in consecutive generations, compared to just seven percent of white families." Discussing the upper end, Sharkey writes: "Among the small number of black families who live in the top quartile, only 35 percent remain there in the second generation. By themselves, these figures reveal the striking persistence of neighborhood disadvantage among black families." This figure of 35 percent remaining in the top quartile across generations for blacks contrasts to 63 percent among whites. Thus, "White families exhibit a high rate of mobility out of the poorest neighborhoods and a low rate of mobility out of the most affluent neighborhoods, and the opposite is true among black families."[17]

The general labor market prospects of African Americans have undergone key changes in the last several decades. Three patterns loom large. There is far more internal differentiation and inequality within the black population than was true at the close of World War II, or even during our baseline of the mid-1960s. The fortunes of men and women have recently diverged within the black community. Black women have considerably narrowed the gap between themselves and white women in terms of educational attainment, major occupational categories, and earnings. Black men have faced a growing problem of economic marginalization. Importantly, this is contingent on levels of education; education has become a far sharper dividing line, shaping life chances more heavily than ever before in the black community.[18]

Several other dimensions of socioeconomic status bear mentioning. Even by conservative estimates, the high school dropout rate among blacks is twice that of whites, at 20 percent versus 11 percent. Blacks also have much lower college completion rates (17 percent vs. 30 percent) and lower advanced degree completion rates (6 percent vs. 11 percent). These differences are enormously consequential. As the essays in this volume by economist James Heckman and social psychologist Richard Nisbett emphasize, educational attainment and achievement increasingly define access to the good life, broadly defined. Moreover, some scholars make a strong case that important inequalities in resources still plague the educational experiences of many black school children, involving such factors as fewer well-trained teachers and less access to AP courses and other curriculum-enriching materials and experiences.[19]

One of the major social trends affecting African Americans over the past several decades has been the sharply punitive and incarceration-focused turn in the American criminal justice system. Between 1980 and 2000, the rate of black incarceration nearly tripled. The black-to-white incarceration ratio increased to above eight to one during this time period. Actuarial forecasts, or lifetime estimates, of the risk of incarceration for black males born in the 1990s approach one in three, as compared to below 1 in 10 for non-Hispanic white males. A recent major study by the Pew Foundation reported that as of 2007, 1 in 15 black males age 18 and above was in jail or prison, and 1 in 9 black males between the ages of 20 and 34 was in jail or prison. Blacks constitute a hugely disproportionate share of those incarcerated relative to their numbers in the general population.[20]

The reach of mass incarceration has risen to such levels that some analysts view it as altering normative life-course experiences for blacks in low-income neighborhoods. Indeed, the fabric of social life changes in heavily policed, low-income urban communities. The degree of incarceration has prompted scholars to describe the change as ushering in a new fourth stage of racial oppression, "the carceral state," constituted by the emergence of "the new Jim Crow" or, more narrowly, racialized mass incarceration. Whichever label one employs, there is no denying that exposure to the criminal justice system touches the lives of a large fraction of the African-American population, especially young men of low education and skill levels. These low levels of education and greater exposure to poverty, along with what many regard as the racially biased conduct of the War on Drugs, play a huge role in black overrepresentation in jails or federal and state prisons.[21]

Processes of racial residential segregation are a key factor in contemporary racial inequality. Despite important declines in overall rates of segregation over the past three decades and blacks' increasing suburbanization, blacks remain highly segregated from whites. Some have suggested that active self-segregation on the part of blacks is now a major factor sustaining residential segregation. A number of careful investigations of preferences for neighborhood characteristics and makeup and of the housing search process strongly challenge such claims. Instead, there is substantial evidence that, particularly among white Americans, neighborhoods and social spaces are strongly racially coded, with negative racial stereotypes playing a powerful role in shaping the degree of willingness to enter (or remain) in racially integrated living spaces. Moreover, careful auditing studies continue to show lower, but still significant, rates of anti-black discrimination on the part of real estate agents, homeowners, and landlords.[22]

Lastly, I want to stress that wealth inequality between blacks and whites remains enormous. Recent scholarship has convincingly argued that wealth (or accumulated assets) is a crucial determinant of quality of life. Blacks at all levels of the class hierarchy typically possess far less wealth than otherwise comparable whites. Moreover, the composition of black wealth is more heavily based in homes and automobiles as compared to white wealth, which includes a more even spread across savings, stocks and bonds, business ownership, and other more readily liquidated assets. Whereas approximately 75 percent of whites own their homes, only 47 percent of blacks do. Looking beyond homeownership to the full range of financial assets, analyses from sociologists Melvin Oliver and Tom Shapiro put the black-to-white wealth gap ratio in the range of 10 or 11 to 1. Other estimates, such as those based on Panel Study of Income Dynamics data, are lower but still represent gaping disparities. . . .[23]

In many respects, these sizable gaps in wealth associated with race are one of the principal ways in which the cumulative and "sedimentary" impact of a long history of racial oppression manifests itself. Research has shown that black and white families do not differ substantially in the extent to which they try to save income. Much wealth is inherited; it is not the product of strictly individual merit or achievement. Furthermore, social policy in many ways played a direct role in facilitating the accumulation of wealth for many generations of white Americans while systematically constraining or undermining such opportunities for African Americans. For example, Oliver and Shapiro and political scientist Ira Katznelson both point to federal home mortgage lending guidelines and practices, which were once openly discriminatory, as playing a crucial role in this process.[24]

What do we know about changes in racial attitudes in the United States? The first and most consistent finding of the major national studies of racial attitudes in the United States has been a steady repudiation of the outlooks that supported the Jim Crow social order. Jim Crow racism once reigned in American society, particularly in the South. Accordingly, blacks were understood as inherently inferior to whites, both intellectually and temperamentally. As a result, society was to be expressly ordered in terms of white privilege, with blacks relegated to secondary status in education, access to jobs, and in civic status such as the right to vote. Above all, racial mixture was to be avoided; hence, society needed to be segregated. The best survey data on American public opinion suggest that this set of ideas has been in steady retreat since the 1940s.[25]

There is one telling illustration of this trend. It shows the percentage of white Americans in national surveys who said that they would *not* be willing to vote for a qualified black candidate for president if nominated by their own party. When first asked in 1958, nearly two out of three white Americans endorsed such an openly discriminatory posture. That trend has undergone unabated decline, reaching the point where roughly only one in five white Americans expressed this view by the time the Reverend Jesse Jackson launched his first bid for the Democratic presidential nomination in 1984. It declined to fewer than 1 in 10 by the time of Obama's campaign in 2008.

In broad sweep, though not necessarily in exact levels, the aforementioned trend is true of most questions on racial attitudes from national surveys that deal with broad principles of whether American society should be integrated or segregated, discriminatory or nondiscriminatory on the basis of race. Whether the specific domain involved school integration, residential integration, or even racial intermarriage, the level of endorsement of discriminatory, segregationist responses has continued to decline. To an important degree, these changes have been led by highly educated whites and those outside the South. African Americans have never endorsed elements of the Jim Crow outlook to any substantial degree, though many of these questions were not initially asked of black respondents out of fear that the questions would be regarded as an insult, or to the assumption that their responses were predictable.

This picture of the repudiation of Jim Crow is complicated somewhat by evidence of significant social distance preferences. To be sure, low and typically declining percentages of whites objected when asked about entering into integrated social settings—neighborhoods or schools—where one or just a small number of blacks might be present. But as the number of blacks involved increased, and as one shifts from more impersonal and public domains of life (workplaces, schools, neighborhoods) to more intimate and personal domains (intermarriage), expressed levels of white resistance rise and the degree of positive change is not as great.

The notion of the 1960s as an inflection point in the struggle for racial change is reinforced by the growing preoccupation of studies of racial attitudes in the post-1960 period with matters of public policy. These studies consider levels of support or opposition to public policies designed to bring about greater racial equality (antidiscrimination laws and various forms of affirmative action) and actual integration (open housing laws and methods of school desegregation such as school busing). The picture that results is complex but has several recurrent features. Blacks are typically far more supportive of social-policy intervention on matters of race than are whites. In general, support for policy or governmental intervention to bring about greater integration or to reduce racial inequality lags well behind endorsement of similar broad principles or ideals. This finding has led many scholars to note a "principle-implementation gap." Some policies, however, have wider appeal than others. Efforts to enhance or improve the human capital attributes of blacks and other minority group members are more popular than policies that call for group preferences. Forms of affirmative action that imply quotas or otherwise disregard meritocratic criteria of reward are deeply unpopular.

One important line of investigation seeking to understand the principle-implementation gap involved assessments of perceptions and causal attributions for racial inequality. To the extent that many individuals do not perceive much racial inequality, or explain it in terms of individual dispositions and choices (as opposed to structural constraints and conditions such as discrimination), then there is little need seen for government action. Table 1 shows responses to a series of questions on possible causes of black-white economic inequality that included "less inborn ability," "lack of motivation and willpower," "no chance for an education," and "mainly due to discrimination." The questions thus span biological basis (ability), cultural basis (motivation), a weak form of structural constraint (education), and finally, a strong structural constraint (discrimination).[26]

There is low and decreasing support among whites for the overtly racist belief that blacks have less inborn ability. The most widely endorsed account among whites points to a lack of motivation or willpower on the part of blacks as a key factor in racial inequality, though this attribution declines over time. Attributions to discrimination as well as to the weaker structural account of lack of a chance for education also decline among whites. Blacks are generally far more likely than whites to endorse structural accounts of racial inequality, particularly the strongest attribution of discrimination. However, like their white counterparts, a declining number of blacks point to discrimination as the key factor, and there is actually a rise in the percentage of African Americans attributing racial inequality to a lack of motivation or willpower on the part of blacks themselves. More detailed multivariate analyses suggest that there has been growth in cultural attributions for racial inequality. Among African Americans this growth seems most prominent among somewhat younger, ideologically conservative, and less well-educated individuals. . . .[27]

We can see trends in whites' stereotype trait ratings of whites as compared to blacks on the dimensions of being hardworking or lazy and intelligent or unintelligent. In 1990, when these trait-rating stereotype questions were first posed in national surveys, more than 60 percent of whites rated whites as more likely to be hardworking than blacks, and just under 60 percent rated blacks as less intelligent. A variety of other trait dimensions were included in this early assessment, such as welfare dependency, involvement in drugs and gangs, and levels of patriotism. Whites usually expressed a substantially negative image of blacks relative to how they rated whites across this array of traits. The trends suggest some slight reduction in negative stereotyping over the past two decades, but such negative images of blacks still remain quite commonplace. To the extent that unfavorable beliefs about the behavioral characteristics of blacks have a bearing on levels of support for policies designed to benefit blacks, these data imply, and much evidence confirms, that negative beliefs about blacks' abilities and behavioral choices contribute to low levels of white support for significant social-policy interventions to ameliorate racial inequality.[28]

A third and perhaps most vigorously considered resolution of the principle-implementation gap involves the hypothesis that a new form of antiblack racism is at the root of much white opposition to policies aimed at reducing racial inequality. This scholarship has focused largely on the emergence of attitudes of resentment toward the demands or grievances voiced by African Americans and the expectation of governmental redress for those demands and grievances. In trends for one question frequently used to tap such sentiments; respondents are asked to agree or disagree with the statement, "Irish, Italian, Jewish and many other minorities overcame prejudice and worked their way up. Blacks should do the same without special favors." Throughout the 1994 to 2008 time span, roughly three-fourths of white Americans agreed with this assertion.

There is no meaningful trend, despite a slight dip in 2004: the lopsided view among whites is that blacks need to make it all on their own.[29]

Throughout the 14-year time span, whites were always substantially more likely to endorse this viewpoint than blacks; however, not only did a nontrivial number of blacks agree with it (about 50 percent), but the black-white gap actually narrowed slightly over time. The meaning and effects of this type of outlook vary in important ways depending on race, usually carrying less potent implications for policy views among blacks than among whites. Indeed, one reason for focusing on this type of attitude is that it and similar items are found to correlate with a wide range of social-policy outlooks. And some evidence suggests that how attitudes and outlooks connect with partisanship and voting behavior may be strengthening and growing.[30]

Judged by the trends considered here and in the essays in this volume, declarations of having arrived at the post-racial moment are premature. Much has changed—and unequivocally for the better—in light of where the United States stood in 1965. Indeed, I will speculate that none of the contributors to the 1965/1966 *Dædalus* volumes would have considered likely changes that have now, a mere four or so decades later, been realized, including the election of an African American President of the United States, the appointment of the first black Chair of the Joint Chiefs of Staff, and the appointment of two different African American Secretaries of State. Similarly, the size and reach of today's black middle class were not easy to forecast from the scholarly perch of mid-1960s data and understandings. At the same time, troublingly entrenched patterns of poverty, segregation, gaps in educational attainment and achievement, racial identity formation, and disparaging racial stereotypes all endure into the present, even if in somewhat less extreme forms. And the scandalous rise in what is now termed racialized mass incarceration was not foreseen but now adds a new measure of urgency to these concerns.

The very complex and contradictory nature of these changes cautions against the urge to make sweeping and simple declarations about where we now stand. But our nation's "mixed" or ambiguous circumstance—suspended uncomfortably somewhere between the collapse of the Jim Crow social order and a post-racial social order that has yet to be attained—gives rise to many intense exchanges over whether or how much "race matters." This is true of scholarly discourse, where many see racial division as a deeply entrenched and tragic American flaw and many others see racial division as a waning exception to the coming triumph of American liberalism.[31]

Average Americans, both black and white, face and wage much of the same debate in their day-to-day lives. One way of capturing this dynamic is illustrated . . . in a 2009 national survey that asked, "Do you think that blacks have achieved racial equality, will soon achieve racial equality, will not achieve racial equality in your lifetime, or will never achieve racial equality?" Fielded after the 2008 election and the inauguration of Obama in early 2009, these results are instructive. Almost two out of three white Americans (61.3 percent) said that blacks have achieved racial equality. Another 21.5 percent of whites endorse the view that blacks will soon achieve racial equality. Thus, the overwhelming fraction of white Americans see the postracial moment as effectively here (83.8 percent). Fewer than one in five blacks endorsed the idea that they have already achieved racial equality. A more substantial fraction, 36.2 percent, believe that they will soon achieve racial equality. African Americans, then, are divided almost evenly between those doubtful that racial equality will soon be achieved (with more than 1 in 10 saying that it will never be achieved) and those who see equality as within reach, at 46.6 percent versus 53.6 percent.[32]

These results underscore why discussions of race so easily and quickly become polarized and fractious along racial lines. The central tendencies of public opinion on these issues, despite real increasing overlap, remain enormously far apart between black and white Americans. When such differences in perception and belief are grounded in, or at least reinforced by, wide economic inequality, persistent residential segregation, largely racially homogeneous family units and close friendship networks, and a popular culture still suffused with negative ideas and images about African Americans, then there should be little surprise that we still find it enormously difficult to have sustained civil discussions about race and racial matters. Despite growing much closer together in recent decades, the gaps in perspective between blacks and whites are still sizable.

The ideas and evidence marshaled in this *Dædalus* issue should help sharpen our focus and open up productive new lines of discourse and inquiry. Four of the essays directly engage central, but changing, features of racial stratification in the United States. Sociologist Douglas S. Massey provides a trenchant, broad map of change in the status of African Americans. Sociologist William Julius Wilson reviews and assesses his field-defining argument about the "declining significance of race." The core framework is sustained, he maintains, by much subsequent careful research; but Wilson stresses now the special importance of employment in the government sector to the economic well-being of many African Americans. Economist James J. Heckman focuses on education, building the case for enhancing the capacities of families and communities to prepare children to get

the most out of schooling. Social psychologist Richard E. Nisbett looks closely at the types of early intervention strategies that evidence suggests are most likely to improve ultimate educational attainment and achievement.

Three essays put the changing status of African Americans in more explicit political, policy-related, and legal perspectives. Political scientist Rogers M. Smith and his colleagues identify the pivotal role played by agents of competing racial policy coalitions, pointing to the differing agendas and degrees of political success and influence of those pursuing a color-blind strategy and those pursuing a color-conscious strategy. Legal scholar Michael J. Klarman challenges the presumption that the U.S. Supreme Court has been a special ally or supporter of African American interests and claims. He suggests that the Court has often, particularly in a string of recent rulings, tilted heavily in the direction of a color-blind set of principles that do little to advance the interests of black communities. Political scientist Daniel Sabbagh traces the impetus for affirmative action and its evolution in the United States and compares that to how affirmative action is now pursued in a number of other countries.

Several essays examine the cultural dynamics of race and racial identities. Anthropologists Marcyliena Morgan and Dionne Bennett examine the remarkable dynamism, worldwide spread, and influence of hip-hop music. Social psychologists Jennifer A. Richeson and Maureen A. Craig examine the psychological dynamics of identity choices facing minority communities and individuals in this era of rapid population change. Political scientist Jennifer L. Hochschild and her colleagues assess how younger cohorts of Americans are bringing different views of race and its importance to politics and social life.

Three essays pivot off the 2008 presidential election. Political scientist Taeku Lee examines the complex role of race, group identity, and immigrant status in forging new political identities, coalitions, and voting behavior. Political scientist Cathy J. Cohen shows the continuing racial consciousness and orientations of black youth. Sociologist Alford A. Young, Jr., examines the special meaning of Obama's candidacy and success for young black men.

Two final essays push in quite different directions. Sociologist Roger Waldinger argues that even as the black-white divide remains an important problem, we as a nation are facing deep contradictions in how we deal with immigration and immigrants themselves, particularly those coming from Latin America. Historian Martha Biondi muses on continuities with and departures from past traditions in recent discourse surrounding the mission of African American studies programs and departments.

This issue is a companion volume to the Winter 2011 issue of *Dædalus*, Race in the Age of Obama, guest edited by Gerald

Early, the Merle Kling Professor of Modern Letters and Director of the Center for the Humanities at Washington University in St. Louis. It has been my privilege to work with Gerald on this project, and I am grateful to the contributors to this volume for their informed analyses.

This essay's epigraphs from Martin Luther King, Jr., John Hope Franklin, and Barack Obama, each in its own fashion, remind us of the depth and complexity of race in the United States. Although it is tempting to seek quick and simple assessments of where we have been and where we are going, it is wise, instead, to wrestle with taking stock of all the variegated and nuanced circumstances underlying the black-white divide and its associated phenomena. Just as 1965 seemed a point of inflection, of contradictory lines of development, future generations may look back and regard 2011 as a similarly fraught moment. At the same time that a nation celebrates the historic election of an African-American president, the cultural production of demeaning antiblack images—postcards featuring watermelons on the White House lawn prior to the annual Easter egg roll, Obama featured in loincloth and with a bone through his nose in ads denouncing the health care bill, a cartoon showing police officers shooting an out-of-control chimpanzee under the heading "They'll have to find someone else to write the next stimulus bill"—are ugly reminders of some of the more overtly racialized reactions to the ascendancy of an African American to the presidency of the United States.

As a result of complex and contradictory indicators, no pithy phrase or bold declaration can possibly do justice to the full body of research, evidence, and ideas reviewed here. One optimistic trend is that examinations of the status of blacks have moved to a place of prominence and sophistication in the social sciences that probably was never imagined by founding figures of the tradition, such as W.E.B. Du Bois. That accumulating body of knowledge and theory, including the new contributions herein, deepens our understanding of the experience of race in the United States. The configuration and salience of the color line some 50 or 100 years from now, however, cannot be forecast with any measure of certainty. Perhaps the strongest general declaration one can make at present is that we stand somewhere between a Jim Crow past and the aspiration of a postracial future.

Notes

1. Martin Luther King, Jr., *Where Do We Go From Here: Chaos or Community?* (New York: Bantam, 1968), 19; John Hope Franklin, *The Color Line: Legacy for the 21st Century* (Columbia: University of Missouri Press, 1993), 36; Barack H. Obama, "A More Perfect Union," speech delivered at the National Constitution Center, Philadelphia, May 18, 2008.

2. I wish to thank Alicia Simmons, Victor Thompson, and Deborah De Laurell for their invaluable assistance in preparing this essay. I am responsible for any remaining errors or shortcomings.

3. St. Clair Drake, "The Social and Economic Status of the Negro in the United States," *Dædalus* 94 (4) (Fall 1965): 3–46; Daniel Patrick Moynihan, "Employment, Income, and the Ordeal of the Negro Family," *Dædalus* 94 (4) (Fall 1965): 134–159.

4. See John McWhorter, *Losing the Race: Self-Sabotage in Black America* (New York: Free Press, 2000); and Charles Johnson, "The End of the Black American Narrative," *The American Scholar* 77 (3) (Summer 2008).

5. See Hua Hsu, "The End of White America?" *The Atlantic*, January/February 2009; and Susan Saulny, "Black? White? Asian? More Young Americans Choose All of the Above," *The New York Times*, January 29, 2011.

6. On laissez-faire racism, see Lawrence D. Bobo, James R. Kluegel, and Ryan A. Smith, "Laissez-Faire Racism: The Crystallization of a Kinder, Gentler, Antiblack Ideology," in *Racial Attitudes in the 1990s: Continuity and Change*, ed. Steven A. Tuch and Jack K. Martin (Greenwood, CT: Praeger, 1997), 15–44; on modern or symbolic racism, see David O. Sears, "Symbolic Racism," in *Eliminating Racism: Profiles in Controversy*, ed. Phyllis A. Katz and Dalmas A. Taylor (New York: Plenum Press, 1988), 53–84; and on color-blind racism, see Eduardo Bonilla-Silva, *Racism without Racists: Colorblind Racism and Racial Inequality in Contemporary America* (Boulder, CO: Rowman and Littlefield, 2010).

7. See C. Matthew Snipp, "Defining Race and Ethnicity: The Constitution, the Supreme Court, and the Census," in *Doing Race: 21 Essays for the 21st Century*, ed. Hazel R. Markus and Paula M.L. Moya (New York: W.W. Norton, 2010), 105–122. It is noteworthy that Obama himself checked only the "Black" category rather than marking more than one race on his 2010 Census form.

8. On the history of "mixing" in the United States, see Gary B. Nash, "The Hidden History of Mestizo America," *Journal of American History* 82 (1995): 941–964; and Victor Thompson, "The Strange Career of Racial Science: Racial Categories and African American Identity," in *The Oxford Handbook of African American Citizenship*, ed. Henry Louis Gates, Jr., et al. (New York: Oxford University Press, forthcoming).

9. David A. Hollinger, "Amalgamation and Hypodescent: The Question of Ethnoracial Mixture in the History of the United States," *American Historical Review* 108 (December 2003): 1305–1390.

10. Melissa R. Herman, "Do You See Who I Am?: How Observers' Background Affects the Perceptions of Multiracial Faces," *Social Psychology Quarterly* 73 (2010): 58–78; see also Arnold K. Ho, Jim Sidanius, Daniel T. Levin, and Mahzarin R. Banaji, "Evidence for Hypo-descent and Racial Hierarchy in the

Categorization and Perception of Biracial Individuals," *Journal of Personality and Social Psychology* 94 (2010): 1–15.

11. Vincent Kang Fu, "How Many Melting Pots?: Intermarriage, Panethnicity, and the Black/Non-Black Divide in the United States," *Journal of Comparative Family Studies* 38 (2007): 215–237. On the point of a racial preference hierarchy, see Vincent Kang Fu, "Racial Intermarriage Pairings," *Demography* 38 (2001): 147–159.

12. Zenchao Qian and Daniel T. Lichter, "Social Boundaries and Marital Assimilation: Interpreting Trends in Racial and Ethnic Intermarriage," *American Sociological Review* 72 (2007): 68–94. See also Zenchao Qian, "Breaking the Last Taboo: Interracial Marriage in America," *Contexts* 4 (2005): 33–37.

13. Herbert J. Gans, "The Possibility of a New Racial Hierarchy in the Twenty-First Century United States," in *The Cultural Territories of Race: Black and White Boundaries,* ed. Michèle Lamont (New York: Russell Sage, 1999), 371–390; and Frank D. Bean et al., "The New U.S. Immigrants: How Do They Affect Our Understanding of the African American Experience?" *Annals of the American Academy of Political and Social Science* 621 (2009): 202–220. For closely related discussions, see Mary C. Waters, *Black Identities: West Indian Immigrant Dreams and American Realities* (Cambridge, MA: Harvard University Press, 1999); and Milton Vickerman, "Recent Immigration and Race: Continuity and Change," *Du Bois Review* 4 (2007): 141–165.

14. See Bart Landry, *The New Black Middle Class* (Berkeley: University of California Press, 1987); Karyn Lacy, *Blue Chip Black: Race, Class and Status in the New Black Middle Class* (Berkeley: University of California Press, 2007); and Mary Pattillo, *Black on the Block: The Politics of Race and Class in the City* (Chicago: University of Chicago Press, 2007).

15. Christian E. Weller, Jaryn Fields, and Folayemi Agbede, "The State of Communities of Color in the U.S. Economy" (Washington, DC: Center for American Progress, January 21, 2011), http://www.americanprogress.org/issues/2011/01/coc_snapshot.html/print.html (accessed January 23, 2011).

16. William Julius Wilson, *The Truly Disadvantaged: The Inner City, the Underclass, and Public Policy* (Chicago: University of Chicago Press, 1987); William Julius Wilson, *When Work Disappears: The World of the New Urban Poor* (New York: Knopf, 1996); and Robert J. Sampson, "Urban Black Violence: The Effect of Male Joblessness and Family Disruption," *American Journal of Sociology* 93 (1987): 348–382.

17. Patrick Sharkey, "The Intergenerational Transmission of Context," *American Journal of Sociology* 113 (4): 931–969. See also Tom Hertz, "Rags, Riches, and Race: The Intergenerational Economic Mobility of Black and White Families in the United States," in *Unequal Chances: Family Background and Economic Success,* ed. Samuel Bowles, Herbert Gintis, and Melissa Osborne Groves (Princeton, NJ: Princeton University Press, 2005).

18. See Michael B. Katz, Mark J. Stern, and Jamie J. Fader, "The New African American Inequality," *The Journal of American History* 92 (1) (2005): 75–108.

19. Linda Darling Hammond, "The Color Line in American Education: Race, Resources, and Student Achievement," *Du Bois Review* 1 (2004): 213–246; and Linda Darling Hammond, "Structured for Failure: Race, Resources, and Student Achievement," in *Doing Race,* ed. Markus and Moya, 295–321.

20. Alfred Blumstein, "Race and Criminal Justice," in *America Becoming: Racial Trends and Their Consequences, Volume II,* ed. Neil J. Smelser, William Julius Wilson, and Faith Mitchell (Washington, DC: National Academies Press, 2001), 21–31; and Pew Center on the States, "One in 100: Behind Bars in America 2008" (Washington, DC: Pew Charitable Trusts, 2008).

21. Generally, see Bruce Western, *Punishment and Inequality in America* (New York: Russell Sage, 2006). On changes in the normative life trajectories, see Becky Pettit and Bruce Western, "Mass Imprisonment and the Life-Course: Race and Class Inequality in U.S. Incarceration," *American Sociological Review* 69 (2004): 151–169. On the social costs of heavy police scrutiny of poor neighborhoods, see Loïc Wacquant, "Deadly Symbiosis: When Ghetto and Prison Meet and Mesh," *Punishment and Society* 3 (2001): 95–135; and Alice Goffman, "On the Run: Wanted Men in a Philadelphia Ghetto," *American Sociological Review* 74 (2009): 339–357. On the rising incarceration rates for blacks more broadly, see Lawrence D. Bobo and Victor Thompson, "Racialized Mass Incarceration: Poverty, Prejudice, and Punitiveness," in *Doing Race,* ed. Markus and Moya, 322–355; and Michelle Alexander, *The New Jim Crow: Mass Incarceration in the Age of Colorblindness* (New York: The New Press, 2010).

22. Generally, see Douglas S. Massey and Nancy A. Denton, *American Apartheid: Segregation and the Making of the Underclass* (Cambridge, MA: Harvard University Press, 1993); Camille Z. Charles, *Won't You Be My Neighbor?: Race, Class, and Residence in Los Angeles* (New York: Russell Sage, 2006); Robert J. Sampson, "Seeing Disorder: Neighborhood Stigma and the Social Construction of 'Broken Windows,'" *Social Psychology Quarterly* 67 (2004): 319–342; Maria Krysan, Mick Couper, Reynolds Farley, and Tyrone A. Forman, "Does Race Matter in Neighborhood Preferences? Results from a Video Experiment," *American Journal of Sociology* 115 (2) (2009): 527–559; and Devah Pager and Hana Shepherd, "The Sociology of Discrimination: Racial Discrimination in Employment, Housing, Credit, and Consumer Markets," *Annual Review of Sociology* 34 (2008): 181–209.

23. Melvin L. Oliver and Thomas M. Shapiro, *Black Wealth/White Wealth: A New Perspective on Racial Inequality* (New York: Routledge, 1995); Dalton Conley, *Being Black, Living in the Red: Race, Wealth, and Social Policy in America* (Berkeley: University of California Press, 1999); and Thomas M. Shapiro, *The Hidden Cost of Being African American: How Wealth Perpetuates Inequality* (New York: Oxford University Press, 2004).

24. See Ira Katznelson, *When Affirmative Action Was White: An Untold Story of Racial Inequality in Twentieth-Century America* (New York: W.W. Norton, 2005).

25. I owe much of this discussion of racial attitudes to Howard Schuman, Charlotte Steeh, Lawrence D. Bobo, and Maria Krysan, *Racial Attitudes in America: Trends and Interpretations* (Cambridge, MA: Harvard University Press, 1997). See also Lawrence D. Bobo, "Racial Attitudes and Relations at the Close of the Twentieth Century," in *America Becoming: Racial Trends and Their Consequences, Volume 1*, ed. Neil J. Smelser, William Julius Wilson, and Faith Mitchell (Washington, DC: National Academies Press, 2001), 264–301; and Maria Krysan, "From Color Caste to Color Blind?: Racial Attitudes Since World War II," in *The Oxford Handbook of African American Citizenship*, ed. Gates.

26. Important early work on attributions for racial inequality appears in Howard Schuman, "Sociological Racism," *Society* 7 (1969): 44–48; Richard Apostle et al., *The Anatomy of Racial Attitudes* (Berkeley: University of California Press, 1983); James R. Kluegel and Eliot R. Smith, *Beliefs About Inequality: Americans' Views of What Is and What Ought to Be* (New York: Aldine de Gruyter, 1986); Paul M. Sniderman and Michael G. Hagen, *Race and Inequality: A Study in American Values* (Chatham, NJ: Chatham House, 1985); and James R. Kluegel "Trends in Whites' Explanations of the Black-White Gap in Socioeconomic Status, 1977–1989," *American Sociological Review* 55 (1990): 512–525.

27. Matthew O. Hunt, "African-American, Hispanic, and White Beliefs about Black/White Inequality, 1977–2004," *American Sociological Review* 72 (2007): 390–415; Lawrence D. Bobo et al., "The Real Record on Racial Attitudes," in *Social Trends in the United States 1972–2008: Evidence from the General Social Survey*, ed. Peter V. Marsden (Princeton, NJ: Princeton University Press, forthcoming).

28. On the stereotype measures, see Tom W. Smith, "Ethnic Images," GSS Technical Report No. 19 (Chicago: National Opinion Research Center, 1990); and Lawrence D. Bobo and James R. Kluegel, "Status, Ideology, and Dimensions of Whites' Racial Beliefs and Attitudes: Progress and Stagnation," in *Racial Attitudes in the 1990s*, ed. Tuch and Martin, 93–120. On the stereotype connection to public policy views, see Martin I. Gilens, *Why Americans Hate Welfare: Race, Media, and the Politics of Antipoverty Policy* (Chicago: University of Chicago Press, 1999); Lawrence D. Bobo and James R. Kluegel, "Opposition to Race-Targeting: Self-Interest, Stratification Ideology, or Racial Attitudes?" *American Sociological Review* 58 (1993): 443–464; and Steven A. Tuch and Michael Hughes, "Whites' Racial Policy Attitudes," *Social Science Quarterly* 77 (1996): 723–745.

29. For one excellent empirical report, see David O. Sears, Collette van Larr, Mary Carillo, and Rick Kosterman, "Is It Really Racism?: The Origins of White American Opposition to Race-Targeted Policies," *Public Opinion Quarterly* 61 (1997): 16–53. For a careful review and assessment of debates regarding the new racism hypothesis, see Maria Krysan, "Prejudice, Politics, and Public Opinion: Understanding the Sources of Racial Policy Attitudes," *Annual Review of Sociology* 26 (2000): 135–168.

30. For a discussion of the growing role of such resentments in partisan outlooks and political behavior, see Nicholas A. Valentino and David O. Sears, "Old Times There Are Not Forgotten: Race and Partisan Realignment in the Contemporary South," *American Journal of Political Science* 49 (2005): 672–688. For differential effects by race, see Lawrence D. Bobo and Devon Johnson, "A Taste for Punishment: Black and White Americans' Views on the Death Penalty and the War on Drugs," *Du Bois Review* 1 (2004): 151–180.

31. Those representative of the "deeply rooted racial flaw" camp would include Derrick Bell, *Faces at the Bottom of the Well: The Permanence of Racism* (New York: Basic Books, 1992); Andrew Hacker, *Two Nations: Black and White: Separate, Hostile, Unequal* (New York: Scribner, 1992); Donald R. Kinder and Lynn M. Sanders, *Divided by Color: Racial Politics and Democratic Ideals* (Chicago: University of Chicago Press, 1996); Charles W. Mills, *The Racial Contract* (Ithaca, NY: Cornell University Press, 1997); Joe R. Feagin, *Racist America: Roots, Current Realities, and Future Reparations* (New York: Routledge, 2000); Michael K. Brown et al., *White-Washing Race: The Myth of a Color-Blind Society* (Berkeley: University of California Press, 2003); and Douglas S. Massey, *Categorically Unequal: The American Stratification System* (New York: Russell Sage, 2006). Those representative of the "triumph of American liberalism" camp would include Nathan Glazer, "The Emergence of an American Ethnic Pattern," in *From Different Shores: Perspectives on Race and Ethnicity in America*, ed. Ronald Takaki (New York: Oxford University Press, 1987), 11–23; Orlando Patterson, *The Ordeal of Integration: Progress and Resentment in America's "Racial" Crisis* (Washington, DC: Basic Civitas, 1997); Paul M. Sniderman and Edward G. Carmines, *Reaching Beyond Race* (Cambridge, MA: Harvard University Press, 1997); Abigail Thernstrom and Stephan Thern-strom, *America in Black and White: One Nation, Indivisible* (New York: Simon & Schuster, 1997); and Richard D. Alba, *Blurring the Color Line: The New Chance for a More Integrated America* (Cambridge, MA: Harvard University Press, 2009).

32. These numbers point to a sharp rise in the percentage of white Americans endorsing the view that we have or will soon achieve racial equality; the figure rose from about 66 percent in 2000 to over 80 percent in 2009. A similar increase occurred among blacks: while 27 percent endorsed this view in 2000, the figure rose to 53 percent in 2009; thus, it nearly doubled. The 2000 survey allowed respondents to answer, "Don't know"; the 2009 survey did not. These percentages are calculated without the "don't know" responses. The 2000 results are reported in Lawrence D. Bobo, "Inequalities that Endure? Racial Ideology, American Politics, and the Peculiar Role of the Social

Sciences," in *The Changing Terrain of Race and Ethnicity,* ed. Maria Krysan and Amanda E. Lewis (New York: Russell Sage, 2004), 13–42.

Critical Thinking

1. Can you list evidences of a racial divide in your own town? Explain your answer.

2. Do you see differences among races regarding expectations of government programs?

3. What can be done to close up the racial divide?

Create Central

www.mhhe.com/createcentral

Internet References

ACLU Criminal Justice Home Page
www.aclu.org/crimjustice/index.html

Human Rights and Humanitarian Assistance
www.etown.edu/vl/humrts.html

New American Studies Web
www.georgetown.edu/crossroads/asw

Sociology—Study Sociology Online
http://edu.learnsoc.org

Sociology Web Resources
http://www.mhhe.com/socscience/sociology/resources/index.htm

Sociosite
http://www.topsite.com/goto/sociosite.net

Socioweb
http://www.topsite.com/goto/socioweb.com

LAWRENCE D. BOBO, a Fellow of the American Academy since 2006, is the W.E.B. Du Bois Professor of the Social Sciences at Harvard University and a founding editor of the *Du Bois Review*. His publications include *Racialized Politics: The Debate about Racism in America* (with David O. Sears and James Sidanius, 2000), *Urban Inequality: Evidence from Four Cities* (with Alice O'Connor and Chris Tilly, 2001), and *Prejudice in Politics: Group Position, Public Opinion, and the Wisconsin Treaty Rights Dispute* (with Mia Tuan, 2006).

From *Daedalus*, Spring 2011, pp. 11–36. Copyright © 2011 by MIT Press Journals/American Academy of Arts and Sciences. Reprinted by permission via Rightslink.

Article   Prepared by: Kurt Finsterbusch, *University of Maryland, College Park*

Black Pathology and the Closing of the Progressive Mind

TA-NEHISI COATES

Learning Outcomes

After reading this article, you will be able to:

- Understand the roles of both the culture of white supremacy and structural conditions in explaining the situation of blacks in the United States.

- Be able to evaluate the strength and weakness of the cultural explanation of the situation of blacks.

- Discuss the strengths of black culture.

Among opinion writers, Jonathan Chait is outranked in my esteem only by Hendrik Hertzberg. This lovely takedown of Robert Johnson is a classic of the genre, one I studied incessantly when I was sharpening my own sword. The sharpening never ends. With that in mind, it is a pleasure to engage Chait in the discussion over President Obama, racism, culture, and personal responsibility. It's good to debate a writer of such clarity—even when that clarity has failed him.

On y va.

Chait argues that I've conflated Paul Ryan's view of black poverty with Barack Obama's. He is correct. I should have spent more time disentangling these two notions, and illuminating their common roots—the notion that black culture is part of the problem. I have tried to do this disentangling in the past. I am sorry I did not do it in this instance and will attempt to do so now.

Need of moral instruction is an old and dubious tradition in America. There is a conservative and a liberal rendition of this tradition. The conservative version eliminates white supremacy as a factor and leaves the question of the culture's origin ominously unanswered. This version can never be regarded seriously. Life is short. Black life is shorter.

On y va.

The liberal version of the cultural argument points to "a tangle of pathologies" haunting black America born of oppression. This argument—which Barack Obama embraces—is more sincere, honest, and seductive. Chait helpfully summarizes:

The argument is that structural conditions shape culture, and culture, in turn, can take on a life of its own independent of the forces that created it. It would be bizarre to imagine that centuries of slavery, followed by systematic terrorism, segregation, discrimination, a legacy wealth gap, and so on did not leave a cultural residue that itself became an impediment to success.

The "structural conditions" Chait outlines above can be summed up under the phrase "white supremacy." I have spent the past two days searArguing that poor black people are not "holding up their end of the bargain," or that they are in ching for an era when black culture could be said to be "independent" of white supremacy. I have not found one. Certainly the antebellum period, when one third of all enslaved black people found themselves on the auction block, is not such an era. And surely we would not consider postbellum America, when freed people were regularly subjected to terrorism, to be such an era.

We certainly do not find such a period during the Roosevelt-Truman era, when this country erected a racist social safety net, leaving the NAACP to quip that the New Deal was "like a sieve with holes just big enough for the majority of Negroes to fall through." Nor do we find it during the 1940s, '50s and '60s, when African-Americans—as a matter of federal policy—were largely excluded from the legitimate housing market. Nor during the 1980s when we began the erection of a prison-industrial complex so vast that black males now comprise 8 percent of the world's entire incarcerated population.

And we do not find an era free of white supremacy in our times either, when the rising number of arrests for marijuana are mostly borne by African-Americans; when segregation drives a foreclosure crisis that helped expand the wealth gap; when big banks busy themselves baiting black people with "wealth-building seminars" and instead offering "ghetto loans" for "mud people"; when studies find that black low-wage applicants with no criminal record "fared no better than a white applicant just released from prison"; when, even after controlling for neighborhoods and crime rates, my son finds himself more likely to be stopped and frisked. Chait's theory of independent black cultural pathologies sounds reasonable. But it can't actually be demonstrated in the American record, and thus has no applicability.

What about the idea that white supremacy necessarily "bred a cultural residue that itself became an impediment to success"? Chait believes that it's "bizarre" to think otherwise. I think it's bizarre that he doesn't bother to see if his argument is actually true. Oppression might well produce a culture of failure. It might also produce a warrior spirit and a deep commitment to attaining the very things which had been so often withheld from you. There is no need for theorizing. The answers are knowable.

There certainly is no era more oppressive for black people than their 250 years of enslavement in this country. Slavery encompassed not just forced labor, but a ban on black literacy, the vending of black children, the regular rape of black women, and the lack of legal standing for black marriage. Like Chait, 19th century Northern white reformers coming South after the Civil War expected to find "a cultural residue that itself became an impediment to success."

In his masterful history, *Reconstruction*, the historian Eric Foner recounts the experience of the progressives who came to the South as teachers in black schools. The reformers "had little previous contact with blacks" and their views were largely cribbed from *Uncle Tom's Cabin*. They thus believed blacks to be culturally degraded and lacking in family instincts, prone to lie and steal, and generally opposed to self-reliance:

Few Northerners involved in black education could rise above the conviction that slavery had produced a "degraded" people, in dire need of instruction in frugality, temperance, honesty, and the dignity of labor . . . In classrooms, alphabet drills and multiplication tables alternated with exhortations to piety, cleanliness, and punctuality.

In short, white progressives coming South expected to find a black community suffering the effects of not just oppression but its "cultural residue."

Here is what they actually found:

During the Civil War, John Eaton, **who, like many whites, believed that slavery had destroyed the sense of family obligation,** was astonished by the eagerness with which former slaves in contraband camps legalized their marriage bonds. The same pattern was repeated when the Freedmen's Bureau and state governments made it possible to register and solemnize slave unions. Many families, in addition, adopted the children of deceased relatives and friends, rather than see them apprenticed to white masters or placed in Freedmen's Bureau orphanages.

By 1870, a large majority of blacks lived in two-parent family households, a fact that can be gleaned from the manuscript census returns but also "quite incidentally" from the Congressional Ku Klux Klan hearings, which recorded countless instances of victims assaulted in their homes, "the husband and wife in bed, and . . . their little children beside them."

The point here is rich and repeated in American history—it was not "cultural residue" that threatened black marriages. It was white terrorism, white rapacity, and white violence. And the commitment among freed people to marriage mirrored a larger commitment to the reconstitution of family, itself necessary because of systemic white violence.

"In their eyes," wrote an official from the Freedmen's Bureau, in 1865. "The work of emancipation was incomplete until the families which had been dispersed by slavery were reunited."

White people at the time noted a sudden need in black people to travel far and wide. "The Negroes," reports one observer, "are literally crazy about traveling." Why were the Negroes "literally crazy about traveling?" Part of it was the sheer joy of mobility granted by emancipation. But there was something more: "Of all the motivations for black mobility," writes Foner, "none was more poignant than the effort to reunite families separated during slavery."

This effort continued as late the onset of the twentieth century, when you could still find newspapers running ads like this:

During the year 1849, Thomas Sample carried away from this city, as his slaves, our daughter, Polly, and son. . . . We will give $100 each for them to any person who will assist them . . . to get to Nashville, or get word to us of their whereabouts.

Nor had the centuries-long effort to destroy black curiosity and thirst for education yielded much effect:

Perhaps the most striking illustration of the freedmen's quest for self-improvement was their seemingly unquenchable thirst for education. . . . The desire for learning led parents to migrate to towns and cities in search of education for their children, and plantation workers to make the establishment of a school-house "an absolute condition" of signing labor contracts . . .

Contemporaries could not but note the contrast **between white families seemingly indifferent to education and blacks who "toil and strive, labour and endure in order that their children 'may have a schooling'."** As one Northern educator remarked: "Is it not significant that after the lapse of

144 years since the settlement [of Beaufort, North Carolina], the Freedmen are building the first public school-house ever erected here."

"All in all," Foner concludes, "the months following the end of the Civil War were a period of remarkable accomplishment for Southern blacks." This is not especially remarkable, if you consider the time. Education, for instance, was not merely a status marker. Literacy was protection against having your land stolen or being otherwise cheated. Perhaps more importantly, it gave access to the Bible. The cultural fruits of oppression are rarely predictable merely through theorycraft. Who would predicted that oppression would make black people hungrier for education than their white peers? Who could predict the blues?

And culture is not exclusive. African-American are Americans, and have been Americans longer than virtually any other group of white Americans. There is no reason to suppose that enslavement cut African-Americans off from a broader cultural values. More likely African-Americans contributed to the creation and maintenance of those values.

The African-Americans who endured enslavement were subject to two and half centuries of degradation and humiliation. Slavery lasted twice as long as Jim Crow and was more repressive. If you were going to see evidence of a "cultural residue" which impeded success you would see it there. Instead you find black people desperate to reconstitute their families, desperate to marry, and desperate to be educated. Progressives who advocate the nineteenth-century line must specifically name the "cultural residue" that afflicts black people, and then offer evidence of it. Favoring abstract thought experiments over research will not cut it.

Progressives who advocate the nineteenth-century line must name the "cultural residue" that afflicts black people, and then offer evidence of it. Abstract thought experiments will not cut it.

Nor will pretending that old debates are somehow new. For some reason there is an entrenched belief among many liberals and conservatives that discussions of American racism should begin somewhere between the Moynihan Report and the Detroit riots. Thus Chait dates our dispute to the fights in the '70s between liberals. In fact, we are carrying on an argument that is at least a century older.

The passage of time is important because it allows us to assess how those arguments have faired. I contend that my arguments have been borne out, and the arguments of progressives like Chait and the president of the United States have not. Either Booker T. Washington was correct when he urged black people to forgo politics in favor eliminating "the criminal and loafing element of our people" or he wasn't. Either W.E.B. Du Bois was correct when he claimed that correcting "the immorality, crime and laziness among the Negroes" should be the "first and primary" goal or he was not. The track record of progressive moral reform in the black community is knowable.

And it's not just knowable from Eric Foner. It can be gleaned from reading the entire Moynihan Report—not just the "tangle of pathologies" section—and then comparing it with Herb Gutman's *The Black Family in Slavery and Freedom.* It can be gleaned from Isabel Wilkerson's history of the Great Migration, *The Warmth of Other Suns.* One of the most important threads in this book is Wilkerson dismantling of the liberal theory of cultural degradation.

I want to conclude by examining one important element of Chait's argument—the role of the president of the United States who also happens to be a black man:

If I'm watching a basketball game in which the officials are systematically favoring one team over another (let's call them Team A and Team Duke) as an analyst, the officiating bias may be my central concern. But if I'm coaching Team A, I'd tell my players to ignore the biased officiating. Indeed, I'd be concerned the bias would either discourage them or make them lash out, and would urge them to overcome it. That's not the same as denying bias. It's a sensible practice of encouraging people to concentrate on the things they can control.

Obama's habit of speaking about this issue primarily to black audiences is Obama seizing upon his role as the most famous and admired African-American in the world to urge positive habits and behavior.

Chait's metaphor is incorrect. Barack Obama isn't the coach of "Team Negro," he is the commissioner of the league. Team Negro is very proud that someone who served on our staff has risen (for the first time in history!) to be commissioner. And Team Negro, which since the dawn of the league has endured biased officiating and whose every game is away, hopes that the commissioner's tenure among them has given him insight into the league's problems. But Team Negro is not—and should not be—confused about the commissioner's primary role.

"I'm not the president of black America," Barack Obama has said. "I'm the president of the United States of America."

Precisely.

And the president of the United States is not just an enactor of policy for today, he is the titular representative of his country's heritage and legacy. In regards to black people, America's heritage is kleptocracy—the stealing and selling of other people's children, the robbery of the fruits of black labor, the pillaging of black property, the taxing of black citizens for schools they can not attend, for pools in which they can not swim, for libraries that bar them, for universities that exclude them, for police who do not protect them, for the marking of whole communities as beyond the protection of the state and thus subject to the purview of outlaws and predators.

Obama-era progressives view white supremacy as something awful that happened in the past. I view it as one of the central organizing forces in American life.

The bearer of this unfortunate heritage feebly urging "positive habits and behavior" while his country imprisons some ungodly number of black men may well be greeted with applause in some quarters. It must never be so among those of us whose love of James Baldwin is true, whose love of Ida B. Wells is true, whose love of Harriet Tubman and our ancestors who fought for the right of family is true. In that fight America has rarely been our ally. Very often it has been our nemesis.

Obama-era progressives view white supremacy as something awful that happened in the past and the historical vestiges of which still afflict black people today. They believe we need policies—though not race-specific policies—that address the affliction. I view white supremacy as one of the central organizing forces in American life, whose vestiges and practices afflicted black people in the past, continue to afflict black people today, and will likely afflict black people until this country passes into the dust.

There is no evidence that black people are less responsible, less moral, or less upstanding in their dealings with America nor with themselves. But there is overwhelming evidence that America is irresponsible, immoral, and unconscionable in its dealings with black people and with itself. Urging African-Americans to become superhuman is great advice if you are concerned with creating extraordinary individuals. It is terrible advice if you are concerned with creating an equitable society. The black freedom struggle is not about raising a race of hyper-moral super-humans. It is about all people garnering the right to live like the normal humans they are.

Critical Thinking

1. How significant is the racism of white supremacy in holding back blacks today?
2. What is your view of the prospects for blacks today?
3. Why is racism still fairly strong?

Create Central

www.mhhe.com/createcentral

Internet References

ACLU Criminal Justice Home Page
www.aclu.org/crimjustice/index.html
Human Rights and Humanitarian Assistance
www.etown.edu/vl/humrts.html
New American Studies Web
www.georgetown.edu/crossroads/asw
Sociology—Study Sociology Online
http://edu.learnsoc.org
Sociology Web Resources
http://www.mhhe.com/socscience/sociology/resources/index.htm
Sociosite
http://www.topsite.com/goto/sociosite.net
Socioweb
http://www.topsite.com/goto/socioweb.com

© 2014 The Atlantic Media Co., as first published in The Atlantic Magazine. All rights reserved. Distributed by Tribune Content Agency, LLC.

Article   Prepared by: Kurt Finsterbusch, *University of Maryland, College Park*

Fear and Loathing of Islam

A decade after 9/11, ordinary life for American Muslims is enough to arouse suspicion.

MOUSTAFA BAYOUMI

Learning Outcomes

After reading this article, you will be able to:

- Describe the situation of Muslims in the United States today.

- Understand that American Arabs and Muslims were very well integrated into U.S. society before 9/11.

- Understand and be sorrowful that many untrue terrible stories about Muslims have spread like wildfire through talk radio, the Internet, and other media that have little regard for the facts.

S omething's gone terribly wrong.

In August 2007, the New York Police Department released a report called "Radicalization in the West: The Homegrown Threat," claiming that the looming danger to the United States was from "unremarkable" Muslim men under 35 who visit "extremist incubators." The language sounds ominous, conjuring up *Clockwork Orange*–style laboratories of human reprogramming, twisting average Muslims into instruments of evil. And yet what are these "incubators"? The report states that they are mosques, "cafes, cab driver hangouts, flophouses, prisons, student associations, nongovernmental organizations, hookah (water pipe) bars, butcher shops and book stores"—in other words, precisely the places where ordinary life happens.

But the report wasn't based on any independent social science research, and actual studies clearly refuted the very claims made by the NYPD. The Rand Corporation found that the number of homegrown radicals here is "tiny." "There are more than 3 million Muslims in the United States, and few more than 100 have joined jihad—about one out of every 30,000—suggesting an American Muslim population that remains hostile to jihadist

ideology and its exhortations to violence," Rand's 2010 report found. "A mistrust of American Muslims by other Americans seems misplaced," it concluded. This year, an analysis by the Triangle Center on Terrorism and Homeland Security also described the number of American Muslims involved in domestic terrorism since 2001 as "tiny." "This study's findings challenge Americans to be vigilant against the threat of homegrown terrorism while maintaining a responsible sense of proportion," it said. And a 2011 Gallup survey found that American Muslims were the least likely of any major U.S. religious group to consider attacks on civilians justified.

Every group has its loonies. And yet the idea that American Muslim communities are foul nests of hatred, where dark-skinned men plot Arabic violence while combing one another's beards, persists. In fact, it's worse than that. In the past few years, another narrative about American Muslims has come along, which sows a different kind of paranoia. While the old story revolves around security, portraying American Muslims as potential terrorists or terrorist sympathizers, the new narrative operates more along the axis of culture. Simple acts of religious or cultural expression and the straightforward activities of Muslim daily life have become suspicious. Building a mosque in Lower Manhattan or in Sheepshead Bay, Brooklyn, or in Murfreesboro, Tennessee, becomes an act of "stealth jihad." Muslims filing for divorce invokes the bizarre charge of "creeping Sharia." A dual-language Arabic-English high school in New York is demonized as a "madrassa." The State Board of Education in Texas determines that reading about Islam is not education but indoctrination. Changing your Muslim-sounding name to one with a more Anglophone tenor triggers an NYPD investigation, according to the Associated Press. Even the fact that some Butterball turkeys are "halal" was enough to fire up the bigotry last Thanksgiving, the most American of holidays.

What happens when ordinary life becomes grounds for suspicion without a hint of wrongdoing; when law enforcement premises its work on spying on the quotidian and policing the unremarkable; and when the everyday affairs of American Muslim life can so easily be transformed into nefarious intent? Something has gone terribly wrong for American Muslims when, more than a decade after the terrorist attacks of September 11, anti-Muslim sentiment in the United States continues to grow.

A *Washington Post*/ABC News poll taken in October 2001 found that 39 percent of Americans held unfavorable opinions of Islam. After dipping for a few years, the number rose to 46 percent in 2006 and reached 49 percent—basically half the population—in 2010, the last year the question was asked. (Other recent polls show similar results.) Such anti-Muslim attitudes are not merely absorbed by law enforcement and the military or reflected on the airwaves and in the words of our politicians. Rather, the idea that American Muslims are to be feared or loathed or excluded from the United States is being actively promoted.

Absent personal contact, most Americans get their views of Islam through TV, talk-radio, the Internet and really bad action movies.

This past September, *Wired* broke the story that the FBI tells its counterterrorism agents in training that mainstream American Muslims are probably terrorist sympathizers, that the Prophet Muhammad was a "cult leader" and that the religiously mandated practice of giving charity in Islam is no more than a "funding mechanism for combat." The training materials, which stated that FBI agents had the "ability to bend or suspend the law and impinge on freedoms of others," identify other insidious techniques Muslims use for promoting jihad, including "immigration" and "law suits"—in other words, the ordinary uses of the American political system. The revelations forced the FBI to remove 876 pages from its manuals.

Another egregious example that recently came to light is that the NYPD, as part of its training, screened *The Third Jihad,* a film that claims "the true agenda of much of Islam in America" is "a strategy to infiltrate and dominate" the country. The film ran on a continuous loop for somewhere between three months and a year of training and was viewed by at least 1,489 officers. Yet another example involved Army Lt. Col. Matthew Dooley, who taught a course at the Pentagon's Joint Forces Staff College that informed senior officers that the United States would have to fight a "total war" against the world's Muslims, including abandoning the international laws of war that protect civilians

(deemed "no longer relevant"), and possibly applying "the historical precedents of Dresden, Tokyo, Hiroshima, Nagasaki" to destroy Islam's holy cities of Mecca and Medina. Claiming "Islam is an ideology rather than solely a religion," the class taught that the United States was "culturally vulnerable" to this threat because of its "'judeo-christian' [*sic*] ethic of reason and tolerance." The Pentagon canceled the course in the wake of the revelations, and Dooley maintains a nonteaching position, pending an investigation.

The consequences of these efforts to promote anti-Muslim beliefs and sentiments influence how American Muslims practice their faith, engage with their neighbors, cooperate with law enforcement, work at their jobs and study at school. Anti-mosque activity, according to the ACLU, has taken place in more than half the states in the country. And American Muslims, who make up 1–2 percent of the population, account for more than 20 percent of religion-based filings with the Equal Employment Opportunity Commission.

There is legitimate concern about future acts of terrorism in the United States. But there is also plenty of reason to be skeptical of many of the plots that the FBI has disrupted, which are usually scripted by a paid informant, often with a criminal record himself [see Petra Bartosiewicz, "The FBI Stings Muslims,"]. Yet the publicity these "plots" receive feeds the anti-Muslim fervor.

Media coverage plays a major role in ramping up anti-Muslim attitudes, for a very simple reason: 62 percent of Americans, according to a 2010 *Time* magazine poll, say they have never met a Muslim. (If you do know a Muslim, you're less likely to harbor anti-Muslim feelings, polls also show.) Absent ordinary personal contact, most Americans will get their views of Islam through television, cable news, talk-radio, the Internet and really bad action movies. Because the counterweight of personal contact is missing, Muslim attitudes are easily ventriloquized and distorted, and Muslims themselves often rendered mute or suspect. The myth that American Muslims haven't spoken out against terrorism, for example, continues to haunt the community, even though they do so loudly and repeatedly.

Then there's the myth, promulgated by Representative Peter King in his radicalization hearings last year, of American Muslim noncooperation with law enforcement. In reality, around 40 percent of Muslim domestic terrorism suspects since September 11, 2001, have been turned in by fellow Muslims, who have sometimes discovered later that the FBI was directing the operation.

Republican politicians, meanwhile, have been falling all over themselves to vilify Muslims, especially during the presidential primary. Herman Cain proclaimed that "a majority of Muslims share the extremist views," initially vowing not to appoint any Muslims to his cabinet. Rick Santorum endorsed religious profiling, saying that "obviously Muslims would be someone [sic] you'd look at." Newt Gingrich compared Muslims to Nazis in 2010, when he opposed building an Islamic center in Lower Manhattan. "Nazis don't have the right to put up a sign next to the Holocaust museum in Washington," he said. And, in 2007, Mitt Romney said, "Based on the numbers of American Muslims [as a percentage] in our population, I cannot see that a cabinet position would be justified. But of course, I would imagine that Muslims could serve at lower levels of my administration." Whatever happened to the matter of qualifications? But hey, if you're a Muslim, that's all you'll ever be. Romney has hired Walid Phares, part of the active anti-Muslim network, as a foreign policy adviser, and GOP voters continue to consider that President Obama is a Muslim in large numbers (52 percent of Mississippi GOP members thought so in March).

It gets stranger still. When media portrayals of everyday American Muslim life are produced, the very ordinariness is attacked as a lie. TLC's show *All-American Muslim* premiered in November to favorable reviews. The show, which focused on five Lebanese-American Shiite Muslim families in the Dearborn, Michigan, area, was a bit of a yawner for racy reality TV, but it was a useful kind of ethnography for Americans unfamiliar with the stuff of daily American Muslim life. Immediately, the organized anti-Muslim network kicked into gear. The Florida Family Association, basically a one-man show run by David Caton, led a boycott of the show via e-mail that was quickly picked up by the extreme right-wing anti-Islamic blogosphere, and led to Lowe's and Kayak.com pulling their ads. Caton's e-mail read, "The show profiles only Muslims that appear to be ordinary folks while excluding many Islamic believers whose agenda poses a clear and present danger to liberties and traditional values that the majority of Americans cherish."

Follow the logic. The only thing accepted as "normal" for a Muslim is to act like an extremist. Ordinary Muslim folk appearing to live ordinary Muslim lives? That's just plain suspicious.

The same belief drives the NYPD's surveillance of American Muslim communities. Police Commissioner Raymond Kelly informed American Muslim audiences in 2007 that the radicalization report of that year was "never intended to be a policy prescriptive for law enforcement actions," but we now know he was lying. In its Pulitzer Prize-winning series published beginning in August 2011, the Associated Press has reported on how American Muslims who were not suspected of any wrongdoing were spied on in New York and beyond by the NYPD, with the CIA's help. The NYPD catalogued the locations of barbershops, cafes and restaurants, noting where the undercover officers—dubbed "rakers"—heard "political and inflammatory rhetoric," though what that means, and the fact that it's free speech, is never stated. Undercover officers chatted up bookstore owners, played cricket with Muslims and

uncovered such unsavory things as a travel agency on Atlantic Avenue in Brooklyn, where an officer "observed a female named 'Rasha' working in the travel agency, she recommended the 'Royal Jordanian Airline.'"

The department also spied on Muslim college students throughout the Tri-State area, including at Brooklyn College, where I teach. Soheeb Amin, president of the college's Islamic Society, told me that the AP reports were more of a confirmation than a revelation. "We know that there are people who are looking for excuses to get you in trouble for your religion," he noted, and so he has adjusted. "I don't talk about politics. I don't talk about anything controversial. I don't do anything that can raise suspicion." Like many American Muslims, he feels his rights to practice his religion and express his ideas have been compromised. He told me he prays the mandatory five daily prayers, "but now I know that there are NYPD reports that mention that people prayed four times a day, and I guess five is worse than that," he added, only half-jokingly. Muslims from New Jersey, including a decorated soldier, recently filed suit against the NYPD for violating their constitutional rights.

Does this mean that the United States is an Islamophobic country? Of course not. Large support for American Muslims exists in many quarters. Polls may suggest that about half the population is anti-Muslim, but that leaves half that isn't. In many quarters of the country, there is genuine, not suspicious, interest in American Muslims and the realities they face, as evidenced by the fact that TLC produced *All-American Muslim.* Aasif Mandvi's contributions to *The Daily Show* routinely deflate the power of this contemporary prejudice, and libraries, museums, classrooms, and houses of worship across the country now regularly include Muslims and Islam in their programming in an attempt to further understanding and combat bigotry.

American Muslims have responded to events over the past decade and the expansion of an anti-Muslim network largely by being more, not less, visible. The number of mosques grew 74 percent over the past decade, despite the opposition Muslims sometimes confront in their construction. Even if a 2011 poll found that 48 percent of American Muslims reported experiencing discrimination in the previous 12 months, they also showed more optimism than other Americans in the poll that their lives would be better in five years (perhaps, in part, because of today's discrimination). The guiding belief in the American Muslim community today is that the country will recognize that Muslims have always been and will continue to be a part of America.

An ordinary life is more meaningful than it sounds. It signifies being able to live your life as you define yourself, not as others define you, and being able to assume a life free of unwarranted government prying. In fact, ordinariness is the foundation of an open society, because it endows citizens with a private life and demands that the government operate openly—not the other way around, which is how closed societies operate.

There is a real danger that the same tools that enable today's Islamophobia will continue to migrate and expand with little or no public outcry. The FBI deploys a strategy of sting operations against Occupy protesters that is eerily familiar to American Muslims, to little outrage. The president enacts a law that allows for the indefinite detention of American citizens, and after a federal judge strikes it down as unconstitutional, Congress rushes in two days later to try to keep it on the books. American citizens can be assassinated by presidential decree, making a mockery of due process. Forget the Muslims. This mission creep is as good a reason as any to pay attention to Islamophobia today—because when the ordinary affairs of the United States include such actions, the stakes are nothing less than extraordinary.

Critical Thinking

1. How have Muslims been treated in the United States since 9/11?
2. Why have beliefs about Arab Americans been so false?
3. What can be done to correct these misperceptions that so adversely affect many loyal Americans?

Create Central

www.mhhe.com/createcentral

Internet References

ACLU Criminal Justice Home Page
www.aclu.org/crimjustice/index.html
Human Rights and Humanitarian Assistance
www.etown.edu/vl/humrts.html
New American Studies Web
www.georgetown.edu/crossroads/asw
Sociology—Study Sociology Online
http://edu.learnsoc.org
Sociology Web Resources
http://www.mhhe.com/socscience/sociology/resources/index.htm
Sociosite
http://www.topsite.com/goto/sociosite.net
Socioweb
http://www.topsite.com/goto/socioweb.com

MOUSTAFA BAYOUMI, a professor of English at Brooklyn College, CUNY, is the author of *How Does It Feel to Be a Problem?: Being Young and Arab in America* (Penguin), which won an American Book Award and the Arab American Book Award for Non-Fiction. He is the editor of *Midnight on the Mavi Marmara* (O/R Books and Haymarket Books) and co-editor of *The Edward Said Reader* (Vintage).

Reprinted by permission from the July 2–9, 2012, pp. 11–12, 14 issue of *The Nation*. Copyright © 2012 by The Nation. For subscription information, call 1-800-333-8536. Portions of each week's Nation magazine can be accessed at www.thenation.com

Article   Prepared by: Kurt Finsterbusch, *University of Maryland, College Park*

Why Women Still Can't Have It All

It's time to stop fooling ourselves, says a woman who left a position of power: the women who have managed to be both mothers and top professionals are superhuman, rich, or self-employed. If we truly believe in equal opportunity for all women, here's what has to change.

ANNE-MARIE SLAUGHTER

Learning Outcomes

After reading this article, you will be able to:

- Understand the tensions between work and family for women but also for men.

- Know why Anne-Marie Slaughter thinks that women cannot have high commitment to both career and family.

- Understand the factors that are influencing women's roles today.

Eighteen months into my job as the first woman director of policy planning at the State Department, a foreign-policy dream job that traces its origins back to George Kennan, I found myself in New York, at the United Nations' annual assemblage of every foreign minister and head of state in the world. On a Wednesday evening, President and Mrs. Obama hosted a glamorous reception at the American Museum of Natural History. I sipped champagne, greeted foreign dignitaries, and mingled. But I could not stop thinking about my 14-year-old son, who had started eighth grade three weeks earlier and was already resuming what had become his pattern of skipping homework, disrupting classes, failing math, and tuning out any adult who tried to reach him. Over the summer, we had barely spoken to each other—or, more accurately, he had barely spoken to me. And the previous spring I had received several urgent phone calls—invariably on the day of an important meeting—that required me to take the first train from Washington, D.C., where I worked, back to Princeton, New Jersey, where he lived. My husband, who has always done everything possible to support my career, took care of him, and his

12-year-old brother during the week; outside of those midweek emergencies, I came home only on weekends.

As the evening wore on, I ran into a colleague who held a senior position in the White House. She has two sons exactly my sons' ages, but she had chosen to move them from California to D.C. when she got her job, which meant her husband commuted back to California regularly. I told her how difficult I was finding it to be away from my son when he clearly needed me. Then I said, "When this is over, I'm going to write an op-ed titled 'Women Can't Have It All.'"

She was horrified. "You *can't* write that," she said. "You, of all people." What she meant was that such a statement, coming from a high-profile career woman—a role model—would be a terrible signal to younger generations of women. By the end of the evening, she had talked me out of it, but for the remainder of my stint in Washington, I was increasingly aware that the feminist beliefs on which I had built my entire career were shifting under my feet. I had always assumed that if I could get a foreign-policy job in the State Department or the White House while my party was in power, I would stay the course as long as I had the opportunity to do work I loved. But in January 2011, when my two-year public-service leave from Princeton University was up, I hurried home as fast as I could.

A rude epiphany hit me soon after I got there. When people asked why I had left government, I explained that I'd come home not only because of Princeton's rules (after two years of leave, you lose your tenure), but also because of my desire to be with my family and my conclusion that juggling high-level government work with the needs of two teenage boys was not possible. I have not exactly left the ranks of full-time career women: I teach a full course load; write regular print and online columns on foreign policy; give 40 to 50 speeches a year; appear regularly on TV and radio; and am working on a new academic book. But I routinely got reactions from other women my age or older that ranged from disappointed ("It's such a pity that you had to leave Washington") to condescending ("I wouldn't generalize from your experience. *I've* never had to compromise, and *my* kids turned out great").

The first set of reactions, with the underlying assumption that my choice was somehow sad or unfortunate, was irksome enough. But it was the second set of reactions—those implying that my parenting and/or my commitment to my profession were somehow substandard—that triggered a blind fury. Suddenly, finally, the penny dropped. All my life, I'd been on the other side of this exchange. I'd been the woman smiling the faintly superior smile while another woman told me she had decided to take some time out or pursue a less competitive career track so that she could spend more time with her family. I'd been the woman congratulating herself on her unswerving commitment to the feminist cause, chatting smugly with her dwindling number of college or law-school friends who had reached and maintained their place on the highest rungs of their profession. I'd been the one telling young women at my lectures that you *can* have it all and do it all, regardless of what field you are in. Which means I'd been part, albeit unwittingly, of making millions of women feel that *they* are to blame if they cannot manage to rise up the ladder as fast as men and also have a family and an active home life (and be thin and beautiful to boot).

Last spring, I flew to Oxford to give a public lecture. At the request of a young Rhodes Scholar I know, I'd agreed to talk to the Rhodes community about "work-family balance." I ended up speaking to a group of about 40 men and women in their mid-20s. What poured out of me was a set of very frank reflections on how unexpectedly hard it was to do the kind of job I wanted to do as a high government official and be the kind of parent I wanted to be, at a demanding time for my children (even though my husband, an academic, was willing to take on the lion's share of parenting for the two years I was in Washington). I concluded by saying that my time in office had convinced me that further government service would be very unlikely while my sons were still at home. The audience was rapt, and asked many thoughtful questions. One of the first was from a young woman who began by thanking me for "not giving just one more fatuous 'You can have it all' talk." Just about all of the women in that room planned to combine careers and family in some way. But almost all assumed and accepted that they would have to make compromises that the men in their lives were far less likely to have to make.

The striking gap between the responses I heard from those young women (and others like them) and the responses I heard from my peers and associates prompted me to write this article. Women of my generation have clung to the feminist credo we were raised with, even as our ranks have been steadily thinned

by unresolvable tensions between family and career, because we are determined not to drop the flag for the next generation. But when many members of the younger generation have stopped listening, on the grounds that glibly repeating "you can have it all" is simply airbrushing reality, it is time to talk.

I still strongly believe that women can "have it all" (and that men can too). I believe that we can "have it all at the same time." But not today, not with the way America's economy and society are currently structured. My experiences over the past three years have forced me to confront a number of uncomfortable facts that need to be widely acknowledged—and quickly changed.

Before my service in government, I'd spent my career in academia: as a law professor and then as the dean of Princeton's Woodrow Wilson School of Public and International Affairs. Both were demanding jobs, but I had the ability to set my own schedule most of the time. I could be with my kids when I needed to be, and still get the work done. I had to travel frequently, but I found I could make up for that with an extended period at home or a family vacation.

I knew that I was lucky in my career choice, but I had no idea how lucky until I spent two years in Washington within a rigid bureaucracy, even with bosses as understanding as Hillary Clinton and her chief of staff, Cheryl Mills. My workweek started at 4:20 on Monday morning, when I got up to get the 5:30 train from Trenton to Washington. It ended late on Friday, with the train home. In between, the days were crammed with meetings, and when the meetings stopped, the writing work began—a never-ending stream of memos, reports, and comments on other people's drafts. For two years, I never left the office early enough to go to any stores other than those open 24 hours, which meant that everything from dry cleaning to hair appointments to Christmas shopping had to be done on weekends, amid children's sporting events, music lessons, family meals, and conference calls. I was entitled to four hours of vacation per pay period, which came to one day of vacation a month. And I had it better than many of my peers in D.C.; Secretary Clinton deliberately came in around 8 A.M. and left around 7 P.M., to allow her close staff to have morning and evening time with their families (although of course she worked earlier and later, from home).

In short, the minute I found myself in a job that is typical for the vast majority of working women (and men), working long hours on someone else's schedule, I could no longer be both the parent and the professional I wanted to be—at least not with a child experiencing a rocky adolescence. I realized what should have perhaps been obvious: having it all, at least for me, depended almost entirely on what type of job I had. The flip side is the harder truth: having it all was not possible in many types of jobs, including high government office—at least not for very long.

I am hardly alone in this realization. Michèle Flournoy stepped down after three years as undersecretary of defense for policy, the third-highest job in the department, to spend more time at home with her three children, two of whom are teenagers. Karen Hughes left her position as the counselor to President George W. Bush after a year and a half in Washington to go home to Texas for the sake of her family. Mary Matalin, who spent two years as an assistant to Bush and the counselor to Vice President Dick Cheney before stepping down to spend more time with her daughters, wrote: "Having control over your schedule is the only way that women who want to have a career and a family can make it work."

Yet the decision to step down from a position of power—to value family over professional advancement, even for a time—is directly at odds with the prevailing social pressures on career professionals in the United States. One phrase says it all about current attitudes toward work and family, particularly among elites. In Washington, "leaving to spend time with your family" is a euphemism for being fired. This understanding is so ingrained that when Flournoy announced her resignation last December, *The New York Times* covered her decision as follows:

> Ms. Flournoy's announcement surprised friends and a number of Pentagon officials, but all said they took her reason for resignation at face value and not as a standard Washington excuse for an official who has in reality been forced out. "I can absolutely and unequivocally state that her decision to step down has nothing to do with anything other than her commitment to her family," said Doug Wilson, a top Pentagon spokesman. "She has loved this job and people here love her."

Think about what this "standard Washington excuse" implies: it is so unthinkable that an official would *actually* step down to spend time with his or her family that this must be a cover for something else. How could anyone voluntarily leave the circles of power for the responsibilities of parenthood? Depending on one's vantage point, it is either ironic or maddening that this view abides in the nation's capital, despite the ritual commitments to "family values" that are part of every political campaign. Regardless, this sentiment makes true work-life balance exceptionally difficult. But it cannot change unless top women speak out.

Only recently have I begun to appreciate the extent to which many young professional women feel under assault by women my age and older. After I gave a recent speech in New York, several women in their late 60s or early 70s came up to tell me how glad and proud they were to see me speaking as a foreign-policy expert. A couple of them went on, however, to contrast my career with the path being traveled by "younger women today." One expressed dismay that many younger women "are just not willing to get out there and do it." Said another, unaware of the circumstances of my recent job change: "They think they have to choose between having a career and having a family."

A similar assumption underlies Facebook Chief Operating Officer Sheryl Sandberg's widely publicized 2011 commencement speech at Barnard, and her earlier TED talk, in which she lamented the dismally small number of women at the top and advised young women not to "leave before you leave." When a woman starts thinking about having children, Sandberg said, "she doesn't raise her hand anymore ... She starts leaning back." Although couched in terms of encouragement, Sandberg's exhortation contains more than a note of reproach. We who have made it to the top, or are striving to get there, are essentially saying to the women in the generation behind us: "What's the matter with you?"

They have an answer that we don't want to hear. After the speech I gave in New York, I went to dinner with a group of 30-somethings. I sat across from two vibrant women, one of whom worked at the UN and the other at a big New York law firm. As nearly always happens in these situations, they soon began asking me about work-life balance. When I told them I was writing this article, the lawyer said, "I look for role models and can't find any." She said the women in her firm who had become partners and taken on management positions had made tremendous sacrifices, "many of which they don't even seem to realize ... They take two years off when their kids are young but then work like crazy to get back on track professionally, which means that they see their kids when they are toddlers but not teenagers, or really barely at all." Her friend nodded, mentioning the top professional women she knew, all of whom essentially relied on round-the-clock nannies. Both were very clear that they did not want that life, but could not figure out how to combine professional success and satisfaction with a real commitment to family.

I realize that I am blessed to have been born in the late 1950s instead of the early 1930s, as my mother was, or the beginning of the twentieth century, as my grandmothers were. My mother built a successful and rewarding career as a professional artist largely in the years after my brothers and I left home—and after being told in her 20s that she could not go to medical school, as her father had done and her brother would go on to do, because, of course, she was going to get married. I owe my own freedoms and opportunities to the pioneering generation of women ahead of me—the women now in their 60s, 70s, and 80s who faced overt sexism of a kind I see only when watching *Mad Men,* and who knew that the only way to make it as a woman was to act exactly like a man. To admit to, much less act on, maternal longings would have been fatal to their careers.

But precisely thanks to their progress, a different kind of conversation is now possible. It is time for women in leadership positions to recognize that although we are still blazing trails and breaking ceilings, many of us are also reinforcing a falsehood: that "having it all" is, more than anything, a function of personal determination. As Kerry Rubin and Lia Macko, the authors of *Midlife Crisis at 30,* their cri de coeur for Gen-X and Gen-Y women, put it:

> What we discovered in our research is that while the empowerment part of the equation has been loudly celebrated, there has been very little honest discussion among women of our age about the real barriers and flaws that still exist in the system despite the opportunities we inherited.

I am well aware that the majority of American women face problems far greater than any discussed in this article. I am writing for my demographic—highly educated, well-off women who are privileged enough to have choices in the first place. We may not have choices about whether to do paid work, as dual incomes have become indispensable. But we have choices about the type and tempo of the work we do. We are the women who could be leading, and who should be equally represented in the leadership ranks.

Millions of other working women face much more difficult life circumstances. Some are single mothers; many struggle to find any job; others support husbands who cannot find jobs. Many cope with a work life in which good day care is either unavailable or very expensive; school schedules do not match work schedules; and schools themselves are failing to educate their children. Many of these women are worrying not about having it all, but rather about holding on to what they do have. And although women as a group have made substantial gains in wages, educational attainment, and prestige over the past three decades, the economists Justin Wolfers and Betsey Stevenson have shown that women are less happy today than their predecessors were in 1972, both in absolute terms and relative to men.

The best hope for improving the lot of all women, and for closing what Wolfers and Stevenson call a "new gender gap"—measured by well-being rather than wages—is to close the leadership gap: to elect a woman president and 50 women senators; to ensure that women are equally represented in the ranks of corporate executives and judicial leaders. Only when women wield power in sufficient numbers will we create a society that genuinely works for all women. That will be a society that works for everyone.

The Half-Truths We Hold Dear

Let's briefly examine the stories we tell ourselves, the clichés that I and many other women typically fall back on when younger women ask us how we have managed to "have it all." They are not necessarily lies, but at best partial truths. We must clear them out of the way to make room for a more honest and productive discussion about real solutions to the problems faced by professional women.

It's possible if you are just committed enough

Our usual starting point, whether we say it explicitly or not, is that having it all depends primarily on the depth and intensity of a woman's commitment to her career. That is precisely the sentiment behind the dismay so many older career women feel about the younger generation. *They are not committed enough,* we say, to make the trade-offs and sacrifices that the women ahead of them made.

Yet instead of chiding, perhaps we should face some basic facts. Very few women reach leadership positions. The pool of female candidates for any top job is small, and will only grow smaller if the women who come after us decide to take time out, or drop out of professional competition altogether, to raise children. That is exactly what has Sheryl Sandberg so upset, and rightly so. In her words, "Women are not making it to the top. A 190 heads of state; nine are women. Of all the people in parliament in the world, 13 percent are women. In the corporate sector, [the share of] women at the top—C-level jobs, board seats—tops out at 15, 16 percent."

Can "insufficient commitment" even plausibly explain these numbers? To be sure, the women who do make it to the top are highly committed to their profession. On closer examination, however, it turns out that most of them have something else in common: they are genuine superwomen. Consider the number of women recently in the top ranks in Washington—Susan Rice, Elizabeth Sherwood-Randall, Michelle Gavin, Nancy-Ann Min DeParle—who are Rhodes Scholars. Samantha Power, another senior White House official, won a Pulitzer Prize at age 32. Or consider Sandberg herself, who graduated with the prize given to Harvard's top student of economics. These women cannot possibly be the standard against which even very talented professional women should measure themselves. Such a standard sets up most women for a sense of failure.

What's more, among those who have made it to the top, a balanced life still is more elusive for women than it is for men. A simple measure is how many women in top positions have children compared with their male colleagues. Every male Supreme Court justice has a family. Two of the three female justices are single with no children. And the third, Ruth Bader Ginsburg, began her career as a judge only when her younger child was almost grown. The pattern is the same at the National Security Council: Condoleezza Rice, the first and only woman national-security adviser, is also the only national-security adviser since the 1950s not to have a family.

The line of high-level women appointees in the Obama administration is one woman deep. Virtually all of us who have stepped down have been succeeded by men; searches for women to succeed men in similar positions come up empty. Just about every woman who could plausibly be tapped is already in government. The rest of the foreign-policy world is not much better; Micah Zenko, a fellow at the Council on Foreign Relations, recently surveyed the best data he could find across the government, the military, the academy, and think tanks, and found that women hold fewer than 30 percent of the senior foreign-policy positions in each of these institutions.

These numbers are all the more striking when we look back to the 1980s, when women now in their late 40s and 50s were coming out of graduate school, and remember that our classes were nearly 50-50 men and women. We were sure then that by now, we would be living in a 50-50 world. Something derailed that dream.

Sandberg thinks that "something" is an "ambition gap"— that women do not dream big enough. I am all for encouraging young women to reach for the stars. But I fear that the obstacles that keep women from reaching the top are rather more prosaic than the scope of their ambition. My longtime and invaluable assistant, who has a doctorate and juggles many balls as the mother of teenage twins, e-mailed me while I was working on this article: "You know what would help the vast majority of women with work/family balance? MAKE SCHOOL SCHEDULES MATCH WORK SCHEDULES." The present system, she noted, is based on a society that no longer exists—one in which farming was a major occupation and stay-at-home moms were the norm. Yet the system hasn't changed.

Consider some of the responses of women interviewed by Zenko about why "women are significantly underrepresented in foreign policy and national security positions in government, academia, and think tanks." Juliette Kayyem, who served as an assistant secretary in the Department of Homeland Security from 2009 to 2011 and now writes a foreign-policy and national-security column for *The Boston Globe,* told Zenko that among other reasons,

> the basic truth is also this: the travel sucks. As my youngest of three children is now 6, I can look back at the years when they were all young and realize just how disruptive all the travel was. There were also trips I couldn't take because I was pregnant or on leave, the conferences I couldn't attend because (note to conference organizers: weekends are a bad choice) kids would be home from school, and the various excursions that were offered but just couldn't be managed.

Jolynn Shoemaker, the director of Women in International Security, agreed: "Inflexible schedules, unrelenting travel, and constant pressure to be in the office are common features of these jobs."

These "mundane" issues—the need to travel constantly to succeed, the conflicts between school schedules and work schedules, the insistence that work be done in the office— cannot be solved by exhortations to close the ambition gap.

I would hope to see commencement speeches that finger America's social and business policies, rather than women's level of ambition, in explaining the dearth of women at the top. But changing these policies requires much more than speeches. It means fighting the mundane battles—every day, every year— in individual workplaces, in legislatures, and in the media.

It's possible if you marry the right person

Sandberg's second message in her Barnard commencement address was: "The most important career decision you're going to make is whether or not you have a life partner and who that partner is." Lisa Jackson, the administrator of the Environmental Protection Agency, recently drove that message home to an audience of Princeton students and alumni gathered to hear her acceptance speech for the James Madison Medal. During the Q&A session, an audience member asked her how she managed her career and her family. She laughed and pointed to her husband in the front row, saying: "There's my work-life balance." I could never have had the career I have had without my husband, Andrew Moravcsik, who is a tenured professor of politics and international affairs at Princeton. Andy has spent more time with our sons than I have, not only on homework, but also on baseball, music lessons, photography, card games, and more. When each of them had to bring in a foreign dish for his fourth-grade class dinner, Andy made his grandmother's Hungarian *palacsinta;* when our older son needed to memorize his lines for a lead role in a school play, he turned to Andy for help.

Still, the proposition that women can have high-powered careers as long as their husbands or partners are willing to share the parenting load equally (or disproportionately) assumes that most women will *feel* as comfortable as men do about being away from their children, as long as their partner is home with them. In my experience, that is simply not the case.

Here I step onto treacherous ground, mined with stereotypes. From years of conversations and observations, however, I've come to believe that men and women respond quite differently when problems at home force them to recognize that their absence is hurting a child, or at least that their presence would likely help. I do not believe fathers love their children any less than mothers do, but men do seem more likely to choose their job at a cost to their family, while women seem more likely to choose their family at a cost to their job.

Many factors determine this choice, of course. Men are still socialized to believe that their primary family obligation is to be the breadwinner; women, to believe that their primary family obligation is to be the caregiver. But it may be more than that. When I described the choice between my children and my job to Senator Jeanne Shaheen, she said exactly what I felt: "There's really no choice." She wasn't referring to social expectations, but to a maternal imperative felt so deeply that the "choice" is reflexive.

Men and women also seem to frame the choice differently. In *Midlife Crisis at 30,* Mary Matalin recalls her days working as President Bush's assistant and Vice President Cheney's counselor:

> Even when the stress was overwhelming—those days when I'd cry in the car on the way to work, asking myself "Why am I doing this??"—I always knew the answer to that question: I believe in this president.

But Matalin goes on to describe her choice to leave in words that are again uncannily similar to the explanation I have given so many people since leaving the State Department:

> I finally asked myself, "Who needs me more?" And that's when I realized, it's somebody else's turn to do this job. I'm indispensable to my kids, but I'm not close to indispensable to the White House.

To many men, however, the choice to spend more time with their children, instead of working long hours on issues that affect many lives, seems selfish. Male leaders are routinely praised for having sacrificed their personal life on the altar of public or corporate service. That sacrifice, of course, typically involves their family. Yet their children, too, are trained to value public service over private responsibility. At the diplomat Richard Holbrooke's memorial service, one of his sons told the audience that when he was a child, his father was often gone, not around to teach him to throw a ball or to watch his games. But as he grew older, he said, he realized that Holbrooke's absence was the price of saving people around the world—a price worth paying.

It is not clear to me that this ethical framework makes sense for society. Why should we want leaders who fall short on personal responsibilities? Perhaps leaders who invested time in their own families would be more keenly aware of the toll their public choices—on issues from war to welfare—take on private lives. (Kati Marton, Holbrooke's widow and a noted author, says that although Holbrooke adored his children, he came to appreciate the full importance of family only in his 50s, at which point he became a very present parent and grandparent, while continuing to pursue an extraordinary public career.) Regardless, it is clear which set of choices society values more today. Workers who put their careers first are typically rewarded; workers who choose their families are overlooked, disbelieved, or accused of unprofessionalism.

In sum, having a supportive mate may well be a necessary condition if women are to have it all, but it is not sufficient. If women feel deeply that turning down a promotion that would involve more travel, for instance, is the right thing to do, then

they will continue to do that. Ultimately, it is society that must change, coming to value choices to put family ahead of work just as much as those to put work ahead of family. If we really valued those choices, we would value the people who make them; if we valued the people who make them, we would do everything possible to hire and retain them; if we did everything possible to allow them to combine work and family equally over time, then the choices would get a lot easier.

It's possible if you sequence it right

Young women should be wary of the assertion "You can have it all; you just can't have it all at once." This twenty-first century addendum to the original line is now proffered by many senior women to their younger mentees. To the extent that it means, in the words of one working mother, "I'm going to do my best and I'm going to keep the long term in mind and know that it's not always going to be this hard to balance," it is sound advice. But to the extent that it means that women can have it all if they just find the right sequence of career and family, it's cheerfully wrong.

The most important sequencing issue is when to have children. Many of the top women leaders of the generation just ahead of me—Madeleine Albright, Hillary Clinton, Ruth Bader Ginsburg, Sandra Day O'Connor, Patricia Wald, Nannerl Keohane—had their children in their 20s and early 30s, as was the norm in the 1950s through the 1970s. A child born when his mother is 25 will finish high school when his mother is 43, an age at which, with full-time immersion in a career, she still has plenty of time and energy for advancement.

Yet this sequence has fallen out of favor with many high-potential women, and understandably so. People tend to marry later now, and anyway, if you have children earlier, you may have difficulty getting a graduate degree, a good first job, and opportunities for advancement in the crucial early years of your career. Making matters worse, you will also have less income while raising your children, and hence less ability to hire the help that can be indispensable to your juggling act.

When I was the dean, the Woodrow Wilson School created a program called Pathways to Public Service, aimed at advising women whose children were almost grown about how to go into public service, and many women still ask me about the best "on-ramps" to careers in their mid-40s. Honestly, I'm not sure what to tell most of them. Unlike the pioneering women who entered the workforce after having children in the 1970s, these women are competing with their younger selves. Government and NGO jobs are an option, but many careers are effectively closed off. Personally, I have never seen a woman in her 40s enter the academic market successfully, or enter a law firm as a junior associate, Alicia Florrick of *The Good Wife* notwithstanding.

These considerations are why so many career women of my generation chose to establish themselves in their careers first and have children in their mid-to-late 30s. But that raises the possibility of spending long, stressful years and a small fortune trying to have a baby. I lived that nightmare: for three years, beginning at age 35, I did everything possible to conceive and was frantic at the thought that I had simply left having a biological child until it was too late.

And when everything does work out? I had my first child at 38 (and counted myself blessed) and my second at 40. That means I will be 58 when both of my children are out of the house. What's more, it means that many peak career opportunities are coinciding precisely with their teenage years, when, experienced parents advise, being available as a parent is just as important as in the first years of a child's life.

Many women of my generation have found themselves, in the prime of their careers, saying no to opportunities they once would have jumped at and hoping those chances come around again later. Many others who have decided to step back for a while, taking on consultant positions or part-time work that lets them spend more time with their children (or aging parents), are worrying about how long they can "stay out" before they lose the competitive edge they worked so hard to acquire.

Given the way our work culture is oriented today, I recommend establishing yourself in your career first but still trying to have kids before you are 35—or else freeze your eggs, whether you are married or not. You may well be a more mature and less frustrated parent in your 30s or 40s; you are also more likely to have found a lasting life partner. But the truth is, neither sequence is optimal, and both involve trade-offs that men do not have to make.

You should be able to have a family if you want one—however and whenever your life circumstances allow—and still have the career you desire. If more women could strike this balance, more women would reach leadership positions. And if more women were in leadership positions, they could make it easier for more women to stay in the workforce. The rest of this essay details how.

Changing the Culture of Face Time

Back in the Reagan administration, a *New York Times* story about the ferociously competitive budget director Dick Darman reported, "Mr. Darman sometimes managed to convey the impression that he was the last one working in the Reagan White House by leaving his suit coat on his chair and his office light burning after he left for home." (Darman claimed that it was just easier to leave his suit jacket in the office so he could put it on again in the morning, but his record of psychological manipulation suggests otherwise.)

The culture of "time macho"—a relentless competition to work harder, stay later, pull more all-nighters, travel around the world and bill the extra hours that the international date line affords you—remains astonishingly prevalent among professionals today. Nothing captures the belief that more time equals more value better than the cult of billable hours afflicting large law firms across the country and providing exactly the wrong incentives for employees who hope to integrate work and family. Yet even in industries that don't explicitly reward sheer quantity of hours spent on the job, the pressure to arrive early, stay late, and be available, always, for in-person meetings at 11 A.M. on Saturdays can be intense. Indeed, by some measures, the problem has gotten worse over time: a study by the Center for American Progress reports that nationwide, the share of all professionals—women and men—working more than 50 hours a week has increased since the late 1970s.

But more time in the office does not always mean more "value added"—and it does not always add up to a more successful organization. In 2009, Sandra Pocharski, a senior female partner at Monitor Group and the head of the firm's Leadership and Organization practice, commissioned a Harvard Business School professor to assess the factors that helped or hindered women's effectiveness and advancement at Monitor. The study found that the company's culture was characterized by an "always on" mode of working, often without due regard to the impact on employees. Pocharski observed:

Clients come first, always, and sometimes burning the midnight oil really does make the difference between success and failure. But sometimes we were just defaulting to behavior that overloaded our people without improving results much, if at all. We decided we needed managers to get better at distinguishing between these categories, and to recognize the hidden costs of assuming that "time is cheap." When that time doesn't add a lot of value and comes at a high cost to talented employees, who will leave when the personal cost becomes unsustainable—well, that is clearly a bad outcome for everyone.

I have worked very long hours and pulled plenty of all-nighters myself over the course of my career, including a few nights on my office couch during my two years in D.C. Being willing to put the time in when the job simply has to get done is rightfully a hallmark of a successful professional. But looking back, I have to admit that my assumption that I would stay late made me much less efficient over the course of the day than I might have been, and certainly less so than some of my colleagues, who managed to get the same amount of work done and go home at a decent hour. If Dick Darman had had a boss who clearly valued prioritization and time management, he might have found reason to turn out the lights and take his jacket home.

Long hours are one thing, and realistically, they are often unavoidable. But do they really need to be spent at the office? To be sure, being in the office *some* of the time is beneficial. In-person meetings can be far more efficient than phone or e-mail tag; trust and collegiality are much more easily built up around the same physical table; and spontaneous conversations often generate good ideas and lasting relationships. Still, armed with e-mail, instant messaging, phones, and videoconferencing technology, we should be able to move to a culture where the office is a base of operations more than the required locus of work.

Being able to work from home—in the evening after children are put to bed, or during their sick days or snow days, and at least some of the time on weekends—can be the key, for mothers, to carrying your full load versus letting a team down at crucial moments. State-of-the-art videoconferencing facilities can dramatically reduce the need for long business trips. These technologies are making inroads, and allowing easier integration of work and family life. According to the Women's Business Center, 61 percent of women business owners use technology to "integrate the responsibilities of work and home"; 44 percent use technology to allow employees "to work off-site or to have flexible work schedules." Yet our work culture still remains more office-centered than it needs to be, especially in light of technological advances.

One way to change that is by changing the "default rules" that govern office work—the baseline expectations about when, where, and how work will be done. As behavioral economists well know, these baselines can make an enormous difference in the way people act. It is one thing, for instance, for an organization to allow phone-ins to a meeting on an ad hoc basis, when parenting and work schedules collide—a system that's better than nothing, but likely to engender guilt among those calling in, and possibly resentment among those in the room. It is quite another for that organization to declare that its policy will be to schedule in-person meetings, whenever possible, during the hours of the school day—a system that might normalize call-ins for those (rarer) meetings still held in the late afternoon.

One real-world example comes from the British Foreign and Commonwealth Office, a place most people are more likely to associate with distinguished gentlemen in pinstripes than with progressive thinking about work-family balance. Like so many other places, however, the FCO worries about losing talented members of two-career couples around the world, particularly women. So it recently changed its basic policy from a default rule that jobs have to be done on-site to one that assumes that some jobs might be done remotely, and invites workers to make the case for remote work. Kara Owen, a career foreign-service officer who was the FCO's diversity director and will soon become the British deputy ambassador to France, writes that she has now done two remote jobs. Before her current maternity leave, she was working a London job from Dublin to be with her partner, using teleconferencing technology and timing her trips to London to coincide "with key meetings where I needed to be in the room (or chatting at the pre-meeting coffee) to have an impact, or to do intensive 'network maintenance.'"

In fact, she writes, "I have found the distance and quiet to be a real advantage in a strategic role, providing I have put in the investment up front to develop very strong personal relationships with the game changers." Owen recognizes that not every job can be done this way. But she says that for her part, she has been able to combine family requirements with her career.

Changes in default office rules should not advantage parents over other workers; indeed, done right, they can improve relations among co-workers by raising their awareness of each other's circumstances and instilling a sense of fairness. Two years ago, the ACLU Foundation of Massachusetts decided to replace its "parental leave" policy with a "family leave" policy that provides for as much as 12 weeks of leave not only for new parents, but also for employees who need to care for a spouse, child, or parent with a serious health condition. According to Director Carol Rose, "We wanted a policy that took into account the fact that even employees who do not have children have family obligations." The policy was shaped by the belief that giving women "special treatment" can "backfire if the broader norms shaping the behavior of all employees do not change." When I was the dean of the Wilson School, I managed with the mantra "Family comes first"—any family—and found that my employees were both productive and intensely loyal.

None of these changes will happen by themselves, and reasons to avoid them will seldom be hard to find. But obstacles and inertia are usually surmountable if leaders are open to changing their assumptions about the workplace. The use of technology in many high-level government jobs, for instance, is complicated by the need to have access to classified information. But in 2009, Deputy Secretary of State James Steinberg, who shares the parenting of his two young daughters equally with his wife, made getting such access at home an immediate priority so that he could leave the office at a reasonable hour and participate in important meetings via videoconferencing if necessary. I wonder how many women in similar positions would be afraid to ask, lest they be seen as insufficiently committed to their jobs.

Revaluing Family Values

While employers shouldn't privilege parents over other workers, too often they end up doing the opposite, usually subtly, and usually in ways that make it harder for a primary caregiver to get ahead. Many people in positions of power seem to place a low value on child care in comparison with other outside activities. Consider the following proposition: An employer has two equally talented and productive employees. One trains for and runs marathons when he is not working. The other takes care of two children. What assumptions is the employer likely to make about the marathon runner? That he gets up in the dark every day and logs an hour or two running before even coming into the office, or drives himself to get out there even after a long day. That he is ferociously disciplined and willing to push himself through distraction, exhaustion, and days when nothing seems to go right in the service of a goal far in the distance. That he must manage his time exceptionally well to squeeze all of that in.

Be honest: Do you think the employer makes those same assumptions about the parent? Even though she likely rises in the dark hours before she needs to be at work, organizes her children's day, makes breakfast, packs lunch, gets them off to school, figures out shopping and other errands even if she is lucky enough to have a housekeeper—and does much the same work at the end of the day. Cheryl Mills, Hillary Clinton's indefatigable chief of staff, has twins in elementary school; even with a fully engaged husband, she famously gets up at four every morning to check and send e-mails before her kids wake up. Louise Richardson, now the vice chancellor of the University of St. Andrews, in Scotland, combined an assistant professorship in government at Harvard with mothering three young children. She organized her time so ruthlessly that she always keyed in 1:11 or 2:22 or 3:33 on the microwave rather than 1:00, 2:00, or 3:00, because hitting the same number three times took less time.

Elizabeth Warren, who is now running for the U.S. Senate in Massachusetts, has a similar story. When she had two young children and a part-time law practice, she struggled to find enough time to write the papers and articles that would help get her an academic position. In her words:

> I needed a plan. I figured out that writing time was when Alex was asleep. So the minute I put him down for a nap or he fell asleep in the baby swing, I went to my desk and started working on something—footnotes, reading, outlining, writing … I learned to do everything else with a baby on my hip.

The discipline, organization, and sheer endurance it takes to succeed at top levels with young children at home is easily comparable to running 20 to 40 miles a week. But that's rarely how employers see things, not only when making allowances, but when making promotions. Perhaps because people *choose* to have children? People also choose to run marathons.

One final example: I have worked with many Orthodox Jewish men who observed the Sabbath from sundown on Friday until sundown on Saturday. Jack Lew, the two-time director of the Office of Management and Budget, former deputy secretary of state for management and resources, and now White House chief of staff, is a case in point. Jack's wife lived in New York when he worked in the State Department, so he would leave the office early enough on Friday afternoon to take the shuttle to New York and a taxi to his apartment before sundown. He would not work on Friday after sundown or all day Saturday.

Everyone who knew him, including me, admired his commitment to his faith and his ability to carve out the time for it, even with an enormously demanding job.

It is hard to imagine, however, that we would have the same response if a mother told us she was blocking out mid-Friday afternoon through the end of the day on Saturday, every week, to spend time with her children. I suspect this would be seen as unprofessional, an imposition of unnecessary costs on co-workers. In fact, of course, one of the great values of the Sabbath—whether Jewish or Christian—is precisely that it carves out a family oasis, with rituals and a mandatory setting-aside of work.

Our assumptions are just that: things we believe that are not necessarily so. Yet what we assume has an enormous impact on our perceptions and responses. Fortunately, changing our assumptions is up to us.

Redefining the Arc of a Successful Career

The American definition of a successful professional is someone who can climb the ladder the furthest in the shortest time, generally peaking between ages 45 and 55. It is a definition well suited to the mid-twentieth century, an era when people had kids in their 20s, stayed in one job, retired at 67, and were dead, on average, by age 71.

It makes far less sense today. Average life expectancy for people in their 20s has increased to 80; men and women in good health can easily work until they are 75. They can expect to have multiple jobs and even multiple careers throughout their working life. Couples marry later, have kids later, and can expect to live on two incomes. They may well retire *earlier*—the average retirement age has gone down from 67 to 63—but that is commonly "retirement" only in the sense of collecting retirement benefits. Many people go on to "encore" careers.

Assuming the priceless gifts of good health and good fortune, a professional woman can thus expect her working life to stretch some 50 years, from her early or mid-20s to her mid-70s. It is reasonable to assume that she will build her credentials and establish herself, at least in her first career, between 22 and 35; she will have children, if she wants them, sometime between 25 and 45; she'll want maximum flexibility and control over her time in the 10 years that her children are 8 to 18; and she should plan to take positions of maximum authority and demands on her time after her children are out of the house. Women who have children in their late 20s can expect to immerse themselves completely in their careers in their late 40s, with plenty of time still to rise to the top in their late 50s and early 60s. Women who make partner, managing director, or senior vice president; get tenure; or establish a medical practice before having children in their late 30s should be coming back on line for the most demanding jobs at almost exactly the same age.

Along the way, women should think about the climb to leadership not in terms of a straight upward slope, but as irregular stair steps, with periodic plateaus (and even dips) when they turn down promotions to remain in a job that works for their family situation; when they leave high-powered jobs and spend a year or two at home on a reduced schedule; or when they step off a conventional professional track to take a consulting position or project-based work for a number of years. I think of these plateaus as "investment intervals." My husband and I took a sabbatical in Shanghai, from August 2007 to May 2008, right in the thick of an election year when many of my friends were advising various candidates on foreign-policy issues. We thought of the move in part as "putting money in the family bank," taking advantage of the opportunity to spend a close year together in a foreign culture. But we were also investing in our children's ability to learn Mandarin and in our own knowledge of Asia.

Peaking in your late 50s and early 60s rather than your late 40s and early 50s makes particular sense for women, who live longer than men. And many of the stereotypes about older workers simply do not hold. A 2006 survey of human-resources professionals shows that only 23 percent think older workers are less flexible than younger workers; only 11 percent think older workers require more training than younger workers; and only 7 percent think older workers have less drive than younger workers.

Whether women will really have the confidence to stair-step their careers, however, will again depend in part on perceptions. Slowing down the rate of promotions, taking time out periodically, pursuing an alternative path during crucial parenting or parent-care years—all have to become more visible and more noticeably accepted as a pause rather than an opt-out. (In an encouraging sign, *Mass Career Customization,* a 2007 book by Cathleen Benko and Anne Weisberg arguing that "today's career is no longer a straight climb up the corporate ladder, but rather a combination of climbs, lateral moves, and planned descents," was a *Wall Street Journal* best seller.)

Institutions can also take concrete steps to promote this acceptance. For instance, in 1970, Princeton established a tenure-extension policy that allowed female assistant professors expecting a child to request a one-year extension on their tenure clocks. This policy was later extended to men, and broadened to include adoptions. In the early 2000s, two reports on the status of female faculty discovered that only about 3 percent of assistant professors requested tenure extensions in a given year. And in response to a survey question, women were much more likely than men to think that a tenure extension would be detrimental to an assistant professor's career.

So in 2005, under President Shirley Tilghman, Princeton changed the default rule. The administration announced that all assistant professors, female and male, who had a new child would *automatically* receive a one-year extension on the tenure clock, with no opt-outs allowed. Instead, assistant professors could request early consideration for tenure if they wished. The number of assistant professors who receive a tenure extension has tripled since the change.

One of the best ways to move social norms in this direction is to choose and celebrate different role models. New Jersey Governor Chris Christie and I are poles apart politically, but he went way up in my estimation when he announced that one reason he decided against running for president in 2012 was the impact his campaign would have had on his children. He reportedly made clear at a fund-raiser in Louisiana that he didn't want to be away from his children for long periods of time; according to a Republican official at the event, he said that "his son [missed] him after being gone for the three days on the road, and that he needed to get back." He may not get my vote if and when he does run for president, but he definitely gets my admiration (providing he doesn't turn around and join the GOP ticket this fall).

If we are looking for high-profile female role models, we might begin with Michelle Obama. She started out with the same résumé as her husband, but has repeatedly made career decisions designed to let her do work she cared about and also be the kind of parent she wanted to be. She moved from a high-powered law firm first to Chicago city government and then to the University of Chicago shortly before her daughters were born, a move that let her work only 10 minutes away from home. She has spoken publicly and often about her initial concerns that her husband's entry into politics would be bad for their family life, and about her determination to limit her participation in the presidential election campaign to have more time at home. Even as first lady, she has been adamant that she be able to balance her official duties with family time. We should see her as a full-time career woman, but one who is taking a very visible investment interval. We should celebrate her not only as a wife, mother, and champion of healthy eating, but also as a woman who has had the courage and judgment to invest in her daughters when they need her most. And we should expect a glittering career from her after she leaves the White House and her daughters leave for college.

Rediscovering the Pursuit of Happiness

One of the most complicated and surprising parts of my journey out of Washington was coming to grips with what I really wanted. I had opportunities to stay on, and I could have tried to work out an arrangement allowing me to spend more time at home. I might have been able to get my family to join me in Washington for a year; I might have been able to get classified technology installed at my house the way Jim Steinberg did; I might have been able to commute only four days a week instead of five. (While this last change would have still left me very little time at home, given the intensity of my job, it might have made the job doable for another year or two.) But I realized that I didn't just *need* to go home. Deep down, I *wanted* to go home. I wanted to be able to spend time with my children in the last few years that they are likely to live at home, crucial years for their development into responsible, productive, happy, and caring adults. But also irreplaceable years for me to enjoy the simple pleasures of parenting—baseball games, piano recitals, waffle breakfasts, family trips, and goofy rituals. My older son is doing very well these days, but even when he gives us a hard time, as all teenagers do, being home to shape his choices and help him make good decisions is deeply satisfying.

The flip side of my realization is captured in Macko and Rubin's ruminations on the importance of bringing the different parts of their lives together as 30-year-old women:

> If we didn't start to learn how to integrate our personal, social, and professional lives, we were about five years away from morphing into the angry woman on the other side of a mahogany desk who questions her staffs work ethic after standard 12-hour workdays, before heading home to eat moo shoo pork in her lonely apartment.

Women have contributed to the fetish of the one-dimensional life, albeit by necessity. The pioneer generation of feminists walled off their personal lives from their professional personas to ensure that they could never be discriminated against for a lack of commitment to their work. When I was a law student in the 1980s, many women who were then climbing the legal hierarchy in New York firms told me that they never admitted to taking time out for a child's doctor appointment or school performance, but instead invented a much more neutral excuse.

Today, however, women in power can and should change that environment, although change is not easy. When I became dean of the Woodrow Wilson School, in 2002, I decided that one of the advantages of being a woman in power was that I could help change the norms by deliberately talking about my children and my desire to have a balanced life. Thus, I would end faculty meetings at 6 P.M. by saying that I had to go home for dinner; I would also make clear to all student organizations that I would not come to dinner with them, because I needed to be home from six to eight, but that I would often be willing to come back after eight for a meeting. I also once told the Dean's Advisory Committee that the associate dean would chair the next session so I could go to a parent-teacher conference.

After a few months of this, several female assistant professors showed up in my office quite agitated. "You *have* to stop talking about your kids," one said. "You are not showing the gravitas that people expect from a dean, which is particularly damaging precisely because you are the first woman dean of the school." I told them that I was doing it deliberately and continued my practice, but it is interesting that gravitas and parenthood don't seem to go together.

Ten years later, whenever I am introduced at a lecture or other speaking engagement, I insist that the person introducing me mention that I have two sons. It seems odd to me to list degrees, awards, positions, and interests and *not* include the dimension of my life that is most important to me—and takes an enormous amount of my time. As Secretary Clinton once said in a television interview in Beijing when the interviewer asked her about Chelsea's upcoming wedding: "That's my real life." But I notice that my male introducers are typically uncomfortable when I make the request. They frequently say things like "And she particularly wanted me to mention that she has two sons"—thereby drawing attention to the unusual nature of my request, when my entire purpose is to make family references routine and normal in professional life.

This does not mean that you should insist that your colleagues spend time cooing over pictures of your baby or listening to the prodigious accomplishments of your kindergartner. It does mean that if you are late coming in one week, because it is your turn to drive the kids to school, that you be honest about what you are doing. Indeed, Sheryl Sandberg recently acknowledged not only that she leaves work at 5:30 to have dinner with her family, but also that for many years she did not dare make this admission, even though she would of course make up the work time later in the evening. Her willingness to speak out now is a strong step in the right direction.

Seeking out a more balanced life is not a women's issue; balance would be better for us all. Bronnie Ware, an Australian blogger who worked for years in palliative care and is the author of the 2011 book *The Top Five Regrets of the Dying*, writes that the regret she heard most often was "I wish I'd had the courage to live a life true to myself, not the life others expected of me." The second-most-common regret was "I wish I didn't work so hard." She writes: "This came from every male patient that I nursed. They missed their children's youth and their partner's companionship."

Juliette Kayyem, who several years ago left the Department of Homeland Security soon after her husband, David Barron, left a high position in the Justice Department, says their joint decision to leave Washington and return to Boston sprang from their desire to work on the *"happiness project,"* meaning quality time with their three children. (She borrowed the term from her friend Gretchen Rubin, who wrote a best-selling book and now runs a blog with that name.)

It's time to embrace a national happiness project. As a daughter of Charlottesville, Virginia, the home of Thomas

Jefferson and the university he founded, I grew up with the Declaration of Independence in my blood. Last I checked, he did not declare American independence in the name of life, liberty, and professional success. Let us rediscover the pursuit of happiness, and let us start at home.

Innovation Nation

As I write this, I can hear the reaction of some readers to many of the proposals in this essay: It's all fine and well for a tenured professor to write about flexible working hours, investment intervals, and family-comes-first management. But what about the real world? Most American women cannot demand these things, particularly in a bad economy, and their employers have little incentive to grant them voluntarily. Indeed, the most frequent reaction I get in putting forth these ideas is that when the choice is whether to hire a man who will work whenever and wherever needed, or a woman who needs more flexibility, choosing the man will add more value to the company.

In fact, while many of these issues are hard to quantify and measure precisely, the statistics seem to tell a different story. A seminal study of 527 U.S. companies, published in the *Academy of Management Journal* in 2000, suggests that "organizations with more extensive work-family policies have higher perceived firm-level performance" among their industry peers. These findings accorded with a 2003 study conducted by Michelle Arthur at the University of New Mexico. Examining 130 announcements of family-friendly policies in *The Wall Street Journal,* Arthur found that the announcements alone significantly improved share prices. In 2011, a study on flexibility in the workplace by Ellen Galinsky, Kelly Sakai, and Tyler Wigton of the Families and Work Institute showed that increased flexibility correlates positively with job engagement, job satisfaction, employee retention, and employee health.

This is only a small sampling from a large and growing literature trying to pin down the relationship between family-friendly policies and economic performance. Other scholars have concluded that good family policies attract better talent, which in turn raises productivity, but that the policies themselves have no impact on productivity. Still others argue that results attributed to these policies are actually a function of good management overall. What is evident, however, is that many firms that recruit and train well-educated professional women are aware that when a woman leaves because of bad work-family balance, they are losing the money and time they invested in her.

Even the legal industry, built around the billable hour, is taking notice. Deborah Epstein Henry, a former big-firm litigator, is now the president of Flex-Time Lawyers, a national consulting firm focused partly on strategies for the retention of female attorneys. In her book *Law and Reorder,* published by the American Bar Association in 2010, she describes a legal profession "where the billable hour no longer works"; where attorneys, judges, recruiters, and academics all agree that this system of compensation has perverted the industry, leading to brutal work hours, massive inefficiency, and highly inflated costs. The answer—already being deployed in different corners of the industry—is a combination of alternative fee structures, virtual firms, women-owned firms, and the outsourcing of discrete legal jobs to other jurisdictions. Women, and Generation X and Y lawyers more generally, are pushing for these changes on the supply side; clients determined to reduce legal fees and increase flexible service are pulling on the demand side. Slowly, change is happening.

At the core of all this is self-interest. Losing smart and motivated women not only diminishes a company's talent pool; it also reduces the return on its investment in training and mentoring. In trying to address these issues, some firms are finding out that women's ways of working may just be better ways of working, for employees and clients alike.

Experts on creativity and innovation emphasize the value of encouraging nonlinear thinking and cultivating randomness by taking long walks or looking at your environment from unusual angles. In their new book, *A New Culture of Learning: Cultivating the Imagination for a World of Constant Change,* the innovation gurus John Seely Brown and Douglas Thomas write, "We believe that connecting play and imagination may be the single most important step in unleashing the new culture of learning."

Space for play and imagination is exactly what emerges when rigid work schedules and hierarchies loosen up. Skeptics should consider the "California effect." California is the cradle of American innovation—in technology, entertainment, sports, food, and lifestyles. It is also a place where people take leisure as seriously as they take work; where companies like Google deliberately encourage play, with Ping-Pong tables, light sabers, and policies that require employees to spend one day a week working on whatever they wish. Charles Baudelaire wrote: "Genius is nothing more nor less than childhood recovered at will." Google apparently has taken note.

No parent would mistake child care for childhood. Still, seeing the world anew through a child's eyes can be a powerful source of stimulation. When the Nobel laureate Thomas Schelling wrote *The Strategy of Conflict,* a classic text applying game theory to conflicts among nations, he frequently drew on child-rearing for examples of when deterrence might succeed or fail. "It may be easier to articulate the peculiar difficulty of constraining [a ruler] by the use of threats," he wrote, "when one is fresh from a vain attempt at using threats to keep a small child from hurting a dog or a small dog from hurting a child."

The books I've read with my children, the silly movies I've watched, the games I've played, questions I've answered, and people I've met while parenting have broadened my world. Another axiom of the literature on innovation is that the more often people with different perspectives come together, the more likely creative ideas are to emerge. Giving workers the ability to integrate their nonwork lives with their work—whether they spend that time mothering or marathoning—will open the door to a much wider range of influences and ideas.

Enlisting Men

Perhaps the most encouraging news of all for achieving the sorts of changes that I have proposed is that men are joining the cause. In commenting on a draft of this article, Martha Minow, the dean of the Harvard Law School, wrote me that one change she has observed during 30 years of teaching law at Harvard is that today many young men are asking questions about how they can manage a work-life balance. And more systematic research on Generation Y confirms that many more men than in the past are asking questions about how they are going to integrate active parenthood with their professional lives.

Abstract aspirations are easier than concrete trade-offs, of course. These young men have not yet faced the question of whether they are prepared to give up that more prestigious clerkship or fellowship, decline a promotion, or delay their professional goals to spend more time with their children and to support their partner's career.

Yet once work practices and work culture begin to evolve, those changes are likely to carry their own momentum. Kara Owen, the British foreign-service officer who worked a London job from Dublin, wrote me in an e-mail:

I think the culture on flexible working started to change the minute the Board of Management (who were all men at the time) started to work flexibly—quite a few of them started working one day a week from home.

Men have, of course, become much more involved parents over the past couple of decades, and that, too, suggests broad support for big changes in the way we balance work and family. It is noteworthy that both James Steinberg, deputy secretary of state, and William Lynn, deputy secretary of defense, stepped down two years into the Obama administration so that they could spend more time with their children (for real).

Going forward, women would do well to frame work-family balance in terms of the broader social and economic issues that affect both women and men. After all, we have a new generation of young men who have been raised by full-time working mothers. Let us presume, as I do with my sons, that they will understand "supporting their families" to mean more than earning money.

I have been blessed to work with and be mentored by some extraordinary women. Watching Hillary Clinton in action makes me incredibly proud—of her intelligence, expertise, professionalism, charisma, and command of any audience. I get a similar rush when I see a frontpage picture of Christine Lagarde, the managing director of the International Monetary Fund, and Angela Merkel, the chancellor of Germany, deep in conversation about some of the most important issues on the world stage; or of Susan Rice, the U.S. ambassador to the United Nations, standing up forcefully for the Syrian people in the Security Council.

These women are extraordinary role models. If I had a daughter, I would encourage her to look to them, and I want a world in which they are extraordinary but not unusual. Yet I also want a world in which, in Lisa Jackson's words, "to be a strong woman, you don't have to give up on the things that define you as a woman." That means respecting, enabling, and indeed celebrating the full range of women's choices. "Empowering yourself," Jackson said in her speech at Princeton, "doesn't have to mean rejecting motherhood, or eliminating the nurturing or feminine aspects of who you are."

I gave a speech at Vassar last November and arrived in time to wander the campus on a lovely fall afternoon. It is a place infused with a spirit of community and generosity, filled with benches, walkways, public art, and quiet places donated by alumnae seeking to encourage contemplation and connection. Turning the pages of the alumni magazine (Vassar is now coed), I was struck by the entries of older alumnae, who greeted their classmates with *Salve* (Latin for "hello") and wrote witty remembrances sprinkled with literary allusions. Theirs was a world in which women wore their learning lightly; their news is mostly of their children's accomplishments. Many of us look back on that earlier era as a time when it was fine to joke that women went to college to get an "M.R.S." And many women of my generation abandoned the Seven Sisters as soon as the formerly all-male Ivy League universities became coed. I would never return to the world of segregated sexes and rampant discrimination. But now is the time to revisit the assumption that women must rush to adapt to the "man's world" that our mothers and mentors warned us about.

I continually push the young women in my classes to speak more. They must gain the confidence to value their own insights and questions, and to present them readily. My husband agrees, but he actually tries to get the young men in his classes to act more like the women—to speak less and listen more. If women are ever to achieve real equality as leaders, then we have to stop accepting male behavior and male choices as the default and the ideal. We must insist on changing social policies and bending career tracks to accommodate *our* choices, too. We have the power to do it if we decide to, and we have many men standing beside us.

We'll create a better society in the process, for *all* women. We may need to put a woman in the White House before we are able to change the conditions of the women working at Walmart. But when we do, we will stop talking about whether women can have it all. We will properly focus on how we can help all Americans have healthy, happy, productive lives, valuing the people they love as much as the success they seek.

Critical Thinking

1. How do you think women should handle work and family?

2. Why do men seem to have much less of a problem regarding work and family? Should they have more of a problem?

3. Where will this issue be 10 years from now?

Create Central

www.mhhe.com/createcentral

Internet References

Marriage and Family Therapy
www.aamft.org/index_nm.asp

Sociology—Study Sociology Online
http://edu.learnsoc.org

Sociology Web Resources
http://www.mhhe.com/socscience/sociology/resources/index.htm

Sociosite
http://www.topsite.com/goto/sociosite.net

Socioweb
http://www.topsite.com/goto/socioweb.com

From *The Atlantic*, July/August 2012. Copyright © 2012 by The Atlantic Media Co. Reprinted by permission of Tribune Media Services. www.theatlantic.com

Article Prepared by: Kurt Finsterbusch, *University of Maryland, College Park*

Human Sex Trafficking

AMANDA WALKER-RODRIGUEZ AND RODNEY HILL

Learning Outcomes

After reading this article, you will be able to:

- Understand the extent of sex slavery in the United States.

- Understand the ways that many prostitutes are forced or manipulated into sex slavery.

- Understand the role of the mob in sex slavery.

Human sex trafficking is the most common form of modern-day slavery. Estimates place the number of its domestic and international victims in the millions, mostly females and children enslaved in the commercial sex industry for little or no money.[1] The terms *human trafficking* and *sex slavery* usually conjure up images of young girls beaten and abused in faraway places, like Eastern Europe, Asia, or Africa. Actually, human sex trafficking and sex slavery happen locally in cities and towns, both large and small, throughout the United States, right in citizens' backyards.

Appreciating the magnitude of the problem requires first understanding what the issue is and what it is not. Additionally, people must be able to identify the victim in common trafficking situations.

Human Sex Trafficking

Many people probably remember popular movies and television shows depicting pimps as dressing flashy and driving large fancy cars. More important, the women—adults—consensually and voluntarily engaged in the business of prostitution without complaint. This characterization is extremely inaccurate, nothing more than fiction. In reality, the pimp *traffics* young women (and sometimes men) completely against their will by force or threat of force; this is human sex trafficking.

The Scope

Not only is human sex trafficking slavery but it is big business. It is the fastest-growing business of organized crime and the third-largest criminal enterprise in the world.[2] The majority of sex trafficking is international, with victims taken from such places as South and Southeast Asia, the former Soviet Union, Central and South America, and other less developed areas and moved to more developed ones, including Asia, the Middle East, Western Europe, and North America.[3]

Unfortunately, however, sex trafficking also occurs domestically.[4] The United States not only faces an influx of international victims but also has its own homegrown problem of interstate sex trafficking of minors.[5]

> **The United States not only faces an influx of international victims but also has its own homegrown problem of interstate sex trafficking of minors.**

Although comprehensive research to document the number of children engaged in prostitution in the United States is lacking, an estimated 293,000 American youths currently are at risk of becoming victims of commercial sexual exploitation.[6] The majority of these victims are runaway or thrown-away youths who live on the streets and become victims of prostitution.[7] These children generally come from homes where they have been abused or from families who have abandoned them. Often, they become involved in prostitution to support themselves financially or to get the things they feel they need or want (like drugs).

Other young people are recruited into prostitution through forced abduction, pressure from parents, or through deceptive agreements between parents and traffickers. Once these children become involved in prostitution, they often are forced to travel far from their homes and, as a result, are isolated from their friends and family. Few children in this situation can develop new relationships with peers or adults other than the person victimizing them. The lifestyle of such youths revolves around violence, forced drug use, and constant threats.[8]

Among children and teens living on the streets in the United States, involvement in commercial sex activity is a problem of epidemic proportion. Many girls living on the street engage in formal prostitution, and some become entangled in nationwide organized crime networks where they are trafficked nationally. Criminal networks transport these children around the United States by a variety of means—cars, buses, vans, trucks, or planes—and often provide them counterfeit identification to use in the event of arrest. The average age at which girls first become victims of prostitution is 12 to 14. It is not only the girls on the streets who are affected; boys and transgender youth enter into prostitution between the ages of 11 and 13 on average.[9]

The Operation

Today, the business of human sex trafficking is much more organized and violent. These women and young girls are sold to traffickers, locked up in rooms or brothels for weeks or months, drugged, terrorized, and raped repeatedly.[10] These continual abuses make it easier for the traffickers to control their victims. The captives are so afraid and intimidated that they rarely speak out against their traffickers, even when faced with an opportunity to escape.

Today, the business of human sex trafficking is much more organized and violent.

Generally, the traffickers are very organized. Many have a hierarchy system similar to that of other criminal organizations. Traffickers who have more than one victim often have a "bottom," who sits atop the hierarchy of prostitutes. The bottom, a victim herself, has been with the trafficker the longest and has earned his trust. Bottoms collect the money from the other girls, discipline them, seduce unwitting youths into trafficking, and handle the day-to-day business for the trafficker.

Traffickers represent every social, ethnic, and racial group. Various organizational types exist in trafficking. Some perpetrators are involved with local street and motorcycle gangs, others are members of larger nationwide gangs and criminal organizations, and some have no affiliation with any one group or organization. Traffickers are not only men—women run many established rings.

Traffickers represent every social, ethnic, and racial group.

Traffickers use force, drugs, emotional tactics, and financial methods to control their victims. They have an especially easy time establishing a strong bond with young girls. These perpetrators may promise marriage and a lifestyle the youths often did not have in their previous familial relationships. They claim they "love" and "need" the victim and that any sex acts are for their future together. In cases where the children have few or no positive male role models in their lives, the traffickers take advantage of this fact and, in many cases, demand that the victims refer to them as "daddy," making it tougher for the youths to break the hold the perpetrator has on them.

Sometimes, the traffickers use violence, such as gang rape and other forms of abuse, to force the youths to work for them and remain under their control. One victim, a runaway from Baltimore County, Maryland, was gang raped by a group of men associated with the trafficker, who subsequently staged a "rescue." He then demanded that she repay him by working for him as one of his prostitutes. In many cases, however, the victims simply are beaten until they submit to the trafficker's demands.

In some situations, the youths have become addicted to drugs. The traffickers simply can use their ability to supply them with drugs as a means of control.

Traffickers often take their victims' identity forms, including birth certificates, passports, and drivers' licenses. In these cases, even if youths do leave they would have no ability to support themselves and often will return to the trafficker.

These abusive methods of control impact the victims both physically and mentally. Similar to cases involving Stockholm Syndrome, these victims, who have been abused over an extended period of time, begin to feel an attachment to the perpetrator.[11] This paradoxical psychological phenomenon makes it difficult for law enforcement to breach the bond of control, albeit abusive, the trafficker holds over the victim.

National Problem with Local Ties
The Federal Level

In 2000, Congress passed the Trafficking Victims Protection Act (TVPA), which created the first comprehensive federal law to address trafficking, with a significant focus on the international dimension of the problem. The law provides a three-pronged approach: *prevention* through public awareness programs overseas and a State Department-led monitoring and sanctions program; *protection* through a new T Visa and services for foreign national victims; and *prosecution* through new federal crimes and severe penalties.[12]

As a result of the passing of the TVPA, the Office to Monitor and Combat Trafficking in Persons was established in October 2001. This enabling legislation led to the creation of a bureau within the State Department to specifically address human trafficking and exploitation on all levels and to take legal action against perpetrators.[13] Additionally, this act was designed to enforce all laws within the 13th Amendment to the U.S. Constitution that apply.[14]

U.S. Immigration and Customs Enforcement (ICE) is one of the lead federal agencies charged with enforcing the TVPA. Human trafficking represents significant risks to homeland security. Would-be terrorists and criminals often can access the same routes and use the same methods as human traffickers. ICE's Human Smuggling and Trafficking Unit works to identify criminals and organizations involved in these illicit activities.

The FBI also enforces the TVPA. In June 2003, the FBI, in conjunction with the Department of Justice Child Exploitation and Obscenity Section and the National Center for Missing and Exploited Children, launched the Innocence Lost National Initiative. The agencies' combined efforts address the growing problem of domestic sex trafficking of children in the United States. To date, these groups have worked successfully to rescue nearly 900 children. Investigations successfully have led to the conviction of more than 500 pimps, madams, and their associates who exploit children through prostitution. These convictions have resulted in lengthy sentences, including multiple 25-year-to-life sentences and the seizure of real property, vehicles, and monetary assets.[15]

Both ICE and the FBI, along with other local, state, and federal law enforcement agencies and national victim-based advocacy groups in joint task forces, have combined resources and expertise on the issue. Today, the FBI participates in approximately 30 law enforcement task forces and about 42 Bureau of Justice Assistance (BJA)-sponsored task forces around the nation.[16]

In July 2004, the Human Smuggling Trafficking Center (HSTC) was created. The HSTC serves as a fusion center for information on human smuggling and trafficking, bringing together analysts, officers, and investigators from such agencies as the CIA, FBI, ICE, Department of State, and Department of Homeland Security.

The Local Level

With DOJ funding assistance, many jurisdictions have created human trafficking task forces to combat the problem. BJA's 42 such task forces can be demonstrated by several examples.[17]

- In 2004, the FBI's Washington field office and the D.C. Metropolitan Police Department joined with a variety of nongovernment organizations and service providers to combat the growing problem of human trafficking within Washington, D.C.

- In January 2005, the Massachusetts Human Trafficking Task Force was formed, with the Boston Police Department serving as the lead law enforcement entity. It uses a two-pronged approach, addressing investigations focusing on international victims and those focusing on the commercial sexual exploitation of children.

- The New Jersey Human Trafficking Task Force attacks the problem by training law enforcement in the methods of identifying victims and signs of trafficking, coordinating statewide efforts in the identification and provision of services to victims of human trafficking, and increasing the successful interdiction and prosecution of trafficking of human persons.

- Since 2006, the Louisiana Human Trafficking Task Force, which has law enforcement, training, and victim services components, has focused its law enforcement and victim rescue efforts on the Interstate 10 corridor from the Texas border on the west to the Mississippi border on the east. This corridor, the basic northern border of the hurricane-ravaged areas of Louisiana, long has served as a major avenue of illegal immigration efforts. The I-10 corridor also is the main avenue for individuals participating in human trafficking to supply the labor needs in the hurricane-damaged areas of the state.

- In 2007, the Maryland Human Trafficking Task Force was formed. It aims to create a heightened law enforcement and victim service presence in the community. Its law enforcement efforts include establishing roving operations to identify victims and traffickers, deputizing local law enforcement to assist in federal human trafficking investigations, and providing training for law enforcement officers.

Anytown, USA

In December 2008, Corey Davis, the ringleader of a sex-trafficking ring that spanned at least three states, was sentenced in federal court in Bridgeport, Connecticut, on federal civil rights charges for organizing and leading the sex-trafficking operation that exploited as many as 20 females, including minors. Davis received a sentence of 293 months in prison followed by a lifetime term of supervised release. He pleaded guilty to multiple sex-trafficking charges, including recruiting a girl under the age of 18 to engage in prostitution. Davis admitted that he recruited a minor to engage in prostitution; that he was the organizer of a sex-trafficking venture; and that he used force, fraud, and coercion to compel the victim to commit commercial sex acts from which he obtained the proceeds.

According to the indictment, Davis lured victims to his operation with promises of modeling contracts and a glamorous lifestyle. He then forced them into a grueling schedule of dancing and performing at strip clubs in Connecticut, New York, and New Jersey. When the clubs closed, Davis forced the victims to walk the streets until 4 or 5 A.M. propositioning customers. The indictment also alleged that he beat many of the victims to force them to work for him and that he also used physical abuse as punishment for disobeying the stringent rules he imposed to isolate and control them.[18]

As this and other examples show, human trafficking cases happen all over the United States. A few instances would represent just the "tip of the iceberg" in a growing criminal enterprise. Local and state criminal justice officials must understand that these cases are not isolated incidents that occur infrequently. They must remain alert for signs of trafficking in their jurisdictions and aggressively follow through on the smallest clue. Numerous websites openly (though they try to mask their actions) advertise for prostitution. Many of these sites involve young girls victimized by sex trafficking. Many of the pictures are altered to give the impression of older girls engaged in this activity freely and voluntarily. However, as prosecutors, the authors both have encountered numerous cases of suspected human trafficking involving underage girls.

> **Local and state criminal justice officials must understand that these cases are not isolated incidents that occur infrequently.**

The article "The Girls Next Door" describes a conventional midcentury home in Plainfield, New Jersey, that sat in a nice middle-class neighborhood. Unbeknownst to the neighbors, the house was part of a network of stash houses in the New York area where underage girls and young women from dozens of countries were trafficked and held captive. Acting on a tip, police raided the house in February 2002, expecting to find an underground brothel. Instead, they found four girls between the ages of 14 and 17, all Mexican nationals without documentation.

However, they were not prostitutes; they were sex slaves. These girls did not work for profit or a paycheck. They were captives to the traffickers and keepers who controlled their every move. The police found a squalid, land-based equivalent of a nineteenth-century slave ship. They encountered rancid, doorless bathrooms; bare, putrid mattresses; and a stash of penicillin, "morning after" pills, and an antiulcer medication that can induce abortion. The girls were pale, exhausted, and malnourished.[19]

Human sex trafficking warning signs include, among other indicators, streetwalkers and strip clubs. However, a jurisdiction's lack of streetwalkers or strip clubs does not mean that it is immune to the problem of trafficking. Because human trafficking involves big money, if money can be made, sex slaves can be sold. Sex trafficking can happen anywhere, however unlikely a place. Investigators should be attuned to reading the signs of trafficking and looking closely for them.

Investigation of Human Sex Trafficking

ICE aggressively targets the global criminal infrastructure, including the people, money, and materials that support human trafficking networks. The agency strives to prevent human trafficking in the United States by prosecuting the traffickers and rescuing and protecting the victims. However, most human trafficking cases start at the local level.

Strategies

Local and state law enforcement officers may unknowingly encounter sex trafficking when they deal with homeless and runaway juveniles; criminal gang activity; crimes involving immigrant children who have no guardians; domestic violence calls; and investigations at truck stops, motels, massage parlors, spas, and strip clubs. To this end, the authors offer various suggestions and indicators to help patrol officers identify victims of sex trafficking, as well as tips for detectives who investigate these crimes.

Patrol Officers

- Document suspicious calls and complaints on a police information report, even if the details seem trivial.
- Be aware of trafficking when responding to certain call types, such as reports of foot traffic in and out of a house. Consider situations that seem similar to drug complaints.
- Look closely at calls for assaults, domestic situations, verbal disputes, or thefts. These could involve a trafficking victim being abused and disciplined by a trafficker, a customer having a dispute with a victim, or a client who had money taken during a sex act.
- Locations, such as truck stops, strip clubs, massage parlors, and cheap motels, are havens for prostitutes forced into sex trafficking. Many massage parlors and strip clubs that engage in sex trafficking will have cramped living quarters where the victims are forced to stay.
- When encountering prostitutes and other victims of trafficking, do not display judgment or talk down to them.

Understand the violent nature in how they are forced into trafficking, which explains their lack of cooperation. Speak with them in a location completely safe and away from other people, including potential victims.

- Check for identification. Traffickers take the victims' identification and, in cases of foreign nationals, their travel information. The lack of either item should raise concern.

Detectives/Investigators

- Monitor websites that advertise for dating and hooking up. Most vice units are familiar with the common sites used by sex traffickers as a means of advertisement.
- Conduct surveillance at motels, truck stops, strip clubs, and massage parlors. Look to see if the girls arrive alone or with someone else. Girls being transported to these locations should raise concerns of trafficking.
- Upon an arrest, check cell phone records, motel receipts, computer printouts of advertisements, and tollbooth receipts. Look for phone calls from the jailed prostitute to the pimp. Check surveillance cameras at motels and toll facilities as evidence to indicate the trafficking of the victim.
- Obtain written statements from the customers; get them to work for you.
- Seek assistance from nongovernmental organizations involved in fighting sex trafficking. Many of these entities have workers who will interview these victims on behalf of the police.
- After executing a search warrant, photograph everything. Remember that in court, a picture may be worth a 1,000 words: nothing else can more effectively describe a cramped living quarter a victim is forced to reside in.
- Look for advertisements in local newspapers, specifically the sports sections, that advertise massage parlors. These businesses should be checked out to ensure they are legitimate and not fronts for trafficking.
- Contact your local U.S. Attorney's Office, FBI field office, or ICE for assistance. Explore what federal resources exist to help address this problem.

Other Considerations

Patrol officers and investigators can look for many other human trafficking indicators as well.[20] These certainly warrant closer attention.

General Indicators

- People who live on or near work premises
- Individuals with restricted or controlled communication and transportation
- Persons frequently moved by traffickers
- A living space with a large number of occupants
- People lacking private space, personal possessions, or financial records
- Someone with limited knowledge about how to get around in a community

Physical Indicators

- Injuries from beatings or weapons
- Signs of torture (e.g., cigarette burns)
- Brands or scarring, indicating ownership
- Signs of malnourishment

Financial/Legal Indicators

- Someone else has possession of an individual's legal/travel documents
- Existing debt issues
- One attorney claiming to represent multiple illegal aliens detained at different locations
- Third party who insists on interpreting. Did the victim sign a contract?

Brothel Indicators

- Large amounts of cash and condoms
- Customer logbook or receipt book (trick book)
- Sparse rooms
- Men come and go frequently

Conclusion

This form of cruel modern-day slavery occurs more often than many people might think. And, it is not just an international or a national problem—it also is a local one. It is big business, and it involves a lot of perpetrators and victims.

Agencies at all levels must remain alert to this issue and address it vigilantly. Even local officers must understand the problem and know how to recognize it in their jurisdictions. Coordinated and aggressive efforts from all law enforcement organizations can put an end to these perpetrators' operations and free the victims.

Notes

1. www.routledgesociology.com/books/Human-Sex-Trafficking-isbn9780415576789 (accessed July 19, 2010).

2. www.unodc.org/unodc/en/human-trafficking/what-is-human-trafficking.html (accessed July 19, 2010).

3. www.justice.gov/criminal/ceos/trafficking.html (accessed July 19, 2010).

4. Ibid.

5. www.justice.gov/criminal/ceos/prostitution.html (accessed July 19, 2010).

6. Richard J. Estes and Neil Alan Weiner, *Commercial Sexual Exploitation of Children in the U.S., Canada, and Mexico* (University of Pennsylvania, Executive Summary, 2001).

7. Ibid.

8. http://fpc.state.gov/documents/organization/9107.pdf (accessed July 19, 2010).

9. Estes and Weiner.

10. www.womenshealth.gov/violence/types/human-trafficking.cfm (accessed July 19, 2010).

11. For additional information, see Nathalie De Fabrique, Stephen J. Romano, Gregory M. Vecchi, and Vincent B. Van Hasselt, "Understanding Stockholm Syndrome," *FBI Law Enforcement Bulletin*, July 2007, 10–15.

12. Trafficking Victims Protection Act, Pub. L. No. 106–386 (2000), codified at 22 U.S.C. § 7101, et seq.

13. Ibid.

14. U.S. CONST. amend. XIII, § 1: "Neither slavery nor involuntary servitude, except as a punishment for crime whereof the party shall have been duly convicted, shall exist within the United States, or any place subject to their jurisdiction."

15. U.S. Department of Justice, "U.S. Army Soldier Sentenced to Over 17 Years in Prison for Operating a Brothel from Millersville Apartment and to Drug Trafficking," www.justice.gov/usao/md/Public-Affairs/press_releases/press10a.htm (accessed September 30, 2010).

16. www.fbi.gov/hq/cid/civilrights/trafficking_initiatives.htm (accessed September 30, 2010).

17. www.ojp.usdoj.gov/BJA/grant/42HTTF.pdf (accessed September 30, 2010).

18. http://actioncenter.polarisproject.org/the-frontlines/recent-federal-cases/435-leader-of-expansive-multi-state-sex-trafficking-ring-sentenced (accessed July 19, 2010).

19. www.nytimes.com/2004/01/25/magazine/25SEXTRAFFIC.html (accessed July 19, 2010).

20. http://httf.wordpress.com/indicators/ (accessed July 19, 2010).

Critical Thinking

1. Are most American prostitutes totally free or are they completely or practically enslaved?

2. How are most prostitutes enslaved or prevented from leaving prostitution until they are useless for making profits on sex services?

3. How can sex slavery be stopped in America?

Create Central

www.mhhe.com/createcentral

Internet References

ACLU Criminal Justice Home Page
www.aclu.org/crimjustice/index.html

Human Rights and Humanitarian Assistance
www.etown.edu/vl/humrts.html

New American Studies Web
www.georgetown.edu/crossroads/asw

Sociology—Study Sociology Online
http://edu.learnsoc.org

Sociology Web Resources
http://www.mhhe.com/socscience/sociology/resources/index.htm

Sociosite
http://www.topsite.com/goto/sociosite.net

Socioweb
http://www.topsite.com/goto/socioweb.com

Walker-Rodriguez, Amanda; Hill, Rodney, "Human Sex Trafficking," *FBI Law Enforcement Bulletin*, March 2011.

Article   Prepared by: Kurt Finsterbusch, *University of Maryland, College Park*

Free and Equal in Dignity and LGBT Rights

"Be on the right side of history."

HILLARY RODHAM CLINTON

Learning Outcomes

After reading this article, you will be able to:

- Evaluate the significance of the Universal Declaration of Human Rights passed by the United Nations in 1948 without a negative vote.

- Understand the progress on human rights that has occurred since the declaration.

- Identify the critical issues that are involved in extending the declaration to LGBT equality.

Good evening, and let me express my deep honor and pleasure at being here. I want to thank Director General Tokayev and Ms. Wyden along with other ministers, ambassadors, excellencies, and UN partners. This weekend, we will celebrate Human Rights Day, the anniversary of one of the great accomplishments of the last century.

Beginning in 1947, delegates from six continents devoted themselves to drafting a declaration that would enshrine the fundamental rights and freedoms of people everywhere. In the aftermath of World War II, many nations pressed for a statement of this kind to help ensure that we would prevent future atrocities and protect the inherent humanity and dignity of all people. And so the delegates went to work. They discussed, they wrote, they revisited, revised, rewrote, for thousands of hours. And they incorporated suggestions and revisions from governments, organizations and individuals around the world.

At three o'clock in the morning on December 10th, 1948, after nearly two years of drafting and one last long night of debate, the president of the UN General Assembly called for a vote on the final text. Forty-eight nations voted in favor; eight abstained; none dissented. And the Universal Declaration of Human Rights was adopted. It proclaims a simple, powerful idea: All human beings are born free and equal in dignity and rights. And with the declaration, it was made clear that rights are not conferred by government; they are the birthright of all people. It doe not matter what country we live in, who our leaders are, or even who we are. Because we are human, we therefore have rights. And because we have rights, governments are bound to protect them.

In the 63 years since the declaration was adopted, many nations have made great progress in making human rights a human reality. Step by step, barriers that once prevented people from enjoying the full measure of liberty, the full experience of dignity, and the full benefits of humanity have fallen away. In many places, racist laws have been repealed legal and social practices that relegated women to second-class status have been abolished, the ability of religious minorities to practice their faith freely has been secured.

In most cases, this progress was not easily won. People fought and organized and campaigned in public squares and private spaces to change not only laws, but hearts and minds. And thanks to that work of generations, for millions of individuals whose lives were once narrowed by injustice, they are now able to live more freely and to participate more fully in the political, economic, and social lives of their communities.

Now, there is still, as you all know, much more to be done to secure that commitment, that reality, and progress for all people. Today, I want to talk about the work we have left to do to protect one group of people whose human rights are still denied in too many parts of the world today. In many ways, they are an invisible minority. They are arrested, beaten, terrorized, even executed. Many are treated with contempt and violence by their fellow citizens while authorities empowered to protect them look the other way or, too often, even join in the abuse. They are denied opportunities to work and learn, driven from their homes and countries, and forced to suppress or deny who they are to protect themselves from harm.

I am talking about gay, lesbian, bisexual, and transgender people, human beings born free and given bestowed equality and dignity, who have a right to claim that, which is now one of the remaining human rights challenges of our time. I speak about this subject knowing that my own country's record on human rights for gay people is far from perfect. Until 2003, it was still a crime in parts of our country. Many LGBT Americans have endured violence and harassment in their own lives, and for some, including many young people, bullying, and exclusion are daily experiences. So we, like all nations, have more work to do to protect human rights at home.

Now, raising this issue, I know, is sensitive for many people and that the obstacles standing in the way of protecting the human rights of LGBT people rest on deeply held personal, political, cultural, and religious beliefs. So I come here before you with respect, understanding, and humility. Even though progress on this front is not easy, we cannot delay acting. So in that spirit, I want to talk about the difficult and important issues we must address together to reach a global consensus that recognizes the human rights of LGBT citizens everywhere.

The first issue goes to the heart of the matter. Some have suggested that gay rights and human rights are separate and distinct; but, in fact, they are one and the same. Now, of course, 60 years ago, the governments that drafted and passed the Universal Declaration of Human Rights were not thinking about how it applied to the LGBT community. They also weren't thinking about how it applied to indigenous people or children or people with disabilities or other marginalized groups. Yet in the past 60 years, we have come to recognize that members of these groups are entitled to the full measure of dignity and rights, because, like all people, they share a common humanity.

This recognition did not occur all at once. It evolved over time. And as it did, we understood that we were honoring rights that people always had, rather than creating new or special rights for them. Like being a woman, like being a racial, religious, tribal, or ethnic minority, being LGBT does not make you less human. And that is why gay rights are human rights, and human rights are gay rights.

It is violation of human rights when people are beaten or killed because of their sexual orientation, or because they do not conform to cultural norms about how men and women should look or behave. It is a violation of human rights when governments declare it illegal to be gay, or allow those who harm gay people to go unpunished. It is a violation of human rights when lesbian or transgendered women are subjected to so-called corrective rape, or forcibly subjected to hormone treatments, or when people are murdered after public calls for violence toward gays, or when they are forced to flee their nations and seek asylum in other lands to save their lives. And it is a violation of human rights when life-saving care is withheld from people because they are gay, or equal access to justice is denied to people because they are gay, or public spaces are out of bounds to people because they are gay. No matter what we look like, where we come from, or who we are, we are all equally entitled to our human rights and dignity.

The second issue is a question of whether homosexuality arises from a particular part of the world. Some seem to believe it is a Western phenomenon, and therefore people outside the West have grounds to reject it. Well, in reality, gay people are born into and belong to every society in the world. They are all ages, all races, all faiths; they are doctors and teachers, farmers and bankers, soldiers and athletes; and whether we know it, or whether we acknowledge it, they are our family, our friends, and our neighbors.

Being gay is not a Western invention; it is a human reality. And protecting the human rights of all people, gay or straight, is not something that only Western governments do. South Africa's constitution, written in the aftermath of Apartheid, protects the equality of all citizens, including gay people. In Colombia and Argentina, the rights of gays are also legally protected. In Nepal, the supreme court has ruled that equal rights apply to LGBT citizens. The Government of Mongolia has committed to pursue new legislation that will tackle antigay discrimination.

Now, some worry that protecting the human rights of the LGBT community is a luxury that only wealthy nations can afford. But in fact, in all countries, there are costs to not protecting these rights, in both gay and straight lives lost to disease and violence, and the silencing of voices and views that would strengthen communities, in ideas never pursued by entrepreneurs who happen to be gay. Costs are incurred whenever any group is treated as lesser than the other, whether they are women, racial, or religious minorities, or the LGBT. Former President Mogae of Botswana pointed out recently that for as long as LGBT people are kept in the shadows, there cannot be an effective public health program to tackle HIV and AIDS. Well, that holds true for other challenges as well.

The third, and perhaps most challenging, issue arises when people cite religious or cultural values as a reason to violate or not to protect the human rights of LGBT citizens. This is not unlike the justification offered for violent practices towards women like honor killings, widow burning, or female genital mutilation. Some people still defend those practices as part of a cultural tradition. But violence toward women isn't cultural; it's criminal. Likewise with slavery, what was once justified as sanctioned by God is now properly reviled as an unconscionable violation of human rights.

In each of these cases, we came to learn that no practice or tradition trumps the human rights that belong to all of us. And this holds true for inflicting violence on LGBT people, criminalizing their status or behavior, expelling them from their families and communities, or tacitly or explicitly accepting their killing.

Of course, it bears noting that rarely are cultural and religious traditions and teachings actually in conflict with the protection of human rights. Indeed, our religion and our culture are sources of compassion and inspiration toward our fellow human beings. It was not only those who've justified slavery who leaned on religion, it was also those who sought to abolish it. And let us keep in mind that our commitments to protect the freedom of religion and to defend the dignity of LGBT people emanate from a common source. For many of us, religious belief and practice is a vital source of meaning and identity, and fundamental to who we are as people. And likewise, for most of us, the bonds of love and family that we forge are also vital sources of meaning and identity. And caring for others is an expression of what it means to be fully human. It is because the human experience is universal that human rights are universal and cut across all religions and cultures.

The fourth issue is what history teaches us about how we make progress towards rights for all. Progress starts with honest discussion. Now, there are some who say and believe that all gay people are pedophiles, that homosexuality is a disease that can be caught or cured, or that gays recruit others to become gay. Well, these notions are simply not true. They are also unlikely to disappear if those who promote or accept them are dismissed out of hand rather than invited to share their fears and concerns. No one has ever abandoned a belief because he was forced to do so.

Universal human rights include freedom of expression and freedom of belief, even if our words or beliefs denigrate the humanity of others. Yet, while we are each free to believe whatever we choose, we cannot do whatever we choose, not in a world where we protect the human rights of all.

Reaching understanding of these issues takes more than speech. It does take a conversation. In fact, it takes a constellation of conversations in places big and small. And it takes a willingness to see stark differences in belief as a reason to begin the conversation, not to avoid it.

But progress comes from changes in laws. In many places, including my own country, legal protections have preceded, not followed, broader recognition of rights. Law have a teaching effect. Laws that discriminate validate other kinds of discrimination. Laws that require equal protections reinforce the moral imperative of equality. And practically speaking, it is often the case that laws must change before fears about change dissipate.

Many in my country thought that President Truman was making a grave error when he ordered the racial desegregation of our military. They argued that it would undermine unit cohesion. And it wasn't until he went ahead and did it that we saw how it strengthened our social fabric in ways even the supporters of the policy could not foresee. Likewise, some worried in my country that the repeal of "Don't Ask, Don't Tell" would have a negative effect on our armed forces. Now, the Marine Corps Commandant, who was one of the strongest voices against the repeal, says that his concerns were unfounded and that the Marines have embraced the change.

Finally, progress comes from being willing to walk a mile in someone else's shoes. We need to ask ourselves, "How would it feel if it were a crime to love the person I love? How would it feel to be discriminated against for something about myself that I cannot change?" This challenge applies to all of us as we reflect upon deeply held beliefs, as we work to embrace tolerance and respect for the dignity of all persons, and as we engage humbly with those with whom we disagree in the hope of creating greater understanding.

A fifth and final question is how we do our part to bring the world to embrace human rights for all people including LGBT people. Yes, LGBT people must help lead this effort, as so many of you are. Their knowledge and experiences are invaluable and their courage inspirational. We know the names of brave LGBT activists who have literally given their lives for this cause, and there are many more whose names we will never know. But often those who are denied rights are least empowered to bring about the changes they seek. Acting alone, minorities can never achieve the majorities necessary for political change.

So when any part of humanity is sidelined, the rest of us cannot sit on the sidelines. Every time a barrier to progress has fallen, it has taken a cooperative effort from those on both sides of the barrier. In the fight for women's rights, the support of men remains crucial. The fight for racial equality has relied on contributions from people of all races. Combating Islamaphobia or anti-Semitism is a task for people of all faiths. And the same is true with this struggle for equality.

Conversely, when we see denials and abuses of human rights and fail to act, that sends the message to those deniers and abusers that they won't suffer any consequences for their actions, and so they carry on. But when we do act we send a powerful moral message. Right here in Geneva, the international community acted this year to strengthen a global consensus around the human rights of LGBT people. At the Human

Rights Council in March, 85 countries from all regions supported a statement calling for an end to criminalization and violence against people because of their sexual orientation and gender identity.

At the following session of the Council in June, South Africa took the lead on a resolution about violence against LGBT people. The delegation from South Africa spoke eloquently about their own experience and struggle for human equality and its indivisibility. When the measure passed, it became the firstever UN resolution recognizing the human rights of gay people worldwide. In the Organization of American States this year, the Inter-American Commission on Human Rights created a unit on the rights of LGBT people, a step toward what we hope will be the creation of a special rapporteur.

Now, we must go further and work here and in every region of the world to galvanize more support for the human rights of the LGBT community. To the leaders of those countries where people are jailed, beaten, or executed for being gay, I ask you to consider this: Leadership, by definition, means being out in front of your people when it is called for. It means standing up for the dignity of all your citizens and persuading your people to do the same. It also means ensuring that all citizens are treated as equals under your laws, because let me be clear—I am not saying that gay people can't or don't commit crimes. They can and they do, just like straight people. And when they do, they should be held accountable, but it should never be a crime to be gay.

And to people of all nations, I say supporting human rights is your responsibility too. The lives of gay people are shaped not only by laws, but by the treatment they receive every day from their families, from their neighbors. Eleanor Roosevelt, who did so much to advance human rights worldwide, said that these rights begin in the small places close to home—the streets where people live, the schools they attend, the factories, farms, and offices where they work. These places are your domain. The actions you take, the ideals that you advocate, can determine whether human rights flourish where you are.

And finally, to LGBT men and women worldwide, let me say this: Wherever you live and whatever the circumstances of your life, whether you are connected to a network of support or feel isolated and vulnerable, please know that you are not alone. People around the globe are working hard to support you and to bring an end to the injustices and dangers you face. That is certainly true for my country. And you have an ally in the United States of America and you have millions of friends among the American people.

The Obama Administration defends the human rights of LGBT people as part of our comprehensive human rights policy and as a priority of our foreign policy. In our embassies, our diplomats are raising concerns about specific cases and laws, and working with a range of partners to strengthen human rights protections for all. In Washington, we have created a task force at the State Department to support and coordinate this work. And in the coming months, we will provide every embassy with a toolkit to help improve their efforts. And we have created a program that offers emergency support to defenders of human rights for LGBT people.

This morning, back in Washington, President Obama put into place the first U.S. Government strategy dedicated to combating human rights abuses against LGBT persons abroad. Building on efforts already underway at the State Department and across the government, the President has directed all U.S. Government agencies engaged overseas to combat the criminalization of LGBT status and conduct, to enhance efforts to protect vulnerable LGBT refugees and asylum seekers, to ensure that our foreign assistance promotes the protection of LGBT rights, to enlist international organizations in the fight against discrimination, and to respond swiftly to abuses against LGBT persons.

I am also pleased to announce that we are launching a new Global Equality Fund that will support the work of civil society organizations working on these issues around the world. This fund will help them record facts so they can target their advocacy, learn how to use the law as a tool, manage their budgets, train their staffs, and forge partnerships with women's organizations and other human rights groups. We have committed more than $3 million to start this fund, and we have hope that others will join us in supporting it.

The women and men who advocate for human rights for the LGBT community in hostile places, some of whom are here today with us, are brave and dedicated, and deserve all the help we can give them. We know the road ahead will not be easy. A great deal of work lies before us. But many of us have seen firsthand how quickly change can come. In our lifetimes, attitudes toward gay people in many places have been transformed. Many people, including myself, have experienced a deepening of our own convictions on this topic over the years, as we have devoted more thought to it, engaged in dialogues and debates, and established personal and professional relationships with people who are gay.

This evolution is evident in many places. To highlight one example, the Delhi High Court decriminalized homosexuality in India two years ago, writing, and I quote, "If there is one tenet that can be said to be an underlying theme of the Indian constitution, it is inclusiveness." There is little doubt in my mind that support for LGBT human rights will continue to climb. Because for many young people, this is simple: All people deserve to be treated with dignity and have their human rights respected, no matter who they are or whom they love.

There is a phrase that people in the United States invoke when urging others to support human rights: "Be on the right side of history." The story of the United States is the story of a nation that has repeatedly grappled with intolerance and inequality. We fought a brutal civil war over slavery. People from coast to coast joined in campaigns to recognize the rights of women, indigenous peoples, racial minorities, children, people with disabilities, immigrants, workers, and on and on. And the march toward equality and justice has continued. Those who advocate for expanding the circle of human rights were and are on the right side of history, and history honors them. Those who tried to constrict human rights were wrong, and history reflects that as well.

I know that the thoughts I've shared today involve questions on which opinions are still evolving. As it has happened so many times before, opinion will converge once again with the truth, the immutable truth, that all persons are created free and equal in dignity and rights. We are called once more to make real the words of the Universal Declaration. Let us answer that call. Let us be on the right side of history, for our people, our nations, and future generations, whose lives will be shaped by the work we do today. I come before you with great hope and confidence that no matter how long the road ahead, we will travel it successfully together. Thank you very much.

Critical Thinking

1. Do you agree with Hillary Clinton that the Universal Declaration of Human Rights should apply to LGBT people?
2. What actions does Clinton advocate at this time?
3. Where is the Obama Administration on this issue?

Create Central

www.mhhe.com/createcentral

Internet References

Human Rights and Humanitarian Assistance
   www.etown.edu/vl/humrts.html
Human Rights Watch
   http://www.hrw.org
Sociology—Study Sociology Online
   http://edu.learnsoc.org
Sociology Web Resources
   http://www.mhhe.com/socscience/sociology/resources/index.htm
Sociosite
   http://www.topsite.com/goto/sociosite.net
Socioweb
   http://www.topsite.com/goto/socioweb.com

Clinton, Hillary Rodham, "Free and Equal in Dignity and LGBT Rights," Speech or Remarks, December 6, 2011.

Article   Prepared by: Kurt Finsterbusch, *University of Maryland, College Park*

Do Boys Face More Sexism Than Girls?

CHRISTINA HOFF SOMMERS

Learning Outcomes

After reading this article, you will be able to:

- Discuss the ways boys and girls are treated differently in school.
- Critically consider the ways that schools function and the unintended consequences of these patterns.

When it comes to education, are boys the new girls? Are they facing more discrimination than their female peers, just because they are sexually different? According to recent studies, boys score as well as or better than girls on most standardized tests, yet they are far less likely to get good grades, take advanced classes or attend college. We asked prominent gender warriors, Michael Kimmel and Christina Hoff Sommers, to hash this one through in HuffPost's latest "Let's Talk" feature.

Michael: Christina, I was really impressed with your recent op-ed in the *Times*.

The first edition of your book, The War Against Boys: How Misguided Policies Are Harming Our Young Men, came out in 2000. Maybe I've optimistically misread, but it seemed to me that the change in your subtitle from "misguided feminism" (2000) to "misguided policies" indicates a real shift in your thinking? Does it? What's changed for boys in the ensuing decade? Have things gotten worse? Why revise it now? And what's changed for feminism that it's no longer their fault that boys are continuing to fall behind?

Christina: Thank you Michael. I am delighted you liked the op-ed. Boys need allies these days, especially in the academy. Yes, I regret the subtitle of the first edition was

"How Misguided Feminism is Harming Our Young Men." My emphasis was on *misguided*—I did not intend to indict the historical feminist movement, which I have always seen as one of the great triumphs of our democracy. But some readers took the book to be an attack on feminism itself, and my message was lost on them. Indeed, many dismissed the book as culture war propaganda. In the new edition (to be published this summer), I have changed the subtitle and sought to make a clear distinction between the humane and progressive feminist movement and a few hard-line women's lobbying groups who have sometimes thwarted efforts to help boys. I have also softened the tone: the problem of male underachievement is too serious to get lost in stale cultural debates of the 1990s.

Groups like the American Association of University Women and the National Women's Law Center continue to promote a girls-are-victims narrative and sometimes advocate policies harmful to boys. But it is now my view that boys have been harmed by many different social trends and there is plenty of blame to go round These trends include the decline of recess, punitive zero-tolerance policies, myths about armies of juvenile "super-predators" and a misguided campaign against single-sex schooling. As our schools become more feelings-centered, risk-averse, competition-free and sedentary, they have moved further and further from the characteristic sensibilities of boys.

What has changed since 2000? Back then almost no one was talking about the problem of male disengagement from school. Today the facts are well known and we are already witnessing the alarming social and economic consequences. (Have a look at a recent report from the Harvard Graduate School of Education—"Pathways to Prosperity"—about the bleak economic future of inadequately educated young men.) The problem of school disengagement is most serious among boys of color and white boys from poor backgrounds—but even middle-class white boys have fallen behind their sisters. My new book focuses on solutions.

The recent advances of girls and young women in school, sports, and vocational opportunities are cause for deep satisfaction. But I am persuaded we can address the problems of boys without undermining the progress of women. This is not a zero-sum contest. Most women, including most feminist women, do not see the world as a Manichean struggle between Venus and Mars. We are all in this together. The current plight of boys and young men is, in fact, a women's issue. Those boys are our sons; they are the people with whom our daughters will build a future. If our boys are in trouble, so are we all.

Now I have a question for you, Michael. In the past, you seem to have sided with a group of gender scholars who think we should address the boy problem by raising boys to be more like girls. Maybe I am being overly optimistic, but does your praise for my *New York Times* op-ed indicate a shift in your own thinking?

Michael: Not at all. I'm not interested in raising boys to be more like girls any more than I want girls to be raised more like boys. The question itself assumes that there is a way to raise boys that is different from the way we raise girls. To me this is stereotypic thinking. I want to raise our children to be themselves, and I think that one of the more wonderful components of feminism was to critique that stereotype that all girls are supposed to act and dress in one way and one way only. Over the past several decades, girls have reduced the amount of gender policing they do to each other: for every "You are such a slut," a young woman is now equally likely to hear "You go girl!" (Note: I am not saying one has replaced the other; this is not some either/or, but a both/and.) The reforms initiated in the 1970s for girls—Title IX, STEM programs—have been an incontesible success. We agree there, I think—and also that we need to pay attention also to boys, because many are falling behind (though not upper- and middle-class white boys as much, as you rightly point out).

I think cultural definitions of masculinity are complex and often offer boys contradictory messages. Just as there are parts that may be unhealthy—never crying or showing your feelings, winning at all costs, etc.—there are also values associated with manhood such as integrity, honor, doing the right thing, speaking truth to power, that are not of "redeemable" but important virtues. I wouldn't want to get rid of them in some wholesale "Etch-a-Sketch" redefinition.

Our disagreement, I think, comes from what we see as the source of that falling behind. My interviews with over 400 young men, aged 6–26, in *Guyland,* showed me that young men and boys are constantly and relentlessly policed by other guys, and pressured to conform to a very narrow definition of masculinity by the constant spectre of being called a fag or gay. So if we're going to really intervene in schools to ensure that boys succeed, I believe that we have to empower boys' resilience in the face of this gender policing. What my interviews taught me is that many guys believe that academic disengagement is a sign of their masculinity. Therefore, re-engaging boys in school requires that we enable them to reconect educational engagement with manhood.

My question to you: In your essay, you list a few reforms to benefit boys that strike me as unproblematic, such as recess, and some that seem entirely regressive, like single-sex classes in public schools or single-sex public schools. Is your educational vision of the future—a return to schools with separate entrances for boys and girls—a return to the past?

Christina: I hereby declare myself opposed to separate entrances for boys and girls at school. And I agree that we should raise children to be themselves. But that will often mean respecting their gender. Increasingly, little boys are shamed and punished for the crime of being who they are. The typical, joyful play of young males is "rough and tumble" play. There is no known society where little boys fail to evince this behavior (girls do it too, but far less). In many schools, this characteristic play of little boys is no longer tolerated. Intrusive and intolerant adults are insisting "tug of war" be changed to "tug of peace"; games such as tag are being replaced with "circle of friends"—in which no one is ever out. Just recently, a seven-year-old Colorado boy named Alex Evans was suspended from school for throwing an imaginary hand grenade at "bad guys" so he could "save the world." Play is the basis of learning. And boys' superhero play is no exception. Researchers have found that by allowing "bad guy" play, children's conversation and imaginative writing skills improved. Mary Ellin Logue (University of Maine) and Hattie Harvey (University of Denver) ask an important question: "If boys, due to their choices of dramatic play themes, are discouraged from dramatic play, how will this affect their early language and literacy development and their engagement in school?"

You seem to think that single-sex education is "regressive." This tells me that you may not have been keeping up with new developments. Take a close look at what is going on at the Irma Rangel Young Women's Leadership School and the Barack Obama Male Leadership Academy in Dallas. There are hundreds of similar programs in public schools around the country and they are working wonders with boys and girls. Far from representing a "return to the past," these schools are cutting edge.

An important new study by three University of Pennsylvania researchers looked at single-sex education in Seoul, Korea. In Seoul, until 2009, students were randomly assigned to single-sex and coeducational schools; parents had little choice on which schools their children attended. After controlling for other variables such as teacher quality, student–teacher ratio, and the proportion of students receiving lunch support, the study found significant advantages in single-sex education. The students earned higher scores on their college entrance exams and were more likely to attend four-year colleges. The authors describe the positive effects as "substantial." With so many boys languishing in our schools, it would be reckless not to pay attention to the Dallas academies and the Korean school study. No one is suggesting these schools be the norm—but they may be an important part of the solution to male underachievement. For one thing, they seem to meet a challenge you identify: connecting male educational engagement with manhood.

Finally, a word about Title IX, which you call an "incontestable success." Tell that to all the young men who have watched their swimming, diving, wrestling, baseball and gymnastic teams eliminated. Title IX was a visionary and progressive law; but over the years it has devolved into a quota regime. If a college's student body is 60 percent female, then 60 percent of the athletes should be female—even if far fewer women than men are interested in playing sports at that college. Many athletic directors have been unable to attract the same proportions of women as men. To avoid government harassment, loss of funding, and lawsuits, they have simply eliminated men's teams.

Michael, I think you focus too much on vague and ponderous abstractions such as "cultural definitions of masculinity." Why not address the very real, concrete and harsh prejudice boys now face every day in our nation's schools? You speak of "empowering boys to resist gender policing." In my view, the most aggressive policing is being carried out by adults who seem to have ruled conventional masculinity out of order.

Michael: Well, my earlier optimism seems somewhat misplaced; it's clear that you changed the subtitle, and want to argue that it's not a zero sum game—these give me hope. But then you characterize Title IX exactly as the zero sum game you say you no longer believe in. I think some of the reforms you suggest—increased recess, for example—are good for both boys and girls. Others, like reading more science fiction, seem to touch the surface, and then only very lightly. Some others, like single-sex schools strike me as, to use your favorite word, misguided. (There is little empirical evidence that the sex of a teacher has a demonstrable

independent effect on educational outcomes.) It seems to me you mistake form for content.

I'd rather my son go to a really great co-ed school than a really crappy single-sex one. (It happens that single sex schools, whether at the secondary or tertiary level, are very resource-rich, with more teacher training and lower student–teacher ratios. Those things actually do matter.) It's not the form, Christina, but the content.

And the content we need is to continue the reforms initiated by feminist women, reforms that suggested *for the first time* that one size doesn't fit all. They didn't change the "one size," and impose it on boys; they expanded the sizes. Those reforms would have us pay attention to differences *among* boys and differences *among* girls, which, it turns out, are far larger than any modest mean difference that you might find between males and females. You'd teach to the stereotype—that rambunctious roll-in-the-mud "boys will be boys" boy of which you are so fond—and not the mean, that is some center of the distribution. Teaching to the stereotype flattens the differences among boys, which will crush those boys who do not conform to that stereotype: the artistic ones, the musical ones, the soft-spoken ones, the ones who aren't into sports.

If you'd actually talked to boys in your research, instead of criticizing Bill Pollack or Carol Gilligan, I think you'd see this. The incredible research by Niobe Way, for example, in her book *Deep Secrets,* shows that prior to adolescence, boys are emotionally expressive and connected in ways that will surprise you. Something happens to those exuberant, expressive, emotional boys in middle school or so, and what happens to them is masculinity, the ideology of gender, which is relentlessly policed by other guys.

In my more than 400 interviews with boys this was made utterly clear to me. I've done workshops with literally thousands of boys, and asked them about the meaning of manhood and where they get those ideas they have. The answer is overwhelming: it is other guys who police them, with the ubiquitous "that's so gay" and other comments.

I've said this above, so I'll use my last word to reiterate. Boys learn that academic disengagement is a sign of their masculinity. If we want to re-engage boys in education, no amount of classroom tinkering and recess and science fiction reading is going to address that. We will need to enable boys to decouple the cultural definition of masculinity from academic disengagement. We need to acknowledge the vast differences among boys; their beauty lies in their diversity. We need to stop trying to force them into a stereotypic paradigm of rambunctiousness and let them be the individuals they are. And the really good research that talks to boys, all sorts of boys, suggests to me that they are waiting for us to do just that.

Critical Thinking

1. Somers establishes that gender sexism goes both ways. In schools boys are disadvantaged. Outside schools girls are disadvantaged. Overall which gender do you think is disadvantaged?
2. How can the schools function more in step with the needs and psychology of boys without being less beneficial to girls?
3. Can some disadvantages in schools be compensated for?

Create Central

www.mhhe.com/createcentral

Internet References

New American Studies Web
www.georgetown.edu/crossroads/asw

Sociology—Study Sociology Online
http://edu.learnsoc.org/

Sociology Web Resources
http://www.mhhe.com/socscience/sociology/resources/index.htm

Sociosite
http://www.topsite.com/goto/sociosite.net

Socioweb
http://www.topsite.com/goto/socioweb.com

The Center for Education Reform
http://edreform.com/school_choice

Sommers, Christina Hoff, "Do Boys Face more Sexism than Girls?," *Huffington Post,* February 20, 2013. Copyright © 2013 by Christina Hoff Sommers. All rights reserved. Used with permission.

Unit 4

UNIT

Prepared by: Kurt Finsterbusch, *University of Maryland, College Park*

Institutional Problems

This unit looks at the problems in four institutional areas: family, education, healthcare, and religion.

The family is the basic institution in society. Politicians and preachers are earnestly preaching this message today as though most people need to be convinced, but everyone already agrees. Nevertheless, families are having real problems, and sociologists should be as concerned as preachers. Unlike the preachers who blame couples who divorce for shallow commitment, sociologists point to additional causes such as the numerous changes in society that have had an impact on the family. For example, women have to work because many men do not make enough income to support a family adequately. So, women are working not only to enjoy a career but also out of necessity. Working women are often less dependent on their husbands. As a result, divorce can be an option for neglected or badly treated wives.

The first section in this unit examines the connection between love and power in marriage and other important relationships and the changing nature of parent–children relationships. The following section deals with the costs of education: Can the United States improve first-through 12th-grade education without increasing costs, and are college costs worth it? The next section discusses the medical advances that can greatly extend life and how the Veterans Health Administration can be reformed. Finally, we look at religious persecution in the world today.

Article   Prepared by: Kurt Finsterbusch, *University of Maryland, College Park*

Hey! Parents, Leave Those Kids Alone

Hanna Rosin

Learning Outcomes

After reading this article, you will be able to:

- Develop an understanding of the proper balance between protecting children and allowing them to take risks and learn for themselves.

- Understand the unintended consequences of parental overprotection.

In the past generation, the rising preoccupation with children's safety has transformed childhood, stripping it of independence, risk-taking, and discovery. What's been gained is unclear: rates of injury have remained fairly steady since the 1970s, and abduction by strangers was as rare then as it is now. What's been lost is creativity, passion, and courage. Now a countermovement is arising, based on mounting evidence that today's parenting norms do children more harm than good.

A trio of boys tramps along the length of a wooden fence, back and forth, shouting like carnival barkers. "The Land! It opens in half an hour." Down a path and across a grassy square, 5-year-old Dylan can hear them through the window of his nana's front room. He tries to figure out what half an hour is and whether he can wait that long. When the heavy gate finally swings open, Dylan, the boys, and about a dozen other children race directly to their favorite spots, although it's hard to see how they navigate so expertly amid the chaos, "is this a junkyard?" asks my 5-year-old son, Gideon, who has come with me to visit. "Not exactly," I tell him, although it's inspired by one. The Land is a playground that takes up nearly an acre at the far end of a quiet housing development in North Wales. It's only two years old but has no marks of newness and could just as well have been here for decades. The ground is muddy in spots and, at one end, slopes down steeply to a creek where a big, faded plastic boat that most people would have thrown away is wedged into the bank. The center of the playground is dominated by a high pile of tires that is growing ever smaller as a redheaded girl and her friend roll them down the hill and into the creek. "Why are you rolling tires into the water?" my son asks. "Because we are," the girl replies.

It's still morning, but someone has already started a fire in the tin drum in the corner, perhaps because it's late fall and wet-cold, or more likely because the kids here love to start fires. Three boys lounge in the only unbroken chairs around it; they are the oldest ones here, so no one complains. One of them turns on the radio—Shaggy is playing (Honey came in and she caught me red-handed, creeping with the girl next door)—as the others feel in their pockets to make sure the candy bars and soda cans are still there. Nearby, a couple of boys are doing mad flips on a stack of filthy mattresses, which makes a fine trampoline. At the other end of the playground, a dozen or so of the younger kids dart in and out of large structures made up of wooden pallets stacked on top of one another. Occasionally a group knocks down a few pallets—just for the fun of it, or to build some new kind of slide or fort or unnamed structure. Come tomorrow and the Land might have a whole new topography.

Other than some walls lit up with graffiti, there are no bright colors, or anything else that belongs to the usual playground landscape: no shiny metal slide topped by a red steering wheel or a tic-tac-toe board; no yellow seesaw with a central ballast to make sure no one falls off; no rubber bucket swing for babies. There is, however, a frayed rope swing that carries you over the creek and deposits you on the other side, if you can make it that far (otherwise it deposits you in the creek). The actual children's toys (a tiny stuffed elephant, a soiled Winnie the Pooh) are ignored, one facedown in the mud, the other sitting behind a green plastic chair. On this day, the kids seem excited by a walker that was donated by one of the elderly neighbors and is repurposed, at different moments, as a scooter, a jail cell, and a gymnastics bar.

The Land is an "adventure playground," although that term is maybe a little too reminiscent of theme parks to capture the vibe. In the UK, such playgrounds arose and became popular in the 1940s, as a result of the efforts of Lady Marjory Allen of Hurtwood, a landscape architect and children's advocate. Allen was disappointed by what she described in a documentary as "asphalt square" playgrounds with "a few pieces of mechanical equipment." She wanted to design playgrounds with loose parts that kids could move around and manipulate, to create their own makeshift structures. But more important, she wanted to encourage a "free and permissive atmosphere" with as little adult supervision as possible. The idea was that kids should face what to them seem like "really dangerous risks" and then conquer them alone. That, she said, is what builds self-confidence and courage.

The playgrounds were novel, but they were in tune with the cultural expectations of London in the aftermath of World War II. Children who might grow up to fight wars were not shielded from danger; they were expected to meet it with assertiveness and even bravado. Today, these playgrounds are so out of sync with affluent and middle-class parenting norms that when I showed fellow parents back home a video of kids crouched in the dark lighting fires, the most common sentence I heard from them was "This is insane." (Working-class parents hold at least some of the same ideals, but are generally less controlling—out of necessity, and maybe greater respect for toughness.) That might explain why there are so few adventure playgrounds left around the world, and why a newly established one, such as the Land, feels like an act of defiance.

If a 10-year-old lit a fire at an American playground, someone would call the police and the kid would be taken for counseling. At the Land, spontaneous fires are a frequent occurrence. The park is staffed by professionally trained "playworkers," who keep a close eye on the kids but don't intervene all that much. Claire Griffiths, the manager of the Land, describes her job as "loitering with intent." Although the playworkers almost never stop the kids from what they're doing, before the playground had even opened they'd filled binders with "risk benefits assessments" for nearly every activity. (In the two years since it opened, no one has been injured outside of the occasional scraped knee.) Here's the list of benefits for fire: "It can be a social experience to sit around with friends, make friends, to sing songs to dance around, to stare at, it can be a cooperative experience where everyone has jobs. It can be something to experiment with, to take risks, to test its properties, its heat, its power, to re-live our evolutionary past." The risks? "Burns from fire or fire pit" and "children accidentally burning each other with flaming cardboard or wood." In this case, the benefits win, because a playworker is always nearby, watching for impending accidents but otherwise letting the children figure out lessons about fire on their own.

"I'm gonna put this cardboard box in the fire," one of the boys says.

"You know that will make a lot of smoke," says Griffiths.

"Where there's smoke, there's fire," he answers, and in goes the box. Smoke instantly fills the air and burns our eyes. The other boys sitting around the fire cough, duck their heads, and curse him out. In my playground set, we would call this "natural consequences," although we rarely have the nerve to let even much tamer scenarios than this one play out. By contrast, the custom at the Land is for parents not to intervene. In fact, it's for parents not to come at all. The dozens of kids who passed through the playground on the day I visited came and went on their own. In seven hours, aside from Griffiths and the other playworkers, I saw only two adults: Dylan's nana, who walked him over because he's only 5, and Steve Hughes, who runs a local fishing-tackle shop and came by to lend some tools.

Griffiths started selling local families on the proposed playground in 2006. She talked about the health and developmental benefits of freer outdoor play, and explained that the playground would look messy but be fenced in. But mostly she made an appeal rooted in nostalgia. She explained some of the things kids might be able to do and then asked the parents to remember their own childhoods. "Ahh, did you never used to do that?" she would ask. This is how she would win them over. Hughes moved to the neighborhood after the Land was already open, but when he stopped by, I asked how he would have answered that question. "When I was a kid, we didn't have all the rules about health and safety," he said. "I used to go swimming in the Dee, which is one of the most dangerous rivers around. If my parents had found out, they would have grounded me for life. But back then we would get up to all sorts of mischief."

Like most parents my age, I have memories of childhood so different from the way my children are growing up that sometimes I think I might be making them up, or at least exaggerating them. I grew up on a block of nearly identical six-story apartment buildings in Queens, New York. In my elementary-school years, my friends and I spent a lot of afternoons playing cops and robbers in two interconnected apartment garages, after we discovered a door between them that we could pry open. Once, when I was about 9, my friend Kim and I "locked" a bunch of younger kids in an imaginary jail behind a low gate. Then Kim and I got hungry and walked over to Alba's pizzeria a few blocks away and forgot all about them. When we got back an hour later, they were still standing in the same spot. They never hopped over the gate, even though they easily could have; their parents never came looking for them, and no one expected them to. A couple of them were pretty upset, but back then, the code between kids ruled. We'd told them they were in jail, so they stayed in jail until we let them out. A parent's opinion on their term of incarceration would have been irrelevant.

I used to puzzle over a particular statistic that routinely comes up in articles about time use: even though women work vastly more hours now than they did in the 1970s, mothers—and fathers—of all income levels spend much more time with their children than they used to. This seemed impossible to me until recently, when I began to think about my own life. My mother didn't work all that much when I was younger, but she didn't spend vast amounts of time with me, either. She didn't arrange my playdates or drive me to swimming lessons or introduce me to cool music she liked. On weekdays after school she just expected me to show up for dinner; on weekends I barely saw her at all. I, on the other hand, might easily spend every waking Saturday hour with one if not all three of my children, taking one to a soccer game, the second to a theater program, the third to a friend's house, or just hanging out with them at home. When my daughter was about 10, my husband suddenly realized that in her whole life, she had probably not spent more than 10 minutes unsupervised by an adult. Not 10 minutes in 10 years.

It's hard to absorb how much childhood norms have shifted in just one generation. Actions that would have been considered paranoid in the '70s—walking third-graders to school, forbidding your kid to play ball in the street, going down the slide with your child in your lap—are now routine. In fact, they are the markers of good, responsible parenting. One very thorough study of "children's independent mobility," conducted in urban, suburban, and rural neighborhoods in the UK, shows that in 1971, 80 percent of third-graders walked to school alone. By 1990, that measure had dropped to 9 percent, and now it's even lower. When you ask parents why they are more protective than their parents were, they might answer that the world is more dangerous than it was when they were growing up. But this isn't true, or at least not in the way that we think. For example, parents now routinely tell their children never to talk to strangers, even though all available evidence suggests that children have about the same (very slim) chance of being abducted by a stranger as they did a generation ago. Maybe the real question is, how did these fears come to have such a hold over us? And what have our children lost—and gained—as we've succumbed to them?

In 1978, a toddler named Frank Nelson made his way to the top of a 12-foot slide in Hamlin Park in Chicago, with his mother, Debra, a few steps behind him. The structure, installed three years earlier, was known as a "tornado slide" because it twisted on the way down, but the boy never made it that far. He fell through the gap between the handrail and the steps and landed on his head on the asphalt. A year later, his parents sued the Chicago Park District and the two companies that had manufactured and installed the slide. Frank had fractured his skull in the fall and suffered permanent brain damage.

He was paralyzed on his left side and had speech and vision problems. His attorneys noted that he was forced to wear a helmet all the time to protect his fragile skull.

The Nelsons' was one of a number of lawsuits of that era that fueled a backlash against potentially dangerous playground equipment. Theodora Briggs Sweeney, a consumer advocate and safety consultant from John Carroll University, near Cleveland, testified at dozens of trials and became a public crusader for playground reform. "The name of the playground game will continue to be Russian roulette, with the child as unsuspecting victim," Sweeney wrote in a 1979 paper published in *Pediatrics*. She was concerned about many things—the heights of slides, the space between railings, the danger of loose S-shaped hooks holding parts together—but what she worried about most was asphalt and dirt. In her paper, Sweeney declared that lab simulations showed children could die from a fall of as little as a foot if their head hit asphalt, or three feet if their head hit dirt.

A federal-government report published around that time found that tens of thousands of children were turning up in the emergency room each year because of playground accidents. As a result, the US Consumer Product Safety Commission in 1981 published the first "Handbook for Public Playground Safety," a short set of general guidelines—the word guidelines was in bold, to distinguish the contents from requirements—that should govern the equipment. For example, no component of any equipment should form angles or openings that could trap any part of a child's body, especially the head.

To turn up the pressure, Sweeney and a fellow consultant on playground safety, Joe Frost, began cataloguing the horrors that befell children at playgrounds. Between them, they had testified in almost 200 cases and could detail gruesome specifics—several kids who had gotten their heads trapped or crushed by merry-go-rounds; one who was hanged by a jump rope attached to a deck railing; one who was killed by a motorcycle that crashed into an unfenced playground; one who fell while playing football on rocky ground. In a paper they wrote together, Sweeney and Frost called for "immediate inspection" of all equipment that had been installed before 1981, and the removal of anything faulty. They also called for playgrounds nationwide to incorporate rubber flooring in crucial areas.

In January 1985, the Chicago Park District settled the suit with the Nelsons. Frank Nelson was guaranteed a minimum of $9.5 million. Maurice Thominet, the chief engineer for the Park District, told the *Chicago Tribune* that the city would have to "take a cold, hard look at all of our equipment" and likely remove all the tornado slides and some other structures. At the time, a reader wrote to the paper:

Do accidents happen anymore? . . .

Can a mother take the risk of taking her young child up to the top of a tornado slide, with every good intention, and have an accident?

Who is responsible for a child in a park, the park district or the parent? . . . Swings hit 1-year-old children in the head, I'm sure with dire consequences in some instances. Do we eliminate swings?

But these proved to be musings from a dying age. Around the time the Nelson settlement became public, park departments all over the country began removing equipment newly considered dangerous, partly because they could not afford to be sued, especially now that a government handbook could be used by litigants as proof of standards that parks were failing to meet. In anticipation of lawsuits, insurance premiums skyrocketed. As the *Tribune* reader had intuited, the cultural understanding of acceptable risk began to shift, such that any known risk became nearly synonymous with hazard.

Over the years, the official consumer-product handbook has gone through several revisions; it is now supplemented by a set of technical guidelines for manufacturers. More and more, the standards are set by engineers and technical experts and lawyers, with little meaningful input from "people who know anything about children's play," says William Weisz, a design consultant who has sat on several committees overseeing changes to the guidelines. The handbook includes specific prescriptions for the exact heights, slopes, and other angles of nearly every piece of equipment. Rubber flooring or wood chips are virtually required; grass and dirt are "not considered protective surfacing because wear and environmental factors can reduce their shock absorbing effectiveness."

It is no longer easy to find a playground that has an element of surprise, no matter how far you travel. Kids can find the same slides at the same heights and angles as the ones in their own neighborhood, with many of the same accessories. I live in Washington, D.C., near a section of Rock Creek Park, and during my first year in the neighborhood, a remote corner of the park dead-ended into what our neighbors called the forgotten playground. The slide had wooden steps, and was at such a steep angle that kids had to practice controlling their speed so they wouldn't land too hard on the dirt. More glorious, a freestanding tree house perched about 12 feet off the ground, where the neighborhood kids would gather and sort themselves into the pack hierarchies I remember from my childhood—little kids on the ground "cooking" while the bigger kids dominated the high shelter. But in 2003, nearly a year after I moved in, the park service tore down the tree house and replaced all the old equipment with a prefab playground set on rubber flooring. Now the playground can hold only a toddler's attention, and not for very long. The kids seem to spend most of their time in the sandbox; maybe they like it because the neighbors have turned it into a mini adventure playground, dropping off an odd mixing spoon or colander or broken-down toy car.

In recent years, Joe Frost, Sweeney's old partner in the safety crusade, has become concerned that maybe we have gone too

far. In a 2006 paper, he gives the example of two parents who sued when their child fell over a stump in a small redwood forest that was part of a playground. They had a basis for the lawsuit. After all, the latest safety handbook advises designers to "look out for tripping hazards, like exposed concrete footings, tree stumps, and rocks." But adults have come to the mistaken view "that children must somehow be sheltered from all risks of injury," Frost writes. "In the real world, life is filled with risks—financial, physical, emotional, and social—and reasonable risks are essential for children's healthy development."

At the core of the safety obsession is a view of children that is the exact opposite of Lady Allen's, "an idea that children are too fragile or unintelligent to assess the risk of any given situation," argues Tim Gill, the author of *No Fear,* a critique of our risk-averse society. "Now our working assumption is that children cannot be trusted to find their way around tricky physical or social and emotional situations."

What's lost amid all this protection? In the mid-1990s, Norway passed a law that required playgrounds to meet certain safety standards. Ellen Sandseter, a professor of early-childhood education at Çhıeen Maud University College in Trondheim, had just had her first child, and she watched as one by one the playgrounds in her neighborhood were transformed into sterile, boring places. Sandseter had written her master's dissertation on young teens and their need for sensation and risk; she'd noticed that if they couldn't feed that desire in some socially acceptable way, some would turn to more-reckless behavior. She wondered whether a similar dynamic might take hold among younger kids as playgrounds started to become safer and less interesting.

Sandseter began observing and interviewing children on playgrounds in Norway. In 2011, she published her results in a paper called "Children's Risky Play from an Evolutionary Perspective: The Anti-Phobic Effects of Thrilling Experiences." Children, she concluded, have a sensory need to taste danger and excitement; this doesn't mean that what they do has to actually be dangerous, only that they feel they are taking a great risk. That scares them, but then they overcome the fear. In the paper, Sandseter identifies six kinds of risky play: (1) Exploring heights, or getting the "bird's perspective," as she calls it—"high enough to evoke the sensation of fear." (2) Handling dangerous tools—using sharp scissors or knives, or heavy hammers that at first seem unmanageable but that kids learn to master. (3) Being near dangerous elements—playing near vast bodies of water, or near a fire, so kids are aware that there is danger nearby. (4) Rough-and-tumble play—wrestling, play-fighting—so kids learn to negotiate aggression and cooperation. (5) Speed—cycling or skiing at a pace that feels too fast. (6) Exploring on one's own.

This last one Sandseter describes as "the most important for the children." She told me, "When they are left alone and can take full responsibility for their actions, and the consequences of their decisions, it's a thrilling experience."

To gauge the effects of losing these experiences, Sandseter turns to evolutionary psychology. Children are born with the instinct to take risks in play, because historically, learning to negotiate risk has been crucial to survival; in another era, they would have had to learn to run from some danger, defend themselves from others, be independent. Even today, growing up is a process of managing fears and learning to arrive at sound decisions. By engaging in risky play, children are effectively subjecting themselves to a form of exposure therapy, in which they force themselves to do the thing they're afraid of in order to overcome their fear. But if they never go through that process, the fear can turn into a phobia. Paradoxically, Sandseter writes, "our fear of children being harmed," mostly in minor ways, "may result in more fearful children and increased levels of psychopathology." She cites a study showing that children who injured themselves falling from heights when they were between 5 and 9 years old are less likely to be afraid of heights at age 18. "Risky play with great heights will provide a desensitizing or habituating experience," she writes.

We might accept a few more phobias in our children in exchange for fewer injuries. But the final irony is that our close attention to safety has not in fact made a tremendous difference in the number of accidents children have. According to the National Electronic Injury Surveillance System, which monitors hospital visits, the frequency of emergency-room visits related to playground equipment, including home equipment, in 1980 was 156,000, or one visit per 1,452 Americans. In 2012, it was 271,475, or one per 1,156 Americans. The number of deaths hasn't changed much either. From 2001 through 2008, the Consumer Product Safety Commission reported 100 deaths associated with playground equipment—an average of 13 a year, or 10 fewer than were reported in 1980. Head injuries, runaway motorcycles, a fatal fall onto a rock—most of the horrors Sweeney and Frost described all those years ago turn out to be freakishly rare, unexpected tragedies that no amount of safety proofing can prevent.

Even rubber surfacing doesn't seem to have made much of a difference in the real world. David Ball, a professor of risk management at Middlesex University, analyzed UK injury statistics and found that as in the United States, there was no clear trend over time. "The advent of all these special surfaces for playgrounds has contributed very little, if anything at all, to the safety of children," he told me. Ball has found some evidence that long-bone injuries, which are far more common than head injuries, are actually increasing. The best theory for that is "risk compensation"—kids don't worry as much about falling on rubber, so they're not as careful, and end up hurting themselves more often. The problem, says Ball, is that "we have come to think of accidents as preventable and not a natural part of life."

The category of risky play on Sandseter's list that likely makes this current generation of parents most nervous is the one involving children getting lost, or straying from adult supervision. "Children love to walk off alone and go exploring away from the eyes of adults," she writes. They "experience a feeling of risk and danger of getting lost" when "given the opportunity to 'cruise' on their own exploring unknown areas; still, they have an urge to do it." Here again Sandseter cites evidence showing that the number of separation experiences before age 9 correlates negatively with separation-anxiety symptoms at age 18, "suggesting an 'inoculation' effect."

But parents these days have little tolerance for children's wandering on their own, for reasons that, much like the growing fear of playground injuries, have their roots in the 1970s. In 1979, nine months after Frank Nelson fell off that slide in Chicago, 6-year-old Etan Patz left his parents' downtown New York apartment to walk by himself to the school-bus stop. Etan had been begging his mother to let him walk by himself; many of his friends did, and that morning was the first time she let him. But, as just about anyone who grew up in New York in that era knows, he never came home. (In 2012, a New Jersey man was arrested for Etan's murder.) I was nearly 10 at the time, and I remember watching the nightly news and seeing his school picture, with a smile almost as wide as Mick Jagger's. I also remember that, sometime during those weeks of endless coverage of the search for Etan, the parents in my neighborhood for the first time organized a walk pool to take us to the bus stop.

The Etan Patz case launched the era of the ubiquitous missing child, as Paula Fass chronicles in *Kidnapped: Child Abduction in America*. Children's faces began to appear on milk cartons, and Ronald Reagan chose the date of Etan's disappearance as National Missing Children's Day. Although no one knew what had happened to Etan, a theory developed that he had been sexually abused; soon *The New York Times* quoted a psychologist who said that the Patz case heralded an "epidemic of sexual abuse of children." In a short period, writes Fass, Americans came to think child molestations were very prevalent. Over time, the fear drove a new parenting absolute: children were never to talk to strangers.

But abduction cases like Etan Patz's were incredibly uncommon a generation ago, and remain so today. David Finkelhor is the director of the Crimes Against Children Research Center and the most reliable authority on sexual-abuse and abduction statistics for children. In his research, Finkelhor singles out a category of crime called the "stereotypical abduction," by which he means the kind of abduction that's likely to make the news, during which the victim disappears overnight, or is taken more than 50 miles away, or is killed. Finkelhor says these cases remain exceedingly rare and do not appear to have increased since at least the mid-'80s, and he guesses the '70s, although he was not keeping track then. Overall, crimes against children have been declining, in keeping with the general crime drop since the '90s. A child from a happy, intact family who walks to the bus stop and never comes home is still a singular tragedy, not a national epidemic.

One kind of crime that has increased, says Finkelhor, is family abduction (which is lumped together with stereotypical abduction in FBI crime reports, accounting for the seemingly alarming numbers sometimes reported in the media). The explosion in divorce in the '70s meant many more custody wars and many more children being smuggled away by one or the other of their parents. If a mother is afraid that her child might be abducted, her ironclad rule should not be Don't talk to strangers. It should be Don't talk to your father.

The gap between what people fear (abduction by a stranger) and what's actually happening (family turmoil and custody battles) is revealing. What has changed since the 1970s is the nature of the American family, and the broader sense of community. For a variety of reasons—divorce, more single-parent families, more mothers working—both families and neighborhoods have lost some of their cohesion. It is perhaps natural that trust in general has eroded, and that parents have sought to control more closely what they can—most of all, their children.

As we parents began to see public spaces—playgrounds, streets, public ball fields, the distance between school and home—as dangerous, other, smaller daily decisions fell into place. Ask any of my parenting peers to chronicle a typical week in their child's life and they will likely mention school, homework, after-school classes, organized playdates, sports teams coached by a fellow parent, and very little free, unsupervised time. Failure to supervise has become, in fact, synonymous with failure to parent. The result is a "continuous and ultimately dramatic decline in children's opportunities to play and explore in their own chosen ways," writes Peter Gray, a psychologist at Boston College and the author of *Free to Learn*. No more pickup games, idle walks home from school, or cops and robbers in the garage all afternoon. The child culture from my Queens days, with its own traditions and codas, its particular pleasures and distresses, is virtually extinct.

In1972, the British-born geography student Roger Hart settled on an unusual project for his dissertation. He moved to a rural New England town and, for two years, tracked the movements of 86 children in the local elementary school, to create what he called a "geography of children," including actual maps that would show where and how far the children typically roamed away from home. Usually research on children is conducted by interviewing parents, but Hart decided he would go straight to the source. The principal of the school lent him a room, which became known as "Roger's room," and he slowly got to know the children. Hart asked them questions about where they went each day and how they felt about those places, but mostly he just wandered around with them. Even now, as a

father and a settled academic, Hart has a dreamy, puckish air. Children were comfortable with him and loved to share their moments of pride, their secrets. Often they took him to places adults had never seen before—playhouses or forts the kids had made just for themselves.

Hart's methodology was novel, but he didn't think he was recording anything radical. Many of his observations must have seemed mundane at the time. For example: "I was struck by the large amount of time children spend modifying the landscape in order to make places for themselves and for their play." But reading his dissertation today feels like coming upon a lost civilization, a child culture with its own ways of playing and thinking and feeling that seems utterly foreign now. The children spent immense amounts of time on their own, creating imaginary landscapes their parents sometimes knew nothing about. The parents played no role in their coming together—"it is through cycling around that the older boys chance to fall into games with each other," Hart observed. The forts they built were not praised and cooed over by their parents, because their parents almost never saw them.

Through his maps, Hart discovered broad patterns: between second and third grade, for instance, the children's "free range"—the distance they were allowed to travel away from home without checking in first—tended to expand significantly, because they were permitted to ride bikes alone to a friend's house or to a ball field. By fifth grade, the boys especially gained a "dramatic new freedom" and could go pretty much wherever they wanted without checking in at all. (The girls were more restricted because they often helped their mothers with chores or errands, or stayed behind to look after younger siblings.) To the children, each little addition to their free range—being allowed to cross a paved road, or go to the center of town—was a sign of growing up. The kids took special pride, Hart noted, in "knowing how to get places," and in finding shortcuts that adults wouldn't normally use.

Hart's research became the basis for a BBC documentary, which he recently showed me in his office at the City University of New York. One long scene takes place across a river where the kids would go to build what they called "river houses," structures made from branches and odds and ends they'd snuck out from home. In one scene, Joanne and her sister Sylvia show the filmmakers the "house" they made, mostly from orange and brown sheets slung over branches. The furniture has been built with love and wit—the TV, for example, is a crate on a rock with a magazine glamour shot taped onto the front. The phone is a stone with a curled piece of wire coming out from under it.

The girls should be self-conscious because they are being filmed, but they are utterly at home, flipping their hair, sitting close to each other on crates, and drawing up plans for how to renovate. Nearby, their 4-year-old brother is cutting down a small tree with a hatchet for a new addition. The girls and their siblings have logged hundreds of hours here over the years; their mother has never been here, not once, they say, because she doesn't like to get her toes wet.

In another scene, Andrew and Jenny, a brother and sister who are 6 and 4, respectively, explore a patch of woods to find the best ferns to make a bed with. Jenny walks around in her knee-high white socks, her braids swinging, looking for the biggest fronds. Her big brother tries to arrange them just so. The sun is shining through the dense trees and the camera stays on the children for a long time. When they are satisfied with their bed, they lie down next to each other. "Don't take any of my ferns," Jenny scolds, and Andrew sticks his tongue out. At this point, I could hear in my head the parent intervening: "Come on, kids, share. There's plenty to go around." But no parents are there; the kids have been out of their sight for several hours now. I teared up while watching the film, and it was only a few days later that I understood why. In all my years as a parent, I have never come upon children who are so inwardly focused, so in tune with each other, so utterly absorbed by the world they've created, and I think that's because in all my years as a parent, I've mostly met children who take it for granted that they are always being watched.

In 2004, Hart returned to the same town to do a follow-up study. His aim was to reconnect with any kids he had written about who still lived within 100 miles of the town and see how they were raising their own children, and also to track some of the kids who now lived in the town. But from the first day he arrived, he knew he would never be able to do the research in the same way. Hart started at the house of a boy he'd known, now a father, and asked whether he could talk to his son outside. The mother said they could go in the backyard, but she followed them, always staying about 200 yards behind them. Hart didn't get the sense that the parents were suspicious of him, more that they'd "gotten used to the idea of always being close to their children, and didn't like them going off." He realized that this time around, he could get to the children only through the adults; even the kids didn't seem that interested in talking to him alone; they got plenty of adult attention already. "They were so used to having their lives organized by their parents," he told me. Meanwhile, the new principal at the school said he didn't want Hart doing any research there, because it was not directly related to the curriculum.

At one point Hart tracked down Sylvia, one of the girls he'd filmed at the river house. "Roger Hart! Oh my God, my childhood existed," she screamed into the phone. "It's just that I'm always telling people what we used to do, and they don't believe me!" Sylvia was now a suburban mom of two kids (ages 5 and 4), and she and her husband had moved into a new house 30 miles away. When Hart went to visit Sylvia, he filmed the exchange. Standing outside in her backyard, Sylvia tells him she bought this house because she wanted to give her own children the kinds of childhood experiences she'd had, and when she saw the little wooded area out back, her "heart leapt." But "there's no way they'd be out in the woods," she adds. "My hometown is now so diverse, with people coming in and out and lots of transients." Hart reminds her how she used to spend most of her time across the river, playing. "There's no river here," she tells him, then whispers, "and I'm really glad about that." There will soon be a fence around the yard—she mentions the fence several times—"so they'll be contained," and she'll always be able to see her kids from the kitchen window. As Sylvia is being interviewed, her son makes some half-hearted attempts to cut the hedges with a pair of scissors, but he doesn't really seem to know how to do it, and he never strays more than a few inches from his father.

When Hart shows Jenny and Andrew the film of themselves playing in the ferns, they are both deeply moved, because they'd never seen a film of themselves as children, and because for them, too, the memories had receded into hazy unreality. They are both parents and are still living in that New England town. Of all the people Hart caught up with, they seem to have tried the hardest to create some of the same recreational opportunities for their own children that they'd had. Jenny bought a house, with a barn, near a large patch of woods; she doesn't let her sons watch TV or play video games all that much, instead encouraging them to go to the barn and play in the hay, or tend the garden. She says she wouldn't really mind if they strayed into the woods, but "they don't want to go out of sight." Anyway, they get their exercise from the various sports teams they play on. Jenny gets some of her girlish self back when she talks about how she and the boys pile up rocks in the backyard to build a ski jump or use sticks to make a fort. But Jenny initiates these activities; the boys usually don't discover them on their own.

Among this new set of kids, the free range is fairly limited. They don't roam all that far from home, and they don't seem to want to. Hart talked with a law-enforcement officer in the area, who said that there weren't all that many transients and that over the years, crime has stayed pretty steady—steadily low. "There's a fear" among the parents, Hart told me, "an exaggeration of the dangers, a loss of trust that isn't totally clearly explainable." Hart hasn't yet published his findings from his more recent research, and he told me he's wary of running into his own nostalgia for the Rousseauean children of his memories. For example, he said he has to be honest about the things that have improved in the new version of childhood. In the old days, when children were left on their own, child power hierarchies formed fairly quickly, and some children always remained on the bottom, or were excluded entirely. Also, fathers were largely absent; now children are much closer to their dads—closer to both their parents than kids were back then. I would add that the 1970s was the decade of the divorce boom, and many children felt neglected by their parents; perhaps today's close supervision is part of a vow not to repeat that mistake. And yet despite all this, Hart can't help but wonder what disappeared with "the erosion of child culture," in which children were "inventing their own activities and building up a kind of community of their own that they knew much more about than their parents."

One common concern of parents these days is that children grow up too fast. But sometimes it seems as if children don't get the space to grow up at all; they just become adept at mimicking the habits of adulthood. As Hart's research shows, children used to gradually take on responsibilities, year by year. They crossed the road, went to the store; eventually some of them got small neighborhood jobs. Their pride was wrapped up in competence and independence, which grew as they tried and mastered activities they hadn't known how to do the previous year. But these days, middle-class children, at least, skip these milestones. They spend a lot of time in the company of adults, so they can talk and think like them, but they never build up the confidence to be truly independent and self-reliant.

Lately parents have come to think along the class lines defined by the University of Pennsylvania sociologist Annette Lareau. Middle-class parents see their children as projects: they engage in what she calls "concerted cultivation," an active pursuit of their child's enrichment. Working-class and poor parents, meanwhile, speak fewer words to their children, watch their progress less closely, and promote what Lareau calls the "accomplishment of natural growth," perhaps leaving the children less prepared to lead middle-class lives as adults. Many people interpret her findings as proof that middle-class parenting styles, in their totality, are superior. But this may be an overly simplistic and self-serving conclusion; perhaps each form of child-rearing has something to recommend it to the other.

When Claire Griffiths, the Land's manager, applies for grants to fund her innovative play spaces, she often lists the concrete advantages of enticing children outside: combatting obesity, developing motor skills. She also talks about the same issue Lady Allen talked about all those years ago—encouraging children to take risks so they build their confidence. But the more nebulous benefits of a freer child culture are harder to explain in a grant application, even though experiments bear them out. For example, beginning in 2011, Swanson Primary School in New Zealand submitted itself to a university experiment and agreed to suspend all playground rules, allowing the kids to run, climb trees, slide down a muddy hill, jump off swings, and play in a "loose-parts pit" that was like a mini adventure playground. The teachers feared chaos, but in fact what they got was less naughtiness and bullying—because the kids were too busy and engaged to want to cause trouble, the principal said.

In an essay called "The Play Deficit," Peter Gray, the Boston College psychologist, chronicles the fallout from the loss of the old childhood culture, and it's a familiar list of the usual ills attributed to Millennials: depression, narcissism, and a decline in empathy. In the past decade, the percentage of college-age kids taking psychiatric medication has spiked, according to a 2012 study by the American College Counseling Association. Practicing psychologists have written (in this magazine and others) about the unique identity crisis this generation faces—a fear of growing up and, in the words of Brooke Donatone, a New York-based therapist, an inability "to think for themselves."

In his essay, Gray highlights the work of Kyung-Hee Kim, an educational psychologist at the College of William and Mary and the author of the 2011 paper "The Creativity Crisis." Kim has analyzed results from the Torrance Tests of Creative Thinking and found that American children's scores have declined steadily across the past decade or more. The data show that children have become:

> less emotionally expressive, less energetic, less talkative and verbally expressive, less humorous, less imaginative, less unconventional, less lively and passionate, less perceptive, less apt to connect seemingly irrelevant things, less synthesizing, and less likely to see things from a different angle.

The largest drop, Kim noted, has been in the measure of "elaboration," or the ability to take an idea and expand on it in a novel way.

The stereotypes about Millennials have alarmed researchers and parents enough that they've started pushing back against the culture of parental control. Many recent parenting books have called for a retreat, among them *Duct Tape Parenting, Baby Knows Best,* and the upcoming *The Kids Will Be Fine.* In her excellent new book, *All Joy and No Fun,* Jennifer Senior takes the route that parents are making themselves miserable by believing they always have to maximize their children's happiness and success.

In the UK, the safety paranoia is easing up. The British equivalent of the Consumer Product Safety Commission recently released a statement saying it "wants to make sure that mistaken health and safety concerns do not create sterile play environments that lack challenge and so prevent children from expanding their learning and stretching their abilities." When I was in the UK, Tim Gill, the author of *No Fear,* took me to a newly built London playground that reminded me of the old days, with long, fast slides down a rocky hill, high drops from a climbing rock, and few fenced-in areas. Meanwhile, the Welsh government has explicitly adopted a strategy to encourage active independent play, rather than book learning, among young children, paving the way for a handful of adventure playgrounds like the Land and other play initiatives.

Whether Americans will pick up on the British vibe is hard to say, although some hopeful signs are appearing. There is rising American interest in European-style "forest kindergartens," where kids receive little formal instruction and have more freedom to explore in nature. And in Washington, D.C., not far from where I live, we finally have our first exciting playground since the "forgotten playground" was leveled. Located at a private school called Beauvoir, it has a zip line and climbing structures that kids of all ages perceive as treacherous. I recently met someone who worked on the playground and asked him why the school board wasn't put off by safety concerns, especially since it keeps the park open to the public on weekends. He said the board was concerned about safety but also wanted an exciting playground; the safety guidelines are, after all these years, still just guidelines.

But the real cultural shift has to come from parents. There is a big difference between avoiding major hazards and making every decision with the primary goal of optimizing child safety (or enrichment, or happiness). We can no more create the perfect environment for our children than we can create perfect children. To believe otherwise is a delusion, and a harmful one; remind yourself of that every time the panic rises.

As the sun set over the Land, I noticed out of the corner of my eye a gray bin, like the kind you'd keep your récycling in, about to be pushed down the slope that led to the creek. A kid's head poked out of the top, and I realized it was my son's. Even by my relatively laissez-faire parenting standards, the situation seemed dicey. The light was fading, the slope was very steep, and Christian, the kid who was doing the pushing, was only 7. Also, the creek was frigid, and I had no change of clothes for Gideon.

I hadn't seen much of my son that day. Kids, unparented, take on pack habits, so as the youngest and newest player, he'd been taken care of by the veterans of the Land. I inched close enough to hear the exchange.

"You might fall in the creek," said Christian.

"I know," said Gideon.

Christian had already taught Gideon how to climb up to the highest slide and manage the rope swing. At this point, he'd earned some trust. "I'll push you gently, okay?" "Ready, steady, go!," Gideon said in response. Down he went, and landed in the creek. In my experience, Gideon is very finicky about water. He hates to have even a drop land on his sleeve while he's brushing his teeth. I hadn't rented a car on this trip, and the woman who'd been driving us around had left for a while. I started scheming how to get him new clothes. Could I knock on one of the neighbors' doors? Ask Christian to get his father? Or, failing that, persuade Gideon to sit a while with the big boys by the fire?

"I'm wet," Gideon said to Christian, and then they raced over to claim some hammers to build a new fort.

Critical Thinking

1. Why has parenting changed from granting children considerable freedom to operate on their own and tighter controls?
2. What are the consequences of greater parental controls today?
3. Do you agree with Rosin that parents should leave their children [more] alone?

Create Central

www.mhhe.com/createcentral

Internet References

Human Rights and Humanitarian Assistance
    www.etown.edu/vl/humrts.html
National Council on Family Relations (NCFR)
    www.ncfr.com
New American Studies Web
    www.georgetown.edu/crossroads/asw
Sociology—Study Sociology Online
    http://edu.learnsoc.org
Sociology Web Resources
    http://www.mhhe.com/socscience/sociology/resources/index.htm
Sociosite
    http://www.topsite.com/goto/sociosite.net
Socioweb
    http://www.topsite.com/goto/socioweb.com
The National Academy for Child Development (NACD)
    www.nacd.org

HANNA ROSIN is an **Atlantic** national correspondent.

© 2014 The Atlantic Media Co., as first published in The Atlantic Magazine. All rights reserved. Distributed by Tribune Content Agency, LLC.

Article Prepared by: Kurt Finsterbusch, *University of Maryland, College Park*

Myths and Reality About Student Debt and the Cost of Higher Education

RICHARD EKMAN

Learning Outcomes

After reading this article, you will be able to:

- Understand how colleges and universities are adapting to changing economic conditions in higher education.

- Learn some useful good advice about college from this article.

- Evaluate Ekman's defense of the costs of higher education as well as the criticism of these costs.

L adies and gentlemen, it's a pleasure to talk with you today about the future of American education, a subject much in the news as an object of criticism by policy makers and consumer groups. Several myths have grown up about American higher education—what works and what doesn't; what college does cost and what it should cost; who goes to college and who cannot. Today I want to address a handful of the most egregious myths. Here they are:

- A college education costs too much and is a bad long-term investment.
- A private college education costs more than a family can afford.
- Colleges have not reduced costs.
- Student debt is out of control.
- The students with the greatest financial need don't receive the greatest amount of financial aid.
- Only the children of wealthy families attend private colleges.
- Liberal arts majors don't get jobs.

The more these myths are repeated, the more people tend to believe them. I've become alarmed by the dangerously inaccurate picture that these caricatures of American higher education present.

If you look at the changing demographics of the 18-year-old population, you will see that today's college-goers are different from those of a generation earlier. They are drawn largely from low- and middle-income families; they are often the first members of their families to go to college; they are increasingly members of racial and ethnic minority groups; and they come increasingly from the southwestern and southeastern regions of the United States. This demographic shift has put enormous pressure on the colleges located in the Southeast and Southwest to increase capacity quickly. Meanwhile, many private and some public colleges in the northern half of the country face shortfalls in enrollment and have underutilized facilities. By the way, the fastest growing enrollments are in community colleges.

We've had 18 years lead time to watch these trends develop. But after the financial meltdown of 2008, the situation took yet another turn. State governments are less able to support public universities. Tuition charges are up in order to close the gap. Meanwhile, private colleges and universities, most with small endowments to begin with, have earned low rates of return on investments, which means that they have trouble supporting the lower-income students who wish to enroll but require financial aid. So here we are today—with nearly 14 million students enrolled in four-year colleges and universities—a remarkable achievement for our country—but facing very difficult circumstances in many of America's four-year colleges and universities. While colleges did not create the economic recession, they along with all Americans have been scrambling to cope with it.

Some people think that college costs too much and wonder whether we too easily dismiss the honorable path to adulthood of learning a trade that does not require a college degree. There are several problems with this perspective. First, over a lifetime a person who has a college degree likely will earn $700,000–$1 million more than a high school graduate. Second, the main reason why the differential in lifetime earnings potential is so huge is that the old economy's jobs that one could qualify for on the basis of a high school diploma simply do not exist any more. Even factory jobs today require training in mathematics and computers. In other words, today's earnings gap is less the result of salary increases for college graduates and more the result of the evaporation of the jobs that could support a middle-class lifestyle but did not require a college education.

Some people believe they can bypass college and still earn a good income—the Bill Gates effect, if you will. Too much has been made of the rare college drop-outs who make good. Bill Gates is a very successful entrepreneur and a socially responsible philanthropist. As a Harvard student, he rarely went to class and eventually dropped out. But it's also the case that he was able to use Harvard's computer facilities in the middle of the night and talk with faculty members he knew. People who knew him as a high school student in Seattle say that he also had friends who were students at the University of Washington and gave him "unofficial" access to computing facilities! Like the occasional star athlete who makes it big, Gates is not a model for most young people. For most people, college is a worthwhile long-term investment.

America's colleges and universities are first-rate. Our 100 research universities dominate every list of the institutions worldwide that are the recognized leaders in research and innovation. The United States, with only 5 percent of the world's population, wins 80–90 percent of the world's scientific prizes year after year, including Nobel Prizes. But there are additional reasons to take pride in the 1,800 other four-year colleges in the United States. Fifty years ago, America began to expand access to higher education from fewer than half of all high school graduates to more than two-thirds today. We can be proud of the sustained generosity of both state and federal governments and of private donors who, over many years, have made possible this expansion of access. The Obama White House and several leading foundations have set the goal of continuing to increase the number of Americans with college degrees.

Despite these achievements, our colleges are criticized for being expensive, for not preparing students for productive lives, and for not being accessible to low-income students. Even in the US Congress—a body that is unable to reach consensus about almost anything—one of the few topics of bipartisan agreement, unfortunately, seems to be that higher education is doing a bad job.

The solutions proposed by public officials to these alleged problems are sometimes bizarre. The governor of one state, observing that recent graduates in engineering have better employment prospects than graduates with humanities majors, proposed earlier this year that the tuition for the state university's engineering program be set at a lower level than the tuition for humanities majors. You would think that differential tuition levels—a flawed concept, in any event—should reflect the large investment in laboratory facilities needed for an engineering program and the tiny investment needed for, say, a philosophy program that requires only a 20-page text by Aristotle and perhaps a eucalyptus tree to sit under.

I recognize that most high school students and their parents dream of an Ivy League education, of a college that will open doors to both great personal success and ample opportunities to play an important role in society. But the Ivy League can accept only so many students. The looming public policy questions at a time when we do need to produce more college graduates to assure future American competitiveness are: what form of massive, large-scale higher education will serve us best? How can we pay for the larger scale of access? Where do students—especially the increasing numbers of low-income, first-generation, and minority college students—have the greatest chance of success?

Contrary to the myth, students in long underrepresented populations on campuses account for about the same percentages in both private and state universities. The graduation rates of these students, however, are significantly higher at private colleges than at state universities, and both of these kinds of traditional institutions have higher graduation rates—for all categories of students—than the for-profit education providers. The five-year graduation rate for students at private nonprofit four-year colleges is 62 percent. For public colleges it is 51 percent. For for-profit education providers, it is 40 percent.

All these rates may strike you as too low compared with graduation rates a generation ago when college students were a smaller percentage of the population, so let us focus for a minute on the sub-groups of particular interest. Only 27 percent of Hispanic students at public universities earn their bachelor's degrees in four years; at private colleges it is 46 percent. For low-income students at public colleges, the five-year graduation rate is only 47 percent; at private colleges, 59 percent. At the end of six years, the numbers for low-income students have risen to 68 percent at private and 61 percent at public institutions, respectively, which is good news, but the six-year graduation rate for low-income students at for-profit colleges is still a shockingly low 18 percent.

Think about the implications of these completion rates: a Latino student who has good but not superstar grades at an inner-city high school in Los Angeles, who comes from a family with little income, and whose parents have no college background has a better chance of graduating from a nonelite private college than he or she does from a branch campus of the state university near his home; and a much better chance of success at either of these traditional kinds of colleges than in a for-profit college.

Actually, quite a few colleges, committed to providing college access to those who truly deserve it, have recently made a specialty of educating these students. Here's an example. Southern Vermont College in Bennington admitted an African American student from a New York City high school a few years ago. He had a B minus average in high school. His family had no money. He was being raised by his grandmother. At Southern Vermont, this young man blossomed. The following year, two students from that high school went to Southern Vermont. The following year Southern Vermont decided to recruit students from several New York city public high schools. Today the college has active recruitment programs underway in high schools in New York, Philadelphia, Washington, Buffalo, and Cleveland.

How can these students afford to go to a private college? The answer to this question also runs counter to popular myths. State universities are heavily subsidized by state governments, so the publicly advertised "sticker" price of tuition can be pretty low. Sadly, many state governments have in recent years reduced appropriations to state universities, although a few states have finally seen the bottom of the effects of the 2008 financial crisis and are now beginning to increase support for state universities again. Happily, New York state is one of these.

Private colleges, of course, often have higher sticker prices, because on average 59 percent of their revenue comes from tuition and fees. But not so well understood is that few students at private college pay the sticker price. Private colleges raise tremendous amounts of money to be used for scholarships. The average student pays about half the sticker price—say, $25,000 rather than $50,000 per year. The result is that low-income students can and do enroll in private colleges in sizable numbers. In fact, nearly 40 percent of all private college students are from low-income backgrounds.

Here's another myth-busting fact: a larger proportion of lower-income students enroll at smaller private colleges than at public research universities. How can that be? The explanation has two parts: First, some of the flagship public universities—Berkeley, Michigan, and Indiana, for example—are excellent universities and some of the students with the strongest high school records will prefer to study there regardless of their ability to pay more elsewhere. But second, most private colleges are truly committed to enrolling all deserving students and these colleges treat fundraising for scholarship money as a top priority—higher priority than new buildings or new faculty positions. Indeed, the amount of private scholarship money awarded to students at private colleges is six times as much as the amount of federal aid that is distributed to private college students.

Still, $25,000 is a lot of money, and some students do need to take out loans. We've all heard about the rare student who

has, quite irresponsibly, taken on $150,000 in loans. But that student is the rare exception—thank goodness. Here are the facts. Fully 28 percent of graduates of private colleges have no debt whatsoever. Another 29 percent have debts of under $20,000. The average amount of debt for all students is $28,000, but the average debt for those who actually graduate is below $20,000. Is this a lot of debt or a little? It is not a large amount of money in relation to the lifetime earnings premium of being a college graduate—up to $1 million more in salary. We need a sense of proportion. $25,000 is not a lot of money in relation to the price of other things—about equal to the price of a modest automobile that depreciates the minute you drive it off the lot, whereas a college degree appreciates in value. Most reassuring is that students with the least amount of debt fall into two categories—those with the lowest family incomes and those who have persisted in their studies and graduated in timely fashion. In other words, colleges follow honorable principles when distributing financial aid. The result has been that 79 percent of all private college graduates finish in four years in comparison with only 50 percent of public college graduates.

Journalists, however, have become fascinated by one statistic: the US total amount of student debt, now more than $1 trillion, is more than the total of credit card debt. But this figure is not evidence that college costs too much; it is instead an indication that more people are going to college than ever before and they are drawn from families without a lot of wealth. This is a good thing, an accomplishment by our society over two generations of which we should be proud, a fulfillment of one aspect of Lyndon Johnson's Great Society vision.

Colleges have tried to reduce costs and have succeeded. Over the past five years, net tuition and fees, adjusted for inflation, has actually declined by 3.5 percent. Many colleges have frozen tuition. Additional scholarship money has been raised and awarded. Several colleges have slashed tuition charges—Converse College in South Carolina, Cabrini College in Pennsylvania, Sewanee in Tennessee, and Hartwick College here in New York State are recent examples. Their assumption is that the "high tuition/high financial aid" model wastes a lot of people's time in negotiations and everyone would be better off getting to the bottom line right away. These colleges also believe that some very bright low-income students don't even apply to college and never learn about the financial aid available because the publicly announced sticker price scares them away.

This fact has some bearing on the national goals for higher education. One major goal is that our country needs more scientists and engineers. In fields of study that are cumulative, such as mathematics, science, and foreign languages, the rate of degree completion is higher in small colleges than at large universities. In fact, small colleges account for a disproportionately large share of those individuals who become career scientists and engineers. Look at the field of physics. In the United States, we produce too few PhD physicists who are Americans. The foreign-born graduate students at US universities, meanwhile, increasingly choose to return home to pursue their careers. The National Academy of Sciences issued reports by blue-ribbon commissions in 2005 and 2010 that express alarm, and call on universities and the federal government to do better.

But there is a cost-effective solution at hand. Think about this comparison. In the past five years, 16 people who were undergraduate physics majors at one large university, Texas A&M, completed PhDs in physics. In the same period, 17 people who did their undergraduate work at Swarthmore College, a much smaller institution, completed PhDs in physics. The same pattern holds true in chemistry. Oberlin College has exactly one-tenth the number of students as the University of Wisconsin at Madison and one-tenth the number of undergraduate chemistry majors. The numbers of those undergraduate chemistry majors who ultimately earn PhDs in chemistry is very small—about two or three per year who were Wisconsin undergraduates and about the same number who were Oberlin undergraduates, not one-tenth the number. If the United States needs more scientists, small colleges are the most cost-effective way to produce them. The same amount of taxpayers' money spent to educate college students who plan to be scientists and engineers will produce many more physicists and chemists if the funds are used to support students at smaller private colleges.

What about the world of work more generally? It's certainly reasonable for students to expect college to give them both a solid general education and the skills to obtain a job in a chosen profession. Are colleges preparing students for jobs? The answer is yes, but there is a caveat because new college graduates in the past few years have found it difficult to obtain jobs. This is not the fault of the colleges, but of an overall weak economy. Even so, it is still the case that the unemployment rate for college graduates is half the unemployment rate of non-graduates—4.6 percent versus 9.4 percent. For college graduates, the unemployment rate even at the depths of the recession never rose above 6.3 percent. The rates of employment of new graduates do vary more by field than by institution, and always have. Right now, petroleum engineers are in great demand; social workers are not. These patterns are cyclical. Today, those who majored in the former boom field of business are struggling to find work—a big change from just few years ago. A new college graduate in social work earns about $30,000; five years later the average salary rises to $46,000. If that person gets an advanced degree, the average salary rises to $60,000. A new college graduate who becomes a chemical engineer earns $51,000; five years later the salary has increased to $94,000.

But a new graduate in computer science earns $50,000; in five years the median salary has increased only to $81,000. We also know from past oil booms that the petroleum engineers who received a broad-based education in the liberal arts are going to fare better when the employment cycle gets to a low point, as it inevitably will, than the engineers whose educational background were narrow and technical.

Employers say that the skills they want in their new employees are those of problem-solving, creativity, clear written and oral expression, and the ability to work in teams. These are precisely the skills that the liberal arts teach and are emphasized in the small classes of liberal arts colleges.

In closing, let me say I hope these comments will help you to recognize inaccurate statements about higher education when you encounter them. If I were to convert the handful of myths I listed at the outset to true statements about the cost of education, here's what I'd say:

- A college education is well worth the cost. Going to college is the best long-term investment one can make to increase earnings potential over a lifetime.
- A private college education is affordable for families across all income brackets. Large numbers of low- and middle-income students enroll in private colleges every year.
- Colleges have gone to great lengths to reduce costs and raise a great deal of private support to offset costs.
- Student debt is not out of control. Taking on some debt to earn a college degree is a wise financial decision.
- The students with the greatest financial need do in fact receive most of the financial aid they need to complete their degrees at private colleges.
- Liberal arts majors do get jobs because they possess the skills that employers say they want most.

I hope everyone here will help to set the record straight. The myths are doing damage. Students are not making well-informed choices. Colleges are distracted by the need to respond to problems that don't exist. And our country is jeopardizing its global leadership by a failure to appreciate how effectively the American approach to higher education has served the nation for a very long time, and continues to do so today.

Thank you.

Critical Thinking

1. Does college cost too much? Is higher education worth the costs?
2. How are the financial issues of higher education affecting community colleges?
3. How should higher education costs change? Can they?

Create Central

www.mhhe.com/createcentral

Internet References

New American Studies Web
www.georgetown.edu/crossroads/asw

Sociology—Study Sociology Online
http://edu.learnsoc.org

Sociology Web Resources
http://www.mhhe.com/socscience/sociology/resources/index.htm

Sociosite
http://www.topsite.com/goto/sociosite.net

Socioweb
http://www.topsite.com/goto/socioweb.com

The American Studies Web
www.lamp.georgetown.edu/asw

The Center for Education Reform
http://edreform.com/school_choice

Ekman, Richard, "Myths and Reality about U.S. Higher Education," *Vital Speeches of the Day*, vol. 79, 12, December 2013, pp. 392–396. Copyright © 2013 by Richard Ekman. All rights reserved. Used with permission.

Article   Prepared by: Kurt Finsterbusch, *University of Maryland, College Park*

Is $600 Billion Enough?

PETER W. COOKSON JR.

Learning Outcomes

After reading this article, you will be able to:

- Understand what is wrong with the US education system and how can it be improved.

- Understand that per pupil investment has doubled but performance has not improved.

- Discuss how technological changes could improve pupils' performance without increasing costs.

Today's new austerity may have an upside if it prods schools to embrace new technologies that cut costs and improve learning.

It is crunch time for public education. Several storms are converging to create a hurricane of educational instability: sharply declining revenues, intense international competition, outdated approaches to teaching and learning, and a significant achievement gap between white students and their African-American and Hispanic peers. Seemingly unable to get to the root causes of what is plaguing the schools, we keep spinning our policy wheels while also spending a great deal of money— $600 billion a year.

The National Center for Education Statistics reports that the nation's per pupil expenditures have doubled in inflation-adjusted terms since 1970, while scores on standardized assessments of student achievement have remained essentially flat. In 1971 the average reading score for nine-year-olds on the National Assessment of Educational Progress was 208 (on a scale of 0 to 500); in 2009 it was 221, an improvement, yes, but still mediocre at best. Moreover, it appears that the longer students stay in school, the smaller the learning gains. Seventeen-year-olds averaged a score of 285 on the NAEP reading test in 1971; nearly 40 years later, they scored only three points better.

Today, the average yearly cost of educating a public school student is more than $10,000. Topping the expenditure scale is

New York state, at $17,000, and at the bottom is Utah, at $6,000. Yet on average, Utah students do as well as their New York counterparts on standardized tests. To be sure, interstate and intradistrict funding inequities are sometimes glaring and very likely contribute to achievement gaps between whites and blacks and between other groups. Few policymakers advocate abandoning the goal of finance equity. But on the whole, simply spending more money is not likely to produce greater student learning.

In any case, money is going to be increasingly hard to come by. Nearly every state and school district is grappling with budget shortfalls, and there is little reason to expect much relief in the foreseeable future. Financial constraints have caused states and districts to experiment with a variety of cost-cutting strategies, including bigger classes, shorter school days, fewer school days per year, and reduced extracurricular and afterschool programs. We don't know yet how these measures will affect student learning, but we can be certain of one thing: They are not going to usher in the era of breakthrough achievement we desperately need.

Today's climate of austerity is forcing us to grapple with the reality that a good deal of our current education spending is ill directed. We keep investing in 19th-century classrooms even though today's students are 21st-century learners. One promising alternative to business as usual is the creation of cost-effective 21st-century classrooms in which new communication technologies are blended with traditional face-to-face instruction. Teachers will always be the key to unlocking students' imaginations, but standing in front of a 21st-century class and lecturing is neither pedagogically sound nor economically efficient.

Integrating technology into the classroom does not mean putting kids in front of computers all day or turning schools into academic call centers where teachers are technicians and students are "end users." Technology can be a trap. In the 1990s, media scholar Neil Postman of New York University warned against "technopoly," a state of mind that "consists in the deification of technology, finds its satisfactions in technology, and takes its orders from technology." But if we treat technology as a partner, it can facilitate individualized learning and thus stimulate intellectual curiosity and academic ambition. We know that students have different learning styles, skills, abilities, and dispositions, and that they progress and mature at different rates. Common sense and research tell us that if we can customize students' educational experiences, achievement will increase. Truly individualized instruction is the age-old dream of education; technology puts it within our grasp.

In the current industrial-era model of education, all students are exposed to the same (or nearly the same) educational treatment, as if they were identical units moving along an assembly line. At the end of the treatment, they are tested competitively in a yearly exercise of what passes for quality control. This is the system that is failing us, as well as the young people it is supposed to prepare for productive and meaningful lives.

Imagine a middle school student named Alicia. She is about to enter the eighth grade and encounter algebra for the first time. Algebra is not just another subject in Alicia's academic career; it is a gatekeeper course. Failure to master the subject means exclusion from advanced mathematics courses and reduces her chances of admission to a selective college.

Let's assume that Alicia is an average math student. In most situations, she would have only two possible pathways: placement in a "real" algebra class with other mathematically competent students or in a general math class, a kind of "algebra for dummies." Tests largely determine which path Alicia will find herself on. If she is placed in the "real" class, she has a good shot at succeeding in high school; if she is placed in the general class, there is a high probability that her academic career will go nowhere. And students placed in lower academic tracks can see the writing on the wall. That is one reason why nearly 50 percent of teenagers in urban areas leave school before graduation, choosing, however unwisely, to look for work rather than see their rather empty education through.

So the stakes are high for Alicia and for us, because in the era of global competition the wasting of talent is not only a personal tragedy, it is a national security issue. We cannot expect to successfully compete internationally if many of our students fail to complete high school while others fail to achieve their full potential even as they hang on to earn a diploma.

What if we had a different approach? It might look like this: When Alicia is about to enter eighth grade, she is given a battery of diagnostic tests to assess her preparedness for the conceptual thinking required by algebra. The results are not used to slot Alicia into column A or column B. Rather, a computer program is able to integrate data about her aptitudes and abilities to create a unique learning profile. Teachers, with the assistance of intelligent software, are then able to create a customized, individualized algebra curriculum for Alicia by drawing on a wide variety of digitized resources, some from online education companies, universities, and other outside sources, and some developed by teachers at her school.

Alicia's individualized algebra course is dynamic; after she completes her assignments every day she takes a short quiz, perhaps in the form of a game, which gauges her level of comprehension. This allows her teacher to adjust Alicia's next lesson in order to address those areas where she needs more work or a different approach. Her teacher has a large library of digitized alternatives from which to choose, and Alicia's program allows her to make certain choices herself. She is participating in the creation of her own education. Unlike weekly tests that have little diagnostic utility.

Alicia's daily quizzes and games are adaptive; that is, they adjust themselves to her strengths and weaknesses and prescribe a course of study to address her specific learning needs. None of this means that students like Alicia are no longer part of a classroom community or that their only learning comes through a computer. Teachers in "blended" classrooms such as these, like police officers using modern community policing methods, do spend more time than their counterparts of old managing and analyzing data, focusing on problem areas, and carefully charting progress. This is what enables them to use their time more effectively on the "street," talking and listening to flesh-and-blood students and guiding them in their education.

Recently I visited Intermediate School 228 in Brooklyn, New York, where an experimental blended math program called the School of One is being implemented. Just outside the big white doors that lead to the School of One wing, an old-fashioned classroom with battered chairs and heavy desks has been preserved as a kind of case study of what the School of One is not. It is a bit unsettling, since such traditional classrooms served generations of earlier students well, and indeed some of their principles still animate places like the School of One.

Beyond the white doors, however, is a classroom that would have been unrecognizable to a teacher or student of 50 years ago. I.S. 228 students come to this classroom only for their math classes. Kids move around, talk, listen to teachers, occasionally talk back to teachers, and, yes, even hack around a little in the open and airy space. Gone are the rows of desks facing the teacher and blackboard. Movable bookshelves create flexible spaces where students can work together or with instructors in groups of various sizes. Some students collaborate, others work alone on computers. A teacher circulates, spending a few minutes with one student, perhaps a larger block of time instructing a group.

Journalist Ta-Nehisi Coates wrote about his visit to a School of One campus in the Bronx in The Atlantic last year, remembering his own experience as a young man who had struggled mightily in school. "By the time I was in high school, we were using the computer lab once a week for math. But we were using it the same way we used pen and paper—a teacher at the front of the class and all of us following along. The computer lab bored me as much as the chalkboard. . . . I thought I was lazy (and maybe I was) and lacking the will to learn. But as

I watched the kids at I.S. 339 working at their own pace and in their own way, I wondered if all I had ever really needed was the equivalent of a warm hug from a cold algorithm."

One of the notable experiments in blended learning is Rocketship Education, a nonprofit charter school network that opened its first school in San Jose, California, in 2007. The five Rocketship elementary schools were designed from the ground up to support customized learning. They are hardly enclaves of privilege. Ninety percent of the students qualify for free or reduced-price lunches, and 75 percent speak English as a second language. With an explicit mission of closing the achievement gap, Rocketship has already seen two of its sites ranked among the 15 top-performing schools serving high-poverty areas in California.

Experiments in blended learning have caught the eye of policymakers and private-sector innovators. President Barack Obama paid a highly publicized visit earlier this year to TechBoston Academy, a blended curriculum public school for grades 6–12 in Boston. The United States Department of Education's 2010 National Education Technology Plan calls for bringing "state-of-the-art technology into learning to enable, motivate, and inspire all students." Education entrepreneur Chris Whittle and his partners are planning to open the first in a planned international network of private schools using a blended curriculum in 2012.

Integrating technology into classrooms will be no easier than it has been in offices and factories. Finding the right ways to shape human–computer interactions is a delicate task, especially when the humans are children. Different approaches will be needed for children of different ages. There will be—and already have been—disappointments and mistakes.

No comprehensive research exists on the impact of computers on education, and those studies that have been conducted yielded conflicting results. That is no surprise. We are only in the early stages of learning how to create effective blended classrooms, and there are many pitfalls—from techno-utopianism and our weakness for thinking that complex problems can be solved with easy technological fixes, to the challenge of identifying the useful technologies amid the mountains of ill-conceived and simply shoddy software and edu-gadgets being peddled by eager companies.

Can we afford such experiments in a time of increasing austerity? Up-front investments will be needed. But over the longer term, blended schools can produce considerable economies. Textbooks are an obvious place to begin. They cost billions of dollars every year—Texas alone budgeted more than $800 million for textbooks in 2010. Information technology, meanwhile, gets radically cheaper every year. Additional savings can be realized through the use of open-source curricula, shared lesson plans, online tutoring, and other measures. In time, fewer teachers will be required as large, unmanageable, industrially organized classrooms disappear. Even in today's classrooms,

research shows that teachers with the right training and support can lead quite large classrooms without diminishing student achievement. (Reducing class size, a perennial favorite reform in public opinion surveys, does not automatically improve student performance. The only consistent evidence of a positive effect indicates that kindergarten and primary-level students do better in classrooms that do not exceed 15 students.)

Exploring how blended classrooms can individualize teaching and learning while saving money is a reform strategy that has several virtues. New technologies coupled with new thinking about education can expand students' opportunities to learn, enable implementation of new forms of teaching more in keeping with the learning styles of today's students, and squeeze much better results from our education funds. Six hundred billion dollars is a lot of money; cutting back spending on nonessentials and investing in innovative teaching and learning may be one way to reduce costs and boost achievement at the same time. Perhaps we can turn the energy of the hurricane that is engulfing public education to positive ends by redirecting that energy toward the future.

A School of One program in New York city is one of many efforts to find effective ways to bring technology into the classroom.

Critical Thinking

1. Is spending more money critical to improving our schools?
2. How will new technologies improve our schools?
3. How should teaching methods change?

Internet References

New American Studies Web
www.georgetown.edu/crossroads/asw
Sociology—Study Sociology Online
http://edu.learnsoc.org
Sociology Web Resources
http://www.mhhe.com/socscience/sociology/resources/index.htm
Sociosite
http://www.topsite.com/goto/sociosite.net
Socioweb
http://www.topsite.com/goto/socioweb.com
The Center for Education Reform
http://edreform.com/school_choice

PETER W. COOKSON JR., a sociologist and educational consultant, is the former president of TC Innovations at Teachers College, Columbia University, and the author of several books, including *School Choice: The Struggle for the Soul of American Education* (1994) and *Sacred Trust: A Children's Education Bill of Rights*, published earlier this year.

From *Washington Monthly*, Autumn 2011. Copyright © 2011 by Washington Monthly Publishing, LLC, 1319 F St. NW, Suite 710, Washington DC 20004. (202)393-5155. Reprinted by permission. www.washingtonmonthly.com

Article Prepared by: Kurt Finsterbusch, *University of Maryland, College Park*

A Thousand Years Young

Aubrey de Grey

Learning Outcomes

After reading this article, you will be able to:

- Understand that Aubrey de Grey's approach to life extension is to constantly rejuvenate the body as it deteriorates.

- Assuming that de Grey is right, consider how people would change their lifestyles.

- Understand the many specific treatments that would together greatly extend life.

An "antiaging activist" identifies the medical and biochemical advances that could eventually eliminate all the wear and tear that our bodies and minds suffer as we grow old. Those who undergo continuous repair treatments could live for millennia, remain healthy throughout, and never fear dying of old age.

Let me first say very explicitly: I don't work on longevity. I work on health. People are going to live longer as a result of the therapies I will describe, but extended longevity is a side effect—a consequence of keeping people healthy. There is no way in hell that we are going to keep people alive for a long time in a frail state. People will live longer only if we succeed in keeping them healthy longer.

The problem of aging is unequivocally humanity's worst medical problem. Roughly 100,000 people worldwide die every day of it, and there's an awful lot of suffering that happens before you die. But I feel that the defeat of aging in the foreseeable future is a realistic proposition. We will have medicine that will get aging under control to the same level that we now have most infectious diseases under control.

This article will describe what aging is, what regenerative medicine is, and what the various alternative approaches are to combat aging and postpone the ill health of old age. I'll then go into the details of the approach that I feel we need to take and what my expectations are for the future.

Regenerative medicine is any medical intervention that seeks to restore some part of the body—or the whole body—to how it was before it suffered some kind of damage. It could be damage that happened as the result of an acute injury, such as spinal cord damage. But it could also be damage that accumulated as a chronic condition over a long period of time.

Aging is a side effect of being alive in the first place. *Metabolism* is the word that biologists use to encompass all the aspects of being alive—all the molecular and cellular and systemic processes that keep us going from one day to the next and from one year to the next.

Ongoing lifelong side effects of metabolism—i.e., *damages*—are created throughout life. For whatever reason, damage is not repaired when it occurs. So damage accumulates. For a long time, the amount of damage is tolerable, and the metabolism just carries on. But eventually, damage becomes sufficiently extensive that it gets in the way of metabolism. Then metabolism doesn't work so well, and *pathologies*—all the things that go wrong late in life, all the aspects of age-related ill health—emerge and progress.

Geriatrics Versus Gerontology

Traditionally, there have been two themes within the study of aging that aim to actually do something about this process. One is the *geriatrics* approach, which encompasses pretty much everything that we have today in terms of medical treatments for the elderly.

The geriatrics approach is all about the pathology. It focuses on old people in whom the pathologies are already emerging, and strives to slow down their progression so that it takes longer for those pathologies to reach a life-threatening stage.

The *gerontology* approach, on the other hand, says that prevention is better than cure. This approach assumes that it will be more effective to dive in at an earlier point in the chain of events and clean up metabolism so that it creates these various types of damage at a slower rate than it naturally would. The effect would be to postpone the age at which damage reaches the level of abundance that is pathogenic.

The two approaches both sound pretty promising, but they're really not. The problem with the geriatrics approach is that aging is awfully chaotic, miserable, and complicated. There are many things that go wrong with people as they get older, and they tend to happen at much the same time. These problems interact, exacerbating each other, and damage accumulates. Even later in life, as damage continues to accumulate, the pathologies of old age become progressively more and more difficult to combat.

The geriatric approach is thus intervening too late in the chain of events. It's better than nothing, but it's not much better than nothing.

So that leaves us with the gerontology approach. Unfortunately, the gerontology approach has its own problem: Metabolism is complicated. What we know about how metabolism works is completely dwarfed by the utterly astronomical amount that we *don't* know about how metabolism works. We have no prospect whatsoever of being able to interfere in this process in a way that does not simply do more harm than good.

A Maintenance Approach

There are some Volkswagen Bugs that are 50 years old or more and still running. And the reason is because those VW Bugs have been extraordinarily well maintained. If you maintain your car only as well as the law requires, then it will only last 15 years or so. But if you do a lot more, then you can do a lot better. Maintenance works.

Now what does that tell us about the human body? Well, quite a lot, because the human body is a machine. It's a really complicated machine, but it's still a machine. So there is a third way of combating aging by postponing age-related ill health. This is the *maintenance* approach. We go in and periodically repair the damage that metabolism creates, so as to prevent that damage from accumulating and reaching the level that causes the pathology of old age to emerge and to progress.

Maintenance is a much more promising approach than either geriatrics or gerontology. First, the maintenance approach is preemptive, so it doesn't have this problem of this downward spiral of the geriatrics approach.

Second, the maintenance approach avoids the problem of the gerontology approach because it does not attempt to intervene with metabolism; we merely fix up the consequences. In other words, we let metabolism create these various types of damage at the rate that it naturally does, and then repair the damages before they cause pathology. We can get away with not understanding very much at all about how metabolism creates damage. We just have to characterize the damage itself and figure out ways to repair it.

That's pretty good news, but it gets better. It also turns out that damage is simpler than its causes or its consequences. All the phenomena that qualify as damage can be classified into one of seven major categories:

- Junk inside cells.
- Junk outside cells.
- Too few cells.
- Too many cells.
- Chromosome mutations.
- Mitochondria mutations.
- Protein crosslinks.

By "junk inside cells," I am referring to the molecular byproducts of normal biologic processes that are created in the cell and that the cell, for whatever reason, does not have the machinery to break down or to excrete. Those byproducts simply accumulate, and eventually the cell doesn't work so well. That turns out to be the main cause of cardiovascular disease and of macular degeneration.

"Junk outside cells" means things like senile plaques in Alzheimer's disease. This creates the same molecular damage, but in this case it is in the spaces between cells.

"Too few cells" simply means cells are dying and not being automatically replaced by the division of other cells. This is the cause of Parkinson's disease, the particular part of the brain in which neurons happen to die more rapidly than in most parts of the brain and they're not replaced. When there are too few of them, that part of the brain doesn't work so well.

But here's the really good news. We actually have a pretty good idea how to fix all of these types of damage. Here is the same list of types of damage, and on the right is the set of approaches that I feel are very promising for fixing them:

Damage	Treatment
Junk inside cells	Transgenic microbial hydrolases
Junk outside cells	Phagocytosis by immune stimulation
Too few cells (cell loss)	Cell therapy
Too many cells (death-resistant cells)	Suicide genes and immune stimulation
Chromosome mutations	Telomerase/ALT gene deletion plus periodic stem-cell reseeding
Mitochondria mutations	Allotopic expression of 13 proteins
Protein crosslinks	AGE-breaking molecules and enzymes

Stem-cell therapy replaces those cells that the body cannot replace on its own. That includes joint degeneration and muscular-skeletal problems. For example, arthritis ultimately comes from the degeneration of the collagen and other extracellular material in the joints, which happens as a result of insufficient regeneration of that tissue.

For some other medical conditions, such as Alzheimer's, we need to restore the functions of those cells that are already there by getting rid of the garbage accumulating outside them. Toward that purpose, there are phase-three clinical trials for the elimination of senile plaques in the brains of Alzheimer's patients. This is a technology using vaccination that we at the SENS Foundation are extending to the elimination of other types of extracellular garbage.

In fact, we now have an enormous amount of detail about how we're going to reverse each of the seven categories of age-related damage, so that's why I feel that my estimates of how long it's going to take to get there are likely to be borne out accurately.

The SENS Foundation: Doing Something About Aging

I'm the chief officer of a 501 (c) 3 public charity based in California. The mission of the SENS Foundation is to develop, promote, and enable widespread access to regenerative medicine as solutions to the disabilities and diseases of aging.

Is there any competition in this work? Are other people trying other things? The short answer is, Not really. There are other people, of course, looking at ways to postpone aging and age-related ill health. But regenerative medicine is really the only game in town when we're talking about serious postponement of age-related ill health. And SENS Foundation really is the hub of that concept.

We are a charity, so if you are a billionaire, please see me! But of course it's not just money we need. We need people's time and expertise. If you're a biologist, work on relevant things. Write to us and ask us for advice about what to work on, because we need more manpower in this area. If you're a conference organizer, have me to speak. If you're a journalist, come and interview me. It's all about getting the word out.

—Aubrey de Grey

Details: The SENS Foundation, www.sens.org; e-mail foundation@sens.org.

Case in Point: Cleaning the Cellular Garbage

I'm going to talk about one example: the garbage that accumulates inside cells. I'm going to explain what *transgenic microbial hydrolases* are.

White blood cells, called macrophages, sweep along a healthy adult's artery walls to clean up miscellaneous detritus, typically lipo-protein particles that were transporting cholesterol around the body from one place to another and that got stuck in the artery wall. Macrophages are very good at coping with cholesterol, but they are not so good at coping with certain derivatives of cholesterol, such as oxysterols. These contaminants end up poisoning macrophages. The macrophages become unable even to cope with native cholesterol, and then they themselves break down, lodging in the artery walls. This is the beginning of an atherosclerotic plaque. The results are cardiovascular disease, heart attacks, or strokes. In the eye, this phenomenon causes macular degeneration.

To combat this problem, we might adapt bioremediation technology from environmental decontamination. The technology that is used to break down pollutants in the environment could be adapted for biomedical purposes, breaking down the body's contaminants.

If we could apply this bioremediation process to our own cells, we could combat the initial process that turns young people into old people in the first place. A very simple idea. The question is, does it work? Bioremediation for getting rid of pollutants works really well: It's a thriving commercial discipline.

There are a number of oxidized derivatives of cholesterol, but the nastiest in abundance and toxicity is 7-ketocholesterol—public enemy number one in atherosclerosis. We have tried "feeding" it to many different strains of bacteria. Most of them can't do anything with it, but we've found two strains of bacteria that gorge themselves on it. After only 10 days, the material is completely gone.

The next step is to figure out how these bacteria are able to do this from a genetic basis. From there, we could try to turn 7-ketocholesterol back into native cholesterol. But there are other steps that we can use—remember that I said we're looking to avoid the problem of things neither being broken down nor excreted. There are modifications that we can make to compounds that are toxic that simply promote their excretion rather than promoting their degradation.

So that's all pretty good news. But don't get me wrong. This is really hard. This is a very ambitious, long-term project. The processes we hope to develop must work in vivo. What we are seeking is a truly definitive, complete cure for cardiovascular disease and for other pathologies caused by the accumulation of molecular garbage inside cells.

Escape Velocity: From Longevity to Immortality?

I do not claim that any of the work I've just described is going to be a "cure" for aging. I claim, rather, that it's got a good chance of adding 30 years of extra healthy life to people's lives. I call that *robust human rejuvenation*. And 30 years is better than nothing, but it sure does not equate to defeating aging completely. So what's the rest of my story?

The rest of the story is that it's not something that's going to work just on people who haven't been conceived yet. It's stuff that is going to work on people who are already middle-aged or older when the therapies arrive.

This is fundamentally what it all comes down to. The maintenance approach is so cool because repairing damage buys time.

At age zero, people start off with not much damage. Time goes on, they age, damage accumulates, reserve is depleted, and eventually, they get down to a certain point—the frailty threshold—and that's when pathologies start to happen. Then they're not long for this world.

Now take someone who is in middle age. You have therapies that are pretty good, but not perfect, at fixing the damage. They can be rejuvenated, but not all the way. These therapies do not reduce the rate at which damage is created. Aging happens at the normal rate.

Then we reapply the same therapies again and again. But consider that the interval between the first and second applications of these therapies to some particular individual may be 15 to 20 years. That's a long time in biomedical technology, and it means that the person is going to get new and improved therapies that will not only fix the types of damage that they could fix 15 years previously, but also fix some types of damage that they could not fix 15 years previously.

So after the second rejuvenation, our hero is not only more thoroughly rejuvenated than he would be if he'd gotten the old therapies, but he's actually more rejuvenated than he was when he got the old therapies, even though at that point he was chronologically younger. Now we see this phenomenon where we don't hit diminishing returns on additional therapies. People over the long term will be getting progressively younger as they're getting chronologically older. They'll remain far away from reaching the frailty threshold, however long that they live. They will only be subjected to the risks of death and ill health that affect young adults. They never become more susceptible to ill health simply as a result of having been born a long time ago.

There's some minimum rate at which we have to improve the comprehensiveness of these therapies in order for the general trend in increased life span to be upwards rather than downwards. And that minimum rate is what I call *longevity escape velocity*. It's the rate at which these rejuvenation therapies need to be improved in terms of comprehensiveness following that first step—the first-generation therapies that give robust human regeneration—in order to stay one step ahead of the problem and to outpace the accumulation of damage that they cannot yet repair.

So is it realistic? Are we likely actually to reach longevity escape velocity and to maintain it? We are. Consider powered flight as an illustrated example: There are very big differences between fundamental breakthroughs and incremental refinements of those breakthroughs. Fundamental breakthroughs are very hard to predict. Mostly people think they're not going to happen right up until they already have happened.

Incremental refinements, meanwhile, are very much more predictable. Leonardo da Vinci probably thought he was only a couple of decades away from getting off the ground. He was wrong. But once the Wright brothers got there, progress was ridiculously rapid. It only took 24 years for someone to fly solo across the Atlantic (that was Lindbergh), 22 more years until the first commercial jet liner, and 20 more years until the first supersonic airlines.

Can we actually give more direct evidence that we are likely to achieve longevity escape velocity? I believe that we can.

An Age-Busting Virtuous Cycle

A few years ago I worked with others on a computer simulation of the aging process to see what the impact would be of these interventions coming in at a realistic schedule. We started by imagining a population of adults who were all born in 1999. Everyone is alive at age zero and almost everyone survives until age 50 or 60, at which point they start dropping like flies; hardly anyone gets beyond 100.

Next, we imagined another population whose intrinsic risk of death at any given age is the same as for the first, but who are receiving these therapies. But they only start receiving them when they are already 80 years old. That population's survival rate will actually mostly coincide with the first population's survival rate, because obviously half the population or so is dead by age 80 and those who are still living are already in a reasonably bad way.

But what if population number two started getting these therapies 10 years earlier, when they're only 70? Initially, the same story is the case—there is not a lot of benefit. But gradually, the therapies get the upper hand. They start to impose genuine rejuvenation on these people so that they become biologically younger and less likely to die. Some of them reach 150, by which time they have very little chance of dying of *any* age-related cause. Eventually, there is exactly no such risk.

And if they're 60 years old when the therapies begin? Then almost half of them will get to that point. So we calculated, group by group.

Here's the real kicker: I was ludicrously over-pessimistic in the parameters that I chose for this simulation. I said that we would assume that the therapy would only be doubled in their efficacy every 42 years. Now, 42 years: That's the difference between Lindbergh's *Spirit of St. Louis* and the *Concorde!* But even then, we unambiguously see longevity escape velocity.

So it's inescapable. If and when we do succeed in developing these rejuvenation therapies that give us those first couple of decades more of health and the postponement of age-related ill health, then we will have done the hard part. The sky is the limit after that.

Here is what it means. At the moment, the world record for life span is 122. We won't be getting anyone who is 150 until such time as we do develop these technologies that give us robust human rejuvenation. But we will have done the hard part, so people not much younger than that will be able to escape aging indefinitely, living even to age 1,000.

A 1,000 is not pulled out of the air. It's simply the average age—plus or minus a factor of two—that people would live to if we already didn't have aging, if the only risks of death were the same risks that currently afflict young adults in the Western world today.

Should we be developing these therapies? We are ignorant about the circumstances within which humanity of the future will be deciding whether to use these technologies or not. It could actually be a no-brainer that they will want to use them. And if we have prevented them from using them by not developing them in time, then future generations won't be very happy. So it seems to me that we have a clear moral obligation to develop these technologies so as to give humanity of the future the choice. And the sooner, the better.

Critical Thinking

1. Would you like to live 1,000 years? Aubrey de Grey says that the technology will be developed to make that happen for you or your grandchildren.
2. What would be the impacts on social life and society if healthy life extended for hundreds of years?
3. Why is de Grey's message largely ignored by the media?

Create Central

www.mhhe.com/createcentral

Internet References

National Institutes of Health (NIH)
   www.nih.gov
Sociology—Study Sociology Online
   http://edu.learnsoc.org
Sociology Web Resources
   http://www.mhhe.com/socscience/sociology/resources/index.htm
Sociosite
   http://www.topsite.com/goto/sociosite.net
Socioweb
   http://www.topsite.com/goto/socioweb.com

AUBREY DE GREY is a biomedical gerontologist and chief science officer of the SENS Foundation (www.sens.org). He is the author (with Michael Rae) of *Ending Aging* (St. Martin's Press, 2007) and editor-in-chief of the journal *Rejuvenation Research*. This article draws from his presentation at WorldFuture 2011 in Vancouver.

Originally published in the May–June 2012, pp. 19–23 issue of *The Futurist*. Copyright © 2012 by World Future Society, Bethesda, MD. Used with permission via Copyright Clearance Center.

Unit 5

UNIT

Prepared by: Kurt Finsterbusch, *University of Maryland, College Park*

Crime, Violence, and Law Enforcement

T his unit deals with criminal behavior and its control by the law enforcement system. The first line of defense against crime is the socialization of the young to internalize norms against harmful and illegal behavior. Thus families, schools, religious institutions, and social pressure are the major crime fighters, but they do not do a perfect job, and the police and courts have to handle their failures. Over the last half-century crime has increased, signaling for some commentators a decline in morality. If the power of norms to control criminal behavior diminishes, the role of law enforcement must increase, and that is what has happened.

The societal response to crime has been threefold: Hire more police, build more prisons, and toughen penalties for crimes. These policies by themselves can have only limited success. For example, putting a drug dealer in prison just creates an opportunity for another person to become a drug dealer. Another approach is to give potential criminals alternatives to crime. The

key factor in this approach is a healthy economy that provides many job opportunities for unemployed young men. To some extent, this has happened and has caused the crime rate to drop. Programs that work with inner-city youth might also help, but budget-tight cities are not funding many programs like this. Amid the policy debates there is one thing we can agree upon: Crime has declined significantly in the past two decades (with a slight increase recently) after rising substantially for a half century.

This unit looks at several aspects of crime, law enforcement, and terrorism. It describes many injustices in the criminal justice system such as the tendency for the poor go to jail and rich go free. Too many people are imprisoned and for too long. Many innocent people are convicted. Gun laws are often inappropriate. The Stand Your Ground law has justified murders. Many reforms are needed but are not likely to be enacted given the public mood and the government impasse.

Article   Prepared by: Kurt Finsterbusch, *University of Maryland, College Park*

Bold Steps To Reform and Strengthen America's Criminal Justice System

The course we are on is far from sustainable. And it is our time—and our duty—to identify those areas we can improve in order to better advance the cause of justice for all Americans.

ERIC HOLDER

Learning Outcomes

After reading this article, you will be able to:

- Understand the degree of injustice in the justice system.

- Understand the roles that prisons have served.

- Understand why petty crimes are severely punished in the United States.

Thank you, Bob Carlson, for those kind words—and for your exemplary service as Chair of the American Bar Association's House of Delegates. It's a pleasure to be with you this morning. And it's a privilege to join so many friends, colleagues, and leaders—including US Attorney for the Northern District of California Melinda Haag—here in San Francisco for the ABA's 2013 Annual Meeting.

I'd like to thank your Delegates for all that they've done to bring us together this week—and for their dedication to serving as faithful stewards of the greatest legal system the world has ever known. From its earliest days, our Republic has been bound together by this system, and by the values that define it. These values—equality, opportunity, and justice under law—were first codified in the US Constitution. And they were renewed and reclaimed—nearly a century later—by this organization's earliest members.

With the founding of the ABA in 1878, America's leading legal minds came together—for the first time—to revolutionize their profession. In the decades that followed, they created new standards for training and professional conduct. And they

established the law as a clear and focused vocation at the heart of our country's identity.

Throughout history, Americans of all backgrounds and walks of life have turned to our legal system to settle disputes, but also to hold accountable those who have done wrong—and even to answer fundamental questions about who we are and who we aspire to be. On issues of slavery and segregation; voting and violence; and equal rights and equal justice—generations of principled lawyers have engaged directly in the work of building a more perfect Union. Today, under the leadership of my good friend, President Laurel Bellows, this organization is fighting against budget cuts that undermine the ability of our courts to administer justice. You're standing with me—and with my colleagues across the Obama Administration—in calling for Congressional action on common-sense measures to prevent and reduce gun violence. And you're advancing our global fight against the heinous crime of human trafficking.

In so many ways, today's ABA is reminding us that, although our laws must be continually updated, our shared dedication to the cause of justice—and the ideals set forth by our Constitution—must remain constant. It is this sense of dedication that brings me to San Francisco today—to enlist your partnership in forging a more just society. To ask for your leadership in reclaiming, once more, the values we hold dear. And to draw upon the ABA's legacy of achievement in calling on every member of our profession to question that which is accepted truth; to challenge that which is unjust; to break free of a tired status quo; and to take bold steps to reform and strengthen America's criminal justice system—in concrete and fundamental ways.

It's time—in fact, it's well past time—to address persistent needs and unwarranted disparities by considering a fundamentally new approach. As a prosecutor; a judge; an attorney in private practice; and now, as our nation's Attorney General, I've seen the criminal justice system firsthand, from nearly every angle. While I have the utmost faith in—and dedication to—America's legal system, we must face the reality that, as it stands, our system is in too many respects broken. The course we are on is far from sustainable. And it is our time—and our duty—to identify those areas we can improve in order to better advance the cause of justice for all Americans.

Even as most crime rates decline, we need to examine new law enforcement strategies—and better allocate resources—to keep pace with today's continuing threats as violence spikes in some of our greatest cities. As studies show that 6 in 10 American children are exposed to violence at some point in their lives—and nearly one in four college women experience some form of sexual assault by their senior year—we need fresh solutions for assisting victims and empowering survivors. As the so-called "war on drugs" enters its fifth decade, we need to ask whether it, and the approaches that comprise it, have been truly effective—and build on the Administration's efforts, led by the Office of National Drug Control Policy, to usher in a new approach. And with an outsized, unnecessarily large prison population, we need to ensure that incarceration is used to punish, deter, and rehabilitate—not merely to warehouse and forget.

Today, a vicious cycle of poverty, criminality, and incarceration traps too many Americans and weakens too many communities. And many aspects of our criminal justice system may actually exacerbate these problems, rather than alleviate them.

It's clear—as we come together today—that too many Americans go to too many prisons for far too long, and for no truly good law enforcement reason. It's clear, at a basic level, that 20th-century criminal justice solutions are not adequate to overcome our 21st-century challenges. And it is well past time to implement common sense changes that will foster safer communities from coast to coast.

These are issues the President and I have been talking about for as long as I've known him—issues he's felt strongly about ever since his days as a community organizer on the South Side of Chicago. He's worked hard over the years to protect our communities, to keep violent criminals off our streets, and to make sure those who break the law are held accountable. And he's also made it part of his mission to reduce the disparities in our criminal justice system. In Illinois, he passed legislation that addressed racial profiling and trained police departments on how they could avoid racial bias. And in 2010, this Administration successfully advocated for the reduction of the unjust 100-to-1 sentencing disparity between crack and powder cocaine.

That's the balance the President and I have tried to strike—because it's important to safeguard our communities and stay true to our values. And we've made progress. But as you heard the President say a few weeks ago when he spoke about the Trayvon Martin case, he also believes—as I do—that our work is far from finished.

That's why, over the next several months, the President will continue to reach out to Members of Congress from both parties—as well as governors, mayors, and other leaders—to build on the great work being done across the country to reduce violent crime and reform our criminal justice system. We need to keep taking steps to make sure people feel safe and secure in their homes and communities. And part of that means doing something about the lives being harmed, not helped, by a criminal justice system that doesn't serve the American people as well as it should.

At the beginning of this year, I launched a targeted Justice Department review of the federal system—to identify obstacles, inefficiencies, and inequities, and to address ineffective policies. Today, I am pleased to announce the results of this review—which include a series of significant actions that the Department has undertaken to better protect the American people from crime; to increase support for those who become victims; and to ensure public safety by improving our criminal justice system as a whole. We have studied state systems and been impressed by the policy shifts some have made.

I hope other state systems will follow our lead and implement changes as well. The changes I announce today underscore this Administration's strong commitment to common sense criminal justice reform. And our efforts must begin with law enforcement.

Particularly in these challenging times—when budgets are tight, federal sequestration has imposed untenable and irresponsible cuts, and leaders across government are being asked to do more with less—coordination between America's federal, state, local, and tribal law enforcement agencies has never been more important. It's imperative that we maximize our resources by focusing on protecting national security; combating violent crime; fighting against financial fraud; and safeguarding the most vulnerable members of our society.

This means that federal prosecutors cannot—and should not—bring every case or charge every defendant who stands accused of violating federal law. Some issues are best handled at the state or local level. And that's why I have today directed the US Attorney community to develop specific, locally-tailored guidelines—consistent with our national priorities—for determining when federal charges should be filed, and when they should not.

I've also issued guidance to ensure that every case we bring serves a substantial federal interest and complements the work of our law enforcement partners. I have directed all US Attorneys to create—and to update—comprehensive antiviolence strategies for badly afflicted areas within their districts. And I've encouraged them to convene regular law enforcement forums with state and local partners to refine these plans, foster greater efficiency, and facilitate more open communication and cooperation.

By targeting the most serious offenses, prosecuting the most dangerous criminals, directing assistance to crime "hot spots," and pursuing new ways to promote public safety, deterrence, efficiency, and fairness—we in the federal government can become both smarter and tougher on crime. By providing leadership to all levels of law enforcement—and bringing intelligence-driven strategies to bear—we can bolster the efforts of local leaders, US Attorneys, and others in the fight against violent crime.

Beyond this work, through the Community Oriented Policing Services—or "COPS"—Office, the Justice Department is helping police departments keep officers on the beat while enhancing training and technical support. Over the last four years, we have allocated more than $1.5 billion through the COPS Hiring Program to save or create over 8,000 jobs in local law enforcement. In the coming weeks, we will announce a new round of COPS grants—totaling more than $110 million—to support the hiring of military veterans and school resource officers throughout the country.

In addition, through our landmark Defending Childhood Initiative and the National Forum on Youth Violence Prevention, we're rallying federal leaders, state officials, private organizations, and community groups to better understand, address, and prevent young people's exposure to violence. We have assembled a new Task Force to respond to the extreme levels of violence faced by far too many American Indian and Alaska Native children. Next month, we will launch a national public awareness campaign—and convene a Youth Violence Prevention Summit—to call for comprehensive solutions. And, through the Department's Civil Rights Division and other components, we'll continue to work with allies—like the Department of Education and others throughout the federal government and beyond—to confront the "school-to-prison pipeline" and those zero-tolerance school discipline policies that do not promote safety, and that transform too many educational institutions from doorways of opportunity into gateways to the criminal justice system. A minor school disciplinary offense should put a student in the principal's office and not a police precinct.

We'll also continue offering resources and support to survivors of sexual assault, domestic violence, and dating violence. Earlier this summer, I announced a new Justice Department initiative—known as Vision 21—which offers an unprecedented snapshot of the current state of victim services. It calls for sweeping, evidence-based changes to bring these services into the 21st century, and to empower all survivors by closing research gaps and developing new ways to reach those who need our assistance the most.

This work shows tremendous promise. I'm hopeful that it will help to bring assistance and healing to more and more crime victims across the country. But it is only the beginning.

More broadly, through the Department's Access to Justice Initiative, the Civil Rights Division, and a range of grant programs, this Administration is bringing stakeholders together—and providing direct support—to address the inequalities that unfold every day in America's courtrooms, and to fulfill the Supreme Court's historic decision in Gideon v. Wainwright. Fifty years ago last March, this landmark ruling affirmed that every defendant charged with a serious crime has the right to an attorney, even if he or she cannot afford one. Yet America's indigent defense systems continue to exist in a state of crisis, and the promise of Gideon is not being met. To address this crisis, Congress must not only end the forced budget cuts that have decimated public defenders nationwide—they must expand existing indigent defense programs, provide access to counsel for more juvenile defendants, and increase funding for federal public defender offices. And every legal professional, every member of this audience, must answer the ABA's call to contribute to this cause through pro bono service—and help realize the promise of equal justice for all.

As we come together this morning, this same promise must lead us all to acknowledge that—although incarceration has a significant role to play in our justice system—widespread incarceration at the federal, state, and local levels is both ineffective and unsustainable. It imposes a significant economic burden—totaling $80 billion in 2010 alone—and it comes with human and moral costs that are impossible to calculate.

As a nation, we are coldly efficient in our incarceration efforts. While the entire US population has increased by about a third since 1980, the federal prison population has grown at an astonishing rate—by almost 800 percent. It's still growing—despite the fact that federal prisons are operating at nearly 40 percent above capacity. Even though this country comprises just 5 percent of the world's population, we incarcerate almost a quarter of the world's prisoners. More than 219,000 federal inmates are currently behind bars. Almost half of them are serving time for drug-related crimes, and many have substance use disorders. Nine to 10 million more people cycle through America's local jails each year. And roughly 40 percent of former federal prisoners—and more than 60 percent of former state prisoners—are rearrested or have their supervision revoked within three years after their release, at great cost to American taxpayers and often for technical or minor violations of the terms of their release.

As a society, we pay much too high a price whenever our system fails to deliver outcomes that deter and punish crime, keep us safe, and ensure that those who have paid their debts have the chance to become productive citizens. Right now, unwarranted disparities are far too common. As President Obama said last month, it's time to ask tough questions about how we can strengthen our communities, support young people, and address the fact that young black and Latino men are disproportionately likely to become involved in our criminal justice system—as victims as well as perpetrators.

We also must confront the reality that—once they're in that system—people of color often face harsher punishments than their peers. One deeply troubling report, released in February, indicates that—in recent years—black male offenders have received sentences nearly 20 percent longer than those imposed on white males convicted of similar crimes. This isn't just unacceptable—it is shameful. It's unworthy of our great country, and our great legal tradition. And in response, I have today directed a group of US Attorneys to examine sentencing disparities, and to develop recommendations on how we can address them.

In this area and many others—in ways both large and small—we, as a country, must resolve to do better. The President and I agree that it's time to take a pragmatic approach. And that's why I am proud to announce today that the Justice Department will take a series of significant actions to recalibrate America's federal criminal justice system.

We will start by fundamentally rethinking the notion of mandatory minimum sentences for drug-related crimes. Some statutes that mandate inflexible sentences—regardless of the individual conduct at issue in a particular case—reduce the discretion available to prosecutors, judges, and juries. Because they oftentimes generate unfairly long sentences, they breed disrespect for the system. When applied indiscriminately, they do not serve public safety. They—and some of the enforcement priorities we have set—have had a destabilizing effect on particular communities, largely poor and of color. And, applied inappropriately, they are ultimately counterproductive.

This is why I have today mandated a modification of the Justice Department's charging policies so that certain low-level, nonviolent drug offenders who have no ties to large-scale organizations, gangs, or cartels will no longer be charged with offenses that impose draconian mandatory minimum sentences. They now will be charged with offenses for which the accompanying sentences are better suited to their individual conduct, rather than excessive prison terms more appropriate for violent criminals or drug kingpins. By reserving the most severe penalties for serious, high-level, or violent drug traffickers, we can

better promote public safety, deterrence, and rehabilitation—while making our expenditures smarter and more productive. We've seen that this approach has bipartisan support in Congress—where a number of leaders, including Senators Dick Durbin, Patrick Leahy, Mike Lee, and Rand Paul have introduced what I think is promising legislation aimed at giving federal judges more discretion in applying mandatory minimums to certain drug offenders. Such legislation will ultimately save our country billions of dollars while keeping us safe. And the President and I look forward to working with members of both parties to refine and advance these proposals.

Secondly, the Department has now updated its framework for considering compassionate release for inmates facing extraordinary or compelling circumstances—and who pose no threat to the public. In late April, the Bureau of Prisons expanded the criteria which will be considered for inmates seeking compassionate release for medical reasons. Today, I can announce additional expansions to our policy—including revised criteria for elderly inmates who did not commit violent crimes and who have served significant portions of their sentences. Of course, as our primary responsibility, we must ensure that the American public is protected from anyone who may pose a danger to the community. But considering the applications of nonviolent offenders—through a careful review process that ultimately allows judges to consider whether release is warranted—is the fair thing to do. And it is the smart thing to do as well, because it will enable us to use our limited resources to house those who pose the greatest threat.

Finally, my colleagues and I are taking steps to identify and share best practices for enhancing the use of diversion programs—such as drug treatment and community service initiatives—that can serve as effective alternatives to incarceration.

Our US Attorneys are leading the way in this regard—working alongside the judiciary to meet safety imperatives while avoiding incarceration in certain cases. In South Dakota, a joint federal-tribal program has helped to prevent at-risk young people from getting involved in the federal prison system—thereby improving lives, saving taxpayer resources, and keeping communities safer. This is exactly the kind of proven innovation that federal policymakers, and state and tribal leaders, should emulate. And it's why the Justice Department is working—through a program called the Justice Reinvestment Initiative—to bring state leaders, local stakeholders, private partners, and federal officials together to comprehensively reform corrections and criminal justice practices.

In recent years, no fewer than 17 states—supported by the Department, and led by governors and legislators of both parties—have directed funding away from prison construction and toward evidence-based programs and services, like treatment and supervision, that are designed to reduce recidivism.

In Kentucky, for example, new legislation has reserved prison beds for the most serious offenders and refocused resources on community supervision and evidence-based alternative programs. As a result, the state is projected to reduce its prison population by more than 3,000 over the next 10 years—saving more than $400 million.

In Texas, investments in drug treatment for nonviolent offenders and changes to parole policies brought about a reduction in the prison population of more than 5,000 inmates last year alone. The same year, similar efforts helped Arkansas reduce its prison population by more than 1,400. From Georgia, North Carolina, and Ohio, to Pennsylvania, Hawaii, and far beyond—reinvestment and serious reform are improving public safety and saving precious resources. Let me be clear: these measures have not compromised public safety. In fact, many states have seen drops in recidivism rates at the same time their prison populations were declining. The policy changes that have led to these welcome results must be studied and emulated. While our federal prison system has continued to slowly expand, significant state-level reductions have led to three consecutive years of decline in America's overall prison population—including, in 2012, the largest drop ever experienced in a single year.

Clearly, these strategies can work. They've attracted overwhelming, bipartisan support in "red states" as well as "blue states." And it's past time for others to take notice.

I am also announcing today that I have directed every US Attorney to designate a Prevention and Reentry Coordinator in his or her district—to ensure that this work is, and will remain, a top priority throughout the country. And my colleagues and I will keep working closely with state leaders, agency partners, including members of the Federal Interagency Reentry Council—and groups like the American Bar Association—to extend these efforts.

In recent years, with the Department's support, the ABA has catalogued tens of thousands of statutes and regulations that impose unwise and counterproductive collateral consequences—with regard to housing or employment, for example—on people who have been convicted of crimes. I have asked state attorneys general and a variety of federal leaders to review their own agencies' regulations. And today I can announce that I've directed all Department of Justice components, going forward, to consider whether any proposed regulation or guidance may impose unnecessary collateral consequences on those seeking to rejoin their communities.

The bottom line is that, while the aggressive enforcement of federal criminal statutes remains necessary, we cannot simply prosecute or incarcerate our way to becoming a safer nation. To be effective, federal efforts must also focus on prevention and reentry. We must never stop being tough on crime. But we must also be smart and efficient when battling crime and the conditions and the individual choices that breed it.

Ultimately, this is about much more than fairness for those who are released from prison. It's a matter of public safety and public good. It makes plain economic sense. It's about who we are as a people. And it has the potential to positively impact the lives of every man, woman, and child—in every neighborhood and city—in the United States. After all, whenever a recidivist crime is committed, innocent people are victimized. Communities are less safe. Burdens on law enforcement are increased. And already-strained resources are depleted even further.

Today—together—we must declare that we will no longer settle for such an unjust and unsustainable status quo. To do so would be to betray our history, our shared commitment to justice, and the founding principles of our nation. Instead, we must recommit ourselves—as a country—to tackling the most difficult questions, and the most costly problems, no matter how complex or intractable they may appear. We must pledge—as legal professionals—to lend our talents, our training, and our diverse perspectives to advancing this critical work. And we must resolve—as a people—to take a firm stand against violence; against victimization; against inequality—and for justice.

This is our chance—to bring America's criminal justice system in line with our most sacred values.

This is our opportunity—to define this time, our time, as one of progress and innovation.

This is our promise—to forge a more just society.

And this is our solemn obligation, as stewards of the law, and servants of those whom it protects and empowers: to open a frank and constructive dialogue about the need to reform a broken system. To fight for the sweeping, systemic changes we need. And to uphold our dearest values, as the ABA always has, by calling on our peers and colleagues not merely to serve their clients, or win their cases—but to ensure that—in every case, in every circumstance, and in every community—justice is done.

This, after all, is the cause that has been our common pursuit for more than two centuries, the ideal that has guided the ABA since its inception, and the goal that will drive additional actions by President Obama—and leaders throughout his Administration—in the months ahead. Of course, we recognize—as you do—that the reforms I've announced today, and others that we must consider, explore, and implement in the coming years, will not take hold overnight. There will be setbacks and false starts. We will encounter resistance and opposition.

But if we keep faith in one another, and in the principles we've always held dear; if we stay true to the ABA's history as a driver of positive change; and if we keep moving forward together—knowing that the need for this work will outlast us, but determined to make the difference that we seek—then I know we can all be confident in where these efforts will lead us. I look forward to everything that we will undoubtedly achieve. And I will always be proud to stand alongside you in building the brighter, more just, and more prosperous future that all of our citizens deserve.

Thank you.

Critical Thinking

1. Why is the US criminal justice system so punitive, resulting in so many people in prison?

2. Why are US gun laws so lax even most murders are by guns?

3. What changes in the criminal justice system are greatly needed?

Create Central

www.mhhe.com/createcentral

Internet References

ACLU Criminal Justice Home Page
www.aclu.org/crimjustice/index.html

New American Studies Web
www.georgetown.edu/crossroads/asw

Sociology—Study Sociology Online
http://edu.learnsoc.org

Sociology Web Resources
http://www.mhhe.com/socscience/sociology/resources/index.htm

Sociosite
http://www.topsite.com/goto/sociosite.net

Socioweb
http://www.topsite.com/goto/socioweb.com

Holder, Eric, "Bold Steps to Reform and Strengthen American's Criminal Justice System," *Vital Speeches of the Day,* vol. 79, 10, October 2013, pp. 308–312. Copyright © 2013 by Vital Speeches of the Day. All rights reserved. Used with permission.

Article　　　　　　　Prepared by: Kurt Finsterbusch, *University of Maryland, College Park*

This Man Was Sentenced to Die in Prison for Shoplifting a $159 Jacket: This Happens More Than You Think

Ed Pilkington

Learning Outcomes

After reading this article, you will be able to:

- Understand the U.S. criminal justice system and how it works.

- Analyze the thesis that the U.S. criminal justice system is too punitive.

- Understand why crazy laws are not removed.

At about 12.40 P.M. on 2 January 1996, Timothy Jackson took a jacket from the Maison Blanche department store in New Orleans, draped it over his arm, and walked out of the store without paying for it. When he was accosted by a security guard, Jackson said: "I just needed another jacket, man."

A few months later Jackson was convicted of shoplifting and sent to Angola prison in Louisiana. That was 16 years ago. Today he is still incarcerated in Angola, and will stay there for the rest of his natural life having been condemned to die in jail. All for the theft of a jacket, worth $159.

Jackson, 53, is one of 3,281 prisoners in America serving life sentences with no chance of parole for nonviolent crimes. Some, like him, were given the most extreme punishment short of execution for shoplifting; one was condemned to die in prison for siphoning petrol from a truck; another for stealing tools from a tool shed and yet another for attempting to cash a stolen cheque.

"It has been very hard for me," Jackson wrote to the American Civil Liberties Union (ACLU) as part of its new report on life without parole for nonviolent offenders. "I know that for my crime I had to do some time, but a life sentence for a jacket value at $159. I have met people here whose crimes are a lot badder with way less time."

Senior officials at Angola prison refused to allow the *Guardian* to speak to Jackson, on grounds that it might upset his victims—even though his crime was victimless. But his sister Loretta Lumar did speak to the *Guardian*. She said that the last time she talked by phone with her brother he had expressed despair. "He told me, 'Sister, this has really broke my back. I'm ready to come out.'"

Lumar said that she found her brother's sentence incomprehensible. "This doesn't make sense to me. I know people who have killed people, and they get a lesser sentence. That doesn't make sense to me right there. You can take a life and get 15 or 16 years. He takes a jacket worth $159 and will stay in jail forever. He didn't kill the jacket!"

The ACLU's report, *A Living Death,* chronicles the thousands of lives ruined and families destroyed by the modern phenomenon of sentencing people to die behind bars for nonviolent offences. It notes that contrary to the expectation that such a harsh penalty would be meted out only to the most serious offenders, people have been caught in this brutal trap for sometimes the most petty causes.

Ronald Washington, 48, is also serving life without parole in Angola, in his case for shoplifting two Michael Jordan jerseys from a Foot Action sportswear store in Shreveport, Louisiana, in 2004. Washington insisted at trial that the jerseys were reduced in a sale to $45 each—which meant that their combined value was below the $100 needed to classify the theft as a felony; the prosecution disagreed, claiming they were on sale for $60 each, thus surpassing the $100 felony minimum and opening him up to a sentence of life without parole.

"I felt as though somebody had just taken the life out of my body," Washington wrote to the ACLU about the moment he learnt his fate. "I seriously felt rejected, neglected, stabbed right through my heart."

He added: "It's a very lonely world, seems that nobody cares. You're never ever returning back into society. And whatever you had or established, its now useless, because you're being buried alive at slow pace."

Louisiana, where both Washington and Jackson are held, is one of nine states where prisoners are serving life without parole sentences for nonviolent offences (other states with high numbers are Alabama, Florida, Mississippi, Oklahoma, and South Carolina). An overwhelming proportion of those sentences—as many as 98 percent in Louisiana—were mandatory: in other words judges had no discretion but to impose the swingeing penalties.

The warden of Angola prison, Burl Cain, has spoken out in forthright terms against a system that mandates punishment without any chance of rehabilitation. He told the ACLU: "It's ridiculous, because the name of our business is 'corrections'—to correct deviant behaviour. If I'm a successful warden and I do my job and we correct the deviant behaviour, then we should have a parole hearing. I need to keep predators in these big old prisons, not dying old men."

The toll is not confined to the state level: most of those nonviolent inmates held on life without parole sentences were given their punishments by the federal government. More than 2,000 of the 3,281 individuals tracked down on these sentences by the ACLU are being held in the federal system. Overall, the ACLU has calculated that taxpayers pay an additional $1.8 billion to keep the prisoners locked up for the rest of their lives.

"It Doesn't Have to Be This Way"

Until the early 1970s, life without parole sentences were virtually unknown. But they exploded as part of what the ACLU calls America's "late-twentieth-century obsession with mass incarceration and extreme, inhumane penalties."

The report's author Jennifer Turner states that today, the United States is "virtually alone in its willingness to sentence nonviolent offenders to die behind bars." Life without parole for non-violent sentences has been ruled a violation of human rights by the European Court of Human Rights. The UK is one

of only two countries in Europe that still metes out the penalty at all, and even then only in 49 cases of murder.

Even within America's starkly racially charged penal system, the disparities in nonviolent life without parole are stunning. About 65 percent of the prisoners identified nationwide by the ACLU are African American. In Louisiana, that proportion rises to 91 percent, including Jackson and Washington, who are both black.

The United States has the highest incarceration rate in the world, with 2.3 million people now in custody, with the war on drugs acting as the overriding push-factor. Of the prisoners serving life without parole for nonviolent offences nationwide, the ACLU estimates that almost 80 percent were for drug-related crimes.

Again, the offences involved can be startlingly petty. Drug cases itemised in the report include a man sentenced to die in prison for having been found in possession of a crack pipe; an offender with a bottle cap that contained a trace of heroin that was too small to measure; a prisoner arrested with a trace amount of cocaine in their pocket too tiny to see with the naked eye; a man who acted as a go-between in a sale to an undercover police officer of marijuana—street value $10.

Drugs are present in the background of Timothy Jackson's case too. He was high when he went to the Maison Blanche store, and he says that as a result he shoplifted "without thinking." Paradoxically, like many of the other prisoners on similar penalties, the first time he was offered drug treatment was after he had already been condemned to spend the rest of his life in jail.

The theft of the $159 jacket, taken in isolation, carries today a six-month jail term. It was combined at Jackson's sentencing hearing with his previous convictions—all for nonviolent crimes including a robbery in which he took $216—that brought him under Louisiana's brutal "four-strikes" law by which it became mandatory for him to be locked up and the key thrown away.

The ACLU concludes that it does not have to be this way—suitable alternatives are readily at hand, including shorter prison terms and the provision of drug treatment and mental health services. The organisation calls on Congress, the Obama administration and state legislatures to end the imposition of mandatory life without parole for nonviolent offenders and to require resentencing hearings for all those already caught in this judicial black hole.

A few months after Timothy Jackson was put away for life, a Louisiana appeals court reviewed the case and found it "excessive," "inappropriate," and "a prime example of an unjust result." Describing Jackson as a "petty thief," the court threw out the sentence.

The following year, in 1998, the state's supreme court gave a final ruling. "This sentence is constitutionally excessive in that it is grossly out of proportion to the seriousness of the offence," concluded Judge Bernette Johnson. However, she found that the state's four strikes law that mandates life without parole could only be overturned in rare instances, and as a result she reinstated the sentence—putting Jackson back inside his cell until the day he dies.

"I am much older and I have learned a lot about myself," Jackson wrote to the ACLU from that cell. "I am sorry for the crime that I did, and I am a changed man."

Jackson expressed a hope that he would be granted his freedom when he was still young enough to make something of his life and "help others." But, barring a reform of the law, the day of his release will never come.

Critical Thinking

1. Laws and law enforcement are supposed to establish justice. In reality it establishes both justice and injustice. Why?

2. It seems that the most poignant cases of the miscarriage of justice applies to poor people. Why?

3. Pilkington argues against overpunishment. Discuss cases of underpunishment and explain the differences.

Create Central

www.mhhe.com/createcentral

Internet References

ACLU Criminal Justice Home Page
www.aclu.org/crimjustice/index.html

Human Rights and Humanitarian Assistance
www.etown.edu/vl/humrts.html

New American Studies Web
www.georgetown.edu/crossroads/asw

Sociology—Study Sociology Online
http://edu.learnsoc.org

Sociology Web Resources
http://www.mhhe.com/socscience/sociology/resources/index.htm

Sociosite
http://www.topsite.com/goto/sociosite.net

Socioweb
http://www.topsite.com/goto/socioweb.com

Pilkington, Ed, "Over 3,000 US prisoners serving life without parole for non-violent crimes," theguardian.com, November 13, 2013. Copyright Guardian News & Media Ltd 2013.

Article   Prepared by: Kurt Finsterbusch, *University of Maryland, College Park*

Crime, Inequality, & Social Justice

GLENN C. LOURY

Learning Outcomes

After reading this article, you will be able to:

- Understand the law enforcement policies that are most heavily relied upon today.

- Describe how crime affects society and estimate its full costs.

- Understand the many ways that the criminal justice system treats blacks and whites differently.

C rime and punishment are certainly contentious topics, and the authors gathered in this issue do not always agree with one another. For my own part, I must confess to having a personal stake in this issue. As an African American male, a baby boomer born and raised on Chicago's South Side, I can identify with the plight of the urban poor because I have lived among them. I am tied to them by the bonds of social and psychic affiliation. I myself have passed through the courtroom and the jailhouse on my way along life's journey. I have twice been robbed at gunpoint. I have known—personally and intimately—men and women who lived their entire lives with one foot on either side of the law. Whenever I step to a lectern to speak about incarceration, I envision voiceless and despairing people—both offenders and victims—who would have me speak on their behalf. Of course, personal biography has no authority to compel agreement about public policy. Still, I prefer candor in such matters to a false pretense of clinical detachment and scientific objectivity. While I recognize that these revelations will discredit me in some quarters, that is a fate which I can live with. Allow me to share a few critical observations of my own about crime, inequality, and social justice.

One principal point of disagreement among contributors to this volume has to do with how the fact of mass incarceration relates to the social problem of crime. Mark Kleiman claims

that mass incarceration is only a partial problem definition; the other part of the problem is crime. This stance is in sharp contrast to that of Loïc Wacquant, who insists that "hyperincarceration" (his preferred term, since only those living in the lower social strata face much risk of imprisonment) isn't really about crime at all. Rather, he says, it's about "managing dispossessed and dishonored populations." There is merit in both viewpoints. There can be no doubt that public ideas about crime—especially fears of violent victimization—have fueled the imprisonment boom. To speak of a crisis of mass imprisonment without reference to crime is, indeed, to address only one part of the problem. After all, declarations of "war" against crime (and, most noticeably, against *criminals*) are a primary means by which political aspirants now signal their bona fides to their electorates. The long upward trend in crime rates from the mid-1960s to the early 1980s "primed the penal pump" by hardening attitudes and discrediting liberal criminal justice policies. It is certainly the case, therefore, that the steep rise of imprisonment in the United States is closely intertwined with the social experience and political salience of crime in American life. We cannot understand the one without thinking carefully about the other. Nor can we persuade voters to undo the one without addressing their concerns about the other.

Yet evidence suggests that changes over time in the scale of incarceration have not been caused in any direct way by changes in the extent of criminal behavior. Indeed, linkages between prisons and crime have been anything but simple and direct. Prison populations have been on the rise steadily for more than three decades. However, crime rates increased in the 1970s; fell, then rose again in the 1980s; and increased before sharply decreasing again in the 1990s. For two generations, crime rates have fluctuated with no apparent relationship to a steady climb in the extent of imprisonment. Today, with prison populations as large as they have ever been in American history, crime rates are about the same as they were in 1970, when a then-falling United States prison population reached its lowest level in a generation.

Prisons and crime cannot be rightly understood simply as opposite sides of the same coin. Incarceration does not exhaust the available means of crime control. Nor does criminal offending directly explain the profound *qualitative* institutional transformation that we have witnessed in the United States over the past two generations.[1]

Furthermore, the trend of racial disparity in imprisonment rates cannot be accounted for as a consequence of changes in rates of offending over time. Crime rates, especially for violent offenses, have always been higher among African Americans than whites in the United States. This long-term disparity goes far toward explaining the historical fact of greater imprisonment for African Americans. Certainly there is little doubt that those who commit violent crimes should be punished, regardless of race. If more African Americans commit such offenses, more will be imprisoned, and no issues of impropriety would be raised thereby. Yet it is significant that the racial disparity of imprisonment rates has increased dramatically since the prison boom began, largely because of the "war on drugs." African Americans were vastly overrepresented among persons incarcerated for drug offenses during the 1980s and 1990s, even as African Americans were no more likely to be using or selling drugs than whites. Moreover, despite a sharp drop in violent crime rates, starting in the early 1990s and extending to the present, racial differences in imprisonment rates have begun a slight decline only in the last few years.

As for the links between imprisonment and public safety, the widely held notion that one prevents crime by incapacitating criminals is simplistic. It fails to take account of the fact that for many crimes—selling drugs, for instance—incapacitated criminals are simply replaced by others, there being no shortage of contenders vying for a chance to enter the illicit trade. (It also ignores the reality of criminal victimization within prisons—no small matter.) Furthermore, by adopting a more holistic view of the complex connections between prisons and communities, we can immediately recognize the significance of the fact that almost everyone who goes to prison is eventually released, most after just two or three years. Evidence suggests that for these hundreds of thousands of exoffenders released each year, time behind bars will have *diminished,* not enhanced, their odds of living crime-free lives: by lowering employability, severing ties to communal supports, and hardening attitudes.

Thus, the impact of high incarceration rates on the sustainable level of public safety over the long term is ambiguous. The fact—amply demonstrated for the case of Chicago by Robert Sampson and Charles Loeffler in this volume—that incarceration in large American cities is so highly concentrated means that the ill effects of having spent time behind bars may diminish the social opportunities of others who reside in the most heavily impacted communities and who themselves have done nothing wrong.

Spatial concentration of imprisonment may foster criminality because it undermines the informal social processes of order maintenance, which are the primary means of sustaining prosocial behavior in all communities. In some poor urban neighborhoods, as many as one in five adult men is behind bars on any given day. As the criminologist Todd Clear has written, "[T]he cycling of these young men through the prison system has become a central factor determining the social ecology of poor neighborhoods, where there is hardly a family without a son, an uncle or a father who has done time in prison."[2] This ubiquity of the prison experience in poor, minority urban neighborhoods has left families in these places less effective at inculcating in their children the kinds of delinquency-resistant self controls and prosocial attitudes that typically insulate youths against law-breaking. As Clear concludes from his review of the evidence, "[D]eficits in informal social controls that result from high levels of incarceration are, in fact, crime-promoting. The high incarceration rates in poor communities destabilize the social relationships in these places and help cause crime rather than prevent it."

The relationship between prison and public safety is complicated in view of the fact that "what happens in San Quentin need not stay in San Quentin." Nor does the evidence afford us much comfort in the thought that, at the very least, a threat of imprisonment will deter future would-be offenders from breaking the law. Among children exposed to an incarcerated parent or sibling—youngsters who can be assumed to have firsthand knowledge of the penalties associated with law-breaking—the likelihood of their eventual incarceration is actually higher, not lower, than is the case for otherwise comparable children with no such exposure, which attests to the weakness of the deterrent effect of the sanction. Furthermore, in a careful review of the econometric evidence on this question, economist Steven Durlauf and public policy expert Daniel Nagin conclude:

> The key empirical conclusion of our literature review is that there is relatively little reliable evidence for variation in the severity of punishment having a substantial deterrent effect, but there is relatively strong evidence that variation in the certainty of punishment has a large deterrent effect. . . . One policy-relevant implication of this conclusion is that lengthy prison sentences, particularly in the form of mandatory minimum type statutes such as California's Three Strikes Law, are difficult to justify on a deterrence-based crime prevention basis.[3]

Disparities by social class in this punishment binge are enormous, and they have far-reaching and often deleterious consequences for the families and communities affected. The prisoners come mainly from the most disadvantaged corners of our unequal society; the prisons both reflect and exacerbate this inequality. The factors that lead young people to crime—the "root causes"—have long been known: disorganized childhoods, inadequate educations, child abuse, limited employability, delinquent peers. These are factors that also have long been more prevalent among the poor than the middle classes, though it has for some time been unfashionable to speak of "root causes." Nevertheless, as Bruce Western stresses in his comprehensive empirical survey of this terrain, "punishment" and "inequality" are intimately linked in modern America, and the causality runs in both directions.[4]

Racial disparities in the incidence of incarceration are also huge. The subordinate status of African American ghetto-dwellers—their social deprivation and spatial isolation in America's cities—puts their residents at great risk of embracing the dysfunctional behaviors that lead to incarceration. Also, it is quite clear that punishment policies serve expressive, not merely instrumental, ends. Americans have wanted to "send a message," and have done so with a vengeance. In the midst of such dramaturgy—necessarily so in America—has lurked a potent racial subplot. Inequalities by race in the realm of punishment exceed those found in just about any other arena of American social life: at roughly seven to one, the black-white ratio of male incarceration rates dwarfs the two to one ratio of unemployment rates, the three to one nonmarital child-bearing ratio, the two to one black-white ratio of infant mortality rates, and the one to five ratio of net worth. (The homicide rate is a noteworthy exception to this generalization about racial disproportions. For 20 to 29-year-old males, the black-white ratio has been in the neighborhood of 10 to 1 in recent years.) It is of some political significance that, for young African American men, coercion is the most salient feature of their encounters with the American state. In this issue, Bruce Western and Becky Pettit report that more African American male high school dropouts are held in prisons than belong to unions or are enrolled in any (other) state or federal social welfare programs. They estimate that nearly 70 percent of African American male dropouts born between 1975 and 1979 will have spent at least one year in prison before reaching the age of 35.

Given the scale of imprisonment for African American men, and the troubled history of race relations in this country, it can be no surprise that some observers see the advent of mass incarceration as the catalyst for a new front in the long, historic, and still incomplete struggle for racial justice.[5] Because history and political culture matter, considering the factor of race is crucial to a full understanding and evaluation of our current policy regime. It is true that slavery ended a long time ago. But it is also true that an ideology of racial subordination accompanied the institution of African slavery, and this racial ideology

has cast a long shadow. Thus, in his recently published history of the entanglement of race with crime in American political culture at the turn of the twentieth century,[6] historian Khalil Muhammad contrasts the treatment of two related, but differently experienced, phenomena: crime by newly arrived European immigrants and crime by African Americans. Looking at the emergent statistical social-science literatures of that period, Muhammad makes clear that the prevailing ideological climate in the United States at that time led analysts and critics to construe the many problems of urbanizing and industrializing America in distinct ways. In essence, poor, white city-dwelling migrants were understood to be committing crimes, but the poor African Americans migrating to those same cities were seen as inherently criminal.

Our unlovely history of race relations is linked to the current situation, both as a matter of social causation—since the structure of our cities, with their massive racial ghettos, is implicated in the production of deviancy among those living there—and as a matter of ethical evaluation—since the decency of our institutions depends on whether they comport with a narrative of national purpose that recognizes and seeks to limit and to reverse the consequences of history's wrongs. It is certainly arguable (take Loïc Wacquant's essay in this volume, for example) that managing social dysfunction via imprisonment has now become the primary instrument for reproducing racial stratification in American society.

What does all this tell us about our purportedly open and democratic society? What manner of people do our punishment policies reveal us Americans to be? Just look at what we have wrought. We have established what, to many an outside observer, looks like a system of social caste in the centers of our great cities. I refer here to millions of stigmatized, feared, and invisible people. The extent of disparity between the children of the middle class and the children of the disadvantaged to achieve their full human potential is virtually unrivaled elsewhere in the industrial, advanced, civilized, and free world. And it is a disparity that is apparently taken for granted in America.

I see the broader society as implicated in the creation and maintenance of these damaged, neglected, feared, and despised communities. People who live in these places know that outsiders view them with suspicion and contempt. The plain historical fact is that North Philadelphia, the West Side of Chicago, the East Side of Detroit, or South Central Los Angeles did not come into being by accident or because of some natural processes. As Wacquant emphasizes in this issue, these social formations are man-made structures that were created and have persisted because the concentration of their residents in such urban enclaves serves the interests of others. The desperate and vile behaviors of some of the people caught in these social structures reflect not merely their personal moral deviance, but also the moral shortcomings of our society as a whole. Yet many Americans have concluded, in effect, that those languishing at the margins of our society are simply reaping what they have sown. Their suffering is seen as having nothing to do with us—as not being evidence of broader, systemic failures that can be corrected through collective action. As a consequence, there is no broadly based demand for reform—no sense of moral outrage, anguished self-criticism, or public reflection—in the face of what is a massive, collective failure. American political culture, it seems, accepts as credible no account of personal malfeasance other than the conclusion that the offending individual is unworthy.

The legal scholar William Stuntz has recently called attention to the close connection in American history between local control, democratic governance, and inequalities of punishment.[7] He suggests, persuasively in my view, that increases in the severity and inequality of American punishment have mainly been due to a shift over the course of the twentieth century in the ways that crime and punishment policies are formulated. Because caseloads have grown alongside reliance on plea bargaining, prosecutors have gained power at the expense of juries; because a thicket of constitutional protections has been elaborated, federal appellate judges exert more influence than trial judges; because of population decentralization trends in large urban areas—with judges now elected mostly on county-wide ballots and police no longer drawn preponderantly from the communities where they make arrests—suburban and exurban voters now have a good deal more to say than do central-city residents about crime control policies, even though they are less affected by those policies.

The law, Stuntz argues, has grown more extensive in its definition of criminality and has left less room for situational discretion. Alienation of urban populations from democratic control over the apparatus of punishment has resulted in more inequality and less leniency. There is too much law and too little (local) politics. Local populations bear the brunt of the misbehavior by the lawbreakers in their midst. Yet, at the same time, they are closely connected to lawbreakers via bonds of social and psychic affiliation. Mass incarceration is a political not a legal crisis, one that arises from a disjunction between the "locus of control" and the "locus of interests" in the formulation of punishment policies.

Following Stuntz, I wish to suggest that punishment, rightly construed, is a communal affair; and that an ambiguity of relationship—involving proximity to both sides of the offender-victim divide and a wealth of local knowledge combined with keen local interests—is essential to doing justice. Viewed in this light, hyperincarceration and the (racial) inequalities that it has bred are more deeply disturbing because urban minority communities, where both the depredations of crime and the enormous costs of its unequal punishment are experienced, have effectively been divorced from any means of influencing the administration of criminal justice.

To the extent that the socially marginal are not seen as belonging to the same general public body as the rest of us, it becomes possible to do just about anything with them. Yet, in my view, a pure ethic of *personal responsibility* could never provide an adequate foundation for justifying the current situation. In making this claim, I am not invoking a "root causes" argument (he did the crime, but only because he had no choice) so much as I am arguing that society as a whole is implicated in the offender's choices. We have acquiesced in structural arrangements that work to our benefit and the offender's detriment and that shape his consciousness and sense of identity such that his choices, which we must condemn, are nevertheless compelling to him.

In his influential treatise, *A Theory of Justice,* the philosopher John Rawls distinguishes between principles that should govern the distribution of primary goods in society and the very different principles that should determine the distribution of the "negative good" of punishment. He explicitly states that justice in the distribution of economic and social advantages is "entirely different" from justice in the realm of criminal punishment. He even refers to "bad character" as relevant to punishment.[8] As I understand Rawls, his famous "difference principle"—arrived at in "reflective equilibrium" from his hypothetical "original position"—presupposes the moral irrelevance of the mechanisms by which inequalities emerge. (For example, Rawls sees "ability" as a morally irrelevant trait, a manifestation of luck. So, unequal individual rewards based on differences in ability cannot be justified on the grounds of desert.) Yet because he does not see the mechanisms that lead to disparities of punishment as being morally irrelevant, he would not apply the difference principle when assessing the (in)justice of such inequalities, since they are linked to wrongdoing.

In my view, justice is complex because the consequences wrought by our responses to wrongdoing also raise questions of justice. The phrase "Let justice be done though the heavens may fall" is, for me, an oxymoron; no concept of justice deserving the name would accept mass suffering simply because of blind adherence to an abstract principle (such as "do the crime, and you'll do the time"). It is common for ethicists to say things such as "social welfare should be maximized subject to deontological constraints," meaning that actions like distributing body parts taken from a healthy person to render 10 other persons healthy cannot be morally justified. But this conviction should go both ways: abstract moral goals should be subjected to constraints that weigh the consequences induced by such pursuits.

In the realm of punishment, retribution against offenders and notions of deserved punishment exemplify deontological principles. But even if current incarceration policies perfectly embodied these principles (and that is an eminently dubious proposition), it still would not be sufficient to justify such rigid adherence to moral obligation. For the reason that the effects of mass incarceration—on families and communities that may themselves have done nothing wrong—can cause sufficient harm, the principled claims that punishment is deserved should not be allowed to dictate policy at whim. A million criminal cases, each one rightly decided, can still add up to a great and historic wrong.

Notes

1. For an illuminating exploration of the deeper roots of this transformation, see David Garland, *The Culture of Control: Crime and Social Order in Contemporary Society* (Chicago: University of Chicago Press, 2001).

2. Todd R. Clear, *Imprisoning Communities: How Mass Incarceration Makes Disadvantaged Neighborhoods Worse* (New York: Oxford University Press, 2009), 10.

3. Steven Durlauf and Daniel Nagin, "The Deterrent Effect of Imprisonment," unpublished working paper (University of Wisconsin-Madison, March 2010).

4. Bruce Western, *Punishment and Inequality in America* (New York: Russell Sage Foundation, 2006).

5. See Michelle Alexander, *The New Jim Crow: Mass Incarceration in the Age of Colorblindness* (New York: New Press, 2010).

6. Khalil Gibran Muhammad, *The Condemnation of Blackness: Race, Crime, and the Making of Modern Urban America* (Cambridge, MA: Harvard University Press, 2010).

7. William Stuntz, "Unequal Justice," *Harvard Law Review* 121 (8) (June 2008): 1969–2040.

8. The full quote from Rawls is: "It is true that in a reasonably well-ordered society those who are punished for violating just laws have normally done something wrong. This is because the purpose of the criminal law is to uphold basic natural duties, those which forbid us to injure other persons in their life and limb, or to deprive them of their liberty and property, and punishments are to serve this end. They are not simply a scheme of taxes and burdens designed to put a price on certain forms of conduct and in this way to guide men's conduct for mutual advantage. It would be far better if the acts proscribed by penal statutes were never done. Thus a propensity to commit such acts is a mark of bad character, and in a just society legal punishments will only fall upon those who display these faults"; John Rawls, *A Theory of Justice,* rev. ed. (1971; Cambridge, MA: Belknap Press of Harvard University Press, 1999), 314–315.

Critical Thinking

1. What do you think are the best criminal justice policies and why?
2. What kinds of crimes are the most costly and why?
3. Why are imprison rates so high?

Create Central

www.mhhe.com/createcentral

Internet References

ACLU Criminal Justice Home Page
www.aclu.org/crimjustice/index.html

Human Rights and Humanitarian Assistance
www.etown.edu/vl/humrts.html

New American Studies Web
www.georgetown.edu/crossroads/asw

Sociology—Study Sociology Online
http://edu.learnsoc.org

Sociology Web Resources
http://www.mhhe.com/socscience/sociology/resources/index.htm

Sociosite
http://www.topsite.com/goto/sociosite.net

Socioweb
http://www.topsite.com/goto/socioweb.com

From *Daedalus,* Summer 2010, pp. 134–140. Copyright © 2010 by MIT Press Journals/American Academy of Arts and Sciences. Reprinted by permission via Rightslink.

Article   Prepared by: Kurt Finsterbusch, *University of Maryland, College Park*

Wrongful Convictions

RADLEY BALKO

Learning Outcomes

After reading this article, you will be able to:

- Describe specific cases of wrongful convictions and understand some of the inexcusable actions by authorities that lead to these wrongful convictions.

- Understand the very large gap between proven wrongful convictions and the actual number of wrongful convictions.

- Understand the main reasons for wrongful convictions.

How many innocent Americans are behind bars? When Paul House was finally released from prison in 2008, he was a specter of the man who had been sentenced to death more than 22 years earlier. When I visit his home in Crossville, Tennessee, in March, House's mother Joyce, who has cared for him since his release, points to a photo of House taken the day he was finally allowed to come home. In that photo and others from his last days in prison, House is all of 150 pounds, ashen and drawn, his fragile frame nearly consumed by his wheelchair. In most of the images he looks days away from death, although in one he wears the broad smile of a man finally escaping a long confinement.

When House's aunt called to congratulate him on his first day back, his mother handed him her cell phone so he could chat. He inspected the phone, gave her a frustrated look, and asked her to find him one that worked. That kind of Rip Van Winkle moment is common among people freed after a long stint in prison. Dennis Fritz, one of the two wrongly convicted men profiled in John Grisham's 2006 book *The Innocent Man,* talks about nearly calling the police upon seeing someone use an electronic key card the first time he found himself in a hotel after his release. He thought he'd witnessed a burglar use a credit card to jimmy open a door.

"Paul's first meal when he got home was chili verde," Joyce House says. "It's his favorite. And I had been waiting a long time to make it for him." And apparently quite a few meals after that. House, now 49, has put on 75 pounds since his release. More important, he has been getting proper treatment for his advanced-stage multiple sclerosis, treatment the Tennessee prison system hadn't given him.

The years of inadequate care have taken a toll. House can't walk, and he needs help with such basic tasks as bathing, feeding himself, and maneuvering around in his wheelchair. His once distinctively deep voice (which had allegedly been heard by a witness at the crime scene) is now wispy and high-pitched. He spends his time playing computer games and watching game shows.

In the hour or so that I visit with House, his mental facilities fade in and out. Communicating with him can be like trying to listen to a baseball game broadcast by a distant radio station. He will give a slurred but lucid answer to one question, then answer the next one with silence, or with the answer to a previous question, or just with a random assortment of words. He frequently falls back on the resigned refrain, "Oh, well," delivered with a shrug. The gesture and phrasing are identical every time he uses them. It's what House says to kill the expectation that he will be able to deliver the words others in the room are waiting for. It's his signal to stop waiting for him and move on.

In 1986 House was convicted of murdering Carolyn Muncey in Union County, Tennessee, a rural part of the state that shoulders Appalachia. He was sentenced to death. His case is a textbook study in wrongful conviction. It includes mishandled evidence, prosecutorial misconduct, bad science, cops with tunnel vision, DNA testing, the near-execution of an innocent man, and an appellate court reluctant to reopen old cases even in the face of new evidence that strongly suggests the jury got it wrong.

House also embodies the tribulations and frustrations that the wrongly convicted encounter once they get out. According to the doctors treating him, his current condition is the direct result of the inadequate care he received in prison. If he is ever granted a formal exoneration—a process that can be as much political as it is judicial—he will be eligible for compensation for his years behind bars, but even then the money comes with vexing conditions and limitations.

Since 1989, DNA testing has freed 268 people who were convicted of crimes they did not commit. There are dozens of other cases, like House's, where DNA strongly suggests innocence but does not conclusively prove it. Convicting and imprisoning an innocent person is arguably the worst thing a government can do to one of its citizens, short of mistakenly executing him. (There's increasing evidence that this has happened too.) Just about everyone agrees that these are unfathomable tragedies. What is far less clear, and still hotly debated, is what these cases say about the way we administer justice in America, what we owe the wrongly convicted, and how the officials who send innocent people to prison should be held accountable.

How Many Are Innocent?

According to the Innocence Project, an advocacy group that provides legal aid to the wrongly convicted, the average DNA exoneree served 13 years in prison before he or she was freed. Seventeen had been sentenced to death. Remarkably, 67 percent of the exonerated were convicted after 2000, the year that marked the onset of modern DNA testing. Each new exoneration adds more urgency to the question that has hovered over these cases since the first convict was cleared by DNA in 1989: How many more innocent people are waiting to be freed?

Given the soundness of DNA testing, we can be nearly certain that the 268 cleared so far didn't commit the crimes for which they were convicted. There are hundreds of other cases where no DNA evidence exists to definitively establish guilt or innocence, but a prisoner has been freed due to lack of evidence, recantation of eyewitness testimony, or police or prosecutorial misconduct. Those convictions were overturned because there was insufficient evidence to overcome reasonable doubt; it does not necessarily mean the defendant didn't commit the crime. It's unclear whether and how those cases should be factored into any attempt to estimate the number of innocent people in prison.

In a country where there are 15,000 to 20,000 homicides each year, 268 exonerations over two decades may seem like an acceptable margin of error. But reform advocates point out that DNA testing is conclusive only in a small percentage of criminal cases. Testing is helpful only in solving crimes where exchange of DNA is common and significant, mostly rape

and murder. (And most murder exonerations have come about because the murder was preceded by a rape that produced testable DNA.) Even within this subset of cases, DNA evidence is not always preserved, nor is it always dispositive to the identity of the perpetrator.

Death penalty cases add urgency to this debate. In a 2007 study published in the *Journal of Criminal Law and Criminology*, the Seton Hall law professor Michael Risinger looked at cases of exoneration for capital murder-rapes between 1982 and 1989, compared them to the total number of murder-rape cases over that period for which DNA would be a factor, and estimated from that data that 3 percent to 5 percent of the people convicted of capital crimes probably are innocent. If Risinger is right, it's still unclear how to extrapolate figures for the larger prison population. Some criminologists argue that there is more pressure on prosecutors and jurors to convict someone, anyone, in high-profile murder cases. That would suggest a higher wrongful conviction rate in death penalty cases. But defendants also tend to have better representation in capital cases, and media interest can also mean more scrutiny for police and prosecutors. That could lead to fewer wrongful convictions.

In a study published in the *Journal of Criminal Law and Criminology* in 2005, a team led by University of Michigan law professor Samuel Gross looked at 328 exonerations of people who had been convicted of rape, murder, and other felonies between 1989 and 2003. They found that while those who have been condemned to die make up just 1 percent of the prison population, they account for 22 percent of the exonerated. But does that mean capital cases are more likely to bring a wrongful conviction? Or does it mean the attention and scrutiny that death penalty cases get after conviction—particularly as an execution date nears—make it more likely that wrongful convictions in capital cases will be discovered?

Many states have special public defender offices that take over death penalty cases after a defendant has exhausted his appeals. These offices tend to be well staffed, with enough funding to hire their own investigators and forensic specialists. That sometimes stands in stark contrast to the public defender offices that handled the same cases at trial. Perversely, this means that in some jurisdictions, a defendant wrongly convicted of murder may be better off with a death sentence than with life in prison.

Even if we were to drop below the floor set in the Risinger study and assume that 2 percent of the 2008 prison population was innocent, that would still mean about 46,000 people have been convicted and incarcerated for crimes they didn't commit. But some skeptics say even that figure is way too high.

Joshua Marquis, the district attorney for Clatsop County, Oregon, is an outspoken critic of the Innocence Project and of academics like Risinger and Gross. He is skeptical of the belief that wrongful convictions are common. "If I thought that 3 to 5 percent of people in prison right now were innocent, I'd quit my job," Marquis says. "I'd become a public defender or something. Maybe an activist. Look, nobody but a fool would say that wrongful convictions don't happen. As a prosecutor, my worst nightmare is not losing a case—I've lost cases; I'll lose cases in the future. My worst nightmare is convicting an innocent person, and I tell my staff that. But the question here is whether wrongful convictions are epidemic or episodic. And I just don't think it's possible that the number could be anywhere near 3 to 5 percent."

Marquis and Gross have been butting heads for several years. In a 2006 *New York Times* op-ed piece, Marquis took the 328 exonerations Gross and his colleagues found between 1989 and 2003, rounded it up to 340, then multiplied it by 10—a charitable act, he wrote, to "give the professor the benefit of the doubt." He then divided that number by 15 million, the total number of felony convictions during the same period, and came up with what he said was an error rate of just 0.027 percent. His column was later quoted in a concurring opinion by U.S. Supreme Court Justice Antonin Scalia in the 2006 case *Kansas v. Marsh,* the same opinion where Scalia made the notorious claim that nothing in the U.S. Constitution prevents the government from executing an innocent person.

Gross responded with a 2008 article in the *Annual Review of Law and Social Science,* pointing out that his original number was by no means comprehensive. Those were merely the cases in which a judicial or political process had exonerated someone. The figure suggested only that wrongful convictions happen. "By [Marquis'] logic we could estimate the proportion of baseball players who've used steroids by dividing the number of major league players who've been caught by the total of all baseball players at all levels: major league, minor league, semipro, college and Little League," Gross wrote, "and maybe throw in football and basketball players as well."

Whatever the total number of innocent convicts, there is good reason to believe that the 268 cases in which DNA evidence has proven innocence don't begin to scratch the surface. For one thing, the pace of these exonerations hasn't slowed down: There were 22 in 2009, making it the second busiest name-clearing year to date. Furthermore, exonerations are expensive in both time and resources. Merely discovering a possible case and requesting testing often isn't enough. With some commendable exceptions . . . prosecutors tend to fight requests for post-conviction DNA testing. (The U.S. Supreme Court held in 2009 that there is no constitutional right to such tests.) So for now, the pace of genetic exonerations appears to be limited primarily by the amount of money and staff that legal advocacy groups have to uncover these cases and argue them in court, the amount of evidence available for testing, and the willingness of courts to allow the process to happen, not by a lack of cases in need of further investigation.

It's notable that one of the few places in America where a district attorney has specifically dedicated staff and resources to seeking out bad convictions—Dallas County, Texas—has produced more exonerations than all but a handful of states. That's partly because Dallas County District Attorney Craig Watkins is more interested in reopening old cases than his counterparts elsewhere, and partly because of a historical quirk: Since the early 1980s the county has been sending biological crime scene evidence to a private crime lab for testing, and that lab has kept the evidence well preserved. Few states require such evidence be preserved once a defendant has exhausted his appeals, and in some jurisdictions the evidence is routinely destroyed at that point.

"I don't think there was anything unique about the way Dallas was prosecuting crimes," Watkins told me in 2008. "It's unfortunate that other places didn't preserve evidence too. We're just in a unique position where I can look at a case, test DNA evidence from that period, and say without a doubt that a person is innocent. . . . But that doesn't mean other places don't have the same problems Dallas had."

If the rest of the country has an actual (but undetected) wrongful conviction rate as high as Dallas County's, the number of innocents in prison for felony crimes could be in the tens of thousands.

The Trial and Conviction of Paul House

As with many wrongful convictions, the case against Paul House once seemed watertight. House was an outsider, having only recently moved to Union County when Carolyn Muncey was murdered in 1985, and he was an ex-con, having served five years in a Utah prison for sexual assault. He got into scuffles with locals, although he considered Muncey and her husband, Hubert, friends. When Muncey turned up dead, House was a natural suspect.

House has claimed he was innocent of the Utah charge. His mother, Joyce, says it was a he said/she said case in which her son pleaded guilty on the advice of his attorney. "He could have been paroled earlier if he had shown some remorse," she says. "But he said, 'I pled guilty the one time, because that's what the lawyer told me I should do. I'm not going to say again that I did something I didn't do.' He said he'd rather serve more time than admit to the rape again." Joyce House and Mike Pemberton, Paul House's attorney, are hesitant to go into much detail about the Utah case, and public records aren't available due to the plea bargain. But while what happened in Utah certainly makes House less sympathetic, it has no bearing on whether House is the man who killed Carolyn Muncey.

House also didn't do himself any favors during the Muncey investigation. In initial questioning, he lied to the police about where he was the night of the murder, saying he was with his girlfriend all night. But he later admitted he had gone for a walk at one point and had come back without his shoes and with scratches on his arms. He initially lied to police about the scratches too, saying they were inflicted by his girlfriend's cats. House later said he'd been accosted by some locals while on his walk, scuffled with them, then fled through a field, where he lost his shoes. (House would learn years later that his shoes were found by police before his trial. There was no blood or other biological evidence on them, potentially exculpatory information that was never turned over to House's lawyers.)

"I think it was a situation where you're on parole, you're an outsider, and this woman has just been killed near where you live," says Pemberton, House's attorney. "It wasn't smart of him to lie to the police. But it was understandable."

Carolyn Muncey's husband, who House's attorneys would later suspect was her killer, also lied about where he was when she was killed. He would additionally claim, falsely, that he had never physically abused her. Still, House was clearly the early suspect.

The strongest evidence against House was semen found on Muncey's clothing, which an FBI agent testified at trial "could have" belonged to House. DNA testing didn't exist in 1986, but the agent said House was a secretor, meaning he produced blood type secretions in other body fluids, including semen, and that the type secreted in semen found on Muncey's nightgown was a match to House's type A blood. About 80 percent of people are secretors, and about 36 percent of Americans have type A blood. The agent also said the semen found on Muncey's panties included secretions that didn't match House's blood type, but added, inaccurately, that House's secretion could have "degraded" into a match. Muncey's husband was never tested.

The other strong evidence against House was some blood stains on his jeans that matched Muncey's blood type, but not his own. Those stains on House's jeans did turn out to have been Muncey's blood; the question is how they got there.

House was never charged with rape; there were no physical indications that Muncey had been sexually assaulted. But the semen was used to put him at the crime scene, and the state used the possibility of rape as an aggravating circumstance in arguing that House should receive the death penalty.

House was convicted in February 1986. The morning after his conviction, just hours before the sentencing portion of his trial, House slashed his wrists with a disposable razor. He left behind a suicide note in which he professed his innocence. Jail officials rushed him to a hospital in Knoxville, where doctors saved his life and stitched up his wounds. He was then sent back to the courthouse, where a jury sentenced him to death.

It wasn't until more than a decade later, in 1999, that the case against House began to erode. New witnesses came forward with accusations against Hubert Muncey, Carolyn's husband. Several said he was an alcoholic who frequently beat her. At an ensuing evidentiary hearing, two other women said Hubert had drunkenly confessed to killing his wife several months after the murder. When one went to the police with the information the next day, she said at the hearing, the sheriff brushed her off. Another witness testified that Hubert Muncey had asked her to lie to back up his alibi.

But it was the forensic evidence presented at that 1999 hearing that really unraveled the state's case. When House's attorneys were finally able to get DNA testing for the semen found on Carolyn Muncey's clothes, it showed that the semen was a match to Muncey's husband, not House. The state responded that rape was never part of their case against House (though it is why he was initially a suspect, it was the only conceivable motive, and it was presented as evidence in the sentencing portion of his trial). Besides, prosecutors argued, there was still the blood on House's jeans.

Except there were problems with that too. Cleland Blake, an assistant chief medical examiner for the state of Tennessee, testified that while the blood did belong to Muncey, its chemical composition indicated it was blood that had been taken after she had been autopsied. Worse still, three-quarters of a test tube of the blood taken during Muncey's autopsy went missing between the time of the autopsy and the time House's jeans arrived at the FBI crime lab for testing. The test tubes with Muncey's blood and House's jeans were transported in the same Styrofoam box. The blood on House's jeans, his attorneys argued, must have either been planted or spilled because of sloppy handling of the evidence.

It is extraordinarily difficult to win a new trial in a felony case, even in light of new evidence, and House's case was no exception. A federal circuit court judge denied his request for post-conviction relief, and the U.S. Court of Appeals for the 6th Circuit affirmed that decision. Somewhat surprisingly, the U.S. Supreme Court agreed to hear House's case, and in 2006 issued a rare, bitterly divided 5-to-3 ruling granting House a new trial.

The Supreme Court has occasionally thrown out death penalty convictions because of procedural errors or constitutional violations, but it's rare for the Court to methodically review the evidence in a capital case. Writing for the majority, Justice Anthony Kennedy did exactly that, finding in the end that "although the issue is close, we conclude that this is the rare case where—had the jury heard all the conflicting testimony—it is more likely than not that no reasonable juror viewing the record as a whole would lack reasonable doubt."

It was a surprising and significant victory for House. But it would be another three years before he would be released from prison.

How Do Wrongful Convictions Happen?

The most significant consequence of the spate of DNA exonerations has been a much-needed reassessment of what we thought we knew about how justice is administered in America. Consider the chief causes of wrongful convictions:

Bad Forensic Evidence

DNA technology was developed by scientists, and it has been thoroughly peer-reviewed by other scientists. Most of the forensic science used in the courtroom, on the other hand, was either invented in police stations and crime labs or has been refined and revised there to fight crime and obtain convictions. Most forensic evidence isn't peer-reviewed, isn't subject to blind testing, and is susceptible to corrupting bias, both intentional and unintentional. The most careful analysts can fall victim to cognitive bias creeping into their work, particularly when their lab falls under the auspices of a law enforcement agency. Even fingerprint analysis isn't as sound as is commonly believed.

A congressionally commissioned 2009 report by the National Academy of Sciences found that many other forensic specialties that are often presented in court with the gloss of science—hair and carpet fiber analysis, blood spatter analysis, shoe print identification, and especially bite mark analysis—lack the standards, peer review, and testing procedures of genuinely scientific research and analysis. Some are not supported by any scientific literature at all. Moreover, the report found, even the forensic specialties with some scientific support are often portrayed in court in ways that play down error rates and cognitive bias.

According to an Innocence Project analysis of the first 225 DNA exonerations, flawed or fraudulent forensic evidence factored into about half of the faulty convictions.

Eyewitness Testimony

Social scientists have known about the inherent weakness of eyewitness testimony for decades. Yet it continues to be the leading cause of wrongful convictions in America; it was a factor in 77 percent of those first 225 cases. Simple steps, such as making sure police who administer lineups have no knowledge of the case (since they can give subtle clues to witnesses, even unintentionally) and that witnesses are told that the actual perpetrator may not be among the photos included in a lineup, can go a long way toward improving accuracy. But such reforms also make it more difficult to win convictions, so many jurisdictions, under pressure from police and prosecutor groups, have been hesitant to embrace them.

False Confessions

Difficult as it may be to comprehend, people do confess to crimes they didn't commit. It happened in about one-quarter of the first 225 DNA exonerations. Confessions are more common among suspects who are minors or are mentally handicapped, but they can happen in other contexts as well, particularly after intense or abusive police interrogations.

In a candid 2008 op-ed piece for the *Los Angeles Times,* D.C. Police Detective Jim Trainum detailed how he unwittingly coaxed a false confession out of a 34-year-old woman he suspected of murder. She even revealed details about the crime that could only have been known to police investigators and the killer. But Trainum later discovered that the woman couldn't possibly have committed the crime. When he reviewed video of his interrogation, he realized that he had inadvertently provided the woman with those very specific details, which she then repeated back to him when she was ready to confess.

Trainum concluded that all police interrogations should be videotaped, a policy that would not just discourage abusive questioning but also provide an incontrovertible record of how a suspect's confession was obtained. Here too, however, there has been pushback from some police agencies, out of fear that jurors may be turned off even by legitimate forms of questioning.

Jailhouse Informants

If you were to take every jailhouse informant at his word, you'd find that a remarkably high percentage of the people accused of felonies boast about their crimes to the complete strangers they meet in jail and prison cells. Informants are particularly valuable in federal drug cases, where helping a prosecutor obtain more convictions is often the only way to get time cut from a mandatory minimum sentence. That gives them a pretty good incentive to lie.

There is some disagreement over a prosecutor's duty to verify the testimony he solicits from jailhouse informants. In the 2006, Church Point, Louisiana, case of Ann Colomb, for example, Brett Grayson, an assistant U.S. Attorney in Louisiana, put on a parade of jailhouse informants whose claims about buying drugs from Colomb and her sons were rather improbable, especially when the sum of their testimony was considered as a whole. According to defense attorneys I spoke with, when one attorney asked him if he actually believed what his informants were telling the jury, Grayson replied that it doesn't matter if he believes his witnesses; it only matters if the jury does. He expressed a similar sentiment in his closing argument.

After indicating that he isn't familiar with the Colomb case and isn't commenting on Grayson specifically, Josh Marquis says that sentiment is wrong. "A prosecutor absolutely has a duty to only put on evidence he believes is truthful," Marquis says. "And that includes the testimony you put on from informants."

In a 2005 study, the Center on Wrongful Convictions in Chicago found that false or misleading informant testimony was responsible for 38 wrongful convictions in death penalty cases.

The professional culture of the criminal justice system. In addition to the more specific causes of wrongful convictions listed above, there is a problem with the institutional culture among prosecutors, police officers, forensic analysts, and other officials. Misplaced incentives value high conviction rates more than a fair and equal administration of justice.

Prosecutors in particular enjoy absolute immunity from civil liability, even in cases where they manufacture evidence that leads to a wrongful conviction. The only time prosecutors can be sued is when they commit misconduct while acting as investigators—that is, while doing something police normally do. At that point they're subject to qualified immunity, which provides less protection than absolute immunity but still makes it difficult to recover damages.

Marquis says this isn't a problem. "Prosecutors are still subject to criminal liability," he says. "In fact, my predecessor here in Oregon was prosecuted for misconduct in criminal cases. State bars will also hold prosecutors accountable."

But criminal charges are few and far between, and prosecutors can make egregious mistakes that still don't rise to the level of criminal misconduct. Professional sanctions are also rare. A 2010 study by the Northern California Innocence Project found more than 700 examples between 1997 and 2009 in which a court had found misconduct on the part of a prosecutor in the state. Only six of those cases resulted in any disciplinary action by the state bar. A 2010 investigation of federal prosecutorial misconduct by *USA Today* produced similar results: Of 201 cases in which federal judges found that prosecutors had committed misconduct, just one resulted in discipline by a state bar association. Prosecutorial misconduct was a factor in about one-quarter of the first 225 DNA exonerations, but none of the prosecutors in those cases faced any significant discipline from the courts or the bar.

There is also a common misconception that appeals courts serve as a check on criminal justice abuse. It is actually rare for an appeals court to review the evidence in a criminal case. Appeals courts make sure trials abide by the state and federal constitutions and by state or federal rules of criminal procedure, but they almost never second-guess the conclusions of juries.

In a 2008 article published in the *Columbia Law Review*, the University of Virginia law professor Brandon L. Garrett looked at the procedural history of the first 200 cases of DNA exoneration. Of those, just 18 convictions were reversed by appellate courts. Another 67 defendants had their appeals denied with no written ruling at all. In 63 cases, the appellate court opinion described the defendant as guilty, and in 12 cases it referred to the "overwhelming" evidence of guilt. Keep in mind these were all cases in which DNA testing later proved actual innocence. In the remaining cases, the appeals courts either found the defendant's appeal without merit or found that the errors in the case were "harmless"—that is, there were problems with the case, but those problems were unlikely to have affected the jury's verdict due to the other overwhelming evidence of guilt.

"We've seen a lot of exoneration cases where, for example, the defendant raised a claim of ineffective assistance of counsel," says Peter Neufeld, co-founder of the Innocence Project of New York. "And in those cases, the appellate courts often found that the defense lawyer provided substandard representation. But they would then say that the poor lawyering didn't prejudice the case because the evidence of guilt was so overwhelming. Well, these people were later proven innocent! If you have a test that is frequently producing erroneous results, there's either something wrong with the test, or there's something wrong with the way it's being implemented."

Life on the Outside

Paul House was diagnosed with multiple sclerosis in 2000, a year after the evidentiary hearing that would eventually lead to his release. But while House was convicted of Carolyn Muncey's murder less than a year after it happened, it took a decade after his conviction was called into serious question for House to get back home to Crossville. During those 10 years, the state's case continued to fall apart. So did House's body.

After the U.S. Supreme Court overturned House's conviction in 2006, Paul Phillips, the district attorney for Tennessee's 8th Judicial District and the man who prosecuted House in 1986, pushed ahead with plans to retry him. In December 2007, after a series of delays, Harry S. Mattice Jr., a U.S. district court judge in Knoxville, finally ordered the state to try House within 180 days or set him free. Those 180 days then came and went without House being freed, thanks to an extension granted by the 6th Circuit.

In another hearing held in May 2008, Phillips argued that House—who by that point couldn't walk or move his wheelchair without assistance—presented a flight risk. Later, Tennessee Associate Deputy Attorney General Jennifer Smith attempted to show that House presented a danger to the public because he was still capable of feeding himself with a fork, which apparently meant he was also capable of stabbing someone with one. House's bail was set at $500,000, later reduced to $100,000. In July 2008, an anonymous donor paid the bail, allowing House to finally leave prison.

That same month, Phillips told the Associated Press that he would send two additional pieces of biological evidence off for DNA testing: a hair found at the crime scene, and blood found under Carolyn Muncey's fingernails. House's defense team had asked to conduct its own testing of any untested biological evidence for years, but had been told that either there was no such evidence or, if there was, the state didn't know where it was. Philips told the A.P. that if the new tests didn't implicate House, he would drop the murder charge and allow House to go home. In February 2009 the results came back. They didn't implicate House, and in fact pointed to a third, unidentified man. In May of that year, Phillips finally dropped the charge. But he still wouldn't clear House's name, telling Knoxville's local TV station WATE, "There is very adequate proof that Mr. House was involved in this crime. We just don't know the degree of culpability beyond a reasonable doubt." (Phillips' office did not respond to my requests for comment.)

By the time House was diagnosed with M.S. in 2000, his symptoms were already severe, although it took his mother, and not a prison doctor, to notice something was wrong. "I was visiting him, and I brought along some microwave popcorn," Joyce House recalls. "He asked me to heat it up, and I said, 'No, you heat it up.' When he got up, he had to prop himself up and drag along the wall to get to the microwave. He couldn't even stand up straight." According to Joyce House, her son's doctors today say that the Tennessee prison system's failure to diagnose House's M.S. earlier—then treat it properly after it was diagnosed—may have taken years off his life. (M.S. is also exacerbated by stress.) The disease has also significantly diminished the quality of the life House has left.

Under Tennessee's compensation law for the wrongly convicted, if House is formally exonerated—and that's still a big if—he will be eligible for $50,000 for each year he was in prison, up to $1 million. But there's a catch. The compensation is given in annual $50,000 installments over 20 years. If House dies before then, the payments stop.

Most of the 27 states with compensation laws similarly pay the money off in installments. Last October, A.P. ran a story about Victor Burnette, a 57-year-old Virginia man who served eight years for a 1979 rape before he was exonerated by DNA testing in 2006. Burnette actually turned down the $226,500 the state offered in compensation in 2010 because he was offended by the stipulation that it be paid out over 25 years. Even after the DNA test confirmed his innocence, it took another three years for Burnette to officially be pardoned, which finally

made him eligible for the money. The installment plans make it unlikely that many exonerees—especially long-timers, who are arguably the most deserving—will ever see full compensation for their years in prison.

Only about half the people exonerated by DNA testing so far have been compensated at all. Most compensation laws require official findings of actual innocence, which eliminates just about any case that doesn't involve DNA. Some states also exclude anyone who played some role in their own conviction, which would disqualify a defendant who falsely confessed, even if the confession was coerced or beaten out of them.

Paul House has yet another predicament ahead of him. Even if he does win an official exoneration, and even if he somehow lives long enough to receive all of his compensation, he'll have to lose his health insurance to accept it. House's medical care is currently covered by TennCare, Tennessee's Medicare program. If he accepts compensation for his conviction, he will be ineligible. His $50,000 per year in compensation for nearly a quarter century on death row will then be offset by a steep increase in what he'll have to pay for his medical care.

These odd, sometimes absurd predicaments aren't intentionally cruel. They just work out that way. Paul House's attorney Mike Pemberton points out that the prosecutors in these cases aren't necessarily evil, either. "Paul Phillips is an honorable man, and an outstanding trial attorney," Pemberton says. "But on this case he was wrong." Pemberton, who was once a prosecutor himself, says the job can lend itself to tunnel vision, especially once a prosecutor has won a conviction. It can be hard to let go. We have a system with misplaced incentives and very little accountability for state actors who make mistakes. That's a system ripe for bad outcomes.

When I ask Paul House why he thinks it has taken so long to clear his name, he starts to answer, then stammers, looks away, and retreats again to Oh well, his cue to move on because he has no answer.

That may be an understandable response from a guy with advanced M.S. who just spent two decades on death row. But for too long our national response to the increasing evidence that our justice system is flawed has been the same sort of resignation. DNA has only begun to show us where some of those flaws lie. It will take a strong public will to see that policymakers address them.

Critical Thinking

1. DNA has proven many convicted murderers innocent. Discuss estimates of the number of wrongful convictions and the reasons for them.

2. Wrongful convictions reveal some of the injustices in the justice system. How should it be reformed?

Create Central

www.mhhe.com/createcentral

Internet References

ACLU Criminal Justice Home Page
www.aclu.org/crimjustice/index.html

Crime Times
www.crime-times.org

Human Rights and Humanitarian Assistance
www.etown.edu/vl/humrts.html

Sociology—Study Sociology Online
http://edu.learnsoc.org

Sociology Web Resources
http://www.mhhe.com/socscience/sociology/resources/index.htm

Sociosite
http://www.topsite.com/goto/sociosite.net

Socioweb
http://www.topsite.com/goto/socioweb.com

RADLEY BALKO (rbalko@reason.com) is a senior editor at reason.

From *Reason Magazine*, July 2011, pp. 20–33. Copyright © 2011 by Reason Foundation, 3415 S. Sepulveda Blvd., Suite 400, Los Angeles, CA 90034. www.reason.com

Article　　　　Prepared by: Kurt Finsterbusch, *University of Maryland, College Park*

License to Kill

Immunity for Stand Your Ground shooters. Packing heat in bars. Gun permits for wife beaters. How radical gun laws spawned by a band of NRA lobbyists and Florida politicians have spread nationwide.

ADAM WEINSTEIN

Learning Outcomes

After reading this article, you will be able to:

- Evaluate the full consequences of the Stand Your Ground Law.
- Explain why Stand Your Ground laws are passed in many states where the majority of the citizens are against it.

T he Florida law made infamous this spring by the killing of unarmed teenager Trayvon Martin was conceived during the epic hurricane season of 2004. That

---

Stand Your Ground, Explained

The three legal concepts that turned a reasonable self-defense law into a recipe for vigilante justice

1. **Hell no, I won't run away.**
   People who believe they are in danger in public spaces are not required to try to retreat from the perceived threat before defending themselves with force.

2. **I'm totally justified in doing this.**
   People acting in self-defense in their homes, vehicles, or other designated areas are assumed to have reasonably believed they were in imminent danger. The burden of proving otherwise falls on the prosecution.

3. **Ha-ha, you can't sue me.**
   People who use justifiable force to defend themselves are protected not only from criminal prosecution but also civil liability. (The former is common in self-defense legislation; the latter is not.)

November, 77-year-old James Workman moved his family into an RV outside Pensacola after Hurricane Ivan peeled back the roof of their house. One night a stranger tried to force his way into the trailer, and Workman killed him with two shots from a .38 revolver. The stranger turned out to be a disoriented temporary worker for the Federal Emergency Management Agency who was checking for looters and distressed homeowners. Workman was never arrested, but three months went by before authorities cleared him of wrongdoing.

That was three months too long for Dennis Baxley, a veteran Republican representative in Florida's state Legislature. Four hurricanes had hit the state that year, and there was fear about widespread looting (though little took place). In Baxley's view, Floridians who defended themselves or their property with lethal force shouldn't have had to worry about legal repercussions. Baxley, a National Rifle Association (NRA) member and owner of a prosperous funeral business, teamed up with then-GOP state Sen. Durell Peaden to propose what would become known as Stand Your Ground, the self-defense doctrine essentially permitting anyone feeling threatened in a confrontation to shoot their way out.

Or at least that's the popular version of how the law was born. In fact, its genesis traces back to powerful NRA lobbyists and right-wing policy groups like the American Legislative Exchange Council (ALEC). And the law's rapid spread—it now exists in various forms in 25 states—reflects the success of a coordinated strategy, cultivated in Florida, to roll back gun control laws everywhere.

Baxley says he and Peaden lifted the law's language from a proposal crafted by Marion Hammer, a former NRA president and founder of the Unified Sportsmen of Florida, a local NRA affiliate. A 73-year-old dynamo who tops off her 4-foot-11 frame with a brown pageboy, Hammer has been a force in the state capital for more than three decades. "There is no more tenacious presence in

Tallahassee," Gov. Jeb Bush's former chief of staff told CNN in April. "You want her on your side in a fight."

Ever since neighborhood watch volunteer George Zimmerman shot Trayvon Martin point-blank in the chest, the term Stand Your Ground has been widely discussed, but what does it really mean? A *Mother Jones* review of dozens of state laws shows that the concept is built on three planks from the pioneering Florida legislation: A person claiming self-defense is not required to retreat from a threat before opening fire; the burden is almost always on prosecutors to prove that a self-defense claim is *not* credible; and finally, the shooter has immunity from civil suits relating to the use of deadly force. While the so-called Castle Doctrine (as in "a man's home is his") has for centuries generally immunized people from homicide convictions if they resorted to deadly force while defending their home, Florida's law was the first to extend such protection to those firing weapons in public spaces-parking lots, parks, and city streets.

Stand Your Ground was shepherded through the Legislature with help from then-state Rep. Marco Rubio and signed into law by Bush on April 26, 2005. It was the "first step of a multi-state strategy," Wayne LaPierre, a long-standing NRA official who is now the group's CEO, told the *Washington Post*. "There's a big tail-wind we have, moving from state legislature to state legislature. The South, the Midwest, everything they call 'flyover land.'" The measure was adopted as model legislation by ALEC, a corporate—sponsored national consortium of lawmakers—which is how it ended up passing in states from Mississippi to Wisconsin. "We are not a rogue state," says Baxley, who was bestowed with the NRA'S Defender of Freedom Award shortly before his bill passed. "But we may be a leader."

Supporters of such laws cite the slippery-slope argument: Seemingly reasonable regulations—waiting periods, licenses, limits on assault weapons and high-capacity magazines—inevitably lead to ever-stricter measures, they argue, until citizens' constitutional right to defend themselves against government tyranny has vanished. Hammer suggests that an assault on gun rights motivated her move to Tallahassee from her native South Carolina in 1974: "Florida was seeing what I would call a burst of gun control measures being filed by Northerners who had moved to South Florida," she told a radio interviewer in 2005. "There was so much gun control being filed that it was very difficult for the NRA to deal with it from over 1,000 miles away."

After leaving work late one night in the mid-1980s, Hammer claims, a group of men in a car threatened her, only to be scared off when she pulled a gun on them. No police report was ever filed, but Hammer maintains that shortly after this incident a local police chief told her that she could have been arrested had she shot them. It was a convenient tale. She soon became a driving force behind Florida's "shall issue" legislation, passed in 1987, which

stripped authorities of the ability to deny a concealed-weapons permit to someone they consider potentially dangerous. The law would allow thousands of ex-convicts and spouse beaters to pack heat; a Florida state attorney called it "one of the dumbest laws I have ever seen." A 1988 investigation by the *St. Petersburg Times* found permits had been given to two fugitives with outstanding arrest warrants, a disgraced cop who'd been convicted of a DUI and turned down for a county gun license, a man charged with fondling an eight-year-old girl, and a dead man. Florida has since issued more than 2 million concealed-weapons permits.

That same year Hammer called a panel of Florida legislators "a modern-day Gestapo" for considering legislation to keep guns away from violent criminals and the mentally ill. ("This is the lowest standard of integrity I have ever seen for a lobbyist in Tallahassee," one pro-gun Republican responded at the time.)

But Hammer's efforts really picked up steam when she served as the NRA'S first female president from 1995 to 1998—by the end of which time Bush had been elected governor and the GOP had taken firm control of the Statehouse. Hammer and her allies have since barred city and county governments from banning guns in public buildings; forced businesses to let employees keep guns in cars parked in company lots; made it illegal for doctors to warn patients about the hazards of gun ownership (this controversial "Docs versus Glocks" law was overturned by a George W. Bush-appointed federal judge); and secured an exemption to Florida's celebrated open—records laws in order to keep gun permit holders' names a secret. (Baxley had cosponsored a similar bill, explaining in its original text that such lists had been used "to confiscate firearms and render the disarmed population helpless in the face of Nazi atrocities" and Fidel Castro's "tyranny.")

As Florida became known to some as the "Gunshine State," it began exporting its laws, with ALEC'S help, to other statehouses. This effort was no doubt aided by the fact that the vice president of Hammer's Unified Sportsmen of Florida is John Patronis, cousin to Republican state Rep. Jimmy Patronis—sponsor of the aforementioned bill that kept names of concealed-weapons license holders secret and ALEC'S current Florida chairman. The organization would also be instrumental to spreading Stand Your Ground nationwide. "We definitely brought that bill forward to ALEC," said Baxley, a

---

Reloaded

Florida enacted Stand Your Ground in 2005. By 2012, with ALEC'S help, 24 more states had similar laws on the books.

member of the group. "It's a place where you can share ideas. I don't see anything nefarious about sharing good ideas." The NRA has served as "corporate co-chair" of ALEC'S Public Safety and Elections task force, which pushed Stand Your Ground and other gun laws. Since 2005, the year Florida's law was passed, gun manufacturers like Beretta, Remington, and Glock have poured as much as $39 million into the NRA'S lobbying coffers.

Hammer Called Lawmakers "A Modern-Day Gestapo" For Wanting To Keep Guns From Violent Criminals And The Mentally Ill.

Baxley defends the NRA'S involvement: "They have lots of members who want this statute. They're people who live in my district. They're concerned about turning back this lawless chaos and anarchy in our society." Records show that the NRA'S Political Victory Fund has long supported Baxley—from a $500 contribution in 2000 (the state's maximum allowable donation) to $35,000 spent on radio ads in support of his state Senate bid in 2007. Peaden received at least $2,500 from the NRA and allied groups over the years. The NRA also maxed out on direct contributions to Jeb Bush's gubernatorial campaigns in 1998 and 2002, and it gave $125,000 to the Florida GOP between 2004 and 2010—more than it gave to any other state party. According to the Center for Media and Democracy, the NRA spent $729,863 to influence Florida politics in the 2010 election cycle alone.

Once fairly open to speaking with the media, Hammer has proved elusive since the Trayvon Martin killing. When I approached her for this story, explaining that I was a third-generation gun collector with a Florida carry permit, she declined to comment on the record. "Unfortunately," she wrote in an email, "if you did a truly honest article on the law, it would either never be printed in *Mother Jones,* or if they did publish it, it would not be believed by the mag's audience!"

A climate of fear helped spread Stand Your Ground, according to the National District Attorneys Association. In 2007, it conducted the first in-depth study on the expansion of the Castle Doctrine and found that it took root in part because "there was a change in perceptions of public safety after the terrorist attacks of 9/11. Many citizens . . . became concerned that government agencies could not protect every citizen in the event of subsequent terror attacks." Indeed, the NRA used 9/11 to promote its legislative agenda, most notably in its unsuccessful push to let all commercial airline pilots pack heat. "What would have made 9/11 impossible?" LaPierre asked a crowd at the 2002 NRA convention in Reno, Nevada. "If those pilots on those four airplanes had the right to be armed."

Steven Jansen, vice president and CEO of the Association of Prosecuting Attorneys and a former prosecutor in Detroit, was one of the study's authors. He first noticed the Stand Your Ground movement in early 2006 when it spread from Florida to Michigan, sponsored there by Republican state Sen. Rick Jones, an ALEC member. The law was "troublesome to me," Jansen told me. "We didn't really see a public safety need for it, and it could only muddy the legal waters."

With a confrontation like the one between Trayvon Martin and George Zimmerman, cops and prosecutors would now be forced to make judgment calls about which participant felt like he was in more peril. That raised serious questions about whether real-world situations would ever be as clear-cut as the lawmakers assumed. Jansen pointed to scenarios ranging from road rage to scuffles between rival fraternities: "To presume

Safety Off

Since 2005, Florida lawmakers have taken aim at gun control with a barrage of deregulation measures.

- Requiring employers to let employees keep guns in their cars while at work
- Requiring city and county governments to allow guns in public buildings and parks
- Lifting a long-standing ban on guns in national forests and state parks
- Allowing military personnel as young as 17 to get concealed-weapons licenses. (Age limit remains 21 for everyone else.)
- Withholding the names of concealed-carry licensees in public records
- Permitting concealed-carry licensees "to briefly and openly display the firearm to the ordinary sight of another person." (The original bill would have allowed guns on college campuses, but it was amended after a GOP lawmaker's friend's daughter was accidentally killed with an AK-47 at a frat party.)
- Prohibiting doctors from asking patients if they keep guns or ammo in the house unless it's "relevant" to their care or safety. (Overturned by a federal judge.)
- Allowing legislators, school board members, and county commissioners to carry concealed weapons at official meetings. (Didn't pass; another bill to let judges pack heat "at any time and in any place" died in 2009.)
- Designating a day for tax-free gun purchases. (Didn't pass.)
- Exempting guns manufactured in Florida from any federal regulations. (Didn't pass.)

—A.W.

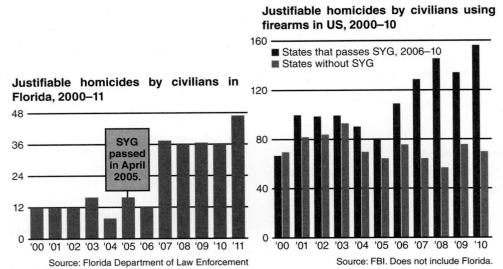

Justifiable homicides by civilians using firearms in US, 2000–10

■ States that passes SYG, 2006–10
■ States without SYG

Justifiable homicides by civilians in Florida, 2000–11

SYG passed in April 2005.

Source: Florida Department of Law Enforcement

Source: FBI. Does not include Florida.

Up in Gunsmoke   Since 2005, justifiable homicides by civilians in Florida have nearly tripled; they've also shot up in other states that adopted Stand Your Ground.

from the outset, as Florida's law arguably does, that a deadly response in these situations is justified would be at best irresponsible; at worst, that assumption could create a new protected set of behaviors that might otherwise be considered hate crimes or vigilantism."

But legislators across the country nevertheless ignored objections from law enforcement. Indeed, stand Your Ground gives armed civilians rights that even cops don't enjoy: "Society hesitates to grant blanket immunity to police officers, who are well trained in the use of deadly force and require yearly testing of their qualifications to carry a firearm," Jansen has written. "Yet the expansion of the Castle Doctrine has given such immunity to citizens."

Back when Florida passed Stand Your Ground, a few legislators did raise concerns. "This could be two gangs, deciding to have a fight in the street in Miami," said then-Rep. Jack Seiler, a Democrat from South Florida. "They both have a right to be standing on Biscayne Boulevard." It was a prescient warning. In 2006, a Miami man avoided prosecution after spraying a car filled with gang members with 14 bullets. In 2008, a 15-year-old Tallahassee boy was killed in a shoot-out between rival gangs; two of the gang members successfully took refuge behind Stand Your Ground.

The cumulative effect of those cases has been staggering: Two years after Stand Your Ground passed in Florida, the number of "justifiable homicides" by civilians more than doubled, and it nearly tripled by 2011, FBI statistics show a similar national trend: Justifiable homicides doubled in states with Florida-style laws, while they remained flat or fell in states that lacked them. Jansen also notes that research has shown that, when it came to domestic-abuse cases, "the only thing Stand Your Ground did

was blur the lines between who was the batterer and who was the victim."

He says the laws have been passed without legislators asking basic questions: What, exacdty, makes a fear of imminent harm reasonable? Do the laws have a disparate negative effect on minorities or juveniles? And, perhaps the simplest question: "Is it worth losing a life over a car radio?"

That's happened, too. In Miami, a man was granted immunity in March for chasing down a burglar and stabbing him after the thief swung a bag of stolen car radios at him. He "was well within his rights to pursue the victim and demand the return of his property," the judge ruled. A state attorney for Miami-Dade County disagreed: "She, in effect, is saying that it's appropriate to chase someone down with a knife to get property back."

For now, Florida has deemed that it is indeed appropriate, and polls taken after the Martin killing show that half of voters agree. But outrage over that case has cost ALEC prime corporate sponsors—including McDonald's, Coca-Cola, Pepsi, Kraft, and Procter & Gamble—and its tax-exempt status has been challenged by Common Cause. In April, ALEC disbanded the panel that pushed Stand Your Ground and redirected funds to "task forces that focus on the economy."

But Hammer and her allies are still pressing for laxer gun laws. This spring, Hammer got Florida to drop the cost of gun permits and lower the age restriction to 17 for military members, and she's still fighting to allow residents to carry their guns openly. And the NRA is pumping millions into the November elections nationally. "America needs us now more than ever as we gather together as one in the most dangerous times in American history," LaPierre told the NRA'S annual convention in St. Louis in April. "By the time I finish this speech, two Americans will be slain, six women will be raped, 27 of us will be robbed, and 50 more will be beaten. That is the harsh reality we face every day." With an unabashed reference to the shooting that brought Stand Your Ground to national attention, LaPierre drove home his point. "But the media, they don't care. Everyday victims aren't celebrities. They don't draw ratings and sponsors, but sensational reporting from Florida does."

Critical Thinking

1. Do the Stand Your Ground laws give an unwarranted licence to kill?
2. Explain how George Zimmerman could chase and shoot Trayvon Martin, and innocent person, to death and expect to be exonerated.
3. Why have Stand Your Ground laws been passed in 25 states and what have been the results?

Create Central

www.mhhe.com/createcentral

Internet References

ACLU Criminal Justice Home Page
   www.aclu.org/crimjustice/index.html
Human Rights and Humanitarian Assistance
   www.etown.edu/vl/humrts.html
New American Studies Web
   www.georgetown.edu/crossroads/asw
Sociology—Study Sociology Online
   http://edu.learnsoc.org
Sociology Web Resources
   http://www.mhhe.com/socscience/sociology/resources/index.htm
Sociosite
   http://www.topsite.com/goto/sociosite.net
Socioweb
   http://www.topsite.com/goto/socioweb.com

From *Mother Jones*, July/August 2012, pp. 45–47, 65. Copyright © 2012 by Mother Jones. Reprinted by permission of the Foundation for National Progress.

Article Prepared by: Kurt Finsterbusch, *University of Maryland, College Park*

Toward Fewer Prisoners and Less Crime

MARK A.R. KLEIMAN

Learning Outcomes

After reading this article, you will be able to:

- Explain why the United States incarcerates the highest percentage of its population compared to the rest of the world.
- Understand the impacts of high incarceration rates on the extent of crime.
- Consider what reforms would improve the prison system.

Introduction: Four Ways of Looking at Mass Incarceration

The topic of this volume is mass incarceration. That problem can be approached from (at least) four perspectives: social science, cultural criticism, advocacy, and policy analysis.

The social scientist wants to know about causes and consequences, to use theories to explain events such as the explosion of incarceration in America over the past generation, and to use events to develop new theories. The cultural critic wants to elucidate meanings, asking both what the participants in the social, administrative, and political processes that produce a given set of results intended and intend by their actions and how they justify those actions to themselves and others and what those processes and their results tell us about the character of the social order that produced them. The advocate searches for persuasive means to the end of ameliorating an already-identified evil. The policy analyst tries to figure out what course of action would best serve the public interest, all things considered, trying to take into account unintended as well as intended consequences.

To a policy-analytic eye, "mass incarceration" looks like only a partial problem definition. The other part of the problem is crime. If the crime problem were trivial, or if incarceration had only a trivial effect on crime, the solution to the mass-incarceration problem would trivially obvious: release those currently locked up, and end the practice of sending offenders to jail or prison. The policy analyst's work would then be complete, and the task of persuasion could then be turned over to the advocate, guided by the social scientist and the cultural critic.

But if crime is a real problem and if incarceration can be one means among many to control crime, then the situation looks more complicated. One would need to measure the harms done by crime as well as the harms done by incarceration, ask about the effects of alternative incarceration policies on the rates of different sorts of crime, and consider the likely results of using more of other crime-control measures, including alternative forms of punishment, along with less incarceration.

For example, it seems clear that increasing levels of police activity can reduce victimization rates. Thus it ought to be possible in principle, given some target level of victimization, to "trade off" policing against incarceration, adding police while reducing imprisonment. Whether that would be desirable is a different question. The extremely aggressive style of the New York Police Department, even if we credit it with reductions in crime (and, unusually, reductions in incarceration as well) has profound impacts on the lives of poor young African—American, Dominican, Puerto Rican, and Haitian New Yorkers.

Is it better to live in a city with fewer prisoners but more police surveillance? The answer is not obvious on its face: resolving the question would require both the collection of facts and the assignment of values to different outcomes. But it is the sort of question that a policy analysis starting from the problem of mass incarceration must try to answer, if crime matters and if incarceration is one means of reducing it. So is the question of which prisoners to release, or not admit in the first place.

Thinking about mass incarceration and crime control as twin problems can create two advantages for those whose focus is on how to reduce mass incarceration. First, since many political actors are concerned about crime and do think that incarceration helps control it, advocates of incarceration-reduction will find a better hearing if they are heard as proposing alternative means of crime control rather than as ignoring the crime issue entirely. Second, there is evidence that support for highly punitive approaches to crime varies—albeit with a substantial lag—with the crime rate, so that success in reducing crime will tend to facilitate the project of incarceration reduction. As the crime explosion of 1962–1994 helped produce the problem of mass incarceration, the crime collapse of 1994–2004 might help ameliorate it, especially if victimization rates continue to fall.

The next section of this essay will argue that, even at current levels, crime—especially in poor African-American communities—remains a first-order social problem, comparable to the problem of mass incarceration. The final section will sketch a system of community corrections (probation and parole supervision) that would allow very large reductions in the prison population while not increasing, or perhaps reducing, crime.

The High Cost of Crime

The measurable losses from crime do not seem to be especially large compared to the measurable losses from other sources of risk: surely not large enough to account for the level of public concern over crime. Averaging across households, the average property lost to burglars comes out to about $4 per month, a small fraction of a typical utility bill. Homicide is a horrible event, but also a rare one; three times as many people die on the highways each year as are deliberately killed by others.

Crime—the risk of being victimized—imposes costs on those who are never actually victimized, because of the costly efforts they make to avoid victimization and the "external costs" of victimization-avoidance measures taken by others. Crime, like incarceration, deprives people of liberty; it does so by making them afraid. The deprivation of liberty is, in general, less profound—though there are certainly people who feel trapped in their homes because they are afraid to go outdoors—but it extends to a much larger group of people. The direct and secondary costs of crime avoidance easily swamp the immediate costs of victimization.

If the bulk of crime-related loss is not victimization loss, then the rate of completed victimization—the crime rate—is not a good proxy for the seriousness of the crime problem. A neighborhood abandoned due in part to crime, or where residents stay inside behind locked doors for fear of muggers, or a park that many people are afraid to enter after dark, may have a lower rate of completed crime than a safer neighborhood or park, simply

because so many more people are at risk. Even before the spectacular crime decrease of the 1994–2004 period, New York city actually had a relatively low burglary rate compared to other big cities, but the public impression that burglary risk was higher in New York was nonetheless probably correct: as a visitor might easily notice, New Yorkers were habituated to being much more careful about burglary proofing their homes than was common in cities where burglary was less on residents' minds.

The extent to which the fear of crime reflects mass-media choices about what sort of "news" to emphasize remains an open question. Certainly, there is no strong tendency for measured fear to shift quickly with, or even in the same direction as, measured crime. But this need not indicate that the fear itself is irrational, or insensitive to the actual crime risks prevalent in various social milieux, insofar as victimization might fall precisely as a result of increased precaution.

If the level of precaution tends to risk with the criminal riskiness of the social environment, and if precaution tends to reduce the rate of being victimized, then the measured changes in the rate of completed crime will tend to understate the changes in the underlying risk, especially when crime is increasing: if the number of robberies doubles even as potential victims are taking greater precautions against being robbed, then the rate of robbery per exposed person-hour—imagining that such a quantity could be measured—must have gone up even more. The flow of population away from high-crime urban neighborhoods and into lower-crime suburbs and exurbs means that the measured crime rate could fall even as the level of risk in every area continued to rise.

So the observation that the Great Crime Decline has left the country with "only" 250 percent of the crime rates prevalent in the early 1960s is less reassuring that it would seem. I am not very old, but I am old enough to recall when American storefronts, unlike European storefronts, did not have metal shutters and when middle-class parents did not regard it as imprudent to allow their young teenage children to take busses through tough neighborhoods late at night. If Americans continued to be as careless about the risks of crime as they were 45 years ago, the rate of completed crime would no doubt be substantially higher. And the loss of that carelessness—or rather, of a social environment which made that carelessness rational—is not a small loss. Blaming that loss on television news shows rather than on muggers makes it no less of a loss.

The fear of crime deprives the residents of high-crime neighborhoods of economic opportunity by driving jobs away from the places where they live. Whether the "spatial mismatch" between the location of the unemployed and the location of unfilled jobs is an important cause of high minority unemployment remains a contested question, but there can be no doubt that having to commute farther to work is, at best, an inconvenience, especially for teenagers who would be working only part-time in any case and whose attachment to the labor market may be weak. And those disadvantages tend to accumulate, since teenagers with less work experience become less attractive employees as young adults. Worst of all, anything that makes licit employment less attractive will tend to make its illicit alternatives more attractive; and a criminal record can be a very substantial barrier to subsequent employment in the licit economy.

Crime to job loss to poverty to crime is a positive-feedback loop: high-crime neighborhoods tend to be low-opportunity neighborhoods, low-opportunity neighborhoods encourage criminal activity by their residents, and that criminal activity makes the neighborhoods even less attractive places in which to live and do business, and some of the residents less attractive as potential employees. Loss of residents, especially the relatively prosperous residents most likely to be able to afford to move out, makes a neighborhood less attractive to retail businesses, and the loss of retail services in turn makes the neighborhood a less attractive place to live for those who have other options.

The economic geography of every metropolitan area provides testimony to the importance of crime as a factor shaping residential and business location decisions. How else could one account for the coexistence of housing abandonment and new housing construction only a few miles apart? There are many reasons for moving to the suburbs, but crime ranks high on the list. The same applies to business—location decisions. It would be unconventional, but it would not be beside the point, to insert a discussion of crime control in a treatise on reducing suburban sprawl.

That poverty is a cause of crime is a commonplace, though the mechanisms involved are complex and poorly understood. That crime is a sustaining cause of poverty is no less true, though in the past it has been much less remarked on. The poor are victimized directly; the probability of criminal victimization rises steadily with income. They are victimized again as a result of crime-avoidance behavior that limits their opportunities and blights their neighborhoods.

The picture is worst for African Americans; even adjusting for overall lower incomes, African Americans suffer much more crime than do members of other ethnic categories. Homicide provides the most dramatic example; representing less than 15 percent of the population, black people suffer more than 50 percent of the murders.

The problem tends to be self-sustaining. Given a constrained criminal-justice system, punishment per crime tends to be lower where crime is more common. Assuming that the threat of punishment has some deterrent effect, growing up where that threat is smaller—and licit economic opportunity less available—should be expected, other things equal, to lead to a higher rate of criminal activity. And indeed that is what we find. African Americans are far more heavily victimized than others, but not as a result of crossethnic aggression; crime is overwhelmingly intraracial.

Paradoxically, then, efforts to reduce the racial disproportion in the prison population are likely to intensify the implicit racial discrimination among victims that results from lower per-crime rates of punishment, leaving African Americans even more exposed to victimization. The critique of the current system in terms of imposing prison terms and the consequent social stigma on a much higher proportion of African Americans than of whites is fully justified by the facts, but the mechanisms involved are far more subtle than conscious, or even systemic, racial discrimination by officials against black perpetrators.

In some ways it would be better if, as is often asserted, systemic racial bias, in the form of more severe punishment for black offenders, lay at the root of problem; then eliminating racial bias could eliminate disproportionate incarceration. But if the actual problem is the positive-feedback loop from high criminal activity to low punishment-per-crime back to high criminal activity, no such fix is available. The standard critique portrays a melodrama; the reality is a tragedy.

Substituting Community Supervision for Incarceration

If crime and mass incarceration are both great evils, then we should look for ways to have less of both at once. One way to do so would be to substitute some other form of punishment for incarceration to serve the twin functions of incapacitation and deterrence. (If, as Useem and Piehl argue, the rising scale of incarceration has brought its marginal crime-control benefits down close to—or in some instances below—zero, then to some extent we could reduce mass incarceration without increasing crime. But the data do not suggest that 50 percent of current incarceration is useless, and cutting our incarceration rate in half would still leave it more than twice its historical norm and more than twice the level in any other advanced polity.)

Probation and parole are the two systems that manage convicted offenders outside the walls. Fines, community service, diversion to drug treatment or mental-health treatment, and "restorative justice" programs all rely on probation and parole supervision as their enforcement mechanism, without which they are no more than helpful hints from the judge. Alas, that enforcement is generally very weak, and compliance with "alternative sanctions" spotty at best. In California's famous Proposition 36 drug-diversion program, only about one entrant in four completed the prescribed course of treatment, and virtually none of them faced any consequence for reneging on the bargain they had made with the court other than the lost opportunity to have their convictions expunged and the risk that an outstanding bench warrant might complicate the course of a future arrest.

That failure does not stem from the laxity or laziness of probation officers—though no doubt some workers in any job are lax and lazy—but from the conditions under which they work. Typically, a big-city probation officer supervises more than 100 clients, and is expected to meet with each of them once a month. That schedule alone largely fills a working week, and the time required to prepare a violation report to send to the supervising judge is measured in hours. So the number of referrals is constrained by the officer's time. The judge and the judge's staff are also busy, and will not thank the probation officer for subjecting them to a flurry of revocation motions.

Short of a revocation motion, the probation officer's leverage over a client is limited. Only the judge can order a term of confinement; the probation officer (generally with the concurrence of supervisor) can only use moral suasion and impose additional requirements, such as more frequent meetings. But what if the client defies those requirements as well?

If a revocation motion is made, the judge, too, has a limited repertoire of sanctions. She can send the offender to prison or jail, usually for a period of months but sometimes for years. She can impose more onerous conditions of supervision (which, again, the probationer may well ignore). She can lengthen the period of supervision, which is a noticeable inconvenience but one that doesn't hit until sometime in the future.

None of these options is attractive. Jails and prisons are crowded, and whatever the probationer did to earn the conviction that underlies his probation term the violation of probation conditions is likely to be relatively trivial: a missed meeting or a "dirty" drug test. To a judge who has just put someone on probation for a burglary, sending someone else away for a mere "technical" violation seems disproportionate, unless that violation comes at the end of a very long string. (Sometimes a new substantive offense is handled as a violation of probation rather than prosecuted afresh; in those cases, a term behind bars is a more likely outcome.)

As a result, the most likely consequence to a probationer of breaking a probation rule is a warning, either by the probation office or (less often) by the judge. If the probationer keeps it up, at some point it will be the case that his previous "last warning" really was the last, and he will be on his way to, or back to, a cell. But such deferred and low-probability risks do little to reduce the violation rate, though they may cumulate to a great deal of punishment. The lack of an immediate and high-probability aversive consequence for a violation helps sustain the high violation rate, and the high violation rate in turn guarantees that most violations will not be sanctioned. This is simply the social trap of the neighborhood with a high crime rate and a low punishment risk per offense, writ small; the community corrections system reproduces the cruel and futile randomized draconianism of the larger criminal-justice system. (Parole supervision is tighter, though it, too over-relies on severe sanctions, but there are about five times as many probationers at any one time as parolees.)

But just as the threat of severe sanctions is largely impotent at controlling behavior if the sanctions are uncertain and deferred, the threat of even a mild sanction can be potent if the consequence follows the act swiftly and certainly. In Hawaii, a judicial warning that the next positive drug test would draw an immediate jail term measured in days succeeded in virtually ending drug use for more than three-quarters of a group of chronically defiant felony probationers, most of them methamphetamine users. The hard part was organizing the judge's staff, the probation department, the sheriff's office, the police, the jail, prosecutors, and defense counsel to actually deliver on that warning when the rules were broken. (That meant, for example, developing a two-page, check-the-box-or-fill-in-the-blank reporting form to replace the elaborate motion-for-revocation paperwork; since only a single violation is in question, very little information is needed.)

Most of the probationers on the program—dubbed HOPE—never faced an actual sanction; the warning alone did the job. On average, the group subjected to tight supervision spent about as many days in jail for probation violations as a comparison group, with more but shorter spells. But they spent only about a third as many days in prison after revocations or new convictions.

The project now covers about 1500 offenders, about one out of five felony probationers on the island of Oahu; the judge plans to expend it to 3000, and intends to manage all of them himself, by contrast with drug-court judge who typically manage caseloads of 50 to 75. Most of the participants are drug users, but by no means all; the process works just as well enforcing a different set of rules on domestic-violence offenders and sex offenders. The process isn't drug-specific; it applies basic principles of behavior change relevant to a wide range of behavior, as long as that behavior can be easily monitored.

Commercial vendors now sell, for $15 per month, a service that tracks the whereabouts of a GPS monitor; parents place them in their young children's backpacks to be able to find them when they stray. One version of that service provides "exception reporting;" after the parent enters a weekly schedule of where the child is supposed to be at given hours of given days, the system sends a text message to the parent's cell phone or email in-box if the child isn't where he is supposed to be.

Now imagine such a unit mounted on an anklet that can't be removed without the GPS unit detecting the change and sending an alert (or merely failing to respond). Put that anklet on a probationer or parolee, and his whereabouts are subject to continuous monitoring. Comparing the position records with the locations of crimes reported to the 9-1-1 system will make it difficult for anyone wearing an anklet to get away with a new predatory offense. Street gangs will not welcome the presence of members whose location is transparent to the police. Such a system makes it feasible to enforce curfews, stay-away orders, "community service" obligations, and requirements to appear as scheduled for employment or therapy. It could even be extended to home confinement, currently used for some sex offenders and for bailees thought to constitute a flight risk.

Unlike the expensive process of monitoring sex offenders, where any straying constitutes a potential emergency and the system must therefore be staffed around the clock, for routine probationers and parolees there would be no urgency about responding to a mere schedule violation; it would suffice for the probation or parole officer to be notified the next morning. As long as the offender is still wearing the device, finding him would pose no challenge, and the next day is soon enough for a sanction to be effective.

It would be an emergency if the offender removed the device; usually that will mean that he plans either to commit a serious crime or to abscond from supervision. But the police department, already staffed 24/7, could respond to those (presumably rare) events.

The operational challenges would be legion: developing rules about imposing and relaxing restrictions, what to do if the GPS unit loses contact with the satellite (perhaps a cell phone, which also transmits its position, would be required as a backup); how to deal with false positives; ensuring that the police respond quickly and vigorously to absconding; and managing the sanctions hearings.

But given the results from HOPE, it's a reasonable guess that 80 percent, perhaps even 90 percent of probationers and parolees would comply with the system in the sense of not shedding the GPS device, and that they would be highly compliant with rules and commit very few new crimes. They would probably also find it much easier to secure employment, despite their criminal histories, once employers found that they were not only certified drug-free but also showed up for work every day. And as a result, many fewer of them would wind up returning to prison.

Once probation and parole involved that sort of monitoring, only a limited number of cases would justify using incarceration instead: people who commit such heinous crimes that justice demands it (the Bernie Madoffs of the world), people whose demonstrated tendency for assault or sexual predation requires their incarceration to protect potential victims, and those who, in effect, *choose* incarceration by absconding. Everyone else could be adequately punished and incapacitated from future offending with monitoring alone, backed by brief jail stays. That could both reduce the inflow to prison (by reducing the number of revocations and persuading judges to sentence more felons to probation instead) and increase the outflow from prison by persuading parole boards to make more early-release decisions.

Moreover, converting probation into a real punishment rather than the placeholder for an absent punishment it now largely is

would be expected to deter crime, reducing the inflows both to prison and to probation.

How far this process might go is anyone's guess. But it would not be unreasonable to hope that the United States might find itself a decade from now with a European incarceration rate and crime rates resembling those of the 1950s.

The change could not be made overnight; each jurisdiction that adopts such a system will need an operational "shakedown" period, and it is essential that the program not outgrow its capacity to monitor and sanction; once offenders come to believe that the threat of quick incarceration is a bluff, their offending will so swamp the system that it will become a bluff.

But other than the need for shaking down and then phasing in, this approach has no natural upper limit. HOPE costs about $1000 per year on top of routine probation supervision, and most of that excess goes to drug treatment for the minority that cannot comply without professional help. It pays for itself several times over in reduced incarceration cost alone.

The implementation of this idea will vary from jurisdiction to jurisdiction and from population to population. In various ways, it could be applied to juvenile offenders, to probationers, to parolees, and to those released while awaiting trial either on bail or on their own recognizance. For juvenile probationers in particular, "outpatient" supervision under tight monitoring backed with the threat of 48 hours' solitary confinement for each violation, might succeed in squaring the circle of finding a punishment adequately aversive to serve as a deterrent without being so damaging as to push a juvenile who might otherwise have recovered from a period of criminal activity into persistent criminality, by reducing his commitment to, and opportunities within, the world of school and licit work.

This proposal of incarceration on the outpatient plan cannot expect to receive a universally warm welcome. In a criminal-justice-policy debate that sometimes seems to take place between the disciples of Michel Foucault and those of the Marquis de Sade, it will be too intrusive for the foucauldians and not retributive enough for the sadists. But for those not overly reluctant to punish lawbreakers with some months or years of a boring, go-to-bed-early-and-show-up-for-work middle-class lifestyle, and unwilling to accept current levels of incarceration or of crime, the virtual prison cell offers the prospect of having less of both.

With respect to the population not currently in prison, including pretrial releasees, and those newly placed on probation who would not have gone to prison otherwise, there is no doubt that the proposed system represents a further extension of state control over individuals. Whether that is desirable or not could be debated, with the answer depending in part on the empirical results in terms of crime, days behind bars, and employment, family, and housing status, and in part on the value one assigns to the liberty and privacy of the recently arrested (including their liberty to commit fresh offenses with impunity). In the somewhat longer run—over a period of a few years—the result might be to reduce the scope of direct state control by discouraging offending and thus reducing the total size of the prison-jail-probation-parole-pretrial release population.

Such a happy ending cannot be guaranteed. Such a program has yet to be tried out on a parolee population; it is possible (though I would rate the probability as small) that massive absconscion and consequent return to prison would make it operationally infeasible. It is more plausible that, in some jurisdictions, a combination of haste, under-resourcing, and administrative noncompliance would lead to program breakdown, with the supervised population discovering that, despite the threat, violation did not in fact lead swiftly and predictably to confinement. If that happened, violation rates would surely soar, thus putting the program into a "death spiral" of increasing violation rates and decreasing swiftness and certainty of sanctions. Managing the behavior of offenders is a much more straightforward task than managing the behavior of officials, and most of all of independent officials such as judges.

The other risk is that some offenders who get away with some minor violations under the current loose supervision systems, finish their assigned terms, and then go straight, will instead find tighter supervision intolerable, commit repeated in technical infractions leading to short confinement terms, abscond, and wind up in prison. That risk would be especially grave if the system were applied to misdemeanants in addition to felons, since the misdemeanants start out with a much lower level of prison risk.

But if the application of "outpatient incarceration" can be restricted to those who would otherwise face, with high probability, repeated spells of actual incarceration, then on balance it promotes not only public safety but the liberty and life prospects of the offender population. There are worse fates than being forced to live a law-abiding life.

Critical Thinking

1. Why does Mark Kleinman conclude that the high imprisonment rates in the United States have a net negative impact?
2. What benefits would result from reducing imprisonment?

Create Central

www.mhhe.com/createcentral

Internet References

ACLU Criminal Justice Home Page
   www.aclu.org/crimjustice/index.html
Human Rights and Humanitarian Assistance
   www.etown.edu/vl/humrts.html
New American Studies Web
   www.georgetown.edu/crossroads/asw
Sociology—Study Sociology Online
   http://edu.learnsoc.org
Sociology Web Resources
   http://www.mhhe.com/socscience/sociology/resources/index.htm
Sociosite
   http://www.topsite.com/goto/sociosite.net
Socioweb
   http://www.topsite.com/goto/socioweb.com

Kleiman, Mark A. R., "Toward Fewer Prisoners and Less Crime," *Daedalus,* Summer 2010, pp. 115–123. Copyright © 2010 by MIT Press Journals. All rights reserved. Used with permission.

Article   Prepared by: Kurt Finsterbusch, *University of Maryland, College Park*

The Year in Hate & Extremism, 2010

MARK POTOK

Learning Outcomes

After reading this article, you will be able to:

- Explain the recent dramatic increase in right-wing extremist groups.
- Be familiar with the number of extremist groups in the past 15 years.

For the second year in a row, the radical right in America expanded explosively in 2010, driven by resentment over the changing racial demographics of the country, frustration over the government's handling of the economy, and the mainstreaming of conspiracy theories and other demonizing propaganda aimed at various minorities. For many on the radical right, anger is focusing on President Obama, who is seen as embodying everything that's wrong with the country.

Hate groups topped 1,000 for the first time since the Southern Poverty Law Center began counting such groups in the 1980s. Anti-immigrant vigilante groups, despite having some of the political wind taken out of their sails by the adoption of hard-line anti-immigration laws around the country, continued to rise slowly. But by far the most dramatic growth came in the antigovernment "Patriot" movement—conspiracy-minded organizations that see the federal government as their primary enemy—which gained more than 300 new groups, a jump of over 60 percent.

Taken together, these three strands of the radical right—the hatemongers, the nativists and the antigovernment zealots—increased from 1,753 groups in 2009 to 2,145 in 2010, a 22 percent rise. That followed a 2008–2009 increase of 40 percent.

What may be most remarkable is that this growth of right-wing extremism came even as politicians around the country, blown by gusts from the Tea Parties and other conservative formations, tacked hard to the right, co-opting many of the issues important to extremists. Last April, for instance, Arizona Gov. Jan Brewer signed S.B. 1070, the harshest anti-immigrant law in memory, setting off a tsunami of proposals for similar laws across the country. Continuing growth of the radical right could be curtailed as a result of this shift, especially since Republicans, many of them highly conservative, recaptured the U.S. House last fall.

But despite those historic Republican gains, the early signs suggest that even as the more mainstream political right strengthens, the radical right has remained highly energized. In an 11-day period this January, a neo-Nazi was arrested

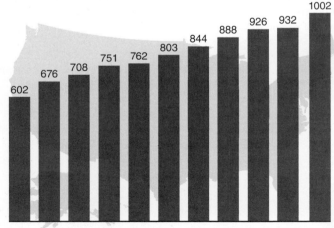

Hate Groups 2000–2010

Editor's note: Since the article below was published, authorities have changed their view of an incident in Dearborn, Mich., that is mentioned. Initially, it was believed that the Michigan suspect was planning an attack based on hatred of Muslims. In fact, it turns out that Roger Stockham is an American convert to Sunni Islam, and reportedly was angry at the mosque in question because it was Shi'ite.

headed for the Arizona border with a dozen homemade grenades; a terrorist bomb attack on a Martin Luther King Jr. Day parade in Spokane, Wash., was averted after police dismantled a sophisticated antipersonnel weapon; and a man who officials said had a long history of antigovernment activities was arrested outside a packed mosque in Dearborn, Mich., and charged with possessing explosives with unlawful intent. That's in addition, the same month, to the shooting of U.S. Rep. Gabrielle Giffords in Arizona, an attack that left six dead and may have had a political dimension.

It's also clear that other kinds of radical activity are on the rise. Since the murder last May 20 of two West Memphis, Ark., police officers by two members of the so-called "sovereign citizens" movement, police from around the country have contacted the Southern Poverty Law Center (SPLC) to report what one detective in Kentucky described as a "dramatic increase" in sovereign activity. Sovereign citizens, who, like militias, are part of the larger Patriot movement, believe that the federal government has no right to tax or regulate them and, as a result, often come into conflict with police and tax authorities. Another sign of their increased activity came early this year, when the Treasury Department, in a report assessing what the IRS faces in 2011, said its biggest challenge will be the "attacks and threats against IRS employees and facilities [that] have risen steadily in recent years."

Extremist ideas have not been limited to the radical right; already this year, state legislators have offered up a raft of proposals influenced by such ideas. In Arizona, the author of the S.B. 1070 law—a man who just became Senate president on the basis of his harshly nativist rhetoric—proposed a law this January that would allow his state to refuse to obey any federal

law or regulation it cared to. In Virginia, a state legislator wants to pass a law aimed at creating an alternative currency "in the event of the destruction of the Federal Reserve System's currency"—a longstanding fear of right-wing extremists. And in Montana, a state senator is working to pass a statute called the "Sheriffs First Act" that would require federal law enforcement to ask local sheriffs' permission to act in their counties or face jail. All three laws are almost certainly unconstitutional, legal experts say, and they all originate in ideas that first came from ideologues of the radical right.

There also are new attempts by nativist forces to roll back birthright citizenship, which makes all children born in the United States citizens. Such laws have been introduced this year in Congress, and a coalition of state legislators is promising to do the same in their states. And then there's Oklahoma, where 70 percent of voters last November approved a measure to forbid judges to consider Islamic law in the state's courtrooms—a completely groundless fear, but one pushed nonetheless by Islamophobes. Since then, lawmakers have promised to pass similar laws in Arizona, Florida, Louisiana, South Carolina, Tennessee, and Utah.

After the Giffords assassination attempt, a kind of national dialogue began about the political vitriol that increasingly passes for "mainstream" political debate. But it didn't seem to get very far. Four days after the shooting, a campaign called the Civility Project—a two-year effort led by an evangelical conservative tied to top Republicans—said it was shutting down because of a lack of interest and furious opposition. "The worst E-mails I received about the Civility Project were from conservatives with just unbelievable language about communists and some words I wouldn't use in this phone call," director Mark DeMoss

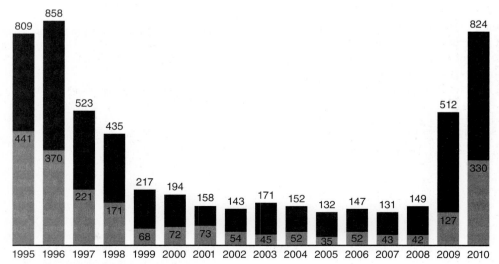

Patriot & Militia Groups 1995–2010

told *The New York Times*. "This political divide has become so sharp that everything is black and white, and too many conservatives can see no redeeming value in any" opponent.

A *Washington Post*/ABC News poll this January captured the atmosphere well. It found that 82 percent of Americans saw their country's political discourse as "negative." Even more remarkably, the poll determined that 49 percent thought that negative tone could or already had encouraged political violence.

Last year's rise in hate groups was the latest in a trend stretching all the way back to the year 2000, when the SPLC counted 602 such groups. Since then, they have risen steadily, mainly on the basis of exploiting the issue of undocumented immigration from Mexico and Central America. Last year, the number of hate groups rose to 1,002 from 932, a 7.5 percent increase over the previous year and a 66 percent rise since 2000.

At the same time, what the SPLC defines as "nativist extremist" groups—organizations that go beyond mere advocacy of restrictive immigration policy to actually confront or harass suspected immigrants or their employers—rose slightly, despite the fact that most of their key issues had been taken up by mainstream politicians. There were 319 such groups in 2010, up 3 percent from 309 in 2009.

But like the year before, it was the antigovernment Patriot groups that grew most dramatically, at least partly on the basis of furious rhetoric from the right aimed at the nation's first black president—a man who has come to represent to at least some Americans ongoing changes in the racial makeup of the country. The Patriot groups, which had risen and fallen once before during the militia movement of the 1990s, first came roaring back in 2009, when they rose 244 percent to 512 from 149 a year earlier. In 2010, they rose again sharply, adding 312 new groups to reach 824, a 61 percent increase. The highest prior count of Patriot groups came in 1996, when the SPLC found 858 (see also chart, above).

It's hard to predict where this volatile situation will lead. Conservatives last November made great gains and some of them are championing a surprising number of the issues pushed by the radical right—a fact that could help deflate some of the even more extreme political forces. But those GOP electoral advances also left the Congress divided and increasingly lined up against the Democratic president, which is likely to paralyze the country on such key issues as immigration reform.

What seems certain is that President Obama will continue to serve as a lightning rod for many on the political right, a man who represents both the federal government and the fact that the racial make-up of the United States is changing, something that upsets a significant number of white Americans. And that suggests that the polarized politics of this country could get worse before they get better.

Critical Thinking

1. Why have extremist groups suddenly increased in the last few years?
2. What kind of beliefs do these groups have?
3. Are the right-wing extremist groups dangerous?

Create Central

www.mhhe.com/createcentral

Internet References

ACLU Criminal Justice Home Page
www.aclu.org/crimjustice/index.html

Human Rights and Humanitarian Assistance
www.etown.edu/vl/humrts.html

New American Studies Web
www.georgetown.edu/crossroads/asw

Sociology—Study Sociology Online
http://edu.learnsoc.org

Sociology Web Resources
http://www.mhhe.com/socscience/sociology/resources/index.htm

Sociosite
http://www.topsite.com/goto/sociosite.net

Socioweb
http://www.topsite.com/goto/socioweb.com

From *Intelligence Report*, Spring 2011. Copyright © 2011 by Southern Poverty Law Center. Reprinted by permission by Mark Potok.

Article   Prepared by: Kurt Finsterbusch, *University of Maryland, College Park*

War in the Fifth Domain

Are the Mouse and Keyboard the New Weapons of Conflict?

THE ECONOMIST

Learning Outcomes

After reading this article, you will be able to:

- Contemplate the ramifications of cyberwar.

- Understand that the United States must develop horrific cyberwar capabilities just to protect itself from cyber threats.

- Understand the amount of cyber-espionage that is going on right now.

At the height of the cold war, in June 1982, an American early-warning satellite detected a large blast in Siberia. A missile being fired? A nuclear test? It was, it seems, an explosion on a Soviet gas pipeline. The cause was a malfunction in the computer-control system that Soviet spies had stolen from a firm in Canada. They did not know that the CIA had tampered with the software so that it would "go haywire, after a decent interval, to reset pump speeds and valve settings to produce pressures far beyond those acceptable to pipeline joints and welds," according to the memoirs of Thomas Reed, a former air force secretary. The result, he said, "was the most monumental nonnuclear explosion and fire ever seen from space."

This was one of the earliest demonstrations of the power of a "logic bomb". Three decades later, with more and more vital computer systems linked up to the internet, could enemies use logic bombs to, say, turn off the electricity from the other side of the world? Could terrorists or hackers cause financial chaos by tampering with Wall Street's computerised trading systems? And given that computer chips and software are produced globally, could a foreign power infect high-tech military equipment

with computer bugs? "It scares me to death," says one senior military source. "The destructive potential is so great."

After land, sea, air and space, warfare has entered the fifth domain: cyberspace. President Barack Obama has declared America's digital infrastructure to be a "strategic national asset" and appointed Howard Schmidt, the former head of security at Microsoft, as his cyber-security tsar. In May, the Pentagon set up its new Cyber Command (Cybercom) headed by General Keith Alexander, director of the National Security Agency (NSA). His mandate is to conduct "full-spectrum" operations—to defend American military networks and attack other countries' systems. Precisely how, and by what rules, is secret.

Britain, too, has set up a cyber-security policy outfit, and an "operations centre" based in GCHQ, the British equivalent of the NSA. China talks of "winning informationised wars by the mid-21st century". Many other countries are organising for cyberwar, among them Russia, Israel, and North Korea. Iran boasts of having the world's second-largest cyber-army.

What will cyberwar look like? In a new book, Richard Clarke, a former White House staffer in charge of counter-terrorism and cyber-security, envisages a catastrophic breakdown within 15 minutes. Computer bugs bring down military e-mail systems; oil refineries and pipelines explode; air-traffic-control systems collapse; freight and metro trains derail; financial data are scrambled; the electrical grid goes down in the eastern United States; and orbiting satellites spin out of control. Society soon breaks down as food becomes scarce and money runs out. Worst of all, the identity of the attacker may remain a mystery.

In the view of Mike McConnell, a former spy chief, the effects of full-blown cyberwar are much like a nuclear attack. Cyberwar has already started, he says, "and we are losing it." Not so, retorts Mr Schmidt. There is no cyberwar. Bruce Schneier, an IT industry security guru, accuses securocrats like

Mr Clarke of scaremongering. Cyberspace will certainly be part of any future war, he says, but an apocalyptic attack on America is both difficult to achieve technically (movie-script stuff) and implausible except in the context of a real war, in which case the perpetrator is likely to be obvious.

For the top brass, computer technology is both a blessing and a curse. Bombs are guided by GPS satellites; drones are piloted remotely from across the world; fighter planes and warships are now huge data-processing centres; even the ordinary foot-soldier is being wired up. Yet growing connectivity over an insecure internet multiplies the avenues for e-attack; and growing dependence on computers increases the harm they can cause.

By breaking up data and sending it over multiple routes, the internet can survive the loss of large parts of the network. Yet some of the global digital infrastructure is more fragile. More than nine-tenths of internet traffic travels through undersea fibre-optic cables, and these are dangerously bunched up in a few choke-points, for instance around New York, the Red Sea or the Luzon Strait in the Philippines. Internet traffic is directed by just 13 clusters of potentially vulnerable domain-name servers. Other dangers are coming: weakly governed swathes of Africa are being connected up to fibre-optic cables, potentially creating new havens for cyber-criminals. And the spread of mobile internet will bring new means of attack.

The internet was designed for convenience and reliability, not security. Yet in wiring together the globe, it has merged the garden and the wilderness. No passport is required in cyberspace. And although police are constrained by national borders, criminals roam freely. Enemy states are no longer on the other side of the ocean, but just behind the firewall. The ill-intentioned can mask their identity and location, impersonate others and con their way into the buildings that hold the digitised wealth of the electronic age: money, personal data and intellectual property.

Mr Obama has quoted a figure of $1 trillion lost last year to cybercrime—a bigger underworld than the drugs trade, though such figures are disputed. Banks and other companies do not like to admit how much data they lose. In 2008 alone, Verizon, a telecoms company, recorded the loss of 285 million personal-data records, including credit-card and bank-account details, in investigations conducted for clients.

About nine-tenths of the 140 billion e-mails sent daily are spam; of these about 16 percent contain moneymaking scams, including "phishing" attacks that seek to dupe recipients into giving out passwords or bank details, according to Symantec, a security-software vendor. The amount of information now available online about individuals makes it ever easier to attack a computer by crafting a personalised e-mail that is more likely to be trusted and opened. This is known as "spear-phishing".

The ostentatious hackers and virus-writers who once wrecked computers for fun are all but gone, replaced by criminal gangs seeking to harvest data. "Hacking used to be about making noise. Now it's about staying silent," says Greg Day of McAfee, a vendor of IT security products. Hackers have become wholesale providers of malware—viruses, worms, and Trojans that infect computers—for others to use. Websites are now the favoured means of spreading malware, partly because the unwary are directed to them through spam or links posted on social-networking sites. And poorly designed websites often provide a window into valuable databases.

Malware is typically used to steal passwords and other data, or to open a "back door" to a computer so that it can be taken over by outsiders. Such "zombie" machines can be linked up to thousands, if not millions, of others around the world to create a "botnet". Estimates for the number of infected machines range up to 100m. Botnets are used to send spam, spread malware or launch distributed denial-of-service (DDoS) attacks, which seek to bring down a targeted computer by overloading it with countless bogus requests.

The Spy Who Spammed Me

Criminals usually look for easy prey. But states can combine the criminal hacker's tricks, such as spear-phishing, with the intelligence apparatus to reconnoitre a target, the computing power to break codes and passwords, and the patience to probe a system until it finds a weakness—usually a fallible human being. Steven Chabinsky, a senior FBI official responsible for cyber-security, recently said that "given enough time, motivation and funding, a determined adversary will always—always—be able to penetrate a targeted system."

Traditional human spies risk arrest or execution by trying to smuggle out copies of documents. But those in the cyberworld face no such risks. "A spy might once have been able to take out a few books' worth of material," says one senior American military source, "Now they take the whole library. And if you restock the shelves, they will steal it again."

China, in particular, is accused of wholesale espionage, attacking the computers of major Western defence contractors and reputedly taking classified details of the F-35 fighter, the mainstay of future American air power. At the end of 2009, it appears to have targeted Google and more than a score of other IT companies. Experts at a cyber-test-range built in Maryland by Lockheed Martin, a defence contractor (which denies losing the F-35 data), say "advanced persistent threats" are hard to fend off amid the countless minor probing of its networks. Sometimes attackers try to slip information out slowly, hidden in ordinary internet traffic. At other times they have tried to break in by leaving infected memory-sticks in the car park, hoping somebody would plug them into the network. Even unclassified e-mails can contain a wealth of useful information about projects under development.

"Cyber-espionage is the biggest intelligence disaster since the loss of the nuclear secrets [in the late 1940s]," says Jim Lewis of the Centre for Strategic and International Studies, a think-tank in Washington, DC. Spying probably presents the most immediate danger to the West: the loss of high-tech know-how that could erode its economic lead or, if it ever came to a shooting war, blunt its military edge.

Western spooks think China deploys the most assiduous, and most shameless, cyberspies, but Russian ones are probably more skilled and subtle. Top of the league, say the spooks, are still America's NSA and Britain's GCHQ, which may explain why Western countries have until recently been reluctant to complain too loudly about computer snooping.

The next step after penetrating networks to steal data is to disrupt or manipulate them. If military targeting information could be attacked, for example, ballistic missiles would be useless. Those who play war games speak of being able to "change the red and blue dots": make friendly (blue) forces appear to be the enemy (red), and vice versa.

General Alexander says the Pentagon and NSA started co-operating on cyberwarfare in late 2008 after "a serious intrusion into our classified networks". Mr Lewis says this refers to the penetration of Central Command, which oversees the wars in Iraq and Afghanistan, through an infected thumb-drive. It took a week to winkle out the intruder. Nobody knows what, if any, damage was caused. But the thought of an enemy lurking in battle-fighting systems alarms the top brass.

That said, an attacker might prefer to go after unclassified military logistics supply systems, or even the civilian infra-structure. A loss of confidence in financial data and electronic transfers could cause economic upheaval. An even bigger worry is an attack on the power grid. Power companies tend not to keep many spares of expensive generator parts, which can take months to replace. Emergency diesel generators cannot make up for the loss of the grid, and cannot operate indefinitely. Without electricity and other critical services, communications systems and cash-dispensers cease to work. A loss of power lasting just a few days, reckon some, starts to cause a cascade of economic damage.

Experts disagree about the vulnerability of systems that run industrial plants, known as supervisory control and data acquisition (SCADA). But more and more of these are being connected to the internet, raising the risk of remote attack. "Smart" grids, which relay information about energy use to the utilities, are promoted as ways of reducing energy waste. But they also increase security worries about both crime (e.g., allowing bills to be falsified) and exposing SCADA networks to attack.

General Alexander has spoken of "hints that some penetrations are targeting systems for remote sabotage". But precisely what is happening is unclear: are outsiders probing SCADA systems only for reconnaissance, or to open "back doors" for future use? One senior American military source said that if any country were found to be planting logic bombs on the grid, it would provoke the equivalent of the Cuban missile crisis.

Estonia, Georgia, and WWI

Important thinking about the tactical and legal concepts of cyber-warfare is taking place in a former Soviet barracks in Estonia, now home to NATO's "centre of excellence" for cyber-defence. It was established in response to what has become known as "Web War 1", a concerted denial-of-service attack on Estonian government, media and bank web servers that was precipitated by the decision to move a Soviet-era war memorial in central Tallinn in 2007. This was more a cyber-riot than a war, but it forced Estonia more or less to cut itself off from the internet.

Similar attacks during Russia's war with Georgia the next year looked more ominous, because they seemed to be coordinated with the advance of Russian military columns. Government and media websites went down and telephone lines were jammed, crippling Georgia's ability to present its case abroad. President Mikheil Saakashvili's website had to be moved to an American server better able to fight off the attack. Estonian experts were dispatched to Georgia to help out.

Many assume that both these attacks were instigated by the Kremlin. But investigations traced them only to Russian "hack-tivists" and criminal botnets; many of the attacking computers were in Western countries. There are wider issues: did the cyber-attack on Estonia, a member of NATO, count as an armed attack, and should the alliance have defended it? And did Estonia's assistance to Georgia, which is not in NATO, risk drawing Estonia into the war, and NATO along with it?

Such questions permeate discussions of NATO's new "strategic concept", to be adopted later this year. A panel of experts headed by Madeleine Albright, a former American secretary of state, reported in May that cyber-attacks are among the three most likely threats to the alliance. The next significant attack, it said, "may well come down a fibre-optic cable" and may be serious enough to merit a response under the mutual-defence provisions of Article 5.

During his confirmation hearing, senators sent General Alexander several questions. Would he have "significant" offensive cyber-weapons? Might these encourage others to follow suit? How sure would he need to be about the identity of an attacker to "fire back"? Answers to these were restricted to a classified supplement. In public, the general said that the president would be the judge of what constituted cyberwar; if America responded with force in cyberspace it would be in keeping with the rules of war and the "principles of military necessity, discrimination, and proportionality."

General Alexander's seven-month confirmation process is a sign of the qualms senators felt at the merging of military and espionage functions, the militarisation of cyberspace and the fear that it may undermine Americans' right to privacy. Cybercommand will protect only the military ".mil" domain. The government domain, ".gov", and the corporate infrastructure, ".com" will be the responsibility respectively of the Department of Homeland Security and private companies, with support from Cybercom.

One senior military official says General Alexander's priority will be to improve the defences of military networks. Another bigwig casts some doubt on cyber-offence. "It's hard to do it at a specific time," he says. "If a cyber-attack is used as a military weapon, you want a predictable time and effect. If you are using it for espionage it does not matter; you can wait." He implies that cyber-weapons would be used mainly as an adjunct to conventional operations in a narrow theatre.

The Chinese may be thinking the same way. A report on China's cyber-warfare doctrine, written for the congressionally mandated US–China Economic and Security Review Commission, envisages China using cyber-weapons not to defeat America, but to disrupt and slow down its forces long enough for China to seize Taiwan without having to fight a shooting war.

Apocalypse or Asymmetry?

Deterrence in cyber-warfare is more uncertain than, say, in nuclear strategy: there is no mutually assured destruction, the dividing line between criminality and war is blurred and identifying attacking computers, let alone the fingers on the keyboards, is difficult. Retaliation need not be confined to cyberspace; the one system that is certainly not linked to the public internet is America's nuclear firing chain. Still, the more likely use of cyber-weapons is probably not to bring about electronic apocalypse, but as tools of limited warfare.

Cyber-weapons are most effective in the hands of big states. But because they are cheap, they may be most useful to the comparatively weak. They may well suit terrorists. Fortunately, perhaps, the likes of al-Qaeda have mostly used the internet for propaganda and communication. It may be that jihadists lack the ability to, say, induce a refinery to blow itself up. Or it may be that they prefer the gory theatre of suicide-bombings to the anonymity of computer sabotage—for now.

Critical Thinking

1. How dangerous is cyberwar?
2. With most things run by computer, think of all the settings that could be changed to cause specific or astronomical damages.
3. What would life be like if almost all computers and chips were destroyed.

Create Central

www.mhhe.com/createcentral

Internet References

ACLU Criminal Justice Home Page
www.aclu.org/crimjustice/index.html
Human Rights and Humanitarian Assistance
www.etown.edu/vl/humrts.html
Sociology—Study Sociology Online
http://edu.learnsoc.org
Sociology Web Resources
http://www.mhhe.com/socscience/sociology/resources/index.htm
Sociosite
http://www.topsite.com/goto/sociosite.net
Socioweb
http://www.topsite.com/goto/socioweb.com
Terrorism Research Center
www.terrorism.com

From *The Economist*, July 3, 2010. Copyright © 2010 by The Economist Newspaper, Ltd, London. All rights reserved. Further reproduction prohibited. Reprinted by permission via Rightslink.

Article   Prepared by: Kurt Finsterbusch, *University of Maryland, College Park*

Low-Tech Terrorism

BRUCE HOFFMAN

Learning Outcomes

After reading this article, you will be able to:

- Understand the dangers of cyberterrorism.

- Describe how the United States can combat cyberterrorism.

Among the more prescient analyses of the terrorist threats that the United States would face in the twenty-first century was a report published in September 1999 by the US Commission on National Security/21st century, better known as the Hart-Rudman commission. Named after its cochairs, former senators Gary Hart and Warren Rudman, and evocatively titled *New World Coming,* it correctly predicted that mass-casualty terrorism would emerge as one of America's preeminent security concerns in the next century. "Already," the report's first page lamented, "the traditional functions of law, police work, and military power have begun to blur before our eyes as new threats arise." It added, "Notable among these new threats is the prospect of an attack on US cities by independent or state-supported terrorists using weapons of mass destruction."

Although hijacked commercial aircraft deliberately flown into high-rise buildings were not the weapons of mass destruction that the commission had in mind, the catastrophic effects that this tactic achieved—obliterating New York City's World Trade Center, slicing through several of the Pentagon's concentric rings and killing nearly 3,000 people—indisputably captured the gist of that prophetic assertion.

The report was also remarkably accurate in anticipating the terrorist organizational structures that would come to dominate the first dozen or so years of the new century. "Future terrorists will probably be even less hierarchically organized, and yet better networked, than they are today. Their diffuse nature will make them more anonymous, yet their ability to coordinate

mass effects on a global basis will increase," the commission argued. Its vision of the motivations that would animate and subsequently fuel this violence was similarly revelatory. "The growing resentment against Western culture and values in some parts of the world," along with "the fact that others often perceive the United States as exercising its power with arrogance and self-absorption," was already "breeding a backlash" that would both continue and likely evolve into new and more insidious forms, the report asserted.

Some of the commission's other visionary conclusions now read like a retrospective summary of the past decade. "The United States will be called upon frequently to intervene militarily in a time of uncertain alliances," says one, while another disconsolately warns that "even excellent intelligence will not prevent all surprises." Today's tragic events in Syria were also anticipated by one statement that addressed the growing likelihood of foreign crises "replete with atrocities and the deliberate terrorizing of civilian populations."

Fortunately, the report's most breathless prediction concerning the likelihood of terrorist use of weapons of mass destruction (WMD) has not come to pass. But this is not for want of terrorists trying to obtain such capabilities. Indeed, prior to the October 2001 US-led invasion of Afghanistan, Al Qaeda had embarked upon an ambitious quest to acquire and develop an array of such weapons that, had it been successful, would have altered to an unimaginable extent our most basic conceptions about national security and rendered moot debates over whether terrorism posed a potentially existential threat.

But just how effective have terrorist efforts to acquire and use weapons of mass destruction actually been? The September 11, 2001, attacks were widely noted for their reliance on relatively low-tech weaponry—the conversion, in effect, of airplanes into missiles by using raw physical muscle and box cutters to hijack them. Since then, efforts to gain access to WMD have been unceasing. But examining those efforts results in some surprising conclusions. While there is no cause for complacency, they do suggest that terrorists face some inherent constraints that will be difficult for them to overcome. It is easier to proclaim the threat of mass terror than to perpetrate it.

The terrorist attacks on September 11 completely recast global perceptions of threat and vulnerability. Long-standing assumptions that terrorists were more interested in publicity than in killing were dramatically swept aside in the rising crescendo of death and destruction. The butcher's bill that morning was without parallel in the annals of modern terrorism. Throughout the entirety of the twentieth century no more than 14 terrorist incidents had killed more than a 100 people, and until September 11 no terrorist operation had ever killed more than 500 people in a single attack. Viewed from another perspective, more than twice as many Americans perished within those excruciating 102 minutes than had been killed by terrorists since 1968—the year widely accepted as marking the advent of modern, international terrorism.

So massive and consequential a terrorist onslaught naturally gave rise to fears that a profound threshold in terrorist constraint and lethality had been crossed. Renewed fears and concerns were in turn generated that terrorists would now embrace an array of deadly nonconventional weapons in order to inflict even greater levels of death and destruction than had occurred that day. Attention focused specifically on terrorist use of WMD, and the so-called Cheney Doctrine emerged to shape America's national-security strategy. The doctrine derived from former vice president Dick Cheney's reported statement that "if there's a one percent chance that Pakistani scientists are helping Al Qaeda build or develop a nuclear weapon, we have to treat it as a certainty in terms of our response." What the "one percent doctrine" meant in practice, according to one observer, was that "even if there's just a one percent chance of the unimaginable coming due, act as if it's a certainty." Countering the threat of nonconventional-weapons proliferation—whether by rogue states arrayed in an "axis of evil" or by terrorists who might acquire such weapons from those same states or otherwise develop them on their own—thus became one of the central pillars of the Bush administration's time in office.

In the case of Al Qaeda, at least, these fears were more than amply justified. That group's interest in acquiring a nuclear weapon reportedly commenced as long ago as 1992—a mere four years after its creation. An attempt by an Al Qaeda agent to purchase uranium from South Africa was made either late the following year or early in 1994 without success. Osama bin Laden's efforts to obtain nuclear material nonetheless continued, as evidenced by the arrest in Germany in 1998 of

a trusted senior aide named Mamdouh Mahmud Salim, who was attempting to purchase enriched uranium. And that same year, the Al Qaeda leader issued a proclamation in the name of the "International Islamic Front for Fighting the Jews and Crusaders." Titled "The Nuclear Bomb of Islam," the proclamation declared that "it is the duty of Muslims to prepare as much force as possible to terrorize the enemies of God." When asked several months later by a Pakistani journalist whether Al Qaeda was "in a position to develop chemical weapons and try to purchase nuclear material for weapons," bin Laden replied: "I would say that acquiring weapons for the defense of Muslims is a religious duty."

Bin Laden's continued interest in nuclear weaponry was also on display at the time of the September 11 attacks. Two Pakistani nuclear scientists named Sultan Bashiruddin Mahmood and Abdul Majeed spent three days that August at a secret Al Qaeda facility outside Kabul. Although their discussions with bin Laden, his deputy Ayman al-Zawahiri and other senior Al Qaeda officials also focused on the development and employment of chemical and biological weapons, Mahmood—the former director for nuclear power at Pakistan's Atomic Energy Commission—claimed that bin Laden's foremost interest was in developing a nuclear weapon.

The movement's efforts in the biological-warfare realm, however, were far more advanced and appear to have begun in earnest with a memo written by al-Zawahiri on April 15, 1999, to Muhammad Atef, then deputy commander of Al Qaeda's military committee. Citing articles published in *Science,* the *Journal of Immunology* and the *New England Journal of Medicine,* as well as information gleaned from authoritative books such as *Tomorrow's Weapons, Peace or Pestilence* and *Chemical Warfare,* al-Zawahiri outlined in detail his thoughts on the priority to be given to developing a biological-weapons capability.

One of the specialists recruited for this purpose was a US-trained Malaysian microbiologist named Yazid Sufaat. A former captain in the Malaysian army, Sufaat graduated from the California State University in 1987 with a degree in biological sciences. He later joined Al Gamaa al-Islamiyya (the "Islamic Group"), an Al Qaeda affiliate operating in Southeast Asia, and worked closely with its military operations chief, Riduan Isamuddin, better known as Hambali, and with Hambali's own Al Qaeda handler, Khalid Sheikh Mohammed—the infamous KSM, architect of the September 11 attacks.

In January 2000, Sufaat played host to two of the 9/11 hijackers, Khalid al-Midhar and Nawaf Alhazmi, who stayed in his Kuala Lumpur condominium. Later that year, Zacarias Moussaoui, the alleged "twentieth hijacker," who was sentenced in 2006 to life imprisonment by a federal district court in Alexandria, Virginia, also stayed with Sufaat. Under KSM's direction, Hambali and Sufaat set up shop at an Al Qaeda camp in Kandahar, Afghanistan, where their efforts focused on the weaponization of anthrax. Although the two made some progress, biowarfare experts believe that on the eve of September 11 Al Qaeda was still at least two to three years away from producing a sufficient quantity of anthrax to use as a weapon.

Meanwhile, a separate team of Al Qaeda operatives was engaged in a parallel research-and-development project to produce ricin and chemical-warfare agents at the movement's Derunta camp, near the eastern Afghan city of Jalalabad. As one senior US intelligence officer who prefers to remain anonymous explained, "Al Qaeda's WMD efforts weren't part of a single program but rather multiple compartmentalized projects involving multiple scientists in multiple locations."

The Derunta facility reportedly included laboratories and a school that trained handpicked terrorists in the use of chemical and biological weapons. Among this select group was Kamal Bourgass, an Algerian Al Qaeda operative who was convicted in British courts in 2004 and 2005 for the murder of a British police officer and of "conspiracy to commit a public nuisance by the use of poisons or explosives." The school's director was an Egyptian named Midhat Mursi—better known by his Al Qaeda nom de guerre, Abu Kebab—and among its instructors were a Pakistani microbiologist and Sufaat. When US military forces overran the camp in 2001, evidence of the progress achieved in developing chemical weapons as diverse as hydrogen cyanide, chlorine and phosgene was discovered. Mursi himself was killed in 2008 by a missile fired from a U.S. Predator drone.

Mursi's death dealt another significant blow to Al Qaeda's efforts to develop nonconventional weapons—but it did not end them. In fact, as the aforementioned senior US intelligence officer recently commented, "Al Qaeda's ongoing procurement efforts have been well established for awhile now . . . They haven't been highlighted in the U.S. media, but that isn't the same as it not happening." In 2010, for instance, credible intelligence surfaced that Al Qaeda in the Arabian Peninsula—widely considered the movement's most dangerous and capable affiliate—was deeply involved in the development of ricin, a bioweapon made from castor beans that the FBI has termed the third most toxic substance known, behind only plutonium and botulism.

Then, in May 2013, Turkish authorities seized two kilograms of sarin nerve gas—the same weapon used in the 1995 attack on the Tokyo subway system—and arrested 12 men linked to Al Qaeda's Syrian affiliate, Al Nusra Front. Days later, another set of sarin-related arrests was made in Iraq of Al Qaeda operatives based in that country who were separately overseeing the production of sarin and mustard blistering agents at two or more locations.

Finally, Israel admitted in November 2013 that for the past three years it had been holding a senior Al Qaeda operative whose expertise was in biological warfare. "The revelations over his alleged biological weapons links," one account noted of the operative's detention, "come amid concerns that Al Qaeda affiliates in Syria are attempting to procure bioweapons—and may already have done so."

Indeed, Syria's ongoing civil war and the prominent position of two key Al Qaeda affiliates—Al Nusra Front and the Islamic State of Iraq and the Levant—along with other sympathetic jihadi entities in that epic struggle, coupled with the potential access afforded to Bashar al-Assad's chemical-weapons stockpiles, suggest that we have likely not heard the last of Al Qaeda's ambitions to obtain nerve agents, poison gas and other harmful toxins for use as mass-casualty weapons.

Nonetheless, a fundamental paradox appears to exist so far as terrorist capabilities involving chemical, biological and nuclear weapons are concerned. As mesmerizingly attractive as these nonconventional weapons remain to Al Qaeda and other terrorist organizations, they have also mostly proven frustratingly disappointing to whoever has tried to use them. Despite the extensive use of poison gas during World War I, for instance, this weapon accounted for only 5 percent of all casualties in that conflict. Reportedly, it required some 60 pounds of mustard gas to produce even a single casualty. Even in more recent times, chemical weapons claimed the lives of less than 1 percent (500) of the 600,000 Iranians who died in the Iran-Iraq war. The Japanese cult Aum Shinrikyo succeeded in killing no more than 13 people in its attack on the Tokyo underground in 1995. And, five years earlier, no fatalities resulted from a Tamil Tigers assault on a Sri Lankan armed forces base in East Kiran that employed chlorine gas. In fact, the wind changed and blew the gas back into the Tigers' lines, thus aborting the attack.

Biological weapons have proven similarly difficult to deploy effectively. Before and during World War II, the Imperial Japanese Army carried out nearly a dozen attacks using a variety of germ agents—including cholera, dysentery, bubonic plague, anthrax and paratyphoid, disseminated through both air and water—against Chinese forces. Not once did these weapons decisively affect the outcome of a battle. And, in the 1942 assault on Chekiang, 10,000 Japanese soldiers themselves became ill, and nearly 2,000 died, from exposure to these agents. "The Japanese program's principal defect, a problem to all efforts so far," the American terrorism expert David Rapoport concluded, was "an ineffective delivery system."

The challenges inherent in using germs as weapons are borne out by the research conducted for more than a decade by Seth Carus, a researcher at the National Defense University.

Carus has assembled perhaps the most comprehensive database of the use of biological agents by a wide variety of adversaries, including terrorists, government operatives, ordinary criminals and the mentally unstable. His exhaustive research reveals that no more than a total of 10 people were killed and less than a 1,000 were made ill as a result of about 200 incidents of bioterrorism or biocrime. Most of which, moreover, entailed the individual poisoning of specific people rather than widespread, indiscriminate attacks.

The formidable challenges of obtaining the material needed to construct a nuclear bomb, along with the fabrication and dissemination difficulties involving the use of noxious gases and biological agents, perhaps account for the operational conservatism long observed in terrorist tactics and weaponry. As politically radical or religiously fanatical as terrorists may be, they nonetheless to date have overwhelmingly seemed to prefer the tactical assurance of the comparatively modest effects achieved by the conventional weapons with which they are familiar, as opposed to the risk of failure inherent in the use of more exotic means of death and destruction. Terrorists, as Brian Jenkins famously observed in 1985, thus continue to "appear to be more imitative than innovative." Accordingly, what innovation does occur tends to take place in the realm of the clever adaptation or modification of existing tactics—such as turning hijacked passenger airliners into cruise missiles—or in the means and methods used to fabricate and detonate explosive devices, rather than in the use of some new or dramatically novel weapon.

Terrorists have thus functioned mostly in a technological vacuum: either aloof or averse to the profound changes that have fundamentally altered the nature of modern warfare. Whereas technological progress has produced successively more complex, lethally effective, and destructively accurate weapons systems that are deployed from a variety of air, land, sea—and space—platforms, terrorists continue to rely, as they have for more than a century, on the same two basic "weapons systems": the gun and the bomb. Admittedly, the guns used by terrorists today have larger ammunition capacities and more rapid rates of fire than the simple revolver the Russian revolutionary Vera Zasulich used in 1878 to assassinate the governor-general of St. Petersburg. Similarly, bombs today require smaller amounts of explosives that are exponentially more powerful and more easily concealed than the sticks of TNT with which the Fenian dynamiters terrorized London more than a century ago. But the fact remains that the vast majority of terrorist incidents continue to utilize the same two attack modes.

Why is this? There are perhaps two obvious explanations: ease and cost. Indeed, as Leonardo da Vinci is said to have observed in a completely different era and context, "Simplicity is the ultimate sophistication." The same can be said about *most* terrorist—and insurgent—weapons and tactics today.

Improvised explosive devices (IED) and bombs constructed of commercially available, readily accessible homemade materials now account for the lion's share of terrorist—and insurgent—attacks. The use of two crude bombs packed in ordinary pressure cookers that killed three people and injured nearly 300 others at last April's Boston Marathon is among the more recent cases in point. Others include the succession of peroxide-based bombs that featured in the July 2005 suicide attacks on London transport, the 2006 plot to blow up seven American and Canadian airliners while in flight from Heathrow Airport to various destinations in North America, and the 2009 attempt to replicate the London transport bombings on the New York City subway system.

The account of the construction of the bombs intended for the New York City attack presented in the book *Enemies Within* vividly illustrates this point. Written by two Pulitzer Prize-winning journalists, Matt Apuzzo and Adam Goldman, the book describes how the would-be bomber, an Afghanistan-born, permanent U.S. resident named Najibullah Zazi, easily purchased the ingredients needed for the device's construction and then, following the instructions given to him by his Al Qaeda handlers in Pakistan, created a crude but potentially devastatingly lethal weapon:

> For weeks he'd been visiting beauty supply stores, filling his carts with hydrogen peroxide and nail polish remover. At the Beauty Supply Warehouse, among the rows of wigs, braids, and extensions, the manager knew him as Jerry. He said his girlfriend owned hair salons. There was no reason to doubt him.

> On pharmacy shelves, in the little brown plastic bottles, hydrogen peroxide is a disinfectant, a sting-free way to clean scrapes. Beauty salons use a more concentrated version to bleach hair or activate hair dyes. At even higher concentrations, it burns the skin. It is not flammable on its own, but when it reacts with other chemicals, it quickly releases oxygen, creating an environment ripe for explosions. . . . Even with a cheap stove, it's easy to simmer water out of hydrogen peroxide, leaving behind something more potent. It takes time, and he had plenty of that.

Preparing the explosive initiator was only slightly more complicated, but considerably more dangerous. Hence, Zazi had to be especially careful. "He added the muriatic acid and watched as the chemicals crystallized," the account continues:

> The crystals are known as triacetone triperoxide, or TATP. A spark, electrical current, even a bit of friction can set off an explosion. . . .

The white crystal compound had been popular among Palestinian terrorists. It was cheap and powerful, but its instability earned it the nickname "Mother of Satan". . . .

When he was done mixing, he rinsed the crystals with baking soda and water to make his creation more stable. He placed the finished product in a wide-rimmed glass jar about the size of a coffee tin and inspected his work. There would be enough for three detonators. Three detonators inside three backpacks filled with a flammable mixture and ball bearings—the same type of weapon that left 52 dead in London in 2005. . . .

He was ready for New York.

These types of improvised weapons are not only devastatingly effective but also remarkably inexpensive, further accounting for their popularity. For example, the House of Commons Intelligence and Security Committee, which investigated the 2005 London transport attacks, concluded that the entire operation cost less than £8,000 to execute. This sum included the cost of a trip to Pakistan so that the cell leader and an accomplice could acquire the requisite bomb-making skills at a secret Al Qaeda training camp in that country's North-West Frontier Province; the purchase of all the needed equipment and ingredients once they were back in Britain; the rental of an apartment in Leeds that they turned into a bomb factory; car rentals and the purchase of cell phones; and other incidentals.

The cost-effectiveness of such homemade devices—and their appeal to terrorists—is of course not new. Decades ago, the Provisional Irish Republican Army (PIRA) demonstrated the disproportionate effects and enormous damage that crude, inexpensive homemade explosive devices could achieve. In what was described as "the most powerful explosion in London since World War II," a PIRA fertilizer bomb made with urea nitrate and diesel fuel exploded outside the Baltic Exchange in April 1992, killing three people, wounding 90 others, leaving a 12-foot-wide crater—and causing $1.25 billion in damage. Exactly a year later, a similar bomb devastated the nearby Bishops Gate, killing one person and injuring more than 40 others. Estimates put the damage of that blast at $1.5 billion.

Long a staple of PIRA operations, in the early 1990s fertilizer had cost the group on average 1 percent of a comparable amount of plastic explosive. Although after adulteration fertilizer is admittedly far less powerful than plastic explosives, it also tends to cause more damage than plastic explosives because the energy of the blast is more sustained and less controlled.

Similarly, the homemade bomb used in the first attack on New York's World Trade Center in 1993—consisting of urea nitrate derived from fertilizer but enhanced by three canisters of hydrogen gas to create a more powerful fuel-air explosion—produced a similarly impressive return on the terrorists' investment. The device cost less than $400 to construct. Yet, it not only killed six people, injured more than a 1,000 others and gouged a 180-foot-wide crater six stories deep, but also caused an estimated $550 million in damages and lost revenue to the businesses housed there. The seaborne suicide-bomb attack seven years later on the USS *Cole,* a U.S. Navy destroyer anchored in Aden, Yemen, reportedly cost Al Qaeda no more than $10,000 to execute. But, in addition to claiming the lives of 17 American sailors and wounding 39 others, it cost the U.S. Navy $250 million to repair the damage caused to the vessel.

This trend toward the increased use of IEDS has had its most consequential and pernicious effects in Iraq and Afghanistan during our prolonged deployments there. As Andrew Bacevich, a retired U.S. Army officer and current Boston University professor, has written, "No matter how badly battered and beaten, the 'terrorists'" on these and other recent battlefields were not "intimidated, remained unrepentant, and kept coming back for more, devising tactics against which forces optimized for conventional combat did not have a ready response." He adds, "The term invented for this was 'asymmetric conflict,' loosely translated as war against adversaries who won't fight the way we want them to."

In Iraq and Afghanistan, both terrorists and insurgents alike have waged low-risk wars of attrition against American, British, allied and host military forces using a variety of IEDS with triggering devices as simple as garage-door openers, cordless phones and car key fobs to confound, if not hobble, among the most technologically advanced militaries in the history of mankind. "The richest, most-trained army got beat by dudes in manjammies and A.K.'s," an American soldier observed to a *New York Times* reporter of one such bloody engagement in Afghanistan five years ago.

Indeed, terrorists and insurgents in both Afghanistan and Iraq have demonstrated the effectiveness of even poorly or modestly armed nonstate adversaries in confronting superior, conventional military forces and waging a deadly war of attrition designed in part to undermine popular support and resolve back home for these prolonged deployments. Equally worrisome, these battle environments have become spawning grounds for continued and future violence: real-life training camps for jihadis and hands-on laboratories for the research and development of new and ever more deadly terrorist and insurgent tactics and techniques. "How do you stop foes who kill with devices built for the price of a pizza?" was the question posed by a *Newsweek* cover story about IEDS in 2007. "Maybe the question is," it continued, "can you stop them?"

At one point, IEDS were responsible for nearly two-thirds of military fatalities caused by terrorists and insurgents in Iraq and a quarter of the military fatalities in Afghanistan. According to one authoritative account, there was an IED incident every 15 minutes in Iraq during 2006. And, after the number of IED attacks had doubled in Afghanistan during 2009, this tactic accounted for three-quarters of military casualties in some areas.

These explosive devices often were constructed using either scavenged artillery or mortar shells, with military or commercial ordnance, or from entirely homemade ingredients. They were then buried beneath roadways, concealed among roadside refuse, hidden in animal carcasses or telephone poles, camouflaged into curbsides or secreted along the guard rails on the shoulders of roadways, put in boxes, or disguised as rocks or bricks strewn by the side of the road. As military vehicle armor improved, the bomb makers adapted and adjusted to these new force-protection measures and began to design and place IEDS in elevated positions, attaching them to road signs or trees, in order to impact the vehicles' unarmored upper structure.

The method of detonation has also varied as United States, allied and host forces have adapted to insurgent tactics. Command-wire detonators were replaced by radio-signal triggering devices such as cell phones and garage-door openers. These devices were remote wired up to 100 meters from the IED detonator to obviate jamming measures. More recently, infrared lasers have been used as explosive initiators. One or more artillery shells rigged with blasting caps and improvised shrapnel (consisting of bits of concrete, nuts, bolts, screws, tacks, ball bearings, etc.) have been the most commonly used, but the makeshift devices have also gradually become larger as multinational forces added more armor to their vehicles, with evidence from insurgent propaganda videos of aviation bombs of 500 lb. being used as IEDS. In some cases, these improvised devices are detonated serially—in "daisy chain" explosions—designed to mow down quick-reaction forces converging on the scene following the initial blast and first wave of casualties.

By 2011, the U.S. Defense Department had spent nearly $20 billion on IED countermeasures—including new technologies, programs, and enhanced and constantly updated training. A "massive new military bureaucracy" had to be created to oversee this effort and itself was forced to create "unconventional processes for introducing new programs," as a 2010 New America Foundation report put it. Yet, as the British Army found in its war against Jewish terrorists in Palestine 70

years ago, there is no easy or lasting solution to this threat, IED attacks had in fact become so pervasive in Palestine that in December 1946 British Army headquarters in Jerusalem issued a meticulously detailed 35-page pamphlet, complete with photographs and diagrams, describing these weapons, their emplacement and their lethal effects. Even so, as military commanders and civilian authorities alike acknowledged at the time, IEDS were then as now virtually impossible to defend against completely.

Perhaps the most novel and innovative use of IEDS, however, has been when they have been paired with toxic chemicals. Much as the Iraq conflict has served as a proving ground for other terrorist weapons and tactics, it has also served this purpose with chemical weapons. Between 2007 and 2010, more than a dozen major truck-bomb attacks occurred in Iraq involving conventional explosions paired with chlorine gas.

The most serious incident, however, was one that was foiled by Jordanian authorities in April 2004. It involved the toxic release of chemicals into a crowded urban environment and was orchestrated by the late Abu Musab al-Zarqawi, the founder and leader of Al Qaeda in Iraq. The Amman plot entailed the use of some 20 tons of chemicals and explosives to target simultaneously the prime minister's office, the General Intelligence Department's headquarters and the U.S. embassy. Although the main purpose of the coordinated operations was to conduct forced-entry attacks by suicide bombers against these three heavily protected, high-value targets, an ancillary intention is believed to have been the infliction of mass casualties on the surrounding areas by the noxious chemical agents deliberately released in the blasts. An estimated 80,000 people, Jordanian authorities claim, would have been killed or seriously injured in the operation.

The above attacks in Iraq and the foiled incident in Amman all underscore the potential for terrorists to attack a domestic industrial chemical facility with a truck bomb or other large explosive device, with the purpose of triggering the release of toxic chemicals. In this respect, the effects of prior industrial accidents involving chemicals may exert a profound influence over terrorists. In 2005, for instance, a train crash and derailment in South Carolina released some 60 tons of liquefied chlorine into the air, killing nine people and injuring 250 others. Considerably more tragic, of course, was the 1984 disaster at a Union Carbide chemical facility in Bhopal, India. Some 40 tons of methyl isocyanate were accidentally released into the environment and killed nearly 4,000 people living around the plant. Methyl isocyanate is one of the more toxic chemicals used in industry, with a toxicity that is only a few percent less than that of sarin.

The war on terrorism today generates little interest and even less enthusiasm. A decade of prolonged military deployments to Iraq and Afghanistan has drained both the treasuries and willpower of the United States, Great Britain, and many other countries, as well as the ardor and commitment that attended the commencement of this global struggle over a dozen years ago. The killings of leading Al Qaeda figures such as bin Laden and Anwar al-Awlaki—along with some 40 other senior commanders and hundreds of the group's fighters—have sufficiently diminished the threat of terrorism to our war-weary, economically preoccupied nations.

But before we simply conclude that the threat from either Al Qaeda or terrorism has disappeared, it would be prudent to pause and reflect on the expansive dimensions of Al Qaeda's WMD research-and-development efforts—and also to consider the continuing developments on the opposite end of the technological spectrum that have likewise transformed the threat against conventionally superior militaries and even against superpowers. Like it or not, the war on terrorism continues, abetted by the technological advances of our adversaries and thus far mercifully countered by our own technological prowess—and all the more so by our unyielding vigilance.

Critical Thinking

1. What kind of damages can cyberterrorists cause?
2. How can the United States defend against cyberterrorists?
3. Could cyberterrorism cause society to literally break down?

Create Central

www.mhhe.com/createcentral

Internet References

ACLU Criminal Justice Home Page
www.aclu.org/crimjustice/index.html
Human Rights and Humanitarian Assistance
www.etown.edu/vl/humrts.html
New American Studies Web
www.georgetown.edu/crossroads/asw
Sociology—Study Sociology Online
http://edu.learnsoc.org
Sociology Web Resources
http://www.mhhe.com/socscience/sociology/resources/index.htm
Sociosite
http://www.topsite.com/goto/sociosite.net
Socioweb
http://www.topsite.com/goto/socioweb.com
Terrorism Research Center
www.terrorism.com

BRUCE HOFFMAN is a contributing editor to *The National Interest,* a senior fellow at the U.S. Military Academy's Combating Terrorism Center, and a professor and director of the Center for Security Studies at Georgetown University.

Hoffman, Bruce, "Low Tech Terrorism," *The National Interest*, March/April 2014, pp. 61–71. Copyright © 2014 by National Interest. All rights reserved. Used with permission.

Unit 6

UNIT

Prepared by: Kurt Finsterbusch, *University of Maryland, College Park*

Problems of Population, Environment, Resources, and the Future

This unit focuses on problems of the future (mostly from a worldwide perspective) and covers topics such as present population and environmental trends, problems with new technologies, and prospects for the future.

Some scholars are very concerned about the worsening state of the environment, and others are confident that technological developments will solve most of these problems. Because the debate is about the future, neither view can be proved or disproved. Nevertheless, it is important to look at the factors that are causing environmental decline and increasing the demands on the environment. One factor is population growth, so future demographics and their implications must be assessed. Another required assessment is a survey of the many environmental problems that need to be addressed. Especially important are food production problems and the current and potential impacts of global warming.

A key issue in predicting the future is how future technology will change conditions and prospects. One author in this unit argues that technology and innovation will save the planet. Another celebrates the potential to genetically design babies to have all desirable attributes and no flaws. Many futurists, however, are not so optimistic. There have been many positive trends in the past century, and many of these are expected to continue, but there have been some negative trends, and they might increase. Especially worrisome are trends in economic and political power and in ideologies that may be creating a world that Americans fear.

Article   Prepared by: Kurt Finsterbusch, *University of Maryland, College Park*

Happy Planet

ROBERT ADLER

Learning Outcomes

After reading this article, you will be able to:

- Understand the present state of the planet.
- Explain recent and probable future land use changes.
- Consider the arguments about the current and probable future effects of human induced global warming.

The system isn't working. Or, depending on your point of view, it's working too well.

Our current economic system has lifted billions of people and entire nations out of poverty, and provides most people in the developed world with a standard of living that royalty couldn't dream of a century or two ago. The problem is that its very success—the intensity with which it motivates and finances the exploitation of nature, the multitudes who consume the cornucopia of goods and services it pours out, and the system's built-in drive for continual growth—is sending us headlong past critical natural boundaries.

The list is long and familiar: too much carbon dioxide warming the atmosphere and acidifying the ocean; too much land being cleared, leading to deforestation and desertification; overfishing causing crashes in one stock after another; and habitat destruction reducing biodiversity so drastically that some consider a sixth mass extinction to be under way. If we don't change course quickly, we will soon face extraordinary risks.

What's the alternative? The answer is simple on the face of it. Live within the limits of what nature can provide and process. Leave the land, ocean, atmosphere and biosphere to the next generation as healthy as we found them.

If we accept such a sustainable future as an important, even urgent, goal, some big questions loom for us in the developed world. What would sustainable living be like? Would it be a drab, subsistence-level existence, or could we still have vibrant lives? Is a sustainable world economically viable, or even possible? And if is it, how can we get there from here?

Not surprisingly, there's a wide range of possible answers to these questions. Some look at the ever-rising greenhouse gases, climate change and species loss and see a stark choice looming between catastrophe and drastic economic cutbacks. The 2 billion of us who are accustomed to a high-consumption lifestyle, together with governments and industries intent on "business as usual", won't voluntarily steer a path towards sustainability, says Richard Heinberg, a senior fellow at the Post Carbon Institute in Santa Rosa, California. The upshot will be a series of crises that will cumulatively "knock civilisation back on its heels", he says. At best, life for most of us in the world's richest countries might resemble that in some of today's poorer countries.

Others, however, argue that with renewable energy, sustainable use, reuse and "upcycling" of resources, and the smart design of everything from candy wrappers to cities, we can have both sustainability and abundance. Although nobody knows for sure what life in such a world would be like, a number of people have tried to envisage it.

Eric Sanderson, a conservation ecologist at the Wildlife Conservation Society in New York, depicts how life in the US might play out in his book, *Terra Nova: The New World after Oil, Cars and Suburbs*. He believes that innovations in four key areas—economics, renewable energy, transportation and urban environments—can work together to bring about rapid change. The book culminates with Sanderson and his wife travelling from New York to San Francisco in 2028 across a transformed country.

Green Vision

They live in a densely populated urban community in which residents travel mostly on foot or by bicycle, supplemented by public transport and shared electric vehicles. They cross the continent not by aeroplane but on energy-efficient, high-speed trains. In place of today's sprawling, gas-guzzling suburbs, they see lots of open country, much of it returning to woodlands and streams. Millions of people have decided to leave the suburbs and instead live in compact, self-sufficient and sustainably designed new towns. Some of these are standalone while others are communities within cities.

As Sanderson crosses the Midwest, instead of today's endless monocultures of corn, wheat and soy, he sees smaller farms using smart, diversified systems to grow crops and animals for local consumption, employing more people while using far fewer fertilisers and pesticides that take a lot of energy to produce.

A radically different energy system is visible everywhere—wind farms, solar fields and geothermal plants feed energy into a continent-spanning smart grid. The problem of storing energy for use when the sky is cloudy or the wind isn't blowing has largely been solved by pumping water from lower to higher reservoirs, then releasing it through turbines to generate power as needed.

Open for Business

Although Sanderson's timescale looks optimistic, his vision is not a utopian one. Use of renewable energy—wind, solar, geothermal and hydro—is surging worldwide. Electric vehicles are increasingly competitive. Homes, public buildings and many industrial processes are becoming far more energy efficient and we are charging ahead in terms of storing energy, sucking CO_2 out of the atmosphere, and generating fuels biologically or from sunlight and CO_2. "The technology that's in the pipeline is astonishing," says British environmentalist and author Jonathon Porritt. "I think we can now speak confidently about delivering the future we need. It's there. It's absolutely there."

Although challenging, the technological part of a transition to sustainability promises to be the easiest. The hard part—and it will be hard—is convincing economists, politicians and ordinary people worldwide to change how they live. To say that such changes are highly charged would be a huge understatement.

To most economists, continual growth is a necessity and a slowly growing economy, or a "steady state" economy that puts the health of the planet first, means catastrophe. Like worried doctors scrutinising an electrocardiogram, they track gross domestic product (GDP)—the market value of goods and services—diagnosing recessions and depressions by its downturns. Many see endless growth as the only way to create jobs and reduce poverty.

Not everyone agrees. Peter Victor, an ecological economist at York University in Toronto, modelled the Canadian economy from 2005 to 2035 under three conditions: business as usual, zeroing out all sources of economic growth, and a managed transition to a steady state—the sustainable option.

Business as usual produced no major surprises. The economy grew, but so did greenhouse gas emissions. Slamming on the economic brakes produced the catastrophe mainstream economists dread—GDP fell while unemployment and poverty soared.

The third scenario, which phased in a carbon tax, boosted anti-poverty programmes and reduced working hours, yielded results that mainstream economists would never have dreamed of: GDP per person rose and stabilised at about 150 percent of current levels, while unemployment, poverty and greenhouse gas emissions all fell. "It is possible for people to live well in a society in which economic stability rather than economic growth is the norm, where all its members flourish and social justice is served," Victor concludes.

On the global scale, the Intergovernmental Panel on Climate Change released a summary in April of the best climate modelling to date. It found that early implementation of policies to reduce climate change, including a global carbon tax and deploying all relevant technologies, could keep CO_2 below 450 parts per million, which would hold global warming below the critical 2°C threshold. Remarkably, those changes reduce economic growth by a maximum of 0.14 percent per year. That's not a misprint—a fraction of 1 percent per year.

The implication is that a sustainable world is economically feasible. It would certainly seem much better than heading full steam ahead into climate disaster. "You can't do business on a dead planet," points out US-based sustainability consultant Hunter Lovins.

Still, that doesn't tell us how to get there from here. Again there's no shortage of ideas. Ecologists, economists and politicians have proposed many initiatives to foster sustainability. Most repurpose tools we are familiar with—international agreements, laws and regulations, taxes and subsidies, plus new technologies. Others are more radical, advocating structural changes to key institutions such as banking and finance, corporations, land and resource ownership, and government. Many individuals, grass-roots groups such as the Transition Network, businesses such as Unilever, universities, cities such as Vancouver, and a few nations, including Iceland and Bhutan, are putting these ideas into practice.

Of course, most of us are not green crusaders. Yet we are already changing our lives, our work patterns and what we consume in ways that suggest the drive for sustainability may be pushing at an open door. For a start, we are driving less. The annual distance travelled by UK car and van drivers fell by 7 percent between 1995 and 2012. Germany, Australia, Japan and even the US all report the same trend. Why is that? Cost is a factor: young people are learning to drive later, put off by the price. We are also driving less to see friends and making fewer trips to the shops and to work by car—the rise in urban living, social media, online shopping and digital homeworking are seeing to that.

Driving less, and walking and cycling more are seen as positive lifestyle choices these days and are increasingly a feature of city living. Dense urban populations make recycling and other resource use more efficient, too. That doesn't mean a return to slums. If building materials can be produced sustainably and houses can be designed to be carbon-neutral, people can still live in ample and comfortable homes, says Mary Ritter, head of the European Union's climate innovation centre Climate KIC.

Porritt believes that the biggest changes will come in response to large popular movements galvanised by droughts, floods, famines and other crises. "Suddenly there's a shock to the system, and re-evaluation kicks in big time," he says. Yet some changes just happen and we hardly notice, such as putting out the recycling or insulating our lofts.

One of the most important is that we are having fewer children. Today the average woman has 2.43 children, fewer than half as many as 40 years ago. There is big population growth still to come in some places, especially sub-Saharan Africa where there is less access to contraception. But after quadrupling in the twentieth century, the world's population, currently at 7 billion, is unlikely to rise by more than 50 percent before settling down. So we can think about how we do sustainability with a stable population, rather than one that is continually growing.

Population is only one part of the equation, of course. Paul Ehrlich, author of *The Population Bomb,* points out that the amount of stuff people use and the resources needed to produce that stuff are the other issues we need to worry about. In the developed world, at least, there is growing evidence that we have reached "peak stuff". Individuals and society have got richer, and the rate at which we use resources has levelled off. Homes and factories are becoming more energy and water efficient and much of our new technology is smaller and lighter, reducing the amount of materials required to make them. So in many ways, the developed world is already dematerialising. The challenge is breaking the historic link between prosperity and energy and resource use fast enough.

Some argue that feeding extra mouths will still trash the planet—but it needn't. We already produce enough food to feed at least 10 billion people. But an estimated 40 percent of it is wasted: in the developing world it rots in warehouses or gets eaten by pests. In the developed world we mostly throw it away uneaten. Our food problems are mainly about distribution and affordability—not overall production. Add in a shift away from industrial agriculture to more local and sustainable alternatives and that's good news for a world that needs lots of food. "We're learning that you can produce more calories per acre with smaller farms", says environmentalist Bill McKibben.

Healthier and Happier

The solutions certainly won't be one-size-fits-all. It's possible to have a sustainable London and a sustainable Amazonia, but they will function very differently. "A renewable world depends on what you have close to hand", says McKibben.

So living sustainably need not be a step backwards. Some things will change, though. Meat will become a luxury, as its cost is pushed up thanks to the huge amounts of energy and water needed to farm livestock. And while we'll still be able

to take holidays, those weekend jaunts on budget airlines are likely to be a thing of the past because there is currently no tax on aircraft fuel.

Porritt believes that doing away with such counterproductive subsidies and tax havens is essential. A global carbon tax and a tax on financial transactions would help to fund ecosystem restoration, public health, education and other crucial steps towards sustainability. "Tax is such a powerful instrument to promote sustainability", he says. "It's absolutely fundamental to the transformation we're talking about".

Porritt and Sanderson are buoyant about the quality of life in a more equitable and sustainable world, without denying the difficulties ahead. "One of the reasons why I think we have failed is that we haven't given a sense of just how good a world it would be", admits Porritt.

All of which adds up to a vision of a sustainable world that is significantly different from the one that critics envisage. It might mean a leaner and slower way of life for some, but also a healthier, happier and more peaceful world for us and future generations to enjoy. We have the tools. What we do with them remains to be seen.

Critical Thinking

1. What have been the many benefits of the current economic system?
2. What have been the negative impacts of the current economic system?
3. What do you think will happen over the next 25 years?

Create Central

www.mhhe.com/createcentral

Internet References

New American Studies Web
www.georgetown.edu/crossroads/asw
Sociology—Study Sociology Online
http://edu.learnsoc.org
Sociology Web Resources
http://www.mhhe.com/socscience/sociology/resources/index.htm
Sociosite
http://www.topsite.com/goto/sociosite.net
Socioweb
http://www.topsite.com/goto/socioweb.com
The Hunger Project
www.thp.org

ROBERT ADLER is a science writer based in northern California and Oaxaca, Mexico.

© 2014 Reed Business Information—UK. All rights reserved. Distributed by Tribune Content Agency, LLC.

Article   Prepared by: Kurt Finsterbusch, *University of Maryland, College Park*

The New Population Bomb: The Four Megatrends That Will Change the World

JACK A. GOLDSTONE

Learning Outcomes

After reading this article, you will be able to:

- Consider that population changes are the foundation for many predictions about the economy and the society.

- Understand that rapid population growth in developing countries and slow or no growth in developed countries rapidly changes the "map" of the world for many other issues.

- Critically examine Goldstone's thesis that the current population dynamics could collapse many governing structures.

Forty-two years ago, the biologist Paul Ehrlich warned in The Population Bomb that mass starvation would strike in the 1970s and 1980s, with the world's population growth outpacing the production of food and other critical resources. Thanks to innovations and efforts such as the "green revolution" in farming and the widespread adoption of family planning, Ehrlich's worst fears did not come to pass. In fact, since the 1970s, global economic output has increased and fertility has fallen dramatically, especially in developing countries.

The United Nations Population Division now projects that global population growth will nearly halt by 2050. By that date, the world's population will have stabilized at 9.15 billion people, according to the "medium growth" variant of the UN's authoritative population database World Population Prospects: The 2008 Revision. (Today's global population is 6.83 billion.) Barring a cataclysmic climate crisis or a complete failure to recover from the current economic malaise, global economic output is expected to increase by two to three percent per year, meaning that global income will increase far more than population over the next four decades.

But twenty-first-century international security will depend less on how many people inhabit the world than on how the global population is composed and distributed: where populations are declining and where they are growing, which countries are relatively older and which are more youthful, and how demographics will influence population movements across regions.

These elements are not well recognized or widely understood. A recent article in *The Economist,* for example, cheered the decline in global fertility without noting other vital demographic developments. Indeed, the same UN data cited by *The Economist* reveal four historic shifts that will fundamentally alter the world's population over the next four decades: the relative demographic weight of the world's developed countries will drop by nearly 25 percent, shifting economic power to the developing nations; the developed countries' labor forces will substantially age and decline, constraining economic growth in the developed world and raising the demand for immigrant workers; most of the world's expected population growth will increasingly be concentrated in today's poorest, youngest, and most heavily Muslim countries, which have a dangerous lack of quality education, capital, and employment opportunities; and, for the first time in history, most of the world's population will become urbanized, with the largest urban centers being in the world's poorest countries, where policing, sanitation, and health care are often scarce. Taken together, these trends will pose challenges every bit as alarming as those noted by Ehrlich. Coping with them will require nothing less than a major reconsideration of the world's basic global governance structures.

Europe's Reversal of Fortunes

At the beginning of the eighteenth century, approximately 20 percent of the world's inhabitants lived in Europe (including Russia). Then, with the Industrial Revolution, Europe's population boomed, and streams of European emigrants set off for the Americas. By the eve of World War I, Europe's population had more than quadrupled. In 1913, Europe had more people than China, and the proportion of the world's population living in Europe and the former European colonies of North America had risen to over 33 percent. But this trend reversed after World War I, as basic health care and sanitation began to spread to poorer countries. In Asia, Africa, and Latin America, people began to live longer, and birthrates remained high or fell only slowly. By 2003, the combined populations of Europe, the United States, and Canada accounted for just 17 percent of the global population. In 2050, this figure is expected to be just 12 percent—far less than it was in 1700. (These projections, moreover, might even understate the reality because they reflect the "medium growth" projection of the UN forecasts, which assumes that the fertility rates of developing countries will decline while those of developed countries will increase. In fact, many developed countries show no evidence of increasing fertility rates.) The West's relative decline is even more dramatic if one also considers changes in income. The Industrial Revolution made Europeans not only more numerous than they had been but also considerably richer per capita than others worldwide. According to the economic historian Angus Maddison, Europe, the United States, and Canada together produced about 32 percent of the world's GDP at the beginning of the nineteenth century. By 1950, that proportion had increased to a remarkable 68 percent of the world's total output (adjusted to reflect purchasing power parity).

This trend, too, is headed for a sharp reversal. The proportion of global GDP produced by Europe, the United States, and Canada fell from 68 percent in 1950 to 47 percent in 2003 and will decline even more steeply in the future. If the growth rate of per capita income (again, adjusted for purchasing power parity) between 2003 and 2050 remains as it was between 1973 and 2003—averaging 1.68 percent annually in Europe, the United States, and Canada and 2.47 percent annually in the rest of the world—then the combined GDP of Europe, the United States, and Canada will roughly double by 2050, whereas the GDP of the rest of the world will grow by a factor of five. The portion of global GDP produced by Europe, the United States, and Canada in 2050 will then be less than 30 percent—smaller than it was in 1820.

These figures also imply that an overwhelming proportion of the world's GDP growth between 2003 and 2050—nearly 80 percent—will occur outside of Europe, the United States, and Canada. By the middle of this century, the global middle class—those capable of purchasing durable consumer products, such as cars, appliances, and electronics—will increasingly be found in what is now considered the developing world. The World Bank has predicted that by 2030 the number of middle-class people in the developing world will be 1.2 billion—a rise of 200 percent since 2005. This means that the developing world's middle class alone will be larger than the total populations of Europe, Japan, and the United States combined. From now on, therefore, the main driver of global economic expansion will be the economic growth of newly industrialized countries, such as Brazil, China, India, Indonesia, Mexico, and Turkey.

Aging Pains

Part of the reason developed countries will be less economically dynamic in the coming decades is that their populations will become substantially older. The European countries, Canada, the United States, Japan, South Korea, and even China are aging at unprecedented rates. Today, the proportion of people aged 60 or older in China and South Korea is 12–15 percent. It is 15–22 percent in the European Union, Canada, and the United States and 30 percent in Japan. With baby boomers aging and life expectancy increasing, these numbers will increase dramatically. In 2050, approximately 30 percent of Americans, Canadians, Chinese, and Europeans will be over 60, as will more than 40 percent of Japanese and South Koreans.

Over the next decades, therefore, these countries will have increasingly large proportions of retirees and increasingly small proportions of workers. As workers born during the baby boom of 1945–65 are retiring, they are not being replaced by a new cohort of citizens of prime working age (15–59 years old).

Industrialized countries are experiencing a drop in their working-age populations that is even more severe than the overall slowdown in their population growth. South Korea represents the most extreme example. Even as its total population is projected to decline by almost 9 percent by 2050 (from 48.3 million to 44.1 million), the population of working-age South Koreans is expected to drop by 36 percent (from 32.9 million to 21.1 million), and the number of South Koreans aged 60 and older will increase by almost 150 percent (from 7.3 million to 18 million). By 2050, in other words, the entire working-age population will barely exceed the 60-and-older population. Although South Korea's case is extreme, it represents an increasingly common fate for developed countries. Europe is expected to lose 24 percent of its prime working-age population (about 120 million workers) by 2050, and its 60-and-older population is expected to increase by 47 percent. In the United States, where higher fertility and more immigration are expected than in Europe, the working-age population will grow by 15 percent over the next four decades—a steep decline from its growth of 62 percent between 1950 and 2010. And by 2050, the United States' 60-and-older population is expected to double.

All this will have a dramatic impact on economic growth, health care, and military strength in the developed world. The forces that fueled economic growth in industrialized countries during the second half of the twentieth century—increased productivity due to better education, the movement of women into the labor force, and innovations in technology—will all likely weaken in the coming decades. College enrollment boomed after World War II, a trend that is not likely to recur in the twenty-first century; the extensive movement of women into the labor force also was a one-time social change; and the technological change of the time resulted from innovators who created new products and leading-edge consumers who were willing to try them out—two groups that are thinning out as the industrialized world's population ages.

Overall economic growth will also be hampered by a decline in the number of new consumers and new households. When developed countries' labor forces were growing by 0.5–1.0 percent per year, as they did until 2005, even annual increases in real output per worker of just 1.7 percent meant that annual economic growth totaled 2.2–2.7 percent per year. But with the labor forces of many developed countries (such as Germany, Hungary, Japan, Russia, and the Baltic states) now shrinking by 0.2 percent per year and those of other countries (including Austria, the Czech Republic, Denmark, Greece, and Italy) growing by less than 0.2 percent per year, the same 1.7 percent increase in real output per worker yields only 1.5–1.9 percent annual overall growth. Moreover, developed countries will be lucky to keep productivity growth at even that level; in many developed countries, productivity is more likely to decline as the population ages.

A further strain on industrialized economies will be rising medical costs: as populations age, they will demand more health care for longer periods of time. Public pension schemes for aging populations are already being reformed in various industrialized countries—often prompting heated debate. In theory, at least, pensions might be kept solvent by increasing the retirement age, raising taxes modestly, and phasing out benefits for the wealthy. Regardless, the number of 80- and 90-year-olds—who are unlikely to work and highly likely to require nursing-home and other expensive care—will rise dramatically. And even if 60- and 70-year-olds remain active and employed, they will require procedures and medications—hip replacements, kidney transplants, and blood-pressure treatments—to sustain their health in old age.

All this means that just as aging developed countries will have proportionally fewer workers, innovators, and consumerist young households, a large portion of those countries' remaining economic growth will have to be diverted to pay for the medical bills and pensions of their growing elderly populations. Basic services, meanwhile, will be increasingly costly because fewer young workers will be available for strenuous and labor-intensive jobs. Unfortunately, policymakers seldom reckon with these potentially disruptive effects of otherwise welcome developments, such as higher life expectancy.

Youth and Islam in the Developing World

Even as the industrialized countries of Europe, North America, and Northeast Asia will experience unprecedented aging this century, fast-growing countries in Africa, Latin America, the Middle East, and Southeast Asia will have exceptionally youthful populations. Today, roughly 9 out of 10 children under the age of 15 live in developing countries. And these are the countries that will continue to have the world's highest birthrates. Indeed, over 70 percent of the world's population growth between now and 2050 will occur in 24 countries, all of which are classified by the World Bank as low income or lower-middle income, with an average per capita income of under $3,855 in 2008.

Many developing countries have few ways of providing employment to their young, fast-growing populations. Would-be laborers, therefore, will be increasingly attracted to the labor markets of the aging developed countries of Europe, North America, and Northeast Asia. Youthful immigrants from nearby regions with high unemployment—Central America, North Africa, and Southeast Asia, for example—will be drawn to those vital entry-level and manual-labor jobs that sustain advanced economies: janitors, nursing-home aides, bus drivers, plumbers, security guards, farm workers, and the like. Current levels of immigration from developing to developed countries are paltry compared to those that the forces of supply and demand might soon create across the world.

These forces will act strongly on the Muslim world, where many economically weak countries will continue to experience dramatic population growth in the decades ahead. In 1950, Bangladesh, Egypt, Indonesia, Nigeria, Pakistan, and Turkey had a combined population of 242 million. By 2009, those six countries were the world's most populous Muslim-majority countries and had a combined population of 886 million. Their populations are continuing to grow and indeed are expected to increase by 475 million between now and 2050—during which time, by comparison, the six most populous developed countries are projected to gain only 44 million inhabitants. Worldwide, of the 48 fastest-growing countries today—those with annual population growth of two percent or more—28 are majority Muslim or have Muslim minorities of 33 percent or more.

It is therefore imperative to improve relations between Muslim and Western societies. This will be difficult given that many Muslims live in poor communities vulnerable to radical appeals and many see the West as antagonistic and militaristic. In the 2009 Pew Global Attitudes Project survey, for example, whereas 69 percent of those Indonesians and Nigerians surveyed reported viewing the United States favorably, just 18 percent of those polled in Egypt, Jordan, Pakistan, and Turkey (all U.S. allies) did. And in 2006, when the Pew survey last asked detailed questions about Muslim-Western relations, more than half of the respondents in Muslim countries characterized those relations as bad and blamed the West for this state of affairs.

But improving relations is all the more important because of the growing demographic weight of poor Muslim countries and the attendant increase in Muslim immigration, especially to Europe from North Africa and the Middle East. (To be sure, forecasts that Muslims will soon dominate Europe are outlandish: Muslims compose just 3 to 10 percent of the population in the major European countries today, and this proportion will at most double by midcentury.) Strategists worldwide must consider that the world's young are becoming concentrated in those countries least prepared to educate and employ them, including some Muslim states. Any resulting poverty, social tension, or ideological radicalization could have disruptive effects in many corners of the world. But this need not be the case; the healthy immigration of workers to the developed world and the movement of capital to the developing world, among other things, could lead to better results.

Urban Sprawl

Exacerbating twenty-first-century risks will be the fact that the world is urbanizing to an unprecedented degree. The year 2010 will likely be the first time in history that a majority of the world's people live in cities rather than in the countryside. Whereas less than 30 percent of the world's population was urban in 1950, according to UN projections, more than 70 percent will be by 2050.

Lower-income countries in Asia and Africa are urbanizing especially rapidly, as agriculture becomes less labor intensive and as employment opportunities shift to the industrial and service sectors. Already, most of the world's urban agglomerations—Mumbai (population 20.1 million), Mexico City (19.5 million), New Delhi (17 million), Shanghai (15.8 million), Calcutta (15.6 million), Karachi (13.1 million), Cairo (12.5 million), Manila (11.7 million), Lagos (10.6 million), and Jakarta (9.7 million)—are found in low-income countries. Many of these countries have multiple cities with over one million residents each: Pakistan has 8, Mexico 12, and China more than 100. The UN projects that the urbanized proportion of sub-Saharan Africa will nearly double between 2005 and 2050, from 35 percent (300 million people) to over 67 percent (1 billion). China, which is roughly 40 percent urbanized today, is expected to be 73 percent urbanized by 2050; India, which is less than 30 percent urbanized today, is expected to be 55 percent urbanized by 2050. Overall, the world's urban population is expected to grow by 3 billion people by 2050.

This urbanization may prove destabilizing. Developing countries that urbanize in the twenty-first century will have far lower per capita incomes than did many industrial countries when they first urbanized. The United States, for example, did not reach 65 percent urbanization until 1950, when per capita income was nearly $13,000 (in 2005 dollars). By contrast, Nigeria, Pakistan, and the Philippines, which are approaching similar levels of urbanization, currently have per capita incomes of just $1,800–$4,000 (in 2005 dollars).

According to the research of Richard Cincotta and other political demographers, countries with younger populations are especially prone to civil unrest and are less able to create or sustain democratic institutions. And the more heavily urbanized, the more such countries are likely to experience Dickensian poverty and anarchic violence. In good times, a thriving economy might keep urban residents employed and governments flush with sufficient resources to meet their needs. More often, however, sprawling and impoverished cities are vulnerable to crime lords, gangs, and petty rebellions. Thus, the rapid urbanization of the developing world in the decades ahead might bring, in exaggerated form, problems similar to those that urbanization brought to nineteenth-century Europe. Back then, cyclical employment, inadequate policing, and limited sanitation and education often spawned widespread labor strife, periodic violence, and sometimes—as in the 1820s, the 1830s, and 1848—even revolutions.

International terrorism might also originate in fast-urbanizing developing countries (even more than it already does). With their neighborhood networks, access to the Internet and digital communications technology, and concentration of valuable targets, sprawling cities offer excellent opportunities for recruiting, maintaining, and hiding terrorist networks.

Defusing the Bomb

Averting this century's potential dangers will require sweeping measures. Three major global efforts defused the population bomb of Ehrlich's day: a commitment by governments and nongovernmental organizations to control reproduction rates; agricultural advances, such as the green revolution and the spread of new technology; and a vast increase in international trade, which globalized markets and thus allowed developing countries to export foodstuffs in exchange for seeds, fertilizers, and machinery, which in turn helped them boost production. But today's population bomb is the product less of absolute growth in the world's population than of changes in its age and distribution. Policymakers must therefore adapt today's global governance institutions to the new realities of the aging of the industrialized world, the concentration of the world's economic and population growth in developing countries, and the increase in international immigration.

During the Cold War, Western strategists divided the world into a "First World," of democratic industrialized countries; a

"Second World," of communist industrialized countries; and a "Third World," of developing countries. These strategists focused chiefly on deterring or managing conflict between the First and the Second Worlds and on launching proxy wars and diplomatic initiatives to attract Third World countries into the First World's camp. Since the end of the Cold War, strategists have largely abandoned this three-group division and have tended to believe either that the United States, as the sole superpower, would maintain a Pax Americana or that the world would become multipolar, with the United States, Europe, and China playing major roles.

Unfortunately, because they ignore current global demographic trends, these views will be obsolete within a few decades. A better approach would be to consider a different three-world order, with a new First World of the aging industrialized nations of North America, Europe, and Asia's Pacific Rim (including Japan, Singapore, South Korea, and Taiwan, as well as China after 2030, by which point the one-child policy will have produced significant aging); a Second World comprising fast-growing and economically dynamic countries with a healthy mix of young and old inhabitants (such as Brazil, Iran, Mexico, Thailand, Turkey, and Vietnam, as well as China until 2030); and a Third World of fast-growing, very young, and increasingly urbanized countries with poorer economies and often weak governments. To cope with the instability that will likely arise from the new Third World's urbanization, economic strife, lawlessness, and potential terrorist activity, the aging industrialized nations of the new First World must build effective alliances with the growing powers of the new Second World and together reach out to Third World nations. Second World powers will be pivotal in the twenty-first century not just because they will drive economic growth and consume technologies and other products engineered in the First World; they will also be central to international security and cooperation. The realities of religion, culture, and geographic proximity mean that any peaceful and productive engagement by the First World of Third World countries will have to include the open cooperation of Second World countries.

Strategists, therefore, must fundamentally reconsider the structure of various current global institutions. The G-8, for example, will likely become obsolete as a body for making global economic policy. The G-20 is already becoming increasingly important, and this is less a short-term consequence of the ongoing global financial crisis than the beginning of the necessary recognition that Brazil, China, India, Indonesia, Mexico, Turkey, and others are becoming global economic powers. International institutions will not retain their legitimacy if they exclude the world's fastest-growing and most economically dynamic countries. It is essential, therefore, despite European concerns about the potential effects on immigration, to take steps

such as admitting Turkey into the European Union. This would add youth and economic dynamism to the EU—and would prove that Muslims are welcome to join Europeans as equals in shaping a free and prosperous future. On the other hand, excluding Turkey from the EU could lead to hostility not only on the part of Turkish citizens, who are expected to number 100 million by 2050, but also on the part of Muslim populations worldwide.

NATO must also adapt. The alliance today is composed almost entirely of countries with aging, shrinking populations and relatively slow-growing economies. It is oriented toward the Northern Hemisphere and holds on to a Cold War structure that cannot adequately respond to contemporary threats. The young and increasingly populous countries of Africa, the Middle East, Central Asia, and South Asia could mobilize insurgents much more easily than NATO could mobilize the troops it would need if it were called on to stabilize those countries. Long-standing NATO members should, therefore—although it would require atypical creativity and flexibility—consider the logistical and demographic advantages of inviting into the alliance countries such as Brazil and Morocco, rather than countries such as Albania. That this seems far-fetched does not minimize the imperative that First World countries begin including large and strategic Second and Third World powers in formal international alliances.

The case of Afghanistan—a country whose population is growing fast and where NATO is currently engaged—illustrates the importance of building effective global institutions. Today, there are 28 million Afghans; by 2025, there will be 45 million; and by 2050, there will be close to 75 million. As nearly 20 million additional Afghans are born over the next 15 years, NATO will have an opportunity to help Afghanistan become reasonably stable, self-governing, and prosperous. If NATO's efforts fail and the Afghans judge that NATO intervention harmed their interests, tens of millions of young Afghans will become more hostile to the West. But if they come to think that NATO's involvement benefited their society, the West will have tens of millions of new friends. The example might then motivate the approximately one billion other young Muslims growing up in low-income countries over the next four decades to look more kindly on relations between their countries and the countries of the industrialized West.

Creative Reforms at Home

The aging industrialized countries can also take various steps at home to promote stability in light of the coming demographic trends. First, they should encourage families to have more children. France and Sweden have had success providing child care, generous leave time, and financial allowances to families with young children. Yet there is no consensus among policymakers—and certainly not among demographers—about what policies best encourage fertility.

More important than unproven tactics for increasing family size is immigration. Correctly managed, population movement can benefit developed and developing countries alike. Given the dangers of young, underemployed, and unstable populations in developing countries, immigration to developed countries can provide economic opportunities for the ambitious and serve as a safety valve for all. Countries that embrace immigrants, such as the United States, gain economically by having willing laborers and greater entrepreneurial spirit. And countries with high levels of emigration (but not so much that they experience so-called brain drains) also benefit because emigrants often send remittances home or return to their native countries with valuable education and work experience.

One somewhat daring approach to immigration would be to encourage a reverse flow of older immigrants from developed to developing countries. If older residents of developed countries took their retirements along the southern coast of the Mediterranean or in Latin America or Africa, it would greatly reduce the strain on their home countries' public entitlement systems. The developing countries involved, meanwhile, would benefit because caring for the elderly and providing retirement and leisure services is highly labor intensive. Relocating a portion of these activities to developing countries would provide employment and valuable training to the young, growing populations of the Second and Third Worlds.

This would require developing residential and medical facilities of First World quality in Second and Third World countries. Yet even this difficult task would be preferable to the status quo, by which low wages and poor facilities lead to a steady drain of medical and nursing talent from developing to developed countries. Many residents of developed countries who desire cheaper medical procedures already practice medical tourism today, with India, Singapore, and Thailand being the most common destinations. (For example, the international consulting firm Deloitte estimated that 750,000 Americans traveled abroad for care in 2008.)

Never since 1800 has a majority of the world's economic growth occurred outside of Europe, the United States, and Canada. Never have so many people in those regions been over 60 years old. And never have low-income countries' populations been so young and so urbanized. But such will be the world's demography in the twenty-first century. The strategic and economic policies of the twentieth century are obsolete, and it is time to find new ones.

Reference

Goldstone, Jack A. "The new population bomb: the four megatrends that will change the world." *Foreign Affairs* 89.1 (2010): 31. *General OneFile*. Web. 23 Jan. 2010. http://0-find.galegroup .com.www.consuls.org/gps/start.do?proId=IPS& userGroupName=a30wc.

Critical Thinking

1. How will aging populations be taken care of?
2. Why does Goldstone call the current demographics a population bomb?
3. What kind of changes are called for by these population issues?

Create Central

www.mhhe.com/createcentral

Internet References

National Center for Policy Analysis
    www.ncpa.org
Sociology—Study Sociology Online
    http://edu.learnsoc.org
Sociology Web Resources
    http://www.mhhe.com/socscience/sociology/resources/index.htm
Sociosite
    http://www.topsite.com/goto/sociosite.net
Socioweb
    http://www.topsite.com/goto/socioweb.com
WWW Virtual Library: Demography & Population Studies
    http://demography.anu.edu.au/VirtualLibrary

Reprinted by permission of FOREIGN AFFAIRS, January/February 2010. Copyright 2010 by the Council on Foreign Relations, Inc. www.ForeignAffairs.com

Article   Prepared by: Kurt Finsterbusch, *University of Maryland, College Park*

The New Geopolitics of Food

From the Middle East to Madagascar, high prices are spawning land grabs and ousting dictators. Welcome to the 21st-century food wars.

LESTER R. BROWN

Learning Outcomes

After reading this article, you will be able to:

- Understand the effects of falling water tables, current lack of improving productivity of the green revolution crops, increasing costs of agricultural inputs, soil depletion, and increasing demand for food on food prices.

- Consider the social, economic, and political consequences of increasing food prices.

- Consider the solutions to these problems.

In the United States, when world wheat prices rise by 75 percent, as they have over the last year, it means the difference between a $2 loaf of bread and a loaf costing maybe $2.10. If, however, you live in New Delhi, those sky-rocketing costs really matter: A doubling in the world price of wheat actually means that the wheat you carry home from the market to hand-grind into flour for chapatis costs twice as much. And the same is true with rice. If the world price of rice doubles, so does the price of rice in your neighborhood market in Jakarta. And so does the cost of the bowl of boiled rice on an Indonesian family's dinner table.

Welcome to the new food economics of 2011: Prices are climbing, but the impact is not at all being felt equally. For Americans, who spend less than one-tenth of their income in the supermarket, the soaring food prices we've seen so far this year are an annoyance, not a calamity. But for the planet's poorest 2 billion people, who spend 50 to 70 percent of their income on food, these soaring prices may mean going from two meals a day to one. Those who are barely hanging on to the lower rungs of the global economic ladder risk losing their grip entirely. This can contribute—and it has—to revolutions and upheaval.

Already in 2011, the U.N. Food Price Index has eclipsed its previous all-time global high; as of March it had climbed for eight consecutive months. With this year's harvest predicted to fall short, with governments in the Middle East and Africa teetering as a result of the price spikes, and with anxious markets sustaining one shock after another, food has quickly become the hidden driver of world politics. And crises like these are going to become increasingly common. The new geopolitics of food looks a whole lot more volatile—and a whole lot more contentious—than it used to. Scarcity is the new norm.

Until recently, sudden price surges just didn't matter as much, as they were quickly followed by a return to the relatively low food prices that helped shape the political stability of the late 20th century across much of the globe. But now both the causes and consequences are ominously different.

In many ways, this is a resumption of the 2007–2008 food crisis, which subsided not because the world somehow came together to solve its grain crunch once and for all, but because the Great Recession tempered growth in demand even as favorable weather helped farmers produce the largest grain harvest on record. Historically, price spikes tended to be almost exclusively driven by unusual weather—a monsoon failure in India, a drought in the former Soviet Union, a heat wave in the U.S. Midwest. Such events were always disruptive, but thankfully infrequent. Unfortunately, today's price hikes are driven by trends that are both elevating demand and making it more difficult to increase production: among them, a rapidly expanding population, crop-withering temperature increases, and irrigation wells running dry. Each night, there are 219,000 additional people to feed at the global dinner table.

More alarming still, the world is losing its ability to soften the effect of shortages. In response to previous price surges, the United States, the world's largest grain producer, was effectively able to steer the world away from potential catastrophe. From the mid-20th century until 1995, the United States had either grain surpluses or idle cropland that could be planted to rescue countries in trouble. When the Indian monsoon failed in 1965, for example, President Lyndon Johnson's administration shipped one-fifth of the U.S. wheat crop to India, successfully staving off famine. We can't do that anymore; the safety cushion is gone.

That's why the food crisis of 2011 is for real, and why it may bring with it yet more bread riots cum political revolutions. What if the upheavals that greeted dictators Zine el-Abidine Ben Ali in Tunisia, Hosni Mubarak in Egypt, and Muammar al-Qaddafi in Libya (a country that imports 90 percent of its grain) are not the end of the story, but the beginning of it? Get ready, farmers and foreign ministers alike, for a new era in which world food scarcity increasingly shapes global politics.

The doubling of world grain prices since early 2007 has been driven primarily by two factors: accelerating growth in demand and the increasing difficulty of rapidly expanding production. The result is a world that looks strikingly different from the bountiful global grain economy of the last century. What will the geopolitics of food look like in a new era dominated by scarcity? Even at this early stage, we can see at least the broad outlines of the emerging food economy.

On the demand side, farmers now face clear sources of increasing pressure. The first is population growth. Each year the world's farmers must feed 80 million additional people, nearly all of them in developing countries. The world's population has nearly doubled since 1970 and is headed toward 9 billion by midcentury. Some 3 billion people, meanwhile, are also trying to move up the food chain, consuming more meat, milk, and eggs. As more families in China and elsewhere enter the middle class, they expect to eat better. But as global consumption of grain-intensive livestock products climbs, so does the demand for the extra corn and soybeans needed to feed all that livestock. (Grain consumption per person in the United States, for example, is four times that in India, where little grain is converted into animal protein. For now.)

At the same time, the United States, which once was able to act as a global buffer of sorts against poor harvests elsewhere, is now converting massive quantities of grain into fuel for cars, even as world grain consumption, which is already up to roughly 2.2 billion metric tons per year, is growing at an accelerating rate. A decade ago, the growth in consumption was 20 million tons per year. More recently it has risen by 40 million tons every year. But the rate at which the United States is converting grain into ethanol has grown even faster. In 2010, the United States harvested nearly 400 million tons of grain, of which 126 million tons went to ethanol fuel distilleries (up from 16 million tons in 2000). This massive capacity to convert grain into fuel means that the price of grain is now tied to the price of oil. So if oil goes to $150 per barrel or more, the price of grain will follow it upward as it becomes ever more profitable to convert grain into oil substitutes. And it's not just a U.S. phenomenon: Brazil, which distills ethanol from sugar cane, ranks second in production after the United States, while the European Union's goal of getting 10 percent of its transport energy from renewables, mostly biofuels, by 2020 is also diverting land from food crops.

This is not merely a story about the booming demand for food. Everything from falling water tables to eroding soils and the consequences of global warming means that the world's food supply is unlikely to keep up with our collectively growing appetites. Take climate change: The rule of thumb among crop ecologists is that for every 1°C rise in temperature above the growing season optimum, farmers can expect a 10 percent decline in grain yields. This relationship was borne out all too dramatically during the 2010 heat wave in Russia, which reduced the country's grain harvest by nearly 40 percent.

While temperatures are rising, water tables are falling as farmers overpump for irrigation. This artificially inflates food production in the short run, creating a food bubble that bursts when aquifers are depleted and pumping is necessarily reduced to the rate of recharge. In arid Saudi Arabia, irrigation had surprisingly enabled the country to be self-sufficient in wheat for more than 20 years; now, wheat production is collapsing because the non-replenishable aquifer the country uses for irrigation is largely depleted. The Saudis soon will be importing all their grain.

Saudi Arabia is only one of some 18 countries with water-based food bubbles. All together, more than half the world's people live in countries where water tables are falling. The politically troubled Arab Middle East is the first geographic region where grain production has peaked and begun to decline because of water shortages, even as populations continue to grow. Grain production is already going down in Syria and Iraq and may soon decline in Yemen. But the largest food bubbles are in India and China. In India, where farmers have drilled some 20 million irrigation wells, water tables are falling and the wells are starting to go dry. The World Bank reports that 175 million Indians are being fed with grain produced by overpumping. In China, overpumping is concentrated in the North China Plain, which produces half of China's wheat and a third of its corn. An estimated 130 million Chinese are currently fed by overpumping. How will these countries make up for the inevitable shortfalls when the aquifers are depleted?

Even as we are running our wells dry, we are also mismanaging our soils, creating new deserts. Soil erosion as a result of overplowing and land mismanagement is undermining the productivity of one-third of the world's cropland. How severe is it? Look at satellite images showing two huge new dust bowls: one stretching across northern and western China and western Mongolia; the other across central Africa. Wang Tao, a leading Chinese desert scholar, reports that each year some 1,400 square miles of land in northern China turn to desert. In Mongolia and Lesotho, grain harvests have shrunk by half or more over the last few decades. North Korea and Haiti are also suffering from heavy soil losses; both countries face famine if they lose international food aid. Civilization can survive the loss of its oil reserves, but it cannot survive the loss of its soil reserves.

Beyond the changes in the environment that make it ever harder to meet human demand, there's an important intangible factor to consider: Over the last half-century or so, we have come to take agricultural progress for granted. Decade after decade, advancing technology underpinned steady gains in raising land productivity. Indeed, world grain yield per acre has tripled since 1950. But now that era is coming to an end in some of the more agriculturally advanced countries, where farmers are already using all available technologies to raise yields. In effect, the farmers have caught up with the scientists. After climbing for a century, rice yield per acre in Japan has not risen at all for 16 years. In China, yields may level off soon. Just those two countries alone account for one-third of the world's rice harvest. Meanwhile, wheat yields have plateaued in Britain, France, and Germany—Western Europe's three largest wheat producers.

In this era of tightening world food supplies, the ability to grow food is fast becoming a new form of geopolitical leverage, and countries are scrambling to secure their own parochial interests at the expense of the common good.

The first signs of trouble came in 2007, when farmers began having difficulty keeping up with the growth in global demand for grain. Grain and soybean prices started to climb, tripling by mid-2008. In response, many exporting countries tried to control the rise of domestic food prices by restricting exports. Among them were Russia and Argentina, two leading wheat exporters. Vietnam, the No. 2 rice exporter, banned exports entirely for several months in early 2008. So did several other smaller exporters of grain.

With exporting countries restricting exports in 2007 and 2008, importing countries panicked. No longer able to rely on the market to supply the grain they needed, several countries took the novel step of trying to negotiate long-term grain-supply agreements with exporting countries. The Philippines, for instance, negotiated a three-year agreement with Vietnam for 1.5 million

tons of rice per year. A delegation of Yemenis traveled to Australia with a similar goal in mind, but had no luck. In a seller's market, exporters were reluctant to make long-term commitments.

Fearing they might not be able to buy needed grain from the market, some of the more affluent countries, led by Saudi Arabia, South Korea, and China, took the unusual step in 2008 of buying or leasing land in other countries on which to grow grain for themselves. Most of these land acquisitions are in Africa, where some governments lease cropland for less than $1 per acre per year. Among the principal destinations were Ethiopia and Sudan, countries where millions of people are being sustained with food from the U.N. World Food Program. That the governments of these two countries are willing to sell land to foreign interests when their own people are hungry is a sad commentary on their leadership.

By the end of 2009, hundreds of land acquisition deals had been negotiated, some of them exceeding a million acres. A 2010 World Bank analysis of these "land grabs" reported that a total of nearly 140 million acres were involved—an area that exceeds the cropland devoted to corn and wheat combined in the United States. Such acquisitions also typically involve water rights, meaning that land grabs potentially affect all downstream countries as well. Any water extracted from the upper Nile River basin to irrigate crops in Ethiopia or Sudan, for instance, will now not reach Egypt, upending the delicate water politics of the Nile by adding new countries with which Egypt must negotiate.

The potential for conflict—and not just over water—is high. Many of the land deals have been made in secret, and in most cases, the land involved was already in use by villagers when it was sold or leased. Often those already farming the land were neither consulted about nor even informed of the new arrangements. And because there typically are no formal land titles in many developing-country villages, the farmers who lost their land have had little backing to bring their cases to court. Reporter John Vidal, writing in Britain's *Observer*, quotes Nyikaw Ochalla from Ethiopia's Gambella region: "The foreign companies are arriving in large numbers, depriving people of land they have used for centuries. There is no consultation with the indigenous population. The deals are done secretly. The only thing the local people see is people coming with lots of tractors to invade their lands."

Local hostility toward such land grabs is the rule, not the exception. In 2007, as food prices were starting to rise, China signed an agreement with the Philippines to lease 2.5 million acres of land slated for food crops that would be shipped home. Once word leaked, the public outcry—much of it from Filipino farmers—forced Manila to suspend the agreement. A similar uproar rocked Madagascar, where a South Korean firm, Daewoo Logistics, had pursued rights to more than 3 million acres of land. Word of the deal helped stoke a political furor that toppled the government and forced cancellation of the agreement. Indeed, few things are more likely to fuel insurgencies than taking land from people. Agricultural equipment is easily sabotaged. If ripe fields of grain are torched, they burn quickly.

Not only are these deals risky, but foreign investors producing food in a country full of hungry people face another political question of how to get the grain out. Will villagers permit trucks laden with grain headed for port cities to proceed when they themselves may be on the verge of starvation? The potential for political instability in countries where villagers have lost their land and their livelihoods is high. Conflicts could easily develop between investor and host countries.

These acquisitions represent a potential investment in agriculture in developing countries of an estimated $50 billion. But it could take many years to realize any substantial production gains. The public infrastructure for modern market-oriented agriculture does not yet exist in most of Africa. In some countries it will take years just to build the roads and ports needed to bring in agricultural inputs such as fertilizer and to export farm products. Beyond that, modern agriculture requires its own infrastructure: machine sheds, grain-drying equipment, silos, fertilizer storage sheds, fuel storage facilities, equipment repair and maintenance services, well-drilling equipment, irrigation pumps, and energy to power the pumps. Overall, development of the land acquired to date appears to be moving very slowly.

So how much will all this expand world food output? We don't know, but the World Bank analysis indicates that only 37 percent of the projects will be devoted to food crops. Most of the land bought up so far will be used to produce biofuels and other industrial crops.

Even if some of these projects do eventually boost land productivity, who will benefit? If virtually all the inputs—the farm equipment, the fertilizer, the pesticides, and the seeds—are brought in from abroad and if all the output is shipped out of the country, it will contribute little to the host country's economy. At best, locals may find work as farm laborers, but in highly mechanized operations, the jobs will be few. At worst, impoverished countries like Mozambique and Sudan will be left with less land and water with which to feed their already hungry populations. Thus far the land grabs have contributed more to stirring unrest than to expanding food production.

And this rich country-poor country divide could grow even more pronounced—and soon. This January, a new stage in the scramble among importing countries to secure food began to unfold when South Korea, which imports 70 percent of its grain, announced that it was creating a new public—private entity that will be responsible for acquiring part of this grain. With an initial office in Chicago, the plan is to bypass the large international trading firms by buying grain directly from U.S. farmers. As the Koreans acquire their own grain elevators, they may well sign multiyear delivery contracts with farmers, agreeing to buy specified quantities of wheat, corn, or soybeans at a fixed price.

Other importers will not stand idly by as South Korea tries to tie up a portion of the U.S. grain harvest even before it gets to market. The enterprising Koreans may soon be joined by China, Japan, Saudi Arabia, and other leading importers. Although South Korea's initial focus is the United States, far and away the world's largest grain exporter, it may later consider brokering deals with Canada, Australia, Argentina, and other major exporters. This is happening just as China may be on the verge of entering the U.S. market as a potentially massive importer of grain. With China's 1.4 billion increasingly affluent consumers starting to compete with U.S. consumers for the U.S. grain harvest, cheap food, seen by many as an American birthright, may be coming to an end.

No one knows where this intensifying competition for food supplies will go, but the world seems to be moving away from the international cooperation that evolved over several decades following World War II to an every-country-for-itself philosophy. Food nationalism may help secure food supplies for individual affluent countries, but it does little to enhance world food security. Indeed, the low-income countries that host land grabs or import grain will likely see their food situation deteriorate.

After the carnage of two world wars and the economic missteps that led to the Great Depression, countries joined together in 1945 to create the United Nations, finally realizing that in the modern world we cannot live in isolation, tempting though that might be. The International Monetary Fund was created to help manage the monetary system and promote economic stability and progress. Within the U.N. system, specialized agencies from the World Health Organization to the Food and Agriculture Organization (FAO) play major roles in the world today. All this has fostered international cooperation.

But while the FAO collects and analyzes global agricultural data and provides technical assistance, there is no organized effort to ensure the adequacy of world food supplies. Indeed, most international negotiations on agricultural trade until recently focused on access to markets, with the United States, Canada, Australia, and Argentina persistently pressing Europe and Japan to open their highly protected agricultural markets. But in the first decade of this century, access to supplies has emerged as the overriding issue as the world transitions from an era of food surpluses to a new politics of food scarcity. At the same time, the U.S. food aid program that once worked to fend off famine wherever it threatened has largely been replaced by the U.N. World Food Program (WFP), where the United States is the leading donor. The WFP now has food-assistance operations in some 70 countries and an annual budget of $4 billion. There is little international coordination otherwise. French President Nicolas Sarkozy—the reigning president of the G-20—is proposing to deal with rising food prices by curbing speculation in commodity markets. Useful though this may be, it treats the symptoms of growing food insecurity, not the causes, such as population growth and climate change. The world now needs to focus not only on agricultural policy, but on a structure that integrates it with energy, population, and water policies, each of which directly affects food security.

But that is not happening. Instead, as land and water become scarcer, as the Earth's temperature rises, and as world food security deteriorates, a dangerous geopolitics of food scarcity is emerging. Land grabbing, water grabbing, and buying grain directly from farmers in exporting countries are now integral parts of a global power struggle for food security.

With grain stocks low and climate volatility increasing, the risks are also increasing. We are now so close to the edge that a breakdown in the food system could come at any time. Consider, for example, what would have happened if the 2010 heat wave that was centered in Moscow had instead been centered in Chicago. In round numbers, the 40 percent drop in Russia's hoped-for harvest of roughly 100 million tons cost the world 40 million tons of grain, but a 40 percent drop in the far larger U.S. grain harvest of 400 million tons would have cost 160 million tons. The world's carryover stocks of grain (the amount in the bin when the new harvest begins) would have dropped to just 52 days of consumption. This level would have been not only the lowest on record, but also well below the 62-day carryover that set the stage for the 2007–2008 tripling of world grain prices.

Then what? There would have been chaos in world grain markets. Grain prices would have climbed off the charts. Some grain-exporting countries, trying to hold down domestic food prices, would have restricted or even banned exports, as they did in 2007 and 2008. The TV news would have been dominated not by the hundreds of fires in the Russian countryside, but by footage of food riots in low-income grain-importing countries and reports of governments falling as hunger spread out of control. Oil-exporting countries that import grain would have been trying to barter oil for grain, and low-income grain importers would have lost out. With governments toppling and confidence in the world grain market shattered, the global economy could have started to unravel.

We may not always be so lucky. At issue now is whether the world can go beyond focusing on the symptoms of the deteriorating food situation and instead attack the underlying causes. If we cannot produce higher crop yields with less water and conserve fertile soils, many agricultural areas will cease to be viable. And this goes far beyond farmers. If we cannot move at wartime speed to stabilize the climate, we may not be able to avoid runaway food prices. If we cannot accelerate the shift to smaller families and stabilize the world population sooner rather than later, the ranks of the hungry will almost certainly continue to expand. The time to act is now—before the food crisis of 2011 becomes the new normal.

Critical Thinking

1. Food prices have recently increased substantially, and future prices will go higher according to Brown. What explains these trends?
2. What are some of the major changes in the environment that are affecting food prices?
3. What are some of the likely economic, social, and political impacts of increasing food prices?

Create Central

www.mhhe.com/createcentral

Internet References

National Center for Policy Analysis
    www.ncpa.org
New American Studies Web
    www.georgetown.edu/crossroads/asw
Sociology—Study Sociology Online
    http://edu.learnsoc.org
Sociology Web Resources
    http://www.mhhe.com/socscience/sociology/resources/index.htm
Sociosite
    http://www.topsite.com/goto/sociosite.net
Socioweb
    http://www.topsite.com/goto/socioweb.com
The Hunger Project
    www.thp.org
WWW Virtual Library: Demography & Population Studies
    http://demography.anu.edu.au/VirtualLibrary

LESTER R. BROWN, president of the Earth Policy Institute, is author of *World on the Edge: How to Prevent Environmental and Economic Collapse.*

Brown, Lester R., "The New Geopolitics of Food," *Foreign Policy,* May/June 2011, pp. 56–58, 61–62. Copyright © 2011 by Foreign Policy. All rights reserved. Used with permission.

Article   Prepared by: Kurt Finsterbusch, *University of Maryland, College Park*

Conservative Climate Panel Warns World Faces "Breakdown of Food Systems" and More Violent Conflict

JOE ROMM

Learning Outcomes

After reading this article, you will be able to:

- Understand that although the IPCC is often attacked, it still is the most authoritative report on global warming and probably the most reliable general report. This article by Romm presents some of the most salient findings of the IPCC report, although he cherry picks the scariest. Know what the pessimists draw from this report.

- Know what risks may be brought on by global warming.

- Separate what are highly speculative and what are highly probable consequences of global warming.

Humanity's choice (via IPCC): Aggressive climate action ASAP minimizes future warming. Continued inaction results in catastrophic levels of warming, 9°F over much of U.S.

The U.N. Intergovernmental Panel on Climate Change (IPCC) has issued its second of four planned reports examining the state of climate science. This one summarizes what the scientific literature says about "Impacts, Adaptation, and Vulnerability". As with every recent IPCC report, it is super-cautious to a fault and yet still incredibly alarming.

It warns that we are doing a bad job of dealing with the climate change we've experienced to date: "Impacts from recent climate-related extremes, such as heat waves, droughts, floods, cyclones, and wildfires, reveal significant vulnerability and exposure of some ecosystems and many human systems to current climate variability."

It warns of the dreaded RFCs ("reasons for concern"—I'm not making this acronym up), such as "breakdown of food systems linked to warming, drought, flooding, and precipitation variability and extremes." You might call them RFAs ("reasons for alarm" or "reasons for action"). Indeed, in recent years, "several periods of rapid food and cereal price increases following climate extremes in key producing regions indicate a sensitivity of current markets to climate extremes among other factors." So warming-driven drought and extreme weather have *already* begun to reduce food security. Now imagine adding another 2 billion people to feed while we are experiencing five times as much warming this century as we did last century!

No surprise, then, that climate change will "prolong existing, and create new, poverty traps, the latter particularly in urban areas and emerging hotspots of hunger." And it will "increase risks of violent conflicts in the form of civil war and inter-group violence"—though for some reason that doesn't make the list of RFCs.

In short, "We're all sitting ducks," as IPCC author and Princeton Prof. Michael Oppenheimer put it to the AP.

An Overly Cautious Report

As grim as the Working Group 2 report on impacts is, it explicitly has very little to say about the catastrophic impacts and vulnerability in the business as usual case where the Earth warms 4–5°C [7–9°F]—and it has nothing to say about even higher warming, which the latest science suggests we are headed toward.

The report states:

- "Relatively few studies have considered impacts on cropping systems for scenarios where global mean temperatures increase by 4°C [7°F] or more.
- ". . . few quantitative estimates [of global annual economic losses] have been completed for additional warming around 3°C [5.4°F] or above."

D'oh! You may wonder why hundreds of the world leading climate experts spend years and years doing climate science and climate projections, but don't bother actually looking at the impacts of merely staying on our current carbon pollution emissions path—let alone looking at the plausible worst-case scenario (which is typically the basis for risk-reducing public policy, such as military spending).

Partly it's because, until recently, climate scientists had naively expected the world to act with a modicum of sanity and avoid at all costs catastrophic warming of 7°F let alone the unimaginable 10°F (or higher) warming we are headed toward. Partly it's because, as a recent paper explained, "climate scientists are biased toward overly cautious estimates, erring on the side of less rather than more alarming predictions."

On top of the overly cautious nature of most climate scientists, we have the overly cautious nature of the IPCC. As the New York Times explained when the IPCC released the Working Group 1 report last fall:

"**The I.P.C.C. is far from alarmist—on the contrary, it is a highly conservative organization,**" said Stefan Rahmstorf of the Potsdam Institute for Climate Impact Research in Germany, whose papers on sea level were among those that got discarded. "That is not a problem as long as the users of the I.P.C.C. reports are well aware of this. **The conservatism is built into its consensus structure, which tends to produce a lowest common denominator on which a large number of scientists can agree.**"

That's why the latest report is full of these sorts of bombshells couched in euphemism and buried deep in the text:

By 2100 for the high-emission scenario RCP8.5, **the combination of high temperature and humidity in some areas for parts of the year is projected to compromise normal human activities, including growing food or working outdoors.**

Yes, "compromise." A clearer word would be "obliterate." And the "high-emission scenario RCP8.5"—an atmospheric concentration of carbon dioxide of about 936 parts per million—is in fact where we are headed by 2100 or soon thereafter on our current do-little path.

Bottom line: We are at risk of making large parts of the planet's currently arable and populated land virtually uninhabitable for much of the year—and irreversibly so for hundreds of years.

The Risk of Creating More Failed States

Here are two important conclusions from the report that the IPCC strangely puts 13 pages apart from each other:

1. **Violent conflict increases vulnerability to climate change.** Large-scale violent conflict harms assets that facilitate adaptation, including infrastructure, institutions, natural resources, social capital, and livelihood opportunities.
2. **Climate change can indirectly increase risks of violent conflicts in the form of civil war and inter-group violence by amplifying well-documented drivers of these conflicts such as poverty and economic shocks.** Multiple lines of evidence relate climate variability to these forms of conflict.

Separately, they are both worrisome. But together, they are catastrophic. Climate change makes violent conflict more likely—and violent conflict makes a country more vulnerable to climate change. So climate change appears poised to help create many more of the most dangerous situations on Earth: failed states. Syria may be turning into an early example.

The High Cost of Inaction

The IPCC's discussion of economic costs is equally muddled:

". . . the incomplete estimates of global annual economic losses for additional temperature increases of ~2°C are between 0.2 percent and 2.0 percent of income. Losses are more likely than not to be greater, rather than smaller, than this range. . . . Losses accelerate with greater warming, but few quantitative estimates have been completed for additional warming around 3°C or above."

It would have been nice if the IPCC had mentioned at this point that keeping additional temperature increases to ~2°C requires very aggressive efforts to slash carbon pollution starting now. As it is, the deniers, confusionists, and easily confused can (incorrectly) assert that this first sentence means global economic losses from climate change will be low. Again, that's only if we act now.

As Climate Science Watch noted Saturday, "Other estimates suggest the high impacts on global GDP with warming of 4°C (For example the Stern Review found impacts of 5–20% of global GDP)."

The costs of even higher warming, which, again, would be nothing more than business as usual, rise exponentially. Indeed, we've known for years that traditional climate cost-benefit analyses are "unusually misleading"—as Harvard economist Martin Weitzman warned colleagues, "we may be deluding ourselves and others." Again, that's because the IPCC is basically a best case analysis—while it largely ignores the business-as-usual case and completely ignores the worst case.

Remember, earlier this month, during the press call for the vastly better written climate report from the American Association for the Advancement of Science, a leading expert on risk analysis explained, "You really do have to think about worst-case scenarios when you are thinking about risk management. When it's a risk management problem, thinking about worst-case scenarios is not alarmist—it's just part of the job. And those worst-case scenarios are part of what drives the price."

So where are we now? The first IPCC report last fall revealed we are as certain that humans are dramatically changing the planet's climate as we are that smoking causes cancer. It found the best estimate is that humans are responsible for *all* of the warming we have suffered since 1950. It warned that on the continued do-little path, we are facing total warming from pre-industrial levels by 2100 headed toward 4°C (7°F), with much more rapid sea level rise than previously reported, and the prospects of large-scale collapse of the permafrost, with resultant release of massive amounts of greenhouse gases.

Now, "the IPCC's new report should leave the world in no doubt about the scale and immediacy of the threat to human survival, health, and wellbeing," which in turn shows the need for "radical and transformative change" in our energy system, as the British Medical Journal editorialized.

Every few years, the world's leading climate scientists and governments identify the ever-worsening symptoms. They give us the same diagnosis, but with ever-growing certainty. And they lay out an ever-grimmer prognosis if we keep ignoring their straightforward and *relatively* inexpensive treatment. Will we act on the science in time?

Critical Thinking

1. Evaluate how important it is to act strongly now to minimize the effects of global warming.

2. Try to determine how to make policies when conditions are uncertain and changing.

3. Is risk adversive the best policy with respect to global warming?

Create Central

www.mhhe.com/createcentral

Internet References

National Center for Policy Analysis
   www.ncpa.org
New American Studies Web
   www.georgetown.edu/crossroads/asw
Sociology—Study Sociology Online
   http://edu.learnsoc.org
Sociology Web Resources
   http://www.mhhe.com/socscience/sociology/resources/index.htm
Sociosite
   http://www.topsite.com/goto/sociosite.net
Socioweb
   http://www.topsite.com/goto/socioweb.com

Romm, Joe, "Conservative Climate Panel Warns World Faces 'Breakdown of Food System' and More Violent Conflict," ThinkProgress.org, March 30, 2014.

Article   Prepared by: Kurt Finsterbusch, *University of Maryland, College Park*

The Moral Case for Designer Babies

RONALD BAILEY

Learning Outcomes

After reading this article, you will be able to:

- Develop your personal view about genetic engineering of embryos.
- Try to provide the basis on which policies about genetic engineering should be determined.
- Understand why religious and secular groups are likely to feel differently about genetic engineering of children.

Should parents be allowed to know if their fetus will get Alzheimer's?

Should prospective parents seek information about gene variants that increase the risk their children will develop diseases as adults? Should physicians provide that information?

Some bioethicists believe that such prebirth testing is wrong, arguing that the information could stigmatize kids or lead parents to terminate pregnancies of genetically at-risk fetuses. Children, they contend, have a right to an "open future" unburdened by the knowledge of their genetic predispositions for adult onset illnesses.

Consider the situation of Amanda and Bradley Kalinsky, as reported on the front page of *The New York* Times in February. Amanda Kalinsky tested positive for the gene that produces Gerstmann–Straussler–Scheinker (GSS) disease, a form of early onset dementia. Several family members, including her father, had already succumbed to the sickness. When she found out that she was a carrier, she initially vowed never to have children.

But then Amanda and her husband learned that they could use preimplantation genetic diagnosis of their embryos to avoid passing the GSS gene to their kids. Fertility clinic specialists induced her to produce several eggs that were removed and then fertilized with her husband's sperm. The resulting embryos were tested for the gene, and only those that did not have it were implanted in her womb.

The happy result is that the Kalinskys are the parents of three children—3-year-old twins, Ava and Cole, and 9-month-old Tatum—who have been spared the prospect of suffering the disease that is likely to kill their mother. The cost for the first round of in vitro and testing was about $20,000, which the Kalinskys paid out of pocket. "I would travel that road a million times over if I had to," Amanda told the *Times,* "because in the end I was given the privilege of being their mother."

In the *Times* article, the Yeshiva University bio-ethicist David Wasserman argued that discarding the GSS-gene embryos is akin to concluding that people like Amanda Kalinsky should have never been born. But decisions about who should be born ought not to be placed in the hands of ethicists or physicians; they should be left up to the people whose lives and values are actually on the line.

For Kalinsky, the prospect of passing on her GSS gene was frightening enough that she initially ruled out reproducing. Preimplantation genetic diagnosis enabled her and her husband to have children that they wouldn't have otherwise. In either scenario, the child with the GSS gene was not going to be born; this way, there are three new humans on the planet.

The Kalinskys were focusing on a single gene. But now a new, much more comprehensive whole-genome screening test is enabling physicians to identify disease risks that parents might not have any reason to suspect, such as genes increasing the possibility of breast cancer or Alzheimer's disease. The new test sequences a fetus's genome based on DNA it sheds into its mother's bloodstream. So researchers can now reveal genetic predispositions ranging from trivial characteristics like eye color and propensity to baldness to the risk of cancer.

Is it ethical for physicians to sequence a fetus's genome and then tell parents what the genetic screening test uncovers?

Yes, argues Ignatia B. Van den Veyver of Baylor College in the January 2014 issue of *Prenatal Diagnosis*. Among other arguments, Van den Veyver wonders "whether we infringe autonomy by shielding information that may allow parents and young adults to make decisions about their future that take into consideration all aspects of their current or future health," adding: "It is not well established that not providing this predictive information is the only direction to preserve the right to an open future."

Indeed not. Apparently, what some bioethicists mean by "open future" is one in which both parents and children are kept ignorant of the ways their complement of genes may expose them to medical risks.

Prenatal whole-genome sequencing will also provide parents with information about their prospective child's genetic susceptibility to illnesses like lung cancer, arteriosclerosis, and diabetes. Armed with such genomic knowledge, mothers and fathers could make sure that they don't smoke around their kid and later explain why it's a really bad idea for him or her to take up a tobacco habit. Warned in advance about their child's heightened risk of diabetes, parents could devise a diet and exercise regimen aimed at preventing its onset.

The American Medical Association (AMA) got it right when it offered ethical guidance to its members on prenatal genetic screening way back in 1994. "If prenatal diagnosis is performed, the principle of patient autonomy requires that all medically relevant information generated from fetal tests be passed along to the parent or parents," the AMA declared. "While the physician should generally discourage requests for information about benign genetic traits, the physician may not ethically refuse to pass along any requested information in his or her possession. The final decision as to what information is deemed appropriate for disclosure can only fall to the parents, informed by the facts and recommendations presented to them by their physician."

More recently, in the January 16 *New England Journal of Medicine*, Ilana Yurkiewicz of Harvard Medical School, Lisa Soleymani Lehmann of Brigham and Women's Hospital, and Bruce Korf of the University of Alabama at Birmingham argue that it is ethical to provide parents with prenatal whole-genome sequencing information, because it is "a basic right of reproductive choice and parental autonomy; people may choose when, with whom, and how to reproduce, and they have the right to data that may inform these decisions." The trio also notes that women in the United States do not have to provide a reason for obtaining an abortion, so it is "difficult to justify restricting abortion in the case of a well-defined reason, such as genetic disease."

The researchers reject the notion that genetic ignorance is somehow liberating. "Instead of limiting a child's potential future, knowledge of genetic risks can offer a greater opportunity to inform possibilities for a good life," they point out.

And that's the essential point. Whatever some bioethicists might believe, autonomy is never enhanced by ignorance.

Critical Thinking

1. Evaluate the degree that genetic modification of embryos should be left to parents and the extent that society should set rules about this.

2. How would you have been improved by genetic engineering?

3. Assuming that the technology will improve, how would you act as a parent with respect to genetic engineering?

Create Central

www.mhhe.com/createcentral

Internet References

National Council on Family Relations (NCFR)
   www.ncfr.com

National Institutes of Health (NIH)
   www.nih.gov

New American Studies Web
   www.georgetown.edu/crossroads/asw

Parenting and Families
   www.cyfc.umn.edu/features/index.html

Sociology—Study Sociology Online
   http://edu.learnsoc.org

Sociology Web Resources
   http://www.mhhe.com/socscience/sociology/resources/index.htm

Sociosite
   http://www.topsite.com/goto/sociosite.net

Socioweb
   http://www.topsite.com/goto/socioweb.com

Science Correspondent **RONALD BAILEY** is the author of Liberation Biology (Prometheus).

Bailey, Ronald, "The Moral Case for Designer Babies," *Reason Magazine*, vol. 46, 2, June 2014. Copyright © 2014 by Reason Foundation. All rights reserved. Used with permission.

Article   Prepared by: Kurt Finsterbusch, *University of Maryland, College Park*

How Innovation Could Save the Planet

Ideas may be our greatest natural resource, says a computer scientist and futurist. He argues that the world's most critical challenges—including population growth, peak oil, climate change, and limits to growth—could be met by encouraging innovation.

RAMEZ NAAM

Learning Outcomes

After reading this article, you will be able to:

- Understand both the benefits and the costs of long-term economic progress.
- Evaluate Ramez Naam's thesis that "Innovation could save the planet."
- Notice the many specific ideas and innovations that could address the major problems.

The Best of Times: Unprecedented Prosperity

There are many ways in which we are living in the most wonderful age ever. We can imagine we are heading toward a sort of science-fiction Utopia, where we are incredibly rich and incredibly prosperous, and the planet is healthy. But there are other reasons to fear that we're headed toward a dystopia of sorts.

On the positive side, life expectancy has been rising for the last 150 years, and faster since the early part of the twentieth century in the developing world than it has in the rich world. Along with that has come a massive reduction in poverty. The most fundamental empowerer of humans—education—has also soared, not just in the rich world, but throughout the world.

Another great empowerer of humanity is connectivity: Access to information and access to communication both have soared. The number of mobile phones on the planet was effectively zero in the early 1990s, and now it's in excess of 4 billion. More than three-quarters of humanity, in the span of one generation, have gotten access to connectivity that, as my

friend Peter Diamand is likes to say, is greater than any president before 1995 had. A reasonably well-off person in India or in Nigeria has better access to information than Ronald Reagan did during most of his career.

With increased connectivity has come an increase in democracy. As people have gotten richer, more educated, more able to access information, and more able to communicate, they have demanded more control over the places where they live. The fraction of nations that are functional democracies is at an all-time high in this world—more than double what it was in the 1970s, with the collapse of the Soviet Union.

Economically, the world is a more equal place than it has been in decades. In the West, and especially in the United States, we hear a lot about growing inequality, but on a global scale, the opposite is true. As billions are rising out of poverty around the world, the global middle classes are catching up with the global rich.

In many ways, this is the age of the greatest human prosperity, freedom, and potential that has ever been on the face of this planet. But in other ways, we are facing some of the largest risks ever.

The Worst of Times: The Greatest Risks

At its peak, the ancient Mayan city of Tikal was a metropolis, a city of 200,000 people inside of a civilization of about 20 million people. Now, if you walk around any Mayan city, you see mounds of dirt. That's because these structures were all abandoned by about the mid-900s A.D. We know now what happened: The Mayan civilization grew too large. It overpopulated.

To feed themselves, they had to convert forest into farmland. They chopped down all of the forest. That, in turn, led to soil erosion. It also worsened drought, because trees, among other things, trap moisture, and create a precipitation cycle.

When that happened, and was met by some normal (not human caused) climate change, the Mayans found they didn't have enough food. They exhausted their primary energy supply, which is food. That in turn led to more violence in their society and ultimately to a complete collapse.

The greatest energy source for human civilization today is fossil fuels. Among those, none is more important than oil. In 1956, M. King Hubbert looked at production in individual oil fields and predicted that the United States would see the peak of its oil production in 1970 or so, and then drop. His prediction largely came true: Oil production went up but did peak in the 1970s, then plummeted.

Oil production has recently gone up in the United States a little bit, but it's still just barely more than half of what it was in its peak in the 1970s.

Hubbert also predicted that the global oil market would peak in about 2000, and for a long time he looked very foolish. But it now has basically plateaued. Since 2004, oil production has increased by about 4 percent, whereas in the 1950s it rose by about 4 percent every three months.

We haven't hit a peak; oil production around the world is still rising a little bit. It's certainly not declining, but we do appear to be near a plateau; supply is definitely rising more slowly than demand. Though there's plenty of oil in the ground, the oil that remains is in smaller fields, further from shore, under lower pressure, and harder to pump out.

Water is another resource that is incredibly precious to us. The predominant way in which we use water is through the food that we eat: 70 percent of the freshwater that humanity uses goes into agriculture.

The Ogallala Aquifer, the giant body of freshwater under the surface of the Earth in the Great Plains of the United States, is fossil water left from the melting and the retreat of glaciers in the end of the last Ice Age, 12,000–14,000 years ago. Its refill time is somewhere between 5,000 and 10,000 years from normal rainfall. Since 1960, we've drained between a third and a half of the water in this body, depending on what estimate you look at. In some areas, the water table is dropping about three feet per year.

If this was a surface lake in the United States or Canada, and people saw that happening, they'd stop it. But because it's out of sight, it's just considered a resource that we can tap. And indeed, in the north Texas area, wells are starting to fail already, and farms are being abandoned in some cases, because they can't get to the water that they once did.

Perhaps the largest risk of all is climate change. We've increased the temperature of the planet by about 2°F in the last 130 years, and that rate is accelerating. This is primarily because of the carbon dioxide we've put into the atmosphere, along with methane and nitrous oxide. CO_2 levels, now at over 390 parts per million, are the highest they've been in about 15 million years. Ice cores go back at least a million years, and we know that they're the highest they've been in that time. Historically, when CO_2 levels are high, temperature is also high. But also, historically, in the lifetime of our species, we've actually never existed as human beings while CO_2 levels have been this high.

For example, glaciers such as the Bear and Pedersen in Alaska have disappeared just since 1920. As these glaciers melt, they produce water that goes into the seas and helps to raise sea levels. Over the next century, the seas are expected to rise about 3 to 6 feet. Most of that actually will not be melting glaciers; it's thermal expansion: As the ocean gets warmer, it gets a little bit bigger.

But 3 to 6 feet over a century doesn't sound like that big a deal to us, so we think of that as a distant problem. The reality is that there's a more severe problem with climate change: its impact on the weather and on agriculture.

In 2003, Europe went through its worst heat wave since 1540. Ukraine lost 75 percent of its wheat crop. In 2009, China had a once-in-a-century level drought; in 2010 they had another once-in-a-century level drought. That's twice. Wells that had given water continuously since the fifteenth century ran dry. When those rains returned, when the water that was soaked up by the atmosphere came back down, it came down on Pakistan, and half of Pakistan was under water in the floods of 2010. An area larger than Germany was under water.

Warmer air carries more water. Every degree Celsius that you increase the temperature value of air, it carries 7 percent more water. But it doesn't carry that water uniformly. It can suck water away from one place and then deliver it in a deluge in another place. So both the droughts are up and flooding is up simultaneously, as precipitation becomes more lumpy and more concentrated.

In Russia's 2010 heat wave, 55,000 people died, 11,000 of them in Moscow alone. In 2011, the United States had the driest 10-month period ever in the American South, and Texas saw its worst wildfires ever. And 2012 was the worst drought in the United States since the Dust Bowl—the corn crop shrank by 20 percent.

So that's the big risk the world faces: that radical weather will change how we grow food, which is still our most important energy source—even more important than fossil fuels.

A number of people in the environmentalist movement are saying that we have to just stop growing. For instance, in his book *Peak Everything: Waking Up to the Century of Declines*, Richard Heinberg of the Post-Carbon Institute says that the Earth is full. Get used to it, and get ready for a world where you live with less wealth, and where your children live with less wealth, than any before.

I don't think this idea of stopping growth is realistic, because there are a top billion people who live pretty well and there are another 6 billion who don't and are hungry for it. We see demand rising for everything—water, food, energy—and that demand is rising not in the United States or Europe or Canada or Australia. It's rising in the developing world. This is the area that will create all of the increased demand for physical resources.

Even if we could, by some chance, say That's enough, sorry, we're not going to let you use these resources, which is doubtful, it wouldn't be just, because the West got rich by using those natural resources. So we need to find a different way.

Ideas as a Resource Expander, Resource Preserver, and Waste Reducer

The best-selling environmental book of all time, *Limits to Growth,* was based on computer modeling. It was a simple model with only about eight variables of what would happen in the world. It showed that economic growth, more wealth, would inevitably lead to more pollution and more consumption of finite resources, which would in turn take us beyond the limits and lead ultimately to collapse.

While it's been widely reported recently that its predictions are coming true, that's actually not the case. If you look at the vast majority of the numbers that the researchers predict in this model, they're not coming true.

Why did they get these things wrong? The most important thing that the forecasters did was underestimate the power of new ideas to expand resources, or to expand wealth while using fewer resources. Ideas have done tremendous things for us. Let's start with food.

In *The Population Bomb* (1968), Paul Ehrlich predicted that food supply could not support the population, just as Malthus did. But what's happened is that we've doubled population since 1960, and we've nearly tripled the food supply in total. We've increased by 30–40 percent the food supply per person since the 1960s.

Let's look at this on a very long time scale. How many people can you feed with an acre of land? Before the advent of agriculture, an acre of land could feed less than a thousandth of a person. Today it's about three people, on average, who can be fed by one acre of land. Preagriculture, it took 3,000 acres for one person to stay alive through hunting and gathering. With agriculture, that footprint has shrunk from 3,000 acres to one-third of one acre. That's not because there's any more sunlight, which is ultimately what food is; it's because we've changed the productivity of the resource by innovation in farming—and then thousands of innovations on top of that to increase it even more.

In fact, the reason we have the forests that we have on the planet is because we were able to handle a doubling of the population since 1960 without increasing farmland by more than about 10 percent. If we had to have doubled our farmland, we would have chopped down all the remaining forests on the planet.

Ideas can reduce resource use. I can give you many other examples. In the United States, the amount of energy used on farms per calorie grown has actually dropped by about half since the 1970s. That's in part because we now only use about a tenth of the energy to create synthetic nitrogen fertilizer, which is an important input.

The amount of food that you can grow per drop of water has roughly doubled since the 1980s. In wheat, it's actually more than tripled since 1960. The amount of water that we use in the United States per person has dropped by about a third since the 1970s, after rising for decades. As agriculture has gotten more efficient, we're using less water per person. So, again, ideas can reduce resource use.

Ideas can also find substitutes for scarce resources. We're at risk of running out of many things, right? Well, let's think about some things that have happened in the past.

The sperm whale was almost hunted into extinction. Sperm whales were, in the mid-1800s, the best source of illumination. Sperm whale oil—spermaceti—was the premier source of lighting. It burned without smoke, giving a clear, steady light, and the demand for it led to huge hunting of the sperm whales. In a period of about 30 years, we killed off about a third of the sperm whales on the planet.

That led to a phenomenon of "peak sperm-whale oil": The number of sperm whales that the fleet could bring in dropped over time as the sperm whales became more scarce and more afraid of human hunters. Demand rose as supply dropped, and the prices skyrocketed. So it looked a little bit like the situation with oil now.

That was solved not by the discovery of more sperm whales, nor by giving up on this thing of lighting. Rather, Abraham Gesner, a Canadian, discovered this thing called kerosene. He found that, if he took coal, heated it up, captured the fumes, and distilled them, he could create this fluid that burned very clear. And he could create it in quantities thousands of times greater than the sperm whales ever could have given up.

We have no information suggesting that Gesner was an environmentalist or that he cared about sperm whales at all. He was motivated by scientific curiosity and by the huge business opportunity of going after this lighting market. What he did was dramatically lower the cost of lighting while saving the sperm whales from extinction.

One more thing that ideas can do is transform waste into value. In places like Germany and Japan, people are mining landfills. Japan estimates that its landfills alone contain 10-year supplies of gold and rare-earth minerals for the world market.

Alcoa estimates that the world's landfills contain a 15-year sup-ply of aluminum. So there's tremendous value.

When we throw things away, they're not destroyed. If we "consume" things like aluminum, we're not really consuming it, we're rearranging it. We're changing where it's located. And in some cases, the concentration of these resources in our land-fills is actually higher than it was in our mines. What it takes is energy and technology to get that resource back out and put it back into circulation.

Ideas for Stretching the Limits

So ideas can reduce resource use, can find substitutes for scarce resources, and can transform waste into value. In that context, what are the limits to growth?

Is there a population limit? Yes, there certainly is, but it doesn't look like we're going to hit that. Projections right now are that, by the middle of this century, world population will peak between 9 billion and 10 billion, and then start to decline. In fact, we'll be talking much more about the graying of civi-lization, and perhaps underpopulation—too-low birthrates on a current trend.

What about physical resources? Are there limits to physi-cal resource use on this planet? Absolutely. It really is a finite planet. But where are those limits?

To illustrate, let's start with energy. This is the most impor-tant resource that we use, in many ways. But when we consider all the fossil fuels that humanity uses today—all the oil, coal, natural gas, and so on—it pales in comparison to a much larger resource, all around us, which is the amount of energy coming in from our Sun every day.

The amount of energy from sunlight that strikes the top of the atmosphere is about 10,000 times as much as the energy that we use from fossil fuels on a daily basis. Ten seconds of sunlight hitting the Earth is as much energy as humanity uses in an entire day; one hour of sunlight hitting the Earth provides as much energy to the planet as a whole as humanity uses from all sources combined in one year.

This is an incredibly abundant resource. It manifests in many ways. It heats the atmosphere differentially, creating winds that we can capture for wind power. It evaporates water, which leads to precipitation elsewhere, which turns into things like rivers and waterfalls, which we can capture as hydropower.

But by far the largest fraction of it—more than half—is pho-tons hitting the surface of the Earth. Those are so abundant that, with one-third of 1 percent of the Earth's land area, using current technology of about 14 percent-efficient solar cells, we could capture enough electricity to power all of current human needs.

The problem is not the abundance of the energy; the prob-lem is cost. Our technology is primitive. Our technology for

building solar cells is similar to our technology for manufac-turing computer chips. They're built on silicon wafers in clean rooms at high temperatures, and so they're very, very expensive.

But innovation has been dropping that cost tremendously. Over the last 30 years, we've gone from a watt of solar power costing $20 to about $1. That's a factor of 20. We roughly drop the cost of solar by one-half every decade, more or less. That means that, in the sunniest parts of the world today, solar is now basically at parity in cost, without subsidies, with coal and natural gas. Over the next 12–15 years, that will spread to most of the planet. That's incredibly good news for us.

Of course, we don't just use energy while the Sun is shin-ing. We use energy at night to power our cities; we use energy in things like vehicles that have to move and that have high energy densities. Both of these need storage, and today's stor-age is actually a bigger challenge than capturing energy. But there's reason to believe that we can tackle the storage problem, as well.

For example, consider lithium ion batteries—the batter-ies that are in your laptop, your cell phone, and so on. The demand to have longer-lasting devices drove tremendous inno-vations in these batteries in the 1990s and the early part of the 2000s. Between 1991 and 2005, the cost of storage in lithium ion batteries dropped by about a factor of nine, and the density of storage—how much energy you can store in an ounce of battery—increased by a little over double in that time. If we do that again, we would be at the point where grid-scale stor-age is affordable and we can store that energy overnight. Our electric vehicles have ranges similar to the range you can get in a gasoline-powered vehicle.

This is a tall order. This represents perhaps tens of billions of dollars in R&D, but it is something that is possible and for which there is precedent.

Another approach being taken is turning energy into fuel. When you use a fuel such as gasoline, it's not really an energy source. It's an energy carrier, an energy storage system, if you will. You can store a lot of energy in a very small amount.

Today, two pioneers in genome sequencing—Craig Venter and George Church—both have founded companies to create next-generation biofuels. What they're both leveraging is that gene-sequencing cost is the fastest quantitative area of progress on the planet.

What they're trying to do is engineer microorganisms that consume CO_2, sunlight, and sugar and actually excrete fuel as a byproduct. If we could do this, maybe just 1 percent of the Earth's surface—or a 30th of what we use for agriculture—could provide all the liquid fuels that we need. We would con-veniently grow algae on saltwater and waste water, so biofuel production wouldn't compete for freshwater. And the possible yields are vast if we can get there.

If we can crack energy, we can crack everything else:

* Water. Water is life. We live in a water world, but only about a tenth of a percent of the water in the world is freshwater that's accessible to us in some way. Ninety-seven percent of the world's water is in the oceans and is salty. It used to be that desalination meant boiling water and then catching the steam and letting it condense.

Between the times of the ancient Greeks and 1960, desalination technology didn't really change. But then, it did. People started to create membranes modeled on what cells do, which is allow some things through but not others. They used plastics to force water through and get only the fresh and not the salty. As a result, the amount of energy it takes to desalinate a liter of water has dropped by about a factor of nine in that time. Now, in the world's largest desalination plants, the price of desalinated water is about a tenth of a cent per gallon. The technology has gotten to the point where it is starting to become a realistic option as an alternative to using up scarce freshwater resources.

* Food. Can we grow enough food? Between now and 2050, we have to increase food yield by about 70 percent. Is that possible? I think it is. In industrialized nations, food yields are already twice what they are in the world as a whole. That's because we have irrigation, tractors, better pesticides, and so on. Given such energy and wealth, we already know that we can grow enough food to feed the planet.

Another option that's probably cheaper would be to leverage some things that nature's already produced. What most people don't know is that the yield of corn per acre and in calories is about 70 percent higher than the yield of wheat. Corn is a C 4 photosynthesis crop: It uses a different way of turning sunlight and CO_2 into sugars that evolved only 30 million years ago. Now, scientists around the world are working on taking these C 4 genes from crops like corn and transplanting them into wheat and rice, which could right away increase the yield of those staple grains by more than 50 percent.

Physical limits do exist, but they are extremely distant. We cannot grow exponentially in our physical resource use forever, but that point is still at least centuries in the future. It's something we have to address eventually, but it's not a problem that's pressing right now.

* Wealth. One thing that people don't appreciate very much is that wealth has been decoupling from physical resource use on this planet. Energy use per capita is going up, CO_2 emissions per capita have been going up a little bit, but they are both widely outstripped by the amount of wealth that we're creating. That's because we can be more efficient in everything—using less energy per unit of food grown, and so on.

This again might sound extremely counterintuitive, but let me give you one concrete example of how that happens. Compare the ENIAC—which in the 1940s was the first digital computer ever created—to an iPhone. An iPhone is billions of times smaller, uses billions of times less energy, and has billions of times more computing power than ENIAC. If you tried to create an iPhone using ENIAC technology, it would be a cube a mile on the side, and it would use more electricity than the state of California. And it wouldn't have access to the Internet, because you'd have to invent that, as well.

This is what I mean when I say ideas are the ultimate resource. The difference between an ENIAC and an iPhone is that the iPhone is embodied knowledge that allows you to do more with less resources. That phenomenon is not limited to high tech. It's everywhere around us.

So ideas are the ultimate resource. They're the only resource that accumulates over time. Our store of knowledge is actually larger than in the past, as opposed to all physical resources.

Challenges Ahead for Innovation

Today we are seeing a race between our rate of consumption and our rate of innovation, and there are multiple challenges. One challenge is the Darwinian process, survival of the fittest. In areas like green tech, there will be hundreds and even thousands of companies founded, and 99 percent of them will go under. That is how innovation happens.

The other problem is scale. Just as an example, one of the world's largest solar arrays is at Nellis Air Force Base in California, and we would need about 10 million of these in order to meet the world's electricity needs. We have the land, we have the solar energy coming in, but there's a lot of industrial production that has to happen before we get to that point.

Innovation is incredibly powerful, but the pace of innovation compared to the pace of consumption is very important. One thing we can do to increase the pace of innovation is to address the biggest challenge, which is market failure.

In 1967, you could stick your hand into the Cuyahoga River, in Ohio, and come up covered in muck and oil. At that time, the river was lined with businesses and factories, and for them the river was a free resource. It was cheaper to pump their waste into the river than it was to pay for disposal at some other sort of facility. The river was a commons that anybody could use or abuse, and the waste they were producing was an externality. To that business or factory, there was no cost to pumping waste into this river. But to the people who depended upon the river, there was a high cost overall.

That's what I mean by a market externality and a market failure, because this was an important resource to all of us. But no one owned it, no one bought or sold it, and so it was treated badly in a way that things with a price are not.

That ultimately culminated when, in June 1969, a railway car passing on a bridge threw a spark; the spark hit a slick of oil a mile long on the river, and the river burst into flames.

The story made the cover of *Time* magazine. In many ways, the environmental movement was born of this event as much as it was of Rachel Carson's *Silent Spring*. In the following three years, the United States created the Environmental Protection Agency and passed the Clean Water and Clean Air acts.

Almost every environmental problem on the planet is an issue of the commons, whether it's chopping down forests that no one owns, draining lakes that no one owns, using up fish in the ocean that no one owns, or polluting the atmosphere because no one owns it, or heating up the planet. They're all issues of the commons. They're all issues where there is no cost to an individual entity to deplete something and no cost to overconsume something, but there is a greater cost that's externalized and pushed on everybody else who shares this.

Now let's come back again to what Limits to Growth said, which was that economic growth always led to more pollution and more consumption, put us beyond limits, and ends with collapse. So if that's the case, all those things we just talked about should be getting worse. But as the condition of the Cuyahoga River today illustrates, that is not the case.

GDP in the United States is three times what it was when the Cuyahoga River caught on fire, so shouldn't it be more polluted? It's not. Instead, it's the cleanest it's been in decades. That's not because we stopped growth. It's because we made intelligent choices about managing that commons.

Another example: In the 1970s, we discovered that the ozone layer was thinning to such an extent that it literally could drive the extinction of all land species on Earth. But it's actually getting better. It's turned a corner, it's improving ahead of schedule, and it's on track to being the healthiest it's been in a century. That's because we've reduced the emissions of CFCs, which destroy ozone; we've dropped the amount of them that we emit into the atmosphere basically to zero. And yet industry has not ground to a halt because of this, either. Economic growth has not faltered.

And one last example: Acid rain—which is primarily produced by sulfur dioxide emitted by coal-burning power plants—is mostly gone as an issue. Emissions of sulfur dioxide are down by about a factor of two. That's in part because we created a strategy called cap and trade: It capped the amount of SO_2 that you could emit, then allowed you to swap and buy emission credits from others to find the optimal way to do that.

The cost, interestingly enough, has always been lower than projected. In each of these cases, industry has said, This will end things. Ronald Reagan's chief of staff said the economy would grind to a halt, and the EPA would come in with lower cost estimates. But the EPA has always been wrong: The EPA cost estimate has always been too high.

Analysis of all of these efforts in the past shows that reducing emissions is always cheaper than you expect, but cleaning up the mess afterwards is always more expensive than you'd guess.

Today, the biggest commons issue is that of climate change, with the CO_2 and other greenhouse gases that we're pumping into the atmosphere. A logical thing to do would be to put a price on these. If you pollute, if you're pumping CO_2 into the atmosphere and it's warming the planet, so you're causing harm to other people in a very diffuse way. Therefore, you should be paying in proportion to that harm you're doing to offset it.

But if we do that, won't that have a massive impact on the economy? This all relates to energy, which drives a huge fraction of the economy. Manufacturing depends on it. Transport depends on it. So wouldn't it be a huge problem if we were to actually put a price on these carbon emissions?

Well, there has been innovative thinking about that, as well. One thing that economists have always told us is that, if you're going to tax, tax the bad, not the good. Whatever it is that you tax, you will get less of it. So tax the bad, not the good.

The model that would be the ideal for putting a price on pollution is what we call a revenue-neutral model. Revenue-neutral carbon tax, revenue-neutral cap and trade. Let's model it as a tax: Today, a country makes a certain amount of revenue for its government in income tax, let's say. If you want to tax pollution, the way to do this without impacting the economy is to increase your pollution tax in the same manner that you decrease the income tax. The government then is capturing the same amount of money from the economy as a whole, so there's no economic slowdown as a result of this.

This has a positive effect on the environment because it tips the scales of price. Now, if you're shopping for energy, and you're looking at solar versus coal or natural gas, the carbon price has increased the price of coal and natural gas to you, but not the cost of solar. It shifts customer behavior from one to the other while having no net impact on the economy, and probably a net benefit on the economy in the long run as more investment in green energy drives the price down.

Toward a Wealthier, Cleaner Future

The number-one thing I want you to take away is that pollution and overconsumption are not inevitable outcomes of growth. While tripling the wealth of North America, for instance, we've gone from an ozone layer that was rapidly deteriorating to one that is bouncing back.

The fundamental issue is not one of limits to growth; it's one of the policy we choose, and it's one of how we structure our economy to value all the things we depend upon and not just those things that are owned privately.

What can we do, each of us? Four things:

First is to communicate. These issues are divisive, but we know that beliefs and attitudes on issues like this spread word of mouth. They spread person to person, from person you trust to person you trust. So talk about it. Many of us have friends or colleagues or family on the other side of these issues, but talk about it. You're better able to persuade them than anyone else is.

Second is to participate. By that I mean politically. Local governments, state and province governments, and national governments are responsive when they hear from their constituents about these issues. It changes their attitudes. Because so few constituents actually make a call to the office of their legislator, or write a letter, a few can make a very large impact.

Third is to innovate. These problems aren't solved yet. We don't have the technologies for these problems today. The trend lines look very good, but the next 10 years of those trend lines demand lots of bright people, lots of bright ideas, and lots of R&D. So if you're thinking about a career change, or if you know any young people trying to figure out what their career is now, these are careers that (A) will be very important to us in the future and (B) will probably be quite lucrative for them.

Last is to keep hope, because we have faced problems like this before and we have conquered them every time. The future isn't written in stone—it could go good or bad—but I'm very optimistic. I know we have the ability to do it, and I think we will. Ultimately, ideas are our most important natural resource.

Critical Thinking

1. Do the facts seem to support an optimistic future or a pessimistic future?
2. What is the potential of new ideas and new technologies?

3. Technologies have brought great benefits and considerable problems. Can technologies and new ideas now solve those problems?

Create Central

www.mhhe.com/createcentral

Internet References

National Center for Policy Analysis
www.ncpa.org
Social Science Information Gateway
http://sosig.esrc.bris.ac.uk
SocioSite
www.pscw.uva.nl/sociosite/TOPICS/Women.html
Sociology—Study Sociology Online
http://edu.learnsoc.org
Sociology Web Resources
http://www.mhhe.com/socscience/sociology/resources/index.htm
Sociosite
http://www.topsite.com/goto/sociosite.net
Socioweb
http://www.topsite.com/goto/socioweb.com
WWW Virtual Library: Demography & Population Studies
http://demography.anu.edu.au/VirtualLibrary

Ramez Naam is a computer scientist and author. He is a former Microsoft executive and current fellow of the Institute for Ethics and Emerging Technologies. He lives in Seattle, Washington.

Naam, Ramez, "How Innovation Could Save the Planet," *The Futurist*, March/April 2013. Copyright © 2013 by World Future Society. All rights reserved. Used with permission.

Article   Prepared by: Kurt Finsterbusch, *University of Maryland, College Park*

Annual Report Card on Our Future

Rick Docksai

Learning Outcomes

After reading this article, you will be able to:

- Better understand the state of the planet.

- Evaluate the significance of massive efforts to assess the state of the planet such as this one.

- Connect these findings to potential new policies.

The Millennium Project assesses where the world is gaining or losing ground.

The world community is in better shape than it should be, states the Millennium Project's leadership team in its 2013–14 State of the Future report. This volume, the international think tank's acclaimed annual "report card on the future of the world," finds that human health and living standards are trending upward but are doing so despite deficient stewardship of the planet and widespread occurrences of poor governance, political corruption, crime, and violence.

"When you consider the many wrong decisions and good decisions not yet taken—day after day and year after year around the world—it is amazing that we are still making as much progress as we are," the authors write.

The Millennium Project has been producing annual State of the Future reports since 1996. Each report makes a full-scale assessment of where life on Earth is heading, based on constantly incoming data from an international network of more than 4,500 contributing researchers. Like its predecessors, this year's report integrates the data into a list of 15 Global Challenges that require collaborative action by the world's leaders, along with a State of the Future Index (SOFI) that marks areas of life in which we are "winning," "losing," or experiencing "unclear or little change."

This report's SOFI cites some encouraging firsts. For the first time, we are "winning" on renewable energy—worldwide renewable capacity has been growing and is on track for a much larger growth spurt this decade. We are also winning for the first time on Gross National Investment Per Capita, Foreign Direct Investment, and Health Expenditures Per Capita.

Also, some positive trends from earlier years are still running strong. The number of physicians per capita is growing worldwide, as it was in 2011. The world is likewise winning on energy efficiency, a winning streak that started in 2012.

Other trends are not good. For the first time, we are losing on forest area. Also, greenhouse-gas emissions and our overall ecological footprint, two areas that have been on the "losing" side of the ledger for the past few years, are still losing areas today. Glaciers are melting and coral reefs are dying at accelerating rates as climate change gathers steam.

"The global situation for humanity continues to improve in general, but at the expense of the environment," the authors write.

All is not trending well for human life, either. The SOFI notes little or no progress on nuclear nonproliferation and HIV prevalence—areas in which we were winning in 2011. Some trends from 2012 or earlier are continuing to worsen, too—namely, income inequality, terrorism, and political corruption.

This year's 15 Global Challenges list additionally notes that global material waste increased 10-fold last century and could double again by 2025. The authors also voice concern over shrinking supplies of potable water. They call for new agricultural approaches that would consume less water, such as new ways to synthesize meat without growing animals, genetic engineering for higher-yielding and more drought-resistant crops, and cultivating insects as animal feed.

On the upside, literacy and IQ scores keep rising, and the growth of online educational resources could accelerate intellectual growth even further. Also, the prospects for a more peaceful world are on the upswing, thanks to democracy, international trade, Internet use, and news media all gaining ground; prosperity rising and poverty declining; crosscultural dialogues flourishing; and NGOs and regional organizations fostering community-led social reforms and peace accords.

Efforts to affirm women's rights are also making crucial gains. New worldwide campaigns to stop violence against women are expanding, while new mobile-phone apps and Internet sites are making it easier to report and publicize incidences of violence. Overall, the report projects that "slow but massive shifts in gender stereotypes will occur in the next few decades."

The Global Challenges section breaks each problem area down to the regional levels, as well. Readers will see specific takes on the energy, governance, and human and environmental health situations of Africa, Europe, North America, Latin America, and Asia and Oceania.

Some new issues have surfaced since 2012, such as poor nutrition. The authors explain that, while hunger is down throughout the world, much of the world's daily caloric intake is "empty calories" that satisfy hunger pangs but do little for overall health and contribute to weight gain and diabetes risk.

"It is not clear that food nutrient density will keep pace with human needs," they write.

The report lists several dozen steps that could remedy the situation. Among them are taxing unhealthy foods more heavily to subsidize healthier ones, posting "low nutritional value" warning labels on food packaging, breaking up agribusiness and food market monopolies, increasing investment in developing countries' agricultural R&D, and organizing school-based campaigns to encourage healthier eating.

Another concern is major construction along the world's coasts, where there is vulnerability to numerous environmental hazards. The authors give several pages of recommendations for safer development, such as more interdisciplinary and participatory urban planning that involves NGOs, ecologists, and the urban poor; building green, floating cities with newer materials; imposing compensation fees and higher taxes on activities that pollute; and organizing youth environmental groups to carry out habitat restoration.

The world has the means to further improve human life while preserving the planet's natural systems and resources, but it must marshal global intelligence and activism across national borders to an entirely new degree, the authors conclude. They stress the value of better information-gathering systems as guides to the process.

"Some of the world's toughest problems affect everyone almost instantly and do not end at national borders. In the future, solutions as well as problems must also cross boundaries—ideological as well as geographic," they write.

The 2013–14 State of the Future is an authoritative compendium of what we know about the future of humanity and our planet. Policy makers and advocates will find it to be a vast yet very readable source of insight on where the world's thorniest problems begin and where they might end.

Critical Thinking

1. Critique the 15 measures selected to measure the State of the Future by the Millennial Project.

2. How authoritative do you consider this report card? Why?

3. No one should be surprised that affluence and health are improving worldwide or that the environment is worsening, but why are governance, crime, and violence worsening?

Create Central

www.mhhe.com/createcentral

Internet References

National Center for Policy Analysis
www.ncpa.org

New American Studies Web
www.georgetown.edu/crossroads/asw

Sociology—Study Sociology Online
http://edu.learnsoc.org

Sociology Web Resources
http://www.mhhe.com/socscience/sociology/resources/index.htm

SocioSite
www.pscw.uva.nl/sociosite/TOPICS/Women.html

Sociosite
http://www.topsite.com/goto/sociosite.net

Socioweb
http://www.topsite.com/goto/socioweb.com

WWW Virtual Library: Demography & Population Studies
http://demography.anu.edu.au/VirtualLibrary

RICK DOCKSAI is senior editor of THE FUTURIST.

Docksai, Rick, "Annual Report Card on Our Future," *The Futurist*, vol. 48, 4, July/August 2014. Copyright © 2014 by World Future Society. All rights reserved. Used with permission.

Article   Prepared by: Kurt Finsterbusch, *University of Maryland, College Park*

The Unruled World

STEWART PATRICK

Learning Outcomes

After reading this article, you will be able to:

- Understand the many weaknesses of many governments today.

- Understand the current difficulties of fixing governments that need to be fixed.

- Evaluate the role of international institutions and aid agencies in supporting improvements in national institutions.

The Case for Good Enough Global Governance

While campaigning for president in 2008, Barack Obama pledged to renovate the dilapidated multilateral edifice the United States had erected after World War II. He lionized the generation of Franklin Roosevelt, Harry Truman, and George Marshall for creating the United Nations, the Bretton Woods institutions, and NATO. Their genius, he said, was to recognize that "instead of constraining our power, these institutions magnified it." But the aging pillars of the postwar order were creaking and crumbling, Obama suggested, and so "to keep pace with the fast-moving threats we face," the world needed a new era of global institution building.

Five years into Obama's presidency, little progress has been made on that front, and few still expect it. Formal multilateral institutions continue to muddle along, holding their meetings and issuing their reports and taking some minor stabs at improving transnational problems at the margins. Yet despite the Obama administration's avowed ambition to integrate rising powers as full partners, there has been no movement to reform the composition of the UN Security Council to reflect new geopolitical realities. Meanwhile, the World Trade Organization (WTO) is comatose, NATO struggles to find its strategic

purpose, and the International Energy Agency courts obsolescence by omitting China and India as members.

The demand for international cooperation has not diminished. In fact, it is greater than ever, thanks to deepening economic interdependence, worsening environmental degradation, proliferating transnational threats, and accelerating technological change. But effective multilateral responses are increasingly occurring outside formal institutions, as frustrated actors turn to more convenient, ad hoc venues. The relative importance of legal treaties and universal bodies such as the UN is declining, as the United States and other states rely more on regional organizations, "minilateral" cooperation among relevant states, codes of conduct, and partnerships with nongovernmental actors. And these trends are only going to continue. The future will see not the renovation or the construction of a glistening new international architecture but rather the continued spread of an unattractive but adaptable multilateral sprawl that delivers a partial measure of international cooperation through a welter of informal arrangements and piecemeal approaches.

"Global governance" is a slippery term. It refers not to world government (which nobody expects or wants anymore) but to something more practical: the collective effort by sovereign states, international organizations, and other nonstate actors to address common challenges and seize opportunities that transcend national frontiers. In domestic politics, governance is straightforward. It is provided by actual governments—formal, hierarchical institutions with the authority to establish and enforce binding rules. Governance in the international or transnational sphere, however, is more complex and ambiguous. There is some hierarchy—such as the special powers vested in the permanent members of the UN Security Council—but international politics remain anarchic, with the system composed of independent sovereign units that recognize no higher authority.

Cooperation under such anarchy is certainly possible. National governments often work together to establish common standards of behavior in spheres such as trade or security, embedding norms and rules in international institutions charged with providing global goods or mitigating global bads. But most cooperative multilateral bodies, even those binding under international law, lack real power to enforce compliance with collective decisions. What passes for governance is thus an ungainly patchwork of formal and informal institutions.

Alongside long-standing universal membership bodies, there are various regional institutions, multilateral alliances and security groups, standing consultative mechanisms, self-selecting clubs, ad hoc coalitions, issue-specific arrangements, transnational professional networks, technical standard-setting bodies, global action networks, and more. States are still the dominant actors, but nonstate actors increasingly help shape the global agenda, define new rules, and monitor compliance with international obligations.

The clutter is unsightly and unwieldy, but it has some advantages, as well. No single multilateral body could handle all the world's complex transnational problems, let alone do so effectively or nimbly. And the plurality of institutions and forums is not always dysfunctional, because it can offer states the chance to act relatively deftly and flexibly in responding to new challenges. But regardless of what one thinks of the current global disorder, it is clearly here to stay, and so the challenge is to make it work as well as possible.

Big Game

The centerpiece of contemporary global governance remains the UN, and the core of the UN system remains the Security Council—a standing committee including the most powerful countries in the world. In theory, the Security Council could serve as a venue for coordinating international responses to the world's most important threats to global order. In practice, however, it regularly disappoints—because the five permanent members (the United States, the UK, France, Russia, and China) often disagree and because their veto power allows the disagreements to block action. This has been true since the UN's inception, of course, but the Security Council's significance has diminished in recent decades as its composition has failed to track shifts in global power.

The Obama administration, like its predecessors, has flirted with the idea of pushing a charter amendment to update the Security Council's membership but has remained wary due to concerns that an enlarged Security Council, with new and more empowered members, might decrease US influence and leverage. But even if Washington were to push hard for change, the status quo would be incredibly hard to overturn. Any expansion plan would require approval by two-thirds of the 193 members of the UN General Assembly, as well as domestic ratification by the five permanent members of the Security Council. And

even those countries that favor expansion are deeply divided over which countries should benefit. So in practice, everyone pays lip service to enlargement while allowing the negotiations to drag on endlessly without any result.

This situation seems likely to persist, but at the cost of a deepening crisis of legitimacy, effectiveness, and compliance, as the Security Council's composition diverges ever further from the distribution of global power. Dissatisfied players could conceivably launch an all-out political assault on the institution, but they are much more likely to simply bypass the council, seeking alternative frameworks in which to address their concerns.

The dysfunction of the UN extends well beyond the Security Council, of course. Despite modest management reforms, the UN Secretariat and many UN agencies remain opaque, and their budgeting and operations are hamstrung by outdated personnel policies that encourage cronyism. Within the UN General Assembly, meanwhile, irresponsible actors who play to the galleries often dominate debates, and too many resolutions reflect encrusted regional and ideological blocs that somehow persist long after their sell-by date.

With the Security Council dominated by the old guard, rising powers have begun eyeing possible alternative venues for achieving influence and expressing their concerns. Shifts in global power have always ultimately produced shifts in the institutional superstructure, but what is distinctive today is the simultaneous emergence of multiple power centers with regional and potentially global aspirations. As the United States courts relative decline and Europe and Japan stagnate, China, India, Brazil, Russia, Turkey, Indonesia, and others are flexing their muscles, expanding their regional influence and insisting on greater voice within multilateral institutions.

Despite these geopolitical shifts, however, no coherent alternative to today's Western order has emerged. This is true even among the much-hyped BRICS: Brazil, Russia, India, China, and, since 2012, South Africa. These countries have always lacked a common vision, but at least initially, they shared a confidence born of economic dynamism and resentment over a global economy they perceived as stacked to favor the West. In recent years, the BRICS have staked out a few common positions. They all embrace traditional conceptions of state sovereignty and resist heavy-handed Western intervention. Their summit communiqués condemn the dollar's privileges as the world's main reserve currency and insist on accelerated governance reforms within the international financial institutions. The BRICS have also agreed to create a full-fledged BRICS bank to provide development aid to countries and for issues the bloc defines as priorities, without the conditionality imposed by Western donors.

Some observers anticipate the BRICS' emerging as an independent caucus and center of gravity within the G-20, rivaling the G-7 nations. But any such bifurcation of the world order between developed and major developing powers seems a distant prospect, for as much divides the BRICS as binds them. China and Russia have no interest in seeing any of their putative partners join them as permanent Security Council members; China and India are emerging strategic competitors with frontier disputes and divergent maritime interests; and China and Russia have their own tensions along the Siberian border. Differences in their internal regimes may also constrain their collaboration. India, Brazil, and South Africa—boisterous multiparty democracies all—have formed a coalition of their own (the India-Brazil-South Africa Dialogue Forum, or IBSA), as have China and Russia (the Shanghai Cooperation Organization). Conflicting economic interests also complicate intra-BRICS relations, something that might increase as the countries' growth slows.

Welcome to the G-X World

The analysts Ian Bremmer and David Gordon have written about the emergence of a "G-Zero world," in which collective global leadership is almost impossible thanks to a global diffusion of power among countries with widely divergent interests. But what really marks the contemporary era is not the absence of multilateralism but its astonishing diversity. Collective action is no longer focused solely, or even primarily, on the UN and other universal, treaty-based institutions, nor even on a single apex forum such as the G-20. Rather, governments have taken to operating in many venues simultaneously, participating in a bewildering array of issue-specific networks and partnerships whose membership varies based on situational interests, shared values, and relevant capabilities.

A hallmark of this "G-X" world is the temporary coalition of strange bedfellows. Consider the multinational antipiracy armada that has emerged in the Indian Ocean. This loosely coordinated flotilla involves naval vessels from not only the United States and its NATO allies but also China, India, Indonesia, Iran, Japan, Malaysia, Russia, Saudi Arabia, South Korea, and Yemen. These countries might disagree on many issues, but they have found common cause in securing sea-lanes off the African coast.

At the same time, the G-X world permits the United States to strengthen its links within the traditional West. Take the surprisingly resilient G-8, composed of the United States, Japan, Germany, France, the UK, Italy, Canada, and Russia (plus the EU). For years, pundits have predicted the G-8's demise, and yet it still moves. The G-8 allows advanced market democracies to coordinate their positions on sensitive political and security issues—just as the parallel financially focused G-7 permits them to harmonize their macroeconomic policies. With

the exception of authoritarian Russia, unwisely added in 1997, G-8 members share similar worldviews and values, strategic interests, and major policy preferences. This like-mindedness facilitates policy coordination on matters ranging from human rights to humanitarian intervention, rogue states to regional stability.

The wealthy G-8 members also possess distinctive assets—financial, diplomatic, military, and ideological—to deploy in the service of their convictions. At the Deauville summit of May 2011, the G-8 moved quickly to offer diplomatic support and material assistance to the Arab Spring countries. That action reaffirmed the G-8 as a practical and symbolic anchor of the Western liberal order while reminding the world that the G-8 remains the overwhelming source of official development assistance.

In global governance, as elsewhere, necessity is the mother of invention, and the global credit crisis that struck with full force in 2008 led to the rise to prominence of a relatively new international grouping, the G-20. Facing the potential meltdown of the international financial system, leaders of the world's major economies—both developed and developing—shared an overriding interest in avoiding a second Great Depression. Stuck in the same lifeboat, they assented to a slew of institutional innovations, including elevating the G-20 finance ministers' group to the leaders' level, creating an exclusive global crisis-response committee.

The G-20 quickly racked up some notable achievements. It injected unprecedented liquidity into the world economy through coordinated national actions, including some $5 trillion in stimulus at the London summit of April 2009. It created the Financial Stability Board, charged with developing new regulatory standards for systemically important financial institutions, and insisted on new bank capital account requirements under the Basel III agreement. It revitalized and augmented the coffers of the once-moribund International Monetary Fund and negotiated governance reforms within the World Bank and the IMF to give greater voice to emerging economies. And its members adopted "standstill" provisions to avoid a recurrence of the ruinous tit-for-tat trade protectionism of the 1930s.

As the immediate panic receded and an uneven global recovery took hold, however, narrow national interests again came to the fore, slowing the G-20's momentum. For the past four years, the G-20—whose heterogeneous members possess diverse values, political systems, and levels of development—has struggled to evolve from a short-term crisis manager to a longer-term steering group for the global economy. The reform of major international financial institutions has also stalled, as established (notably European) powers resist reallocating voting weight and governing board seats. So what looked for a brief moment like the dawn of a newly preeminent global forum proved to be just one more outlet store in the sprawl.

Governance in Pieces

For much of the past two decades, UN mega-conferences dominated multilateral diplomacy. But when it comes to multilateralism, bigger is rarely better, and the era of the mega-conference is ending as major powers recognize the futility of negotiating comprehensive international agreements among 193 UN member states, in the full glare of the media and alongside tens of thousands of activists, interest groups, and hangers-on. Countries will continue to assemble for annual confabs, such as the Conference of the Parties to the UN Framework Convention on Climate Change (UNFCCC), in the Sisyphean quest to secure "binding" commitments from developed and developing countries. But that circus will increasingly become a sideshow, as the action shifts to less formal settings and narrower groupings of the relevant and capable. Already, the 17 largest greenhouse gas emitters have created the Major Economies Forum on Energy and Climate, seeking breakthroughs outside the lumbering UNFCCC. To date, the forum has underdelivered. But more tangible progress has occurred through parallel national efforts, as states pledge to undertake a menu of domestic actions, which they subsequently submit to the forum for collective review.

There is a more general lesson here. Faced with fiendishly complex issues, such as climate change, transnational networks of government officials now seek incremental progress by disaggregating those issues into manageable chunks and agreeing to coordinate action on specific agenda items. Call it "global governance in pieces." For climate change, this means abandoning the quest for an elusive soup-to-nuts agreement to mitigate and adapt to global warming. Instead, negotiators pursue separate initiatives, such as phasing out wasteful fossil fuel subsidies, launching minilateral clean technology partnerships, and expanding the UN Collaborative Program on Reducing Emissions from Deforestation and Forest Degradation in Developing Countries, among other worth-while schemes. The result is not a unitary international regime grounded in a single institution or treaty but a cluster of complementary activities that political scientists call a "regime complex."

Something similar is happening in global health, where the once-premier World Health Organization now shares policy space and a division of labor with other major organizations, such as the World Bank; specialized UN agencies, such as UNAIDS; public–private partnerships, such as the GAVI Alliance (formerly called the Global Alliance for Vaccines and Immunization); philanthropic organizations, such as the Bill and Melinda Gates Foundation; consultative bodies, such as the eight-nation (plus the EU) Global Health Security Initiative; and multi-stakeholder bodies, such as the Global Fund to Fight AIDS, Tuberculosis and Malaria. The upshot is a disaggregated system of global health governance.

Sometimes, the piecemeal approach maybe able to achieve more than its stagnant universalist alternative. Given the failure of the WTO's Doha Round, for example, the United States and other nations have turned to preferential trade agreements in order to spur further liberalization of commerce. Some are bilateral, such as the United States–South Korean pact. But others involve multiple countries. These include two initiatives that constitute the centerpiece of Obama's second-term trade agenda: the Trans-Pacific Partnership and the Transatlantic Trade and Investment Partnership. The administration describes each as a steppingstone toward global liberalization. And yet future WTO negotiations will likely take a disaggregated form, as subsets of WTO members move forward on more manageable specific issues (such as public procurement or investment) while avoiding those lightning-rod topics (such as trade in agriculture) that have repeatedly stymied comprehensive trade negotiations.

The Rise of the Regions

Ad hoc coalitions and minilateral networks are not the only global governance innovations worthy of mention. Regional organizations are also giving universal membership bodies a run for their money, raising the question of how to make sure they harmonize and complement the UN system rather than undermine it.

This dilemma is older than often assumed. In the months leading up to the San Francisco conference of 1945, at which the UN was established, US and British postwar planners debated whether regional bodies ought to be given formal, even independent, standing within the UN (something British Prime Minister Winston Churchill, among others, had proposed). Most US negotiators were adamantly opposed, fearing that an overtly regional thrust would detract from the UN's coherence or even fracture it into rival blocs. In the end, the Americans' universal vision prevailed. Still, Chapter 8 of the UN Charter acknowledges a legitimate subordinate role for regional organizations.

What few in San Francisco could have envisioned was the dramatic proliferation and increasingly sophisticated capabilities of regional and subregional arrangements, which today number in the hundreds. These bodies play an ever more important role in managing crossborder challenges, facilitating trade, and promoting regional security, often in partnership with the UN and other universal organizations. Consider peacekeeping on the African continent. Alongside classic UN operations, we now see a variety of hybrid models, in which the UN Security Council authorizes an observer or peacekeeping mission, which is then implemented by an ad hoc coalition (as in the NATO-led mission in Libya), a regional organization (as in the African Union Mission in Somalia, or AMISOM), or some combination of the two.

This budding role for regional organizations poses policy conundrums. One is whether regional organizations ought to be allowed to serve as gatekeepers for UN-mandated enforcement actions. This contentious issue arose in 2011 after NATO launched Operation Unified Protector in Libya, with the authorization of the UN Security Council and the diplomatic support of the Arab League but not, critically, of the African Union. In January 2012, South African President Jacob Zuma, with South Africa occupying the rotating presidency of the UN Security Council, blasted the Western powers for exceeding the intent of Resolution 1973 in treating their mandate to protect Libyan civilians as a license for regime change. "Africa," he insisted, "must not be a playground for furthering the interests of other regions ever again." Seeking to tighten the relationship between the UN Security Council and regional organizations, Zuma introduced a resolution proposing a system of codetermination for authorizing enforcement actions. Predictably, this gambit met with solid opposition from the five permanent members, and some dismissed the move as populist showboating. But Zuma had given voice to a larger concern: the perceived legitimacy and practical success of international interventions increasingly depends on support from relevant regional organizations.

Given how overstretched the UN and other global bodies can become, rising regionalism has distinct benefits. Regional bodies are often more familiar with the underlying sources of local conflicts, and they may be more sensitive to and invested in potential solutions. But they are in no position to replace the UN entirely. To begin with, regional organizations vary widely in their aspirations, mandates, capabilities, and activities. They are also vulnerable to the same collective-action problems that bedevil the UN. Their members are often tempted to adopt bland, lowest-common-denominator positions or to try to free-ride on the contributions of others. Local hegemons may seek to hijack them for narrow purposes. The ambitions of regional organizations can also outstrip their ability to deliver. Although the African Union has created the Peace and Security Council, for instance, the organization's capacity to conduct peacekeeping operations remains hamstrung by institutional, professional, technical, material, and logistical shortcomings. Accordingly, burden sharing between the UN and regional organizations can easily devolve into burden shifting, as the world invests unprepared regional bodies with unrealistic expectations.

Governing the Contested Commons

If one major problem in contemporary global governance is the floundering of existing institutions when dealing with traditional challenges, another and equally worrisome problem is the lack of any serious institutional mechanism for dealing with untraditional challenges. The gap between the demand for and the supply of global governance is greatest when it comes to the global commons, those spaces no nation controls but on which all rely for security and prosperity. The most important of these are the maritime, outer space, and cyberspace domains, which carry the flows of goods, data, capital, people, and ideas on which globalization rests. Ensuring free and unencumbered access to these realms is therefore a core interest not only of the United States but of most other nations as well.

For almost seven decades, the United States has provided security for the global commons and, in so doing, has bolstered world order. Supremacy at sea—and, more recently, in outer space and online—has also conferred strategic advantages on the United States, allowing it to project power globally. But as the commons become crowded and cutthroat, that supremacy is fading. Rising powers, as well as nonstate actors from corporations to criminals, are challenging long-standing behavioral norms and deploying asymmetric capabilities to undercut US advantages. Preserving the openness, stability, and resilience of the global commons will require the United States to forge agreement among like-minded nations, rising powers, and private stakeholders on new rules of the road.

From China to Iran, for example, rising powers are seeking blue-water capabilities or employing asymmetric strategies to deny the United States and other countries access to their regional waters, jeopardizing the freedom of the seas. The greatest flashpoint today is in the South China Sea, through which more than $5 trillion worth of commerce passes each year. There, China is locked in dangerous sovereignty disputes with Brunei, Malaysia, the Philippines, Taiwan, and Vietnam over some 1.3 million square miles of ocean, the contested islands therein, and the exploitation of undersea oil and gas reserves. Beijing's assertiveness poses grave risks for regional stability. Most dangerous would be a direct US-Chinese naval clash, perhaps in response to US freedom-of-navigation exercises in China's littoral waters or the reckless actions of a US treaty ally or strategic partner.

Geopolitical and economic competition has also heated up in the warming Arctic, as nations wrangle over rights to extended continental shelves, new sea routes over Asia and North America, and the exploitation of fossil fuel and mineral deposits. To date, cooler heads have prevailed. In 2008, the five Arctic nations—Canada, Denmark, Norway, Russia, and the United States—signed the Ilulissat Declaration, affirming their commitment to address any overlapping claims in a peaceful and orderly manner. Some experts contend that the Arctic needs a comprehensive multilateral treaty to reconcile competing sovereignty claims, handle navigational issues, facilitate collective energy development, manage fisheries, and address environmental concerns. A more productive strategy would be to bolster the role of the Arctic Council, composed of the five Arctic nations plus Finland, Iceland, Sweden, and several indigenous peoples' organizations. Although this forum has historically avoided contentious boundary and legal disputes, it could help codify guidelines on oil and gas development, sponsor collaborative mapping of the continental shelf, create a regional monitoring network, and modernize systems for navigation, traffic management, and environmental protection.

The single most important step the United States could take to strengthen ocean governance, including in the Arctic, would be to finally accede to the UN Convention on the Law of the Sea, as recommended by the last four US presidents, US military leaders, industry, and environmental groups. Beyond defining states' rights and responsibilities in territorial seas and exclusive economic zones and clarifying the rules for transit through international straits, UNCLOS provides a forum for dispute resolution on ocean-related issues, including claims to extended continental shelves. As a nonmember, the United States forfeits its chance to participate in the last great partitioning of sovereign space on earth, which would grant it jurisdiction over vast areas along its Arctic, Atlantic, Gulf, and Pacific coasts. Nor can it serve on the International Seabed Authority, where it would enjoy a permanent seat with an effective veto. By remaining apart, the United States not only undercuts its national interests but also undermines its perceived commitment to a rule-based international order and emboldens revisionist regional powers. Both China in East Asia and Russia in the Arctic have taken advantage of the United States' absence to advance outrageous sovereignty claims.

At the same time, US accession to the treaty would be no panacea. This is particularly true in East Asia, where China has been unwilling to submit its claims to binding arbitration under UNCLOS. Ultimately, the peaceful resolution of competing regional claims will require China and its neighbors in the Association of Southeast Asian Nations to agree on a binding code of conduct addressing matters of territorial jurisdiction and joint exploitation of undersea resources. This is something that Beijing has strenuously resisted, but it seems inevitable if the Chinese government wants to preserve the credibility of its "peaceful rise" rhetoric.

The Final Frontier

The international rules governing the uses of outer space have also become outdated, as that domain becomes, in the words of former US Deputy Secretary of Defense William Lynn, more "congested, contested, and competitive." As nations and private corporations vie for scarce orbital slots for their satellites and for slices of a finite radio-frequency spectrum, the number of actors operating in space has skyrocketed. Already, nine countries and the European Space Agency have orbital launch capabilities, and nearly 60 nations or government consortiums regulate civil, commercial, and military satellites. The proliferation of vehicles and space debris—including more than 22,000 orbiting objects larger than a softball—has increased the risk of catastrophic collisions. More worrisome, geopolitical competition among spacefaring nations, both established and emerging, raises the specter of an arms race in space.

Yet so far at least, there is little global consensus on what kind of regulatory regime would best ensure the stability and sustainable use of earths final frontier. The basic convention governing national conduct in outer space remains the Outer Space Treaty of 1967. Although it establishes useful principles (such as a prohibition on sovereignty claims in space), that treaty lacks a dispute-resolution mechanism, is silent on space debris and how to avoid collisions, and inadequately addresses interference with the space assets of other countries.

To address these shortcomings, various parties have suggested options ranging from a binding multilateral treaty banning space weapons to an informal agreement on standards of behavior. Given the problems with a treaty-based approach, the Obama administration has wisely focused on seeking a nonbinding international code of conduct for outer space activities that would establish broad principles and parameters for responsible behavior in space. Such a voluntary code would carry a lesser obligation than a legally binding multilateral treaty, but it offers the best chance to establish new behavioral norms in the short term. Washington should also consider sponsoring a standing minilateral consultative forum of spacefaring nations.

Lost in Cyberspace

Cyberspace differs from the oceans or outer space in that its physical infrastructure is located primarily in sovereign states and in private hands—creating obvious risks of interference by parties pursuing their own interests. Since the dawn of the digital age, the United States has been the premier champion of an open, decentralized, and secure cyberspace that remains largely private. This posture is consistent with the long-standing US belief that the free flow of information and ideas is a core component of a free, just, and open world and an essential bulwark against authoritarianism. But this vision of global governance in cyberspace is now under threat from three directions.

The first is the demand by many developing and authoritarian countries that regulation of the Internet be transferred from ICANN, the Internet Corporation for Assigned Names and Numbers—an independent, nonprofit corporation based in Los Angeles, loosely supervised by the US Department of Commerce—to the UN's ITU (International Telecommunication Union). The second is a growing epidemic of cybercrime, consisting mostly of attempts to steal proprietary information from private-sector actors. Thanks to sophisticated computer viruses, worms, and botnets, what might be termed "cyber public health" has deteriorated dramatically. And there is no cyberspace equivalent to the World Health Organization for dealing with such dangers.

The third major flashpoint is the growing specter of cyberwar among sovereign states. Dozens of nations have begun to develop doctrines and capabilities for conducting so-called information operations, not only to infiltrate but if necessary to disrupt and destroy the critical digital infrastructure (both military and civilian) of their adversaries. Yet there is no broadly accepted definition of a cyberattack, much less consensus on the range of permissible responses; the normative and legal framework governing cyberwar has lagged behind cyberweapons' development and use. Traditional forms of deterrence and retaliation are also complicated, given the difficulty of attributing attacks to particular perpetrators.

No single UN treaty could simultaneously regulate cyberwarfare, counter cybercrime, and protect the civil liberties of Internet users. Liberal and authoritarian regimes disagree on the definition of "cyber-security" and how to achieve it, with the latter generally seeing the free exchange of ideas and information not as a core value but as a potential threat to their stability, and there are various practical hurdles to including cyberweapons in traditional arms control and nonproliferation negotiations. So a piecemeal approach to governance in cyberspace seems more realistic. States will need to negotiate norms of responsibility for cyberattacks and criteria for retaliation. They should also develop transparency and confidence-building measures and agree to preserve humanitarian fundamentals in the event of a cyberwar, avoiding attacks on "root" servers, which constitute the backbone of the Internet, and prohibiting all denial-of-service attacks, which can cripple the Internet infrastructure of the targeted countries. Washington might start advancing such an agenda through a coalition of like-minded states—akin to the Financial Action Task Force or the Proliferation Security Initiative—expanding membership outward as feasible.

Technology and the Frontiers of Global Governance

The history of global governance is the story of adaptation to new technologies. As breakthroughs have been made, sovereign governments have sought common standards and rules to facilitate cooperation and mitigate conflict. For example, we now take for granted the world's division into 24 separate time zones, with Greenwich Mean Time as the base line, but in the middle of the nineteenth century, the United States alone had

144 local time zones. It was only the need to standardize train and shipping schedules in the late nineteenth century that convinced major countries to synchronize their time.

Today, the furious pace of technological change risks leaving global governance in the dust. The growing gap between what technological advances permit and what the international system is prepared to regulate can be seen in multiple areas, from drones and synthetic biology to nanotechnology and geoengineering.

When it comes to drones, the United States has struggled mightily to develop its own legal rationale for targeted assassinations. Initial foreign objections to US drone strikes were concentrated within the target countries, but increasingly, their use has been challenged both domestically and internationally, and the rapid spread of drone technology to both state and nonstate actors makes it imperative to create clear rules for their use—and soon.

Rapid advances in biotechnology could pose even greater long-term threats. Scientists today are in a position to create new biological systems by manipulating genetic material. Such "synthetic biology" has tremendous therapeutic and public health potential but could also cause great harm, with rogue states or rogue scientists fabricating deadly pathogens or other bioweapons. At present, only an incomplete patchwork of regulations exist to prevent such risks. Nor are there any international regulatory arrangements to govern research on and uses of nanotechnology: the process of manipulating materials at the atomic or molecular level. Where regulation exists, it is performed primarily on a national basis; in the United States, for example, this function is carried out jointly by the Environmental Protection Agency, the Food and Drug Administration, and the National Institute of Standards and Technology. To make things even more complicated, most research and investment in this area is currently carried out by the private sector, which has little incentive to consider potential threats to public safety.

Finally, the threat of uncoordinated efforts at geoengineering—the attempt to slow or reverse global warming through large-scale tinkering with the planet s climate system—also demands regulation. Such schemes include seeding the world's oceans with iron filings (as one freelancing US scientist attempted in 2012), deflecting solar radiation through a system of space-based mirrors, and preventing the release of methane held in tundras and the ocean. Long dismissed as fanciful, such attempts to reengineer the earth's atmosphere are suddenly being taken seriously by at least some mainstream experts. As warming proceeds, countries and private actors will be increasingly tempted to take matters into their own hands. Only proper regulation has a chance of ensuring that these uncoordinated efforts do not go badly awry, with potentially disastrous consequences.

"Good Enough" Global Governance

As all these examples highlight, demand for effective global governance continues to outstrip supply, and the gap is growing. Absent dramatic crises, multilateral institutions have been painfully slow and lumbering in their response. So even as they try to revitalize the existing international order, diplomats and other interested parties need to turn to other, complementary frameworks for collective action, including ad hoc coalitions of the willing, regional and subregional institutions, public–private arrangements, and informal codes of conduct. The resulting jerry-rigged structure for global cooperation will not be aesthetically pleasing, but it might at least get some useful things done.

A decade ago, the Harvard scholar Merilee Grindle launched a broadside against the lengthy list of domestic good-governance reforms that the World Bank and other agencies insisted were necessary to encourage growth and reduce poverty in developing countries. She implored international donors to put their long, well-intentioned checklists aside and focus instead on "good enough governance." Rather than try to tackle all problems at once, she suggested, aid agencies should focus on achieving the minimal institutional requirements for progress. This advice to lower expectations and start with the necessary and possible is even more applicable in the international sphere, given all the obstacles in the way of sweeping institutional reform there. For the Obama administration and its colleagues and successors, achieving some measure of "good enough" global governance might be less satisfying than trying to replay the glory days of the Truman administration. But it would be much better than nothing, and it might even work.

Critical Thinking

1. Do you agree with the title that the world is unruled, or in other words, "badly ruled"?
2. Why does Patrick advocate "good enough governance" rather than really good governance?

Create Central

www.mhhe.com/createcentral

Internet References

National Center for Policy Analysis
www.ncpa.org

New American Studies Web
www.georgetown.edu/crossroads/asw

Social Science Information Gateway
http://sosig.esrc.bris.ac.uk

Sociology—Study Sociology Online
http://edu.learnsoc.org

Sociology Web Resources
http://www.mhhe.com/socscience/sociology/resources/index.htm

Sociosite
http://www.topsite.com/goto/sociosite.net

Socioweb
http://www.topsite.com/goto/socioweb.com

STEWART PATRICK is a Senior Fellow and Director of the International Institutions and Global Governance Program at the Council on Foreign Relations.

Reprinted by permission of *foreign affairs*, January/February 2014. Copyright 2014 by the Council on Foreign Relations, Inc. www.ForeignAffairs.com

Article   Prepared by: Kurt Finsterbusch, *University of Maryland, College Park*

The Future of History: Can Liberal Democracy Survive the Decline of the Middle Class?

FRANCIS FUKUYAMA

Learning Outcomes

After reading this article, you will be able to:

- Try to judge the prospects for democracy in the world today.

- Explain the current threats to democracy.

- Consider how technology and globalization threaten (and support) democracy.

Something strange is going on in the world today. The global financial crisis that began in 2008 and the ongoing crisis of the euro are both products of the model of lightly regulated financial capitalism that emerged over the past three decades. Yet despite widespread anger at Wall Street bailouts, there has been no great upsurge of left-wing American populism in response. It is conceivable that the Occupy Wall Street movement will gain traction, but the most dynamic recent populist movement to date has been the right-wing Tea Party, whose main target is the regulatory state that seeks to protect ordinary people from financial speculators. Something similar is true in Europe as well, where the left is anemic and right-wing populist parties are on the move.

There are several reasons for this lack of left-wing mobilization, but chief among them is a failure in the realm of ideas. For the past generation, the ideological high ground on economic issues has been held by a libertarian right. The left has not been able to make a plausible case for an agenda other than a return to an unaffordable form of old-fashioned social democracy. This absence of a plausible progressive counter-narrative is unhealthy, because competition is good for intellectual—debate just as it is for economic activity. And serious intellectual debate is urgently needed, since the current form of globalized capitalism is eroding the middle-class social base on which liberal democracy rests.

The Democratic Wave

Social forces and conditions do not simply "determine" ideologies, as Karl Marx once maintained, but ideas do not become powerful unless they speak to the concerns of large numbers of ordinary people. Liberal democracy is the default ideology around much of the world today in part because it responds to and is facilitated by certain socioeconomic structures. Changes in those structures may have ideological consequences, just as ideological changes may have socioeconomic consequences.

Almost all the powerful ideas that shaped human societies up until the past 300 years were religious in nature, with the important exception of Confucianism in China. The first major secular ideology to have a lasting worldwide effect was liberalism, a doctrine associated with the rise of first a commercial and then an industrial middle class in certain parts of Europe in the seventeenth century. (By "middle class," I mean people who are neither at the top nor at the bottom of their societies in terms of income, who have received at least a secondary education, and who own either real property, durable goods, or their own businesses.)

As enunciated by classic thinkers such as Locke, Montesquieu, and Mill, liberalism holds that the legitimacy of state authority derives from the state's ability to protect the individual rights of its citizens and that state power needs to be limited by the adherence to law. One of the fundamental rights to be protected is that of private property; England's Glorious Revolution of 1688–89 was critical to the development of modern liberalism because it first established the constitutional principle that the state could not legitimately tax its citizens without their consent.

At first, liberalism did not necessarily imply democracy. The Whigs who supported the constitutional settlement of 1689 tended to be the wealthiest property owners in England; the parliament of that period represented less than 10 percent of the whole population. Many classic liberals, including Mill, were highly skeptical of the virtues of democracy: they believed that responsible political participation required education and a stake in society—that is, property ownership. Up through the end of the nineteenth century, the franchise was limited by property and educational requirements in virtually all parts of Europe. Andrew Jackson's election as US president in 1828 and his subsequent abolition of property requirements for voting, at least for white males, thus marked an important early victory for a more robust democratic principle. In Europe, the exclusion of the vast majority of the population from political power and the rise of an industrial working class paved the way for Marxism. The Communist Manifesto was published in 1848, the same year that revolutions spread to all the major European countries save the UK. And so began a century of competition for the leadership of the democratic movement between communists, who were willing to jettison procedural democracy (multiparty elections) in favor of what they believed was substantive democracy (economic redistribution), and liberal democrats, who believed in expanding political participation while maintaining a rule of law protecting individual rights, including property rights.

At stake was the allegiance of the new industrial working class. Early Marxists believed they would win by sheer force of numbers: as the franchise was expanded in the late nineteenth century, parties such as the United Kingdom's Labour and Germany's Social Democrats grew by leaps and bounds and threatened the hegemony of both conservatives and traditional liberals. The rise of the working class was fiercely resisted, often by nondemocratic means; the communists and many socialists, in turn, abandoned formal democracy in favor of a direct seizure of power.

Throughout the first half of the twentieth century, there was a strong consensus on the progressive left that some form of socialism—government control of the commanding heights of the economy in order to ensure an egalitarian distribution of wealth—was unavoidable for all advanced countries. Even a conservative economist such as Joseph Schumpeter could write in his 1942 book, *Capitalism, Socialism, and Democracy*, that

socialism would emerge victorious because capitalist society was culturally self-undermining. Socialism was believed to represent the will and interests of the vast majority of people in modern societies. Yet even as the great ideological conflicts of the twentieth century played themselves out on a political and military level, critical changes were happening on a social level that undermined the Marxist scenario. First, the real living standards of the industrial working class kept rising, to the point where many workers or their children were able to join the middle class. Second, the relative size of the working class stopped growing and actually began to decline, particularly in the second half of the twentieth century, when services began to displace manufacturing in what were labeled "postindustrial" economies. Finally, a new group of poor or disadvantaged people emerged below the industrial working class—a heterogeneous mixture of racial and ethnic minorities, recent immigrants, and socially excluded groups, such as women, gays, and the disabled. As a result of these changes, in most industrialized societies, the old working class has become just another domestic interest group, one using the political power of trade unions to protect the hard-won gains of an earlier era. Economic class, moreover, turned out not to be a great banner under which to mobilize populations in advanced industrial countries for political action. The Second International got a rude wake-up call in 1914, when the working classes of Europe abandoned calls for class warfare and lined up behind conservative leaders preaching nationalist slogans, a pattern that persists to the present day. Many Marxists tried to explain this, according to the scholar Ernest Gellner, by what he dubbed the "wrong address theory":

> Just as extreme Shi'ite Muslims hold that Archangel Gabriel made a mistake, delivering the Message to Mohamed when it was intended for Ali, so Marxists basically like to think that the spirit of history or human consciousness made a terrible boob. The awakening message was intended for classes, but by some terrible postal error was delivered to nations.

Gellner went on to argue that religion serves a function similar to nationalism in the contemporary Middle East: it mobilizes people effectively because it has a spiritual and emotional content that class consciousness does not. Just as European nationalism was driven by the shift of Europeans from the countryside to cities in the late nineteenth century, so, too, Islamism is a reaction to the urbanization and displacement taking place in contemporary Middle Eastern societies. Marx's letter will never be delivered to the address marked "class." Marx believed that the middle class, or at least the capital-owning slice of it that he called the bourgeoisie, would always remain a small and privileged minority in modern societies. What happened instead was that the bourgeoisie and the middle class more generally ended up constituting the vast majority of the populations of most advanced countries, posing problems for socialism. From the days of Aristotle, thinkers have believed that stable democracy rests on a broad middle class and that societies with extremes of wealth and poverty are susceptible either to oligarchic domination or populist revolution. When much of the developed world succeeded in creating middle-class societies, the appeal of Marxism vanished. The only places where leftist radicalism persists as a powerful force are in highly unequal areas of the world, such as parts of Latin America, Nepal, and the impoverished regions of eastern India.

What the political scientist Samuel Huntington labeled the "third wave" of global democratization, which began in southern Europe in the 1970s and culminated in the fall of communism in Eastern Europe in 1989, increased the number of electoral democracies around the world from around 45 in 1970 to more than 120 by the late 1990s. Economic growth has led to the emergence of new middle classes in countries such as Brazil, India, Indonesia, South Africa, and Turkey. As the economist Moises Naim has pointed out, these middle classes are relatively well educated, own property, and are technologically connected to the outside world. They are demanding of their governments and mobilize easily as a result of their access to technology. It should not be surprising that the chief instigators of the Arab Spring uprisings were well-educated Tunisians and Egyptians whose expectations for jobs and political participation were stymied by the dictatorships under which they lived.

Middle-class people do not necessarily support democracy in principle: like everyone else, they are self-interested actors who want to protect their property and position. In countries such as China and Thailand, many middle-class people feel threatened by the redistributive demands of the poor and hence have lined up in support of authoritarian governments that protect their class interests. Nor is it the case that democracies necessarily meet the expectations of their own middle classes, and when they do not, the middle classes can become restive.

The Least Bad Alternative?

There is today a broad global consensus about the legitimacy, at least in principle, of liberal democracy. In the words of the economist Amartya Sen, "While democracy is not yet universally practiced, nor indeed uniformly accepted, in the general climate of world opinion, democratic governance has now achieved the status of being taken to be generally right." It is most broadly accepted in countries that have reached a level of material prosperity sufficient to allow a majority of their citizens to think of themselves as middle class, which is why there tends to be a correlation between high levels of—development and stable democracy.

Some societies, such as Iran and Saudi Arabia, reject liberal democracy in favor of a form of Islamic theocracy. Yet these regimes are developmental dead ends, kept alive only because they sit atop vast pools of oil. There was at one time a large Arab exception to the third wave, but the Arab Spring has shown that Arab publics can be mobilized against dictatorship just as readily as those in Eastern Europe and Latin America were. This does not of course mean that the path to a well-functioning democracy will be easy or straightforward in Tunisia, Egypt, or Libya, but it does suggest that the desire for—political freedom and participation is not a cultural peculiarity of Europeans and Americans.

The single most serious challenge to liberal democracy in the world today comes from China, which has combined authoritarian government with a partially marketized economy. China is heir to a long and proud tradition of high-quality bureaucratic government, one that stretches back over two millennia. Its leaders have managed a hugely complex transition from a centralized, Soviet-style planned economy to a dynamic open one and have done so with remarkable competence—more competence, frankly, than US leaders have shown in the management of their own macroeconomic policy recently. Many people currently admire the Chinese system not just for its economic record but also because it can make large, complex decisions quickly, compared with the agonizing policy paralysis that has struck both the United States and Europe in the past few years. Especially since the recent financial crisis, the Chinese themselves have begun touting the "China model" as an alternative to liberal democracy.

This model is unlikely to ever become a serious alternative to liberal democracy in regions outside East Asia, however. In the first place, the model is culturally specific: the Chinese government is built around a long tradition of meritocratic recruitment, civil service examinations, a high emphasis on education, and deference to technocratic authority. Few developing countries can hope to emulate this model; those that have, such as Singapore and South Korea (at least in an earlier period), were already within the Chinese cultural zone. The Chinese themselves are skeptical about whether their model can be exported; the so-called Beijing consensus is a Western invention, not a Chinese one. It is also unclear whether the model can be sustained. Neither export-driven growth nor the top-down approach to decision-making will continue to yield good results forever. The fact that the Chinese government would not permit open discussion of the disastrous high-speed rail accident last summer and could not bring the Railway Ministry responsible for it to heel suggests that there are other time bombs hidden behind the facade of efficient decision-making.

Finally, China faces a great moral vulnerability down the road. The Chinese government does not force its officials to respect the basic dignity of its citizens. Every week, there are new protests about land seizures, environmental violations, or gross corruption on the part of some official. While the country is growing rapidly, these abuses can be swept under the carpet. But rapid growth will not continue forever, and the government will have to pay a price in pent-up anger. The regime no longer has any guiding ideal around which it is organized; it is run by a Communist Party supposedly committed to equality that presides over a society marked by dramatic and growing inequality.

So the stability of the Chinese system can in no way be taken for granted. The Chinese government argues that its citizens are culturally different and will always prefer benevolent, growth-promoting dictatorship to a messy democracy that threatens social stability. But it is unlikely that a spreading middle class will behave all that differently in China from the way it has behaved in other parts of the world. Other authoritarian regimes may be trying to emulate China's success, but there is little chance that much of the world will look like today's China 50 years down the road.

Democracy's Future

There is a broad correlation among economic growth, social change, and the hegemony of liberal democratic ideology in the world today. And at the moment, no plausible rival ideology looms. But some very troubling economic and social trends, if they continue, will both threaten the stability of contemporary liberal democracies and dethrone democratic ideology as it is now understood. The sociologist Barrington Moore once flatly asserted, "No bourgeois, no democracy." The Marxists didn't get their communist Utopia because mature capitalism generated middle-class societies, not working-class ones. But what if the further development of technology and globalization undermines the middle class and makes it impossible for more than a minority of citizens in an advanced society to achieve middle-class status?

There are already abundant signs that such a phase of development has begun. Median incomes in the United States have been stagnating in real terms since the 1970s. The economic impact of this stagnation has been softened to some extent by the fact that most US households have shifted to two income earners in the past generation. Moreover, as the economist Raghuram Rajan has persuasively argued, since Americans are reluctant to engage in straightforward redistribution, the United States has instead attempted a highly dangerous and inefficient form of redistribution over the past generation by subsidizing mortgages for low-income households. This trend, facilitated by a flood of liquidity pouring in from China and other countries, gave many ordinary Americans the illusion that their standards of living were rising steadily during the past decade. In this respect, the bursting of the housing bubble in 2008–9 was

nothing more than a cruel reversion to the mean. Americans may today benefit from cheap cell phones, inexpensive clothing, and Facebook, but they increasingly cannot afford their own homes, or health insurance, or comfortable pensions when they retire.

A more troubling phenomenon, identified by the venture capitalist Peter Thiel and the economist Tyler Cowen, is that the benefits of the most recent waves of technological innovation have accrued disproportionately to the most talented and well-educated members of society. This phenomenon helped cause the massive growth of inequality in the United States over the past generation. In 1974, the top one percent of families took home nine percent of GDP; by 2007, that share had increased to 23.5 percent.

Trade and tax policies may have accelerated this trend, but the real villain here is technology. In earlier phases of industrialization—the ages of textiles, coal, steel, and the internal combustion engine—the benefits of technological changes almost always flowed down in significant ways to the rest of society in terms of employment. But this is not a law of nature. We are today living in what the scholar Shoshana Zuboff has labeled "the age of the smart machine," in which technology is increasingly able to substitute for more and higher human functions. Every great advance for Silicon Valley likely means a loss of low-skill jobs elsewhere in the economy, a trend that is unlikely to end anytime soon. Inequality has always existed, as a result of natural differences in talent and character. But today's technological world vastly magnifies those differences. In a nineteenth-century agrarian society, people with strong math skills did not have that many opportunities to capitalize on their talent. Today, they can become financial wizards or software engineers and take home ever-larger proportions of the national wealth.

The other factor undermining middle-class incomes in developed countries is globalization. With the lowering of transportation and communications costs and the entry into the global work force of hundreds of millions of new workers in developing countries, the kind of work done by the old middle class in the developed world can now be performed much more cheaply elsewhere. Under an economic model that prioritizes the maximization of aggregate income, it is inevitable that jobs will be outsourced.

Smarter ideas and policies could have contained the damage. Germany has succeeded in protecting a significant part of its manufacturing base and industrial labor force even as its companies have remained globally competitive. The United States and the UK, on the other hand, happily embraced the transition to the postindustrial service economy. Free trade became less a theory than an ideology: when members of the US Congress tried to retaliate with trade sanctions against China for keeping its currency undervalued, they were indignantly charged with protectionism, as if the playing field were already level. There was a lot of happy talk about the wonders of the knowledge economy, and how dirty, dangerous manufacturing jobs would inevitably be replaced by highly educated workers doing creative and interesting things. This was a gauzy veil placed over the hard facts of deindustrialization. It overlooked the fact that the benefits of the new order accrued disproportionately to a very small number of people in finance and high technology, interests that dominated the media and the general political conversation.

The Absent Left

One of the most puzzling features of the world in the aftermath of the financial crisis is that so far, populism has taken primarily a right-wing form, not a left-wing one.

In the United States, for example, although the Tea Party is antielitist in its rhetoric, its members vote for conservative politicians who serve the interests of precisely those financiers and corporate elites they claim to despise. There are many explanations for this phenomenon. They include a deeply embedded belief in equality of opportunity rather than equality of outcome and the fact that cultural issues, such as abortion and gun rights, crosscut economic ones.

But the deeper reason a broad-based populist left has failed to materialize is an intellectual one. It has been several decades since anyone on the left has been able to articulate, first, a coherent analysis of what happens to the structure of advanced societies as they undergo economic change and, second, a realistic agenda that has any hope of protecting a middle-class society.

The main trends in left-wing thought in the last two generations have been, frankly, disastrous as either conceptual frameworks or tools for mobilization. Marxism died many years ago, and the few old believers still around are ready for nursing homes. The academic left replaced it with postmodernism, multiculturalism, feminism, critical theory, and a host of other fragmented intellectual trends that are more cultural than economic in focus. Postmodernism begins with a denial of the possibility of any master narrative of history or society, undercutting its own authority as a voice for the majority of citizens who feel betrayed by their elites. Multiculturalism validates the victimhood of virtually every out-group. It is impossible to generate a mass progressive movement on the basis of such a motley coalition: most of the working- and lower-middle-class citizens victimized by the system are culturally conservative and would be embarrassed to be seen in the presence of allies like this.

Whatever the theoretical justifications underlying the left's agenda, its biggest problem is a lack of credibility. Over the past two generations, the mainstream left has followed a social democratic program that centers on the state provision of a variety of services, such as pensions, health care, and education. That model is now exhausted: welfare states have become big, bureaucratic, and inflexible; they are often captured by the very organizations that administer them, through public-sector unions; and, most important, they are fiscally unsustainable given the aging of populations virtually everywhere in the developed world. Thus, when existing social democratic parties come to power, they no longer aspire to be more than custodians of a welfare state that was created decades ago; none has a new, exciting agenda around which to rally the masses.

An Ideology of the Future

Imagine, for a moment, an obscure scribbler today in a garret somewhere trying to outline an ideology of the future that could provide a realistic path toward a world with healthy middle-class societies and robust democracies. What would that ideology look like?

It would have to have at least two components, political and economic. Politically, the new ideology would need to reassert the supremacy of democratic politics over economics and legitimate a new government as an expression of the public interest. But the agenda it put forward to protect middle-class life could not simply rely on the existing mechanisms of the welfare state. The ideology would need to somehow redesign the public sector, freeing it from its dependence on existing stakeholders and using new, technology empowered approaches to delivering services. It would have to argue forth-rightly for more redistribution and present a realistic route to ending interest groups' domination of politics.

Economically, the ideology could not begin with a denunciation of capitalism as such, as if old-fashioned socialism were still a viable alternative. It is more the variety of capitalism that is at stake and the degree to which governments should help societies adjust to change. Globalization need be seen not as an inexorable fact of life but rather as a challenge and an opportunity that must be carefully controlled politically. The new ideology would not see markets as an end in themselves; instead, it would value global trade and investment to the extent that they contributed to a flourishing middle class, not just to greater aggregate national wealth.

It is not possible to get to that point, however, without providing a serious and sustained critique of much of the edifice of modern neoclassical economics, beginning with fundamental assumptions such as the sovereignty of individual preferences and that aggregate income is an accurate measure of national well-being. This critique would have to note that people's incomes do not necessarily represent their true contributions to society. It would have to go further, however, and recognize that even if labor markets were efficient, the natural distribution of talents is not necessarily fair and that individuals are not sovereign entities but beings heavily shaped by their surrounding societies.

Most of these ideas have been around in bits and pieces for some time; the scribbler would have to put them into a coherent package. He or she would also have to avoid the "wrong address" problem. The critique of globalization, that is, would have to be tied to nationalism as a strategy for mobilization in a way that defined national interest in a more sophisticated way than, for example, the "Buy American" campaigns of unions in the United States. The product would be a synthesis of ideas from both the left and the right, detached from the agenda of the marginalized groups that constitute the existing progressive movement. The ideology would be populist; the message would begin with a critique of the elites that allowed the benefit of the many to be sacrificed to that of the few and a critique of the money politics, especially in Washington, that overwhelmingly benefits the wealthy.

The dangers inherent in such a movement are obvious: a pullback by the United States, in particular, from its advocacy of a more open global system could set off protectionist responses elsewhere. In many respects, the Reagan–Thatcher revolution succeeded just as its proponents hoped, bringing about an increasingly competitive, globalized and friction-free world. Along the way, it generated tremendous wealth and created rising middle classes all over the developing world, and the spread of democracy in their wake. It is possible that the developed world is on the cusp of a series of technological breakthroughs that will not only increase productivity but also provide meaningful employment to large numbers of middle-class people.

But that is more a matter of faith than a reflection of the empirical reality of the last 30 years, which points in the opposite direction. Indeed, there are a lot of reasons to think that inequality will continue to worsen. The current concentration of wealth in the United States has already become self-reinforcing: as the economist Simon Johnson has argued, the financial sector has used its lobbying clout to avoid more onerous forms of regulation. Schools for the well off are better than ever; those for everyone else continue to deteriorate. Elites in all societies use their superior access to the political system to protect their interests, absent a countervailing democratic mobilization to rectify the situation. American elites are no exception to the rule.

That mobilization will not happen, however, as long as the middle classes of the developed world remain enthralled by the narrative of the past generation: that their interests will be best served by ever-freer markets and smaller states. The alternative narrative is out there, waiting to be born.

Source

Fukuyama, Francis. "The future of history: can liberal democracy survive the decline of the middle class?" *Foreign Affairs* 91.1 (2012). *General Reference Center GOLD.* Web. 25 Jan. 2012.

Critical Thinking

1. What does your crystal ball say about the future of the world?
2. Why is a healthy middle class necessary to the sustainability of liberal democracy?
3. What are the causes of the increasing inequality that threatens democracy?

Create Central

www.mhhe.com/createcentral

Internet References

National Center for Policy Analysis
www.ncpa.org
New American Studies Web
www.georgetown.edu/crossroads/asw
Social Science Information Gateway
http://sosig.esrc.bris.ac.uk
Sociology—Study Sociology Online
http://edu.learnsoc.org
Sociology Web Resources
http://www.mhhe.com/socscience/sociology/resources/index.htm
Sociosite
http://www.topsite.com/goto/sociosite.net
Socioweb
http://www.topsite.com/goto/socioweb.com

Francis Fukuyama is a Senior Fellow at the Center on Democracy, Development, and the Rule of Law at Stanford University and the author, most recently, of *The Origins of Political Order: From Prehuman Times to the French Revolution.*

From *Foreign Affairs*, January–February, 2012, pp. 1–7. Copyright © 2012 by Council on Foreign Relations, Inc. Reprinted by permission of Foreign Affairs. www.ForeignAffairs.com